ÖSTERREICH
- ✪ Hauptstadt
- ◉ Landeshauptstadt
- • Stadt
- ▲ Berg
-)(Tunnel/Pass

TSCHECHIEN

DEUTSCHLAND

Passau

NIEDERÖSTERREICH

die Donau

Linz

Melk

SLOWAKEI

WIEN

Pressburg

OBERÖSTERREICH

St.Pölten

Wien

Steyr

Eisenstadt

der Inn

Salzburg

Wiener Neustadt

der Bodensee

die ZUGSPITZE
2.963 m

Kitzbühel

die Salzach

▲ der DACHSTEIN
2.995m

BURGENLAND

der Neusiedler See

Bregenz

A L P E N

Leoben

VORARLBERG

der Inn

Innsbruck

SALZBURG

STEIERMARK

Vaduz

TIROL

der GROSSGLOCKNER
3.798 m
(Zu Tirol)

der BRENNER PASS

der TAUERN TUNNEL

KÄRNTEN

Graz

LIECHTENSTEIN

die Mur

die SCHWEIZ

Lienz

der Wörther See

UNGARN

Villach

Klagenfurt

die Drau

Meilen

0   50

ITALIEN

Kilometer

0   50

SLOWENIEN

die Schweiz
- ✪ Hauptstadt
- ◉ Landeshauptstadt
- • Stadt
- ▲ Berg
-)(Tunnel/Pass

der Rhein

DEUTSCHLAND

SCHAFFHAUSEN
Schaffhausen

Frauenfeld

der Bodensee

BASEL-STADT

ZÜRICH

THURGAU

Basel

Liestal

AARGAU

Winterthur

St Gallen

Delémont

BASEL-LAND

Aarau

Zürich

Herisau

APPENZELL AUSSERRHODEN

Appenzell

FRANKREICH

JURA

SOLOTHURN

der Zürichsee

APPENZELL INNERRHODEN

Biel

Solothurn

Zug

SCHWYZ

SANKT GALLEN

LIECHTENSTEIN

NEUENBURG

Neuenburg

der Bieler See

BERN

LUZERN

ZUG

Glarus

Vaduz

ÖSTERREICH

der Neuenburger See

Freiburg

Luzern

Schwyz

GLARUS

Sarnen

Stans

der Vierwaldstätter See

Chur

Davos

WAADT

FREIBURG

Thun

NIDW.

UNTERWALDEN OBW.

Altdorf

A

der Rhein

GRAUBÜNDEN

Lausanne

der Thuner See

Interlaken

URI

L

der Inn

die JUNGFRAU
4.158 m

Grindelwald

P

St. Moritz

Montreux

der Genfer See

die Rhône

E

ST. GOTTHARD-TUNNEL

N

GENF

WALLIS

TESSIN

ITALIEN

Genf

Sion

Saas-Fee

der SIMPLON-TUNNEL

Locarno

Bellinzona

das MATTERHORN
4.478 m

Zermatt

Lugano

Meilen

0   40

der MONT BLANC
4.807 m

der Lago Maggiore

Kilometer

FRANKREICH

ITALIEN

0   40

EUROPA und NORDAFRIKA
☆ Hauptstadt
◉ Landeshauptstadt
• Stadt

ISLAND
Reykjavik

NORWEGEN
SCHWEDEN
FINNLAND
Oslo
Stockholm
Helsinki
Tallinn
St. Petersburg

die NORDSEE
die OSTSEE
ESTLAND
LETTLAND
Riga
RUSSLAND
Moskau

NORDIRLAND
SCHOTTLAND
Edinburgh
Belfast
Dublin
IRLAND
GROSSBRITANNIEN
DÄNEMARK
Kopenhagen
Königsberg
LITAUEN
Vilnius
(ZU RUSSLAND)
BELARUS
Minsk

WALES
Cardiff
ENGLAND
London
der ÄRMELKANAL
die NIEDERLANDE
Amsterdam
Den Haag
Brüssel
Bonn
Berlin
DEUTSCHLAND
POLEN
Warschau
Kiew
die UKRAINE

der ATLANTIK

BELGIEN
LUXEMBURG
Luxemburg
Paris
Prag
TSCHECHIEN
die SLOWAKEI
Bratislava
MOLDAU
Chisinau

FRANKREICH
LIECHTENSTEIN
Bern
Vaduz
die SCHWEIZ
Wien
ÖSTERREICH
Budapest
UNGARN
RUMÄNIEN
Belgrad
Bukarest
das SCHWARZE MEER

ITALIEN
SLOWENIEN
Ljubljana
Zagreb
KROATIEN
BOSNIEN-HERZEGOWINA
Sarajevo
SERBIEN
BULGARIEN
Sofia
Istanbul
Ankara

PORTUGAL
Madrid
Lissabon
SPANIEN
KORSIKA
MALLORCA
SARDINIEN
Rom
MONTENEGRO
Tirana
Skopje
MAZEDONIEN
ALBANIEN
GRIECHENLAND
Athen
die TÜRKEI

die STRASSE von GIBRALTAR
Rabat
Algier
Tunis
SIZILIEN
das MITTELMEER
KRETA

MAROKKO
ALGERIEN
TUNESIEN
Tripoli
LIBYEN

Meilen
0   400
Kilometer
0   400

A F R I K A

EIGHTH EDITION

Wie geht's?

An Introductory German Course

Dieter Sevin
Vanderbilt University

Ingrid Sevin

THOMSON
HEINLE

Australia Brazil Canada Mexico Singapore Spain United Kingdom United States

Wie geht's?
Eighth Edition
Sevin | Sevin

Executive Editor: Carrie Brandon
Development Editor: Paul Listen
Senior Project Manager, Editorial Production: Esther Marshall
Assistant Editor: Arlinda Shtuni
Editorial Assistant: Morgen Murphy
Marketing Manager: Lindsey Richardson
Marketing Assistant: Marla Nasser
Advertising Project Manager: Stacey Purviance
Managing Technology Project Manager: Sacha Laustsen
Manufacturing Manager: Marcia Locke
Compositor: Pre-Press Company

Project Management: Tunde Dewey & Roberta Peach, Pre-Press Company
Text Designer: Joyce Weston
Photo Manager: Sheri Blaney
Photo Reseacher: Sharon Donahue
Senior Permissions Editor: Isabel Alves
Text Permissions Editor: Cheri Throop
Senior Art Director: Bruce Bond
Cover Designer: Ha Nguyen
Cover Printer: Transcontinental
Printer: Transcontinental

Cover photos: left to right: © Sean Gallyp/Reportage/Getty Images; © Silvio Fiore/SuperStock; © Kevin Forest/Photodisc/Getty; © Mollenhauer/Getty

Thomson Higher Education
25 Thomson Place
Boston, MA 02210-1202
USA

Printed in Canada
2 3 4 5 6 7   09 08 07 06

For more information about our products, contact us at:
Thomson Learning Academic Resource Center
1-800-423-0563
For permission to use material from this text or product, submit a request online at http://www.thomsonrights.com.
Any additional questions about permissions can be submitted by email to **thomsonrights@thomson.com.**

Library of Congress Control Number: 2005933935

Student Edition ISBN 1-4130-1282-5

Credits appear on pages C1_C3, which constitute a continuation of the copyright page.

Inhalt

To the Student

Welcome to **Wie geht's?**, a program for Introductory German that focuses on all four skills—listening, speaking, reading, and writing—and promotes cultural proficiency.

Organization of *Wie geht's?*

The main text is divided into five pre-units *(Schritte)*, fifteen chapters *(Kapitel)*, and an appendix *(Anhang)*.

The Pre-Units *(Schritte)*

The purpose of the *Schritte* is to acquaint you with the German language and the language learning process by focusing on listening and speaking. When you have completed the last *Schritt*, you should be able to greet each other, describe your classroom and your clothes, use numbers, discuss the weather, and tell time, all in German.

The Fifteen Chapters *(Kapitel)*

Each chapter opens with a summary of the learning objectives *(Lernziele)* for that chapter. This is followed by a cultural preview in English *(Vorschau)* that provides you with background information on the chapter topic. The first section of the learning material is called **Zum Thema.** It includes one or two dialogues that focus on the chapter topic and function as models for conversation. For your reference, English translations for these dialogues can be found in the Appendix.

Next comes *Wortschatz 1*, which contains most of the new chapter vocabulary; it is arranged thematically, with nouns listed in alphabetical order according to gender. That list of active vocabulary is followed by a brief list of vocabulary intended for recognition only *(Zum Erkennen)* containing words and phrases from the dialogue and exercises that might make it easier to keep classroom conversation in German. The vocabulary list is followed by exercises and activities on the chapter theme *(Aktives zum Thema)* that foster communication and help you learn the new words and expressions. A pronunciation section *(Aussprache)*, recorded in your lab program, is included as well and is coordinated with more extensive practice in the supplementary summary of pronunciation *(Zur Aussprache)* of your Workbook *(Arbeitsbuch)*. At the end of *Aktives zum Thema*, and again after the reading text, you will find an activity *(Hörverständnis)* that will help improve your listening comprehension. To complete it, you will need to listen to the CD that accompanies the book.

The subsequent **Struktur** section introduces two or three major points of grammar. A variety of exercises *(Übungen)* provides practice of the principles presented.

The grammar explanations and activities are followed by an author-generated reading section **(Einblicke).** It is introduced by a second active vocabulary list *(Wortschatz 2)*, followed by a brief suggestion *(Lesetipp)* for how to approach the reading text , and a prereading section *(Vor dem Lesen)* with a variety of activities. The reading passage itself features one or more cultural aspects related to the chapter topic. It offers additional examples of the new grammar and a review of the chapter vocabulary. The reading text is followed by postreading exercises and activities *(Aktives zum Text)* that check comprehension and provide additional grammar, speaking, and writing practice. They are followed by a second listening activity *(Hörverständnis)*. Starting with Chapter 8, a literature (**Litera-tur**) section offers short literary readings for your enrichment and enjoyment. Cultural notes *(Fokus)* are interspersed throughout every *Kapitel*, as well as the *Schritte*; they point out or explain differences between life in North America and in countries where German is spoken.

In each chapter, you will also find a reference to the accompanying **Video** in the chapter-opening *(Vorschau)*. Near the *Zusammenfassung* activities, there is a reference to the **iLrn** Website pointing to additional practice. Finally, near the end of the chapter, you will find a margin note directing you to the ***Wie geht's?*** **Website** at __http://wiegehts.heinle.com__ where you will find online activities related to the chapter theme. Using the video, the iLrn, and the Website will enrich your language learning, add to cultural insights, and open new vistas of direct contact to the German-speaking countries.

The Appendix

The Appendix includes information on predicting the gender of some nouns, a grammar summary in chart form, tables of all basic verb forms, lists of irregular verbs, translations of dialogues, supplementary charts for the information-gap activities (**Hoppla, hier fehlt was!**), answers to the optional English-to-German activities in the margins, a German-English and English-German vocabulary, and a grammar index.

Visual Icons for *Wie geht's?*

 This icon designates an activity where you'll be working with a partner.

 Activities marked with this icon are designed for work in small groups of perhaps 3–5 students.

 This icon points to audio material that is recorded on the Textbook Audio CD. This includes listening comprehension activities (**Hörverständnis**) that appears twice in each chapter, as well as various pieces of original literature featured in Chapters 8–15. The track number is indicated next to the icon.

 This icon references the Lab Audio CDs. The number on the sleeve indicates the CD, followed by the track number.

 This icon indicates a writing activity.

 This symbol marks a reference to the accompanying video.

 This symbol marks a reference to the accompanying Website activities.

 This symbol marks references to the iLrn™ Website.

Student Program Components

- *Wie geht's!* comes packaged with a **Text Audio CD** that contains the thirty-one listening texts of the *Hörverständnis* sections (one for the *Schritte* and two for each regular *Kapitel*) as well as the original pieces of literature in *Kapitel* 8–15.

- The **Lab Audio CD program** provides additional practice in listening and speaking. On the CDs, you will find the chapter dialogues and pronunciation practice, supplementary grammar activities, the chapter reading text, and a new listening-comprehension exercise *(Verstehen Sie!)*. The program is accompanied by a lab section printed in each chapter of the *Arbeitsbuch*.

- The **Videos** consist of a *Minidrama* that presents authentic dialogues and a *Blickpunkt* that gives cultural insights into the various aspects of life in the German-speaking countries. The latter is more spontaneous and challenging; it appears only in every other chapter. The videos are accompanied by extensive pre-viewing and post-viewing activities printed in the *Arbeitsbuch*.

- The **Workbook *(Arbeitsbuch)*** is introduced by a complete summary of pronunciation *(Zur Aussprache)* that shows brief explanations of correct sound production; corresponding exercises are available on the first lab audio CD. It is followed by practice for the various *Schritte* and *Kapitel*. Each *Kapitel* consists of three components:
    - a) lab manual—The **Zum Hören** section provides activities correlated to the text audio CD program; it contains instructions and examples of the recorded activities.
    - b) video manual—The **Video-aktiv** section provides activities correlated to the *Wie geht's!* video.
    - c) written exercises—The **Zum Schreiben** section focuses on vocabulary building, structure, and cultural enrichment.

  After the *Schritte* as well as *Kapitel* 3, 7, 11, and 15, you will find review sections (**Rückblicke**) that summarize the grammatical structures you have learned. They are accompanied by extensive exercises to review vocabulary and grammar; an answer key can be found at the end of the *Arbeitsbuch*.

- A text-specific **Multimedia CD-ROM for Macintosh® and Windows®** offers interactive activities that will help to improve your listening comprehension skills, and provide further exposure to the culture of German-speaking countries.

- Taking advantage of the new possibilities of the Internet, *Wie geht's!* has its own Website, where you'll find **online activities** specifically tailored to the book. The Transparency Masters are also available on the Website. Go to **http://wiegehts.heinle.com**.

- The **iLrn™ German** Website **http://iLrn.heinle.com**: Everything you need to master the skills and concepts of the course is built right into this dynamic audio- and video-enhanced learning environment (diagnostic activities, an audio-enhanced **e-Book** with integrated activities, companion **videos,** and interactive **VoiceBoard,** an online **Workbook,** an online **Lab Manual** with audio, interactive enrichment **activities,** access to online tutoring with a German teaching expert through **vMentor™**).

- The online **WebTutor™ / WebCT™** and **Blackboard™** let you practice and review the topics in the book on your own; error analysis will guide you to correct answers.

We hope that you will find the *Wie geht's!* program enjoyable. You will be surprised at the rapid progress you will make in just one year. Many students have been able to study abroad after their first year of studying German!

Acknowledgments

We would like to thank the following colleagues who reviewed the manuscript during its various stages of development:

Zsuzsanna Abrams
University of Texas at Austin

Gabriela Appel
Pennsylvania State University

Prisca Augustyn
Florida Atlantic University

Shana Bell
Arizona State University at Tempe

Elise Brayton
California State University, San Diego

Francis Brévart
University of Pennsylvania

Johannes Bruestle
Grossmont College

Bettina F Cothram
Georgia Technical University

Karl-Georg Federhofer
University of Michigan

Ingrid Fry
Texas Tech University

Christine M. Goulding
California State University, Chico

Yvonne Ivory
Duke University

Julia Karolle
Purdue University

Peter Meister
University of Alabama, Huntsville

George Mower
Allegheny County Community College

Lisa Parkes
University of California, Los Angeles

Hartmut Rastalsky
University of Michigan

Christine Staininger
San Diego University

Cordelia Stroinigg
University of Cincinnati

We would like to thank Carrie Brandon, Executive Editor, for putting together such an excellent team and for her support of the **Wie geht's?** project throughout. The great professional support we received from members of the Heinle editorial staff is hereby gratefully acknowledged. We are especially appreciative of Esther Marshall, Senior Production Project Manager, and Paul Listen, Development Editor. Esther Marshall was shepherding the project through its various stages with unusual dedication and great professional expertise. She was always available for consultation, even on weekends. Paul Listen was a most creative and thorough editor who guided **Wie geht's?** through to publication. His skill and expertise touched on all aspects of the editorial process of **Wie geht's?**. Our thanks also go to Sheri Blaney, Photo Manager, and to the freelancers who worked on the different stages of the production and in particular to: Tunde Dewey for her very thorough copyediting and dedicated work in project management along with Roberta Peach on behalf of PrePress Company; Ulrike Rapp, Native Reader, Lorene Sorensen and Anneliese Z. Hall, Proofreaders.

Others who contributed in the early stages of revision were Franziska Unger, Katherine Gilbert and Cécile Hoene.

Last but not least, we would like to express our appreciation to our co-author of the early editions, Katrin T. Bean, whose valuable contribution continues to be an integral part of this text.

Beginnen wir!

Lernziele *(Learning objectives)*

The *Schritte ("pre-units")* will help you take your first steps in German. You will learn to:

introduce yourself and greet others.
say the alphabet and spell.
describe your classroom, clothing, and other things around you.
count, tell prices, and do math.
talk about the calendar, the weather, and time.

Kultur-Fokus

The history of the German language and its place in the world
German names, fashions, and climate
Descendants of German-speaking immigrants in North America

Hallo, wie geht's?

Vorschau   The German Language

Minidrama: *Was darf's sein?*

Over 120 million people worldwide speak German as their native tongue. It is the official language in Germany, Austria, and Liechtenstein as well as one of the official languages of Switzerland and Luxembourg; it is also spoken in parts of eastern Belgium and in Italy's South Tyrol region. In addition, there are significant German-speaking minorities in Denmark (northern Schleswig), France (Alsace), Poland (Silesia), the Czech Republic, and Hungary as well as in Estonia, Lithuania, Latvia, Bosnia, Herzegovina, Russia, and the Ukraine. German is also the native tongue of many people in Australia, Canada, the United States, and some South American countries.

German belongs to the Germanic branch of the Indo-European language family and is closely related to Dutch, English, the Scandinavian languages, Flemish, Frisian, Yiddish, and Afrikaans. For various political, literary, and linguistic reasons, we speak of Germans and the German language as dating from around the year 800. At that time, at least six major dialects with numerous variations were spoken. During the twelfth and thirteenth centuries, efforts were made to write a standardized form of German; thus, the years 1170–1250 saw great literary achievements. However, this use of German as a literary language declined and Latin was preferred for writing important documents. Around the year 1500, Martin Luther's translation of the Bible into German and Johann Gutenberg's invention of the printing press were major impetuses toward the development of a common, written German language. Nonetheless, Latin remained the sole language of instruction at German universities until the 1700s. Because of political fragmentation, a standard language was slow to develop in Germany. As late as the early 1900s, many people spoke only their regional dialects. The use of standard German (**Hochdeutsch**) in both newspapers and magazines and in radio and television broadcasts helped foster the widespread use of standard German, but regional accents and dialects are still common.

Because German and English are members of the same branch of the Indo-European language family, they share a considerable number of words. Some of these related words, called *cognates,* are identical in spelling in both languages (e.g., **Arm, Hand, Finger**), while others are similar (e.g., **Vater, Mutter, Haus**). As the two languages developed, certain cognates acquired different meanings, such as **Hose** (in German, *a pair of pants*) versus "hose" (in English, *nylon stockings*). For those cognates that came to be spelled differently, the differences between English and German often developed systematically. Note the following patterns:

	English	German
t → z	*ten*	zehn
	salt	Salz
p → pf	*pound*	Pfund
	apple	Apfel
t → ss	*water*	Wasser
	white	weiß
p → f	*ship*	Schiff
	help	helfen
k → ch	*book*	Buch
	make	machen
d → t	*bed*	Bett
	dance	tanzen
th → d	*bath*	Bad
	thank	danken

Lippe Rose bitter Ring Nest Gold mild Sack Witz sitzen Land Pfanne Hammer Plan Seite Ellbogen warm Fuß dick Pfeife Milch Silber weiß storch danken gleiten

CD 1, Track 9

■ The following dialogues are recorded for you on the Lab Audio CD. Listen to them and then read them aloud until you can do so fluently. Be prepared to answer questions about them. If necessary, you may consult the translations in the Appendix. ■

Guten Tag!

HERR SANDERS	Guten Tag!
FRAU LEHMANN	Guten Tag!
HERR SANDERS	Ich heiße Sanders, Willi Sanders. Und Sie, wie heißen Sie?
FRAU LEHMANN	Mein Name ist Erika Lehmann.
HERR SANDERS	Freut mich.

HERR MEIER	Guten Morgen, Frau Fiedler! Wie geht es Ihnen?
FRAU FIEDLER	Danke, gut. Und Ihnen?
HERR MEIER	Danke, es geht mir auch gut.

HEIDI	Hallo, Ute! Wie geht's?
UTE	Tag, Heidi! Ach, ich bin müde.
HEIDI	Ich auch. Zu viel Stress. Bis später!
UTE	Tschüss! Mach's gut!

 Was sagen Sie? *(What do you say?)* Read the following cue lines and prepare appropriate responses. Then role-play the scenes with a partner.

1. **Freut mich.** Two people meet for the first time and introduce themselves to each other.

   S1 Guten Tag!
   S2 . . .
   S1 Ich heiße . . . Und Sie, wie heißen Sie?
   S2 Ich heiße . . .
   S1 Freut mich.
   S2 Freut mich auch. Auf Wiedersehen!
   S1 . . .

2. **Wie geht's?** Two friends meet and ask each other how they are doing.

   S1 Hallo, . . . ! Wie geht's?
   S2 Tag, . . . ! . . .
   S1 . . .
   S2 Tschüss!
   S1 Mach's gut! . . .

Lerntipp
Using *Wie geht's?*

Take a few minutes to get acquainted with *Wie geht's!* Read the table of contents, and see how each chapter is organized. See how the audio activities in your book correspond to your Text CD and the Lab Audio CDs. You can also watch the *Minidramas* and the *Blickpunkt* segments on the Video, or explore the chapter themes online through the website, where you can also find self-assessment tests to help you review what you've learned. The web address is http://wiegehts.heinle.com.

Ich bin müde!

Wortschatz *(Vocabulary)*

■ You are responsible for knowing all the vocabulary of the *Wortschatz* (literally, "treasure of words"), including the headings. Be sure to learn the gender and plural forms of nouns! Words and phrases listed under *Zum Erkennen* are intended for comprehension only; you will not be asked to produce them actively. ■

- In German, all nouns are capitalized.
- The pronoun **ich** *(I)* is not capitalized unless it occurs at the beginning of a sentence. The pronoun **Sie** *(you)* is always capitalized.

Wie geht's? *(casual: How are you?)*

der Herr, die Herren *(pl.)*	*Mr.; gentleman*
die Frau, die Frauen *(pl.)*	*Mrs., Ms.; woman; wife*
Guten Morgen!	*Good morning.*
Guten Tag!	*Hello.*
Tag!	*Hi! (casual)*
Guten Abend!	*Good evening.*
Wie heißen Sie?	*What's your name? (formal)*
Mein Name ist . . .	*My name is . . .*
heißen	*to be called*
ich heiße . . .	*my name is . . .*
Sie heißen . . .	*your name is . . . (formal)*
Freut mich.	*Pleased to meet you.*
Wie geht es Ihnen?	*How are you? (formal)*
wie?	*how?*
Es geht mir gut.	*I'm fine.*
gut / schlecht	*good, fine / bad(ly)*
wunderbar	*wonderful(ly), great*
Ich bin müde.	*I'm tired.*
ja / nein	*yes / no*
danke / bitte	*thank you / please*
auch	*also, too*
nicht	*not*
und	*and*
Auf Wiedersehen!	*Good-bye.*
Tschüss!	*Good-bye. Bye. (colloquial)*
Mach's gut!	*Take care! (colloquial)*
Bis später!	*See you later! (colloquial)*

Zum Erkennen: Hallo! *(Hi! Hello!)*; ach *(oh)*; ich auch *(me too)*; zu viel Stress *(too much stress)*; AUCH: Lesen Sie laut! *(Read aloud!)*; Wie schreibt man das? *(How do you write that?)*; Buchstabieren Sie auf Deutsch! *(Spell in German!)*; Schreiben Sie, was ich buchstabiere! *(Write down what I spell!)*; Was sagen sie? *(What do they say?/ What are they saying?)*

◉ In modern German, the title **Frau** *(Mrs., Ms.)* is generally used for any adult woman regardless of her age or marital status. The title **Fräulein** *(Miss)* has more or less disappeared from use, although some people—especially older people in southern Germany—still use it to address young women under age 18.

◉ The words in *Zum Erkennen* are for recognition only, that is, passive vocabulary. They are listed in order of appearance in the dialogue(s). Following "AUCH" are other words or expressions from the chapter that will facilitate classroom instruction in German.

Fokus Greeting and Leave-taking

When greeting someone, **Guten Morgen!** is usually used until about 10:00 A.M., **Guten Tag!** between then and early evening, and **Guten Abend!** from about 5 P.M. on. Casual greetings (equivalent to *Hi!*) include **Tag!, Hallo!,** and **Grüß dich!** In Switzerland and Liechtenstein, people also say **Grüezi!,** and in southern Germany and Austria, **Servus!** or **Grüß Gott!** (lit. *Greetings in the name of God!*). The parting expressions **Tschüss!** or **Ciao [Tschau]!** are more informal than **Auf Wiedersehen!.** Note that **Gute Nacht!** *(Good night!)* is never used for leave-taking, but rather to wish someone a good night's sleep.

When you ask **Wie geht's?** or **Wie geht es Ihnen?,** expect a detailed answer about the other person's well-being. This is different from the English question *How are you?,* which elicits only a short response. Most German speakers pose this question only to people they already know well.

Mündliche Übungen *(Oral exercises)*

A. Mustersätze *(Patterns and cues)*

■ These pattern drills provide an opportunity to practice phrases from the dialogues and the vocabulary of each *Schritt*. Listen carefully and repeat the sentences until you can say them fluently. ■

1. Ich heiße ____.
   Willi Sanders → Ich heiße Willi Sanders.
   Robert Schmidt, Franziska Kleese, Anna Peters . . .
2. Wie geht es Ihnen, ____?
   Frau Fiedler → Wie geht es Ihnen, Frau Fiedler?
   Frau Lehmann, Herr Sanders, Herr und Frau Bauer . . .
3. Es geht mir ____.
   gut → Es geht mir gut.
   auch gut, nicht schlecht, wunderbar . . .

B. Das Alphabet

1. **Lesen Sie laut!** *(Read aloud.)*

a	ah	**g**	geh	**m**	emm	**s**	ess	**y**	üppsilon
b	beh	**h**	hah	**n**	enn	**t**	teh	**z**	tsett
c	tseh	**i**	ih	**o**	oh	**u**	uh	**ä**	äh (a-umlaut)
d	deh	**j**	yot	**p**	peh	**v**	fau	**ö**	öh (o-umlaut)
e	eh	**k**	kah	**q**	kuh	**w**	veh	**ü**	üh (u-umlaut)
f	eff	**l**	ell	**r**	err	**x**	iks	**ß**	ess-tsett

For capital letters, say **großes A (B, C . . .)**, for lower-case letters, **kleines D (E, F . . .)**. For further explanation of the **ß**-sound, see III A.6 in the Summary of Pronunciation section of the *Arbeitsbuch*. Note that there is also a specific pronunciation section (**Aussprache**) for each *Schritt* on your Lab Audio CD, each focusing on particular vowels and consonants. Make it a point to listen to it and to repeat what you hear.

2. **Ihr Name bitte!** *(Your name please.)* Ask classmates for their name and then how to spell it.

   BEISPIEL   S1 Wie heißen Sie?
   　　　　　 S2 Ich heiße Stefan Nentwig.
   　　　　　 S1 Wie schreibt man das?
   　　　　　 S2 . . . *(Spell Nentwig in German.)*

3. **Wie schreibt man das?** *(How do you write that?)* Ask your partner to spell the following words in German.

   BEISPIEL   S1 Wie schreibt man Autobahn?
   　　　　　 S2 A-U-T-O-B-A-H-N

Audi	Mercedes	Volkswagen
danke	Strudel	wunderbar
Gesundheit	tschüss	Zwieback
Kindergarten		

4. **Schreiben Sie, was ich buchstabiere!** *(Write down what I am spelling.)* Pick one of the words from the *Wortschatz* or the name of a famous German-speaking person and spell it. A partner listens, writes down what you spell, and reads it back to you. Take turns.

Aussprache *(Pronunciation):* a, e, er, i, o, u

CD 1, Track 11

■ The words listed below are either familiar words, cognates (words related to English), or proper names (**Erika, Amerika**). A simplified phonetic spelling for each sound is given in brackets. The colon (:) following a vowel means that the vowel is long. Pay particular attention to word stress as you hear it from your instructor or the recording. For a while, you may want to mark words for stress. ■

● The *Aussprache* section is closely tied to the Summary of Pronunciation in the front of the *Arbeitsbuch*. Be sure to see Part II, subsections 1–21.

Hören Sie zu und wiederholen Sie! *(Listen and repeat.)*

1. [a:] **A**bend, T**a**g, Ban**a**ne
2. [a] **A**nna, **A**lbert, w**a**s
3. [e:] **E**rika, P**e**ter, Am**e**rika
4. [e] **E**llen, H**e**rmann, **es**
5. [ə] *(unstressed* **e***)* Ut**e,** dank**e,** heiß**e**
6. [ʌ] *(final* **-er***)* Diet**er** Fiedl**er,** Rain**er** Mei**er**
7. [i:] **Ih**nen, Mar**i**a, Sab**i**ne
8. [i] **i**ch b**i**n, b**i**tte
9. [o:] M**o**nika, H**o**se, s**o**
10. [o] **O**skar, **o**ft, M**o**rgen
11. [u:] Ute, G**u**drun, g**u**t
12. [u] **u**nd, w**u**nderbar, Ges**u**ndheit

- As you may have noticed, double vowels (**Tee, Boot**), vowels followed by **h** (**geht, Schuh**), and the combination **ie** (**wie, Sie**) are long. Vowels followed by double consonants (two identical consonants as in **Anna, Sommer**) are short.

Schritt 2

 ## Was und wie ist das?

CD 1, Track 12

DEUTSCHPROFESSORIN	Hören Sie jetzt gut zu und antworten Sie auf Deutsch! Was ist das?
JIM MILLER	Das ist der Bleistift.
DEUTSCHPROFESSORIN	Welche Farbe hat der Bleistift?
SUSAN SMITH	Gelb.
DEUTSCHPROFESSORIN	Bilden Sie bitte einen Satz!
SUSAN SMITH	Der Bleistift ist gelb.
DEUTSCHPROFESSORIN	Ist das Heft auch gelb?
DAVID JENKINS	Nein, das Heft ist nicht gelb. Das Heft ist hellblau.
DEUTSCHPROFESSORIN	Gut!
SUSAN SMITH	Was bedeutet *hellblau*?
DEUTSCHPROFESSORIN	*Hellblau* bedeutet *light blue* auf Englisch.
SUSAN SMITH	Und wie sagt man *dark blue*?
DEUTSCHPROFESSORIN	*Dunkelblau.*
SUSAN SMITH	Ah, der Kuli ist dunkelblau.
DEUTSCHPROFESSORIN	Richtig! Das ist alles für heute. Für morgen lesen Sie bitte das Gespräch noch einmal und lernen Sie auch die Wörter!

 ### Jetzt sind Sie dran! *(Now it's your turn.)* Once you have familiarized yourself with the new vocabulary in the *Wortschatz* that follows, create your own dialogue with a partner. Take turns pointing at and identifying things and telling their colors.

BEISPIEL
S1 Was ist das?
S2 Das ist die Tafel.
S1 Richtig! Welche Farbe hat die Tafel?
S2 Die Tafel ist grün.
S1 Richtig!

Wortschatz

- In English, the DEFINITE ARTICLE has just one form: *the*. The German singular definite article has three forms: **der, das, die.** Some nouns take **der** and are called MASCULINE; some take **das** and are called NEUTER; and some take **die** and are called FEMININE. This is a grammatical distinction and has little to do with biological gender, although it is true that most nouns referring to female beings are feminine and most referring to male beings are masculine.

der Herr, die Frau, BUT das Kind (child)

Objects without biological gender, such as *table, book,* and *blackboard,* are by no means necessarily neuter. Many inanimate objects are masculine and many others are feminine.

das Buch, BUT der Tisch, die Tafel

Because the gender of many nouns is unpredictable, you must always learn the article with the noun.

Abbreviation	Listing	Plural Form
- *(add nothing)*	das Fenster, **-**	die Fenster
¨ *(add umlaut)*	der Mantel, **¨**	die Mäntel
-e *(add e)*	der Tisch, **-e**	die Tische
¨e *(add umlaut + e)*	der Stuhl, **¨e**	die Stühle
-er *(add er)*	das Bild, **-er**	die Bilder
¨er *(add umlaut + er)*	das Buch, **¨er**	die Bücher
-n *(add n)*	die Farbe, **-n**	die Farben
-en *(add en)*	die Frau, **-en**	die Frauen
-nen *(add nen)*	die Professorin, **-nen**	die Professorinnen
-s *(add s)*	der Kuli, **-s**	die Kulis

Die Farbe, -n *(color)*

blau   rot   orange   gelb

grün

braun   grau   rosa   schwarz   weiß

Das Zimmer, - *(room)*

der Bleistift, -e	*pencil*	das Heft, -e	*notebook*
Kuli, -s	*pen*	Papier, -e	*paper*
Stuhl, ¨e	*chair*	die Kreide	*chalk*
Tisch, -e	*table*	Tafel, -n	*blackboard*
das Bild, -er	*picture*	Tür, -en	*door*
Buch, ¨er	*book*	Wand, ¨e	*wall*
Fenster, -	*window*		

In German, the plural of nouns is formed in various ways that are often unpredictable. You must therefore learn the plural together with the article and the noun. Plurals are given in an abbreviated form in vocabulary lists and in dictionaries. These are the most common plural forms and their abbreviations.

These vocabulary sections are organized by topic, with the nouns listed alphabetically by gender.

The plural article for all nouns is **die.** In this book, when the noun being taught is not followed by one of the plural endings, it either does not have a plural or the plural is rarely used.

Weiteres *(Additional words and phrases)*

auf Deutsch / auf Englisch	*in German / in English*
für morgen	*for tomorrow*
hier / da	*here / there*
noch einmal	*again, once more*
richtig / falsch	*correct, right / wrong, false*
Was ist das?	*What is that?*
Das ist (nicht) . . .	*That is (not) . . .*
Welche Farbe hat . . . ?	*What color is . . . ?*
Was bedeutet . . . ?	*What does . . . mean?*
Wie sagt man . . . ?	*How does one say . . . ?*
Wo ist . . . ?	*Where is . . . ?*
antworten	*to answer*
fragen	*to ask*
hören	*to hear*
lernen	*to learn; to study*
lesen	*to read*
sagen	*to say*
wiederholen	*to repeat*
sein	*to be*
ich bin	*I am*
es ist	*it is*
sie sind	*they are*
Sie sind	*you (formal) are*

8er Pack Bleistifte,
mit Radiergummi

0.⁴⁹

1 Pckg. ✳

Zum Erkennen: Hören Sie gut zu! *(Listen carefully!)*; Bilden Sie einen Satz! *(Form a sentence.)*; hell(grün) / dunkel(blau) *(light[green] / dark[blue])*; Das ist alles für heute. *(That's all for today.)*; das Gespräch, -e *(dialogue, conversation)*; das Wort, ¨er *(word)*; AUCH: der Artikel, - (von) *(article [of])*; der Plural, -e (von) *(plural [of])*; Alle zusammen! *(All together!)*; Jetzt sind Sie dran! *(Now it's your turn.)*

◆ Mündliche Übungen

CD 1, Track 13

A. Mustersätze

1. Das ist ____.
   der Tisch → Das ist der Tisch.
   das Zimmer, die Tür, der Stuhl . . .
2. Wo ist ____? Da ist ____.
   das Papier → Wo ist das Papier? Da ist das Papier.
   der Kuli, die Kreide, das Bild . . .
3. Ist das ____? Nein, das ist nicht ____.
   die Tafel → Ist das die Tafel? Nein, das ist nicht die Tafel.
   der Tisch, das Papier, der Stuhl . . .
4. Das ist ____.
   schwarz → Das ist schwarz.
   rot, gelb, weiß . . .

B. Fragen und Antworten *(Questions and answers)*

1. Ist das Papier weiß? **Ja, das Papier ist weiß.**
   Ist das Buch gelb? die Tafel grün? die Kreide weiß? der Kuli rot?
2. Ist die Kreide grün? **Nein, die Kreide ist nicht grün.**
   Ist die Tafel rot? der Bleistift weiß? das Buch rosa? das Papier braun?
3. Die Kreide ist weiß. Ist das richtig? **Ja, das ist richtig.**
   Das Heft ist schwarz. Ist das richtig? **Nein, das ist nicht richtig.**
   Das Papier ist weiß. Die Tür ist orange. Der Kuli ist blau. Das Buch ist rosa. Der Tisch ist braun.
4. Ist das richtig? *(Is that correct?)* Ask a partner whether certain items are indeed the color you say they are. Take turns.

Lerntipp

Techniques for Building New Vocabulary

To remember vocabulary, you must use it. Name things in German as you see them in the course of your day. Label objects in your room or home using sticky notes. Practice new words aloud—the use of your auditory and motor memory will greatly enhance your learning efficiency. Be sure to learn the gender and plural with each noun. For some, the gender and plural are predictable; study Part 1 in the Appendix.

C. Wiederholung *(Review)*

1. **Was sagen sie?** *(What are they saying?)*

a. b. c.

2. **Wie schreibt man das?** Ask a partner to spell the names of the following animals in German.

Elefant	Maus	Tiger	Löwe
Katze	Hund	Giraffe	Hamster
Ratte	Goldfisch	Dinosaurier	Känguru

3. **Was buchstabiere ich?** *(What am I spelling?)* Think of any German word or name and spell it in German without saying the word. Let your partner write it down and read it back to you.

D. Artikel, Plurale und Farben
Determine the articles and plurals of the nouns listed below and ask questions about the colors of your German textbook.

1. Was ist der Artikel? Tür → die Tür
   Zimmer, Bleistift, Bild, Kreide, Kuli, Stuhl, Tafel, Buch, Tisch, Fenster, Farbe, Papier, Wand, Heft, Wort, Herr, Frau
2. Was ist der Plural? Kuli → die Kulis
   Tür, Bild, Bleistift, Buch, Heft, Tisch, Fenster, Tafel, Stuhl, Wort, Farbe
3. Welche Farben hat das Deutschbuch?

Aussprache: e, ä, ö, ü, eu, au, ai, ei, ie

CD 1, Track 14
Hören Sie zu und wiederholen Sie!

1. [e:]	Erika, Käthe, geht	6. [ü]	Jürgen Müller, Günter, müssen
2. [e]	Wände, Hände, hängen	7. [oi]	Deutsch, freut, Europa
3. [ö:]	Öl, hören, Österreich	8. [au]	Frau Paula Bauer, auf, auch
4. [ö]	Ötker, Pöppel, Wörter	9. [ai]	Rainer, Kreide, weiß
5. [ü:]	Tür, für, Stühle		

- Pay special attention to the pronunciation of **ei** and **ie** (as in *Einstein's niece*):

10. [ai]	heißen, Heidi Meier	[ai / i:]	Beispiel, Heinz Fiedler
[i:]	Sie, wie, Wiedersehen		

For further review, see the Summary of Pronunciation in the front of your Arbeitsbuch. Study Part II, subsections 22–36 and 37–41.

Fokus ## What's in a Name?

German society has become more multicultural in recent decades, a development reflected in German given names. In addition to traditional names such as Stefan, Michael, Thomas, and Philipp for boys, or Julia, Sara, Anna, and Maria for girls, there are more and more foreign names as a result of immigration and the media, such as Dennis, Kevin, Marco, Saskia, Timo, Aaliyah, Yannick, and Yasemin. In Germany, parents must get local government approval for the name they choose for their child. The reason for this is to prevent children from having names that might cause them embarrassment or cause others confusion. The name chosen must be perceived as a "real" name and the gender must be recognizable. Hence, you aren't likely to find anyone in Germany with a name as unique as Moon Unit, which is what Frank Zappa, the late US rock musician, called his daughter.

10 / Schritte / **Beginnen wir!**

Schritt 3

CD 2,
Track 1

VERKÄUFERIN	Na, wie ist die Hose?
CHRISTIAN	Zu groß und zu lang.
VERKÄUFERIN	Und der Pulli?
MEIKE	Zu teuer.
CHRISTIAN	Aber die Farben sind toll. Schade!
VERKÄUFERIN	Guten Tag! Was darf's sein?
SILVIA	Ich brauche ein paar Bleistifte und Papier. Was kosten die Bleistifte?
VERKÄUFERIN	Fünfundfünfzig Cent (€ 0,55).
SILVIA	Und das Papier hier?
VERKÄUFERIN	Zwei Euro vierzig (€ 2,40).
SILVIA	Gut. Ich nehme sechs Bleistifte und das Papier.
VERKÄUFERIN	Ist das alles?
SILVIA	Ja, danke.
VERKÄUFERIN	Fünf Euro siebzig (€ 5,70).

 Jetzt sind Sie dran! *(Now it's your turn.)* Once you have familiarized yourself with the new vocabulary in the *Wortschatz* that follows, create your own dialogue. Ask a partner about certain items in a store or other shopping wishes.

BEISPIEL
S1 Na, wie ist . . . ?   S1 . . . Ist das alles?
S2 Zu . . . / Wunderbar!   S2 Ja, . . . / Nein, ich brauche . . .

Wortschatz

Die Zahl, -en *(number)*

1	eins	11	elf	21	einundzwanzig	0	null
2	zwei	12	zwölf	22	zweiundzwanzig	10	zehn
3	drei	13	dreizehn	30	dreißig	100	hundert
4	vier	14	vierzehn	40	vierzig	101	hunderteins
5	fünf	15	fünfzehn	50	fünfzig	200	zweihundert
6	sechs	16	se**ch**zehn	60	se**ch**zig	1 000	tausend
7	sieben	17	sie**b**zehn	70	sie**b**zig	1 001	tausendeins
8	acht	18	achtzehn	80	achtzig	10 000	zehntausend
9	neun	19	neunzehn	90	neunzig	100 000	hunderttausend
10	zehn	20	zwanzig	100	hundert	1 000 000	eine Million

🔸 To reduce confusion with **drei**, speakers sometimes use the term **zwo** as a substitute for **zwei**, especially on the phone.

As a memory aid, note these similarities between English and German:

-zehn = *-teen*   **vierzehn** = *fourteen*   **-zig** = *-ty*   **vierzig** = *forty*

- 21–29, 31–39, and so on to 91–99 follow the pattern of "four-and-twenty **(vierundzwanzig)** blackbirds baked in a pie."

- German numbers above twelve are seldom written out, except on checks. When they are written out, however, they are written as one word, no matter how long:

  234 567: **zweihundertvierunddreißigtausendfünfhundertsiebenundsechzig**

- German uses a period or a space, where English uses a comma.

  € 2,75   BUT $2.75
  € 1 600,00 (or 1.600,00) BUT $1,600.00

- The numbers 1 and 7 are written differently, as shown at right.

1
EINS

7
SIEBEN

Note that **die Hose** is singular in German; **die Jeans,** however, is plural.

Die Kleidung *(clothing)*

der Mantel, ¨

das T-Shirt, -s

das Sweatshirt, -s

das Hemd, -en

die Jeans *(pl.)*
die Hose, -n

die Bluse, -n

der Schuh, -e

der Rock, ¨e

die Jacke, -n   das Kleid, -er   der Pullover, -; der Pulli, -s

Das Gegenteil, -e *(opposite)*

dick / dünn	*thick, fat / thin, skinny*
groß / klein	*tall, big, large / short, small, little*
lang / kurz	*long / short*
langsam / schnell	*slow(ly) / fast, quick(ly)*
neu / alt	*new / old*
sauber / schmutzig	*clean, neat / dirty*
teuer / billig	*expensive / inexpensive, cheap*

Weiteres

aber	*but, however*
oder	*or*
zu	*too (+ adjective or adverb)*
wie viel? / wie viele?	*how much / how many?*
kosten	*to cost, come to (a certain amount)*
Was kostet / kosten . . . ?	*How much is / are . . . ?*
Das kostet . . .	*That comes to . . .*
brauchen	*to need*
nehmen	*to take*

zählen	*to count*
ich zähl**e**	*I count*
wir	*we count*
sie } zähl**en**	*they count*
Sie	*you* (formal) *count*

der Cent, -s (ein Cent, fünf Cent)	*cent (one cent, five cents)*
der Euro, -s (ein Euro, zehn Euro)	*euro (one euro, ten euros)*

Zum Erkennen: im Kaufhaus *(in the department store)*; der Verkäufer, - / die Verkäuferin, -nen *(sales clerk)*; na *(well)*; toll *(super)*; Schade! *(Too bad!)*; Was darf's sein? *(May I help you?)*; ein paar *(a couple of)*; Ist das alles? *(Is that all?)*; AUCH: von . . . bis *(from . . . to)*; die Seite, -n *(page)*; auf Seite . . . *(on page . . .)*; der Preis, -e *(price)*; Wie ist die Telefonnummer / Adresse (von) . . . ? *(What's the phone number / address [of] . . . ?)*; das Beispiel, -e *(example)*; Wie geht's weiter? *(What comes next?)*

Mündliche Übungen

CD 2, Track 2 **A. Mustersätze**

1. Das ist ____.
   der Schuh → Das ist der Schuh.
   die Jacke, das Hemd, der Mantel, der Pulli . . .
2. Ist ____ ____? Ja, ____ ist ____.
   die Jacke / grau → Ist die Jacke grau? Ja, die Jacke ist grau.
   die Hose / braun; der Rock / blau; die Bluse / rosa; der Pullover / rot . . .
3. Ist ____ ____? Nein, ____ ist nicht ____.
   der Mantel / lang → Ist der Mantel lang? Nein, der Mantel ist nicht lang.
   das Hemd / schmutzig; das Kleid / neu; der Pulli / dick; das Sweatshirt / teuer . . .
4. Sind ____ ____? Nein, ____ sind nicht ____.
   die Schuhe / groß → Sind die Schuhe groß? Nein, die Schuhe sind nicht groß.
   die Röcke / kurz; die Mäntel / dünn; die T-Shirts / blau; die Jeans / schwarz . . .
5. Was kostet ____?
   das Papier → Was kostet das Papier?
   das Heft, der Mantel, die Jacke, der Pulli . . .
6. Was kosten ____?
   die Bleistifte → Was kosten die Bleistifte?
   die Kulis, die Bücher, die Bilder, die Schuhe, die Jeans . . .

B. Hören Sie gut zu und wiederholen Sie!

1. Wir zählen von eins bis zehn: eins, zwei, drei, vier, fünf, sechs, sieben, acht, neun, zehn.
2. Wir zählen von zehn bis zwanzig: zehn, elf, zwölf, dreizehn, vierzehn, fünfzehn, sechzehn, siebzehn, achtzehn, neunzehn, zwanzig.
3. Wir zählen von zwanzig bis dreißig: zwanzig, einundzwanzig, zweiundzwanzig, dreiundzwanzig, vierundzwanzig, fünfundzwanzig, sechsundzwanzig, siebenundzwanzig, achtundzwanzig, neunundzwanzig, dreißig.
4. Wir zählen von zehn bis hundert: zehn, zwanzig, dreißig, vierzig, fünfzig, sechzig, siebzig, achtzig, neunzig, hundert.
5. Wir zählen von hundert bis tausend: hundert, zweihundert, dreihundert, vierhundert, fünfhundert, sechshundert, siebenhundert, achthundert, neunhundert, tausend.

C. Seitenzahlen *(Page numbers):* Lesen Sie laut auf Deutsch!

Seite 1, 7, 8, 9, 11, 12, 17, 21, 25, 32, 43, 54, 66, 89, 92, 101

 D. Inventar With an employee, played by a partner, take inventory of the items you have in stock in your store.

BEISPIEL   Jacke / 32
           S1 Wie viele Jacken?
           S2 Zweiunddreißig Jacken.

1. Pullover / 42
2. Rock / 14
3. Hemd / 66
4. Kleid / 19
5. Hose / 21
6. Jeans / 102
7. Sweatshirt / 89
8. T-Shirt / 37
9. Schuh / 58

E. Preise: Lesen Sie laut!

€ 0,25 / € 0,75 / € 1,10 / € 2,50 / € 8,90 / € 30,00 / € 45,54 / € 80,88

F. Telefonnummern und Adressen

1. **Wie ist die Telefonnummer und die Adresse?** Ask each other for the phone number and address of persons listed below.

BEISPIEL   Wie ist die Telefonnummer von *(of)* Jutta Scheurer und was ist ihre *(her)* Adresse?
Die Nummer ist 4 27 18 12 (vier zwei sieben eins acht eins zwei or vier siebenundzwanzig achtzehn zwölf) und die Adresse ist Wolfszugstraße 33.

● Note that in German telephone books a hyphen following a name usually indicates "street", e.g., **Bach-** = **Bachstraße.**

Scheufler Heike, Schiller-2	8 02 25 75	**Schiebel Renate,** Haydn-20	8 30 64 63
-Gisela, Dresdner-51	8 41 26 74	**Schiebold Heinz,** Hofmann-16	8 80 19 77
-Gustav, Schumann-8	4 11 65 75	**-Katja,** Busch-30	2 81 53 22
Scheumann Ulf, Zwingli-7	4 27 29 69	**-Joachim,** Lange-5	2 59 83 55
Scheurer Ingo, Schul-20b	2 84 48 43	**Schiebschick Kai,** Berliner-3	2 51 49 51
-Jutta, Wolfszug-33	4 27 18 12	**Schiedmeier Ina,** Torgauer 11	4 95 63 56
-Werner, Meißner- 8	4 41 46 40	**Schiedewitz Elke,** Schlüter-2	3 11 83 85
Scheurich Sven, Neue-5b	4 16 04 71	**Schiefer Birgit,** Ring-1	2 02 07 43
Scheuring Jan, Scheriner-9	2 59 15 91	**-Christel,** Park-17	2 84 13 08
-Jochen, Böttger-4	8 03 12 63	**-Wolfgang,** Werft-2	2 70 58 19
Schewe Cornelia, Tannen-3	8 80 82 35	**Schiefner Jobst,** Bahnhof-5	3 11 77 71
-Uwe, Blumen-1	2 81 34 51	**-Manfred,** Dom-3	3 13 93 62
Schibalski Paul, Bach-2a	4 21 94 83	**Schiffer Arndt,** Hohe-19	4 41 92 91
Schicht Carsten, Haupt-27	4 40 16 69	**-Cornelia,** Dürer-9	4 71 26 22
-Eberhard, Azaleenweg-3	8 38 72 78	**-Dorothea,** Niederauer-28	2 52 30 50
Schick Bettina, Görlitzer-12	8 36 33 78	**-Torsten,** Platanen-13	4 76 10 28
Schicke Detlef, Kant-16	2 01 24 71	**Schiffke Jens,** Oschatzer-33	4 96 79 83
-Oliver, Schäfer-10	2 61 01 96	**Schlachter Karl,** Leipziger-2	3 11 77 16
Schickedanz Ute, Bach-17	4 12 48 75	**Schlampi Mario,** Hofwiesen-7	3 10 49 18
Schickmann Udo, Park-31	4 11 26 61	**Schlaumann Hans,** Suttner-9	2 54 25 14

2. **Wie ist Ihre Telefonnummer?** Ask other students about their phone number.

BEISPIEL   S1 Wie ist Ihre Telefonnummer?
S2 Meine Telefonnummer ist 781–555–4601.

G. Wiederholung

1. **Fragen und Antworten** Ask each other the following questions.
   a. Wie geht es Ihnen? Sind Sie müde?
   b. Wie heißen Sie? Heißen Sie . . . ?
   c. Was ist das? Ist das . . . ? *(Point to items in the classroom.)*
   d. Welche Farbe hat der Tisch? die Tafel? . . .
   e. Was ist auch grün? blau? . . .

2. **Wie schreibt man das?** Ask your partner how to spell the following names. You can also add names to the list.

Mozart	Dürer	Nietzsche	Röntgen
Beethoven	Barlach	Aichinger	Zeppelin
Strauß	Kandinsky	Wohmann	Schwarzenegger

H. Artikel, Plurale und Adjektive Ask your partner questions about the articles, plurals, and adjectives below.

1. Was ist der Artikel von Mantel? Kleidung? Pulli? Bluse? Hemd? Rock? Hose? Kleid? Jacke? Schuh? T-Shirt? . . .
2. Was ist der Plural von Schuh? Jacke? Rock? Kleid? Hemd? Bluse? Pullover? Mantel?
3. Sprechen Sie langsam oder schnell? Hören Sie gut oder schlecht? Sind Sie groß oder klein? Sind meine Schuhe sauber oder schmutzig? . . .
4. Was ist das Gegenteil von richtig? alt? schlecht? schnell? billig? dick? nein? danke? . . .

I. Beschreiben Sie bitte! Describe some of your clothing or one or two items you have with you.

BEISPIEL   *Die Hose ist blau. Die Schuhe sind . . .*

J. Kettenreaktion: Rechnen wir! *(Chain reaction: Let's count!)*

1. **Wie viel ist das?** Lesen Sie laut!

BEISPIEL $4 + 4 = 8$ *Vier plus vier ist acht.*
                  $8 - 4 = 4$ *Acht minus vier ist vier.*

a. $3 + 2 = 5$ d. $8 + 1 = 9$ g. $8 - 2 = 6$
b. $7 + 3 = 10$ e. $10 - 2 = 8$ h. $7 - 6 = 1$
c. $1 + 1 = 2$ f. $9 - 4 = 5$ i. $5 - 5 = 0$

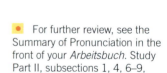

2. **Wie geht's weiter?** *(What comes next?)*

a. $100 - 10 = $ ___   b. $70 - 7 = $ ___
   $90 - 10 = $ ___ $63 - 7 = $ ___
   . . .   . . .

K. Was sagen Sie? Read the dialogue in the left-hand column below. Then be prepared to act out a similar dialogue with a partner using objects in the classroom.

S1 Ist das die Tafel?	S1 Ist das . . . ?
S2 Nein, das ist nicht die Tafel.	S2 Nein, das ist nicht . . .
Das ist die Wand.	Das ist . . .
S1 Wo ist die Tafel?	S1 Wo ist . . . ?
S2 Da ist die Tafel.	S2 . . .
S1 Welche Farbe hat die Tafel?	S1 Welche Farbe hat . . . ?
S2 Die Tafel ist grün.	S2 . . . ist . . .
S1 Was ist auch grün?	S1 Was ist auch . . . ?
S2 Das Buch ist auch grün.	S2 . . . ist auch . . .
S1 Wie ist das Buch? Ist das Buch alt?	S1 Wie ist . . . ?
S2 Nein, das Buch ist neu.	S2 . . .

Aussprache: l, s, st, sp, sch, f, v, z

CD 2,
Track 3
Hören Sie gut zu und wiederholen Sie!

For further review, see the Summary of Pronunciation in the front of your *Arbeitsbuch*. Study Part II, subsections 1, 4, 6–9, and 11–12.

1. [l]   lernen, lesen, Pullover
2. [z]   sie sind, sieben, sauber
3. [s]   Professorin, heißen, Preis
4. [st]   Fenster, kosten, ist
5. [št]   Stefan, Stuhl, Stein
6. [šp]   Sport, Beispiel, Gespräch

7. [š]   schnell, schlecht, schwarz
8. [f]   fünf, fünfzehn, fünfzig
   [f]   vier, vierzehn, vierzig
9. [ts]   Zimmer, Zahl, zählen
10. [z / ts]   sieben, siebzig,
                  siebenundsiebzig

Fokus   Trendsetters of the Fashion World

German fashion has always been known for outstanding quality and workmanship, but it is also beginning to have more of an impact on international fashion trends. Today, Jil Sander, Wolfgang Joop, Hugo Boss, Karl Lagerfeld, Escada, and Strenesse are well-known names in every major city. Fresh ideas are also coming from the German "eco-fashion" scene: Britta Steilmann, for example, has explored new and interesting directions with her collections made of environmentally friendly materials. Twice a year, fashion takes center stage in the trade fair metropolises of Berlin, Düsseldorf, Cologne, and Munich. There, international designers and manufacturers meet with retail buyers to set the latest styles for the coming season.

Das Wetter im April

CD 2, Track 4	

NORBERT   Es ist schön heute, nicht wahr?
JULIA   Ja, wirklich. Die Sonne scheint wieder!
RUDI   Nur der Wind ist kühl.
JULIA   Ach, das macht nichts.
NORBERT   Ich finde es toll.

HANNES   Mensch, so ein Sauwetter! Es schneit schon wieder.
MARTIN   Na und?
HANNES   In Mallorca ist es schön warm.
MARTIN   Wir sind aber hier und nicht in Mallorca.
HANNES   Schade!

LEA   Das Wetter ist furchtbar, nicht wahr?
HEIKO   Das finde ich auch. Es regnet und regnet!
SARA   Und es ist wieder so kalt. Nur 7 Grad!
HEIKO   Ja, typisch April.

Jetzt sind Sie dran! Based on the new vocabulary in the *Wortschatz* that follows, create your own dialogue talking about the weather and how you like it.

BEISPIEL   S1 Es ist . . . heute, nicht wahr?
　　　　　　S2 Ja, . . . / Nein, . . .

Wortschatz

 Note that the names of the **Jahreszeiten** are all masculine.

Das Jahr, -e *(year)*
Die Jahreszeit, -en *(season)*

der Frühling	der Sommer	der Herbst	der Winter

Tage und Monate *(days and months)*

 Note that the names of the **Tage** and **Monate** are all masculine.

For *Saturday,* people in northern and central Germany generally use **Sonnabend,** while those in southern Germany say **Samstag** (derived from the Hebrew word *Sabbat*).

der Tag, -e	*day*		der Monat, -e	*month*
Montag	*Monday*		Januar	*January*
Dienstag	*Tuesday*		Februar	*February*
Mittwoch	*Wednesday*		März	*March*
Donnerstag	*Thursday*		April	*April*
Freitag	*Friday*		Mai	*May*
Samstag	*Saturday*		Juni	*June*
Sonntag	*Sunday*		Juli	*July*
			August	*August*
			September	*September*
			Oktober	*October*
			November	*November*
			Dezember	*December*

Das Wetter *(weather)*

Es ist . . .	It's . . .	heiß / kalt	*hot / cold*
Es regnet.	*It's raining.*	warm / kühl	*warm / cool*
Es schneit.	*It's snowing.*	furchtbar	*awful, terrible*
Die Sonne scheint.	*The sun is shining.*	prima	*great, wonderful*
		schön	*nice, beautiful*
		super	*superb, super*
		toll	*great, terrific*
		windig	*windy*

Weiteres

die Woche, -n	*week*	nicht wahr?	*isn't it? isn't that*
Die Woche hat	*The week has*		*right?*
sieben Tage.	*seven days.*	Wann sind Sie	*When were you*
heute / morgen	*today / tomorrow*	geboren?	*born?*
nur	*only*	Ich bin <u>im Mai</u>	*I was born in*
sehr	*very*	geboren.	*May.*
(schon) wieder	*(already) again*	finden	*to find*
wirklich	*really, indeed*	Ich finde es . . .	*I think it's . . .*
Schade!	*Too bad!*	Das finde ich auch.	*I think so, too.*

> ● **Im** is used with the names of the months and seasons: **im Mai, im Winter.**

Zum Erkennen: der Wind *(wind)*; Das macht nichts. *(It doesn't matter. That's okay.)*; Mensch, so ein Sauwetter! *(Man, what lousy weather!)*; Na und? *(So what?)*; wir sind *(we are)*; Grad *(degrees)*; typisch *(typically)*; AUCH: Hören Sie gut zu! *(Listen carefully!)*; die Temperatur, -en *(temperature)*

Mündliche Übungen

CD 2, Track 5

A. Wie heißen die Jahreszeiten, Monate und Tage?

1. Die Jahreszeiten heißen der Frühling, der Sommer, der Herbst, der Winter.
2. Die Monate heißen Januar, Februar, März, April, Mai, Juni, Juli, August, September, Oktober, November, Dezember.
3. Die Tage heißen Montag, Dienstag, Mittwoch, Donnerstag, Freitag, Samstag, Sonntag.

B. Mustersätze

1. Es ist heute ____.
   schön → Es ist heute schön.
   kühl, windig, warm . . .

2. Ich finde es ____.
   toll → Ich finde es toll.
   gut, prima, wunderbar, furchtbar . . .

3. Ich bin im ____ geboren.
   Juli → Ich bin im Juli geboren.
   März, Sommer, Winter . . .

C. Wiederholung

1. **Antworten Sie mit JA!**

   BEISPIEL   Wiederholen Sie das noch einmal?
   Ja, ich wiederhole das noch einmal.

   a. Lesen Sie das auf Deutsch?   c. Brauchen Sie das Buch?
   b. Lernen Sie das für morgen?   d. Nehmen Sie das Heft?

2. **Antworten Sie mit NEIN!**

   BEISPIEL   Ist das die Kreide?
   Nein, das ist nicht die Kreide.

   a. Ist das die Wand?   c. Sind das die Schuhe?
   b. Ist das der Pulli?   d. Sind das die Klassenzimmer?

   BEISPIEL   Ist die Kreide gelb?
   Nein, die Kreide ist nicht gelb.

   e. Ist die Antwort richtig?   g. Ist das Wetter gut?
   f. Ist die Farbe schön?   h. Ist das typisch?

3. **Zahlen: Wie geht's weiter?** One person states an addition or subtraction problem. A classmate gives the answer, then turns to another student and adds or subtracts another number. Follow the model.

BEISPIEL S1 Sieben plus vier?
S2 Sieben plus vier ist elf. Elf minus acht?
S3 Elf minus acht ist drei. Drei plus . . . ?

4. **Was kostet das?** Write prices on the board for others to read aloud.

5. **Gegenteile** Choose the pair of German adjectives that describe each drawing.

___ kurz / lang   ___ neu / alt   ___ schmutzig / sauber
___ dünn / dick   ___ klein / groß

a.

b.

c.

d.

e.

D. Fragen

1. Wie ist das Wetter hier im Winter? im Sommer? im Frühling? im Herbst?
2. Was ist der Artikel von Montag? September? Herbst? Juni? Monat? Jahr? Woche?
3. Welcher Tag ist heute? morgen?
4. Wie viele Tage hat die Woche? Wie heißen die Tage?
5. Wie viele Tage hat der September? der Oktober? der Februar?
6. Wie viele Monate hat das Jahr? Wie heißen die Monate?
7. Wie viele Wochen hat das Jahr?
8. Wie viele Jahreszeiten hat das Jahr? Wie heißen die Jahreszeiten?
9. Wie heißen die Wintermonate? die Sommermonate? die Herbstmonate?
10. Wie ist das Wetter heute? Scheint die Sonne oder regnet es?

Fokus The German Climate

Although Germany lies between the 47th and 55th parallel north, roughly as far north as northern New England and southern Canada, its climate is generally far milder because of the effect of the warming Gulf Stream. Overall, Germany enjoys a temperate climate, ample rainfall throughout the year, and an absence of extreme heat and cold. In the north-west, summers tend to be cool and winters mild. Toward the east and south, the climate becomes more continental, with greater temperature differences between day and night, and summer and winter. Average daytime temperatures in Berlin are 30°F in January and 64°F in July; in Munich, they are 33°F in January and 73°F in July. Autumns are usually mild, sunny, and drier than other seasons. Between December and March, the mountainous regions of Germany can always expect snow. At the **Zugspitze**, the highest point in the German Alps, snow may pile up from 13 to 16 feet. In the Black Forest, it may average 5 feet. (For information on the current weather in Germany, visit *www.wetter.de*.)

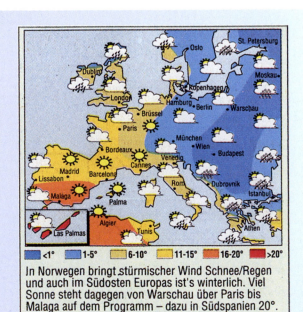

In Norwegen bringt stürmischer Wind Schnee/Regen und auch im Südosten Europas ist's winterlich. Viel Sonne steht dagegen von Warschau über Paris bis Malaga auf dem Programm – dazu in Südspanien 20°.

E. Temperaturen European thermometers use the Celsius scale. On that scale, water freezes at 0°C and boils at 100°C. Normal body temperature is about 37°C, and fever starts at about 37.6°C. To convert Fahrenheit units into Celsius, subtract 32, multiply by 5, then divide by 9. To convert Celsius degrees into Fahrenheit, multiply by 9, divide by 5, then add 32.

1. **Wie viel Grad Celsius sind das?** *(How many degrees Celsius is that?)* Use the thermometer as a reference.

   BEISPIEL   32°F = 0°C
   Zweiunddreißig Grad Fahrenheit sind null Grad Celsius.

   100°F, 96°F, 84°F, 68°F, 41°F, 23°F, −4°F, −13°F

2. **Wie ist das Wetter?** *(What's the weather like?)*

   BEISPIEL   12°C (zwölf Grad Celsius) *Es ist kühl.*

   21°C, 0°C, 30°C, 38°C, −10°C, −25°C

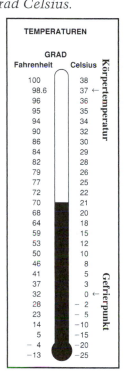

TEMPERATUREN		
GRAD		
Fahrenheit	Celsius	Körpertemperatur
100	38	
98.6	37 ←	
96	36	
95	35	
94	34	
90	32	
86	30	
84	29	
82	28	
79	26	
77	25	
72	22	
70	21	
68	20	
64	18	
59	15	
53	12	
50	10	
46	8	
41	5	
37	3	
32	0	Gefrierpunkt
28	−2	
23	−5	
14	−10	
5	−15	
−4	−20	
−13	−25	

Aussprache: r; p, t, k; final b, d, g; j, h

CD 2, Track 6

Hören Sie zu und wiederholen Sie!

1. [r]   **r**ichtig, **r**egnet, **r**ot
2. [ʌ]   wi**r**, vie**r**, nu**r**
   BUT [ʌ / r] Tü**r** / Tü**r**en;
   Papie**r** / Papie**r**e; Jah**r** / Jah**r**e
3. [p]   **P**ulli, **P**lural, **p**lus
   AND [p] Herb**st**, Jako**b**, gel**b**
   BUT [p / b] gel**b** / gel**b**e
4. [t]   **Th**eo, **T**ür, Doro**th**ea
   AND [t] un**d**, **t**ausend, Bil**d**
   BUT [t / d] Bil**d** / Bil**d**er
5. [k]   **k**ühl, **k**urz, **K**uli, dan**k**e
   AND [k] sa**g**t, fra**g**t, Ta**g**
   BUT [k / g] sa**g**t / sa**g**en;
   fra**g**t / fra**g**en; Ta**g** / Ta**g**e
6. [j]   **j**a, **J**ahr, **J**anuar
7. [h]   **h**ören, **h**eiß, **h**at
8. [:]   **z**ählen, **n**ehmen, **I**hnen

● For further review, see the Summary of Pronunciation in the front of your *Arbeitsbuch.* Study Part III, subsections 1–3, 10, and 17.

Fokus   The Benefits of Learning German

Learning German will bring you benefits you may not have thought of before. In professional terms, you will be at an advantage regardless of whether your interests are in business, law, or academics. After all, the German economy is the largest in Europe. Germany and Austria are active partners in the European Union, and many fields (such as music, art, literature, archaeology, philosophy, physics—to name just a few) reflect the creative work of artists and researchers from the German-speaking world. In personal terms, knowing German will open the doors to another culture. Because German and English are closely related Germanic languages, it is probable that in the course of your studies you will gain new insights into your own language as well.

Wie spät ist es?

CD 2,
Track 7

RITA	Hallo, Axel! Wie spät ist es?
AXEL	Hallo, Rita! Es ist zehn vor acht.
RITA	Oje, in zehn Minuten habe ich Philosophie.
AXEL	Dann mach's gut, tschüss!
RITA	Ja, tschüss!

PHILLIP	Hallo, Steffi! Wie viel Uhr ist es denn?
STEFFI	Tag, Phillip! Es ist halb zwölf.
PHILLIP	Gehen wir jetzt essen?
STEFFI	Okay, die Vorlesung beginnt erst um Viertel nach eins.

HERR RICHTER	Wann sind Sie denn heute fertig?
HERR HEROLD	Um zwei. Warum?
HERR RICHTER	Spielen wir heute Tennis?
HERR HEROLD	Ja, prima! Es ist jetzt halb eins. Um Viertel vor drei dann?
HERR RICHTER	Gut! Bis später!

Jetzt sind Sie dran! Based on the new vocabulary in the *Wortschatz* that follows, create your own dialogue with a partner. Ask for the time and talk about your plans for the rest of the day.

BEISPIEL   S1 Hallo, wie spät ist es? / Wie viel Uhr ist es?
S2 Es ist . . .

Wortschatz

- German has a formal (see Chapter 7) and informal way of telling time. The informal system is used in everyday speech and varies somewhat from region to region. The standard system below is certain to be understood everywhere.

die Uhrzeit, -en (time of day)

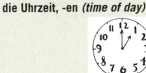

Es ist ein Uhr. Es ist eins.	Es ist zwei Uhr. Es ist zwei.	Es ist Viertel nach zwei.	Es ist halb drei.
Es ist Viertel vor drei.	Es ist zehn (Minuten) vor drei.	Es ust fünf nach vier.	Es ist zwanzig (Minuten) nach sieben.

Glockenturm (bell tower) *in Innsbruck*

Stunde refers to *duration* or to a *particular class:* **Eine Stunde hat 60 Minuten. Die Deutschstunde ist von acht bis neun.** The noun **Uhr** refers to clock time: **Es ist 9 Uhr.** *It is nine o'clock.*

die Minute, -n	*minute*	morgens	*in the morning*
Sekunde, -n	*second*	mittags	*at noon*
Stunde, -n	*hour*	nachmittags	*in the afternoon*
Uhr, -en	*watch, clock; o'clock*	abends	*in the evening*
		Wie spät ist es?	*How late is it?*
Zeit, -en	*time*	Wie viel Uhr ist es?	*What time is it?*

Weiteres

der Student, -en	*student (male)*
die Studentin, -nen	*student (female)*
der Kurs, -e	*course*
die Vorlesung, -en	*lecture, (university) class*
Es ist <u>ein Uhr</u> (zwei Uhr).	*It's one o'clock (two o'clock).*
Es ist eins (zwei).	*It's one (two).*
<u>(um) eins</u>	*(at) one o'clock*
(um) Viertel nach eins, 1.15	*(at) quarter past one, 1:15*
(um) halb zwei, <u>1.30</u>	*(at) half past one, 1:30*
(um) Viertel vor zwei, 1.45	*(at) quarter to two, 1:45*
fertig	*finished, done*
jetzt	*now*
Bitte!	*here: You're welcome.*
beginnen	*to begin*
essen	*to eat*
gehen	*to go*
Tennis spielen	*to play tennis*
haben	*to have*
ich habe	*I have*
es hat	*it has*
wir	*we have*
sie } haben	*they have*
Sie	*you (formal) have*
Ich habe eine Frage.	*I have a question.*
Ich habe keine Zeit.	*I don't have time.*

Zum Erkennen: Oje! *(Oh, no!)*; denn *(flavoring particle used for emphasis)*; erst *(only, not until)*; warum? *(why?)*; AUCH: Was tun Sie wann? *(What do you do when?)*

> ● **Ein Uhr,** BUT **Um eins.**
>
> ● Expressions of time used to be punctuated differently in German than in English: *1:30* vs. **1.30.** Today both styles are used in German. While digital clocks separate hours from minutes with a colon, newspapers and magazines commonly use a simple period.

Mündliche Übungen

CD 2, Track 8

A. Wie spät ist es?

1. 1.00: **Es ist** ein **Uhr.**
   3.00, 5.00
2. 1.05: **Es ist** fünf **nach** eins.
   3.05, 9.10
3. 1.15: **Es ist Viertel nach** eins.
   2.15, 6.15
4. 1.30: **Es ist halb** zwei.
   4.30, 6.30

5. 1.40: **Es ist** zwanzig **vor** zwei.
   5.40, 9.50
6. 1.45: **Es ist Viertel vor** zwei.
   3.45, 9.45
7. 9.00: **Die Vorlesung ist um** neun.
   12.15, 1.30

B. Mustersätze

1. ____ Sie jetzt? Ja, ich ____ jetzt.
   essen → Essen Sie jetzt? Ja, ich esse jetzt.
   gehen, fragen, lernen, antworten, beginnen . . .
2. Ich spiele ____ Tennis.
   heute → Ich spiele heute Tennis.
   jetzt, morgens, nachmittags, abends, wieder . . .
3. Wann ____ ____ heute fertig?
   Sie → Wann sind Sie heute fertig?
   Mark, ich, Niels und Alexandra . . .
4. ____ ____ keine Zeit.
   ich → Ich habe keine Zeit.
   wir, Maria, Sophie und Sascha . . .

Visit the **Wie geht's?** iLrn website for more review and practice.

C. Wiederholung

1. **Wie ist das Wetter?**

   a.   b.   c.   d.

2. **Wie fragen Sie?** Formulate a logical question for each answer.

> BEISPIEL   Ja, ich bin müde.
> *Sind Sie müde?*

a. Danke, gut.
b. Das Buch ist grau.
c. Nein, ich heiße nicht Fiedler.
d. Da ist die Tür.
e. Ja, ich spreche langsam.
f. Das Papier kostet € 1,50.
g. Heute ist es furchtbar heiß.
h. Ich finde das nicht schön.
i. Fünf plus sechzehn ist einundzwanzig.
j. Nein, heute ist Dienstag.

3. **Und Sie?** Answer, then ask someone else.

  a. S1 Wie alt sind Sie?
      S2 Ich bin _____. Und Sie?

  b. S1 Wo sind Sie geboren?
      S2 Ich bin in _____ geboren. Und Sie?

  c. S1 Wann sind Sie geboren?
      S2 Ich bin im _____ *[month]* geboren. Und Sie?

4. **Was tun Sie wann?** *(What do you do when?)* Use the drawings to discuss with another student what you like to do in various months and seasons.

> BEISPIEL   S1 Was tun Sie im Sommer?
>   S2 Im Sommer spiele ich Tennis. Und Sie?

Ski laufen   angeln   segeln   campen   Tennis spielen

joggen   reiten   schwimmen   Golf spielen

D. Fragen und Antworten

1. **Wie viele?**

Wie viele Stunden hat der Tag?   Wie viele Sekunden hat die Minute?
Wie viele Minuten hat die Stunde?   Wie viele Jahreszeiten hat das Jahr?

2. **Lesen Sie laut: Wie spät ist es?**

8.45 9.30 10.15 1.05 2.20 2.45 6.59

3. **Wann essen Sie?** Ask each other when you eat your meals.

> BEISPIEL   S1 Wann essen Sie morgens?
>   S2 Morgens esse ich um . . .

E. Meine Kurse Read the cue lines below, then use them to ask about your partner's schedule and to relate your own.

Biologie, Chemie, Deutsch, Englisch, Französisch (French), Geographie, Geologie, Geschichte (history), Informatik (computer science), Kunst (art), Latein, Mathe(matik), Musik, Philosophie, Physik, Politik, Psychologie, Soziologie, Spanisch, Sport

S1 Welche Kurse haben Sie heute?
S2 Ich habe heute . . .
S1 Und morgen? Welche Kurse haben Sie morgen?
S2 Ich habe morgen . . .
S1 Wann haben Sie . . . ?
S2 Ich habe . . . um . . .
S1 Wie heißt der Professor/die Professorin?
S2 Er/sie heißt . . .
S1 Ist der . . .kurs gut?
S2 . . .
S1 Wann sind Sie heute fertig?
S2 Ich bin heute um . . . fertig.

F. Spiel: Unterschreiben Sie bitte hier! *(Game: Please sign here!)* Circulate around the room asking other students the following questions. As soon as someone truthfully answers **Ja,** ask for his or her signature. When someone answers **Nein,** thank him or her and ask someone else the same question until someone answers **Ja.** The first person with signatures for all questions wins.

BEISPIEL   S1 Geht es Ihnen gut?
            S2 Ja. / Nein.
            S1 Unterschreiben Sie bitte hier. / Danke!

1. Geht es Ihnen gut?
2. Sind Sie müde?
3. Haben Sie zu viel Stress?
4. Finden Sie das Wetter heute schön?
5. Finden Sie Deutsch toll?
6. Sprechen Sie Spanisch?
7. Spielen Sie Tennis?
8. Sind Sie im Juli geboren?
9. Haben Sie abends Kurse?

G. Praktische Ausdrücke im Klassenzimmer *(Useful classroom expressions)*
You should be able to use the following phrases.

Das verstehe ich nicht.	*I don't understand that.*
Ich habe eine Frage.	*I have a question.*
Ich weiß nicht.	*I don't know.*
Ist das richtig?	*Is that correct!*
Öffnen Sie das Buch auf Seite . . . !	*Open the book to page . . .*
Sagen Sie das bitte noch einmal!	*Say that again, please.*
Schreiben Sie das bitte!	*Please write that!*
(Sprechen Sie) bitte langsam!	*(Speak) slowly please!*
Was bedeutet . . . ?	*What does . . . mean?*
Wie bitte?	*I beg your pardon!*
Wiederholen Sie das bitte!	*Please repeat that!*
Wie sagt man . . . auf Deutsch?	*How do you say . . . in German?*
Wie schreibt man das?	*How do you spell that?*

A vertical bar to the left of a list signals that the material is important and must be learned. You already know most of these expressions. Those in **boldface** are new.

H. Was sagen Sie wann? What would you say in these situations?

1. You got called on in class and didn't hear the question.
2. You were unable to follow your instructor's explanation.
3. You have to ask your instructor to repeat something.
4. You want to let your instructor know that you have a question.
5. You have asked your new neighbor for his/her telephone number, but he/she is speaking much too fast.
6. You also did not understand his/her name and ask him/her to spell it.
7. In a conversation, the word **Geschwindigkeitsbegrenzung** keeps coming up. You want to ask for clarification.
8. You want to know how to say *first name* and *last name* in German.
9. You try to repeat the word and want to make sure that what you said is right.

Aussprache: ch, ig, ck, ng, gn, kn, qu, pf, ps, w

CD 2, Track 9 · **Hören Sie gut zu und wiederholen Sie!**

For further review, see the Summary of Pronunciation in the front of your *Arbeitsbuch*. Study Part III, subsections 5, 13–15, 19, and 20–23.

1. [k]   **Ch**ristine, **Ch**ristian, **Ch**aos
2. [x]   a**ch**t, au**ch**, brau**ch**en
3. [ç]   i**ch**, ni**ch**t, wirkli**ch**
4. [iç] richt**ig**, wind**ig**, bill**ig**
5. [ks] se**chs**, se**chs**undse**ch**zig
6. [k]   Ja**ck**e, Ro**ck**, Pi**ck**ni**ck**
7. [ŋ]   E**ng**lisch, Frühli**ng**, la**ng**
8. [gn] re**gn**et, resi**gn**ieren, Si**gn**al
9. [kn] **Kn**irps, **Kn**ie
10. [kv] **Qu**alität, **Qu**antität, **Qu**artett
11. [pf] **Pf**efferminz, A**pf**el
12. [ps] **Ps**ychologie, **Ps**ychiater, **Ps**ychoanalyse
13. [v] **W**ort, **w**ie, **w**as

Hörverständnis

■ The *Hörverständnis* listening comprehension activities go with the Text Audio CD that is packaged with this book. These activities let you listen to natural language by native speakers. Listen to each recording several times. Note that it is not essential to understand every word in order to follow the gist of the conversation or report and answer the questions. ■

There is an extensive review section following the *Schritte* in the *Arbeitsbuch*. The accompanying exercises and answer key will help you prepare for the test.

Das Klassenzimmer Listen to the description of this class and classroom. Then select the correct response from those given below.

1. Das Klassenzimmer ist _____.
   a. kühl   b. groß   c. schmutzig
2. Das Zimmer hat _____ Fenster.
   a. vier   b. fünf   c. sieben
3. Die Wände sind _____.
   a. grau   b. blau   c. schwarz
4. Die _____ sind rot.
   a. Türen   b. Bücher   c. Stühle
5. Der Professor heißt _____.
   a. Theo Seidl   b. Oskar Thieme c. Otto Brockmann
6. Die Bilder sind _____.
   a. alt   b. schön   c. furchtbar
7. Die Studenten lernen _____.
   a. Deutsch   b. Spanisch   c. Englisch

For online activities on the weather in Germany and in Europe, visit: http://wiegehts.heinle.com.

Fokus — Descendants of German-speaking Immigrants in North America

German-speaking immigrants are one of the largest, yet least conspicuous ethnic groups in the United States and Canada. Names of towns like Frankfort, Bremen, Dresden, Heidelberg, Hanover, Berlin, Zurich, and Salzburg bear witness to their influence. The role played by German-speaking immigrants in shaping US and Canadian life has been enormous: Anheuser, Boeing, Chrysler, Eisenhower, Guggenheim, Hammerstein, Heinz, Hershey, Pershing, Rockefeller, Sousa, Steinway, Weyerhaeuser, Westinghouse—the list of companies with German, Austrian, or Swiss names goes on and on. Blue jeans? Thank German immigrant Levi Strauss for them. The hamburger? It is generally attributed to German-Americans in St. Louis. The Republicans' elephant, the Democrats' donkey, and Uncle Sam himself? They sprang from the pen of Thomas Nast, a German-born cartoonist whose drawing of Santa Claus has delighted many over the years. The values of hard work and thrift, commitment to workers' rights, interest in the arts, and love of good living are all attributed to those immigrants, who have all left indelible marks on US and Canadian society.

The first organized group of German immigrants to come to the New World founded Germantown, now part of Philadelphia, in 1683. Thirteen Mennonite families had fled religious persecution in Germany. Their descendants came to be known as the Pennsylvania "Dutch", a misconstrual of the word **Deutsch.** Many other German speakers followed in the years to come, primarily for economic reasons, although religion and politics sometimes played roles as well. While the great majority of German immigrants were farmers, baking, brewing, and carpentry were also prominent skills among these new Americans. Between 1820 and 1930, 5.9 million people of German descent came to America. By 1900, a quarter of all Chicago residents had been born in Germany or had parents who had been born in Germany. Between 1933 and 1937, there was a large exodus of German-speaking immigrants to the United States and Canada, fleeing Hitler's fascist regime, including **Bauhaus** architect Walter Gropius, physicist Albert Einstein, authors Thomas Mann and Bertolt Brecht, and composers Arnold Schönberg and Paul Hindemith. During the 1950s and 1960s, another large wave of immigrants from Germany, Austria, and Switzerland entered the United States and Canada, hoping for a fresh start abroad.

Today, we find German descendants not only in cities with a traditionally high German-speaking population, such as Milwaukee, Cincinnati, St. Louis, Toronto, and Vancouver, but in every state of the Union and in all Canadian provinces. Nearly one-fourth of the US population claims some German ancestry; in Canada, German is the third largest ethnic group after English and French.

Jetzt geht's nach Amerika! Abfahrt von (departure from) *Bremerhaven.*

Familie, Länder, Sprachen

Lernziele

In this chapter you will learn about:

Zum Thema

The family, geographical terms, country names, nationalities, and languages

Kultur-Fokus

Germany and its place in the world, institutions that represent German culture abroad, and ways Germans address one another

Struktur

The present tense of regular verbs
The nominative case
Sentence structure
Compound nouns

Einblicke

Deutschland in Europa

For more information, go to http://iLrn.heinle.com

Was, du kommst auch aus Vancouver?

Vorschau   Spotlight on Germany

Minidrama: *Ganz international*
Blickpunkt: *Am Goethe-Institut*

Size: Approximately 135,800 square miles, comparable to the size of Montana; would fit twenty times into the area of the continental United States; divided into 16 federal states (**Länder**).

Population: 82.5 million (including 7.5 million foreigners). After Russia, Germany is the most populous country of Europe, followed by Italy, the United Kingdom, and France.

Religion: 38% Protestant, 34% Catholic, 28% unaffiliated (see *Fokus* note in Chapter 4, "Diversity in Religious Traditions"). Three million Moslems now form the largest non-Christian group in Germany; approximately 2.5 million of them are Turkish or of Turkish descent.

Geography: Divided into three major regions: the flat lowlands in the north, the central mountain region, and the southern highlands, including a narrow band of the Alps.

Currency: Euro = 100 Cents. The former currency, the Mark (= 100 Pfennig), was phased out in 2002.

Principal cities: Berlin (pop. 3.4 million, capital); Hamburg (pop. 1.7 million); Munich (*München*, pop. 1.3 million); Cologne (*Köln*, pop. 1 million); Frankfurt am Main (pop. 660,000); Essen (pop. 600,000); Stuttgart (pop. 590,000); Düsseldorf (pop. 572,000); Hanover (*Hannover*, pop. 515,000); Leipzig (pop. 497,000); Dresden (pop. 478,000); Bonn (pop. 313,000)

Germany's sometimes turbulent history spans nearly 2,000 years. Unlike its neighbors, it did not become a centralized state until relatively recently. Originally, the population of what is now Germany consisted of various Germanic tribes, and even now their heritage gives the different regions of Germany their particular identity. The Holy Roman Empire, a loose federation of states under an emperor, lasted from 962 to 1806. During this time, the country was divided further until there were almost 350 individual political entities, some of them minuscule. During the reign of Napoleon I, they were consolidated into about 40 states. In 1871, under Prussian Chancellor Otto von Bismarck, Germany became a unified state for the first time. This monarchy lasted until the end of World War I, when Germany became a republic (**die Weimarer Republik,** 1919–1933).

   After the horrors of the Holocaust and World War II, brought about by the Nazi dictatorship (1933–1945), the country was divided into the Federal Republic of Germany, or FRG (**die B**undes**r**epublik **D**eutschland = **BRD**), in the west, and the German Democratic Republic, or GDR (**die D**eutsche **D**emokratische **R**epublik = **DDR**), in the east. The line between the West and Communist Europe, a heavily fortified border, ran through the middle of Germany. The symbol of this division, the infamous Berlin Wall built in 1961 by the GDR, came down on November 9, 1989. On October 3, 1990, the two Germanys were officially reunited. Since then, Germans have been trying to overcome more than 40 years of living in diametrically opposed political and economic systems. Many Germans are still waiting for the day when "the wall in the minds" of people will finally fall. The cost of reunification, both socially and economically, has been much higher than anticipated. In the East, the closing of obsolete socialist enterprises has resulted in massive unemployment; in the West, taxes have increased in order to finance the high cost of reunification. The massive transfer of public funds is showing results. The federal government signed a pact with the new **Länder** granting them a total of 250 billion euros, to be distributed through 2019. The telephone, rail, and road systems of the new states have been almost completely rebuilt, all important steps in the economic development of eastern Germany. But the region's economy remains weak, as new industries have not replaced the old ones rapidly enough, resulting in a massive westward migration of workers. (For pictures and information on a specific German city, visit www.*[city name]*.de.)

27

Am Goethe-Institut

CD 2,
Track 11

■ Listen to the dialogue. Then, with a partner, act out the dialogue together. ■

● The basic purpose of these dialogues is to present the chapter topic, not the grammar!

SHARON   Roberto, woher kommst du?
ROBERTO   Ich bin aus Rom. Und du?
SHARON   Ich komme aus Sacramento, aber jetzt wohnt meine Familie in Seattle.
ROBERTO   Hast du Geschwister?
SHARON   Ja, ich habe zwei Schwestern und zwei Brüder. Und du?
ROBERTO   Ich habe nur eine Schwester. Sie wohnt in Montreal, in Kanada.
SHARON   Wirklich? So ein Zufall! Mein Onkel wohnt auch da.

Später

ROBERTO   Sharon, wann ist die Prüfung?
SHARON   In zehn Minuten. Du, wie heißen ein paar Flüsse in Deutschland?
ROBERTO   Im Norden ist die Elbe, im Osten die Oder, im Süden . . .
SHARON   . . . die Donau?
ROBERTO   Richtig! Und im Westen der Rhein. Wo liegt Düsseldorf?
SHARON   Düsseldorf? Hm. Wo ist eine Landkarte?
ROBERTO   Oh, hier. Im Westen von Deutschland, nördlich von Bonn, am Rhein.
SHARON   Ach ja, richtig! Na, viel Glück!

A. Fragen

1. Woher kommt Roberto? 2. Woher kommt Sharon? 3. Wo wohnt Sharons Familie? 4. Wie groß ist Sharons Familie? 5. Wann ist die Prüfung? 6. Was sind die Elbe, die Oder, die Donau und der Rhein? 7. Wo ist die Elbe? die Oder? die Donau? der Rhein? 8. Wo liegt Düsseldorf?

B. Jetzt sind Sie dran! Use the dialogue above as a model and the *Wortschatz* that follows to create your own dialogue with a partner. Talk about geography or about your family and where they live.

BEISPIEL   S1 Woher kommst du?
            S2 Ich bin aus . . . Und du?

Fokus   The Goethe Institute

The Goethe Institute (**Goethe Institut Inter Nationes**) is the official representative of German culture abroad. With approximately 144 branches in 80 countries, it offers German language courses and organizes lectures, exhibitions, movie screenings, and readings by poets and authors. The combination of language instruction and lively cultural exchange makes the Goethe Institutes important intermediaries in international dialogue and in communicating a comprehensive image of Germany. (For further information, visit www.goethe.de.)

Wortschatz 1

Die Familie, -n *(family)*

der Bruder, ⸚	*brother*	die Schwester, -n	*sister*
der Cousin, -s	*cousin*	die Kusine, -n / Cousine, -n	*cousin*
der Junge, -n	*boy*	das Mädchen, -	*girl*
der Mann, ⸚er	*man; husband*	die Frau, -en	*woman; wife*
der Onkel, -	*uncle*	die Tante, -n	*aunt*
der Sohn, ⸚e	*son*	die Tochter, ⸚	*daughter*
der Vater, ⸚	*father*	die Mutter, ⸚	*mother*
der Großvater, ⸚	*grandfather*	die Großmutter, ⸚	*grandmother*
das Kind, -er	*child*		
die Geschwister *(pl.)*	*siblings; brother and/or sister*		
die Eltern *(pl.)*	*parents*		
die Großeltern *(pl.)*	*grandparents*		

Das Land, ⸚er (country, state)	**Die Leute** (pl.) (people)	**Die Sprache, -n** (language)
Deutschland	der Deutsche, -n/die Deutsche, -n	Deutsch
Frankreich	der Franzose, -n/die Französin, -nen	Französisch
Österreich	der Österreicher, -/die Österreicherin, -nen	Deutsch
die Schweiz	der Schweizer, -/die Schweizerin, -nen	Deutsch, Französisch, Italienisch
Italien	der Italiener, -/die Italienerin, -nen	Italienisch
Spanien	der Spanier, -/die Spanierin, -nen	Spanisch
England	der Engländer, -/die Engländerin, -nen	Englisch
Amerika	der Amerikaner, -/die Amerikanerin, -nen	Englisch
Kanada	der Kanadier, -/die Kanadierin, -nen	Englisch, Französisch

Weiteres

der Satz, ⸚e	*sentence*	die Frage, -n	*question*
Berg, -e	*mountain*	Landkarte, -n	*map*
Fluss, ⸚e	*river*	Prüfung, -en	*test, exam*
See, -n	*lake*	Stadt, ⸚e	*city*
		Hauptstadt, ⸚e	*capital city*

kommen	*to come*
liegen	*to lie (be located)*
wohnen	*to live, reside*
amerikanisch / kanadisch	*American / Canadian*
woher?	*from where?*
Ich bin / komme aus . . .	*I'm from . . . (a native of)*
im Norden / Süden / Osten / Westen	*in the north / south / east / west*
nördlich / südlich / östlich / westlich von	*north / south / east / west of*
mein(e)	*my*
dein(e) / Ihr(e)	*your (informal / formal)*

Zum Erkennen: So ein Zufall! *(What a coincidence!)*; Na, viel Glück! *(Well, good luck!)*; Dir auch! *(To you, too!)*; AUCH: das Pronomen, - *(pronoun)*; das Subjekt, -e *(subject)*; ersetzen *(to replace)*; kombinieren *(to combine)*; Hier fehlt was. *(Something is missing.)*; Was fehlt? *(What's missing?)*; Sagen Sie es anders! *(Say it differently!)*; usw. = und so weiter *(etc.)*; z. B. = zum Beispiel *(e.g., for example)*; Das ist leicht zu verstehen. *(That's easy to understand.)*

● In case you're curious: *Dad / Mom / Grandma / Grandpa =* **Vati, Papa / Mutti, Mama / Oma / Opa;** *step- =* **Stief- (Stiefbruder, Stiefschwester,** etc.**);** *-in-law =* **Schwieger- (Schwiegervater, Schwiegermutter,** etc.**), BUT Schwager, -** *(brother-in-law)* and **Schwägerin, -nen** *(sister-in-law)*; *nephew / niece =* **Neffe, -n / Nichte, -n;** *grandchild =* **Enkelkind, -er;** *great-grand- =* **Urgroß- (Urgroßeltern).**

● ARTICLES: All countries and cities are neuter unless indicated otherwise **(die Schweiz).**

● Many feminine nouns can be derived from masculine nouns by adding **-in,** in which case their plurals end in **-nen (der Schweizer > die Schweizerin, -nen).** BUT: **der Deutsche > die Deutsche, -n; der Franzose > die Französin, -nen.**

● Adjectives denoting nationality are not capitalized: Typisch **deutsch!** *(Typically German!)*, BUT: Ich spreche **Deutsch.** *(the German language)*; Antworten Sie auf **Deutsch** *(in German!)*

● **Im** is used with months, seasons, and points of the compass **(im Mai, im Winter, im Norden); in** is used with names of cities, countries, and continents **(in Berlin, in Deutschland, in Europa).**

● **Mein, dein,** and **Ihr** have no ending when used before masculine and neuter nouns that are sentence subjects: **mein Vater, dein Bruder, Ihr Kind.** Before feminine and plural nouns, **meine, eine,** and **Ihre** are used: **meine Mutter, deine Schwester, Ihre Eltern.**

Fokus — Du or Sie?

German has more than one way of saying *you*. **Du**, corresponding in form to the archaic English word *thou*, is used primarily for addressing children, family members, and friends. **Sie** is used with adults who are not close friends or relatives. Today, young people and university students tend to address each other automatically with the informal **du**-form; but it is still considered rude to address older people, or even colleagues, with **du**. When in doubt, use **Sie**. The general custom is that it is up to the person of higher age or status to suggest **Duzen** instead of **Siezen**. Similarly, you address a German speaker "on a first-name basis" only after you begin using the **du**-form. Up to that point, it is **Herr** . . . or **Frau** . . . to you.

Aktives zum Thema *(Topical activities)*

● The function of the *Mustersätze* is to drill new phrases and to introduce the pronunciation of some new vocabulary.

A. Mustersätze

1. Woher kommt ____?
   Ihre Familie → Woher kommt Ihre Familie?
   Ihr Vater, Ihre Mutter, Ihre Tante . . .
2. Ich bin aus ____.
   Rom → Ich bin aus Rom.
   Frankfurt, Österreich, Amerika, Berlin . . .
3. ____ liegt im ____.
   Hamburg / Norden → Hamburg liegt im Norden.
   Leipzig / Osten; München / Süden; Düsseldorf / Westen; Rostock / Norden . . .
4. ____ liegt ____ von Deutschland.
   die Schweiz / südlich → Die Schweiz liegt südlich von Deutschland.
   Dänemark / nördlich; Polen / östlich; Österreich / südlich; Luxemburg / westlich . . .
5. In ____ sprechen die Leute ____.
   Österreich / Deutsch → In Österreich sprechen die Leute Deutsch.
   Frankreich / Französisch; England / Englisch; Italien / Italienisch . . .

B. Was sind sie? Identify the following people.

CAUTION: Unlike English, German does not use an indefinite article before nationalities or references to membership in a group: **Sie ist Amerikanerin** *(an American)*; **Sie ist Studentin** *(a student)*; **Er ist Berliner** *(a Berliner)*.

1. **Ländernamen**

   BEISPIEL   Juan ist Spanier. Und Juanita?
   Juanita ist Spanierin.

   a. Antonio ist Italiener. Und Luisa?
   b. Hugo ist Österreicher. Und Lilo?
   c. Walter ist Schweizer. Und Monique?
   d. Pierre ist Franzose. Und Claire?

2. **Städtenamen**

   BEISPIEL   Uwe und Margit sind aus Frankfurt.
   Uwe ist Frankfurter und Margit ist Frankfurterin.

   a. Robert und Evi sind aus Berlin.
   b. Klaus und Inge sind aus Hamburg.
   c. Rolf und Katrin sind aus Wien.
   d. Bert und Romy sind aus Zürich.

3. **Kettenreaktion: Was sind Sie?** Ask your classmates where they are from.

BEISPIEL   S1 Ich bin aus Amerika und wohne in New York. Ich bin
              Amerikaner(in) und New Yorker(in). Und Sie?
            S2 Ich bin . . .

 **C. Familien**

1. **Elkes Stammbaum** Look at Elke's family tree and explain who each person is.

BEISPIEL   *Elke ist die Tochter von Jens und Ute.*
            Elke ist Arndts Schwester.

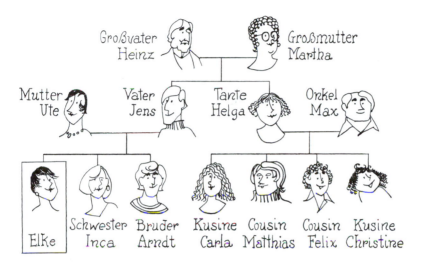

 2. **Familiennamen: Wer ist das?** Write down various names of your immediate
and extended family and pass the list on to your partner, who then asks who
these different people are. Take turns inquiring about each other's family. For
extra vocabulary, see the list in *Zum Erkennen* under *Wortschatz 1.*

 3. **Zwei Familien**
  a. **Meine Familie** Taking turns, ask your partner details about his/her
     family, covering questions like the ones below.

     Wie heißt du?
     Woher kommst du? *(name of your state)*
     Wie groß ist deine Familie? Wie heißen sie und wie alt sind sie?
     Wo in . . . *(name of your state)* wohnt deine Familie?
     Wo liegt . . . *(name of your state)*? (z. B. **Kalifornien liegt südlich von
        Oregon.**)
     Wie heißt die Hauptstadt von . . . *(name of your state)*?
     Wie schreibt man das? *(spell the name of your capital)*
     Ist . . . *(name of your city)* groß oder klein? Wie viele Leute wohnen da?
     Ist da ein Fluss oder ein See? der Ozean *(ocean)*? Wenn ja *(if so)*, wie heißt
        der Fluss / See / Ozean?
     Sind da Berge? Wenn ja, wie heißen die Berge?
     Wie ist das Wetter da im Frühling? im Sommer? im Herbst? im Winter?
        (z. B. **kalt, warm, wunderbar,** . . .)
     Wie findest du es *(how do you like it)* in . . . *(name your city or state)*?
        (z. B. **schön, langweilig, toll,** . . .)

  b. **Deine Familie** *(Your family)* Take turns reporting what you found out
     about your partner's family.

Lerntipp
**Developing Listening and
Comprehension Skills**

Being able to understand
spoken German is probably
your most important skill.
You cannot learn to speak
German unless you under-
stand it. Use class time
well and listen carefully to
your instructor and your
classmates. Play the Lab
and Text Audio CDs as of-
ten as you need to in order
to understand the dialogues
and listening comprehen-
sion texts, and to complete
the exercises correctly. Be
sure to listen to the reading
texts with the book closed.
Take advantage of opportunities to hear German spoken at the German Club or
German House on campus.
Listen to German CDs and
watch plays or movies
(some can be rented in
video stores). Even if you
can't understand much of it
in the beginning, you will
be able to pick out key
words and learn to "tune
in" to German.

D. Was passt? *(What fits?)* For each question or statement on the left, select one or more appropriate responses from the right-hand column, or give your own.

____ 1. Woher kommst du?
____ 2. Wie groß ist deine Familie?
____ 3. Meine Schwester wohnt in Seattle.
____ 4. Wann ist die Prüfung?
____ 5. Wo liegt Erfurt?

a. Sehr klein. Ich habe keine Geschwister.
b. Am Rhein.
c. Mein Onkel wohnt auch da.
d. Aus Seattle, und du?
e. Um Viertel nach zehn.
f. In zwanzig Minuten.
g. Westlich von Weimar.
h. Ich bin aus Rom.
i. Wir sind sechs.
j. Wirklich?
k. Ich weiß nicht.
l. . . .

Aussprache: i, a, u

CD 2, Track 12

A. Laute *(sounds)*

1. [i:] **Ih**nen, l**ie**gen, w**ie**der, W**ie**n, Berl**i**n
2. [i] **i**ch b**i**n, b**i**tte, K**i**nd, Geschw**i**ster, r**i**chtig
3. [a:] Fr**a**ge, Spr**a**che, Amerik**a**ner, Sp**a**nier, V**a**ter
4. [a] St**a**dt, L**a**nd, K**a**nada, S**a**tz, T**a**nte
5. [u:] g**u**t, Br**u**der, K**u**li, Min**u**te, d**u**
6. [u] St**u**nde, J**u**nge, M**u**tter, Fl**u**ss, schm**u**tzig, k**u**rz

- For further review, see the Summary of Pronunciation in the front of your *Arbeitsbuch*. Study Part II, subsections 1, 3–4, 11–13, 17, and 19–20.

- All pronunciation exercises are recorded on the Lab Audio CDs. See the *Zum Hören* section of the *Arbeitsbuch*.

B. Wortpaare

1. still / Stil
2. Stadt / Staat
3. Kamm / komm
4. Schiff / schief
5. Rum / Ruhm
6. Ratte / rate

Hörverständnis

Track 2

Guten Morgen! Listen to the conversation between Hugo Schmidt and Monika Müller. Then decide whether the statements below are true or false according to the dialogue. Remember that you may listen as often as you wish.

Zum Erkennen: die Assistentin; die Arbeit *(work)*

____ 1. Hugo Schmidt ist Professor.
____ 2. Monika Müller ist Professorin.
____ 3. Monika spricht *(speaks)* Deutsch, Englisch und Spanisch.
____ 4. Monika ist aus Spanien.
____ 5. Monikas Mutter ist aus Deutschland.
____ 6. Monika ist 23.
____ 7. Der Professor braucht Monika von 2 Uhr bis 6 Uhr.
____ 8. Monika braucht Arbeit.
____ 9. Monika ist zwei Monate da.

Struktur

1.1 The present tense of regular verbs

1. You are already familiar with some of the PERSONAL PRONOUNS; there are four others: **du, er, sie,** and **ihr.**

	singular	plural	singular / plural
1st person	ich *(I)*	wir *(we)*	
2nd person	**du** *(you,* fam.*)*	**ihr** *(you,* fam.*)*	Sie *(you,* formal*)*
3rd person	**er** / es / **sie** *(he, it, she)*	sie *(they)*	

- **du** and **ihr** are intimate forms of address used with family members, close friends, fellow students, children up to the age of sixteen, and animals.
- **Sie,** which is always capitalized when it means *you,* is used with strangers, casual acquaintances, and people addressed with a title, e.g., **Herr** and **Frau.** It is used to address one or more persons. **Sie** *(you)* and **sie** *(they,* not capitalized) can be distinguished in conversation only through context.

    Herr Schmidt, wo wohnen **Sie?** Und Ihre Eltern, wo wohnen **sie?**
    Mr. Schmidt, where do you live? And your parents, where do they live?

- The subject pronouns **sie** *(she, it)* and **sie** *(they)* can be distinguished through the personal endings of the verb.

    Sie komm**t** im Mai und **sie** komm**en** im Juni.
    She comes in May, and they come in June.

2. The infinitive is the form of the verb that has no subject and takes no personal ending (e.g., *to learn*). Almost every German infinitive ends in **-en: lernen, antworten.** The stem of the verb is the part that precedes the infinitive ending **-en.** Thus, the stem of **lernen** is **lern-,** and that of **antworten** is **antwort-.**

    English verbs have at most one personal ending in the present tense, *-s: I (you, we, they) learn,* but *he (it, she) learns.* In German, endings are added to the verb stem for all persons.

    stem + personal ending = present tense verb form

    German verb endings vary, depending on whether the subject is in the FIRST, SECOND, or THIRD PERSON and in the SINGULAR or PLURAL. The verb must agree with the subject. You have already learned the endings used for some persons. Here is the complete list of endings:

	singular	plural	formal *(sg. / pl.)*
1st person	ich lern**e**	wir lern**en**	
2nd person	du lern**st**	ihr lern**t**	Sie lern**en**
3rd person	er / es / sie lern**t**	sie lern**en**	

NOTE: The verb forms for formal *you* **(Sie)** and plural *they* **(sie)** are identical. The same holds true for **er / es / sie.** For that reason **Sie** and **es / sie** will not be listed in charts in future chapters.

Lerntipp
Studying Grammar

Don't let the idea of grammar scare you. It is a shortcut to learning, providing you with the patterns native speakers follow when they use the language. The fact that German and English are closely related will be very helpful. However, you must make sure to note the instances when German patterns differ from English. As a bonus, your study of German will make you more aware of the fine points of English grammar.

German speakers find it rude if, when talking about yourself and others, you name yourself first, e.g., *I and my brother.* You yourself should always come last in the list, e.g., **Mein Bruder, meine Schwester und ich.**

The following verbs, which you already know from the *Schritte* and from this chapter, follow the model of **lernen.** Be sure to review them:

beginnen	*to begin*	sagen	*to say, tell*
brauchen	*to need*	schreiben	*to write*
fragen	*to ask*	spielen	*to play*
gehen	*to go*	verstehen	*to understand*
hören	*to hear*	wiederholen	*to repeat, review*
kommen	*to come*	wohnen	*to live, reside*
liegen	*to lie; be located*	zählen	*to count*

NOTE: The bar on the left signals that a list is important.

3. When a verb stem ends in **-d** or **-t** (**antwort-, find-**), or in certain consonant combinations with **-m** or **-n** (**öffn-, regn-**), an **-e** is inserted between the stem and the **-st** and **-t** endings.

	singular	plural	formal *(sg. / pl.)*
1st person	ich antworte	wir antworten	
2nd person	du antwortest	ihr antwortet	Sie antworten
3rd person	er / es / sie antwortet	sie antworten	

These familiar verbs follow the model of **antworten:**

finden	*to find*
kosten	*to cost*
öffnen	*to open*
regnen	*to rain*

4. The **du**-form of verbs with a stem ending in any **s**-sound (**-s, -ss, -ß, -tz, -z**) adds only a **-t** instead of **-st: ich heiße, du heißt.** Thus, the **du**-form is identical with the **er**-form of these verbs: **du heißt, er heißt.**

5. German has only one verb form to express what can be said in English in several ways.

Ich wohne in Köln.
$\begin{cases} \textit{I live in Cologne.} \\ \textit{I'm living in Cologne.} \\ \textit{I do live in Cologne.} \end{cases}$

Wo wohnst du?
$\begin{cases} \textit{Where are you living?} \\ \textit{Where do you live?} \end{cases}$

6. Even more than in English, in German the present tense is very frequently used to express future time, particularly when a time expression clearly indicates the future.

In dreißig Minuten **gehe** ich in die Stadt.

I'm going downtown in thirty minutes.

Er **kommt** im Sommer.

He'll come in the summer.

Übungen

● For additional exercises on any of the grammar topics, see the exercises in the *Arbeitsbuch*.

A. *Du, ihr* oder *Sie*? How would you generally address these people: in the singular familiar, the plural familiar, or in a formal fashion?

> BEISPIEL   your brother
> *(I would address him with)* **du**

1. your father 2. members of your family 3. your German professor 4. a store clerk 5. two police officers 6. your roommate 7. friends of your three-year-old niece 8. your classmates 9. a group of strangers who are older than you

B. Ersetzen Sie das Subjekt! Replace the subject by using the words in parentheses.

> BEISPIEL   Ich sage das noch einmal. (wir, Maria)
> *Wir sagen das noch einmal.*
> *Maria sagt das noch einmal.*

1. Wir antworten auf Deutsch. (Roberto, du, ich, die Mutter)
2. Ich wiederhole die Frage. (er, wir, ihr, Sie)
3. Ihr lernt die Wörter. (ich, du, die Kinder, wir)
4. Du öffnest das Buch auf Seite 3. (der Franzose, ich, ihr, sie/*sg.*)
5. Lea Bauer geht an die Tafel. (ihr, sie/*pl.*, ich, du)
6. Brauchst du Papier und Bleistifte? (wir, ich, Sie, ihr)
7. Wie finden Sie das? (ihr, du, Ihre Familie, die Leute)

C. Kombinieren Sie! Create sentences by combining items from each column.

> BEISPIEL   *Er kommt aus Kanada.*

● Optional English-to-German practice: 1. We're learning German. 2. I'm counting slowly. 3. Where do you *(pl. fam.)* come from? 4. They come from Canada. 5. I'm from America. 6. Do you *(sg. fam.)* answer in English? 7. No, I'll speak German. 8. She's opening the book. 9. I do need the book. 10. What does she say? 11. Do you *(sg. fam.)* understand (that)? 12. Is she repeating that? 13. Her name is Sabrina. 14. They do live in Wittenberg. (See answer key in the Appendix.)

1	2	3
ich	beginnen	auf Deutsch
du	brauchen	auf Englisch
er	hören	aus . . .
es	kommen	(das) nicht
sie	kosten	Deutsch
das	lernen	heute
die Deutschvorlesung	regnen	in . . .
das Mädchen	schreiben	jetzt
wir	spielen	morgen
ihr	wohnen	(nicht) gut
Sie	zählen	Tennis
sie		um . . . Uhr
		vier Euro
		von zehn bis zwanzig

D. Was fehlt? (What's missing?) Fill in the missing verb forms.

SVEN   Danny und Laura, woher _____ ihr? (kommen)
LAURA   Ich _____ aus Heidelberg. (kommen)
DANNY   Und ich _____ aus Berlin. (sein)
SVEN   Wirklich? Meine Großmutter _____ auch aus Berlin. (kommen) Aber sie _____ jetzt in Hamburg. (wohnen) Wie _____ ihr es hier? (finden)
LAURA   Wir _____ es hier in Bregenz prima. (finden)
DANNY   Ich _____ den Bodensee wunderbar. (finden)
SVEN   Ich auch!

1.2 The nominative case

To show the function of nouns or pronouns in a sentence, German uses a system called CASE. There are four cases in German: nominative, accusative, dative, and genitive. The NOMINATIVE CASE is the case of the subject and of the predicate noun. (The predicate noun is discussed in Section 1.3–2 below).

In the English sentence *The boy asks the father*, the SUBJECT of the sentence is *the boy*; he does the asking. We know that *the boy* is the subject of the sentence because in English the subject precedes the verb. This is not always true in German, where the function of a word or phrase frequently depends on its form rather than on its position. In the sentence **Der Junge fragt den Vater,** the phrase **der Junge** indicates the subject, whereas **den Vater** represents a direct object (more about this in Chapter 2). In dictionaries and vocabulary lists, nouns are given in the nominative. The nominative answers the questions *who?* for persons or *what?* for objects and ideas.

Der Junge fragt den Vater.	*The boy asks the father.*
Der See ist schön.	*The lake is beautiful.*

1. The forms of the INTERROGATIVE PRONOUNS are **wer?** *(who?)* and **was?** *(what?).*

	persons	things and ideas
nom.	wer?	was?

Wer fragt den Vater?	→	**Der Junge.**
Who is asking the father?	→	*The boy.*
Was ist schön?	→	**Der See.**
What is beautiful?	→	*The lake.*

2. The nominative forms of the DEFINITE ARTICLE **der** *(the)* are already familiar. Note that the INDEFINITE ARTICLE **ein** *(a, an)* is the same for masculine and neuter nouns; it has no ending. It also has no plural:
I have a pencil, but *I have pencils.*

	SINGULAR			PLURAL	
	masc.	**neut.**	**fem.**		
	der	das	die	die	*the*
nom.	ein	ein	eine	—	*a, an*
	kein	kein	keine	keine	*no, not a, not any*

The POSSESSIVE ADJECTIVES **mein** *(my)*, **dein** *(your)*, and **Ihr** *(your,* formal) follow the pattern of **ein** and **kein**.

Die Frau, der Junge und das Mädchen sind aus Österreich.
Mein Onkel und **meine** Tante wohnen auch da. Wo wohnen **deine** Eltern?

3. Nouns can be replaced by personal pronouns. In English, we replace persons with *he, she,* or *they,* and objects and ideas with *it* or *they.* In German, the pronoun used depends on the gender of the noun.

Wer ist **der Mann?**	**Er** heißt Max.	*He's called Max.*
Wie heißt **das Kind?**	**Es** heißt Susi.	*She's called Susi.*
Wer ist **die Frau?**	**Sie** heißt Ute.	*She's called Ute.*
Wie ist **der See?**	**Er** ist groß.	*It's big.*
Wie ist **das Land?**	**Es** ist klein.	*It's small.*
Wie heißt **die Stadt?**	**Sie** heißt Ulm.	*It's called Ulm.*

- Note that German uses three pronouns (**er, es, sie**) for objects where English uses only one *(it).*
- Note also how similar these pronouns are to the forms of the articles:

$$der \rightarrow er; das \rightarrow es; die \rightarrow sie$$

- In the plural, there are no gender distinctions, as the definite article for all plural nouns is **die.** The pronoun for all plural nouns is **sie.**

die Männer		die Seen	
die Kinder	} **sie** *(they)*	die Länder	} **sie** *(they)*
die Frauen		die Städte	

Übungen

E. Ersetzen Sie die Wörter mit Pronomen! *(Replace the words with pronouns.)*

BEISPIEL Fritz *er*
die Landkarte *sie*

der Vater	der Bleistift	Deutschland
der Berg	der Pulli	das Kind
das Land	Österreich	die Geschwister
die Großmutter	der Österreicher	die Töchter
der Junge	die Schweiz	die Söhne
die Stadt	die Schweizerin	

F. Die Geographiestunde

1. **Was ist das?** Describe some features of Europe, using the appropriate form of **ein.**

   BEISPIEL Frankfurt / Stadt
   Frankfurt ist eine Stadt.

   Österreich / Land; die Donau / Fluss; Italienisch / Sprache; Berlin / Stadt; der Main / Fluss; das Matterhorn / Berg; Französisch / Sprache; Luxemburg / Land; der Bodensee *(Lake Constance)* / See; Bremen / Stadt

2. **Ist das richtig?**
   a. **Geographische Namen in Europa** *(Geographical names in Europe)* Ask and answer some questions about Europe, using the appropriate form of **kein.**

   BEISPIEL die Donau / Land
   Ist die Donau ein Land?
   Nein, die Donau ist kein Land. Die Donau ist ein Fluss.

   Frankfurt / Fluss; Frankreich / Sprache; Heidelberg / Berg; der Rhein / Stadt; die Schweiz / See; Spanien / Sprache; Bonn / Land

   b. **Geographische Namen irgendwo** *(Geographical names anywhere)* Make your own statements about any geographical location and have your classmates react to them.

   BEISPIEL Die Smokys sind Berge. *Ja, das sind Berge.*
   Der Hudson ist ein See. *Nein, das ist kein See. Das ist ein Fluss.*

G. Ersetzen Sie das Subjekt!

1. **Antworten Sie mit JA!** A curious neighbor asks you questions about the new family in the neighborhood. Answer positively, using pronouns.

   BEISPIEL   Die Eltern kommen aus Italien, nicht wahr?
   Ja, sie kommen aus Italien.

   a. Der Sohn antwortet auf Italienisch, nicht wahr? b. Die Tochter versteht Deutsch, nicht wahr? c. Das Kind ist fünf Jahre alt, nicht wahr? d. Die Groß-mutter heißt Maria, nicht wahr? e. Der Großvater wohnt auch da, nicht wahr? f. Die Familie kommt aus Rom, nicht wahr?

 2. **Antworten mit Pronomen** *(Answers with pronouns)* Ask another student the following types of questions, which can vary. He or she answers and then returns the question.

   BEISPIEL   S1 Wann beginnt . . . (z. B. dein Tag)?
             S2 Mein Tag? Er beginnt morgens um sechs.
                 Und dein Tag?
             S1 Er beginnt morgens um halb sieben.

   a. Wann beginnt . . . (z. B. die Deutschvorlesung)?
   b. Wie heißt . . . (z. B. das Deutschbuch)?
   c. Welche Farbe hat . . . (z. B. dein Kuli / deine Jacke)?
   d. Wo ist . . . (z. B. das Fenster)?
   e. Wie viele . . . hat . . . (z. B. Monate / das Jahr)?

 3. **Blitzreaktionen** *(Fast responses)* Say one of the German nouns you have learned. Someone else will quickly repeat the word with its article and make a statement about it, using the proper pronoun.

   BEISPIEL   Hemd
             Das Hemd. Es ist weiß.

Fokus   German in Europe

As a result of geography, history, and economics, German is one of the principal languages of Europe, with some 95 million Europeans who are native speakers and millions more who speak German as a second language. In many schools in western and northern Europe—in Scandinavia and France in particular—German is a required foreign language. In Greece, Spain, and Turkey, German is widely spoken, mainly because of southern European "guest work-ers" (**Gastarbeiter**) who have brought German back to their countries, and also as a result of the millions of German tourists who flock to the Mediterranean every year.

Farther east, German has a long tradition. The Austro-Hungarian Empire, in which German was the official language, encompassed large areas of central and eastern Europe. Today, after decades of Soviet domination, young people in Poland, the Czech Republic, Slovakia, and Hungary are rediscovering old links to German culture. Of course, the opportunities offered by the powerful economies of neighboring Austria and Germany are an added incentive to learn German. In Russia alone, 4.7 million students are learning German; in the rest of the former Soviet bloc, German is generally the most frequently studied second language.

At the beginning of the twentieth century, German—not English—was the primary language of science, philosophy, and psychology. Although the German language has since seen growing competition from English, it still remains one of the most widely understood languages in Europe.

1.3 Sentence structure

1. In English, the subject usually precedes the verb, and more than one element may do so.

$\overset{1}{}\quad\overset{2}{}$

*They **are learning** German at the Goethe Institute.*
*At the Goethe Institute they **are learning** German.*

As you know, in German statements and information questions, the verb is always the second sentence element.

$\overset{1}{}\quad\overset{2}{}$

Sie **lernen** Deutsch am Goethe-Institut.

In contrast to English, however, only one sentence element may precede the verb, and this element is not necessarily the subject. If an element other than the subject precedes the verb, *the verb stays* in the second position and *the subject follows* the verb. This pattern is called INVERTED WORD ORDER.

$\overset{2}{}\quad\overset{1}{}$

Deutsch **lernen** sie am Goethe-Institut.
Am Goethe-Institut **lernen** sie Deutsch.

2. The verbs **sein** *(to be)* and **heiß**en *(to be called)* are LINKING VERBS. They normally link two words referring to the same person or thing, both of which are in the nominative: the first is the subject, the other a PREDICATE NOUN.

subject   predicate noun
Der Herr **ist**   Schweizer.
Er **heißt**   Stefan Wolf.

The verb **sein** can be complemented not only by a predicate noun, but also by a PREDICATE ADJECTIVE. Both are considered part of the verb phrase. This is an example of a typical and important feature of German sentence structure: when the verb consists of more than one part, the inflected part (V1)—that is, the part of the verb that takes a personal ending—is the second element in the sentence, as always. However, the uninflected part (V2) stands at the very end of the sentence as a verb complement.

Stefan Wolf **ist** auch **Schweizer.**
Er **ist** heute **sehr müde.**
V1   V2

REMEMBER: In German, no indefinite article is used before nationalities: **Er ist Schweizer** *(an inhabitant of Switzerland).*

Übungen

H. Sagen Sie es anders! *(Say it differently!)* Begin each sentence with the word or phrase in boldface.

> BEISPIEL   Mein Cousin kommt **morgen.**
> *Morgen kommt mein Cousin.*

1. Ich bin **jetzt** am Goethe-Institut.
2. Die Leute sprechen **hier** nur Deutsch.
3. Wir haben **in zehn Minuten** eine Prüfung in Geographie.
4. Du findest die Landkarte **auf Seite 6.**
5. Die Donau ist **im Süden.**
6. Düsseldorf liegt **nördlich von Bonn.**
7. Es geht **mir** gut.
8. Wir spielen **um halb drei** Tennis.
9. Es regnet oft **im April.**
10. Die Sonne scheint **heute** wieder.

I. Welche Nationalität? Professor Händel of the Goethe Institute is determining the nationality of his summer-school students. Follow the model.

BEISPIEL   Pierre kommt aus Marseille.
Er ist Franzose.

1. Roberto kommt aus Florenz.
2. Sam kommt aus Houston.
3. Carla kommt aus Madrid.
4. James kommt aus Manchester.
5. Maria und Caroline kommen aus Nashville.
6. Monique und Simone kommen aus Lausanne.
7. John und Donna kommen aus Montreal.
8. Felix kommt aus Bern.
9. Eva kommt aus Wien.
10. Mirjam kommt aus Vaduz.

1.4 Compound nouns

For additional practice on word compounds, see the *Zum Schreiben* section in Chapters 1 and 7 of the *Arbeitsbuch*.

In German, two or three simple words are frequently combined to create a new one, like **Fingerhut** (a "hat" that protects your finger = *thimble*), **Menschenfreund** (a friend of human beings = *philanthropist*), or **Stinktier** (an animal that stinks = *skunk*). The last component determines the gender and the plural form.

das Land + **die Karte** = **die** Land**karte, -n**
die Kinder + **das Mädchen** = **das** Kinder**mädchen, -**
der Arm + das Band + **die Uhr** = **die** Armband**uhr, -en**
schreiben + **der Tisch** = **der** Schreib**tisch, -e**
klein + **die Stadt** = **die** Klein**stadt, ¨e**

Fokus   Frankfurt am Main

Located on the Main River, Frankfurt is Germany's principal transportation hub. The city has been valued for its strategic position since Roman times. Beginning in 1356, the emperors of the Holy Roman Empire were crowned here. The poet Johann Wolfgang von Goethe (1749–1832), for whom the city's university is named, was born in Frankfurt, and the first German national assembly met here in Saint Paul's Church in 1848.

The city boasts the country's largest train station and an airport that is one of the busiest in Europe. Nicknamed "Mainhattan" because of its modern skyline, Frankfurt is one of Europe's leading financial centers. Some 430 banks (including the seat of the European Central Bank), 75 consulates, and more than 3,000 international businesses have set up shop in the Frankfurt area. Frankfurt's cosmopolitan atmosphere is reflected in its population, eight international schools, and 180 non-German professional and cultural clubs. Almost one-third of its residents have non-German passports. Thanks to its central location, Frankfurt hosts two trade shows every fall of major international importance: the International Book Fair **(die Frankfurter Buchmesse)** and the International Motor Show **(die Frankfurter Autoausstellung, IAA).** Visitors from around the world attend these shows annually.

Frankfurt ist alt und modern. Hier wohnen viele Menschen aus aller Welt.

Übung

J. Was bedeuten die Wörter und was sind die Artikel? Determine the meaning and gender of the following words.

> BEISPIEL Schokoladentafel *die Schokoladentafel; chocolate bar*

Wochentag	Wörterbuch	Hemdbluse
Neujahr	Sprechübung	Hausschuh
Sommerbluse	Familienvater	Handschuh
Herbstwetter	Jungenname	Deutschstunde
Altstadt	Zimmertür	Wanduhr
Bergsee	Hosenrock	Uhrzeit

Zusammenfassung *(Summary)*

K. Hoppla, hier fehlt was! *(Oops, something is missing here!)*

■ This is the first of many activities in which you will try to find missing information with the help of a partner. Each of you has a chart—one appears below, the other in Section 11 of the Appendix. Each chart has information the other person needs. Do not look at your partner's chart! Always start by asking about the first blank on the left; fill it in, and then proceed to the next. Take turns asking questions until both charts are complete. ■

Wer sind sie? Take turns asking each other for the missing names, nationalities, places of residence, and ages of the persons listed. Follow the model.

Name	Nationalität	Wohnort	Alter
	Schweizer	Bern	
	Deutsche		21
Pia		Graz	
Nicole			26
	Franzose	Dijon	52
Mario	Italiener	Rimini	
	Spanierin		17
Tom		Halifax	
	Amerikanerin		49

> BEISPIEL S1 Wer ist Schweizer?
> S2 Toni ist Schweizer. Und woher kommt Toni?
> S1 Toni kommt aus Bern. Wie alt ist er?
> S2 Er ist 32.

Bregenz am Bodensee

L. Sprachstudenten: Auf Deutsch bitte!

■ The translation exercises in this summary section always include material introduced in this chapter and possibly previous ones. Watch carefully for differences between English and German patterns. ■

1. Tomorrow my parents are coming. 2. My father is (a) French(man), and my mother is (an) Austrian. 3. In France they speak French, and in Austria they speak German. 4. France is west of Germany, and Austria is south of Germany. 5. I do understand French and German, but I answer in English. 6. Where are you *(fam.)* from? 7. I'm from Texas. 8. There's Thomas. Thomas is (an) American. 9. He's learning Spanish. 10. I think it's beautiful here, but I am very tired.

> Dein Christus ein **Jude,**
> dein Auto ein **Japaner,**
> deine Pizza *italienisch,*
> deine Demokratie GRIECHISCH,
> dein Kaffee brasilianisch,
> dein Urlaub *türkisch,*
> deine Zahlen **arabisch,**
> deine Schrift *lateinisch,*
> und dein Nachbar nur ein Ausländer?

🔶 For a list of all the previous and current EU members, see the map that accompanies Activity E in *Aktives zum Text.*

Fokus — Germany and the European Union

Germany is part of the European Union, which expanded to 25 member countries in May 2004 with the accession of Poland, Hungary, the Czech Republic, Slovenia, Slovakia, Latvia, Lithuania, Estonia, Cyprus (represented by the Greek Cypriot government), and Malta. The EU's population now totals more than 450 million, compared with close to 300 million in the United States. In terms of gross domestic product, the two are roughly equal.

European integration, which began in the 1950s, has gone furthest in the economic sphere: Since 2002, Germany and eleven other EU members have a common currency, called the euro (**der Euro).** This means that capital, services, and goods can move freely, without restrictions, within the **Euroland.** Today, EU citizens can travel, study, and work in other EU countries. The EU has been less successful in coordinating its members' foreign policy, since individual countries are still reluctant to have their sovereignty infringed upon. In October 2004, a new EU constitution was signed in Rome, but still needs to be ratified by the national parliaments, which might take some time. This, and the eastward shift of the EU's geographical center, should benefit Germany. Some observers believe that the expanded EU is getting too large and diverse to work well. Though inspired by the US federal model in its search for political unity, Europe is working on its own model for unification with respect for its richest asset: the historical, cultural, and linguistic diversity of the European nations.

Einblicke *(Insights)*

■ The reading texts expand on the chapter topic. All vocabulary that is to become active is listed under *Wortschatz 2*. Learn these words well; they will recur in future exercises and activities. Following *Wortschatz 2*, a pre-reading section *(Vor dem Lesen)* introduces each reading selection. It proceeds from one to several activities composed of all sorts of general and personal questions to *Das ist leicht zu verstehen!*, a short set of cognates and compounds from the reading that you should be able to pronounce and recognize but do not have to master actively. The post-reading section *(Aktives zum Text)* includes a variety of exercises and activities, including one or two brief conversations and a writing exercise with a corresponding *Schreibtipp*. ■

Wortschatz 2

der Ausländer, -	*foreigner*
Mensch, -en	*human being, person;* (pl.) *people*
Nachbar, -n/die Nachbarin, -nen	*neighbor*
Staat, -en	*state*
Teil, -e	*part*
die Europäische Union	*European Union (EU)*
arbeiten	*to work*
so . . . wie . . .	*as . . . as . . .*
ungefähr	*about, approximately*
wichtig	*important*

Vor dem Lesen *(Prereading section)*

 A. Die Europakarte Look at the map of Europe in front of the book, then answer the questions below.

1. Wie viele Nachbarn hat Deutschland? Wie heißen sie?
2. Wo liegt Dänemark? Belgien? Spanien? Frankreich? Italien? Schweden? . . .
3. Wie heißt die Hauptstadt von Deutschland? Österreich? England? Finnland? Norwegen? Polen? Litauen? Ungarn? Griechenland? Von der *(of)* Schweiz? Von der Tschechischen Republik? Von den *(of the)* Niederlanden? . . .
4. Wo in Europa sprechen Leute Deutsch als Muttersprache *(as their native tongue)*?

B. Das ist leicht zu verstehen! *(That's easy to understand!)* As your instructor pronounces the following words, underline the stressed syllable in each. Then guess their meaning in English.

der Bankier, Europäer, Großteil, Partner, Service, Tourismus; (das) Europa, Kapital, Mitteleuropa, Osteuropa, Sprachenlernen, Zentrum; die Internationalität, Politik; *(pl.)* die Chancen, Kulturen, Millionen, Personen, USA, Waren; Dänisch, Finnish, Flämisch, Griechisch, Holländisch, Luxemburgisch, Norwegisch, Polnisch, Portugiesisch, Schwedisch, Tschechisch, Ungarisch; studieren; europäisch, interessant, lange, traditionell

Deutschland in Europa

CD 2,
Track 14

^{of course}

^{by far not}

^{as}
^{of the}
ⁱⁿ
^{this way}
^{trade}

^{member states}
^{population / of more than}
^{in the / in the}
^{open to the}
^{trade partners}
^{growth markets}
^{move freely / for}
^{economy / diversity}
^{abroad}
^{tells}
^{interpreter}

^{at home / in school / fluently}
^{as never before}

Europa hat viele Länder und viele Sprachen. In Deutschland hören Sie natür-
lich° Deutsch. Aber die Nachbarn im Norden sprechen Dänisch, Schwedisch,
Norwegisch und Finnisch. Die Nachbarn im Osten sprechen Polnisch und
Tschechisch und im Westen sprechen sie Holländisch, Flämisch und Französisch. Im Süden von Europa sprechen die Menschen Italienisch, Spanisch, Portugiesisch und Griechisch; und das sind noch lange nicht° alle Sprachen!

Deutsch ist sehr wichtig. Ungefähr 95 Millionen Europäer sprechen Deutsch
als° Muttersprache: die Deutschen, Österreicher, Liechtensteiner, ein Großteil
der° Schweizer und ein Teil der Luxemburger und Belgier. Viele Ausländer arbeiten oder studieren in Deutschland, Österreich und in der° Schweiz und lernen
so° auch Deutsch. Sehr viele Menschen in Europa sprechen zwei oder drei
Sprachen. Sie finden das interessant und auch wichtig für Tourismus, Handel°
und Politik.

Die Europäische Union (EU) hat jetzt 25 Mitgliedstaaten° und eine Bevöl-
kerung° von mehr als° 450 Millionen Menschen. Das sind mehr Menschen als
in den° USA, in Kanada und in Mexiko zusammen. Deutschland liegt im°
Zentrum von Europa. Die Tür ist offen zu den° Kulturen im Norden, Süden,
Osten und Westen. Sie ist auch offen zu den traditionellen Handelspartnern° in
Westeuropa und zu den Wachstumsmärkten° in Mitteleuropa und Osteuropa.
Kapital und Service bewegen sich frei° in der EU. Das bringt Chancen für° die
Wirtschaft°, Internationalität und Vielfalt°.

Viele Deutsche arbeiten im Ausland° und viele Ausländer arbeiten in
Deutschland. Ein Beispiel ist Familie Breughel. Marcel Breughel erzählt°: „Ich
bin aus Brüssel und meine Frau Nicole ist Französin. Sie ist Dolmetscherin° und
ich bin Bankier. Wir wohnen schon zwei Jahre in Frankfurt. Wir finden es hier
sehr schön. Wir haben zwei Kinder, Maude und Dominique. Sie sprechen zu
Hause° Französisch, aber in der Schule° sprechen sie fließend° Deutsch. Das
finde ich toll. Das Sprachenlernen ist heute so wichtig wie nie zuvor°."

Aktives zum Text *(Postreading activities)*

A. Richtig oder falsch?

_____ 1. In Europa hören Sie viele Sprachen.

_____ 2. Ungefähr 920 000 Europäer sprechen Deutsch.

_____ 3. Die Liechtensteiner sprechen Deutsch als Muttersprache.

_____ 4. In Westeuropa wohnen so viele Menschen wie in Kanada und in den
USA zusammen.

_____ 5. Alle Länder in Europa sind ein Teil der EU.

_____ 6. In den USA und in Kanada wohnen mehr Menschen als in Europa.

_____ 7. Die Wachstumsmärkte im Osten sind Chancen für die Wirtschaft in
Deutschland.

_____ 8. In Deutschland arbeiten viele Ausländer.

_____ 9. Herr und Frau Breughel sind Bankiers.

_____ 10. Herr Breughel ist Franzose.

_____ 11. Familie Breughel wohnt schon fünf Jahre in Frankfurt.

_____ 12. Die Eltern und die Kinder sprechen zu Hause Deutsch.

B. Die Deutschlandkarte Look at the map of Germany on the inside cover of the book. Then answer these questions.

1. Welche Flüsse, Seen und Berge gibt es *(are there)* in Deutschland? *(Name three each.)*
2. Wo liegt die Nordsee? die Ostsee? die Insel *(island)* Rügen? die Insel Helgoland? Wo liegen die Ostfriesischen Inseln?
3. Wo liegt . . . *(Ask each other about the location of various towns in Germany.)*

C. Kurzgespräch *(A brief conversation)* Imagine you are being interviewed. How do you respond to the reporter's questions?

1. Guten Tag! Wie heißen Sie? 2. Woher kommen Sie? 3. Was ist Ihre Muttersprache? 4. Sprechen Ihre Eltern oder Großeltern Deutsch? 5. Sprechen Sie noch andere Sprachen? 6. Wie heißt Ihr Deutschbuch? 7. Wie heißt Ihr Professor? 8. Lernen Sie viel? 9. Wie finden Sie Deutsch?

D. Zusammenfassung: Deutschland heute Using the following key words taken from the reading text, summarize the passage in five or six sentences.

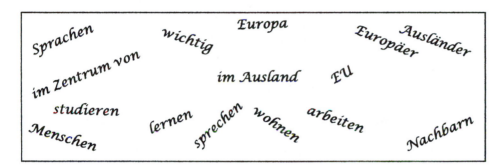

Schreibtipp

Writing a Summary

When writing a summary, keep the following in mind: (1) Be brief and try not to be repetitious; (2) Include key words from the passage; (3) Use pronouns where appropriate: *Viele Europäer sprechen zwei oder drei Sprachen.* **Sie** *finden das interessant.*

Fokus   German Throughout the World

Even though Germany was never an important colonial power, German language and culture have reached all regions of the globe. Looking for new opportunities, millions of Germans emigrated to the Americas, especially to the United States, Canada, Chile, Argentina, and Brazil. Nearly a fourth of the US population claims German ancestry, and some 300 German-language periodicals are still published here.

In Asia, German language, literature, and philosophy continue to be popular subjects at universities; thousands of exchange scholars and students from the Far East have studied in Germany. When Japan opened up to the West in the late 1800s, it borrowed heavily from German law and science. At the turn of the century, the Chinese city of Qingdao was under German administration and consequently has many German buildings—and the best beer in China.

Although Germany only briefly controlled a handful of African colonies—Togo, Cameroon, and Namibia (formerly South-West Africa)—the impact of those years as well as the influence of German missionaries and doctors can still be found in some regions. German is taught at all levels throughout Africa. Worldwide, 20 million people are learning German as a second language.

E. Die EU-Karte Look at the map of Europe, showing the old and new members of the EU, then answer the following questions.

1. Wie heißen die alten EU-Mitgliedstaaten (blau)?
2. Wie heißen die neuen EU-Mitgliedstaaten (grün)?
3. Welche Länder sind nicht in der EU?
4. Welche Sprachen sprechen die Menschen in der Europäischen Union?

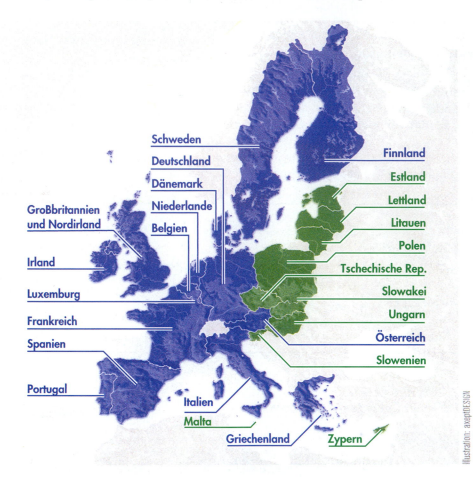

Bisherige Mitglieder
Belgien, Dänemark, Deutschland, Finnland, Frankreich, Griechenland, Irland, Italien, Luxemburg, Niederlande, Österreich, Portugal, Schweden, Spanien, Vereinigtes Königreich

F. Die neuen Mitgliedstaaten: Wie groß sind sie? How big are the new members? Read aloud in German the numbers relating to their size and population.

● F: One km² = 247.11 acres = 0.3861 square miles. Note: die Tschechische Republik, **in der** Tschechischen Republik; die Slowakei, **in der** Slowakei.

BEISPIEL Fläche: 93 000 km²
Ungarn hat dreiundneunzigtausend Quadratkilometer.
Bevölkerung: 10,2 Mio.
Ungarn hat zehn Komma zwei Millionen Menschen.

● In 2007, **Rumänien (238.400 km², 22,33 Mio.)** and **Bulgarien (111.900 km², 9,8 Mio.)** are scheduled to become members, too.

Neue Mitgliedstaaten
ab 1. Mai 2004

Malta
Fläche: 385.000 km²
Bevölkerung: 385.000

Zypern
Fläche: 9.251 km²
Bevölkerung: ca. 710.000

Estland
Fläche: 45.227 km²
Bevölkerung: 1,36 Mio.

Slowenien
Fläche: 20.723 km²
Bevölkerung: 2,0 Mio.

Lettland
Fläche: 64.597 km²
Bevölkerung: 2,36 Mio.

Litauen
Fläche: 65.000 km²
Bevölkerung: 3,69 Mio.

Slowakei
Fläche: 49.030 km²
Bevölkerung: 5,4 Mio.

Ungarn
Fläche: 93.000 km²
Bevölkerung: 10,2 Mio.

Tschechische Republik
Fläche: 78.866 km²
Bevölkerung: 10,3 Mio.

Polen
Fläche: 312.678 km²
Bevölkerung: 38,6 Mio.

 ## Hörverständnis

Track 3

Europäer in Deutschland Many foreign nationals have chosen to live in Germany. Listen to the four speakers, and then circle the letter of the response that correctly completes the statement.

Zum Erkennen: zuerst *(first of all)*; komisch *(strange)*

VITTORIO   1. Vittorio ist ____.
    a. 20   b. 29   c. 21
    2. Seine Eltern sind aus ____.
    a. Portugal   b. Italien   c. Spanien

WLOZIMIERZ 3. Wlozimierz ist aus ____.
    a. Polen   b. Portugal   c. Italien
    4. Er wohnt schon ____ Jahr(e) in Deutschland.
    a. 1   b. 2   c. 5

MARIA   5. Maria wohnt in ____.
    a. Frankfurt   b. Dresden   c. Düsseldorf
    6. Sie und ihre Familie sind ____.
    a. Griechen   b. Italiener   c. Türken

JOSÉ   7. José ist Professor in ____.
    a. Frankfurt   b. Bonn   c. Düsseldorf
    8. Seine Frau ist aus ____.
    a. Berlin   b. Erfurt   c. Köln

● When the passage includes vocabulary items that you have not yet learned, they are listed after the instructions, for recognition only.

Families on the Internet; three German cities; Germany's neighbors and the EU: http://wiegehts.heinle.com.

Lebensmittel und Geschäfte

Lernziele

In this chapter you will learn about:

Zum Thema

Food and grocery shopping

Kultur-Fokus

Shopping styles, weights and measures, the euro, pedestrian areas, and Regensburg

Struktur

The present tense of **sein** *(to be)* and **haben** *(to have)*

The accusative case and n-nouns

Sentence structure *(continued)*

Einblicke

Geschäfte und Einkaufen

Im Supermarkt

Vorschau   Shopping and Store Hours

As much as the development of American-style supermarkets and discount chains has changed the way Europeans shop, customs still differ considerably from those in North America. Many people shop daily or several times a week, frequently going on foot or by bicycle rather than by car. With competition from supermarket chains, grocery sections (**Lebensmittelabteilungen**) in department stores, and large discount stores in shopping centers (**Einkaufszentren**) on the outskirts of towns, the traditional corner grocery store (**der Tante-Emma-Laden**) is disappearing rapidly. Specialty stores such as butcher shops, bakeries, or fruit and vegetable stores continue to thrive, however, and many towns have retained open-air farmers' markets. Consumers value the freshness of the products and the personal atmosphere. Customers usually bring their own shopping bags (**Einkaufstaschen**) to stores and shops or buy reusable cloth bags or plastic bags (**Plastiktüten**) at the check-out counter. They also bag their purchases themselves. Grocery store clerks sit rather than stand when checking out customers. The amount shown on the price tag always includes tax. People generally pay in cash (**das Bargeld**). In big cities, credit cards are becoming increasingly accepted, but it is still preferable to ask before ordering a meal or shopping in a store. The most popular pieces of plastic are the EC-debit card (**die EC-Karte**) and the **Eurocard**, along with other credit cards like Mastercard and Visa.

Recycling laws require stores to take back all packaging materials; completely recyclable products are marked with a green dot (**der grüne Punkt**). Most glass beverage containers have a deposit on them (**Mehrwegflaschen**). Since January 2003, even containers like beverage cans have a 25-cent deposit on them (**das Dosenpfand**).

Germany used to be regulated by Europe's most restrictive closing law. Over vigorous opposition from owners of small shops, retail workers, and trade unions, the law was finally liberalized in 1996. Stores can now be open from 6 A.M. to 8 P.M., Monday through Saturday. Many shops and supermarkets in bigger cities are taking advantage of this change. However, many small neighborhood stores still close earlier in the evening and even for one or two hours around lunchtime. Sunday and holiday shopping have been banned since 1891, although pharmacies, bakeries, pastry shops, and news and flower stands were exempt. A few stores are now open also on Sunday afternoon, such as the grocery chain ALDI. However, the only stores that can do business round-the-clock are at airports, train stations, and gas stations.

Minidrama: *Martin geht einkaufen.*

Es gibt immer weniger (fewer and fewer) *Tante-Emma-Läden.*

Zum Thema

 ## Im Lebensmittelgeschäft

CD 3,
Track 1

■ Listen to the dialogue. Then act out the dialogue with a partner. ■

VERKÄUFER	Guten Tag! Was darf's sein?
OLIVER	Ich hätte gern etwas Obst. Haben Sie denn keine Bananen?
VERKÄUFER	Doch, da drüben.
OLIVER	Was kosten sie?
VERKÄUFER	90 Cent das Pfund.
OLIVER	Und die Orangen?
VERKÄUFER	45 Cent das Stück.
OLIVER	Gut, zwei Pfund Bananen und sechs Orangen bitte!
VERKÄUFER	Sonst noch etwas?
OLIVER	Ja, zwei Kilo Äpfel bitte!
VERKÄUFER	€ 8,10 bitte! Danke! Auf Wiedersehen!

In der Bäckerei

VERKÄUFERIN	Guten Morgen! Was darf's sein?
SIMONE	Guten Morgen! Ein Schwarzbrot und sechs Brötchen bitte!
VERKÄUFERIN	Sonst noch etwas?
SIMONE	Ja, ich brauche etwas Kuchen. Ist der Apfelstrudel frisch?
VERKÄUFERIN	Natürlich, ganz frisch.
SIMONE	Gut, dann nehme ich vier Stück.
VERKÄUFERIN	Ist das alles?
SIMONE	Ich möchte auch ein paar Plätzchen. Was für Plätzchen haben Sie heute?
VERKÄUFERIN	Zitronenplätzchen, Schokoladenplätzchen, Butterplätzchen . . .
SIMONE	Hm . . . Ich nehme 300 Gramm Schokoladenplätzchen.
VERKÄUFERIN	Noch etwas?
SIMONE	Nein, danke. Das ist alles.
VERKÄUFERIN	Das macht dann € 9,55 bitte.

● On the Continent, a "pound" is about 10% heavier than an American pound (500 g rather than 454 g). For a quick approximation, deduct 10% from US pounds to get European pounds (120 lbs. − 12 = 108 lbs.) and add 10% to European pounds to get American pounds (108 lbs + 11 = 119 lbs).

● 125 g = 1 Viertelpfund, 250 g = 1 halbes Pfund, 500 g = 1 Pfund, 1000 g = 1 Kilo(gramm). As a quick-and-easy measurement guide, some cookbooks render the following approximations: 1 oz. = 30 g; 1 lb. = 500 g; 2 lbs. = 1 kg; 4 cups = 1 liter.

A. Fragen

1. Was braucht Oliver? 2. Was kosten die Bananen? die Orangen? 3. Wie viele Bananen und wie viele Orangen kauft er? 4. Was kauft er noch? 5. Was kostet alles zusammen? 6. Wie viele Brötchen möchte Simone? 7. Was ist ganz frisch? 8. Wie viel Stück Apfelstrudel kauft sie? 9. Was für Plätzchen kauft sie? 10. Kauft sie sonst noch etwas?

 B. Jetzt sind Sie dran! Working with a partner, use the dialogues above as models and the *Wortschatz* that follows to create your own dialogue between a customer and a salesperson.

BEISPIEL	S1 Guten Tag! Was darf's sein?
	S2 Ich möchte . . . / Ich hätte gern etwas . . .
	S1 Noch etwas?

In Europe—as in most of the world—the metric system is used to measure distance, volume, and weight. One exception is the older measurement, **das Pfund**, which is half a kilogram (500 grams), or a little more than a US pound (454 grams). When shopping for food at the market, you can ask for **100 Gramm Leberwurst, ein halbes Pfund Salami,** or **ein Kilo Äpfel.** Liquids are measured by the liter, which is a little more than a quart. In cooking or baking, scales are preferred over cups and spoons, as weighing is more precise: a cup of sugar weighs about 200 grams. A cup of flour weighs about 150 grams, while a tablespoon **(ein Esslöffel)** weighs about 12 grams, and a teaspoon **(ein Teelöffel)** weighs 5 grams. One ounce equals 28.3 grams.

Wortschatz 1

Die Lebensmittel *(pl.)* *(groceries)*

der	Apfel, ⁒	apple	die	Banane, -n	banana
	Fisch, -e	fish		Bohne, -n	bean
	Jogurt, -s	yoghurt		Butter	butter
	Kaffee, -s	coffee		Cola	cola drink
	Käse, -	cheese		Erbse, -n	pea
	Kuchen, -	cake		Erdbeere, -n	strawberry
	Saft, ⁒e	juice		Gurke, -n	cucumber
	Salat, -e	lettuce; salad		Karotte, -n	carrot
	Tee, -s	tea		Limonade, -n	soft drink
	Wein, -e	wine		Limo, -s	
				Marmelade, -n	jam
das	Bier, -e	beer		Milch	milk
	Brot, -e	bread		Orange, -n	orange
	Brötchen, -	roll		Tomate, -n	tomato
	Ei, -er	egg		Wurst, ⁒e	sausage
	Fleisch	meat		Zitrone, -n	lemon
	Gemüse, -	vegetable(s)			
	Obst	fruit			
	Plätzchen, -	cookie			
	Wasser	water			

● **Limonade** (or **Limo**) is a carbonated soft drink similar to Sprite or 7-UP. It is quite different from North American *lemonade.* What North Americans call *lemonade* is **Zitronensaft.**

Weiteres

der	Markt, ⁒e	(farmers') market
	Supermarkt, ⁒e	supermarket
	Verkäufer, -	salesperson
das	Geschäft, -e	department store
	Pfund, -e; ein Pfund	pound; one pound (of)
	Stück, -e; ein Stück	piece; one piece (of)
die	Bäckerei, -en	bakery
	Buchhandlung, -en	bookstore

allerlei	all sorts of, various
alles	everything, all
Das ist alles.	That's all. That's it.
dann	then (temporal)
doch	yes, sure, certainly, of course
es gibt	there is, there are
etwas . . .	a little, some . . . (used with sg. collective nouns)

● Units of measure are always in the singular **(ein Pfund, ein Stück),** even with a plural noun: **zwei Pfund Fleisch, drei Stück Kuchen.** This applies to money as well: **vier Euro.**

Nutella Nuss-Nougat-Creme *jedes 750-g-Glas*

2⁄ 19

Grundpreis: 1000 g = 2,92

nutella

frisch	*fresh*
gern	*gladly*
Ich esse / trinke gern . . .	*I like to eat / drink . . .*
Ich esse / trinke nicht gern . . .	*I don't like to eat / drink . . .*
Ich hätte gern . . .	*I would like (to have) . . .*
Ich möchte . . .	*I would like (to have) . . .*
glauben	*to believe; to think*
kaufen / verkaufen	*to buy / to sell*
machen	*to make; to do*
suchen	*to look for*
natürlich	*of course*
was für (ein) . . . ?	*what kind of (a) . . . ?*
zusammen	*together*

Zum Erkennen: Was darf's sein? *(May I help you?)*; da drüben *(over there)*; Sonst noch etwas? *(Anything else?)*; das Kilo / zwei Kilo *(kilogram / two kilos)*; der Apfelstrudel *(apple strudel)*; AUCH: der Akkusativ, -e; verneinen *(to negate)*; jemand *(somebody)*; Das stimmt (nicht). *(That's [not] true)*; Nennen Sie . . . ! *(Name . . . !)*; Welche Silbe ist betont? *(Which syllable is stressed?)*

Aktives zum Thema

A. Mustersätze

1. Ich esse gern ____.
   Bananen → Ich esse gern Bananen.
   Äpfel, Erdbeeren, Orangen, Gurken, Jogurt . . .
2. Die Kinder essen nicht gern ____.
   Fisch → Die Kinder essen nicht gern Fisch.
   Salat, Tomaten, Karotten, Gemüse, Eier . . .
3. Wir trinken gern ____.
   Cola → Wir trinken gern Cola.
   Limo, Kaffee, Tee, Bier, Wein . . .
4. Ich hätte gern etwas ____.
   Obst → Ich hätte gern etwas Obst.
   Brot, Fleisch, Marmelade, Käse, Wurst . . .
5. Haben Sie keine ____?
   Bananen → Haben Sie keine Bananen?
   Erdbeeren, Bohnen, Erbsen, Zitronen, Brötchen . . .

B. Was passt nicht? Which item does not belong in each list?

1. die Butter—der Käse—die Milch—die Bohne
2. das Brötchen—die Zitrone—das Plätzchen—der Kuchen
3. die Karotte—die Erdbeere—die Gurke—der Salat
4. das Gemüse—der Apfel—die Orange—die Banane
5. das Obst—das Gemüse—der Salat—der Tee
6. der Wein—das Bier—die Erbse—die Milch
7. das Geschäft—die Lebensmittel—die Bäckerei—das Kaufhaus

C. Was bedeuten die Wörter und was sind die Artikel? Determine the meaning and gender of these words.

Bohnensalat, Buttermilch, Delikatessengeschäft, Erdbeermarmelade, Fischbrötchen, Kaffeemilch, Milchkaffee, Obstsalat, Orangenlimonade, Zitronenlimonade, Zitronensaft, Schreibwarengeschäft, Teewasser, Wurstbrot

D. Allerlei Lebensmittel durcheinander In this shopping cart, you'll find all sorts of groceries thrown together. With a partner, place these foods into their appropriate categories, i.e., fruits and vegetables, dairy products, meats, baked goods, beverages, or other.

OBST UND GEMÜSE:

MILCHPRODUKTE:

FLEISCHWAREN:

BACKWAREN:

GETRÄNKE:

ANDERES *(other):*

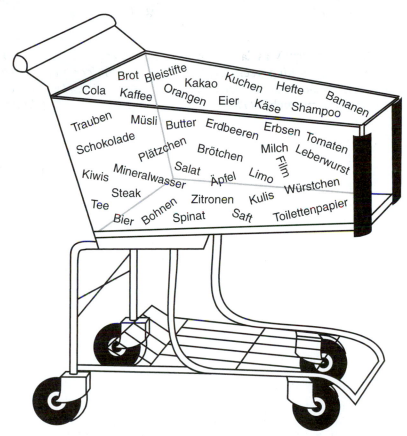

E. Was passt?

_____ 1. Ich glaube, der Fisch ist nicht frisch.

_____ 2. Möchten Sie etwas Obst?

_____ 3. Die Bäckerei verkauft Wurst, nicht wahr?

_____ 4. Wir kaufen auch Kuchen.

_____ 5. Ich trinke morgens gern Cola.

a. Wirklich?

b. Wie bitte?

c. Ich nicht.

d. Ja, gern.

e. Ja, bitte.

f. Natürlich nicht.

g. Prima!

h. Wir auch.

i. Richtig.

j. Nein, danke.

k. Doch.

l. Nein, das ist alles.

m. Schade.

n. . . .

Breads, Sausages, and Cheeses

When Germans think of **Brot**, they probably think first of a firm, heavy loaf of rye bread (**Schwarzbrot**) and not of the soft white bread so common in North America. In Germany, white loaves and rolls are prized for their crisp crust. There are more than 300 varieties of bread in Central Europe, including bread made from a mixture of wheat and rye (**Graubrot**) or of cracked rye and wheat grains (**Vollkornbrot**), as well as bread with linseed (**Leinsamenbrot**) or sunflower seeds (**Sonnenblumenkernbrot**).

For Germans, bread is the most important staple and the central focus of both the morning and evening meals. On average they eat four slices of bread and one roll per day. The traditional German supper, appropriately called **das Abendbrot**, usually consists of bread with cheese, sausage, or cold cuts (**der Aufschnitt**). Germany offers a wide variety of cheeses and sausages, which often carry the name of their place of origin: **Allgäuer** (cheese), **Frankfurter**, **Thüringer** (both sausages). Others are named after ingredients: **Butterkäse**, **Kräuterkäse** (cheese with herbs), **Leberwurst**. Many Germans also eat bread, cold cuts, and cheese for breakfast.

Die Deutschen, Österreicher und Schweizer essen gern Brot.

F. Interview: Ich esse gern . . . Interview a classmate to find out what foods he/she likes and what his/her eating habits are.

1. Was für Obst essen Sie gern (nicht) gern?
2. Was für Gemüse essen Sie (nicht) gern?
3. Essen Sie viel Fisch und Fleisch?
4. Essen Sie gern Süßigkeiten? Wenn ja, was?
5. Was trinken Sie oft?

Aussprache: e, o

CD 3,
Track 2

A. Laute

1. [e:] **geh**en, **neh**men, **K**äse, **G**egenteil, **A**merika, **T**ee
2. [e] **es**, **sp**rechen, **G**eschäft, **M**ensch, **H**emd
3. [o:] **ohn**e **Boh**nen, **o**der, **gr**oß, **O**bst, **B**rot
4. [o] **k**ommen, **d**och, **O**sten, **N**orden, **S**onne

For further review, see the Summary of Pronunciation in the front of your *Arbeitsbuch*. Study Part II, subsections 2, 5, 14–16, 18, and 21.

B. Wortpaare

1. *gate* / geht
2. *shown* / schon
3. zähle / Zelle
4. den / denn
5. Ofen / offen
6. Bonn / Bann

Hörverständnis

Track 4 **Essen und Trinken** Listen to three students tell what they like and don't like to eat and drink. Then note which foods and beverages each student mentions. Write *H* for Hanjo, *M* for Martina, and *D* for Dirk. Not all the available slots will be filled.

Zum Erkennen: also *(well)*; manchmal *(sometimes)*; Kartoffeln *(potatoes)*

ESSEN			
gern		**nicht gern**	
_____	Äpfel	_____	Gemüse
_____	Bananen	_____	Gurken
_____	Kartoffeln	_____	Karotten
_____	Kuchen	_____	Erbsen
_____	Erdbeeren	_____	Fisch
_____	Orangen	_____	Bananen
_____	Gemüse	_____	Jogurt
_____	Fisch	_____	Pizza
_____	Fleisch	_____	Käsebrot

TRINKEN			
gern		**nicht gern**	
_____	Tee	_____	Kaffee
_____	Kaffee	_____	Bier
_____	Kakao	_____	Wein
_____	Milch	_____	Milch
_____	Saft	_____	Cola
_____	Bier	_____	Wasser
_____	Cola	_____	Tee
_____	Mineralwasser	_____	Kakao
_____	Limonade	_____	Eiswasser

Fokus   Flower Power

Germans are very fond of having fresh flowers in their homes. When invited for coffee, tea, or dinner, guests usually bring their hosts a bouquet (**der Strauß, ⸚e**). The flowers, however, have to be carefully chosen: red roses, for example, carry the message of romantic love, while white chrysanthemums are considered funeral flowers. The gift of flowers (or some other small present) eliminates the need for a thank-you note, but a follow-up telephone call is very much appreciated.

Struktur

2.1 The present tense of *sein (to be)* and *haben (to have)*

	sein		haben	
1st person	ich bin	wir sind	ich habe	wir haben
2nd person	du bist	ihr seid	du hast	ihr habt
3rd person	er ist	sie sind	er hat	sie haben

Übung

A. Ersetzen Sie das Subjekt!

BEISPIEL   Haben Sie Zeit? (du)
Hast du Zeit?

1. Ich bin schon fertig. (er, wir, sie/*sg.*)
2. Sind Sie müde? (du, ihr, sie/*pl.*)
3. Sie hat die Landkarte. (ich, er, wir)
4. Haben Sie Papier? (sie/*sg.*, ihr, du)
5. Wir sind Amerikaner. (er, sie/*pl.*, ich)
6. Er hat eine Frage. (ich, wir, Sie)
7. Seid ihr aus Düsseldorf? (Sie, du, sie/*sg.*)
8. Er hat Orangensaft. (sie/*pl.*, ich, ihr)

Fokus   The Euro

In January 2002, the euro (**der Euro**) was introduced as the common currency (**die Währung**) of the European Union. There are seven denominations of bills (5, 10, 20, 50, 100, 200, and 500 euros) and eight different coins (1, 2, 5, 10, 20, 50 cents, as well as 1 and 2 euros). The bills (**der Schein, -e**) have different colors and increase in size along with their value; they are the same throughout the EU. On one side, they show all sorts of historic arches symbolizing bridges to be built between the nations; on the other side, they show a variety of national windows and portals symbolizing Europe as gateway to the rest of the world. With the coins, only the front (showing a map of Europe) is the same for all countries; the back side differs from one country to another to reflect national diversity.

While a few of the EU countries have not introduced the euro, most of them already enjoy the benefits of a single market using the same currency. This represents a tremendous advantage for consumers when traveling or buying goods or services abroad, as well as for the new economy founded on e-commerce. A single currency also allows investors to do business throughout the euro area (**das Euroland**) with minimal disruptions and to take advantage of a more stable economic environment.

2.2 The accusative case and n-nouns

The accusative case has two major functions: it is the case of the direct object and it follows certain prepositions.

1. In the English sentence *The boy asks the father,* the DIRECT OBJECT of the sentence is *the father.* He is being asked; he is the target of the verb's action. We determine the direct object by asking *who* or *what* is directly affected by the verb's action. In other words, the person you see, hear, or ask, or the thing you have, buy, or eat is the direct object.

Der Junge fragt **den Vater.**	*The boy asks the father.*
Ich kaufe **den Kuchen.**	*I buy the cake.*

a. The accusative forms of the INTERROGATIVE PRONOUN are **wen?** *(whom?)* and **was?** *(what?).* You now know two cases for this pronoun.

	persons	things and ideas
nom.	wer?	was?
acc.	**wen?**	**was?**

Wen fragt der Junge?	→	**Den Vater.**
Whom does the boy ask?	→	*The father.*
Was kaufe ich?	→	**Den Kuchen.**
What am I buying?	→	*The cake.*

b. Of the articles, only those for masculine nouns have special forms for the accusative. In the other genders, the nominative and the accusative forms are identical.

	SINGULAR			**PLURAL**
	masc.	**neut.**	**fem.**	
nom.	der	das	die	die
	ein	ein	eine	—
	kein	kein	keine	keine
acc.	**den**	**das**	**die**	**die**
	einen	**ein**	**eine**	**—**
	keinen	**kein**	**keine**	**keine**

PETER Der Käse, das Obst, die Wurst und die Brötchen sind frisch.
KATJA Dann kaufe ich **den** Käse, **das** Obst, **die** Wurst und **die** Brötchen.
PETER Aber wir brauchen **keinen** Käse, **kein** Obst, **keine** Wurst und **keine** Brötchen!

- The POSSESSIVE ADJECTIVES **mein, dein,** and **Ihr** follow the pattern of **ein** and **kein:**

> Brauchen Sie mein**en** Bleistift?
> Nein danke, ich brauche Ihr**en** Bleistift nicht.

c. German has a few masculine nouns that have an **-n** or **-en** ending in all cases (singular and plural) except in the nominative singular. They are called N-NOUNS. Note on the following page how they are listed in vocabularies and dictionaries: the first ending refers to the singular for cases other than the nominative, the second one to the plural.

You are already familiar with all of the n-nouns below.

der Franzose, **-n,** -n	*Frenchman*
Herr, **-n,** -en	*gentleman*
Junge, **-n,** -n	*boy*
Mensch, **-en,** -en	*human being, person*
Nachbar, **-n,** -n	*neighbor*
Student, **-en,** -en	*student*

	singular	plural
nom.	der Student	die Studenten
acc.	**den Studenten**	die Studenten

Der Herr heißt Müller.
Da kommt ein Student.

Fragen Sie Herr**n** Müller!
Fragen Sie den Student**en!**

d. Verbs that elicit accusative objects are called TRANSITIVE. (Some verbs are INTRANSITIVE, i.e., they cannot take a direct object: **gehen** *to go.*) Here are some familiar transitive verbs.

brauchen	*to need*	mögen / möcht-	*would like*
essen	*to eat*	nehmen	*to take*
finden	*to find*	öffnen	*to open*
fragen	*to ask*	sagen	*to say*
haben	*to have*	schreiben	*to write*
hören	*to hear*	sprechen	*to speak; to talk*
kaufen	*to buy*	suchen	*to look for*
lernen	*to learn*	trinken	*to drink*
lesen	*to read*	verkaufen	*to sell*
machen	*to make; to do*	verstehen	*to understand*
es gibt	*there is, there are*		

Sie kauft den Rock und die Bluse.
Schreiben Sie den Satz!
Ich esse einen Apfel und eine Banane.
Wir haben einen Supermarkt und ein Kaufhaus.
Das Geschäft verkauft keinen Fisch und kein Fleisch.

• The idiom **es gibt** is always followed by the accusative case in the singular or in the plural.

Es gibt in Altdorf einen Markt.
Es gibt auch Lebensmittelgeschäfte.

There's a market in Altdorf.
There are also grocery stores.

The pronoun **es** is the subject of the sentence. What "there is," is in the accusative. **Es gibt** implies a general, unspecified existence—unlike **hier ist** or **da ist**, which points to a specific item.

Gibt es in Altdorf einen Markt?
Ja, es gibt einen Markt.
Wo ist der Markt?
Da ist der Markt.

Is there a market in Altdorf?
Yes, there's a market.
Where is the market?
There's the market. (There it is.)

2. ACCUSATIVE PREPOSITIONS are always followed by the accusative case. Here are the ones used most frequently.

durch	*through*	Britta kommt **durch die Tür.**
für	*for*	Das Obst ist **für den Kuchen.**
gegen	*against*	Was hast du **gegen meinen Bruder?**
ohne	*without*	Ich esse das Brötchen **ohne den Käse.**
um	*around*	Wir gehen **um den See.**
	at (time)	Sie kommen **um 12 Uhr.**

• Some prepositions may be contracted with the definite article. These forms are especially common in everyday speech.

durch + das = **durchs**
für + das = **fürs**
um + das = **ums**

NOTE: A sentence can contain two accusatives, one the direct object and the other the object of a preposition.

Sie kauft den Fisch für den Fischsalat.

Übungen

B. Wiederholen Sie die Sätze noch einmal mit *ein* und *kein*!

BEISPIEL   Er kauft den Bleistift, das Buch und die Landkarte.
Er kauft einen Bleistift, ein Buch und eine Landkarte.
Er kauft keinen Bleistift, kein Buch und keine Landkarte.

1. Sie möchte den Rock, das Kleid und die Bluse.
2. Du brauchst das Hemd, die Hose und den Pullover.
3. Ich esse das Brötchen, die Orange und den Apfel.
4. Wir fragen den Herrn, die Frau und das Mädchen.
5. Öffnen Sie bitte die Tür und das Fenster!

C. Einkaufen You're making small talk while shopping with friends. Substitute the nouns in parentheses.

BEISPIEL   Wir kaufen den Saft. (Salat)
Wir kaufen den Salat.

1. Möchtest du das Fleisch? (Gemüse, Obst, Schwarzbrot)
2. Die Wurst essen wir nicht. (Marmelade, Tomate, Gurke)
3. Meine Schwester trinkt keinen Saft. (Limonade, Cola, Wasser)
4. Gibt es hier eine Buchhandlung? (Markt, Delikatessengeschäft, Kaufhäuser)
5. Fragen Sie den Herrn! (Junge, Mensch, Student, Studenten/*pl.*)
6. Den Verkäufer verstehe ich nicht! (Verkäuferin, Nachbar, Kind)
7. Haben Sie keinen Jogurt? (Saft, Eier, Limo)

D. Umzug *(Moving)* You are giving instructions to the movers who are bringing your belongings into your new apartment. Use the cues.

BEISPIEL   durch / Zimmer
Durch das Zimmer bitte!

1. gegen / Wand
2. um / Tisch
3. ohne / Bücher
4. durch / Tür
5. ohne / Stuhl
6. für / Kinderzimmer *(pl.)*
7. gegen / Fenster *(sg.)*
8. um / Ecke *(f.)*

E. Sagen Sie es noch einmal! Replace the noun following the preposition with another noun.

BEISPIEL Ich suche etwas für meinen Vater. (Mutter, Kind)
Ich suche etwas für meine Mutter.
Ich suche etwas für mein Kind.

1. Wir gehen durch die Geschäfte. (Supermarkt, Kaufhaus, Bäckerei)
2. Er kommt ohne das Bier. (Wein, Cola, Kaffee, Käsebrot, Salat)
3. Was haben Sie gegen den Herrn? (Verkäuferin, Mädchen, Junge, Nachbarin)
4. Wiederholen Sie das für Ihren Großvater! (Bruder, Schwester, Nachbar, Eltern)

 F. Was darf's sein? Kombinieren Sie! You are a salesperson in a clothing store. Ask your customers—(a) a friend, (b) a stranger, and (c) two of your relatives— what kind of items they need.

BEISPIEL *Was für einen Pullover möchtest du?*
Was für einen Pullover möchten Sie?
Was für Pullover möchtet ihr?

1	2	3	4
was für (ein)	Rock	brauchen	du
	Hemd	möchten	ihr
	Jacke	suchen	Sie
	Schuhe		
	. . .		

 G. Was kaufen Sie? Working with a partner, answer each question with four to six items, drawing on all the vocabulary you have had so far. Use articles whenever necessary.

BEISPIEL S1 Sie sind im Supermarkt. Was kaufen Sie?
S2 Wir kaufen einen Kuchen, eine Cola, ein Pfund Erdbeeren, ein Stück Käse, etwas Obst, etwas Jogurt . . .

1. Sie sind in der Bäckerei. Was kaufen Sie?
2. Sie sind im Kaufhaus. Was kaufen Sie?
3. Sie sind in der Buchhandlung. Was kaufen Sie?

H. Wie bitte?

1. **Großvater hört schlecht.** Your grandfather, who is hard of hearing and forgetful, always wants you to repeat whatever you say. What questions does he ask?

BEISPIEL Benjamin hat heute eine Prüfung.
Wer hat eine Prüfung?
Was hat Benjamin?

a. Vater hört den Nachbarn.
b. Matthias fragt Tante Martha.
c. Die Mutter kauft Obst.
d. Die Kinder möchten einen Apfel.
e. Helga und Britta verstehen die Engländer nicht.
f. Wir lernen Deutsch.
g. Ich suche eine Landkarte.

 2. **Auch Sie hören schlecht.** You are having difficulty understanding your partner. As he or she makes statements about shopping or anything else, ask for details.

BEISPIEL Bei *(at)* ALDI gibt es heute Vollkornbrot für 99 Cent.
Wo gibt es Brot?
Was für Brot gibt es?
Was kostet es?

I. Einkaufen für eine Party You are organizing a party for a friend. At the grocery store, buy the ingredients for a fruit salad, soft drinks, and so on. Always ask the clerk for the price of each item to make sure that anything you are buying is within your limited budget. Include these or similar expressions.

ein halbes Pfund *(half a pound)*   ein Kilo *(a kilo)*

ein Viertelpfund *(quarter of a pound)*   ein Dutzend *(a dozen)*

S1 Guten Tag! Was darf's sein?
S2 Ich brauche . . . und . . . Was kosten/kostet . . . ?
S1 . . .
S2 Und was kosten/kostet . . . ?
S1 . . .
S2 Gut, dann nehme ich . . . und . . .
S1 Sonst noch etwas?
S2 . . .
S1 . . . Euro bitte!

2.3 Sentence structure *(continued)*

1. Verb complements

   As you know from Chapter 1, predicate nouns and predicate adjectives are verb complements (V2). Sometimes objects or another verb also become part of the verb phrase, i.e., VERB COMPLEMENTS, and in that combination they complete the meaning of the main verb (V1). Verb complements usually stand at the end of the sentence.

Sie **sprechen Deutsch.**		Wir **gehen essen.**	
Sie **sprechen** gut **Deutsch.**		Wir **gehen** gern **essen.**	
Sie **sprechen** wirklich gut **Deutsch.**		Wir **gehen** mittags gern **essen.**	
V1	V2	V1	V2

2. Negation

   a. **Kein**

      Kein *(no, not a, not any)* is the negative of **ein** and, therefore, takes the same endings as **ein.** It negates nouns that in an affirmative statement or question would be preceded by **ein** or by no article at all.

      preceded by **ein:**   Hast du **einen** Bleistift?
                                   Nein, ich habe **keinen** Bleistift.
                                   No, I don't have a pencil.

      unpreceded: Haben Sie Geschwister?
                                   Nein, ich habe **keine** Geschwister.
                                   No, I don't have any brothers or sisters.

b. **Nicht**

Nicht *(not)* is used when **kein** cannot be used. It can negate an entire sentence or just part of it. Its position is determined as follows:

- When negating an entire statement, **nicht** generally stands at the end of that sentence or clause. It always follows the *subject and verb;* also, it usually follows *noun and pronoun objects* and expressions of *definite time.*

subject and verb:	*Sie schreiben* **nicht.**
noun object:	Ich brauche *die Landkarte* **nicht.**
pronoun object:	Ich brauche *sie* **nicht.**
definite time:	Ich brauche sie *heute* **nicht.**

- When **nicht** negates a particular sentence element, it usually comes right before that element. Such elements commonly include: *adverbs,* including adverbs of general time, *prepositional phrases,* and *verb complements (V2).*

adverbs:	Ich kaufe das **nicht** *gern.*
	Ich kaufe das **nicht** *hier.*
	Ich kaufe das **nicht** *oft.*
prepositional phrase:	Ich kaufe das **nicht** *im Geschäft.*
	Ich kaufe das **nicht** *auf dem Markt.*
verb complements:	Ich gehe heute **nicht** *essen.*
	Ich spiele heute **nicht** *Tennis.*
	Ich heiße **nicht** *Beyer.*
	Das ist **nicht** *mein Buch.*
	Das Obst ist **nicht** *billig.*

- The following chart shows the most frequent pattern for the placement of **nicht:**

S	V1	O	definite time expression	other adverbs or adverbial phrases	V2.
			↑		
			nicht		

Wir spielen heute **nicht** mit den Kindern Tennis.

c. **Kein** vs. **nicht**

- Use **kein** when the noun has an indefinite article or no article at all.

noun + indefinite article:	Ich kaufe *ein Brot.*
	Ich kaufe **kein** Brot.
unpreceded noun:	Ich kaufe *Milch.*
	Ich kaufe **keine** Milch.

- Use **nicht** when the noun is preceded by a definite article or a possessive adjective.

noun + definite article:	Ich kaufe *das Brot.*
	Ich kaufe *das Brot* **nicht.**
noun + possessive adjective:	Das ist *mein Buch.*
	Das ist **nicht** *mein Buch.*

d. **Ja, nein, doch**

COMPARE: Hast du das Buch?   **Ja!**   *Yes.*
                                            Nein!   *No.*
            Hast du das Buch **nicht?**   **Doch!**   *Of course, I do.*

- **Doch** is an affirmative response to a negative question or statement.

Wohnt Erika Schwarz **nicht** in Salzburg?   **Doch!**
Haben Sie **keine** Swatch-Uhren?   **Doch,** hier sind sie.
Ich glaube, sie sind **nicht** teuer.   **Doch,** sie sind teuer.

3. Coordinating conjunctions

Two independent clauses can be joined into one sentence by using COORDINATING CONJUNCTIONS. Each of the two clauses keeps the original word order.

aber	*but, however*	Wir essen Fisch, aber sie essen Fleisch.
denn	*because, for*	Sie kauft Obst, denn es ist frisch.
oder	*or*	Nehmen Sie Brot oder möchten Sie Brötchen?
und	*and*	Ich kaufe Wurst und er kauft Käse.

Übungen

J. Die Nachbarin Every time you visit your elderly neighbor, she insists that you eat or drink something. Politely refuse, using the negative **kein.**

BEISPIEL   Möchten Sie eine Banane?
            Nein, ich möchte keine Banane.

1. Nehmen Sie Erdbeeren? 2. Essen Sie Gurkensalat? 3. Trinken Sie Limo?
4. Essen Sie Jogurt? 5. Möchten Sie ein Stück Brot? 6. Nehmen Sie ein Wurstbrötchen? 7. Trinken Sie ein Glas Milch? 8. Möchten Sie einen Apfel?

K. Das stimmt nicht! *(That's not true!)* A recent acquaintance has confused you with someone else. Correct his/her misconceptions using **nicht.** Act out this situation with a partner, then switch roles. You may use the cues in brackets or your own.

BEISPIEL   Ihr Name ist [Fiedler], nicht wahr?
            Nein, mein Name ist nicht [Fiedler]. Mein Name ist [Fiedel].

1. Sie heißen [Watzlik], nicht wahr? 2. Sie kommen aus [Polen], nicht wahr? 3. Ihre Familie wohnt in [Sachsen], nicht wahr? 4. Ihr Onkel und Ihre Tante sprechen [Sächsisch], nicht wahr? 5. Ihr Bruder wohnt in [Thüringen], nicht wahr? 6. Sie studieren [Musik], nicht wahr? 7. Sie trinken gern [Tomatensaft], nicht wahr? 8. Sie essen gern [Fleischsalat], nicht wahr?

L. Nein!!!

1. **Mein kleiner Bruder verneint alles.** To get your attention, your little brother—played by your partner—contradicts everything you say. Use either **nicht** or **kein**.

   BEISPIEL   S1 Heute ist es heiß.
                         S2 Nein, heute ist es nicht heiß.

   a. Heute ist es heiß. b. Die Sonne scheint. c. Da drüben *(over there)* ist ein Geschäft. d. Das Geschäft verkauft Limonade und Eistee. e. Die Cola ist kalt. f. Ich möchte ein Käsebrötchen. g. Ich esse das Käsebrötchen! h. Ich bin Vegetarier *(vegetarian)*. i. Ich esse gern Käse. j. Käse ist gesund *(healthy / healthful)*. k. Wir gehen jetzt in eine Buchhandlung. l. Vater braucht eine Landkarte und einen Stadtplan *(city map)*. m. Er braucht die Landkarte. n. Ich finde das Amerikabuch schön. o. Wir haben Zeit. p. Ich lese gern Bücher. q. Das ist ein Spanischbuch. r. Heinz lernt Spanisch. s. Er studiert in Madrid. t. Ich brauche einen Kalender *(calendar)*. u. Ich finde den Städtekalender gut. v. Der Kalender ist billig. w. Ich möchte den Kalender. x. Wir brauchen Bleistifte und Kulis.

2. **Meinst du?** *(Do you think so?)* This time, make your own statements, which your partner may confirm or contradict. Take turns.

M. *Ja, nein* oder *doch?*

BEISPIEL   Ist der Rhein im Westen von Deutschland?   *Ja!*
                      Ist der Rhein im Osten von Deutschland?   *Nein!*
                      Ist der Rhein nicht im Westen von Deutschland?   *Doch!*

1. Sprechen die Österreicher nicht Deutsch?
2. Hat Deutschland viele Nachbarn?
3. Ist Bonn die Hauptstadt von Deutschland?
4. Ist Wien nicht die Hauptstadt von Österreich?
5. Hamburg liegt in Norddeutschland, nicht wahr?
6. Gibt es in Deutschland keine Einkaufszentren *(malls)*?
7. Sind 600 Gramm ein Pfund?
8. Ein Viertelpfund ist nicht 125 Gramm, oder?
9. Ein Kilogramm ist ein halbes Pfund, nicht wahr?

Fokus   Pedestrian Areas

Fußgängerzone in Regensburg

Most European cities have developed a pedestrian area **(die Fußgängerzone)** in the center of town. Since cars are prohibited, these areas are free of traffic noise and exhaust fumes—a great improvement in the quality of life in dense urban centers. During business hours, and especially on Saturdays, pedestrian areas are packed with shoppers. During the summer, cafés spill out onto the sidewalks, and street musicians add to the atmosphere. The prime real estate along pedestrian areas has provided property owners with an incentive to refurbish older buildings, which typically combine apartments in the upper stories and businesses on the ground floor.

N. Blitzreaktionen *(Quick reactions)* Ask your partner all sorts of questions, which he/she quickly answers with **ja, nein,** or **doch.**

BEISPIEL   S1 Du kommst aus . . . , nicht wahr?
S2 Ja! / Nein!
S1 Du hast keine Geschwister, oder?
S2 Doch! / Nein!

O. Eine Postkarte After your first week in Bremen, you are writing a brief postcard to a friend. Join the two sentences with the conjunctions indicated.

Hallo Frank,

1. Ich schreibe nicht viel. Ich habe keine Zeit. *(because)*
2. Ich finde es hier schön. Ich lerne auch sehr viel. *(and)*
3. Meine Zimmerkolleginnen/Zimmerkollegen *(roommates)* kommen aus Kanada und sprechen Französisch. Sie verstehen nicht viel Deutsch. *(but)*
4. Am Sonntag spielen wir zusammen Minigolf. Wir gehen in die Stadt. *(or)*

Zusammenfassung

P. Auf dem Marktplatz: Auf Deutsch bitte!

1. What would you like? 2. What kind of vegetables do you have today? 3. I think I'll take two pounds of beans. 4. The eggs are fresh, aren't they? —Of course. 5. We don't need (any) eggs. 6 But we need some fish and lettuce. 7. I'm not eating any fish. 8. Do you have any carrot juice? 9. Don't you like (to drink) carrot juice? —No! 10. Do you have any coke? I like to drink coke. 11. She's buying a coke and some orange juice. 12. Is that all? —No, I'd also like two pieces of strawberry cake.

Q. Hoppla, das haben sie hier wohl nicht! *(Oops, it looks as if they don't have that here!)* You and your partner are looking for certain groceries in the supermarket, but discover that you can't find them right away. Ask your partner questions about items that might or might not be visible in the picture below. Take turns and keep track of what you find.

BEISPIEL   S1   Hier gibt es kein Brot, oder?
            S2   Doch, da gibt es Brot. Aber ich sehe keinen Wein.
            S1   Nein, ich sehe auch keinen Wein. Gibt es hier . . . ?

Hier gibt es . . .	Hier gibt es kein/keine/keinen . . .

Wortschatz 2

der	Durst	thirst
	Hunger	hunger
das	Glas, ⸚er; ein Glas	glass; a glass (of)
	Würstchen, -	hot dog
die	Apotheke, -n	pharmacy
	Blume, -n	flower
	Drogerie, -n	drugstore
	Tasse, -n; eine Tasse	cup; a cup (of)

Ach du liebes bisschen!	Good grief! My goodness! Oh, dear!
Bitte, bitte!	You're welcome.
ein paar	a few, some (used with plural nouns)
montags (dienstags . . .)	on Mondays (Tuesdays, . . .)
offen / zu	open / closed
warum?	why?
Ich gehe . . . einkaufen.	I go shopping . . .
Ich habe Hunger / Durst.	I'm hungry / thirsty.

● All nouns ending in the suffix **-chen** are neuter (**das Würstchen**). The suffix makes diminutives of nouns, i.e., it makes them smaller. They often have an umlaut, but no additional plural ending: **die Tasse, das Tässchen,** *(pl.)* **zwei Tässchen.**

● An **Apotheke** sells prescription and nonprescripton drugs and is staffed by a university-trained pharmacist (**Apotheker/in**) and trained assistants. A **Drogerie** sells over-the-counter drugs, toiletries, and other items found in US drugstores and is headed by a druggist (**Drogist/in**) trained in a three-year apprenticeship.

● **Ein paar Tomaten, ein paar Äpfel** *(pl.)*; BUT **etwas Kaffee, etwas Butter** *(sg., collective noun).*

Vor dem Lesen

A. Die Einkaufsliste In the following text you'll meet Carolyn, an American student in Germany. Consult her shopping list, where she has checked what she needs, then complete the sentences. Several correct answers are possible.

1. Was hat Carolyn und was braucht sie nicht?
   Sie hat noch etwas _____ und ein paar _____. Sie braucht kein(e/en) _____.
2. Was hat sie nicht und was kauft sie?
   Carolyn hat kein(e/en) _____. Sie kauft ein paar _____, ein Pfund _____ und etwas _____.

B. Allerlei Geschäfte Ask your partner questions about the various stores. Take turns.

1. Wo gibt es Kaffee und Kuchen? Was gibt es da noch? Ab wann sind sie morgens offen?
2. Wohin gehst du, wenn du ein paar Blumen brauchst? Von wann bis wann ist das Blumengeschäft offen? Kannst du die E-Mail-Adresse buchstabieren?
3. Wo gibt es Medizin? Von wann bis wann sind sie offen? Gibt es eine Telefonnummer oder eine E-Mail-Adresse?
4. Wo verkaufen sie Weine? Kannst du das buchstabieren? Von wann bis wann sind sie offen? Wann haben sie zu? Haben sie eine Internetseite?
5. Welches Geschäft entwickelt *(develops)* Filme? Wie ist ihre Telefonnummer? Haben sie eine Internetseite?

C. Das ist leicht zu verstehen! *(That's easy to understand!)* As your instructor pronounces the following words, underline the stressed syllable in each. Then guess their meaning in English.

das Auto, Café, Einkaufen, Einkaufszentrum, Spezialgeschäft; die Boutique, Medizin; romantisch

Geschäfte und Einkaufen

Carolyn ist Studentin. Sie studiert ein Jahr in Regensburg. In der Studenten-
wohnheimküche° trifft° sie zwei Regensburger Studenten, Ursula und Peter.

dorm kitchen / meets

CD 3,
Track 4

CAROLYN	Guten Morgen! Mein Name ist Carolyn.	
URSULA	Freut mich. Das ist Peter und ich heiße Ursula.	
PETER	Guten Morgen, Carolyn! Woher kommst du?	
CAROLYN	Ich komme aus Colorado.	
5 PETER	Du, wir frühstücken° gerade°. Möchtest du eine Tasse Kaffee?	are eating breakfast / just now
CAROLYN	Ja, gern. Ich habe wirklich Hunger.	
URSULA	Hier hast du ein Stück Brot, etwas Butter und Marmelade.	
CAROLYN	Danke!	
PETER	Etwas Milch für den Kaffee?	
10 CAROLYN	Ja, bitte.	
PETER	Auch ein Ei?	
CAROLYN	Nein, danke.—Hm, das Brot ist gut! . . . Wo gibt es hier Geschäfte?	
URSULA	Um die Ecke° gibt es ein Lebensmittelgeschäft, eine Metzgerei° und auch eine Drogerie.	corner / butcher shop

🔴 In the south, the word **Metzgerei** is prevalent. Elsewhere you commonly hear **Fleischerei.**

15 CAROLYN	Prima! Ich brauche auch Medizin.	
URSULA	Da findest du auch eine Apotheke.	
CAROLYN	Ist das Lebensmittelgeschäft sehr teuer?	
PETER	Billig ist es nicht. Wir gehen oft in die Stadt, denn da findest du alles. Da gibt es Spezialgeschäfte, Supermärkte und auch	
20	Kaufhäuser. Es gibt auch ein Einkaufszentrum.	
URSULA	Regensburg ist wirklich sehr schön. Es ist alt und romantisch und um den Dom° gibt es viele Boutiquen.	cathedral
PETER	Ich finde die Fußgängerzone prima, denn da gibt es keine Autos, nur Fußgänger. Da beobachte° ich gern die Leute.	watch
25 URSULA	Du meinst° die Mädchen.	mean
PETER	Na und°!	So what!
URSULA	Wir gehen auch manchmal in ein Café und essen ein Stück Kuchen.	
PETER	Oder wir gehen an die Donau zur° „Wurstküche", essen ein paar	to the
30	Würstchen und trinken ein Glas Bier.	
URSULA	Samstags ist Markt. Da verkaufen die Bauern° Obst, Gemüse, Eier und Blumen. Alles ist sehr frisch.	farmers
CAROLYN	Und wann sind die Geschäfte offen?	
PETER	Die Kaufhäuser sind von morgens um neun bis abends um acht	
35	offen, ein paar Boutiquen nur bis um halb sieben.	
CAROLYN	Gut, dann gehe ich heute Abend einkaufen.	
PETER	Das geht nicht.°	That won't work.
CAROLYN	Warum nicht?	
PETER	Heute ist Samstag. Samstags sind die Geschäfte hier draußen° nur	out here
40	bis um vier offen und sonntags sind sie zu.	
CAROLYN	Aber nicht die Kaufhäuser, oder?	
PETER	Doch!	
CAROLYN	Ach du liebes bisschen! Dann gehe ich jetzt einkaufen. Danke fürs Frühstück!	
45 PETER	Bitte, bitte!	

Fokus Regensburg

Regensburg (pop. 125,000) is one of the few larger medieval cities in Germany not seriously damaged during World War II. Founded by the Celts around 500 B.C., it was later the site of a Roman military outpost called *Castra Regina,* dating back to A.D. 179. During the Middle Ages, the imperial diet of the Holy Roman Empire held occasional sessions there. After 1663, the city was the seat of a perpetual diet, the first attempt to establish a permanent German parliament.

Today Regensburg's old city center is largely intact and contains fine examples of Romanesque, Gothic, and baroque architecture. Its two most famous landmarks are the Gothic cathedral and a twelfth-century stone bridge that spans the Danube. The city's main sources of income are tourism, the electronics industry, and a BMW plant. The university, founded in 1962, has a significant impact on the cultural and economic life of the city.

Aktives zum Text

A. Was passt wo? Complete the sentences using the following words.

Apotheke, einkaufen, Hunger, Kaffee, Kuchen, Kaufhäuser, Lebensmittelgeschäft, samstags, Studenten, Studentin

1. Carolyn ist _____ . 2. Peter und Ursula sind auch _____ .
3. Carolyn hat wirklich _____ . 4. Um die Ecke gibt es ein _____ und eine _____ . 5. Die Leute im Café essen _____ und trinken _____ . 6. Von Montag bis Freitag sind die _____ bis abends um acht offen. 7. _____ sind die Geschäfte da draußen nur bis um vier offen. 8. Carolyn geht jetzt _____ .

B. Verneinen Sie die Sätze!

1. Sie möchte ein Ei.
2. Sie möchte Milch für den Kaffee.
3. Die Kaufhäuser sind samstags zu.
4. Verkauft die Drogerie Medizin?
5. Das Lebensmittelgeschäft ist billig.
6. Gibt es da Autos?
7. Das glaube ich.
8. Die Blumen sind frisch.
9. Ich brauche Blumen.

C. Was bedeuten die Wörter und was sind die Artikel?

Söhnchen, Töchterchen, Stühlchen, Tischchen, Heftchen, Flüsschen, Mäntelchen, Höschen, Stündchen, Teilchen, Blümchen

D. Kurzgespräch: Im Kaufhaus With your partner, prepare the following brief dialogue, then present it to the class. You want to buy an item of clothing in a department store. Describe to the salesperson what you are looking for. After viewing and commenting on several items the clerk has shown you (they may be too small, too big, too expensive, etc.), decide whether to buy any of them. If you decide not to make a purchase, explain your reasons. If you do buy something, of course, you must pay for it before you leave!

 Food shopping; Regensburg; and converting kilometers into miles: http://wiegehts.heinle.com.

 E. Dialog: Einkaufsfragen Write a brief dialogue that includes answers to the following questions about Regensburg.

Welche Geschäfte gibt es um die Ecke? Ist das Lebensmittelgeschäft sehr teuer? Wann ist Markt? Was verkaufen die Bauern da? Wie sind ihre Produkte? Wann sind die Geschäfte auf? Wann sind sie zu?

 ## Hörverständnis

Track 5

Neu in Regensburg Listen to the conversation between two students. Decide whether the statements are true or false according to the information in the dialogue.

Zum Erkennen: Sag mal! *(Say)*; nachher *(afterwards)*

_____ 1. Ursula wohnt schon zwanzig Jahre in Regensburg.
_____ 2. Claudia ist aus Passau.
_____ 3. Claudia braucht Schuhe.
_____ 4. Ursula geht heute Nachmittag einkaufen.
_____ 5. Sie geht um drei Uhr.
_____ 6. Ursula braucht Jeans und ein Sweatshirt.
_____ 7. Dann gehen sie ein paar Würstchen essen.

Im Restaurant

Lernziele

In this chapter you will learn about:

Zum Thema

Food *(continued)* and restaurants

Kultur-Fokus

Where to eat, table manners, food specialties, wine, as well as friends and acquaintances

Struktur

Verbs with vowel changes
The dative case

Einblicke

Man ist, was man isst.

For more information, go to http://iLrn.heinle.com

Mittagspause in der Fußgängerzone

Vorschau   Eating In and Out

Minidrama: *Und für Sie die Nummer 27!*
Blickpunkt: *Was gibt's zu essen?*

Until the end of World War II, cooking in the German-speaking countries varied substantially from region to region. Each region's cuisine was noticeably influenced by its neighbors. Austrian cooking, for example, had a strong Hungarian component, and Bavarian cooks in turn borrowed from Austria. Swiss-German cuisine, on the other hand, incorporated many aspects of French and Italian culinary arts.

While retaining its regional flavors, modern German cooking has been influenced by cuisines from around the world. Indeed, Germans have developed a sophisticated palate and a sharp awareness of variety and quality in their diet. Health-food stores (**Reformhäuser**) and organic grocery stores (**Bio-Läden**) can be found almost everywhere.

Food preparation is no longer the sole domain of women. More and more German men have ventured into the kitchen, and many assume responsibility for shopping and cooking (especially on weekends). Those Germans who prefer to eat out can choose from a wide range of international restaurants, including Greek, Italian, Turkish, Spanish, Chinese, and Thai. However, fast food has also gained great popularity. Pizza delivery and American hamburger outlets are available in almost every city. Other favorite ethnic foods include tacos, burritos, pasta, and **Dönerkebabs.** The traditional German fast food (**der Imbiss**) continues to offer a quick snack of sausage with potato salad (**Bratwurst mit Kartoffelsalat**).

Restaurant customs in Germany, Austria, and Switzerland differ somewhat from those of North America. Guests usually seat themselves. Before eating, diners wish each other a pleasant meal (**Guten Appetit!** or **Mahlzeit!**), even if they are strangers seated at the same table. The appropriate response is **Danke, gleichfalls!** *(Thanks, the same to you!).* Salads are not eaten before, but with the main course. Germans, like most Europeans, don't drink coffee with a meal, only afterwards. Also, water is never served automatically (and not with ice); guests are expected to order mineral water or another beverage. There are no free refills. Service (**die Bedienung**) and the value-added tax (**die Mehrwertsteuer**) are included in the price of the meal. Although a tip (**das Trinkgeld**) is not necessary, it is customary to round up the total; how much is added depends on the diner's perception of the friendliness and quality of service. After asking for the bill (**Zahlen, bitte!**), diners tell the server what they ate and then let him or her figure out what they owe. Often diners are asked if they want to pay the bill together or split it (**Zusammen oder getrennt?**). If you intend to pay by credit card, ask if they are accepted before you start your meal; if they are, it's likely to be the electronic debit card (**die EC-Karte**).

● First introduced by Turkish immigrants, the **Dönerkebab** is extremely popular in Europe. The classical **Döner** consists of pita bread split open and filled with shredded lettuce, red onion, cucumber, tomatoes, green pickled chilis, and red chili sauce, as well as long strips of freshly carved, thinly sliced pieces of lamb preferably cooked on a revolving spit. Dönerkebabs generally taste nothing like gyros in the US. Gyros are seasoned quite differently.

Zum Thema

 Im Restaurant

CD 3, Track 6 ■ Listen to the dialogue. Then act out the dialogue with a partner. ■

AXEL Herr Ober, die Speisekarte bitte!
OBER Hier bitte!
AXEL Was empfehlen Sie heute?
OBER Die Menüs sind alle sehr gut.
AXEL Gabi, was nimmst du?
GABI Ich weiß nicht. Was nimmst du?
AXEL Ich glaube, ich nehme Menü 1: Schnitzel und Kartoffelsalat.
GABI Und ich hätte gern Menü 2: Rindsrouladen mit Kartoffelklößen.
OBER Möchten Sie etwas trinken?
GABI Ein Glas Apfelsaft, und du?
AXEL Mineralwasser. *(Der Ober kommt mit dem Essen.)* Guten Appetit!
GABI Danke, gleichfalls . . . Hm, das schmeckt.
AXEL Das Schnitzel auch.

Später

GABI Wir möchten zahlen, bitte!
OBER Ja, bitte. Alles zusammen?
GABI Ja. Geben Sie mir die Rechnung bitte!
AXEL Nein, nein, nein!
GABI Doch, Axel! Heute bezahle ich.
OBER Also, einmal Menü 1, einmal Menü 2, ein Apfelsaft, ein Mineralwasser, zwei Tassen Kaffee. Sonst noch etwas?
AXEL Ja, ein Brötchen.
OBER Das macht € 30,30 bitte.
GABI *(Sie gibt dem Ober € 40,–.)* 32 Euro bitte.
OBER Und acht Euro zurück. Vielen Dank!

A. Fragen

1. Wer bringt die Speisekarte? 2. Was empfiehlt der Ober? 3. Was bestellen Gabi und Axel? 4. Was trinken sie? 5. Was bringt der Ober am Ende? 6. Wer zahlt? 7. Was kostet alles zusammen? 8. Wie viel Trinkgeld *(tip)* gibt *(gives)* Gabi dem Ober? Ist das viel? 9. Wie viel Trinkgeld geben Sie normalerweise *(normally)*? **(Ich gebe normalerweise . . . Prozent.)**

 B. Jetzt sind Sie dran! Working with a partner, use the dialogue above as a model and the *Wortschatz* that follows to create your own dialogue between a waiter and a customer.

Wortschatz 1

Das Restaurant, -s *(restaurant)*

der **Kellner**, -	*waiter*	die **Bedienung**	*server; service*
Ober, -		Gabel, -n	*fork*
Löffel, -	*spoon*	Mensa	*student cafeteria*
Teller, -	*plate*	Rechnung, -en	*check; bill*
das Café, -s	*café*	Serviette, -n	*napkin*
Messer, -	*knife*	**Speisekarte, -n**	*menu*

Das Essen *(food, meal)*

der Nachtisch	*dessert*	die **Pommes (frites)** *(pl.)*	*(French) fries*
Pfeffer	*pepper*	Suppe, -n	*soup*
Pudding	*pudding*	das **Eis**	*ice cream*
Reis	*rice*	Salz	*salt*
Zucker	*sugar*	Frühstück	*breakfast*
die Kartoffel, -n	*potato*	Mittagessen	*lunch, midday meal*
Nudel, -n	*noodle*	Abendessen	*supper*
Pizza, -s	*pizza*		

Weiteres

Herr Ober!	*Waiter!*
Bedienung!	*Waiter! / Waitress!*
Was gibt's zum Frühstück (Mittagessen . . .)?	*What's for breakfast (lunch . . .)?*
Guten Appetit!	*Enjoy your meal!*
Danke, gleichfalls!	*Thanks, the same to you!*
etwas (zu essen)	*something (to eat)*
nichts (zu trinken)	*nothing (to drink)*
noch ein(e)	*another*
viel / viele	*much / many*
wie viel? / wie viele?	*how much? / how many?*
zu Hause / nach Hause	*at home / (toward) home*
bestellen	*to order*
(be)zahlen	*to pay (for)*
bleiben	*to remain, stay*
bringen	*to bring*
empfehlen	*to recommend*
frühstücken	*to eat breakfast*
schmecken	*to taste*
Das schmeckt (gut)!	*That's good! That tastes good!*
Das schmeckt (mir).	*I like it; i.e., I like the way it tastes.*
Ich mag kein(e/en) . . .	*I don't like (any) . . . (+ acc. noun)*
Ich möchte / hätte gern . . .	*I would like to have . . .*
(Ich möchte) zahlen bitte!	*I'd like to pay.*

Zum Erkennen: das (Tages)menü, -s *(daily special)*; das Schnitzel, - *(veal cutlet)*; der Kartoffelsalat; die Rindsroulade, -n *(stuffed beef roll)*; der Kartoffelkloß, ̈e *(potato dumpling)*; das Mineralwasser; einmal (here: one order of); AUCH: der Dativ; das Objekt, -e; die Präposition, -en; vergleichen *(to compare)*; Was noch? *(What else?)*; zurück *(back)*

- In upscale restaurants, the server is usually referred to as **der Kellner / die Kellnerin** or **der Ober**. Diners usually say **Herr Ober!, Entschuldigen Sie!, Hallo!, Bedienung bitte!** or use a hand signal to catch a server's attention. There is no equivalent to **Ober** for a female server. Don't use **Oberin** for *waitress*, as that means *Mother Superior* and also *head nurse!*

- **Die Speisekarte** *(à la carte menu)* is not the same thing as **das Menü** *(complete, fixed-price menu, usually including soup and dessert)*.

- **Die [pom frits]**, BUT **die [pommes]**

- **Eis** means both *ice* and *ice cream*. If you ask for **Eis** in a restaurant, you will get ice cream. Ice water is generally not served in German-speaking countries.

- **Viel Obst** *(sg. collective noun)*, **Wie viel Obst?** BUT: **Viele Äpfel, Wie viele Äpfel?**

- Ich bin **zu Hause.** BUT: Ich gehe **nach Hause.** (See Struktur 3.2–3.)

- The verbs **zahlen** and **bezahlen** are mostly used interchangeably. They both mean *to pay for* as well as *to pay:* **Er (be)zahlt die Rechnung.** Although most Germans would say **Zahlen bitte!**, you might also hear **Ich möchte (be)zahlen.**

Frühstück mit Meerblick? Selbstverständlich! Zu einem guten Frühstück laden wir Sie ins Kurhaus / Restaurant recht herzlich ein.

Frühstücksbüfett und Kaffee 9.- €

Täglich von 09:00 -11:00 Uhr

Deciding Where to Eat

In smaller towns, hotels are often the best place to eat. A **Gasthof** or **Gasthaus** can be a restaurant or a hotel that has a restaurant serving complete meals. Since many restaurants serve hot food only at lunch and dinner times, the selection in the afternoon or late at night is usually limited. Whereas older people still like to have coffee and cake in cafés (**das Café, -s**) and pastry shops (**die Konditorei, -en**), young people flock to pubs (**die Kneipe, -n**) for a drink or small meal, or to tearooms (**die Teestube, -n**) for a cup of tea. To avoid fancy places with astronomical prices, check the menus that are usually posted outside by the entrance.

Aktives zum Thema

A. Mustersätze

1. Herr Ober, ____ bitte!
   die Speisekarte → Herr Ober, die Speisekarte bitte!
   ein Glas Mineralwasser, eine Tasse Kaffee, ein Stück Kuchen, ein Eis, die Rechnung . . .

2. Ich brauche ____.
   eine Tasse → Ich brauche eine Tasse.
   einen Teller, einen Löffel, ein Messer, eine Gabel . . .

3. Ich hätte gern ____.
   ein Glas Mineralwasser → Ich hätte gern ein Glas Mineralwasser.
   eine Tasse Kaffee, eine Tasse Tee, ein Glas Limonade, einen Teller Suppe . . .

4. Das Schnitzel schmeckt ____.
   gut → Das Schnitzel schmeckt gut.
   auch gut, wunderbar, nicht schlecht, furchtbar . . .

5. Zum Nachtisch nehme ich ____.
   ein Eis → Zum Nachtisch nehme ich ein Eis.
   Schokoladenpudding, etwas Käse, ein Stück Apfelkuchen, ein paar Erdbeeren . . .

B. Was passt nicht?

1. der Teller—das Messer—die Speisekarte—die Gabel
2. das Frühstück—der Nachtisch—das Mittagessen—das Abendessen
3. das Salz—der Zucker—der Pfeffer—die Serviette
4. die Rechnung—die Kartoffeln—die Nudeln—der Reis
5. das Café—der Appetit—das Restaurant—die Mensa
6. bestellen—empfehlen—sein—zahlen

C. Was bedeuten die Wörter und was sind die Artikel?

Frühstückstisch	Teelöffel	Schokoladenpudding
Kaffeetasse	Suppenlöffel	Jogurteis
Fleischgabel	Suppenteller	Zitroneneis
Buttermesser	Kartoffelsuppe	

Ratskeller

Tagesmenü:
I. Nudelsuppe, Schnitzel und Kartoffelsalat, Eis .... € 12,20
II. Gemüsesuppe, Rindsrouladen mit Kartoffelklößen, Eis 14,60

Tagesspezialitäten:
Bratwurst, Sauerkraut und Kartoffeln 6,50
Marinierter Hering mit Zwiebeln, Äpfeln, Gurken und Kartoffeln 7,90
Omelett mit Schinken, Bratkartoffeln und Salat 8,–
Putensteak mit Mais, Preiselbeeren und Pommes frites 8,80
Kalbsleber, Erbsen mit Karotten und Kartoffelbrei 9,75
Hühnchen mit Weinsoße, Reis und Salat 10,50
Schweinebraten, Kartoffelklöße und Rotkraut 11,20
Sauerbraten, Spätzle und Salat 12,75
Gemischte Fischplatte, Kartoffeln und Salat 13,25

Suppen:
Gulaschsuppe, Bohnensuppe, Erbsensuppe, Linsensuppe,
Kartoffelsuppe, Tomatensuppe 2,50

Salate:
Grüner Salat, Tomatensalat, Gurkensalat, Bohnensalat 2,80

Getränke:

Mineralwasser	1,–	Tee	1,80
Apfelsaft	1,75	Kaffee	2,–
Limonade	1,75	Espresso	2,50
Cola	1,80	Cappuccino	3,50
Bier **(0,2 l)**	1,40		
Wein (0,2 l)	2,20		

Nachtisch:

Schokoladenpudding	1,80	Käsekuchen	2,55
Apfelkompott	1,80	Apfelstrudel	2,80
Vanilleeis mit Erdbeeren	2,50	Kirschtorte	3,60
Rote Grütze mit Sahne	3,25	Sachertorte	3,80

🔸 In case you are curious: **der marinierte Hering, -e** (marinated herring); **das Omelett, -s** (omelet); **der Schinken, -** (ham); **die Bratkartoffeln (pl.)** (fried potatoes); **das Putensteak, -s** (turkey steak); **die Preiselbeeren (pl.)** (type of cranberries); **die Kalbsleber** (calf's liver); **das Hühnchen, -** (chicken); **die Soße, -n** (sauce, gravy); **der Schweinebraten** (pork roast); **der Kartoffelbrei** (mashed potatoes); **der Sauerbraten** (marinated pot roast); **die Spätzle (pl.)** (tiny Swabian dumplings); **die . . . -platte, -n** (. . . platter); **die Linsen (pl.)** (lentils); **der Espresso, -s;** **der Cappuccino, -s;** **das Kompott, -e** (stewed fruit); **die Rote Grütze** (berries in a thick sauce); **Rotkraut** (red cabbage); **die (Schlag)Sahne** ([whipped] cream).

🔸 A liter is a little more than a quart. Therefore, **0,2 liters of beer** is approximately three-fourths of a cup.

1. **Wir möchten bestellen!** *(We would like to order!)* In groups of two to four students, take turns ordering from the menu. One student plays the server and writes the orders down.

2. **Zahlen bitte!** Ask for the check. Tell the server what you had, e.g., **Einmal Bratwurst . . .,** and let him/her figure out what you owe. Round up your bill to include an appropriate tip.

E. Was passt?

_____ 1. Die Suppe ist eiskalt.
_____ 2. Der Kartoffelsalat schmeckt prima.
_____ 3. Möchten Sie etwas zum Nachtisch?
_____ 4. Guten Appetit!
_____ 5. Möchtest du nichts trinken?

a. Danke schön!
b. Wirklich?
c. Freut mich.
d. Das finde ich auch.
e. Ja, bitte.
f. Ja, wirklich.
g. Doch!
h. Nein, danke.
i. Ja, sie schmeckt furchtbar.
j. Ja, gern.
k. Natürlich.
l. Danke, gleichfalls.
m. Ja, ich hätte gern ein Eis.
n. . . .

F. Was noch? (What else?) With a partner, see how many items you can find for each word or phrase below. Compare your results with those of others.

BEISPIEL   ein Stück . . .
            Ich möchte ein Stück Brot.

1. ein Stück . . .
2. ein Glas . . .
3. eine Tasse . . .
4. ein paar . . .
5. etwas . . .
6. ein Pfund . . .
7. viel . . .
8. viele . . .

G. Kombinieren Sie! With your partner, make compound nouns with the following words. Then compare your list with that of others.

BEISPIEL   der Kuchen
            der Kirschkuchen, die Kuchengabel

1. die Wurst
2. der Pudding
3. die Suppe
4. der Wein
5. das Obst
6. das Wasser
7. der Kaffee

● For further review, see the Summary of Pronunciation in the front of your *Arbeitsbuch*. Study section II, subsections 22–28.

Aussprache: ü

CD 3,
Track 7

A. Laute

1. [ü:] über, Tür, für, Frühling, Prüfung, Gemüse, südlich, grün, natürlich, müde
2. [ü] Flüsse, Würste, Stück, Jürgen Müller, München, fünf, fünfundfünfzig

B. Wortpaare

1. vier / für
2. missen / müssen
3. Stuhl / Stühle
4. Mutter / Mütter
5. fühle / Fülle
6. Goethe / Güte

Hörverständnis

Track 6 **Im Gasthaus** Find out what Jürgen, Helga, and Michael are ordering for dinner. Put their initials by the foods and beverages they order. Then add up their total bill to see whether the waitress calculated it correctly.

Zum Erkennen: früh *(early)*; das Getränk, -e *(beverages)*; einmal *(one order of)*

Getränke	Essen	Nachtisch
_____ Limonade	_____ Schnitzel	_____ Apfelkuchen
_____ Apfelsaft	_____ Rindsroulade	_____ Vanilleeis
_____ Bier	_____ Pizza	_____ Reispudding
_____ Mineralwasser	_____ Würstchen	_____ Schokoladenpudding
_____ Cola	_____ Fisch	_____ Käsekuchen

Das kostet:

_____	_____	_____
_____	_____	_____
		_____
	Alles zusammen:	_____

Guten Appetit!

Struktur

3.1 Verbs with vowel changes

Some very common verbs have a stem-vowel change in the SECOND and THIRD PERSON singular. These changes will be clearly noted in all vocabulary lists like this: **sprechen (spricht).**

	e → i **sprechen** *to speak*	e → ie **sehen** *to see*	a → ä **fahren** *to drive*	au → äu **laufen** *to walk, run*
ich	spreche	sehe	fahre	laufe
du	**sprichst**	**siehst**	**fährst**	**läufst**
er	**spricht**	**sieht**	**fährt**	**läuft**
wir	sprechen	sehen	fahren	laufen
ihr	sprecht	seht	fahrt	lauft
sie	sprechen	sehen	fahren	laufen

Siehst du Dresden auf der Landkarte?
Dieter **fährt** nach Dresden.

A few verbs in this group have additional consonant changes:

	nehmen *to take*	**werden** *to become, get*
ich	nehme	werde
du	**nimmst**	**wirst**
er	**nimmt**	**wird**
wir	nehmen	werden
ihr	nehmt	werdet
sie	nehmen	werden

You need to know the following common verbs with stem-vowel changes:

essen	**isst**	*to eat*	lesen	**liest**	*to read*
empfehlen	**empfiehlt**	*to recommend*	nehmen	**nimmt**	*to take; to have (food)*
fahren	**fährt**	*to drive*			
geben	**gibt**	*to give*	sehen	**sieht**	*to see*
gefallen	**gefällt**	*to please, be pleasing*	sprechen	**spricht**	*to speak*
			tragen	**trägt**	*to carry; to wear*
helfen	**hilft**	*to help*	werden	**wird**	*to become, get*
laufen	**läuft**	*to walk, run*			

Note that the second and third person singular forms of **essen** and **lesen** are identical (**du/er isst, du/er liest**). As you know from Chapter 1, the **du-**form of verbs with a stem ending in any s-sound (**-s, -ß, ss, -tz, -z**) adds only a **t-**ending instead of an **-st**: lese → du lies**t**; heißen → du heiß**t**.

Übungen

A. Ersetzen Sie das Subjekt!

> **BEISPIEL**   Der Ober trägt die Teller. (ich)
> *Ich trage die Teller.*

1. Fahren Sie zum Kaufhaus? (wir, er, ihr, du)
2. Wir nehmen Nudelsuppe. (er, ich, sie/*pl.*, du)
3. Ich werde müde. (das Kind, wir, sie/*sg.*, sie/*pl.*)
4. Sie empfehlen das Schnitzel. (der Ober, ich, du, Axel)
5. Sehen Sie die Apotheke nicht? (du, ihr, er, die Leute)
6. Sprechen Sie Deutsch? (er, du, sie/*pl.*)
7. Hilfst du heute nicht? (ihr, Sie, sie/*sg.*)
8. Lesen Sie gern Bücher? (du, ihr, er, sie/*pl.*)

B. Was tun sie?   Answer the questions in your own words to tell what others do. Use pronouns and stem-changing verbs in your answers.

> **BEISPIEL**   Ich esse schnell. Und Ihr Großvater?
> *Er isst sehr langsam.*

1. Ich helfe gern. Und Ihr Nachbar?
2. Ich nehme Apfelstrudel. Und Gabi?
3. Ich empfehle den Schweinebraten *(pork roast)*. Und der Ober?
4. Ich laufe langsam. Und Ihr Bruder oder Ihre Schwester?
5. Ich lese gern. Und Ihre Mutter?
6. Ich fahre im Sommer nach Deutschland. Und Ihre Familie?
7. Ich sehe alles. Und Ihre Nachbarin?
8. Ich gebe gern Hausaufgaben. Und Ihr(e) [Englisch]professor(in)?

 C. Und du?   Choose a classmate whom you don't know well and find out what he/she likes. Follow the model and try to vary your responses. At the end, report to the class what you found out.

1. **Was isst du gern?** Before doing this exercise, glance at the menu and the food vocabulary in this chapter and in Chapter 2.

> **BEISPIEL**   S1 Ich esse gern . . . (z. B. Fischbrötchen).
> Und du, isst du gern . . . ?
> S2 Ja, ich esse gern . . . / Nein, ich esse nicht gern . . .
> S1 Magst du . . . (z. B. Erbsensuppe)?
> S2 Ja, ich mag . . . / Nein, ich mag kein(e/en) . . . ?
> S1 Was magst du auch nicht gern?
> S2 Ich mag auch kein(e/en) . . .

2. **Was trägst du gern?** Before doing this exercise, review the list of clothing in *Schritt 3.*

> **BEISPIEL**   S1 Ich trage gern . . . (z. B. Jeans). Und du, trägst du auch
> gern . . . ?
> S2 Natürlich trage ich gern . . . (z. B. Jeans). / Nein, ich trage
> keine . . . (z. B. Jeans).
> S1 Was trägst du noch / nicht gern?
> S2 Ich trage (nicht) gern . . . / Ich mag kein(e/en) . . . / Ich hasse
> *(hate)* . . .

Biergarten in München

 D. Umfrage *(Survey)* In small groups, ask the following questions and afterwards report back to the class. (Note: *everybody* = **jeder,** *nobody* = **niemand.**)

1. Wer spricht hier . . . (z. B. Französisch, Spanisch, Chinesisch)?
2. Wer läuft hier sehr gern?
3. Wer liest den/das/die . . . (z. B. *das Wallstreet Journal* oder *die New York Times*)?
4. Wer sieht gern . . . (z. B. „Survivor", „Smallville")?
5. Wer isst gern . . . (z. B. Bratwurst, Pommes frites)?
6. Wer isst nicht gern . . . (z. B. Fisch, Sauerkraut)?
7. Wer trinkt gern . . . (z. B. Buttermilch, Latte, Cappuccino)?
8. Wer trinkt kein(e/en) . . . (z. B. Alkohol, Cola)?
9. Wer trägt gern . . . (z. B. Lila, Gelb, Schwarz)?
10. Wer hat ein(e/en) . . . (z. B. Auto, Skateboard, Motorrad)?
11. Wer isst kein(e/en) . . . (z. B. Fleisch, Milchprodukte)?

3.2 The dative case

The dative case has three major functions in German: it is the case of the INDIRECT OBJECT, it follows certain verbs, and it follows certain prepositions.

1. In English the INDIRECT OBJECT is indicated in two ways:

- through word order: *The boy gives **the father** the plate.*
- with a preposition: *The boy gives the plate **to the father.***

In German this function is expressed through case and word order. You can determine the indirect object by asking *for whom* or *in reference to whom* (or occasionally *what*) the action of the verb is taking place.

Der Junge gibt **dem Vater** den Teller.   *The boy gives the father the plate.*

a. The dative form of the INTERROGATIVE PRONOUN is **wem?** *(to whom?).*

	persons	things and ideas
nom.	wer?	was?
acc.	wen?	was?
dat.	**wem?**	—

Wem gibt der Junge den Teller?   →   **Dem Vater.**
To whom does the boy give the plate?   →   *To the father.*

b. The dative forms of the DEFINITE and INDEFINITE ARTICLES are as follows:

	SINGULAR			PLURAL
	masc.	**neut.**	**fem.**	
nom.	der / ein / kein	das / ein / kein	die / eine / keine	die / — / keine
acc.	den / einen / keinen			
dat.	**dem** / **einem** / **keinem**	**dem** / **einem** / **keinem**	**der** / **einer** / **keiner**	**den** / **—** / **keinen**

Der Ober empfiehlt **dem** Vater, **der** Mutter und **den** Kindern das Schnitzel. Er bringt **dem** Kind einen Löffel, aber er gibt **einem** Kind kein Messer und keine Gabel.

- The POSSESSIVE ADJECTIVES **mein, dein,** and **Ihr** follow the pattern of **ein** and **kein:**

  Was empfiehlt er Ihr**em** Vater und Ihr**er** Mutter?
  Er empfiehlt mein**em** Vater und mein**er** Mutter den Fleischsalat.

- In the dative plural, all nouns add an **-n** ending, unless the plural form already ends in **-n** or **-s.**

  die Väter / den Väter**n**
  die Kinder / den Kinder**n**
  die Äpfel / den Äpfel**n**
  BUT: die Eltern / den Elter**n**
  die Mädchen / den Mädche**n**
  die Kulis / den Kuli**s**

- N-nouns also have an **-n** or **-en** ending in the dative singular, as they do in the accusative singular:

  Das Eis schmeckt dem Herr**n** und dem Student**en.**

c. Many verbs can have both accusative and dative objects.

  Der Ober bringt dem Kind den Apfelstrudel.
  The waiter brings the child the apple strudel.

  Er empfiehlt der Studentin den Sauerbraten.
  He recommends the marinated pot roast to the student.

Note the difference in meaning:

Der Onkel trägt der Tante die Lebensmittel. BUT Der Onkel trägt die Tante.

d. In sentences with two objects, the direct object, <u>if it is a noun</u>, generally follows the indirect object.

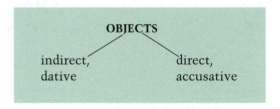

OBJECTS

indirect,   direct,
dative   accusative

Der Kellner bringt dem Herrn den Tee.

2. Dative verbs

Some verbs take only dative objects; a few such verbs are:

antworten	*to answer*	**glauben**	*to believe*
danken	*to thank*	helfen	*to help*
gefallen	*to please, be pleasing*	schmecken	*to taste*
gehören	*to belong to*		

CAUTION: Gefallen is usually not used to talk about food but rather to say that a city, a picture, an item of clothing, or a person is pleasing to you. **Schmecken** is used with food and beverages.

Der Bruder antwortet der Kusine.	*The brother answers (gives an answer to) the cousin.*
Alex dankt der Kellnerin.	*Alex thanks (gives thanks to) the waitress.*
Der Mantel gehört dem Mädchen.	*The coat belongs to the girl.*
Ich glaube dem Jungen.	*I believe the boy.*
Ich helfe dem Nachbarn.	*I'm helping (giving help to) the neighbor.*
Die Mensa gefällt den Studenten.	*The students like the cafeteria (the cafeteria pleases the students).*
Das Schnitzel schmeckt den Leuten.	*People like the schnitzel (i.e., the way it tastes).*

3. Dative prepositions

These prepositions are always followed by the dative case:

aus	*out of*	Sie kommt **aus** dem Geschäft.
	from (a place of origin)	Er ist **aus** Berlin.
außer	*besides*	**Außer** dem Café ist alles zu.
bei	*at, for (a company)*	Sie arbeitet **bei** VW.
	near, by	Die Drogerie ist **beim** Markt.
	at the home of, with	Er wohnt **bei** Familie Angerer.
mit	*with*	Ich schreibe **mit** einem Kuli.
	together with	Alex kommt **mit** Gabi.
nach	*after (time)*	Kommst du **nach** dem Mittagessen?
	to (cities, countries, continents)	Fahrt ihr auch **nach** Österreich?
	to (in certain expressions)	Gehen Sie **nach** Hause!
seit	*since*	Sie wohnen **seit** Mai in Ulm.
	for (time)	Sie wohnen **seit** drei Tagen da.
von	*of*	Das Gegenteil **von** billig ist teuer.
	from	Wir fahren **von** Ulm nach Hamburg.
	by (origin)	Das Bild ist **von** Albrecht Dürer.
zu	*to (in the direction of)*	Sie fährt **zum** Supermarkt.
	at (in certain expressions)	Sie sind **zu** Hause.
	for (purpose)	Was gibt es **zum** Nachtisch?

🔴 **Seit** translates as *for* in English when it expresses a duration of time (e.g., three minutes, one year) that began in the past and continues into the present: *They have been living there for three years.*

• Some dative prepositions are frequently contracted with the definite article.

bei + dem = **beim**	zu + dem = **zum**
von + dem = **vom**	zu + der = **zur**

• Pay particular attention to the contrasting use of these pairs of prepositions:

Sie fährt **zum** *(to the)* Supermarkt.
Fahrt ihr **nach** *(to)* Deutschland?
Wir fahren **von** *(from)* Salzburg **nach** München.
Er kommt **aus** *(from)* Salzburg.
Gehen Sie **nach** Hause *(home)!*
Sie sind nicht **zu** Hause *([at] home).*

Übungen

E. Sagen Sie die Sätze im Plural! Restate the sentences, making the phrases in boldface plural.

BEISPIEL Wir sprechen mit **dem Kanadier.**
Wir sprechen mit den Kanadiern.

1. Er lernt seit **einem Jahr** Deutsch. (drei) 2. Das Restaurant gehört **dem Schweizer.** 3. Sie kommen aus **dem Geschäft.** 4. Nach **einem Monat** bezahlt er die Rechnung. (zwei) 5. Ich gehe nur mit **dem Kind.** 6. Die Stadt gefällt **dem Engländer.** 7. Der Ober kommt mit **der Serviette.** 8. Wir sprechen mit **dem Nachbarn.** 9. Das Geschäft ist bei **dem Restaurant.** 10. Der Kuchen schmeckt **dem Studenten.**

F. Ersetzen Sie das Dativobjekt!

BEISPIEL   Die Bedienung bringt dem Kind ein Eis. (Großvater)
            Die Bedienung bringt dem Großvater ein Eis.

1. Die Kellnerin empfiehlt dem Vater die Rouladen. (Bruder, Spanier, Schweizer)
2. Der Junge gibt der Mutter ein Bild. (Schwester, Herr, Frau)
3. Der Ober bringt den Eltern das Essen. (Leute, Amerikaner/*pl.*, Studenten/*pl.*)
4. Die Drogerie gehört meiner Großmutter. (Nachbar, Eltern, Familie)
5. Axel dankt dem Bruder. (Schwester, Franzose, Leute)
6. Meine Großmutter hilft meinem Vater. (Mutter, Kusinen, Cousins)

G. Sagen Sie es noch einmal! Replace the nouns following the prepositions with the words in parentheses.

BEISPIEL   Eva geht zum Lebensmittelgeschäft. (Apotheke)
            Eva geht zur Apotheke.

1. Paula kommt aus dem Kaufhaus. (Drogerie, Café, Mensa)
2. Seit Sonntag ist er wieder hier. (zwei Tage, eine Stunde, ein Monat)
3. Wir sprechen mit dem Großvater. (Frau, Mädchen, Großeltern)
4. Ich wohne bei meinen Eltern. (Bruder, Schwester, Familie)
5. Er möchte etwas Salat zu den Rouladen. (Schnitzel, Suppe, Würstchen/*pl.*, Fleisch)
6. Nach dem Mittagessen spielen sie Tennis. (Frühstück, Kaffee, Deutschstunde)
7. Außer meinem Bruder sind alle hier. (Vater, Mutter, Tante, Geschwister)
8. Kommst du von der Drogerie? (Markt, Café, Nachbarn)

H. *Wer, wem* oder *was?* You are talking to a friend at a graduation party. Because of the loud music, you can't hear him/her very well. Ask what he/she said three different ways and provide the answer he/she gives for each one.

BEISPIEL   Oskar gibt dem Bruder die Bücher.
            Wer gibt dem Bruder die Bücher?   — *Oskar!*
            Wem gibt Oskar die Bücher?   — *Dem Bruder!*
            Was gibt Oskar dem Bruder?   — *Die Bücher!*

1. Der Nachbar verkauft Onkel Willi den BMW.
2. Onkel Willi gibt dem Jungen den BMW.
3. Großmutter empfiehlt Irene ein paar Tage Ferien *(vacation)*.
4. Die Kinder zahlen der Mutter die Hotelrechnung.
5. Der Vater glaubt den Leuten die Geschichte *(story)* nicht.

Fokus Cafés and Coffee Houses

Cafés and pastry shops are favorite places for conversation or for breaks in shopping excursions. They serve coffee, tea, and hot chocolate, along with a great variety of delicious cakes and pastries. In Austria, many people have a favorite café (**das Kaffeehaus**) where they can relax over such items as **Kaffee mit Schlag** *(coffee with whipped cream)* or a piece of **Linzertorte** *(jam-filled tart)*. The tradition of the coffee house goes back to the early 1700s. Since then, it has been the preferred meeting place not only of the literati, reformers, artists, and philosophers, but also of middle-class society.

Hm, da bekommt man Appetit.

I. Hoppla, hier fehlt was! Freunde helfen auspacken. You and your partner are helping another friend unpack after a family move. Work together to figure out what belongs to whom. One of you looks at and completes the chart below, the other one works with the chart in Section 11 of the Appendix.

Was gehört wem?

	Bruder	Schwester	Mutter	Vater	Großeltern
Bild	x				
Bücher					
Tennishose				x	
Hausschuhe					
Pulli		x			
Ringe *(pl.)*			x		
T-Shirts					
Mantel					
Messer *(sg.)*					
Gläser					x

> BEISPIEL   S1 Wem gehören die Hausschuhe?
> S2 Die Hausschuhe gehören dem Vater. Und wem gehört das Bild?
> S1 Das Bild gehört dem Bruder.

J. Was gefällt wem?

1. **Ersetzen Sie das Dativobjekt!**
   a. Das Restaurant gefällt dem Onkel. (Tante, Großmutter, Kinder, Geschwister, Student, Studentin, Studenten)
   b. Die Preise gefallen der Familie nicht. (Frau, Leute, Nachbar, Herren)

2. **Gefallen, schmecken, mögen: Auf Deutsch bitte!**

> BEISPIEL   My cousin likes Hamburg.
> *Hamburg gefällt meinem Cousin.*

a. Ms. Bayer likes the country. b. My father likes the city. c. My mother likes the South. d. My sister likes the lakes. e. My brothers and sisters like the mountains. f. My grandparents like the student. g. The student likes my grandparents. h. I like German. i. I like the Bratwurst. j. Julia likes the pork roast. k. My friends like the fish. l. I don't like fish. m. Do you like fish? n. I love to eat fish. o. The fish platter tastes especially good.

K. Was kaufen wir wem? The holiday season is approaching, and you and your partner are coming up with ideas for presents for the whole family: brothers and sisters, parents and grandparents, uncles, and aunts. Draw on all the vocabulary you have had so far plus any from the gift box below. Respond to each other's suggestions.

BEISPIEL   S1   Braucht deine Mutter Schreibpapier?
             S2   Nein. Sie hat Schreibpapier. Ich kaufe meiner Mutter kein Schreibpapier.
             S1   Gefallen deinem Vater Kochbücher?
             S2   Ja, sehr. Gut, ich kaufe meinem Vater ein Kochbuch.

die Kamera
das Handy *(cell phone)*
der Gürtel *(belt)*   die Kassette
das Parfüm
die Krawatte *(tie)*   die Bluse   die Blumen
das Video   das Fotoalbum
das Schreibpapier   das Kochbuch *(cookbook)*
die Ohrringe   die DVD   der Ring
die Handtasche *(handbag)*
eine Flasche Wein *(a bottle of wine)*   der Kalender
der Pullover   das Portemonnaie *(wallet)*
die Uhr   die CD
das Taschenmesser *(pocket knife)*   die Kette *(necklace)*

L. *Nach Hause* und *zu Hause*

1. **Was fehlt?**

   a. Heute essen wir _____.
   b. Jürgen ist nicht _____.
   c. Er kommt oft spät _____.
   d. Morgen bleibt er _____.
   e. Wir arbeiten gern _____.
   f. Geht ihr um sechs _____?
   g. Bringst du die Großeltern _____?

2. **Umfrage (Survey)** In small groups, ask the following questions and then report back to the class. In case you need it: *everybody* = **jeder,** *nobody* = **niemand.**

   a. Wer wohnt bei den Eltern?
   b. Wer kommt nur ab und zu *(once in a while)* nach Hause?
   c. Wer hat zu Hause einen Hund *(dog)?* eine Katze *(cat)?* einen Vogel *(bird)?*
   d. Wer hilft zu Hause gern in der Küche *(in the kitchen)?*
   e. Wer arbeitet zu Hause viel im Garten *(in the yard)?*
   f. Wer schreibt oder emailt viel nach Hause?
   g. Wer geht zu Hause einkaufen?
   h. Wem schmeckt das Essen zu Hause besonders gut?
   i. Wer kommt oft spät nach Hause?

The animals are not active vocabulary!

M. Die Präpositionen *aus, bei, mit, nach, von* und *zu* Use contractions when appropriate.

1. Gehst du _____ Buchhandlung? —Nein, ich gehe _____ Kaufhaus. *(to the / to the)*
2. Das Kaufhaus ist _____ Café Engel. *(by)*
3. Christl arbeitet _____ VW. *(at)*
4. Julia fährt heute _____ Leipzig und Philipp _____ Dresden. *(to)*
5. Sind Sie auch _____ Norddeutschland? *(from)*
6. Antonio kommt _____ Rom und wohnt _____ Familie Dinkelacker. *(from / at the home of)*
7. Herr Dinkelacker fährt morgen _____ Frankfurt _____ Stuttgart. *(from / to)*
8. Er fährt _____ der Familie. *(together with)*

Zusammenfassung

N. Bilden Sie Sätze!

BEISPIEL   das / sein / für / Onkel
Das ist für den Onkel.

1. Ober / kommen / mit / Speisekarte
2. Mutter / kaufen / Kind / Apfelsaft
3. Student / empfehlen / Studentin / Apfelkuchen
4. er / sehen / Großvater / nicht
5. kommen / du / von / Mensa?
6. Familie / fahren / nicht / nach / Berlin
7. arbeiten / du / auch / bei / Delikatessengeschäft Dallmayr?
8. Vater / kaufen / Kinder / schnell / ein paar / Pommes frites

O. Guten Appetit: Was fehlt? Complete the articles and contractions if needed.

1. Zu_____ Essen braucht man ein_____ Messer und ein_____ Gabel. 2. Suppe isst man mit ein_____ Esslöffel *(tablespoon)* und für d_____ Kaffee braucht man ein_____ Kaffeelöffel. 9. D_____ Restaurant gefällt d_____ Studenten *(pl.).* 10. Aber sie haben etwas gegen d_____ Preise. 11. Wir sprechen von d_____ Professor und von d_____ Prüfung. 12. Ich bestelle noch ein_____ Cola. 13. Hier trinke ich d_____ Cola aus ein_____ Glas, aber zu Hause aus d_____ Flasche *(f., bottle).* 14. Da kommt der Ober mit d_____ Rechnung. 15. Ohne d_____ Rechnung geht's nicht. 16. Danke für d_____ Mittagessen!

P. In der Mensa: Auf Deutsch bitte!

1. Paul and Helga are walking to the cafeteria. 2. They're from Hamburg. They're Hamburgers. 3. Paul lives with *(at the home of)* a family, and Helga lives at home. 4. Helga, what are you having? 5. I think I'll take the roast **(der Braten),** peas, carrots, and a glass of juice. 6. Would you *(formal)* like a piece of cake for dessert? 7. No, I'm not eating any cake, because I am on a diet **(auf Diät).** 8. I have no knife, no fork, and no spoon. 9. Paul brings the student *(f.)* a knife, a fork, a spoon, and (some) ice cream. 10. Whose ice cream is that? (To whom does the ice cream belong?) 11. Would you *(fam.)* like some ice cream with a cookie? 12. She thanks the student *(m.).* 13. Who's paying for (the) lunch?

iLrn

Visit the *Wie geht's?* iLrn website for more review and practice of the grammar points you have just learned.

Fokus | Regional Specialties

"Food and drink are the glue that keep body and soul together," claims an old Viennese saying. This sentiment is popular in all German-speaking countries.

German cooking has many regional specialties. In addition to excellent hams and sausages, there are numerous fish dishes, such as Helgoland lobster, **Hamburger Matjestopf** *(pickled herring with sliced apples and onion rings in a sour-cream sauce)*, Berlin eel soup, and Black Forest trout. Other regional dishes include **Sauerbraten** *(marinated pot roast)* from the Rhineland, **Kasseler Rippchen** *(smoked loin of pork)*, Bavarian **Spanferkel** *(suckling pig)*, and **Leberkäs** *(meat loaf made with minced meat and liver, eggs, and spices)*. In the South, dumplings and pasta dishes (e.g., **Spätzle**) are popular. Germany also boasts a large variety of pastries, such as **Schwarzwälder Kirschtorte** *(Black Forest cake)*, **Frankfurter Kranz** *(a rich cake ring decorated with whipped cream and nuts)*, and **Thüringer**

Mohnkuchen *(poppy-seed cake)*. A favorite summer dessert is **Rote Grütze** *(berries and their juices thickened with sago starch and served with vanilla sauce or cream)*.

Most famous among Austrian dishes are **Schnitzel**, **Gulasch**, and a variety of salted and smoked meats, as well as dumplings. But desserts like **Strudel**, **Palatschinken** *(dessert crêpes)*, **Kaiserschmarren** *(pancakes pulled to pieces and sprinkled with powdered sugar and raisins)*, and **Sacher-torte** delight visitors even more. Swiss cooking has also developed many specialties of its own, such as **Geschnetzeltes** *(minced veal in a cream sauce)*, **Berner Platte** *(dish with a variety of hams and sausages)*, and **Rös(ch)ti** *(fried potatoes with bacon cubes)*. The most famous Swiss dish is probably cheese fondue **(Käsefondue)**, a reminder that Switzerland produces a great variety of excellent cheeses (e.g., **Gruyère, Emmentaler, Appenzeller**).

Lerntipp
Reviewing for Tests

If you have taken full advantage of all class sessions, kept up with your work, and reviewed your lessons regularly, you should not have to spend much time preparing for tests. Concentrate on the areas that give you the most trouble. Use the *Rückblicke* sections in the *Arbeitsbuch* for efficient reviewing. Go over the vocabulary lists of the chapters that will be covered by the test; make sure you know genders and plurals of nouns. Mark any words you seem to have trouble remembering; review them again. Begin your review early enough so that you can clarify any questions with your instructor.

Schnitzel à la Holstein mit Bratkartoffeln und Ei

Einblicke

Wortschatz 2

der Freund, -e	(close) friend; boyfriend
die Freundin, -nen	(close) friend; girlfriend
Flasche, -n; eine Flasche . . .	bottle; a bottle of . . .
Hand, ⁼e	hand
besonders	especially
gewöhnlich	usual(ly)
man	one (they, people), you
manchmal	sometimes
nicht nur . . . , sondern auch	not only . . . but also . . .
überall	everywhere
vielleicht	perhaps
dick machen	to be fattening
schlafen (schläft)	to sleep

Vor dem Lesen

A. Persönliche Fragen *(Personal questions)* At the exit of your cafeteria, a marketing specialist who is studying what college students eat and drink asks you to answer some questions. Work in pairs and play each role in turns.

1. Wann frühstückst du morgens? Wann isst du mittags und wann abends?
2. Wann isst du warm, mittags oder abends?
3. Wenn du Wasser trinkst, trinkst du Mineralwasser oder Leitungswasser *(tap water)*?
4. Trinkst du dein Wasser mit oder ohne Eiswürfel *(ice cubes)*?
5. Isst du gewöhnlich Nachtisch? Wenn ja *(if so)*, was besonders gern?
6. Zählst du beim Essen die Kalorien?
7. Isst du schnell oder langsam?
8. Gehst du manchmal ins Café, ins Restaurant, in eine Teestube *(tearoom)* oder in eine Kneipe *(pub)*? Wenn ja, wo, wann und was bestellst du gern?
9. Trinkst du Wein oder Bier? Wenn ja, wann? Wenn nicht, was trinkst du auf *(at)* Partys?
10. Ist das, was du isst, immer gesund *(always healthy)*? Wenn nein, warum isst du es?

● Optional tongue twisters **(Zungenbrecher):** 1. Selten ess' ich Essig *(vinegar)*. Ess' ich Essig, ess' ich Essig mit Salat. 2. Klaus Knopf liebt Knödel, Klöße, Klöpse *(meat balls)*. Knödel, Klöße, Klöpse liebt Klaus Knopf.

Fokus   Friends and Acquaintances

Germans consciously distinguish between friends **(Freunde)** and acquaintances **(Bekannte).** This is based on the belief that there are only a few real friends among so many people. Genuine friendships are considered special and often last for a lifetime.

B. Allerlei Restaurants What do these ads tell you about the various restaurants?

1. Wie heißen die fünf Restaurants? 2. Von wann bis wann sind sie offen? 3. Gibt es Telefonnummern? Wenn ja, lesen Sie sie bitte laut 4. Wo gibt es deutsche Küche? chinesische Spezialitäten? französische Delikatessen? 5. Wo bekommt man Bier vom Fass *(beer on tap)?* 6. Wo essen Studenten besonders billig? Was kostet für sie das Buffet? Was gibt es vielleicht beim Buffet? Was denken Sie? 7. Welches Restaurant verkauft auch außer Haus *(has take-out orders)?* 8. Welches Restaurant ist besonders alt? 9. Welche Reklame *(ad)* gefällt Ihnen besonders gut? Warum? 10. Wo möchten Sie gern einmal essen? Warum?

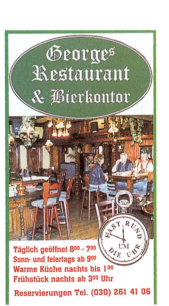

NOTE: As you can see in the advertisement for LA CORNICHE, the German spelling reform is not followed everywhere. Frequently, you will still find the old "ß" where it now should be an "ss," e.g., In Berlin **läßt** es sich leben wie „Gott in Frankreich" *(In Berlin, you can live like a king, lit.: "like God in France").*

C. Das ist leicht zu verstehen! *(That's easy to understand!)* As your instructor pronounces the following words, underline the stressed syllable. Then guess their meaning in English.

der Kaffeeklatsch; die Pasta, Schule; die Kartoffelchips *(pl).*; genetisch modifiziert, relativ, voll

Gemütlich frühstücken ist wichtig.

Man ist, was man isst.

CD 3, Track 9

Die Deutschen, Österreicher und Schweizer beginnen den Tag gewöhnlich mit einem guten° Frühstück. Zum Frühstück gibt es Brot oder Brötchen, Butter, Marmelade, vielleicht auch ein Ei, etwas Schinken oder Käse und manchmal auch etwas Jogurt oder Müsli. Dazu° trinkt man Kaffee, Milch, Obstsaft, Tee oder Kakao.

Mittags isst man warm. Um die Zeit sind viele Schulen aus und die Kinder kommen zum Mittagessen nach Hause. Manche Büros° machen mittags zu. Viele Leute essen mittags zu Hause. Andere° gehen nicht nach Hause, sondern in die Kantine° oder in ein Restaurant. Im Restaurant gibt es gewöhnlich ein Tagesmenü. Das ist oft besonders gut und billig. Außer Bratwurst, Omelett oder Hähnchen° findet man natürlich auch Lokalspezialitäten, wie zum Beispiel Hamburger Matjestopf° oder bayrische Schweinshax'n° mit Knödeln°. Zum Mittagessen trinkt man gern Saft, Limonade oder Mineralwasser, vielleicht auch ein Glas Wein oder Bier, aber kein Leitungswasser° und auch keinen Kaffee. Kaffee trinkt man manchmal nach dem Essen. Egal wo°, überall findet man etwas Besonderes°. Probieren° Sie die Spezialitäten! Nehmen Sie auch das Messer in die rechte° Hand und die Gabel in die linke° Hand, und dann Guten Appetit! Fürs Mittagessen braucht man gewöhnlich Zeit. Leute mit nur wenig° Zeit gehen zur Imbissbude°. Da gibt es Bratwurst, Fischbrötchen°, Tacos, Burritos, Pizza, Pasta, Döner° oder Hamburger mit Pommes frites. Schnell essen ist manchmal nicht schlecht, aber ein Mittagessen ist das für die meisten° Leute nicht.

Lesetipp
Identifying the Topic of a Passage

The first sentence of a paragraph often summarizes what will come next. Make sure you understand these thematic introductions clearly, and the rest of the passage should be easier to follow.

good

With it

Some offices
Others
company cafeteria

(grilled) chicken
pickled herring / Bavarian pig's knuckles / dumplings
tap water
no matter where
something special / try
right / left
little
fast-food stand / fish sandwich
gyros
most

leisurely
talk
pastry shop

evening meal
full stomach
curd cheese

pretzel sticks

as we do here
food coloring / preservatives
unpopular

Nachmittags sieht man viele Menschen in Cafés. Da sitzen sie gemütlich°
bei einer Tasse Kaffee und reden°. Kaffeeklatsch gibt es aber nicht nur im Café
oder einer Konditorei°, sondern auch zu Hause. Besonders sonntags kommt man
25 oft mit Freunden zusammen zu einer Tasse Kaffee und einem Stück Kuchen.
Abends zum Abendbrot° isst man gewöhnlich kalt und nicht so viel wie
mittags. Man sagt: Mit einem vollen Bauch° schläft man schlecht; und was man
abends isst, macht dick. So gibt es nur etwas Brot mit Quark° oder Käse, Wurst
oder Fisch, ein paar Tomaten oder saure Gurken. Dazu gibt es vielleicht eine
30 Tasse Tee oder ein Bier. Abends öffnet man auch gern eine Flasche Wein für
Freunde. Dazu gibt es Salzstangen° oder Kartoffelchips.
Den meisten Deutschen, Österreichern und Schweizern ist wichtig, was sie
essen. Wie bei uns° essen sie relativ viel Obst, Salat und Gemüse. Auch haben
sie etwas gegen Farbstoffe° und Konservierungsmittel°. Genetisch modifizierte
35 Lebensmittel sind unbeliebt°—und das nicht nur in Deutschland, sondern auch
in den anderen EU-Ländern. Was man isst, ist heute wichtig. Wie heißt es? „Man
ist, was man isst!"

Aktives zum Text

A. Welche Antwort passt? Fill in the correct answer according to the text.

1. Zum Frühstück gibt es ___.
   a Sauerbraten c. viel Obst und Gemüse
   b. Kuchen und Plätzchen d. Brot, Butter und Marmelade
2. Mittags essen viele Schulkinder ___.
   a. in der Schule c. im Restaurant
   b. zu Hause d. etwas Besonderes
3. Zum Mittagessen trinkt man gern ___.
   a. Kaffee, Milch oder Tee c. Mineralwasser
   b. Eiswasser d. Kakao
4. Zum Abendessen isst man gewöhnlich ___.
   a. Kaffee und Kuchen c. Suppe, Fleisch und Gemüse
   b. Brot, Wurst und Käse d. Salzstangen und Kartoffelchips
5. Die Deutschen, Österreicher und Schweizer essen ___ Obst und Gemüse.
   a. nicht viel c. nur
   b. kein d. gern
6. Genetisch modifizierte Lebensmittel ___ in Deutschland.
   a. sind besonders teuer c. sind unbeliebt
   b. isst man gern d. gibt es nicht

Fokus Wines from Germany, Austria, and Switzerland

All in all, there are thirteen German wine-growing regions, but most of Germany's wine is produced in western and southwestern Germany. The wines from the Rhine and Moselle rivers (**Rheinwein** and **Moselwein**), as well as from Franconia (**Franken**) and Baden-Württemberg, are especially famous around the world. In Switzerland, 18 of the 23 cantons grow wine. It seems that wine is to the Swiss what beer is to the Bavarians. In Austria, there are excellent vineyards along the Danube around Vienna. Wines are classified as **Tafelwein** *(table or ordinary wine)*, **Qualitätswein** *(quality wine)*, or **Qualitätswein mit Prädikat** *(superior wine)*.

B. Guten Appetit: Was fehlt?

1. Ich beginne den Tag gewöhnlich mit ein____ guten Frühstück: mit ein____ Brötchen, ein____ Ei und ein____ Tasse Tee. 2. Gehst du mittags ____ Hause? 3. Ja, ____ Hause ist es nicht so teuer. 4. Bei d____ Preisen esse ich gern ____ Hause. 5. Warum gehst du nicht zu ____ Mensa? 6. D____ Essen schmeckt mir nicht. 7. Manchmal gehe ich zu ein____ Imbissbude *(f.).* 8. Dann esse ich nichts außer ein____ Bratwurst und die Cola trinke ich schnell aus d____ Flasche. 9. Oft habe ich kein____ Hunger. 10. Dann esse ich nur ein____ Apfel oder ein____ Banane. 11. Möchtest du etwas Brot mit ein____ Stück Käse? 12. Es ist von d____ Bio-Laden und hat kein____ Konservierungsmittel *(pl.)!*

 ## C. Vergleichen Sie! With a classmate, make two lists that compare German and North American food and drink preferences. Draw on all the vocabulary you have learned so far.

	DEUTSCHLAND, SCHWEIZ, ÖSTERREICH	NORDAMERIKA
Zum Frühstück:		
Zum Mittagessen:		
Zum Abendessen:		

 ## D. Die Pizzeria Taking turns, ask your partner about DANTE's pizza ad, and find out how he/she likes pizza.

1. Wie heißt die Pizzeria? 2. Wo ist sie? 3. Wie ist die Telefonnummer? 4. Wie ist die Faxnummer? 5. Gibt es eine E-Mail-Adresse? 6. Was ist der Mindestbestellwert *(minimum order)?* 7. Was macht das Pizza-Taxi? 8. Wer sitzt und wer flitzt *(is rushing)?* 9. Von wann bis wann sind sie offen? 10. Haben Sie einen Ruhetag *(a day when they're closed)?* 11. Bestellen Sie manchmal auch Pizza? Wenn ja, wo? 12. Welche Pizza bestellen Sie gern? 13. Was kostet eine Pizza? 14. Essen Sie Pizza mit Messer und Gabel oder mit der Hand?

Fokus | Table Manners

Whenever Europeans eat something that needs to be cut, they hold the knife in the right hand and the fork in the left throughout the meal—rather than shifting the fork to the right hand after cutting. (It is said that American spies during World War II could be identified by their different food-cutting habits.) If no knife is needed, the left hand rests on the table next to the plate, not in the lap. To signal that a person is finished eating, the knife and fork are placed parallel and diagonally on the plate.

Beim Mittagessen

 E. Wie isst man das? Working in groups or pairs, show each other how you would eat the following foods.

Suppe, Salat, Bratwurst, Hähnchen, Putenfleisch *(turkey meat)*, Sauerbraten, Schnitzel, Spagetti, Erbsen, Spargel *(asparagus)*, Kartoffelbrei *(mashed potatoes)*, Fondue, Eis, Erdbeeren

 Compound nouns can be either plain (**Obstsaft**) or linked (**Tagesmenü, Konservierungsmittel**). The **-es-** or **-s-** are genitive links. There are also **-e-**, **-en-**, and **-n-** links for plural forms. Which link will be used in a compound is not predictable (See *Arbeitsbuch*, Chapter 8).

F. Zusammengesetzte Wörter (compound nouns) Welche finden Sie im Lesetext? Was sind ihre Artikel?

> BEISPIEL Mittagessen
> *der Mittag + das Essen = das Mittagessen*

G. Textanalyse

1. Welche Sätze im Text beginnen mit dem Subjekt? Finden Sie fünf!

> BEISPIEL *Die Deutschen, Österreicher und Schweizer beginnen den Tag mit einem guten Frühstück.*

2. Welche Sätze beginnen mit . . . ?

   a. einem Adverb: z. B. **Mittags** isst man gewöhnlich warm.
   b. einem Objekt: z. B. **Kaffeeklatsch** gibt es aber nicht nur im Café.
   c. etwas anderem *(something else):* **So** gibt es nur etwas Brot.

 H. Kurzgespräche Working with a partner, prepare one of the following brief dialogues. Then present it to the class.

1. **An der Uni**

   You have just met another student in the cafeteria for the first time and inquire how he/she likes it here. Very much, he/she answers. The other student then asks you whether the soup tastes good. You reply that it is not bad, but . . . *(add your own comment)*. You ask how your fellow student likes the chicken. He/she replies that . . . *(let him/her add their own comment)*.

2. **Im Restaurant**

You and a friend are in a German restaurant. The server asks what you would like, and you ask what he/she recommends. He/she mentions a particular dish. Both you and your friend order, each choosing a soup, a main dish, and a salad. The server asks what you would like to drink, and you order beverages. Use the menu in *Aktives zum Thema*.

I. **Aufsatz: Meine Essgewohnheiten** *(My eating habits)* Pretend you are explaining your eating habits to someone from Germany. Write 8–10 sentences describing what you usually like and dislike eating and drinking at various meals. Include the key words below.

> nachmittags   gewöhnlich   morgens
>
>   vielleicht   manchmal
>
> abends   nicht nur ... sondern auch   mittags

Hörverständnis

Track 7   **Gäste zum Wochenende** Listen to Kai and Gerda's plans for their weekend guests, Ruth and Uwe. Then read the questions below and select the correct response.

Zum Erkennen: die Forelle *(trout)*; genug *(enough)*

1. Ruth und Uwe kommen am _____.
   a. Sonntag um vier   b. Samstagnachmittag   c. Sonntag zum Kaffee
2. Sandra macht einen _____.
   a. Quarkkuchen   b. Apfelkuchen   c. Erdbeerkuchen
3. Zum Abendessen gibt es _____.
   a. Kartoffelsalat und Würstchen   b. Fondue, Brot und Wein   c. Eier, Wurst und Käse
4. Uwe isst gern _____.
   a. Jogurt   b. Schwarzbrot   c. Erdbeerkuchen
5. Zum Mittagessen machen sie _____.
   a. eine Nudelsuppe   b. Fleisch und Gemüse   c. Fisch mit Kartoffeln
6. Zum Nachtisch gibt es _____.
   a. Äpfel und Orangen   b. Quark   c. Obstsalat
7. Kai fährt _____.
   a. zum Supermarkt   b. zum Markt   c. zur Bäckerei
8. Sandra kauft Eier, Obst, _____.
   a. Jogurt und Kaffee   b. Obstsalat und Plätzchen   c. Gemüse und Blumen

Schreibtipp
Writing a Composition and Choosing Word Order

When writing a composition (**der Aufsatz**), no matter how long, first think about a basic outline. What will your introduction be? What points are going to be mentioned in the middle? What is your conclusion?

Note that word order in German is quite flexible. To reduce repetition in style, avoid starting too many sentences with the subject, especially with the pronoun **ich.** Bring some variety into the composition by introducing sentences with an adverb, an object, or some other element. Remember, the verb is always the second element in a sentence.

● Following this chapter, there is an extensive review section in the *Arbeitsbuch (Rückblick: Kapitel 1–3).* The accompanying exercises and answer key should help you prepare for the test.

Restaurants; converting currencies into dollars: http://wiegehts.heinle.com.

Feiertage und Feste

Lernziele

In this chapter you will learn about:

Zum Thema

Ordinal numbers, dates, holidays, and congratulations

Kultur-Fokus

Holiday customs, vacations, celebrations, festivals, and tourist destinations

Struktur

The present perfect with **haben**
The present perfect with **sein**
Subordinating conjunctions

Einblicke

Deutsche Feste

For more information, go to http://iLrn.heinle.com

Weihnachtsbummel in Essen

Vorschau   Holidays and Vacations

Minidrama: *Das hat es bei uns nicht gegeben.*

One of the most pleasant aspects of life in Germany, Switzerland, and Austria is the large number of secular and religious holidays (**Feiertage**) that are celebrated. These are days on which stores are closed and people don't work, which is not always the case in the US or in Canada. There are, for example, two vacation days each for Christmas (**Weihnachten**) and for Easter (**Ostern**). When these holidays are combined with a weekend or with a couple of vacation days, Germans find it easy to visit family in other parts of the country, to go skiing, or to go to the countryside for a few days.

Secular holidays include New Year's Eve and New Year's Day (**Silvester** and **Neujahr**), May Day or Labor Day (**Maifeiertag** or **Tag der Arbeit**), and national holidays marked by parades, speeches, and fireworks. On October 3 (**Tag der deutschen Einheit**), Germany commemorates its reunification in 1990. Austria, in turn, celebrates its independence from the Allied occupation in 1955 on October 26 (**Nationalfeiertag**). Switzerland's **Bundesfeiertag** on August 1 is based on the country's founding in 1291. Besides Christmas, Good Friday (**Karfreitag**), and Easter, religious holidays include Ascension Day (**Christi Himmelfahrt**) and Pentecost (**Pfingsten**), celebrated throughout the German-speaking countries. Additional religious holidays, such as Epiphany (**Heilige Drei Könige**), Corpus Christi (**Fronleichnam**), and All Saints' Day (**Allerheiligen**) are observed only in those states and areas where the majority of the population is Catholic. Reformation Day (**Reformationstag**), on October 31, is a public holiday in the predominantly Protestant areas, that is, in the northern and eastern parts of Germany.

The combination of generous vacation allowances—up to six weeks of vacation (**der Urlaub**) for nonsalaried employees—and many holidays has reduced the average number of working days in Germany to less than 200 per year, compared to 230 in the United States and 238 in Japan. Germans feel that frequent holidays and generous vacations improve efficiency and productivity. However, some concerns have arisen about the competitiveness of German workers in the global economy, especially as some unions have succeeded in reducing the workweek to less than 40 hours. Today, as the debate goes on about moving back toward longer hours, employers are also trying to whittle away at holidays and vacations.

German enthusiasm for vacation travel has created some problems, such as overcrowding on highways when school vacations (**Ferien**) begin and end. To alleviate this situation, a system of rotating and staggered school vacations was developed in the various federal states, so that no state—with the exception of Bavaria—always has very late or very early vacations.

● The **Reformationstag** commemorates the reformation of the church by Martin Luther in the 16th century, which led to the formation of a new religious group, the Protestant-Lutheran Church.

Lebkuchenherzen als Geschenk für den Freund oder die Freundin

Zum Thema

 Am Telefon

CD 4,
Track 1

NADJA	Hallo, Simon!
SIMON	Hallo, Nadja! Wie geht's dir denn?
NADJA	Nicht schlecht, danke. Was machst du am Wochenende?
SIMON	Nichts Besonderes. Warum?
NADJA	Erik hat übermorgen Geburtstag und wir geben eine Party.
SIMON	Super! Aber bist du sicher, dass Erik übermorgen Geburtstag hat? Ich glaube, sein Geburtstag ist am siebten Mai.
NADJA	Quatsch! Erik hat am dritten Mai Geburtstag. Und Samstag ist der dritte.
SIMON	Na gut. Wann und wo ist die Party?
NADJA	Samstag um sieben bei mir. Aber nichts sagen! Es ist eine Überraschung.
SIMON	Okay! Also, bis dann!
NADJA	Tschüss! Mach's gut!

Erik klingelt bei Nadja.

NADJA	Grüß dich, Erik! Herzlichen Glückwunsch zum Geburtstag!
ERIK	Wie bitte?
SIMON	Ich wünsche dir alles Gute zum Geburtstag.
ERIK	Tag, Simon! . . . Hallo, Silke! Tobias und Sabine, ihr auch?
ALLE	Wir gratulieren dir zum Geburtstag!
ERIK	Danke! So eine Überraschung! Aber ich habe nicht heute Geburtstag, mein Geburtstag ist am siebten.
NADJA	Echt? Na, dann hat Simon doch Recht gehabt. Ach, das macht nichts. Wir feiern heute.

A. Richtig oder falsch?

_____ 1. Simon hat Geburtstag.

_____ 2. Erik hat vor einem Monat Geburtstag gehabt.

_____ 3. Am 3. Mai gibt es eine Party.

_____ 4. Erik hat am 7. Mai Geburtstag.

_____ 5. Die Party ist bei Nadja.

_____ 6. Zum Geburtstag sagt man: „Grüß dich!"

_____ 7. Erik gratuliert zum Geburtstag.

_____ 8. Alle gratulieren.

 B. Jetzt sind Sie dran! With a partner, create your own dialogue. Talk about weekend plans and any upcoming events, possibly a birthday party.

Fokus Congratulations

Herzlichen Glückwunsch! (or its plural, **Herzliche Glückwünsche!**) suits almost any occasion, be it a birthday, an engagement, a wedding, the birth or christening of a baby, church confirmation or communion, or an anniversary. Germans make a lot of fuss over the celebration of birthdays. Contrary to US custom, the "birthday kid" in Germany is expected to throw his or her own party. Surprise parties, however, are popular with students. Coming-of-age and special birthdays (18, 25, 30, 40, 50, and so forth) are considered particularly important—the older you get, the more elaborate the celebration. Other occasions for congratulations are **Muttertag** and **Vatertag**, traditions that are more or less similar to those in North America.

Wortschatz 1

Die (Ordinal)zahl, -en ([ordinal] number)

1. **erste**	9. neunte	17. **siebzehnte**
2. zweite	10. zehnte	18. achtzehnte
3. **dritte**	11. elfte	19. neunzehnte
4. vierte	12. zwölfte	20. zwanzigste
5. fünfte	13. dreizehnte	21. einundzwanzigste
6. sechste	14. vierzehnte	22. zweiundzwanzigste
7. **siebte**	15. fünfzehnte	30. dreißigste
8. **achte**	16. **sechzehnte**	

From 1 to 19, the ordinal numbers have a **-te(n)** ending. Starting with 20, they end in **-ste(n).** Note the boldface irregularities within the numbers.

Das Datum, die Daten (calendar date)

Welches Datum ist heute?	*What's the date today?*
Heute ist **der erste Mai (1.5.).**	*Today is the first of May (5/1).*
Wann haben Sie Geburtstag?	*When is your birthday?*
Ich habe **am ersten Mai** (1.5.) Geburtstag.	*My birthday is on the first of May.*
Wann sind Sie geboren?	*When were you born?*
Ich bin **1980 geboren.**	*I was born in 1980.*
Ich bin am 1.5.1980 geboren.	*I was born on May 1, 1980.*
Die Ferien sind vom . . . bis zum . . .	*The vacation is from . . . until . . .*

In writing dates, Americans give the month and then the day: *5/1 (May 1), 1/5 (January 5).* Germans give the day first and then the month. The ordinal number is followed by a period: **1.5. (1. Mai), 5.1. (5. Januar).** Thus **1.5.** reads **der erste Mai,** and **5.1.** reads **der fünfte Januar.** Note the **-en** after am, vom, and zum: **am ersten Mai,** vom neunt**en** Juli bis zum achtzehnt**en** August.

Das Fest, -e (fest, festival)

der **Feiertag, -e**	holiday	die Feier, -n	celebration, party
Geburtstag, -e	birthday		
Sekt	champagne	Party, -s	party
das Geschenk, -e	present, gift	Überraschung, -en	surprise
bekommen	to get, receive	die **Ferien** (pl.)	vacation
dauern	to last (duration), take		
denken	to think	singen	to sing
feiern	to celebrate, party	tanzen	to dance
gratulieren	to congratulate	**tun**	to do
nennen	to name, call	überraschen	to surprise
schenken	to give (a present)	wünschen	to wish

German traditionally does not use a preposition when simply naming a year: **Ich bin 1980 geboren.** *I was born in 1980.*

Feiertag refers to a special day, a holiday, and can be in either the singular or the plural, whereas **Ferien** (always in the plural) refers to school or university vacation time. A (paid) vacation from work is **der Urlaub.**

The present tense forms of **tun** are: **ich tue, du tust, er tut, wir tun, ihr tut, sie tun.**

Weiteres

gerade	*just, right now*
noch	*still; else*
sicher	*sure(ly), certain(ly)*
gestern / vorgestern	*yesterday / the day before yesterday*
morgen / übermorgen	*tomorrow / the day after tomorrow*
am Wochenende	*on the weekend*
Wie lange?	*How long?*
vor einer Woche	*a week ago*
Das gibt's doch nicht!	*I don't believe it! That's impossible!*
Echt?	*Really?*
So eine Überraschung!	*What a surprise!*
Vielen / Herzlichen Dank!	*Thank you very much!*
Danke schön! / Bitte schön!	*Thanks a lot! / You're welcome!*
Nichts zu danken!	*You're welcome! My pleasure!*
zu Ostern / Weihnachten / Silvester	*at/for Easter / Christmas / New Year's Eve*
zum Geburtstag	*on/for one's birthday*
Alles Gute!	*All the best!*
Alles Gute zum Geburtstag!	*Happy birthday!*
Herzlichen Glückwunsch (zum Geburtstag)!	*Congratulations (on your birthday)!*
Ich gratuliere dir/Ihnen . . . !	*Congratulations . . . !*
Ich wünsche dir/Ihnen . . . !	*I wish you . . . !*

vor meaning *ago* is PREpositional rather than POSTpositional as it is in English: **vor einer Woche** *(a week ago),* **vor zwei Tagen** *(two days ago).*

Herzliche Glückwünsche!	*Best wishes!*
Viel Glück!	*Good luck!*
Gute Besserung!	*Get well soon!*
Frohe / Fröhliche Weihnachten!	*Merry Christmas!*
Ein gutes neues Jahr!	*Have a good New Year!*
(Ein) schönes Wochenende!	*Have a nice weekend!*

Zum Erkennen: nichts Besonderes *(nothing special)*; Quatsch! *(Nonsense!)*; na gut *(all right)*; klingeln *(here: to ring the doorbell)*; Grüß dich! *(Hi! Hello!)*; Recht haben *(to be correct)*; AUCH: das Sternzeichen, - *(sign of the zodiac)*; der Ferienkalender, - *(vacation schedule)*; das Partizip, -ien *(participle)*; der Infinitiv, -e; das Hilfsverb, -en *(auxiliary verb)*; der Nebensatz, ⁼e *(subordinate clause)*; verbinden *(to connect)*

● For Chicago's version of Nuremberg's Christmas market, see www.christkindlmarket.com.

Fokus The Christmas Season

During the weeks before Christmas, outdoor Christmas markets add to the spirit of the season in many cities. Nuremberg's **Christkindlmarkt** is the best-known Christmas market in Germany. In the month leading up to Christmas, more than 2 million visitors from all over the world stroll by the market's booths, which offer Christmas decorations, candy, and toys. The smells of mulled wine, toasted almonds, and roasted chestnuts are in the air, as well as the festive music of choirs and instrumentalists. Nuremberg is home to the fancy gingerbread called **Nürnberger Lebkuchen.** The traditional **Weihnachtsplätzchen** *(Christmas cookies)* and **Stollen**—a buttery bread filled with almonds, currants, raisins, and candied fruit—are other favorites at Christmas.

The feast of **Sankt Nikolaus** falls on December 6. Until the 16th century, it was Saint Nicholas who brought children holiday gifts on his feast day, a custom still followed in the Netherlands. In some areas, he was accompanied by his fearsome helper **Knecht Ruprecht,** who ensured that children who had misbehaved during the year got a good spanking or even disappeared into the big sack he carried. When Saint Nicholas was unable to deliver his presents in person, children would put their shoes in front of the door or hang their stockings from the chimney, where they would be filled the night of December 5. During the Reformation, German Protestants, in an effort to suppress devotion to saints, tried to transfer their children's adoration from Saint Nicholas to the Christ Child by letting Him bring Christmas presents on Christmas Eve. Later, the figure of Santa Claus or Father Christmas was introduced as the giver of gifts, a change intended to separate gift-giving from the religious symbolism of Christmas. Today, the **Christkind** is more likely to bring gifts in the predominantly Catholic South, while the **Weihnachtsmann** brings gifts in the predominantly Protestant North. During the four weeks before Christmas, the Advent wreath **(der Adventskranz)** with its four candles is a symbol of preparation for the birth of Christ. In the German-speaking countries, Christmas Eve **(Heiligabend)** stands at the center of the Christmas celebration. Many attend late-afternoon or midnight church services on this day, and gifts are exchanged in the evening. The Christmas tree **(der Tannenbaum)** is traditionally lit for the first time on Christmas Eve and remains up until January 6, the feast of the Epiphany, or the Three Kings **(Heilige Drei Könige).** December 25 and 26 are holidays when everything is closed, freeing time for family and friends. (For more on the tradition of Saint Nicholas, Santa, and the Christmas tree, see www.historychannel.com.)

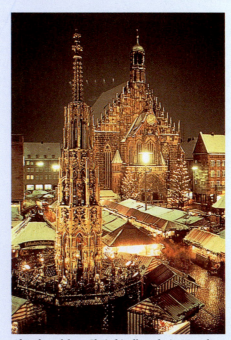

Abends auf dem Christkindlmarkt in Nürnberg

Aktives zum Thema

A. Nennen Sie das Datum!

1. **Kettenreaktion *(Chain reaction):* Das Datum** Start with any date, then name the next two.

   BEISPIEL   Heute ist der 2. Juli.
   Morgen ist der 3. Juli und übermorgen ist der 4. Juli.

2. **Nationalfeiertage in Europa** Say when these European countries celebrate their national holidays.

   BEISPIEL   Irland (3.3.)
   Der Nationalfeiertag in Irland ist am dritten März.

   a. Griechenland (25.3.) b. England (23.4.) c. Italien (2.6.) d. Dänemark (5.6.)
   e. Portugal (10.6.) f. Luxemburg (23.6.) g. Frankreich (14.7.) h. Belgien (21.7.)
   i. Deutschland (3.10.) j. Spanien (12.10.)

B. Was sagen Sie? Find out how your partner would respond to the following situations. Take turns.

1. Ein Freund oder eine Freundin hat heute Geburtstag.
2. Sie haben Geburtstag. Ein Freund oder eine Freundin aus der Schule telefoniert und gratuliert Ihnen.
3. Sie schreiben Ihrer Großmutter zu Weihnachten.
4. Sie haben einen Aufsatz *(paper)* geschrieben. Sie haben nicht viel Zeit gebraucht und doch *(still)* ein „A" bekommen.
5. Sie haben mit einer Freundin in einem Restaurant gegessen. Die Freundin zahlt fürs Essen.
6. Sie sind im Supermarkt gewesen und haben viel gekauft. Die Tür zu Ihrem Studentenwohnheim ist zu. Ein Student öffnet Ihnen die Tür.
7. Ihre Eltern haben Ihnen etwas Schönes zu Weihnachten geschenkt.
8. Sie haben in der Lotterie eine Million Euro gewonnen.
9. Sie danken Ihrem Zimmernachbarn, weil er Ihnen geholfen hat. Was antwortet der Nachbar?
10. Ein Freund fragt, ob Sie zu einer Party kommen möchten.
11. Ihre beste Freundin sagt, dass sie im Herbst ein Jahr nach Deutschland geht.
12. Sie studieren in Deutschland. Ein Regensburger Student fragt, ob Sie Weihnachten bei seiner *(his)* Familie feiern möchten.
13. Sie haben Weihnachten bei Familie Huber gefeiert. Sie fahren wieder nach Hause. Was sagen Sie zu Herrn und Frau Huber?
14. Ihr Cousin hat die Grippe *(flu).*

Zwei Musikanten mit Gitarre und Akkordeon

C. Der Spielplan *(Performance Schedule):* **Im Theater** You work at a ticket office representing four of Bremen's theaters. Give patrons information about dates and times of upcoming performances. Read aloud!

BEISPIEL S1 Am zweiten um achtzehn Uhr gibt es im Theater am Goetheplatz *Die Zauberflöte,* ein Film von Ingmar Bergmann.
S2 Und im Schauspielhaus oder in der Concordia?
S1 Im Schauspielhaus um zwanzig Uhr *Die Gerechten* von Albert Camus und in der Concordia um zwanzig Uhr *Appetit* von Urs Dietrich.

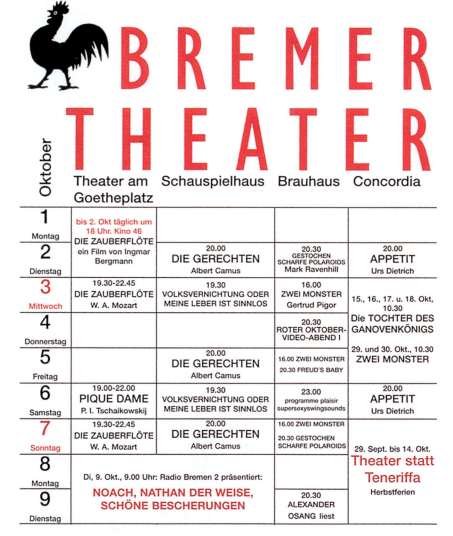

BREMER THEATER

Oktober

	Theater am Goetheplatz	Schauspielhaus	Brauhaus	Concordia
1 Montag	bis 2. Okt täglich um 18 Uhr. Kino 46 DIE ZAUBERFLÖTE ein Film von Ingmar Bergmann			
2 Dienstag		20.00 DIE GERECHTEN Albert Camus	20.30 GESTOCHEN SCHARFE POLAROIDS Mark Ravenhill	20.00 APPETIT Urs Dietrich
3 Mittwoch	19.30–22.45 DIE ZAUBERFLÖTE W. A. Mozart	19.30 VOLKSVERNICHTUNG ODER MEINE LEBER IST SINNLOS	16.00 ZWEI MONSTER Gertrud Pigor	15., 16., 17. u. 18. Okt, 10.30 Die TOCHTER DES GANOVENKÖNIGS
4 Donnerstag			20.30 ROTER OKTOBER-VIDEO-ABEND I	
5 Freitag		20.00 DIE GERECHTEN Albert Camus	16.00 ZWEI MONSTER 20.30 FREUD'S BABY	29. und 30. Okt., 10.30 ZWEI MONSTER
6 Samstag	19.00–22.00 PIQUE DAME P. I. Tschaikowskij	19.30 VOLKSVERNICHTUNG ODER MEINE LEBER IST SINNLOS	23.00 programme plaisir supersexyswingsounds	20.00 APPETIT Urs Dietrich
7 Sonntag	19.30–22.45 DIE ZAUBERFLÖTE W. A. Mozart	20.00 DIE GERECHTEN Albert Camus	16.00 ZWEI MONSTER 20.30 GESTOCHEN SCHARFE POLAROIDS	29. Sept. bis 14. Okt. **Theater statt Teneriffa** Herbstferien
8 Montag	Di, 9. Okt., 9.00 Uhr: Radio Bremen 2 präsentiert: **NOACH, NATHAN DER WEISE, SCHÖNE BESCHERUNGEN**			
9 Dienstag			20.30 ALEXANDER OSANG liest	

 D. Ferien in Deutschland Ask each other about vacations in Germany and elsewhere using the chart on the facing page. Take turns.

1. Welche Ferien gibt es in Deutschland?
2. Von wann bis wann sind die Osterferien in Bayern? die Pfingstferien *(Pentecost holidays)* in Baden-Württemberg? die Sommerferien in Berlin und Mecklenburg-Vorpommern? die Herbstferien in Niedersachsen und Thüringen? die Weihnachtsferien in Hessen und Sachsen-Anhalt?
3. Welche Ferien gibt es hier (in den USA, in Kanada . . .)? Wann sind sie? Wie lange dauern sie?
4. Wann beginnen die nächsten *(next)* Ferien? Wann enden sie? Was tun Sie dann?

Land	Winter	Frújahr/ Ostern	Himmelfahrt/ Pfingsten	Sommer	Herbst	Weihnachten
Baden-Württemberg	-	25.04. - 29.04.	02.06. - 13.06.	27.07. - 09.09.	02.11. - 03.11.	23.12. - 05.01.
Bayern	-	17.04. - 29.04.	13.06. - 24.06.	27.07. - 11.09.	30.10. - 04.11.	27.12. - 08.01.
Berlin	29.01. - 09.02.	20.04. - 06.05.	02.06./10.06. - 13.06.	20.07. - 02.09.	28.10. - 04.11.	23.12. - 02.01.
Brandenburg	31.01. - 12.02.	25.04. - 04.05.	-	20.07. - 02.09.	30.10. - 04.11.	23.12. - 02.01.
Bremen	-	03.04. - 25.04.	-	13.07. - 26.08.	23.10. - 01.11.	22.12. - 06.01.
Hamburg	-	06.03. - 18.03.	29.05. - 03.06.	20.07. - 30.08.	16.10. - 28.10.	21.12. - 02.01.
Hessen	-	10.04. - 20.04.	-	23.06. - 04.08.	02.10. - 14.10.	27.12. - 13.01.
Mecklenburg-Vorp.	07.02. - 19.02.	15.04. - 25.04.	09.06. - 13.06.	20.07. - 30.08.	23.10. - 28.10.	20.12. - 02.01.
Niedersachen	-	14.04. - 29.04.	02.06. - 13.06.	13.07. - 23.08.	19.10. - 01.11.	22.12. - 06.01.
Nordhein-Westfalen	-	17.04. - 29.04.	-	29.06. - 12.08.	02.10. - 14.10.	22.12. - 06.01.
Rheinland-Pfalz	-	17.04. - 28.04.	-	23.06. - 04.08.	02.10. - 13.10.	22.12. - 05.01.
Saarland	-	14.04. - 29.04.	-	22.06. - 02.08.	02.10. - 14.10.	23.12. - 06.01.
Sachsen	14.02. - 26.02.	20.04. - 28.04.	10.06. - 13.06.	13.07. - 23.08.	16.10. - 27.10.	22.12. - 02.01.
Sachsen-Anhalt	17.02. - 26.02.	17.04. - 20.04.	02.06. - 10.06.	13.07. - 23.08.	23.10. - 30.10.	27.12. - 02.01.
Schleswig-Holstein	-	08.04. - 25.04.	-	20.07. - 02.09.	23.10. - 04.11.	27.12. - 06.01.
Thüringen	07.02. - 12.02.	17.04. - 29.04.	10.06. - 13.06.	13.07. - 23.08.	16.10. - 21.10.	22.12. - 06.01.

 E. Geburtstage und Sternzeichen *(Birthdays and signs of the zodiac)* Find out about your partner's birthday and those of his/her family members. What are their signs of the zodiac?

BEISPIEL S1 Wann hast du Geburtstag und was bist du?
S2 Ich habe am 25. Dezember Geburtstag. Ich bin Steinbock. Und du?
S1 Mein Geburtstag ist am 21. Januar. Ich bin Wassermann.
S2 Wann ist dein Vater (deine Mutter usw.) geboren?
S1 Er ist am 21. Juni geboren. Er ist Zwilling.

Note **die Waage, die Jungfrau.** All other signs of the zodiac are masculine.

F. Deutsche Länder und Hauptstädte Look at the map of the various federal states of Germany. Then take turns asking each other questions about their location and their respective capitals.

BEISPIEL S1 Wo liegt Brandenburg?
S2 Brandenburg liegt südlich von Mecklenburg-Vorpommern und östlich von Sachsen-Anhalt.
S1 Und was ist die Hauptstadt von Brandenburg?
S2 Magdeburg!

Aussprache: ch, ck

CD 4,
Track 2

A. Laute

1. [ç] i**ch**, ni**ch**t, fur**ch**tbar, vollei**ch**t, man**ch**mal, spre**ch**en, Re**ch**nung, Mäd**ch**en, Mil**ch**, dur**ch**, gewöhnli**ch**, ri**ch**tig, wi**ch**tig
2. [x] a**ch**, a**ch**t, ma**ch**en, Weihna**ch**ten, au**ch**, brau**ch**en, Wo**ch**e, no**ch**, do**ch**, Bu**ch**, Ku**ch**en, Ba**ch**, Ba**ch**ara**ch**
3. [ks] se**chs**, se**chs**te
4. [k] di**ck**, Zu**ck**er, Bä**ck**er, Ro**ck**, Ja**ck**e, Frühstü**ck**, schme**ck**en

 For further review, see the Summary of Pronunciation in the front of your *Arbeitsbuch*. Study section II, subsections 13–15.

B. Wortpaare

1. mich / misch
2. Kirche / Kirsche
3. nickt / nicht
4. lochen / locken
5. Nacht / nackt
6. möchte / mochte

Hörverständnis

Die Geburtstagsparty Listen to the conversation between Anke and Paul. Then answer the questions below by jotting down key words.

Zum Erkennen: Gute Idee! *(That's a good idea!)*; es geht sicher *(it's probably all right)*

1. Wer hat am 10. Oktober Geburtstag? _____
2. Wer hat am 12. Oktober Geburtstag? _____
3. Was möchte Paul machen? _____
4. Was tut Claire samstags bis um drei? _____
5. Wo wollen sie feiern? _____
6. Was bringt Paul? _____ und _____
7. Was bringt Klaus? _____
8. Wer telefoniert mit Peter und Claire? _____
9. Wann beginnt die Party? _____

Fokus   Diversity in Religious Traditions

Germany has traditionally been a predominantly Christian society; for this reason, almost all official holidays are of Christian origin. Today, as a result of immigration, new ethnic and religious communities have settled in Germany, each bringing its own traditions with it. These include about 3.7 million Moslems, 1.6 million Eastern Orthodox, 150,000 Buddhists, 100,000 Hindus, and more than 150,000 people of the Jewish faith.

Moslems constitute the largest non-Christian group in Germany today. They have come to Germany from many countries, most notably Turkey. The most important date in the Moslem calendar is the three-day celebration of Id al-Fitr **(Fest des Fastenbrechens)**, which occurs at the end of the month of Ramadan. The once-thriving Jewish community in Germany celebrates numerous holidays: Passover **(Pessach)** in the spring; Yom Kippur **(Jom Kippur**, the day of atonement) and Rosh Hashanah **(Rosch ha-Schanah**, Jewish New Year), both observed in the fall; and Hanukkah **(Chanukka**, the festival of lights) in December. The German Constitution allows for religious education to be taught in the public schools. Because non-Christian celebrations are not official holidays in Germany, Moslem and Jewish students in public schools, for example, can request a day off from school to attend religious celebrations.

On the basis of a long-standing agreement between church and state, a special tax levy of 8 to 10 percent of an individual's income tax is collected by the state for the "established churches." However, only major Christian denominations and the Jewish faith are recognized as "established churches." Having a choice, some people discontinued their affiliation with a church. In the East, where the communist regime had discouraged church membership, many people never rejoined after reunification. They often continue the East German ritual of a nonreligious dedication of young people **(die Jugendweihe)** instead of the traditional religious confirmation ceremony **(die Konfirmation).** The families of these young people are among the 28 percent of Germans who are officially unaffiliated with any church and, thus, are not required to pay the church tax collected from all church members.

Moschee am Columbiadamm in Berlin-Neukölln

Struktur

4.1 The present perfect with *haben*

1. The German PRESENT PERFECT corresponds closely in form to the English present perfect. In both languages it consists of an inflected auxiliary verb (or "helping verb") and an unchanging past participle.

You **have learned** that well.	Du **hast** das gut **gelernt.**
She **has brought** the books.	Sie **hat** die Bücher **gebracht.**
We **haven't spoken** any English.	Wir **haben** kein Englisch **gesprochen.**

2. In the use of this tense, however, there is a considerable difference between English and German. In everyday conversation, English makes more use of the simple past, whereas German prefers the present perfect.

Du **hast** das gut **gelernt.**	You **learned** that well.
Sie **hat** die Bücher **gebracht.**	She **brought** the books.
Wir **haben** kein Englisch **gesprochen.**	We **didn't speak** any English.

The German present perfect corresponds to four past-tense forms in English:

Wir haben das gelernt.
$\begin{cases} \text{We have learned that.} \\ \text{We learned that.} \\ \text{We did learn that.} \\ \text{We were learning that.} \end{cases}$

3. Most German verbs form the present perfect by using the present tense of **haben** (V1) with the past participle (V2). The past participle is placed at the end of the sentence or clause.

ich	**habe**	. . . gelernt	wir	**haben**	. . . gelernt
du	**hast**	. . . gelernt	ihr	**habt**	. . . gelernt
er	**hat**	. . . gelernt	sie	**haben**	. . . gelernt

4. German has two groups of verbs that form their past participles in different ways:

   - T-VERBS (also called "WEAK VERBS") with the participle ending in **-t** (**gelernt**).
   - N-VERBS (also called "STRONG VERBS") with the participle ending in **-en** (**gesprochen**).

   Any verb not specifically identified as an irregular t-verb or as an n-verb can be assumed to be a regular t-verb.

   a. The majority of German verbs are regular t-verbs. They form their past participles with the prefix **ge-** and the ending **-t.** They correspond to such English verbs as *learn, learned,* and *ask, asked.*

   $$\boxed{\textbf{ge + STEM + t}} \quad \text{lernen} \rightarrow \quad \boxed{\text{ge lern t}}$$

   Familiar verbs that follow this pattern include: brauchen, danken, dauern, feiern, fragen, glauben, hören, kaufen, machen, sagen, schenken, schmecken, spielen, suchen, tanzen, wohnen, zählen.

🔸 Although lists of familiar verbs such as these are not printed in boldface, they are important. Please review these verbs.

- Verbs with stems ending in **-d, -t,** or with certain consonant combinations with **-m** or **-n** insert an **-e-.**

  | **ge +** STEM **+ et** | kosten → | **ge kost et** |

  Other familiar verbs that follow this pattern include: antworten, arbeiten, öffnen, regnen.

- A few t-verbs are IRREGULAR (MIXED VERBS), i.e., they usually change their stem. They can be compared to such English verbs as *bring, brought,* and *think, thought.*

  | **ge +** STEM *(change)* **+ t** | bringen → | **ge brach t** |

  Here are the participles of familiar irregular t-verbs:

  | bringen | **gebracht** | haben | **gehabt** |
  | denken | **gedacht** | nennen | **genannt** |

b. A smaller but extremely important group of verbs, the N-VERBS, form their past participles with the prefix **ge-** and the ending **-en.** They correspond to such English verbs as *write, written,* and *speak, spoken.* The n-verbs frequently have a stem change in the past participle. Their forms are not predictable and therefore must be memorized. Many of them also have a stem change in the second and third person singular of the present tense: **sprechen, du sprichst, er spricht.**

   NOTE: Those that do have this change are always n-verbs.

   | **ge +** STEM *(change)* **+ en** | geben → | **ge geb en** |
   | | finden → | **ge fund en** |

   You will need to learn the past participles of these n-verbs:

   For a complete alphabetical listing, see Appendix, Section 7.

essen	**gegessen**	schlafen	**geschlafen**
finden	**gefunden**	schreiben	**geschrieben**
geben	**gegeben**	sehen	**gesehen**
heißen	**geheißen**	singen	**gesungen**
helfen	**geholfen**	sprechen	**gesprochen**
lesen	**gelesen**	tragen	**getragen**
liegen	**gelegen**	trinken	**getrunken**
nehmen	**genommen**	tun	**getan**
scheinen	**geschienen**		

5. Two groups of verbs have no **ge-**prefix for the past participle.

- Inseparable-prefix verbs

  In English as in German, many verbs have been formed by the use of inseparable prefixes, e.g., *to belong, to impress, to proceed.* In both languages, the stress is on the verb, not on the prefix. The German inseparable prefixes are **be-, emp-, ent-, er-, ge-, ver-,** and **zer-.**

Gesagt. Getan.

Note: These verbs do not have a **ge**-prefix.

bestellen	→	be stell t
verstehen	→	ver stand en

Familiar t-verbs that also follow this pattern include: bedeuten, bezahlen, gehören, verkaufen, überraschen, wiederholen. Note: **über-** and **wieder-** are not always inseparable prefixes.

You will need to learn the past participles of these familiar n-verbs:

beginnen	**begonnen**	gefallen	**gefallen**
bekommen	**bekommen**	verstehen	**verstanden**
empfehlen	**empfohlen**		

- Verbs ending in **-ieren** (all of which are t-verbs):

gratulieren	**gratuliert**
studieren	**studiert**

Übungen

A. Nennen Sie das Partizip!

BEISPIEL   fragen   *gefragt*

1. dauern, feiern, danken, wohnen, tanzen, antworten, bedeuten, kosten, öffnen, regnen, schmecken, verkaufen, bezahlen, gratulieren, denken, bringen, nennen, studieren
2. essen, finden, tun, helfen, lesen, heißen, trinken, schlafen, scheinen, singen, bekommen, empfehlen, beginnen, gefallen, verstehen

B. Nennen Sie den Infinitiv!

BEISPIEL   gebracht   *bringen*

begonnen, bekommen, bezahlt, empfohlen, geantwortet, gedacht, gefallen, gefeiert, gefunden, gegessen, geglaubt, gehabt, geholfen, gelegen, genannt, genommen, geschienen, geschrieben, gesprochen, gesucht, gesungen, getan, getrunken, gratuliert, überrascht, verkauft, verstanden

C. Ersetzen Sie das Subjekt!

BEISPIEL   Ich habe eine Flasche Sekt gekauft. (er)
Er hat eine Flasche Sekt gekauft.

1. Du hast nichts gesagt. (ihr, man, ich)
2. Ich habe auf Englisch geantwortet. (wir, du, er)
3. Er hat Klaus Geschenke gebracht. (ihr, sie/pl., ich)
4. Ihr habt das Partizip genannt. (ich, sie/sg., du)
5. Sie haben nur Deutsch gesprochen. (du, ihr, Marko und Silva)

Optional English-to-German practice: 1. She was still sleeping. 2. They helped, too. 3. Have you (3rd) already eaten? 4. Did you (formal) find it? 5. I didn't understand that. 6. Have you (sg. fam.) read that? 7. I repeated the question. 8. Who took it? 9. They bought winter coats. 10. My aunt recommended the store. 11. Did you (pl. fam.) sell the books? 12. I was paying the bills. (See answer key in Appendix.)

D. Was habt ihr gemacht? Tell your roommate what happened at Klaus's party.

> BEISPIEL   Ich habe Klaus ein Buch gegeben. (schenken)
> *Ich habe Klaus ein Buch geschenkt.*

1. Wir haben viel gefeiert. (tanzen, spielen, essen, tun, servieren)
2. Christa und Joachim haben Kuchen gekauft. (bestellen, nehmen)
3. Susanne hat Klaus gratuliert. (danken, glauben, helfen, überraschen, suchen)
4. Klaus hat viel gegessen. (arbeiten, trinken, singen, bekommen)
5. Wie gewöhnlich hat Peter nur gelesen. (schlafen, lernen, sprechen)
6. Sabine hat Helmut nicht gesehen. (fragen, antworten, schreiben)

E. Allerlei Fragen Ask your partner all sorts of questions, using only verbs that form the present perfect with **haben.**

> BEISPIEL   S1 Was hast du zuletzt *(the last time)* zum Geburtstag
> bekommen?
> S2 Ich habe . . . bekommen.
> S1 Wie hat dir . . . gefallen?

Fokus   Tourist Destinations

While most of Germany's annual celebrations are rooted firmly in its long history, some of the best-known ones play an important role in the nation's tourism industry, which contributes significantly to the German economy.

Each year, millions of visitors flock to Munich's **Oktoberfest,** the world's largest beer festival—which actually starts at the end of September. The Munich Oktoberfest offers visitors the chance to order **eine Maß** (a large glass holding about one liter of beer) and enjoy sausage and sauerkraut, grilled chicken, or fish, while listening to Bavarian music. Some Oktoberfest celebrations take place annually elsewhere in Germany and throughout the German-speaking world (even in the United States!), but on a much smaller scale.

One of the largest annual events in Germany is **Karneval** (as it is known in the North; it is called **Fasching** in the South). The best-known carnival celebrations are in Cologne and Mainz, both of which draw tourists from around the world. Carnival time (celebrated as Mardi Gras by North Americans in New Orleans) takes place the last few weeks before Ash Wednesday, which occurs sometime in February or March, six weeks before Easter. The celebration has its roots in the pre-Christian era. (It featured a rite intended to cast out the demons of winter.) When the celebration was incorporated into the Christian calendar, it became an occasion for parties, rich food, and generous drink, all to be enjoyed before the start of the six-week Lenten fast leading up to Easter. In Cologne, carnival time is a holiday. Revelers at carnival often dress up in costumes, engage in merrymaking in the streets, and enjoy the annual parade on **Rosenmontag** (the Monday before Ash Wednesday).

Another annual event is the **Wurstmarkt** in Bad Dürkheim (not far from Mannheim), which dates back to 1442. This wine festival **(Winzerfest)** attracts more than 500,000 visitors annually. In late summer and early autumn, there are many wine festivals in towns along the Rhine, Main, and Moselle rivers—areas where wine production plays an important economic role.

Beim Karneval

4.2 The present perfect with *sein*

Whereas most German verbs use **haben** as the auxiliary in the perfect tenses, a few common verbs use **sein.** You will probably find it easiest to memorize **sein** together with the past participles of those verbs requiring it. However, you can also determine which verbs take **sein** by remembering that they must fulfill two conditions:

- They are INTRANSITIVE, i.e., they cannot take an accusative (direct) object. Examples of such verbs are: **gehen, kommen,** and **laufen.**
- They express a CHANGE OF PLACE OR CONDITION. **Sein** and **bleiben** are exceptions to this rule.

Wir **sind** nach Hause **gegangen.**	*We went home.*
Er **ist** müde **geworden.**	*He got tired.*
Ich **bin** zu Hause **geblieben.**	*I stayed home.*

CAUTION: A change in prefix or the addition of a prefix may cause a change in auxiliary because the meaning of the verb changes. Ich **bin** nach Hause **gekommen.** *I came home.* Ich **habe** ein Geschenk **bekommen.** *I received a present.*

The present perfect of the following n-verbs is formed with the present tense of **sein** (V1) and the past participle (V2).

sein	**ist gewesen**	kommen	**ist gekommen**
bleiben	**ist geblieben**	laufen	**ist gelaufen**
fahren	**ist gefahren**	werden	**ist geworden**
gehen	**ist gegangen**		

ich **bin**	. . . gekommen		wir **sind**	. . . gekommen
du **bist**	. . . gekommen		ihr **seid**	. . . gekommen
er **ist**	. . . gekommen		sie **sind**	. . . gekommen

Occasionally, **fahren** takes an object. In that case, the auxiliary **haben** is used:

Sie **sind** nach Hause **gefahren.**	*They drove home.*
Sie **haben** mein Auto nach Hause **gefahren.**	*They drove my car home.*

Übungen

F. *Sein* oder *haben*: Nennen Sie das Partizip und das Hilfsverb *(auxiliary)!*

BEISPIEL   empfehlen   *hat empfohlen*
           gehen   *ist gegangen*

essen, bringen, werden, sein, gefallen, bleiben, liegen, sprechen, laufen, helfen

G. Hoppla, hier fehlt was! Wie ist das gewesen? Yesterday's party went very late and you don't remember all the details. With a partner, piece together the picture. One of you looks at and completes the chart below, the other works with the chart in Section 11 of the Appendix.

S1:

	Kai	Eva	Max	Sven	ich	Partner/in
an alles denken		x				
mit dem Essen helfen	x					x
Getränke bringen			x		x	
den Sekt öffnen		x				
viel essen			x		x	
viel trinken			x			
schön singen				x		
etwas tanzen	x					x
mit allen sprechen						x
nichts tun				x		
nicht lange bleiben				x	x	

BEISPIEL   S1 Was hat Kai gemacht?
            S2 Kai hat mit dem Essen geholfen und etwas getanzt. Und Eva?
            S1 Eva hat . . .

H. Ferien

1. **Michaels Sommerferien** Michael is explaining what he did during his last summer vacation. Use the present perfect. In each case, decide whether to use the auxiliary **haben** or **sein.**

   BEISPIEL   Im August habe ich Ferien.
              Im August habe ich Ferien gehabt.

   a. In den Ferien fahre ich nach Zell.
   b. Ich nehme zwei Wochen frei *(take off)*.
   c. Ich wohne bei Familie Huber.
   d. Das Haus liegt direkt am See.
   e. Zell gefällt mir gut.
   f. Nachmittags laufe ich in die Stadt.
   g. Manchmal gehen wir auch ins Café.
   h. Das Café gehört Familie Huber.
   i. Mittwochs hilft Renate da.
   j. Renate bringt oft Kuchen nach Hause.
   k. Ich bekomme alles frei.
   l. Sie empfiehlt die Sahnetorte.
   m. Die schmeckt wirklich gut.
   n. Den Apfelstrudel finde ich besonders gut.
   o. Renate ist in den Sommerferien bei uns.
   p. Wir werden gute Freunde.
   q. Leider regnet es viel.
   r. Wir lesen viel und hören Musik.

 2. **Meine Ferien** Tell your partner what you did during your vacation last summer or any other time, using the present perfect with **haben** or **sein.**

   BEISPIEL   *Ich bin nach Miami geflogen und habe da Freunde besucht.*

4.3 Subordinating conjunctions

You already know how to join sentences with a coordinating conjunction (**aber, denn, oder, und**). Clauses can also be joined with SUBORDINATING CONJUNCTIONS. Subordinating conjunctions introduce a subordinate or dependent clause, i.e., a statement with a subject and a verb that cannot stand alone as a complete sentence.

because it's his birthday
that they have left already

Whereas coordinating conjunctions do not affect word order, subordinating conjunctions do. German subordinate clauses are always set off by a comma, and the inflected verb (V1) stands at the very end.

1. Six common subordinating conjunctions are:

bevor	*before*
dass	*that*
ob	*if, whether*
obwohl	*although*
weil	*because*
wenn	*if, when(ever)*

> When it is possible to replace *if* with *whether*, use **ob**; otherwise use **wenn**.

Ich kaufe ein Geschenk.
Ich frage Helga, **bevor** ich ein Geschenk **kaufe.**
I'll ask Helga before I buy a present.

Klaus hat Geburtstag.
Sie sagt, **dass** Klaus morgen Geburtstag **hat.**
She says that Klaus has his birthday tomorrow.

Ist sie sicher?
Ich frage, **ob** sie sicher **ist.**
I'll ask whether she is sure.

Sie hat nicht viel Zeit.
Sie kommt zur Party, **obwohl** sie nicht viel Zeit **hat.**
She's coming to the party although she doesn't have much time.

Er trinkt gern Sekt.
Wir bringen eine Flasche Sekt, **weil** er gern Sekt **trinkt.**
We are bringing a bottle of champagne because he likes to drink champagne.

Ich habe Zeit.
Ich komme auch, **wenn** ich Zeit **habe.**
I'll come, too, if I have time.

NOTE: The subject of the dependent clause almost always follows the subordinating conjunction. When a sentence with inverted word order becomes a dependent clause, the subject moves to the position immediately after the conjunction.

Morgen hat **Klaus** Geburtstag.
Ich glaube, dass **Klaus morgen** Geburtstag hat.

2. Information questions can become subordinate clauses by using the question word (**wer? was? wie? wo?** etc.) as a conjunction and putting the verb last.

> Wie schmeckt der Sekt?
> Sie fragt, **wie** der Sekt **schmeckt.**
> *She asks how the champagne tastes.*

> Wo sind die Brötchen?
> Sie fragt, **wo** die Brötchen **sind.**
> *She asks where the rolls are.*

Note the similarity with English:

> *Where are the rolls?*
> *She asks **where** the rolls **are.***

3. Yes/No questions require **ob** as a conjunction.

> Schmeckt der Sekt gut?
> Sie fragt, **ob** der Sekt gut **schmeckt.**
> *She asks whether the champagne tastes good.*

> Sind die Würstchen heiß?
> Sie fragt, **ob** die Würstchen heiß **sind.**
> *She asks whether the franks are hot.*

4. Subordinate clauses as the first sentence element

If the subordinate clause precedes the main clause, the inflected verb of the main clause—the second sentence element—comes right after the comma. In that case, the entire subordinate clause is the first sentence element.

>   1   2
> Ich **komme,** wenn ich Zeit habe.
> Wenn ich Zeit habe, **komme** ich.

5. The present perfect in subordinate clauses

In subordinate clauses in the present perfect, the inflected verb **haben** or **sein** (V1) stands at the end of the sentence.

> Er hat eine Geburtstagskarte bekommen.
> Er sagt, **dass** er eine Geburtstagskarte bekommen **hat.**

> Er ist überrascht gewesen.
> Er sagt, **dass** er überrascht gewesen **ist.**

Übungen

I. Verbinden Sie die Sätze!

BEISPIEL   Eva geht zur Bäckerei. Sie braucht noch etwas Brot. *(because)*
                   Eva geht zur Bäckerei, weil sie noch etwas Brot braucht.

1. Der Herr fragt die Studentin. Kommt sie aus Amerika? *(whether)*
2. Die Stadt gefällt den Amerikanern. Sie ist alt und romantisch. *(because)*
3. Eine Tasse Kaffee tut gut. Man ist müde. *(when)*
4. Rechnen Sie alles zusammen! Sie bezahlen die Rechnung. *(before)*
5. Wir spielen nicht Tennis. Das Wetter ist schlecht. *(if)*
6. Sie hat geschrieben. Sie ist in Österreich gewesen. *(that)*
7. Ich habe Hunger. Ich habe gerade ein Eis gegessen. *(although)*
8. Ich arbeite bei Tengelmann. Ich brauche Geld. *(because)*

Struktur / 115

Lerntipp

Having the Last Word

When listening or reading, pay special attention to the end of the sentence, which often contains crucial sentence elements. As Mark Twain wrote in *A Connecticut Yankee in King Arthur's Court:* "Whenever the literary German dives into a sentence, that is the last we are going to see of him till he emerges on the other side of the Atlantic with his verb in his mouth."

J. Beginnen Sie mit dem Nebensatz! *(Begin with the subordinate clause.)*

BEISPIEL Ich trinke Wasser, wenn ich Durst habe.
Wenn ich Durst habe, trinke ich Wasser.

1. Ich habe ein Stück Käse gegessen, weil ich Hunger gehabt habe.
2. Ich verstehe nicht, warum die Lebensmittel Farbstoffe brauchen.
3. Ihr habt eine Party gegeben, weil ich 21 geworden bin.
4. Ich finde (es) prima, dass ihr nichts gesagt habt.
5. Ich bin nicht müde, obwohl wir bis morgens um sechs gefeiert haben.

K. Sagen Sie die Sätze noch einmal!

1. **Er sagt, dass . . .** A friend has just come back from Luxembourg. Tell the class what he has observed. Follow the model.

BEISPIEL Luxemburg ist wirklich schön.
Er sagt, dass Luxemburg wirklich schön ist.

a. Die Luxemburger sprechen Französisch, Deutsch und Letzeburgisch.
b. Letzeburgisch ist der Luxemburger Dialekt.
c. Er hat den Geburtstag auf einer Burg *(in a castle)* gefeiert.
d. Das ist einfach toll gewesen.
e. In Luxemburg gibt es viele Banken.
f. Den Leuten geht es wirklich sehr gut.
g. Überall sieht man BMWs und Citroëns.

 A Citroën is a car of French manufacture, common in Luxembourg and other European countries.

2. **Sie fragt, . . .** Your mother wants to know about Carla's graduation party. Follow the model.

BEISPIEL Wer ist Carla?
Sie fragt, wer Carla ist.

a. Wo wohnt Carla? b. Wie viele Leute sind da gewesen? c. Wie lange hat die Party gedauert? d. Was habt ihr gegessen und getrunken? e. Mit wem hast du getanzt? f. Wie bist du nach Hause gekommen?

3. **Sie fragt, ob . . .** Your parents are celebrating their 30th anniversary, and your sister is in charge of the party. Now she asks whether you and your brothers have completed the tasks she assigned a week ago.

BEISPIEL Hast du Servietten gekauft?
Sie fragt, ob du Servietten gekauft hast.

a. Seid ihr gestern einkaufen gegangen? b. Hat Alfred Sekt gekauft? c. Haben wir jetzt alle Geschenke? d. Habt ihr den Kuchen beim Bäcker *(baker)* bestellt? e. Hat Peter mit den Nachbarn gesprochen? f. Hat Alfred die Kamera gefunden?

L. Interview Find out the following information from a classmate and then tell the class what he/she said.

1. wann er/sie gestern ins Bett *(to bed)* gegangen ist
2. ob er/sie viel für die Deutschstunde gelernt hat
3. wie er/sie geschlafen hat und wie lange
4. was er/sie heute zum Frühstück gegessen und getrunken hat
5. wie er/sie zur Uni(versität) gekommen ist, ob er/sie gelaufen oder gefahren ist
6. wie viele Kurse er/sie heute schon gehabt hat und welche

Traditional Folk Celebrations

Germans don't have a Thanksgiving holiday with traditional foods like cranberry sauce and pumpkin pie. Instead, churches and rural communities celebrate Harvest Thanksgiving (**Erntedankfest**) with special services and harvest wreaths.

Some towns attract visitors by recreating historical events in their carefully preserved surroundings. The **Meistertrunk** in Rothenburg ob der Tauber recalls an event from the Thirty Years' War (1618–1648). Landshut recruits many of its residents in the reenactment of the 1475 wedding of the son of Duke Ludwig to a Polish princess (**die Fürstenhochzeit**). The "Rattenfänger von Hameln" (*"The Pied Piper of Hamelin"*) commemorates the Children's Crusade of 1284, when 130 of the town's children mysteriously vanished.

While no longer everyday attire, traditional folk costumes (**Trachten**) are still worn in rural areas of Germany, Switzerland, and Austria for church holidays, weddings, and other special occasions. Special clubs (**Trachtenvereine**) endeavor to keep the tradition alive.

Der Rattenfänger von Hameln

Zusammenfassung

 M. Rückblick auf die Gespräche Looking back on the dialogues with your partner, pick any of them in the *Schritte* or *Kapitel* you have read so far and report what people talked about.

> KAPITEL 1: *Sharon hat Roberto gefragt, woher er kommt. Er hat gesagt, dass er aus Rom kommt und dass er eine Schwester in Montreal hat. Dann hat Roberto Sharon gefragt, wann die Prüfung ist. Sie hat gesagt, dass sie in zehn Minuten ist und sie hat Roberto viel Glück gewünscht.*

 N. Das habe ich gestern gemacht: Schreiben Sie 8–10 Sätze im Perfekt!

> BEISPIEL *Ich habe bis 10 Uhr geschlafen. Dann . . .*

 O. Die Abschlussparty

1. **Wir planen eine Abschlussparty** With one or several partners, work out a plan for your cousin's graduation party. Be prepared to outline your ideas.

   Sagen Sie, . . . !

   a. wann und wo die Party ist b. wie lange sie dauert c. wer kommt
   d. was Sie trinken und essen e. was Sie noch brauchen

   a. _____

   b. _____

   c. _____

   d. _____

   e. _____

iLrn

Visit the *Wie geht's?* iLrn website for more review and practice of the grammar points you have just learned.

2. **Wie ist die Party gewesen?** Describe what happened at the party.

P. Die Geburtstagsfeier: Auf Deutsch bitte!

1. The day before yesterday I gave a birthday party. 2. Did Volker and Bettina come? 3. Yes, they came, too. 4. My friends brought presents. 5. My father opened some bottles of wine. 6. How long did you *(pl. fam.)* celebrate? 7. Until three o'clock. We danced, ate well, and drank a lot of Coke. 8. The neighbors said that the music was too loud **(laut)**. 9. Did you *(sg. fam.)* hear the music? 10. Yesterday a neighbor came and spoke with my parents. 11. I liked the party.

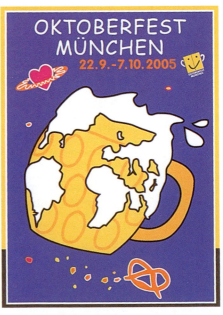

Wortschatz 2

das Lied, -er	*song*
die Kerze, -n	*candle*
dort	*(over) there*
eigentlich	*actual(ly)*
ein bisschen	*some, a little bit of* (+sing.)
immer	*always*
laut	*loud, noisy*
lustig	*funny, amusing*
(noch) nie	*never (before)*
verrückt	*crazy*
fallen (fällt), ist gefallen	*to fall*
studieren	*to study a particular field, be a student at a university*
Glück / Pech haben	*to be lucky / unlucky.*
Glück / Pech gehabt!	*I was (you were, she was, etc.) lucky / unlucky.*
Spaß machen	*to be fun*
Das macht (mir) Spaß.	*That's fun.*

»Ich tue, was mir Spaß macht«

🟡 **Ich studiere** *(I am a student)* in Heidelberg. **Ich studiere** Kunst *(i.e., art is my major).* BUT **Ich lerne** Deutsch *(i.e., I'm taking German).* **Ich lerne** die Vokabeln *(i.e., I'm learning / studying the vocabulary, possibly for a test).*

🟡 Learn this as an idiom: **Lesen macht Spaß.** *(Reading is fun.)* **Das macht mir/ihm/uns/ ihnen Spaß.** *(I/he/we/they love [to do] it.);* **Macht es dir Spaß?** *(Do you enjoy [doing] it?)*

Vor dem Lesen

A. Fragen

1. Welche religiösen Feste feiern wir hier (in den USA, in Kanada . . .)? 2. Gibt es hier historische Feste? Wenn ja, welche? 3. Wann gibt es hier Karussells, Buden (booths), Spaß für alle? 4. Was machen die Leute hier gern am 4. Juli? Was machen Sie/haben Sie gemacht?

Nussknacker aus dem Erzgebirge

B. Wohin gehen wir? There are all sorts of musical entertainment during the Christmas season. Look at the Leipzig calendar of events and then discuss with your partner what performances might interest you and why. Compare the theater program with what is typically offered in your home town or on campus during that time.

BEISPIEL S1 Welche Oper möchtest du sehen?
S2 Ich möchte . . . sehen. / Ich möchte keine Oper sehen, aber ich gehe gern ins Konzert.

Spielpläne

Oper Leipzig

29. 11.	19.30 Uhr	**Les Contes d'Hoffmann**
30. 11.	10.30 Uhr	**Salome**
1. 12.	19.00 Uhr	**Bruckner 8** (Ballet)
2. 12.	18.00 Uhr	**Tannhäuser**
5. 12.	19.30 Uhr	**Hänsel und Gretel**
6. 12.	19.30 Uhr	**Bruckner 8** (Ballet)
7. 12.	19.30 Uhr	**Hänsel und Gretel**
8. 12.	19.00 Uhr	**Bruckner 8** (Ballet)
9. 12.	18.00 Uhr	**Salome**
12. 12.	19.30 Uhr	**Bruckner 8** (Ballet)
13. 12.	19.30 Uhr	**Rigoletto**
14. 12.	19.30 Uhr	**Salome**
15. 12.	19.00 Uhr	**Carmen**
16. 12.	11.00 Uhr	**Hänsel und Gretel**
	17.00 Uhr	**Hänsel und Gretel**
20. 12.	19.30 Uhr	**Schwanensee** (Ballet)
21. 12.	19.30 Uhr	**Hänsel und Gretel**
22. 12.	17.00 Uhr	**Hänsel und Gretel**
23. 12.	18.00 Uhr	**Schwanensee** (Ballet)

Neues Gewandhaus

1. 12.	16.00 Uhr	**Salonorchester CAPPUCCINO** Vorweihnachtliche Impressionen
	17.00 Uhr	**Orgelstunde zum 1. Advent**
2. 12.	11.00 Uhr	**Salonorchester CAPPUCCINO** Vorweihnachtliche Impressionen
	20.00 Uhr	**Großes Konzert für UNICEF**
3. 12.	16.00 Uhr	**Adventskonzert**
6./7./8. 12.	19.30 Uhr	**Großes Konzert**
	19.00 Uhr	G. F. Händel: Messias (Teil I – III)
8. 12.	16.00 Uhr	**Orgelstunde zum 2. Advent**
9. 12.	18.00 Uhr	**Kammermusik**
10. 12.	16.00 Uhr	**Adventskonzert**
12. 12.	20.00 Uhr	**Konzert für den American Football Club „Leipzig Lions"** J. S. Bach: Weihnachtsoratorium (I–III)
15. 12.	16.00 Uhr	**Familienkonzert: Hänsel und Gretel**
16. 12.	18.00 Uhr	**Kammermusik**
17. 12.	16.00 Uhr	**Adventskonzert**
20./21. 12.	20.00 Uhr	**Musik aus Hollywood-Filmen**

Frohe Weihnachten und viel Glück im neuen Jahr

C. Das ist leicht zu verstehen! Welche Silbe ist betont? Was ist das auf Englisch?:

der Prinz, Studentenball, Vampir; das Kostüm, Musikinstrument, Weihnachtsessen, Weihnachtslied; die Adventszeit, Brezel, Flamme (in Flammen), Kontaktlinse, Konversationsstunde, Prinzessin, Weihnachtsdekoration, Weihnachtspyramide, Weihnachtszeit; Ende Juli; ins Bett fallen; authentisch, enorm viel, exakt, historisch, Hunderte von, wunderschön

Deutsche Feste

(Carolyn berichtet° für die Konversationsstunde.)　　　　　　　　　　　reports

Wie ihr gehört habt, habe ich gerade ein Jahr in Deutschland studiert. Ich bin
erst° vor einem Monat wieder nach Hause gekommen, weil ich dort mit der　　　only
Uni erst Ende Juli fertig geworden bin. Es ist wunderschön gewesen. Ich habe
viel gesehen und viel gelernt. Heute habe ich ein paar Bilder gebracht.

5　　　Im September bin ich mit Freunden beim Winzerfest° in Bacharach am Rhein　　vintage festival
gewesen. Da haben wir Wein getrunken und gesungen. Abends haben wir von
einem Schiff den „Rhein in Flammen" gesehen, mit viel Feuerwerk°　　　　　　fireworks
und Rotlicht°. Ich habe immer gedacht, dass die Deutschen etwas steif° sind. Aber　　red light of torches / rigid
nicht, wenn sie feiern! So lustig und verrückt habe ich sie° noch nie gesehen.　　them

10　Zwei Wochen später sind wir zum Oktoberfest nach München gefahren. Im
Bierzelt° haben wir Brezeln gegessen und natürlich auch Bier getrunken. Die　　　. . . tent
Musik ist mir° ein bisschen zu laut gewesen. Was mir aber besonders gefallen　　for me
hat, war° der Trachtenzug° zur Wies'n°.　　　　　　　　　　　　　　　　　　was / parade in traditional
　　　　　　　　　　　　　　　　　　　　　　　　　　　　　　　　　　　　　　garb / festival grounds

CD 4,
Track 4

Im Oktoberfestzelt

Im Februar gibt's den Fasching. Das ist so etwas wie° Mardi Gras in New　　　like
15　Orleans, mit Umzügen° und Kostümen. Ich bin als Vampir zu einem Studenten-　　parades
ball gegangen. Wir haben lange getanzt und morgens bin ich dann todmüde° ins　　dead tired
Bett gefallen. Halloween kommt in Deutschland auch immer mehr in Mode°,　　　into vogue
jedenfalls° für die Geschäfte. Das finde ich lustig.　　　　　　　　　　　　　　at least

　　　Außer diesen° Festen gibt es natürlich noch viele Feiertage. Weihnachten　　these
20　war besonders schön. Auf dem Christkindlmarkt in Nürnberg gibt es Hunderte
von Buden° mit Weihnachtsdekorationen, Kerzen, Spielzeug°, Lebkuchen und　　　booths / toys
auch Buden mit Glühwein°. Den Weihnachtsengel° habe ich dort gekauft; der　　　mulled wine / . . . angel
Nussknacker° und die Weihnachtspyramide kommen aus dem Erzgebirge. In der　　nutcracker
Adventszeit hat man nur einen Adventskranz° und Weihnachtsdekorationen,　　　Advent wreath
25　aber noch keinen° Weihnachtsbaum. Den Weihnachtsbaum sehen die Kinder erst　　still no
am 24. Dezember, am Heiligabend. Aber dann bleibt er gewöhnlich bis zum 6.
Januar im Zimmer.

　　　Zu Weihnachten bin ich bei Familie Fuchs gewesen. Bevor das Christkind die
Geschenke gebracht hat, haben wir Weihnachtslieder gesungen. Am 25. und 26.
30　Dezember sind alle Geschäfte zu. Die zwei Feiertage sind nur für Familie und
Freunde. Das finde ich eigentlich gut. Zum Weihnachtsessen hat es Gans°　mit　　goose
Rotkraut° und Knödeln gegeben. Die Weihnachtsplätzchen und der Stollen haben　　red cabbage
mir besonders gut geschmeckt.

Silvester habe ich mit Freunden gefeiert. Um Mitternacht° haben alle
35 Kirchenglocken° geläutet° und wir haben mit Sekt und „Prost Neujahr!"° das
neue Jahr begonnen.

at midnight
church bells / rang / Happy New Year!

Landshuter Fürstenhochzeit

Das Bild hier ist von der Fürstenhochzeit in Landshut. Da bin ich im Juni
gewesen. Das vergesse° ich nie. Viele Landshuter haben mittelalterliche°
Kleidung getragen und alles ist sehr authentisch gewesen: die Ritter°, Prinzen
40 und Prinzessinnen, die Musikinstrumente und Turniere°. Man ist historisch so
exakt, dass Leute mit Brillen° Kontaktlinsen tragen, weil es im Mittelalter° noch
keine Brillen gegeben hat. Übrigens habe ich Glück gehabt, weil man das Fest
nur alle° vier Jahre feiert.
Ich habe immer gedacht, dass die Deutschen viel arbeiten. Das tun sie, aber
45 sie haben auch enorm viele Feiertage, viele mehr als° wir. Und Feiern in
Deutschland macht Spaß.

forget / medieval
knights
tournaments
glasses / in the Middle Ages

every

more than

Aktives zum Text

A. Was hat Carolyn gesagt? Match the sentence fragments from the two groups.

_____ 1. Wie ihr gehört habt, . . .

_____ 2. Ich bin erst vor einem Monat wieder
nach Hause gekommen, . . .

_____ 3. Ich habe immer gedacht, . . .

_____ 4. Im Bierzelt haben wir . . .

_____ 5. Der Weihnachtsbaum bleibt . . .

_____ 6. Bevor das Christkind die Geschenke
gebracht hat, . . .

_____ 7. Was mir besonders gut gefallen hat, . . .

_____ 8. Man ist historisch so exakt, . . .

a. haben wir Weihnachtslieder
gesungen.

b. war die Fürstenhochzeit in
Landshut.

c. Brezeln gegessen.

d. bis zum 6. Januar im Zimmer.

e. weil ich dort mit der Uni erst
Ende Juli fertig geworden bin.

f. habe ich gerade ein Jahr in
Deutschland studiert.

g. dass die Deutschen etwas zu
steif sind.

h. dass Leute mit Brillen
Kontaktlinsen tragen.

B. Feiern in Deutschland Complete these sentences with the appropriate verb in the present perfect. Use each verb once.

bringen, fahren, feiern, gefallen, gehen, haben, kaufen, kommen, sein, studieren

1. Carolyn _____ vor einem Monat nach Hause _____. 2. Sie _____ ein Jahr in Deutschland _____. 3. Es _____ wunderbar _____. 4. Sie _____ ein paar Bilder zur Deutschstunde _____. 5. Im September _____ sie mit Freunden zum Winzerfest nach Bacharach _____. 6. Zum Fasching _____ sie als Vampir zu einem Studentenball _____. 7. Die Weihnachtszeit _____ Carolyn besonders gut _____. 8. In Nürnberg _____ sie einen Weihnachtsengel _____. 9. Sie _____ Weihnachten bei der Familie Fuchs _____. 10. Mit der Landshuter Fürstenhochzeit _____ sie Glück _____, weil man das Fest nur alle vier Jahre feiert.

C. Interview: *Fragen Sie einen Nachbarn/eine Nachbarin, . . .!*

1. ob man in seiner/ihrer Familie Vatertag, Mutter, und/oder Valentinstag feiert; wenn ja, wie
2. ob er/sie zum 4. Juli Kracher *(firecrackers)* gekauft hat oder ein Feuerwerk gesehen hat; wenn ja, wo
3. ob er/sie noch Halloween feiert; wenn ja, wie? wenn nein, warum nicht?
4. wie und wo er/sie gewöhnlich Thanksgiving feiert; was man dann isst und trinkt
5. welche religiösen Feste seine/ihre Familie feiert; ob es dann Geschenke gibt; wenn ja, wer bekommt oft was?
6. wie und wo er/sie das letzte *(last)* Silvester gefeiert hat; wie man Silvester auch feiern kann

SILVESTER 2005/2006 IN LEIPZIG

1 Eintrittskarte der Preisgruppe II	für das Konzert zum Jahreswechsel am 31.12., 17.00 Uhr, Gewandhausorchester, Herbert Blomstedt, Ludwig van Beethoven, 9. Sinfonie
1 Abendessen	3-Gänge-Menü ohne Getränkein einem Innenstadtrestaurant
Preis pro Person	85,–€

D. Kurzgespräche With a partner, prepare a brief dialogue using one of the situations. Then role-play your dialogue to the class.

1. **Krankenbesuch** *(call on someone who is ill)*
   One of your very best friends has been quite sick. You stop by to visit. Your friend expresses his/her surprise. You have also brought a little present (e.g., a book, flowers, cookies). Your friend is very pleased and thanks you. You respond appropriately and wish him/her a speedy recovery.

2. **Ich komme!**
   Your Mom (**Mutti**) calls you and asks whether you have plans for the weekend. She is driving through the town where you are studying and would like to see you (**dich**). You are surprised and pleased. It is your mother's birthday, and you wish her a happy birthday. Tell her you have bought a present and that she will get it when she comes. You conclude the conversation.

 E. Eine Postkarte: Gruß aus München Read the following postcard written to a friend you know in Germany, Austria, or Switzerland. Your friend mentions some of the experiences with holiday celebrations described in the text. Using her postcard as a model, write your own postcard.

Schreibtipp
Writing a Postcard

Greetings to friends and relatives usually start with *Dear . . .* (**Liebe Eva / Lieber Axel**) or *Hi . . .* (**Hallo Luca**), and mostly end with *Greetings, your . . .* (**Viele [liebe] Grüße, Dein(e)/Euer(e) . . .**) Other informal good-byes are *Bye!* (**Tschüss!**), *See you then!* (**Bis dann!**), or *See you soon!* (**Bis bald!**).

In addressing the postcard, you may use the person's name alone, or else precede it with **Herrn** or **Frau.** A card might also be addressed **An Familie [Norbert Fuchs].** Note the last line of the address shows the country code + postal code + the name of the city. Common country codes are **D** for Germany (**Deutschland**), **A** for Austria (**Österreich**), and **CH** for Switzerland (**Confoederatio Helvetica = Schweiz**).

Lieber Axel,
meine Freunde und ich sind gerade in München und haben viel Spaß. Die Stadt ist echt interessant, das Wetter ist prima und die Leute sind nett. Gestern sind wir beim Oktoberfest gewesen. Verrückt! So viel Bier und Brezeln habe ich schon lange nicht mehr gesehen. Der Trachtenzug zur Wies'n hat mir besonders gefallen. Wenn ihr Deutschen feiert, feiert ihr richtig. Habe viele Fotos gemacht. Viele Grüße,

    Deine Michelle

 51-H3275

Herrn
Axel Fitzke
Am Neuen Teiche 37
D–31139 Hildesheim

0,55 €
DEUTSCHLAND ALTE OPER FRANKFURT

 ## Hörverständnis

Track 9 **Das Straßenfest** Listen to what Bibi tells Matthias about their local street fair. Then select the correct response from those given below.

Zum Erkennen: Was gibt's? *(What's up?)*; niemand *(nobody)*; Krimskrams *(this and that)*; Spiele *(games)*; Jung und Alt *(all ages, young and old)*

1. Matthias ist bei Bibi gewesen, aber niemand hat ____ geöffnet.
   a. das Fenster
   b. die Garage
   c. die Tür

2. Bei Bibi hat es am ____ ein Straßenfest gegeben.
   a. Freitag
   b. Samstag
   c. Sonntag

3. Bibi findet das eigentlich ____ sehr schön.
   a. nie
   b. immer
   c. noch

4. Bibi hat mit ____ beim Straßenfest geholfen.
   a. Matthias
   b. den Eltern
   c. dem Bruder

5. Der Vater hat ____ .
   a. Würstchen verkauft
   b. mit den Kindern gespielt
   c. mit den Tischen und Stühlen geholfen

6. Abends haben die Leute ein bisschen ____ .
   a. Pech gehabt
   b. getanzt
   c. geschlafen

Carnival; Oktoberfest; the Landshut Wedding and the Rhine in Flames: http://wiegehts.heinle.com.

In der Stadt

Lernziele

In this chapter you will learn about:

Zum Thema

Viennese landmarks and asking for directions

Kultur-Fokus

Austria; Viennese life, music, art, architecture, sights, and history

Struktur

Personal pronouns
Modal auxiliary verbs
Sondern vs. **aber**

Einblicke

Grüße aus Wien

For more information, go to http://iLrn.heinle.com

Schloss Belvedere in Wien

Vorschau **Spotlight on Austria**

Minidrama: *Wie komme ich zur Staatsoper?*
Blickpunkt: *Besuch in Österreich*

Area: Approximately 32,400 square miles, about the size of Maine.

Population: About 8.1 million, 98% German-speaking; ethnic minorities include some 50,000 Croats in the Burgenland, 20,000 Slovenes in southern Carinthia, and small groups of Hungarians, Czechs, Slovaks, and Italians.

Religion: 78% Catholic, 5% Protestant, 17% other (including 2% Moslem)

Geography: The Alps are the dominant physical feature, covering all of the narrow western part of the country and much of its central and southern regions. The Danube Valley and the Vienna Basin lie in the northeastern part of the country.

Currency: Euro, 1 € = 100 Cents. The former Austrian currency, the Schilling (= 100 Groschen), was phased out in 2002.

Principal cities: Vienna (*Wien*, pop. 1.6 million, capital); Graz (pop. 250,000), Linz (pop. 203,000); Salzburg (pop. 143,000); Innsbruck (pop. 120,000).

The history of Austria and of the Habsburg family, who ruled Austria through much of its history, were closely linked for more than 650 years. Rudolf von Habsburg started the dynasty in 1273 when he was elected emperor of the Holy Roman Empire, which existed in some form from 962 until 1806. Over the course of several centuries, the Habsburg empire grew to include Flanders, Burgundy, Bohemia, Hungary, and large areas of the Balkans. These acquisitions were made not only through war, but also through shrewdly arranged marriages (**Heiratspolitik**) with other European ruling houses. The Holy Roman Empire ended with the Napoleonic wars in the early 1800s, yet members of the Habsburg family ruled until the end of World War I. In 1918, the defeated Austro-Hungarian Empire was carved up into independent countries: Austria, Hungary, Czechoslovakia, Yugoslavia, and Romania. In 1938, after several political and economic crises, Hitler annexed the young Austrian republic into the Third Reich. After World War II, the country was occupied by the Allies until 1955, when Austria regained its sovereignty and pledged neutrality. During the Cold War, the country belonged to neither the Warsaw Pact nor to NATO.

Since the end of World War II, Austria has been actively involved in international humanitarian efforts. Hungary's decision in 1989 to allow East German refugees to cross its border into Austria was a contributing factor in the fall of the Berlin Wall. In 1995, the country became a member of the European Union. (For pictures and information on Austrian cities, visit www.[city name].at.)

In der Innenstadt von Innsbruck

Zum Thema

 Entschuldigen Sie! Wo ist . . . ?

CD 4, Track 6

TOURIST	Entschuldigen Sie! Können Sie mir sagen, wo das Hotel Sacher ist?
WIENER	Erste Straße links hinter der Staatsoper.
TOURIST	Und wie komme ich von da zum Stephansdom?
WIENER	Geradeaus, die Kärntner Straße entlang.
TOURIST	Wie weit ist es zum Dom?
WIENER	Nicht weit. Sie können zu Fuß gehen.
TOURIST	Danke!
WIENER	Bitte schön!

● **Hotel Sacher** is probably the best-known hotel in Vienna. One of the reasons for its popularity is its famous café, for which a rich, delicious cake (**die Sachertorte**) is named.

Da drüben!

TOURIST	Entschuldigung! Wo ist das Burgtheater?
HERR	Es tut mir Leid. Ich bin nicht aus Wien.
TOURIST	Verzeihung! Ist das das Burgtheater?
DAME	Nein, das ist nicht das Burgtheater, sondern die Staatsoper. Fahren Sie mit der Straßenbahn zum Rathaus! Gegenüber vom Rathaus ist das Burgtheater.
TOURIST	Und wo hält die Straßenbahn?
DAME	Da drüben links.
TOURIST	Vielen Dank!
DAME	Bitte sehr!

A. Fragen

1. Wo ist das Hotel Sacher? 2. Wie kommt man von der Staatsoper zum Stephansdom? 3. Wen fragt der Tourist im zweiten Gespräch? 4. Ist der Herr Wiener? 5. Wie kommt der Tourist zum Burgtheater? 6. Wo ist die Haltestelle? 7. Was ist gegenüber vom Burgtheater?

 B. Jetzt sind Sie dran! With a partner, create your own dialogue asking for directions to any place in your city.

BEISPIEL   S1 Entschuldigung. Wo ist . . . ?
                  S2 . . .

Fokus Viennese Landmarks

Vienna is an old city, filled with reminders of its history. It is also a very walkable city, and its residents are frequently reminded of its past by the famous buildings that they pass each day. In addition to the Sacher Hotel with its famous café—for which the delicious **Sachertorte** was named—the three following famous landmarks are mentioned in the dialogue.

- Vienna's Opera (**die Staatsoper**), inaugurated in 1869, was built in the style of the early French Renaissance and is one of the foremost European opera houses.
- A masterpiece of Gothic architecture, Saint Stephen's Cathedral (**der Stephansdom**) dates from the 12th century. Its roof of colored tile and its 450-foot-high spire (nicknamed "Steffi") make it the principal landmark of Vienna.

There is an excellent panoramic view of the city at the top of the spire's 438 steps. It is possible to take an elevator from the lower, unfinished tower to the top, which houses the **Pummerin,** a bell that weighs over 4 tons. It was made out of the metal melted down from the cathedral's former bells, all of which were smashed to the ground during World War II.

- In 1776, Emperor Joseph II declared Vienna's **Burgtheater** Austria's national theater. The Burgtheater has always devoted itself to classical drama. Over the years, its actors have developed a stylized mode of diction that gives an aura of conservatism to their performances. Most of the ensemble, numbering more than a hundred, have lifetime contracts.

Das Wiener Burgtheater

Wortschatz 1

Der Stadtplan, ⸚e *(city map)*

der Bahnhof, ⸚e	*train station*	die Bank, -en	*bank*
Bus, -se	*bus*	Bibliothek, -en	*library*
Dom, -e	*cathedral*	Brücke, -n	*bridge*
Park, -s	*park*	Haltestelle, -n	*(bus, etc.) stop*
Platz, ⸚e	*place; square*	Kirche, -n	*church*
Weg, -e	*way; trail*	Post	*post office*
das Auto, -s	*car*	Schule, -n	*school*
Fahrrad, ⸚er	*bike*	Straße, -n	*street*
Hotel, -s	*hotel*	Straßenbahn, -en	*streetcar*
Kino, -s	*movie theater*	**U-Bahn**	*subway*
Museum, Museen	*museum*	Universität, -en	*university*
Rathaus, ⸚er	*city hall*	Uni, -s	
Schloss, ⸚er	*palace*		
Taxi, -s	*taxi*		
Theater, -	*theater*		

Weiteres

der Tourist, -en, -en	*tourist*
die Dame, -n	*lady*
besichtigen	*to tour, visit (palace, etc.)*
halten (hält), gehalten	*to stop; to hold*
zeigen	*to show*

⦿ U-Bahn stands for **Untergrundbahn,** and S-Bahn for **Schnellbahn** *(a suburban commuter train).*

⦿ When halten is intransitive (that is, without an accusative object), it means *to come to a stop:* **Der Bus hält da drüben.** When it is transitive, it means *to hold:* **Halten Sie mir bitte das Buch!**

zu Fuß gehen, ist zu Fuß gegangen	*to walk*
Entschuldigen Sie!	*Excuse me!*
Entschuldigung! / Verzeihung!	*Excuse me!*
Es tut mir Leid.	*I'm sorry.*
Ich möchte zum/zur . . .	*I would like to go to . . .*
Können Sie mir sagen, wo . . . ist?	*Can you tell me where . . . is?*
Wie kommt man von hier zum/zur . . . ?	*How do you get from here to . . . ?*
Gibt es hier in der Nähe . . . ?	*Is there . . . nearby?*
in der Nähe von (+ *dat.*)	*near, in the vicinity of*
die erste Straße links / rechts	*first street to the left / right*
(immer) geradeaus	*(keep) straight ahead*
an/am . . . vorbei	*past the . . .*
(den Fluss) entlang	*along (the river)*
bis Sie . . . sehen	*until you see . . .*
da drüben	*over there*
dorthin	*to there*
gegenüber von (+ *dat.*)	*across from*
nah / weit	*near / far*
sondern	*but (on the contrary)*
Sie können zu Fuß gehen.	*You can walk.*
Fahren Sie mit dem Bus!	*Take the bus!*

Zum Erkennen: hinter *(behind)*; die Oper, -n *(opera house)*; AUCH: das Hauptwort, ¨er *(noun)*; das Modalverb, -en *(modal auxiliary)*; variieren *(to vary)*; direkt dorthin *(right to it)*

Aktives zum Thema

A. Mustersätze

1. Das ist nicht ____, sondern ____.
   das Theater / die Oper → Das ist nicht das Theater, sondern die Oper.
   das Rathaus / die Universität; das Museum / die Bibliothek; die Bank / die Post; die Bushaltestelle / die Straßenbahnhaltestelle . . .
2. Können Sie mir sagen, wie ich ____ komme?
   zur Universität → Können Sie mir sagen, wie ich zur Universität komme?
   zum Rathaus, zur Bibliothek, zum Museum, zur Schulstraße . . .
3. Die ____ Straße ____.
   erste / links → Die erste Straße links.
   zweite / rechts; dritte / links; vierte / rechts . . .
4. Fahren Sie mit ____!
   die Straßenbahn → Fahren Sie mit der Straßenbahn!
   der Bus, das Auto, das Fahrrad, die U-Bahn, das Taxi . . .
5. Die Straßenbahn hält ____.
   da drüben → Die Straßenbahn hält da drüben.
   da drüben rechts, beim Bahnhof, in der Nähe vom Park, gegenüber vom Theater . . .

B. Was bedeuten die Wörter und was sind die Artikel?

Domplatz, Fußgängerweg, Fahrradweg, Schlosshotel, Touristenstadt, Kirchenfest, Schulferien, Studentenkino, Bahnhofsdrogerie, Universitätsparkplatz, Parkuhr

C. Was passt nicht?

1. der Bus—das Taxi—das Fahrrad—das Kino
2. das Theater—der Weg—das Museum—die Bibliothek
3. die U-Bahn—die Bank—die Post—das Rathaus
4. die Straße—die Brücke—der Stadtplan—der Platz
5. da drüben—gegenüber von—in der Nähe von—schade
6. fahren—zu Fuß gehen—halten—laufen

D. Wo ist . . . ? Working with a partner, practice asking for and giving directions to various places on campus.

S1 Entschuldigen Sie! Wo ist . . . ?
S2 . . .
S1 Und wie komme ich dorthin?
S2 . . .
S1 Vielen Dank!
S2 . . . !

E. Fragen zum Stadtplan von Winterthur With your partner, using the formal **Sie,** practice asking for and giving directions from one place to another. Start out at the information office at the train station.

● Winterthur is in Switzerland. The Swiss don't use the letter **ß,** therefore the spelling **Strasse** instead of **Straße.**

BEISPIEL   S1 Entschuldigung! Können Sie mir sagen, wie ich zum Technikum *(technical university)* komme?
S2 Das Technikum ist in der Technikumstrasse. Gehen Sie am Bahnhof vorbei und links in die Technikumstrasse. Dann gehen Sie immer geradeaus, bis Sie rechts das Technikum sehen.

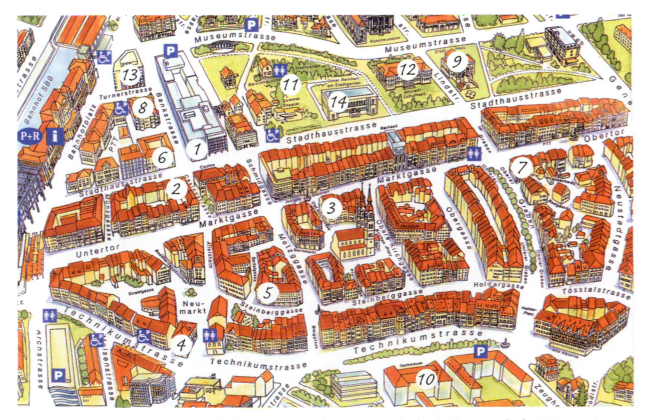

1. Kaufhaus 2. Metzgerei 3. Möbelladen 4. Hotel 5. Fotogeschäft 6. Sportgeschäft 7. Drogerie
8. Bank 9. Theater 10. Technikum 11. Stadtpark 12. Schule 13. Post 14. Museum

 **For further review,** see the Summary of Pronunciation in the front of your *Arbeitsbuch*. Study Part II, subsections 29–36.

 ## Aussprache: ö

CD 4, Track 7 **A. Laute**

1. [ö:] **Ö**sterreich, Br**ö**tchen, G**oe**the, sch**ö**n, gew**ö**hnlich, franz**ö**sisch, h**ö**ren
2. [ö] **ö**ffnen, **ö**stlich, k**ö**nnen, L**ö**ffel, zw**ö**lf, n**ö**rdlich, m**ö**chten

B. Wortpaare

1. kennen / können
2. Sehne / Söhne
3. große / Größe
4. schon / schön
5. Sühne / Söhne
6. Höhle / Hölle

Hörverständnis

Track 10 **Touristen in Innsbruck** Listen to this conversation between two tourists and a woman from Innsbruck. Then complete the sentences below with the correct information from the dialogue.

Zum Erkennen: uns *(us)*; das Goldene Dachl *(The Golden Roof, a 15th-century burgher house)*; das Konzert *(concert)*; erst *(only)*; Viel Spaß! *(Have fun!)*

1. Die Touristen fragen, wo _____ ist.
2. Es ist _____ sehr weit. Sie können _____ gehen.
3. Bei der Brücke _____ die Fußgängerzone.
4. Da geht man _____, bis man links zum Dachl kommt.
5. Der Dom ist _____ Dachl.
6. Das Konzert beginnt _____.
7. Vor dem Konzert möchten die Touristen _____.
8. Von der Maria-Theresia-Straße sieht man wunderbar _____.
9. Sie sollen nicht *(are not supposed to)* zu spät zum Dom gehen, weil

   _____.

Das Goldene Dachl in Innsbruck

Struktur

5.1 Personal pronouns

1. In English the PERSONAL PRONOUNS are *I, me, you, he, him, she, her, it, we, us, they,* and *them.* Some of these pronouns are used as subjects, others as direct or indirect objects, or objects of prepositions.

SUBJECT:	**He** *is coming.*
DIRECT OBJECT:	*I see* **him.**
INDIRECT OBJECT:	*I give* **him** *the book.*
OBJECT OF A PREPOSITION:	*We'll go without* **him.**

The German personal pronouns are likewise used as subjects, direct or indirect objects, or objects of prepositions. Like the definite and indefinite articles, personal pronouns have special forms in the various cases. You already know the nominative case of these pronouns. Here are the nominative, accusative, and dative cases together.

		singular					plural			sg. / pl.
nom.	ich	du	er	es	sie	wir	ihr	sie		Sie
acc.	**mich**	**dich**	**ihn**	**es**	**sie**	**uns**	**euch**	**sie**		**Sie**
dat.	**mir**	**dir**	**ihm**	**ihm**	**ihr**	**uns**	**euch**	**ihnen**		**Ihnen**

SUBJECT:	**Er** kommt.
DIRECT OBJECT:	Ich sehe **ihn.**
INDIRECT OBJECT:	Ich gebe **ihm** das Buch.
OBJECT OF A PREPOSITION:	Wir gehen ohne **ihn.**

- Note the similarities between the definite article of the noun and the pronoun that replaces it.

	masc.	neut.	fem.	pl.
nom.	der Mann = **er**	das Kind = **es**	die Frau = **sie**	die Leute = **sie**
acc.	den Mann = **ihn**	das Kind = **es**	die Frau = **sie**	die Leute = **sie**
dat.	dem Mann = **ihm**	dem Kind = **ihm**	der Frau = **ihr**	den Leuten = **ihnen**

2. As in English, the dative object usually precedes the accusative object, unless the accusative object is a pronoun. If that is the case, the accusative object pronoun comes first.

Ich gebe **dem Studenten**	den Kuli.	*I'm giving the student the pen.*
Ich gebe **ihm**	den Kuli.	*I'm giving him the pen.*
Ich gebe ihn	**dem Studenten.**	*I'm giving it to the student.*
Ich gebe ihn	**ihm.**	*I'm giving it to him.*

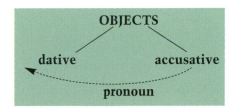

Übungen

A. Ersetzen Sie die Hauptwörter durch Pronomen! Replace each noun with a pronoun in the appropriate case.

BEISPIEL   den Bruder   *ihn*

1. der Vater, dem Mann, den Großvater, dem Freund, den Ober
2. die Freundin, der Großmutter, der Dame, die Frau, der Familie
3. die Eltern, den Herren, den Frauen, die Freundinnen, den Schweizern
4. für die Mutter, mit den Freunden, gegen die Studenten, außer dem Großvater, ohne den Ober, von den Eltern, zu dem Mädchen, bei der Großmutter

B. Kombinieren Sie mit den Präpositionen! Was sind die Akkusativ- und Dativformen?

BEISPIEL   ich (ohne, mit)
ohne mich, mit mir

1. er (für, mit)   5. ihr (für, außer)
2. wir (durch, von)   6. sie/*sg.* (um, nach)
3. Sie (gegen, zu)   7. sie/*pl.* (für, aus)
4. du (ohne, bei)   8. es (ohne, außer)

C. Was fehlt?

1. **Nennen Sie die Pronomen!** Complete the sentences with the appropriate German case forms of the suggested pronouns.

   BEISPIEL   Sie kauft _____ das Buch. *(me)*
   Sie kauft mir das Buch.

   a. Siehst du _____? *(them, him, her, me, us)*
   b. Geben Sie es _____! *(him, me, her, us, them)*
   c. Sie braucht _____. *(you/sg. fam.; you/pl. fam.; you/formal; me, him, them, us)*
   d. Wie geht es _____? *(him, them, you/formal; her, you/sg. fam.; you/pl. fam.)*
   e. Der Ober hat _____ das Eis gebracht. *(you/sg. fam.; you/pl. fam.; us, him, her, me, you/formal)*
   f. Hat die Party _____ überrascht? *(you/formal; me, you/sg. fam.; us, her, him, you/pl. fam.)*

2. **Fragen und Antworten** Working with a partner, complete the following sentences.

   S1   Siehst du _____? *(them)*
   S2   Nein, aber sie sehen _____. *(us)*
   S1   Gehört das Buch _____? *(you/sg. fam.)*
   S2   Nein, es gehört _____. *(him)*
   S1   Glaubst du _____? *(him)*
   S2   Nein, aber ich glaube _____. *(you/pl. fam.)*
   S1   Sie sucht _____. *(you/sg. fam.)*
   S2   Ich suche _____. *(her)*
   S1   Hilft er _____? *(us)*
   S2   Nein, aber er hilft _____. *(them)*
   S1   Zeigst du _____ die Kirche? *(us)*
   S2   Ja, ich zeige sie _____. *(you/pl. fam.)*

D. Variieren Sie die Sätze!

1. **Es tut mir Leid.**

   a. He's sorry. b. She's sorry. c. They're sorry. d. Are you *(3×)* sorry? e. We aren't sorry. f. Why are you *(sg. fam.)* sorry? g. I was sorry. h. We weren't sorry.

2. **Wien gefällt mir.**

   a. They like Vienna. b. Do you *(3×)* like Vienna? c. He doesn't like Vienna. d. We like Vienna. e. I liked Vienna. f. How did you *(sg. fam.)* like Vienna? g. Who didn't like Vienna? h. She didn't like Vienna.

E. Antworten Sie und Ersetzen Sie die Hauptwörter!

> **BEISPIEL**   Wo ist **das Hotel? Es** ist da drüben. (Bank)
> *Wo ist **die Bank? Sie** ist da drüben.*

1. Wo ist **die Post?** Da ist **sie.** (Dom, Rathaus, Apotheke)
2. Ist **das Museum** weit von hier? Nein, **es** ist nicht weit von hier. (Kirche, Geschäft, Platz)
3. Zeigen Sie **der Dame** den Weg? Ja, ich zeige **ihr** den Weg. (Mann, Leute, Touristin)
4. Helfen Sie **dem Herrn?** Ja, ich helfe **ihm.** (Kind, Damen, Touristin)
5. Haben Sie **die Straßenbahn** genommen? Ja, ich habe **sie** genommen. (Bus, U-Bahn, Taxi)
6. Wie hat dir **die Stadt** gefallen? **Sie** hat mir gut gefallen. (Hotel, Universität, Park)

F. Fragen und Antworten mit Pronomen   Ask your partner all sorts of questions which he/she answers freely with the proper pronouns. Take turns.

> **BEISPIEL**   S1 Wie geht es . . . (dir, deiner Freundin)?
> S2 Es geht mir gut. / Es geht ihr nicht so gut.

1. Wie geht es . . . (Andreas, Stefanie, Mario und Antje usw.)?
2. Hast du mit . . . (Kevin, Miriam, Sabine und Karin usw.) gesprochen?
3. Wie gefällt/gefallen dir . . . (die Uni, Björn, Paul und Paula usw.)?
4. Wie findest du . . . (die Restaurants, Toni, Tobias und Anne usw.)?
5. Habt ihr schon einmal . . . (den Park, das Rathaus, die Museen usw.) besichtigt?
6. Zeigst du . . . (deinem Onkel, deinem Onkel und deiner Tante, Sara und mir usw.) die Stadt?
7. Glaubst du alles, was . . . (ich, wir, er und ich, die Leute usw.) sage/sagt/sagen?

> ● Optional English-to-German practice: 1. Did you *(3 ×)* thank him? 2. We congratulated her. 3. I surprised them. 4. We'll show you *(3 ×)* the palace. 5. Did they answer you *(pl. fam.)?* 6. I wrote (to) you *(sg. fam.)*. 7. Are you *(sg. fam.)* going to give him the present? 8. She doesn't believe me.

G. Wer bekommt was?

1. **Wem gibt sie was?** Carolyn has just cleaned out her closet and is going to give away all the souvenirs from her European trip. Explain to whom she is going to give them.

> **BEISPIEL**   ihrer Schwester / die Bilder
> *Sie gibt ihrer Schwester die Bilder.*
> *Sie gibt ihr die Bilder.*
> *Sie gibt sie ihrer Schwester.*
> *Sie gibt sie ihr.*

   a. ihrem Vater / den Stadtplan   b. ihren Großeltern / die Landkarte   c. ihrer Mutter / den Zuckerlöffel   d. ihrer Schwester / das Kleingeld *(small change)*   e. Eva / die CD von Mariah Carey   f. Moritz und Merle / die Poster   g. dir / das T-Shirt

In addition to the places mentioned in the *Zum Thema,* numerous other Viennese landmarks are known around the world.

- The **Hofburg** is almost a self-contained city within the city of Vienna. Although it started life as a medieval castle, it later became the imperial palace of the Habsburgs, who resided there until 1918. It now houses the Museum of Art and Ethnography (**das Völkerkundemuseum**), the portrait collection of the National Library (**die Nationalbibliothek**), the Imperial Treasury (**die Schatzkammer**), the Spanish Riding Academy (**die Spanische Reitschule**), and the federal chancellor's residence.
- **Schönbrunn** was the favorite summer residence of the Empress Maria Theresa (**Maria Theresia**), who ruled Austria, Hungary, and Bohemia from 1740 to 1780. Her daughter Marie Antoinette, who became queen of France, spent her childhood there. It was at Schönbrunn where Mozart dazzled the empress with his talents. During the wars of 1805 and 1809, Napoleon used it as his headquarters. Franz Joseph I, emperor of Austria from 1848 to 1916, was born and died at Schönbrunn, and Charles I, the last of the Habsburgs, abdicated there in 1918, when Austria became a republic. To this day, the parks of Schönbrunn feature some of the best-preserved French-style baroque gardens in the world.
- The **Prater** is a large amusement park with a 220-foot-tall Ferris wheel and many modern rides, a stadium, fairgrounds, race tracks, bridle paths, pools, and ponds.

Das Riesenrad im Prater

 2. **Wem schenkst du was?** Ask your partner what presents he/she is giving for Christmas, Hanukkah, or other holiday. Follow the pattern.

     BEISPIEL   S1   Was schenkst du deinem Vater?
                     S2   Ich schenke ihm ein Wörterbuch.

5.2   Modal auxiliary verbs

Ich soll
Sie schön
grüßen…

1. Both English and German have a small group of MODAL AUXILIARY VERBS that modify the meaning of another verb. Modal verbs express such ideas as permission, ability, necessity, obligation, or desire to do something.

dürfen	*to be allowed to, may*	sollen	*to be supposed to*
können	*to be able to, can*	wollen	*to want to*
müssen	*to have to, must*	mögen	*to like*

- The German modals are irregular in the singular of the present tense:

	dürfen	können	müssen	sollen	wollen	mögen / möchten	
ich	darf	kann	muss	soll	will	mag	möchte
du	darfst	kannst	musst	sollst	willst	magst	möchtest
er	darf	kann	muss	soll	will	mag	möchte
wir	dürfen	können	müssen	sollen	wollen	mögen	möchten
ihr	dürft	könnt	müsst	sollt	wollt	mögt	möchtet
sie	dürfen	können	müssen	sollen	wollen	mögen	möchten

- The **möchte**-forms of **mögen** occur more frequently than the **mag**-forms.

Ich **möchte** eine Tasse Tee. *I would like (to have) a cup of tea.*
Ich **mag** Kaffee nicht. *I don't like coffee.*

2. Modals are another example of the two-part verb phrase. In statements and information questions, the modal is the inflected second element of the sentence (V1). The modified verb (V2) appears at the very end of the sentence in its infinitive form.

Er **geht** nach Hause. *He's going home.*
Er **darf** nach Hause | gehen. | *He may (is allowed to) go home.*
Er **kann** nach Hause | gehen. | *He can (is able to) go home.*
Er **muss** nach Hause | gehen. | *He must (has to) go home.*
Er **soll** nach Hause | gehen. | *He is supposed to go home.*
Er **will** nach Hause | gehen. | *He wants to go home.*
Er **möchte** nach Hause | gehen. | *He would like to go home.*

V1 V2

CAUTION:
- The English set of modals is frequently supplemented by such forms as *is allowed to, is able to, has to.* The German modals, however, do not use such supplements. They follow the pattern of *may, can,* and *must:* **Ich muss gehen.** *(I must go.)*

- The subject of the modal and of the infinitive are always the same: **Er will nach Hause gehen.** *(He wants to go home.)* The English construction *to want somebody to do something,* e.g., *He wants you to go home,* cannot be imitated in German. The correct way to express this idea is **Er will, dass du nach Hause gehst.**

3. Modals can be used without an infinitive, provided the omitted infinitive can be inferred from the context. This structure is common with verbs of motion.

Musst du zum Supermarkt? —Ja, ich **muss,** aber ich **kann** nicht.
Do you have to (go) to the supermarket? —*Yes, **I have to,** but I **can't.***

4. Watch these important differences in meaning:

a. *Gern vs. möchten*

Ich **esse gern** Kuchen. BUT Ich **möchte** ein Stück Kuchen **(haben).**

The first sentence says that I am generally fond of cake *(I like to eat cake).* The second sentence implies a desire for a piece of cake at this particular moment *(I'd like a piece of cake).*

Wir wollen mehr Feiertage!

b. *Wollen* vs. *möchten*

Notice the difference in tone and politeness between these two sentences:

Ich **will** Kuchen. BUT Ich **möchte** Kuchen.

The first might be said by a spoiled child *(I want cake)*, the second by a polite adult *(I would like cake)*.

> **Wenn du dein ganzes Leben lang glücklich sein willst, musst du gute Freunde haben.**

5. Modals in subordinate clauses

   a. Remember that the inflected verb stands at the very end of clauses introduced by subordinate conjunctions such as **bevor, dass, ob, obwohl, wenn,** and **weil.**

   Sie sagt, **dass** du nach Hause gehen **kannst.**
   Du kannst nach Hause gehen, **wenn** du **möchtest.**

   b. If the sentence starts with the subordinate clause, then the inflected verb of the main sentence (the modal) follows right after the comma.

   Du **kannst** nach Hause gehen, wenn du möchtest.
   Wenn du möchtest, **kannst** du nach Hause gehen.

Übungen

H. Ersetzen Sie das Subjekt!

BEISPIEL   Wir sollen zum Markt fahren. (ich)
Ich soll zum Markt fahren.

1. Wir wollen zu Hause bleiben. (er, sie/*pl.*, du, ich)
2. Sie müssen noch die Rechnung bezahlen. (ich, ihr, du, Vater)
3. Du darfst zum Bahnhof kommen. (er, ihr, die Kinder, ich)
4. Möchtet ihr ein Eis haben? (sie/*pl.*, du, er, das Mädchen)
5. Können Sie mir sagen, wo das ist? (du, ihr, er, die Damen)

I. Am Sonntag Say what these people will do on Sunday.

BEISPIEL   Carolyn spricht nur Deutsch. (wollen)
Carolyn will nur Deutsch sprechen.

1. Frank und Margit spielen Tennis. (wollen)
2. Christoph fährt mit ein paar Freunden in die Berge. (möchten)
3. Janina bezahlt Rechnungen. (müssen)
4. Ronny hilft Vater zu Hause. (sollen)
5. Herr und Frau Ahrendt besichtigen Schloss Schönbrunn. (können)
6. Die Kinder gehen in den Zoo. (dürfen)

J. Besucher *(Visitors)*

1. **Stadtbesichtigung *(Sightseeing in town)*** Mitzi and Sepp are visiting their friends Heike and Dirk in Salzburg. Dirk tells Mitzi and Sepp what Heike wants to know.

   Beginnen Sie mit **Heike fragt, ob . . . !**

   a. Könnt ihr den Weg in die Stadt allein finden?
   b. Wollt ihr einen Stadtplan haben?
   c. Möchtet ihr zu Fuß gehen?
   d. Soll ich euch mit dem Auto zum Stadtzentrum bringen?
   e. Müsst ihr noch zur Bank?

2. **Fragen** Mitzi has several questions. Report what she is asking.

   Beginnen Sie mit **Mitzi fragt, wo (was, wie lange, wann, wer)** . . .

   a. Wo kann man hier in der Nähe Blumen kaufen?
   b. Was für ein Geschenk sollen wir für den Vater kaufen?
   c. Wie lange dürfen wir hier bleiben?
   d. Wann müssen wir abends wieder hier sein?
   e. Wer will mit in die Stadt?

 K. Hoppla, hier fehlt was! Wer möchte was tun? You and your partner are checking out Vienna's calendar of events. You've each talked with different friends about preferences. One of you looks at and completes the chart below, while the other one works with the chart in Section 11 of the Appendix.

S1:

WER?	WAS?	WARUM?	WANN?	INFORMATION?
	bei den Wiener Festwochen in Wien sein		10.5.–1.6.	www.festwochen.at
Dieter + ich	Silvester in Wien feiern	Es ist eine Mega-Open-Air-Party mit Walzermusik. (müssen)		
	das Museum moderner Kunst besichtigen		ab *(starting)* 15.9.	www.mumok.at
Karen	zum Christkindlmarkt am Rathausplatz	Sie kauft Weihnachtsdekorationen. (wollen)		
	zum Wiener Eistraum gehen		sechs Wochen ab Ende Januar	www.wien-event.at

BEISPIEL   S1 Wer möchte bei den Wiener Festwochen in Wien sein?
                S2 Dieter möchte bei den Wiener Festwochen in Wien sein.
                S1 Und warum?
                S2 Er kann nicht genug Opern und Theaterstücke sehen.

L. Welches Modalverb passt? Work with a partner to complete the dialogue. Often several answers are possible.

UWE   Uta, _____ du mit mir gehen? Ich _____ einen Stadtplan kaufen.
UTA   Wo _____ wir einen Stadtplan bekommen?
UWE   Die Buchhandlung _____ Stadtpläne haben.
UTA   Gut, ich gehe auch. Ich _____ zwei Bücher für meinen Bruder kaufen.
UWE   _____ wir zu Fuß gehen oder _____ wir mit dem Fahrrad fahren?
UTA   Ich _____ mit dem Fahrrad fahren. Dann _____ wir noch zur Bank. Die Bücher sind bestimmt nicht billig. _____ du nicht auch zur Bank?
UWE   Ja, richtig. Ich _____ eine Rechnung bezahlen.

● Optional English-to-German practice: 1. He wants to see the cathedral. 2. They have to go to the post office. 3. I can't read that. 4. You *(pl. fam.)* are supposed to speak German. 5. You *(sg. fam.)*, may order a piece of cake. 6. She's supposed to study **(lernen).** 7. We have to find the way. 8. Can't you *(3×)* help me? 9. We'd like to drive to Vienna. 10. Are we allowed to see the palace? (See answer key in the Appendix.)

M. Was machst du morgen? Using modal verbs, ask a partner what he/she wants to, has to, is supposed to, or would like to do tomorrow. In the responses, you may use some of the phrases below or choose your own expressions.

BEISPIEL   S1 Was möchtest du morgen tun?
           S2 Ich möchte morgen Tennis spielen.

einen Pulli kaufen   einkaufen gehen   nach . . . fahren
Pizza essen gehen   Rechnungen bezahlen   zu Hause bleiben
viel lernen   ein Geschenk für . . . kaufen ins Kino gehen
ein Buch lesen   meine Eltern überraschen

Fokus   The Sezessionsstil Movement

Known as *Art Nouveau* in France and as **Jugendstil** in Germany, the Austrian variant on this modern art movement was the **Sezessionsstil**, or the *Vienna Secession.* It was so called because its practitioners hoped to break off entirely ("to secede") from traditional art conventions. It was a style of art that emerged toward the end of the 19th century and flourished until World War I. Breaking with previous historical styles, it combined romantic and almost sentimental fidelity to nature with symbolic and abstract ornamentation. The school's influence brought about changes not only in art, but in the applied arts, including fashion, architecture, jewelry, sculpture, poetry, music, theater, and dance. Munich, Darmstadt, Brussels, Paris, Nancy, and Vienna were all centers of the movement. Gustav Klimt emerged as the leader of the Secession in Austria from 1897 until 1905, when he himself broke off from the Secession to develop his own style.

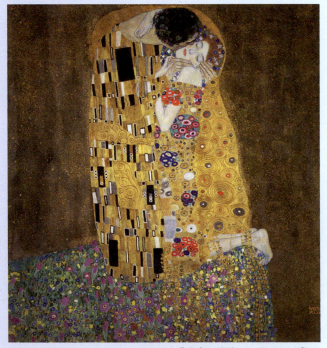

„Der Kuss" (The Kiss) von Gustav Klimt

5.3 *Sondern* vs. *aber*

German has two coordinating conjunctions corresponding to the English *but*.

aber	*but, however*
sondern	*but on the contrary, but rather*

- **Sondern** implies *but on the contrary* and occurs frequently with opposites. It must be used when the first clause is negated and the two ideas are mutually exclusive.

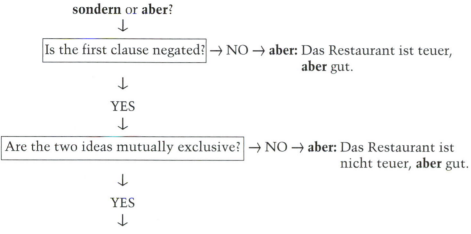

sondern or **aber**?
↓
Is the first clause negated? → NO → **aber:** Das Restaurant ist teuer, **aber** gut.
↓
YES
↓
Are the two ideas mutually exclusive? → NO → **aber:** Das Restaurant ist nicht teuer, **aber** gut.
↓
YES
↓
sondern: Das Restaurant ist nicht teuer, **sondern** billig.

- **Nicht nur . . . , sondern auch . . .**

  Das Restaurant ist **nicht nur** gut, **sondern auch** billig.
  The restaurant is not only good, but also inexpensive.

Übungen

N. *Sondern* oder *aber*? Insert the appropriate conjunction.

1. Till wohnt nicht in Salzburg, _____ in Wien.
2. Er geht heute nicht mit seiner *(his)* Frau, _____ mit seiner Tochter Lisa einkaufen.
3. Lisa geht gern einkaufen, _____ sie will nicht so viel laufen.
4. Der Kinderwagen ist nicht groß, _____ sehr praktisch.
5. Im *(in the)* Kinderwagen transportiert Till nicht nur seine Tochter, _____ auch Lebensmittel.
6. Da ist Platz für vieles, _____ nicht für alles.
7. _____ Till hat ja einen Rucksack *(backpack)*!
8. Wenn Till will, kann er auch mit dem Bus nach Hause fahren, _____ das will er nicht.
9. Till kauft gewöhnlich nicht nur Lebensmittel, _____ oft auch ein Eis für Lisa.
10. Einkaufen macht Spaß, _____ man braucht Zeit.

Zusammenfassung

O. Kombinieren Sie! Create questions by combining items from each column. Then ask different classmates and have them give you an answer using a modal.

BEISPIEL   S1 Wann möchtet ihr essen gehen?
           S2 Ich möchte jetzt gehen. Und ihr?
           S3 Wir möchten um halb eins gehen.

1	2	3	4
wann	dürfen	du	nach Österreich fahren
warum	können	man	nach Hause gehen
was	möchten	wir	in die Stadt (Mensa . . .) gehen
wem	müssen	ihr	schön (billig . . .) essen
wen	sollen	sie	zu Fuß gehen
wer	wollen	Sie	mit dem Bus fahren
wie lange		das	jetzt tun
		. . .	schenken
			dauern
			haben
			sein
			kommen
			bleiben
			. . .

P. Wie geht's weiter? Use the statements below as models to complete a thought logically using the conjunction **aber** or **sondern**.

BEISPIEL   Ich esse nicht gern Karotten, aber . . .
           Ich esse nicht gern Karotten, aber Bohnen finde ich gut.

 1. Ich trinke nicht gern Cola, aber . . .
 2. Wir besichtigen nicht das Museum, sondern . . .
 3. Die Straßenbahn hält nicht hier, sondern . . .
 4. Es gibt keinen Bus, aber . . .
 5. Er kann uns heute die Stadt nicht zeigen, aber . . .
 6. Ich bin nicht in Wien geblieben, sondern . . .
 7. Ihr lernt nicht Spanisch, sondern . . .
 8. Es tur mir Leid, aber . . .
 9. Sie möchte nicht zu Fuß gehen, sondern . . .
10. Ich darf nicht lange schlafen, aber . . .
11. Man geht nicht geradeaus, sondern . . .
12. Das ist nicht das Theater, sondern . . .

Q. Die Bank: Auf Deutsch bitte!

1. Excuse me *(formal),* can you tell me where there's a bank? 2. I'm sorry, but I'm not from Vienna. 3. Whom can I ask? 4. Who can help me? 5. May I help you? 6. I'd like to find a bank. 7. Near the cathedral (there) is a bank. 8. Can you tell me whether that's far from here? 9. You can walk (there), but the banks close (are closed) in 20 minutes. 10. Take the subway or a taxi!

The Gateway City

Originally, Vienna **(Wien)** was a Roman settlement. The city's fate was linked to its geographic location on the Danube and at the gateway to the plains of eastern Europe. Here merchants met where ancient trade routes crossed; crusaders passed through on their way to the Holy Land; and in 1683, at the walls and gates of this city, the Turks abandoned their hopes of conquering the heart of Europe.

The center of Vienna **(die Innenstadt)** dates back to medieval times. As late as the 1850s, it was surrounded by horseshoe-shaped walls. The city reached its zenith of power and wealth as the capital of the Austro-Hungarian Empire during the reign of Emperor Franz Josef (1848–1916), when it developed into one of Europe's most important cultural centers. Composers such as Haydn, Mozart, Beethoven, Schubert, Brahms, Bruckner, Johann and Richard Strauss, Mahler, and Schönberg have left a lasting imprint on the city's cultural life. The psychoanalyst Freud, the writers Schnitzler, Zweig, and von Hofmannsthal, as well as the painters Klimt, Schiele, and Kokoschka laid the intellectual and artistic foundation of the 20th century.

Today, Vienna ranks among the leading convention cities in the world. It houses the headquarters for the International Atomic Energy Agency (IAEA), the Organization of Petroleum Exporting Countries (OPEC), and the United Nations Industrial Development Organization (UNIDO). It is also one of the three headquarters of the United Nations, along with New York City and Geneva. When the Iron Curtain was in place from the 1960s to the 1980s, Vienna served as a bridge between the West and the Communist countries of eastern Europe. Although the city's pivotal role in East–West relations has diminished since the fall of the Iron Curtain in 1989, Austria's accession to the European Union in 1995 has meant new political and economic opportunities for Vienna.

Fußgängerzone am Stephansdom

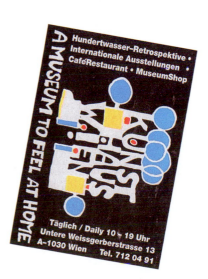

Einblicke

Wortschatz 2

- **Einmal** (once), **zweimal** (twice), **dreimal** (three times), etc.; BUT: Ich habe ihr **mal** geschrieben; sie hat auch **mal** geantwortet. *I wrote her once; she also answered at one time.*

- Lieb**e** Eltern, lieb**e** Elisabeth, lieb**er** Michael

- Like **stundenlang**: jahrelang, monatelang, wochenlang, tagelang, etc.

bekannt	*well-known*
Das macht nichts.	*That doesn't matter.*
(ein)mal	*once, (at) one time*
gemütlich	*pleasant, cozy, convivial*
genug	*enough*
hoffentlich	*hopefully; I hope*
interessant	*interesting*
leider	*unfortunately*
lieb	*dear*
stundenlang	*for hours*
bummeln, ist gebummelt	*to stroll*

Vor dem Lesen

A. Auf Reisen *(Traveling)* Read the list below and pick out the five most important things you like to do when you travel. Compare your travel interests with those of your partner. What do you have in common? Where do you differ?

_____ zu Fuß durch die Stadt gehen	_____ Kirchen besichtigen
_____ mit Leuten sprechen	_____ Karten schreiben
_____ Souvenirs kaufen	_____ tanzen gehen
_____ in Museen gehen	_____ lange schlafen
_____ in die Oper gehen	_____ mit dem Taxi fahren
_____ in Restaurants gehen	_____ fotografieren
_____ ins Konzert gehen	_____ ins Theater gehen
_____ mit der Familie telefonieren	_____ Fahrrad fahren
_____ zum Park gehen	_____ einkaufen gehen
_____ in Musicals gehen	_____ mit dem Bus fahren
_____ die Bibliothek besichtigen	_____ mit der U-Bahn fahren
_____ Schlösser besichtigen	_____ ?

B. Wohin gehen wir? Look over the following entertainment offers with your partner. Then tell each other where you would like to go and why.

BEISPIEL   S1 Ich möchte in die Dinner Show gehen. Ich tanze gern. Und du?
S2 Ich möchte zum Burggarten gehen. Schmetterlinge sind toll!

C. Das ist leicht zu verstehen! Welche Silbe ist betont? Was ist das auf Englisch?

der Sport, Stopp, Walzer; das Gästehaus; die Studentengruppe, Winterresidenz; fantastisch, zentral

Grüße° aus Wien

greetings

CD 4,
Track 9

Liebe Eltern!
Jetzt muss ich euch aber wirklich wieder mal schreiben! Ich habe so viel gesehen, dass ich nicht weiß, wo ich beginnen soll. Vor einer Woche bin ich mit unserer Studentengruppe noch in Passau gewesen. Von dort sind wir mit dem Schiff
5   die Donau hinuntergefahren°. Wir haben einen Stopp in Linz gemacht und haben   traveled down
die Stadt, das Schloss und den Dom besichtigt. Dann sind wir mit dem Schiff
weiter bis nach Wien gefahren. Die Weinberge°, Burgen° und besonders Kloster°   vineyards / castles / monastery
Melk haben mir sehr gut gefallen. Das Wetter ist auch sehr schön gewesen.
Glück gehabt!

10 Jetzt sind wir schon ein paar Tage in Wien. Ach°, ich finde es toll hier! Unser Gästehaus liegt sehr zentral und wir können alles zu Fuß oder mit der U-Bahn erreichen°. Einfach° super! So viel bin ich noch nie gelaufen! Am Freitag sind wir stundenlang durch die Innenstadt gebummelt. Die Geschäfte in der° Kärntner Straße sind sehr teuer, aber man muss ja° nichts kaufen. Wir haben natürlich

15 auch den Stephansdom besichtigt und sind mit dem Aufzug° im Turm hinaufgefahren°. Von dort kann man Wien gut sehen. Am Abend haben wir Mozarts *Zauberflöte*° in der Oper gesehen. Fantastisch!

Am Samstag haben wir die Hofburg besichtigt. Das ist einmal die Winterresidenz der° Habsburger Kaiser° gewesen. Dort ist auch die Spanische Reitschule

20 und man kann die Lipizzaner° beim Training sehen. Das haben wir auch getan. Wirklich prima! Da ist das Reiten° kein Sport, sondern Kunst°. Am Abend sind wir mit der Straßenbahn nach Grinzing gefahren und haben dort Marks Geburtstag mit Musik und Wein gefeiert. Die Weinstube° ist sehr gemütlich gewesen.

Lipizzaner beim Training in der Spanischen Reitschule

Johann Strauß

Tja°, und heute besichtigen wir das Museum für Völkerkunde° und die

25 Sezession° und später wollen ein paar von uns noch zum Prater. Das Riesenrad° dort soll toll sein. Morgen früh wollen wir noch zum Schloss Schönbrunn, der Sommerresidenz der Habsburger; und dann ist unsere Zeit in Wien auch schon fast um°. Schade!

Wien ist wirklich interessant. Überall findet man Denkmäler° oder Straßen

30 mit bekannten Namen wie Mozart, Beethoven, Johann Strauß usw. Aber ihr dürft nicht denken, dass man hier nur Walzer hört und alles romantisch ist. Wien ist auch eine Großstadt mit vielen Menschen und viel Verkehr°. Es gefällt mir hier so gut, dass ich gern noch ein paar Tage bleiben möchte. Das geht leider nicht, weil wir noch nach Salzburg und Innsbruck wollen. Eine Woche ist einfach nicht

35 lange genug für so eine Reise. Nach Budapest können wir leider auch nicht. Nun, das macht nichts. Hoffentlich komme ich im Frühling einmal nach Ungarn°.

So, jetzt muss ich aber schnell frühstücken und dann geht's wieder los°! Tschüss und viele liebe Grüße!

Euer Michael

Fokus   Heurigen Wine

Due to the relatively mild climate, vineyards flourish on the hillsides of the Danube valley north of Vienna. There you can find the traditional **Heurige**, the young, fresh wine sold by wine growers in their courtyards or houses. Some of these places, identified by a wreath of vines or a branch hanging over the door, have been turned into restaurants (**Weinstuben** or **Heurigenschänken**). The more tourist-oriented ones also have **Schrammelmusik** with violins, guitars, and accordions. Located on the outskirts of Vienna, Grinzing is probably the best-known **Heurigen** wine village.

Aktives zum Text

A. Wer, was oder wo ist das? Match the descriptions with the places or people in the list below.

die Donau, Grinzing, die Hofburg, die Kärntner Straße, Linz, Melk, Passau, der Prater, Schloss Schönbrunn, die Spanische Reitschule, die Staatsoper, der Turm vom Stephansdom

1. Hier hat die Flussfahrt nach Wien begonnen.
2. Auf diesem (*on this*) Fluss kann man mit dem Schiff bis nach Wien fahren.
3. Hier haben die Habsburger Kaiser im Sommer gelebt.
4. Hier gibt es ein Barockkloster. Es ist sehr bekannt.
5. Da haben die Studenten einen Stopp gemacht und die Stadt besichtigt.
6. Hier kann man schön bummeln, aber die Geschäfte sind sehr teuer.
7. Von dort kann man ganz Wien sehen.
8. Das ist einmal die Winterresidenz der (*of the*) Habsburger Kaiser gewesen.
9. Hier kann man die Lipizzaner trainieren sehen.
10. Hier kann man Mozarts *Zauberflöte* sehen.
11. Hier gibt es ein Riesenrad.
12. Dort kann man gemütlich essen und Wein trinken.

B. *Sondern* oder *aber*? Insert the appropriate conjunction.

1. Das Gästehaus ist nicht sehr elegant, _____ es liegt zentral.
2. Wir sind nicht mit dem Bus gefahren, _____ viel gelaufen.
3. Bei der Spanischen Reitschule ist das Reiten kein Sport, _____ eine Kunst.
4. Die Geschäfte in der Kärntner Straße sind teuer, _____ sie gefallen mir.

C. Fahrt *(trip)* nach Österreich Mr. Schubach is talking about his travel plans. Phrase his statements using modal verbs as indicated in parentheses.

> BEISPIEL Ihr fahrt mit uns mit dem Schiff bis nach Wien. (müssen)
> *Ihr müsst mit uns mit dem Schiff bis nach Wien fahren.*

 Passau is a German city situated at the border with Austria. It is the starting point for regular steamer service down the Danube to Vienna and the Black Sea.

1. Unsere Fahrt beginnt in Passau. (sollen)
2. In Linz machen wir einen Stopp. (wollen)
3. Vom Schiff sieht man viele Weinberge und Burgen. (können)
4. Wir bleiben fünf Tage in Wien. (wollen)
5. Dort gibt es viel zu sehen. (sollen)
6. Man hat natürlich bequeme *(comfortable)* Schuhe. (müssen)
7. Ich laufe aber nicht so viel. (dürfen)
8. Meine Frau bummelt gemütlich durch die Kärntner Straße. (möchten)

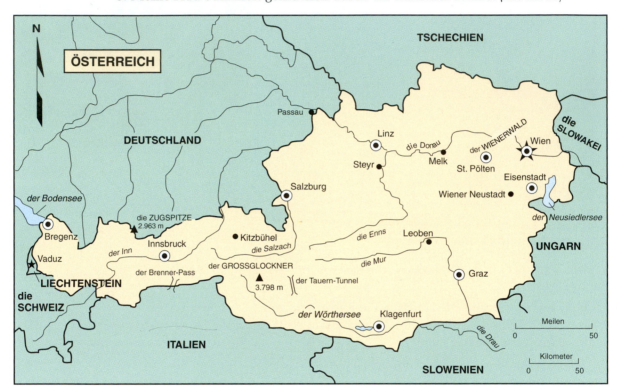

D. Landkarte von Österreich: Beantworten Sie die Fragen!

1. Wie viele Nachbarländer hat Österreich? Wie heißt sie und wo liegen sie?
2. Wie heißen ein paar Städte in Österreich? Wie heißt die Hauptstadt?
3. Welche Flüsse gibt es in Österreich? An welchem Fluss liegt Wien? Salzburg? Innsbruck? Linz? Graz? (. . . liegt am/an der . . .)
4. Welcher See liegt nicht nur in Österreich, sondern auch in Deutschland und in der Schweiz? Welcher See liegt zum Teil in Österreich und zum Teil in Ungarn? An welchem See liegt Klagenfurt?
5. Wo liegt der Brenner-Pass? der Großglockner? der Tauern-Tunnel?

E. Stadtplan von Wien

1. **Wo ist das?** In small groups, make a list of all the locations in Vienna mentioned throughout this chapter. Find them on the map on the facing page and ask each other about their location, giving a brief description.

> BEISPIEL S1 Wo ist die Oper?
> S2 Am Opernring, in der Nähe vom Burggarten.

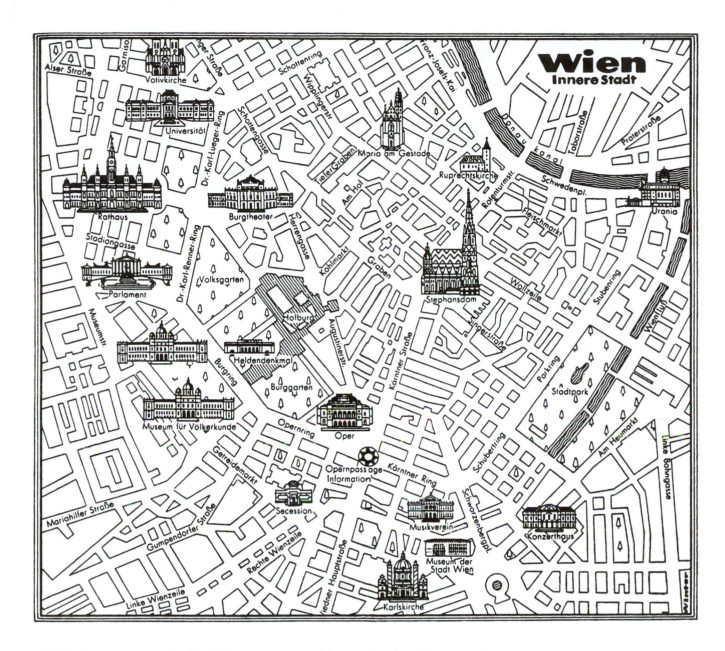

2. **Wie kommt man dorthin?** Now practice asking and giving directions from one place to another.

BEISPIEL   vom Stephansdom zur Oper

    S1   Entschuldigen Sie bitte! Können Sie mir sagen, wie ich von hier zur Oper komme?

    S2   Gern. Gehen Sie immer geradeaus die Kärntner Straße entlang! Sie sehen dann die Oper rechts.

  a. von der Oper zur Hofburg
  b. von der Hofburg zur Uni
  c. von der Uni zum Parlament
  d. vom Parlament zum Musikverein
  e. vom Musikverein zum Donaukanal
  f. vom Konzerthaus zur Praterstraße

F. Interview: Fragen Sie einen Partner/eine Partnerin, . . . !

1. ob er/sie schon einmal in Wien gewesen ist; wenn ja, was ihm/ihr in Wien besonders gut gefallen hat (**Was hat dir . . . ?**); wenn nein, was er/sie einmal in Wien sehen möchte
2. wie die Hauptstadt in seinem/ihrem Bundesstaat oder in seiner/ihrer Provinz heißt
3. ob die Stadt eine Altstadt hat und ob sie schön ist
4. ob es dort eine Straßenbahn, eine U-Bahn oder Busse gibt
5. welche Denkmäler und Straßen mit bekannten Namen es gibt
6. was ihm/ihr dort besonders gefällt und was nicht
7. ob er/sie schon einmal in einem Schloss gewesen ist; wenn ja, wo; wenn nein, welches Schloss er/sie einmal sehen möchte

G. Kurzgespräche With a partner choose one of the situations and prepare a brief dialogue. Then present it to the class.

1. **Im Kaffeehaus** You and a friend are in a Viennese coffee house. Your friend suggests visiting the *Museum für Völkerkunde.* You ask someone at the table next to yours where the museum is located. You find out that it is not too far away, but that unfortunately it is closed today. You respond politely. Your friend suggests an alternative activity (strolling along the *Kärntner Straße,* visiting the *Spanische Reitschule* or the *Stephansdom,* etc.). Discuss how to reach your destination. Then consider what you might want to do in the evening (**heute Abend**): Perhaps go to *Grinzing* or the *Prater?*

2. **Souvenirs aus Wien** Before leaving Vienna, you and a friend are hunting for souvenirs but have a hard time finding something. What could one bring home? You might end up buying some **Mozartkugeln** or a piece of **Sacher-torte,** but instead of taking them home, you eat them yourselves. You decide that's O.K. and that it was delicious. Some postcards (**Karten**) would be fine, too, but of what?

H. Brief: Grüße an die Gastfamilie in Regensburg Pretend you are with Michael's group in Vienna. Write eight to ten sentences to your host family in Regensburg.

Wien, den 11. 9. 2005

Liebe Herr und Frau Fuchs,

jetzt wird es Zeit, dass ich Ihnen einmal schreibe. Wir sind schon eine Woche in Wien. Alles ist sehr interessant. Bin noch nie so viel gelaufen! Wir haben viele Museen gesehen und sind auch einmal in die Oper gegangen. Sie haben „Die Zauberflöte" gespielt. Fantastisch! Heute Abend wollen wir in Grinzing gemütlich Geburtstag feiern. Morgen fahren wir nach Salzburg und Innsbruck und dann geht's wieder nach Hause. Wir sind Samstagnachmittag um 4 Uhr 15 wieder in Regensburg.

Viele liebe Grüße, auch an die Kinder!

Ihr Oliver

Abs. Oliver Smith
Singerstraße 11
A-1010 Wien

An Familie
Norbert Fuchs
Bogenstraße 30
D-93051 Regensburg

Schreibtipp
Writing a Letter

Letters should start with the name of the city and a date. Less formal letters may begin with the salutation **Liebe(r) . . .** followed by a name, but more formal letters start with **Sehr geehrte Frau Schulz/Sehr geehrter Herr Schulz/Sehr geehrte Damen und Herren).** If either salutation is followed by a comma, the first word of the paragraph that follows is not capitalized. End your letter with a closing such as **Mit freundlichem Gruß! Ihr(e)/Dein(e)/Euer(e)** + your name. Until the spelling reform a few years ago, the 2nd person familiar **du** and **ihr,** as well as all cases of those pronouns, were always capitalized in letters. It is no longer necessary to capitalize them, but many people still prefer to do so. Note that the return address is always preceded by **Abs. (= Absender).**

Hörverständnis

Track 11 **Schon lange nicht mehr gesehen!** Listen to the conversation between Uwe and Erika, then answer the questions. You do not need to write complete sentences.

Zum Erkennen: schon lange nicht mehr *(not for a long time)*; Bergwanderungen *(mountain hikes)*

1. Wo ist Uwe gewesen? _____
2. Mit wem ist er gefahren? _____
3. Wie ist das Wetter gewesen? _____
4. Wo ist Maria Alm? _____
5. Was haben sie dort gemacht? _____
6. Wo sind sie noch gewesen? _____
7. Was haben sie dort besichtigt? _____
8. Wann will Uwe nach Wien? _____
9. Warum muss Erika gehen? _____

Visit Vienna and Salzburg; a trip from Passau to Linz: http://wiegehts.heinle.com.

Wohnen

Lernziele

In this chapter you will learn about:

Zum Thema
Homes and home furnishings

Kultur-Fokus
Living arrangements, city life,
  public transportation,
  architecture, and German dialects

Struktur
Two-way prepositions
Imperatives
Wissen vs. **kennen**

Einblicke
Schaffen, sparen, Häuschen bauen

For more information,
go to
http://iLrn.heinle.com

Familie Hauser vorm Kachelofen (tiled stove) *im Wohnzimmer*

Vorschau Housing

After World War II, West Germany suffered an acute housing shortage, not only because so many buildings had been destroyed, but also because of the large number of refugees coming from the east. Rebuilding in the 1960s and 1970s created high-rise apartment clusters (**Wohnsilos**) that mushroomed around the old cities, often contrasting sharply with the traditional architecture. Fortunately, many people have rediscovered the beauty of older buildings. Government subsidies and tax incentives have made it possible to restore and modernize many of them. More recently, builders have attempted to harmonize new housing developments with the landscape and to conform to local building styles. Strict zoning laws prevent the loss of open space and agricultural land, but they also make it more difficult to add housing.

With the end of the Cold War and the collapse of the East Bloc economies, another wave of people moved west, which created a housing crisis once again. Students, young couples, large families, and foreign nationals often have difficulties finding affordable accommodations, especially in the larger cities of southern Germany, such as Stuttgart and Munich.

In the former German Democratic Republic (GDR, East Germany), two-thirds of the housing units in existence in 1989 dated back to the time before World War II and often lacked modern sanitary facilities and heating systems. In the early 1970s, the GDR instituted an important housing program that created standardized high-rise apartment buildings on the outskirts of towns, the so-called **Plattenbauten.** These cheaply produced apartments were a quick solution to the housing shortage, and the uniform satellite settlements (**Plattenbausiedlungen**) became a typical feature of Eastern urban planning. For most families, they were a luxury because they had central heating and bathroom facilities! Since reunification in 1990, more and more people have been leaving these housing projects to move into newly renovated older housing units (**Altbauwohnungen**) or newly built modern homes and apartments, leaving 30 percent of the cheap GDR apartments empty—many of them being either left abandoned or torn down; few are being rehabilitated.

Although real estate is expensive in Germany, home ownership is encouraged by various forms of governmental help, such as tax incentives. In contrast to the situation in North America, only 43 percent of households are made up of homeowners (36 percent in Switzerland), which places Germany behind most of the European countries. Interestingly enough, the percentage of homeowners is higher in the former East Germany than in West Germany.

Apartments are advertised in terms of the number of rooms. Those who want to rent a three-bedroom apartment with a living room and a dining room need a **Fünfzimmerwohnung;** bathroom and kitchen are excluded from the room count. Furnished apartments are relatively rare. "Unfurnished" is usually to be taken literally, since there are no built-in closets, kitchen cabinets, appliances, light fixtures, or other conveniences. Tenants are responsible for furnishing and maintaining their apartments (including interior painting and decorating) and may have to pay monthly maintenance fees (**Betriebskosten**) for a janitor, garbage removal, and the like. Heat may or may not be included in the rent or maintenance fees; the apartment is advertised accordingly as being either **warm** or **kalt.**

Eine Neubausiedlung (new housing addition) *in Deutschland*

Minidrama: *Kein Zimmer für Studenten*
Blickpunkt: *Bei Viktor zu Hause*

Zum Thema

Wohnung zu vermieten

CD 5, Track 1

ANNA   Hallo, mein Name ist Anna Moser. Ich habe gehört, dass Sie eine Zweizimmerwohnung zu vermieten haben. Stimmt das?

VERMIETER   Ja, in der Nähe vom Dom, mit Blick auf den Marktplatz.

ANNA   Wie alt ist die Wohnung?

VERMIETER   Ziemlich alt, aber sie ist renoviert und schön groß und hell. Sie hat sogar einen Balkon.

ANNA   Ein Balkon? Das ist ja toll. Ich habe viele Pflanzen. In welchem Stock liegt sie?

VERMIETER   Im dritten Stock.

ANNA   Ist sie möbliert oder unmöbliert?

VERMIETER   Unmöbliert.

ANNA   Und was kostet die Wohnung?

VERMIETER   550 Euros.

ANNA   Ist das kalt oder warm?

VERMIETER   Kalt.

ANNA   Oje, das ist mir ein bisschen zu teuer. Na ja, vielen Dank! Auf Wiederhören!

VERMIETER   Auf Wiederhören!

In der WG (Wohngemeinschaft)

ANNA   Euer Haus gefällt mir!

JÖRG   Wir haben noch Platz für dich. Komm, ich zeige dir alles! . . . Hier links ist unsere Küche. Sie ist klein, aber praktisch.

ANNA   Wer kocht?

JÖRG   Wir alle: Benno, Verena und ich.

ANNA   Und das ist das Wohnzimmer?

JÖRG   Ja. Es ist ein bisschen dunkel, aber das ist okay.

ANNA   Eure Sessel gefallen mir.

JÖRG   Sie sind alt, aber echt bequem . . . So, und hier oben sind dann vier Schlafzimmer und das Bad.

ANNA   Mm, das Schlafzimmer ist sehr gemütlich, aber nur ein Bad?

JÖRG   Ja, leider! Aber unten ist noch eine Toilette.

ANNA   Was bezahlt ihr im Monat?

JÖRG   Jeder 200 Euro.

ANNA   Nicht schlecht! Und wie kommst du zur Uni?

JÖRG   Kein Problem. Ich gehe zu Fuß.

ANNA   Klingt gut!

A. Richtig oder falsch?

_____ 1. In der Nähe vom Dom gibt es eine Wohnung zu vermieten.

_____ 2. Die Wohnung hat vier Zimmer.

_____ 3. Die Wohnung ist etwas dunkel.

_____ 4. Die Wohnung liegt im Parterre.

_____ 5. Jörg wohnt in einer WG.

_____ 6. Das Haus hat drei Schlafzimmer.

_____ 7. Sie fahren mit der U-Bahn zur Uni.

_____ 8. Für das Haus bezahlen die Studenten 100 Euro pro Person.

_____ 9. Jörg möchte, dass Anna auch dort wohnt.

_____ 10. Aber das gefällt Anna nicht.

Fokus | Shared Living Arrangements

Rooms in dormitories (**Studentenwohnheime**) are typically quite scarce and often allocated by lottery, so students and other young people often choose instead to live in **WGs** or **Wohngemeinschaften** (*shared housing or "co-op"*). Moving into an apartment or house with others—who are often complete strangers—is quite common, as even studio apartments are often too expensive for student budgets.

 B. Jetzt sind Sie dran! With a partner, create your own dialogue. Pretend you are hunting for an apartment or house. Talk about prices, individual rooms, whether utilities are included or not, location, and how to get from there to the university.

Wortschatz 1

Das Haus, ⸚er *(house)*
Das Studentenwohnheim, -e *(dorm)*
Die Wohnung, -en *(apartment)*

der Balkon, -s	*balcony*	die Ecke, -n	*corner*
Baum, ⸚e	*tree*	Garage, -n	*garage*
Flur, -e	*hallway*	Küche, -n	*kitchen*
Garten, ⸚	*garden, yard*	Toilette, -n	*toilet*
Keller, -	*basement, cellar*		
das Bad, ⸚er	*bathroom*		
Dach, ⸚er	*roof*	im Bad / in der Küche	*in the bathroom / kitchen*
Zimmer, -	*room*		
Arbeitszimmer, -	*study*	im Keller	*in the basement*
Esszimmer, -	*dining room*	im Parterre	*on the first floor (ground level)*
Schlafzimmer, -	*bedroom*		
Wohnzimmer, -	*living room*	im ersten Stock	*on the second floor*

⦿ **Das** Parterre, BUT **der** Stock.

Die Möbel (pl.) *(furniture)*

der Fernseher, -	*TV set*	das Bett, -en	*bed*
Kühlschrank, ⸚e	*refrigerator*	Radio, -s	*radio*
Schrank, ⸚e	*closet, cupboard*	Regal, -e	*shelf, bookcase*
Schreibtisch, -e	*desk*	Sofa, -s	*sofa*
Sessel, -	*armchair*	Telefon, -e	*telephone*
Stuhl, ⸚e	*chair*	die Kommode, -n	*dresser*
Teppich, -e	*carpet*	Lampe, -n	*lamp*
Tisch, -e	*table*		
Vorhang, ⸚e	*curtain*		

Weiteres

im Monat	*per month*
oben / unten	*up(stairs) / down(stairs)*
hell / dunkel	*bright, light / dark*
praktisch	*practical(ly)*
(un)bequem	*(un)comfortable; (in)convenient*
sogar	*even*
ziemlich	*quite, rather*
baden	*to take a bath; to swim*
duschen	*to take a shower*
hängen, gehängt	*to hang (up)*
hängen, gehangen	*to hang (be hanging)*
kochen	*to cook*
legen	*to lay, put (flat)*

⦿ Note that translations in these lists focus on the use of these words in the dialogue, e.g., **sogar** could be translated in many other ways.

⦿ There are two verbs with the infinitive **hängen.** The t-verb means *to hang (up)* something somewhere; the n-verb, that something *is hanging* somewhere.

liegen, gelegen	*to lie (be lying flat)*
mieten / vermieten	*to rent / to rent out*
setzen	*to set, put*
sitzen, gesessen	*to sit (be sitting)*
stehen, gestanden	*to stand (be standing)*
stellen	*to stand, put (upright)*
waschen (wäscht), gewaschen	*to wash*
das Problem, -e	*problem*
(Das ist) kein Problem.	*(That's) no problem.*
(Das) klingt gut!	*(That) sounds good.*
(Das) stimmt!	*(That's) true. / (That's) right.*
Auf Wiederhören!	*Good-bye!* (on the phone)

Zum Erkennen: die Pflanze, -n *(plant)*; renoviert *(renovated)*; (un)möbliert *([un]furnished)*; die WG, -s / Wohngemeinschaft, -en *(shared housing)*; Oje! *(Oh no! Good gracious!)*; na ja *(oh well, all right then)*; echt *(really)*; jeder *(each one)*; AUCH: der Imperativ, -e; der Blick auf *(+ acc.) (view of)*; im Dachgeschoss *(in the attic)*; im Erdgeschoss *(on the ground level)*; beschreiben *(to describe)*; markieren *(to mark)*

Aktives zum Thema

A. Mustersätze

1. Wie gefällt dir _____?
   der Sessel → Wie gefällt dir der Sessel?
   das Sofa, der Teppich, das Regal, das Radio . . .
2. _____ gefällt mir sehr.
   das Haus → Das Haus gefällt mir sehr.
   das Wohnzimmer, die Küche, das Bad, der Garten . . .
3. _____ gefallen mir nicht.
   die Möbel → Die Möbel gefallen mir nicht.
   Sessel, Stühle, Vorhänge, Schränke . . .
4. Die Wohnung ist _____.
   sehr praktisch → Die Wohnung ist sehr praktisch.
   schön hell, ziemlich dunkel, zu klein, schön sauber, sehr gemütlich, furchtbar schmutzig, wirklich bequem . . .
5. Die Wohnung ist _____.
   unten → Die Wohnung ist unten.
   oben, im Parterre, im ersten Stock, im zweiten Stock, im dritten Stock . . .

Fokus | Homes and Houses

When German-speakers say "first floor" (**erste Etage** or **erster Stock**), they mean what North Americans usually call the *second floor.* Either **das Parterre** or **das Erdgeschoss** is used to denote the ground floor, or North American first floor. In elevators, remember to press "E" (for **Erdgeschoss**) or "0" to get to the exit.

Homes and apartments usually have a foyer (**die Diele**) and a hallway (**der Flur**), with doors leading to the various rooms. For the sake of privacy, many Germans prefer to keep doors shut—this also holds true in the workplace and institutions like the university, where people prefer to work with doors closed. Sheer, pretty curtains (**Gardinen**) are also a typical feature that permits people to see out, but prevents others from looking in. In addition, some houses have outside shutters (**Rolläden** or **Rollos**) that can be rolled down over the windows at night. Traditional half-timbered houses (**Fachwerkhäuser**) often have colorful shutters that swing shut on hinges. Another difference you may notice in Germany is that the toilet (**die Toilette**) is often in a separate room from the bathroom (**das Badezimmer**), where the bathtub is located.

B. Beschreiben Sie die Wohnung! With a partner, take turns describing what furniture you see in the various rooms of this apartment. Don't forget to use the accusative case!

> BEISPIEL   *Im Bad gibt es ein Klo, ein Waschbecken . . .*

⬤ In case you are curious: *bathtub* **die Badewanne, -n;** *closet* **der Kleiderschrank, ⁻e;** *computer* **der Computer, -;** *dining room cabinet* **das Büfett, -s;** *dishwasher* **die Spülmaschine, -n;** *fireplace* **der Kamin, -e;** *kitchen cabinet* **der Küchenschrank, ⁻e;** *microwave* **die Mikrowelle, -n (coll.);** *mirror* **der Spiegel, -;** *night stand* **der Nachttisch, -e;** *oven* **der Ofen ⁻;** *patio* **die Terrasse, -n;** *piano* **das Klavier, -e;** *range, cooktop* **der Herd, -e;** *shower* **die Dusche, -n;** *(bathroom) sink* **das Waschbecken, -;** *(kitchen) sink* **das Spülbecken, -**

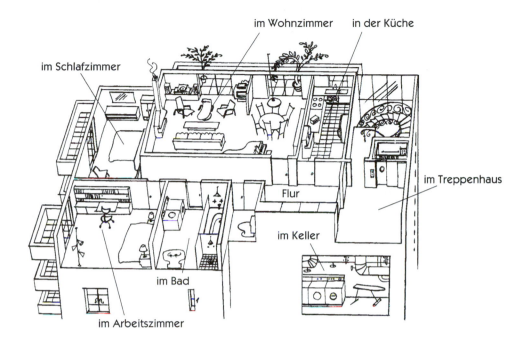

 C. Kein Haus / keine Wohnung ohne Maschinen Working in small groups, report what machines or appliances you have or don't have, what you need, and what you would like to have in your house or apartment.

D. Was bedeuten die Wörter? Was ist ihr Artikel und ihr Plural?

Balkontür, Bücherregal, Dachgeschosswohnung, Duschvorhang, Elternschlafzimmer, Kinderbad, Farbfernseher, Küchenfenster, Kochecke, Liegestuhl, Schlafsofa, Schreibtischlampe, Sitzecke, Stehlampe, Wandlampe, Waschecke, Wohnzimmerteppich

 E. Interview: Fragen Sie einen Nachbarn/eine Nachbarin, . . . !

1. ob er/sie eine Wohnung hat oder ob er/sie zu Hause, im Studentenwohnheim oder in einer WG wohnt; wenn nicht zu Hause, wie viel Miete er/sie im Monat bezahlt
2. ob er/sie Mitbewohner *(housemates)*, einen Zimmerkollegen oder eine Zimmerkollegin *(roommate)* hat; wenn ja, wie sie heißen
3. wie sein/ihr Zimmer ist und was für Möbel er/sie im Zimmer hat
4. ob er/sie eine Küche hat; wenn ja, was es in der Küche gibt und wer kocht
5. was man vom Zimmerfenster sehen kann
6. wie lange er/sie schon da wohnt
7. wie er/sie zur Uni kommt

For further review, see the Summary of Pronunciation in the front of your *Arbeitsbuch*. Study Part II, subsections 37–39.

 CD 5, Track 2

Aussprache: ei, au, eu, äu

A. Laute

1. [ai] w**ei**t, l**ei**der, **ei**gentlich, z**ei**gen, f**ei**ern, bl**ei**ben
2. [au] **au**f, bl**au**grau, B**au**m, K**au**fh**au**s, br**au**chen, l**au**fen
3. [oi] **eu**ch, h**eu**te, t**eu**er, L**eu**te, Fr**eu**nde, H**äu**ser, B**äu**me

B. Wortpaare

1. *by* / bei
2. *Troy* / treu
3. *mouse* / Maus
4. Haus / Häuser
5. aus / Eis
6. euer / Eier

Hörverständnis

Track 12 **Hier Müller!** Listen to the conversation between Inge and Mrs. Müller. Then decide whether the statements below are true or false according to the dialogue.

Zum Erkennen: nett *(nice)*; teilen *(to share)*; na gut *(well, good)*; Bis bald! *(See you soon!)*

_____ 1. Inge ist Frau Müllers Tochter.
_____ 2. Frau Müller hat ein Zimmer gefunden.
_____ 3. Das Zimmer ist in der Schillerstraße.
_____ 4. Inges Telefonnummer ist 91 68.
_____ 5. Wohnungen sind sehr teuer.
_____ 6. Inge hat Horst vor ein paar Tagen gesehen.
_____ 7. Sie teilt jetzt ein Zimmer mit Horst.
_____ 8. Inge zahlt 140 Euro im Monat.
_____ 9. Sie kann mit dem Fahrrad zur Uni fahren.
_____ 10. Am Wochenende kommt sie nach Hause.

Die Dreiflüssestadt Passau liegt an der Grenze zu Österreich.

6.1 Two-way prepositions

You have learned some prepositions that are always followed by the dative and some that are always followed by the accusative. You will now learn a set of prepositions that sometimes take the dative and sometimes the accusative.

1. The basic meanings of the nine TWO-WAY PREPOSITIONS are:

an	*to, up to, at (the side of), on (vertical surface)*
auf	*on (top of; horizontal surface), onto*
hinter	*behind*
in	*in, into, inside of*
neben	*beside, next to*
über	*over, above; about*
unter	*under, below*
vor	*before, in front of*
zwischen	*between*

über
auf
hinter
vor
in
an
neben
zwischen
unter

9

Most of these prepositions may be contracted with articles in colloquial German. The following are the most common contractions that are acceptable even in written German:

an + das = **ans**	in + das = **ins**
an + dem = **am**	in + dem = **im**
auf + das = **aufs**	

CAUTION: Be careful to distinguish between **vor** and **bevor**. The preposition **vor** precedes a noun (**vor dem Haus**). The conjunction **bevor** introduces a clause (. . . , **bevor du das Haus mietest**).

2. **Wo?** vs. **wohin?**

   a. German has two words to ask *where:* **wo?** *(in what place?)* and **wohin?** *(to what place?).* **Wo** asks about LOCATION, where something is or an activity within a place. **Wohin** asks about DESTINATION OR A CHANGE OF PLACE.

   LOCATION: **Wo** ist Horst?   *Where's Horst? (in what place)*
   DESTINATION: **Wohin** geht Horst?   *Where's Horst going? (to what place)*

   b. The difference between location and destination also plays a role in determining the case following two-way prepositions. If the question is **wo?**, the <u>dative</u> is used. If the question is **wohin?**, the <u>accusative</u> is used.

Wo ist Horst?   → **In der** Küche.   *Where's Horst?*   → *In the kitchen.*
Wohin geht Horst?   → **In die** Küche.   *Where's Horst going?* → *To the kitchen.*

wo?	LOCATION	→	<u>dative</u>
wohin?	DESTINATION	→	<u>accusative</u>

• **woher** *(from where),* introduced in Chapter 1, denotes origin.

3. The difference lies entirely with the verb!

- Some verbs denoting LOCATION OR ACTIVITY WITHIN A PLACE (**wo?** → <u>dative</u>) are: hängen, kaufen, kochen, lesen, liegen, schlafen, sein, sitzen, spielen, stehen, studieren, tanzen, trinken, wohnen
- Typical verbs implying DESTINATION OR A CHANGE OF PLACE OR MOTION TOWARD a point (**wohin?** → <u>accusative</u>) are: bringen, fahren, gehen, hängen, kommen, laufen, legen, setzen, stellen, tragen

4. Some important verb pairs

N-VERBS / LOCATION → <u>dative</u>	T-VERBS / CHANGE OF PLACE → <u>accusative</u>
hängen, gehangen *(to be hanging)*	hängen, gehängt *(to hang up)*
liegen, gelegen *(to be lying [flat])*	legen, gelegt *(to lay down, put [flat])*
sitzen, gesessen *(to be sitting)*	setzen, gesetzt *(to set down)*
stehen, gestanden *(to be standing)*	stellen, gestellt *(to put [upright])*

- Note that the four n-verbs are all intransitive (that is, they do not take a direct object). The four t-verbs, on the other hand, are transitive (that is, they do take a direct object).

> Der Mantel hat **im** Schrank gehangen.
> Ich habe den Mantel **in den** Schrank gehängt.

CAUTION: Although **legen, setzen,** and **stellen** are all sometimes translated as *to put,* they are <u>not interchangeable</u>!

> Sie **stellt** den Stuhl an die Wand. *(upright position)*
> Sie **legt** das Heft auf den Tisch. *(flat position)*
> Er **setzt** das Kind auf den Stuhl. *(sitting position)*

5. Summary

● ALSO: Das Kind legt den Teddy auf die Bank *(bench).* Der Teddy liegt auf der Bank. / Das Huhn läuft unter die Bank. Es sitzt unter der Bank.

WOHIN?

Die Tante hängt den Teppich **über das** Balkongeländer (. . . *banister).*
Die Mutter stellt die Leiter *(ladder)* **an die** Wand.
Das Auto fährt **neben das** Haus.
Das Kind läuft **hinter die** Mutter.
Der Hund läuft **vor das** Auto.
Der Großvater nimmt die Pfeife *(pipe)* **in den** Mund *(mouth).*

WO?

Der Teppich hängt **über dem** Balkongeländer.
Die Leiter steht **an der** Wand.

Das Auto steht **neben dem** Haus.
Das Kind steht **hinter der** Mutter.
Der Hund steht **vor dem** Auto.
Der Großvater hat die Pfeife **im** Mund.

Note also these uses of **an, auf,** and **in!** You are already familiar with most of them:

Die Stadt liegt **am** Rhein / **an der** Donau.	*The city is on the Rhine / on the Danube.*
Sie spielen **auf der** Straße.	*They're playing in the street.*
Sie leben **in** Deutschland / **in der** Schweiz.	*They live in Germany / in Switzerland.*
Sie leben **in** Stuttgart / **im** Süden.	*They live in Stuttgart / in the South.*
Sie wohnen **in der** Schillerstraße.	*They live on Schiller Street.*
Sie wohnen **im** Parterre / **im** ersten Stock.	*They live on the first / second floor.*

- With feminine or plural names of countries, **in** is used rather than **nach** to express *to.*

  Wir fahren **in die Schweiz / in die Bundesrepublik.**
  Wir fahren **in die USA / in die Vereinigten Staaten.**
  BUT: Wir fahren **nach Österreich / nach Deutschland.**

- If you plan to see a film or play, or to attend a church service, **in** must be used; **zu** implies going *in the direction of, up to,* BUT NOT *into a place.*

Wir gehen **zum Kino.**	*(To go just to look outside and see what's playing, or to meet somebody there)*
Wir gehen **ins Kino.**	*(To go inside to see a movie)*

Übungen

A. Sagen Sie es noch einmal! Replace the nouns following the prepositions with the words suggested.

> BEISPIEL   Der Bleistift liegt unter dem Papier. (Jacke)
> *Der Bleistift liegt unter der Jacke.*

1. Die Post ist neben der Bank. (Bahnhof, Kino, Apotheke)
2. Melanie kommt in die Wohnung. (Küche, Esszimmer, Garten)
3. Die Mäntel liegen auf dem Bett. (Sofa, Kommode, Stühle)
4. Mein Schlafzimmer ist über der Küche. (Wohnzimmer, Garage, Bad)
5. Willi legt den Pullover auf die Kommode. (Bett, Schreibtisch, Sessel)

B. Wo bekommt man das? *(Where can you get that?)* Start with the boldface phrase. Repeat the information by saying where each of the people below is going to get those items.

> BEISPIEL   Frau Müller braucht etwas **Butter und Käse.** (Supermarkt)
> *Butter und Käse bekommt man im Supermarkt.*
> *Frau Müller geht in den Supermarkt.*

1. Silvia sucht ein paar **Bücher.** (Bibliothek)
2. Oliver will ein paar **CDs.** (Kaufhaus)
3. Bettina braucht **Parfüm** *(perfume)* **und Shampoo.** (Drogerie)
4. Andreas braucht **Medizin.** (Apotheke)
5. Maren sucht ein paar **Schuhe.** (Schuhgeschäft)
6. Christian hat viele Bücher, aber keine **Regale.** (Möbelgeschäft)
7. Oma Schütz ist müde vom Einkaufen und möchte eine Tasse **Kaffee und Kuchen.** (Café)

C. Wo sind Sie wann? Report where you are at certain times. You may use the locations in the last column or come up with ideas of your own.

> BEISPIEL   morgens
> *Morgens bin ich gewöhnlich in der Bibliothek.*

1	2	3	4	5
morgens	fahren	gern	an	Badewanne *(f.)*
mittags	gehen	gemütlich	auf	Berge
abends	liegen	gewöhnlich	in	Bett
am Wochenende	sein	manchmal	vor	Bibliothek
(über)morgen	sitzen	nicht		Computer *(m.)*
im Sommer / Winter	sprechen	oft		Fernseher
wenn ich Hunger habe	. . .	stundenlang		Garten
wenn ich faul *(lazy)* bin		tagelang		Sofa
wenn ich lernen muss		. . .		Kühlschrank
wenn ich baden will				Swimmingpool
wenn ich müde bin				Kino
wenn ich keine Zeit habe				Vorlesung(en)
. . .				. . .

D. Wieder zu Hause After you and your family come home from a camping trip, your mother has many questions. Form her questions with **wo** or **wohin!**

> BEISPIEL   Vater ist in der Garage.   *Wo ist Vater?*
> Jochen geht in den Garten.   *Wohin geht Jochen?*

1. Das Handy ist im Auto.
2. Der Rucksack *(backpack)* liegt im Flur.
3. Sandra legt die Schlafsäcke *(sleeping bags)* aufs Bett.
4. Kristina hängt den Mantel über den Stuhl.
5. Die Regenmäntel sind auf dem Balkon.
6. Die Jacken liegen in der Ecke.
7. Kristina und Niels haben die Lebensmittel in die Küche gebracht.
8. Niels hat die Milch in den Kühlschrank gestellt.
9. Kristina hat den Schuh unter dem Baum gefunden.
10. Der Hund liegt auf dem Sofa.

E. Ein paar Fragen, bevor Sie gehen! Before you leave for a vacation, answer the questions your house sitter is asking you.

> BEISPIEL   Wo ist das Telefon? (an / Wand)
> *An der Wand!*

1. Wo darf ich schlafen? (auf / Sofa; in / Arbeitszimmer)
2. Wohin soll ich meine Kleider hängen? (in / Schrank; an / Wand; über / Stuhl)
3. Wo gibt es ein Lebensmittelgeschäft? (an / Ecke; neben / Bank; zwischen / Apotheke und Café)
4. Wo können die Kinder spielen? (hinter / Haus; unter / Baum; auf / Spielplatz)
5. Wohin gehen sie gern? (in / Park; an / Fluss; in / Kino)
6. Wohin soll ich die Katze tun? (vor / Tür [outside]; in / Garten; auf / Balkon; in / Garage)

F. Bei Lotte

1. **Wohin sollen wir das stellen?** Lotte is moving into a new house. She is telling the movers where they are supposed to put things.

   > BEISPIEL   Schreibtisch / an / Wand
   > *Stellen Sie den Schreibtisch an die Wand!*

   a. Computer (*m.*) / auf / Schreibtisch
   b. Schrank / in / Ecke
   c. Lampe / neben / Bett
   d. Stuhl / an / Tisch
   e. Regal / unter / Uhr
   f. Bild / auf / Regal
   g. Nachttisch / vor / Fenster
   h. Bett / zwischen / Tür / und / Fenster

2. **Was ist wo?** Make ten statements about the picture of Lotte's house, telling where things are standing, lying, or hanging.

   > BEISPIEL   *Der Schreibtisch steht an der Wand.*

3. **Wo sind nur meine Schlüssel?** Lotte has lost her keys. Looking at the drawing of the house, work with a partner to help her find them. One of you plays Lotte and the other asks her about specific places she may have left them. Lotte will answer each question negatively until you finally get it right. Ask at least five questions using two-way prepositions.

   > BEISPIEL   S1 Hast du sie auf den Schreibtisch gelegt?
   >   S2 Nein, sie liegen nicht auf dem Schreibtisch.

Lottes Zimmer

Willkommen

G. Wir bekommen Besuch Your visitors will arrive soon. You still have a lot to prepare. Fill in the blanks with the correct form of the definite article. Use contractions where possible.

1. Die Gläser sind _____ Küche. *(in the)* 2. Ich muss die Gläser _____ Wohnzimmer bringen und sie _____ Tisch stellen. *(into the; on the)* 3. Der Wein ist noch _____ Keller. *(in the)* 4. Wir müssen die Gläser _____ Teller stellen. *(next to the)* 5. Ich muss _____ Küche gehen und die Wurst und den Käse _____ Teller *(sg.)* legen. *(into the; on the)* 6. Haben wir Blumen _____ Garten? *(in the)* 7. Wir stellen die Blumen _____ Tischchen *(sg.)* _____ Sofa. *(on the; in front of the)* 8. Sind die Kerzen _____ Schrank? *(in the)* 9. Nein, sie stehen _____ Kommode. *(on the)*

 H. Mensch, wo ist mein Handy (cell phone)? Your partner can't find his/her cell phone. Looking at the drawing of Lotte's home or just simply around the classroom, ask him/her about specific places where it might have been put. Your partner will answer each question negatively until you finally guess right. Ask at least five questions using two-way prepositions.

BEISPIEL   S1 Hast du es neben die Blumen im Flur gelegt?
                S2 Nein, es liegt nicht neben den Blumen im Flur.

 I. Mein Zimmer / meine Wohnung / mein Studentenwohnheim Describe your room, apartment, or dorm in 8 to 10 sentences. Use a two-way preposition in each sentence.

BEISPIEL   *Mein Schreibtisch steht neben der Tür.*

Fokus Friedensreich Hundertwasser

Friedensreich Hundertwasser, born Friedrich Stowasser (1928–2000), was a well-known Austrian painter, graphic artist, and architect. In his ecologically oriented writings, he vehemently protested contemporary architecture, which he described as "an aesthetic void," "a desert of uniformity," and as having a "criminal sterility." Since no straight lines exist in nature, he also rejected them in his art, referring to them as "something cowardly drawn with a ruler, without thought or feeling." His architecture echoes that conviction, as exemplified by the Hundertwasser House in Vienna and the Hundertwasser Church in Bärnbach near Graz, the exterior of which is uneven and constructed of various materials that symbolize the vicissitudes of life. Its processional path leads through multiple gates that bear symbols taken from a variety of religions, their inclusion intended to show respect for all faiths. (See www.hundertwasserhaus.com or www.hundertwasserhaus.at.)

Das Hundertwasser-Haus in Wien

6.2 Imperatives

You are already familiar with the FORMAL IMPERATIVE which addresses one individual or several people. You know that the verb is followed by the pronoun **Sie:**

> Herr Schmidt, **lesen Sie** das bitte!
> Herr und Frau Müller, **kommen Sie** später wieder!

1. The FAMILIAR IMPERATIVE has two forms: one for the singular and one for the plural.

   a. The singular usually corresponds to the **du**-form of the verb *without* the pronoun **du** and *without* the **-st** ending:

du schreibst	du tust	du antwortest	du fährst	du nimmst	du isst	du liest
Schreib!	**Tu!**	**Antworte!**	**Fahr!**	**Nimm!**	**Iss!**	**Lies!**

   NOTE: **Lesen** and **essen** retain the **s** or **ss** of the verb stem. **Lies! Iss!**

   - Verbs ending in **-d, -t, -ig,** or in certain other consonant combinations *usually* have an **-e** ending in the **du**-form.

     Finde es! **Antworte** ihm! **Entschuldige** bitte! **Öffne** die Tür!

   - Verbs with vowel changes from **a → ä** in the present singular *do not* make this change in the imperative. Verbs that change from **e → i(e)** do retain this change, however.

     Fahr langsam! **Lauf** schnell!
     Nimm das! **Iss** nicht so viel! **Sprich** Deutsch! **Lies** laut! **Sieh** mal!

   b. The plural corresponds to the **ihr**-form of the verb *without* the pronoun **ihr.**

ihr schreibt	ihr tut	ihr antwortet	ihr fahrt	ihr nehmt	ihr esst	ihr lest
Schreibt!	**Tut!**	**Antwortet!**	**Fahrt!**	**Nehmt!**	**Esst!**	**Lest!**

Legt den Teppich vor das Sofa!	*Put the carpet in front of the couch.*
Stellt die Kommode an die Wand!	*Put the dresser against the wall.*
Hängt das Bild neben die Tür!	*Hang the picture next to the door.*

2. English imperatives beginning with *Let's . . .* are expressed in German as follows:

Sprechen wir Deutsch!	*Let's speak German.*
Gehen wir nach Hause!	*Let's go home.*

3. Here is a summary chart of the imperative.

Schreiben Sie!	Schreib!	Schreibt!	Schreiben wir!
Antworten Sie!	Antworte!	Antwortet!	Antworten wir!
Fahren Sie!	**Fahr!**	Fahrt!	Fahren wir!
Nehmen Sie!	**Nimm!**	Nehmt!	Nehmen wir!
Essen Sie!	**Iss!**	Esst!	Essen wir!
Lesen Sie!	**Lies!**	Lest!	Lesen wir!

   Frau Schmidt, **schreiben Sie** mir!
   Helga, **schreib** mir!
   Kinder, **schreibt** mir!
   Schreiben wir Lisa!

   NOTE: The German imperative is usually followed by an EXCLAMATION POINT.

Übungen

J. Nennen Sie den Imperativ! First form the singular and then the plural familiar.

BEISPIEL   Bleiben Sie bitte!
Bleib bitte!
Bleibt bitte!

1. Fragen Sie ihn!
2. Entschuldigen Sie bitte!
3. Bitte helfen Sie uns!
4. Zeigen Sie uns den Weg!
5. Geben Sie mir die Landkarte!
6. Fahren Sie immer geradeaus!
7. Wiederholen Sie das bitte!
8. Halten Sie da drüben!
9. Hören Sie mal!
10. Schlafen Sie gut!
11. Essen Sie einen Apfel!
12. Trinken Sie eine Cola!

K. Geben Sie Befehle! Form formal and familiar commands, using the phrases below.

BEISPIEL   an die Tafel gehen
Gehen Sie an die Tafel!
Geh an die Tafel!
Geht an die Tafel!

1. die Kreide nehmen 2. ein Wort auf Deutsch schreiben 3. von 1 bis 10 zählen 4. wieder an den Platz gehen 5. das Deutschbuch öffnen 6. auf Seite 150 lesen 7. mit dem Nachbarn auf Deutsch sprechen 8. mir einen Kuli geben 9. nach Hause gehen 10. das nicht tun

L. Was tun? Decide with your friend what to do with the rest of the day.

BEISPIEL   zu Hause bleiben
Bleiben wir zu Hause!

1. in die Stadt gehen 2. an den See fahren 3. durch die Geschäfte bummeln 4. eine Pizza essen 5. das Schloss besichtigen 6. ins Kino gehen

M. Noch mehr Befehle! Address three commands to each of the following below. Use whatever verbs you wish.

BEISPIEL   an einen Touristen
Fahren Sie mit dem Bus!
Gehen Sie immer geradeaus!
Fragen Sie dort noch einmal!

1. an einen Taxifahrer/eine Taxifahrerin
2. an einen Kellner/eine Kellnerin
3. an ein paar Freunde oder Klassenkameraden (*classmates*)
4. an einen Bruder/eine Schwester
5. an ein paar Kinder

N. Bitte tu, was ich sage! Ask your partner to do what you say. Give each other 5–10 different classroom commands that are to be followed, for example, opening the book to a certain page, reading something fast or slowly, and so forth.

6.3 *Wissen* vs. *kennen*

In German, two verbs correspond to the English *to know.*

kennen, gekannt	*to know, to be acquainted with (a person, place, or thing)*
wissen, gewusst	*to know (a fact)* (The fact is most often expressed in a subordinate clause.)

Whereas **kennen** is regular in the present tense, the forms of **wissen** are very similar to the forms of the modals.

ich	weiß
du	weißt
er	weiß
wir	wissen
ihr	wisst
sie	wissen

Volkswagen –
da weiß man, was man hat.

WO BITTE GEHT'S HIER ZUR GESUNDHEIT?

IHR APOTHEKER KENNT DEN WEG.

Ich **kenne** das Buch.	BUT	Ich **weiß, dass** es gut ist.
Ich **kenne** den Lehrer.	BUT	Ich **weiß, dass** er aus Salzburg ist.
		Ich **weiß** seine Telefonnummer.

Übungen

O. *Kennen* oder *wissen*? These young people are looking for a place to eat in Vienna. Fill in the appropriate forms in the dialogue.

ANGELIKA Entschuldigen Sie! _____ Sie, wo die Wipplinger Straße ist?
DAME Nein. Ich _____ Wien gut, aber das _____ ich nicht.
MICHAEL Danke! Du, Angelika, _____ du, wie spät es ist?
ANGELIKA Nein, aber ich _____, dass ich Hunger habe.
MICHAEL Hallo, Holger und Sabine! Sagt mal, _____ ihr Angelika?
SABINE Ja, natürlich.
MICHAEL Wir haben Hunger. _____ ihr, wo es hier ein Restaurant gibt?
HOLGER Ja, da drüben ist die „Bastei Beisl". Wir _____ es nicht, aber wir _____, dass es gut sein soll.
MICHAEL _____ ihr was? Gehen wir essen!

 P. Was weißt du und wen kennst du? Ask your partner ten questions about certain people or certain things, which he/she will answer in a complete German sentence. Also include questions in the present perfect.

BEISPIEL S1 Kennst du den Herrn da?
S2 Natürlich kenne ich ihn.
S1 Weißt du, dass er Deutsh spricht?
S2 Nein, das habe ich nicht gewusst.

Public Transportation and City Life

Visitors from North America are often astounded by the efficient and extensive public transportation networks in German cities. Their existence is one reason why Germans consume only one-third of the per capita energy used by Americans. Most large cities have extensive subway lines (**U-Bahn-Linien**) that connect with suburban commuter trains (**S- Bahn**). Bikes are usually permitted on trains and subways during off-peak hours.

German urban transportation systems typically operate on the honor system. Passengers are required to validate their own tickets (**Fahrkarten entwerten**) upon boarding by inserting them into machines that stamp the time and date. People who evade paying (**Schwarzfahrer**) have to reckon with random checks by plainclothes employees and stiff fines. Buses and streetcars complement the subway system, making for dense networks that reach outlying suburbs. At each stop, a schedule is posted, and buses usually arrive within a few minutes of the posted time. Most large cities also have night buses (**Nachtbusse**), which run on special routes all night long.

All cities have some form of public transportation, usually heavily subsidized, in an effort to limit pollution and congestion in city centers. Monthly and yearly passes are available with reduced rates for students and senior citizens. Large companies also offer their employees a reduced-rate transportation ticket (**das Firmenticket**).

Zum ersten Mal in Dresden und Sie kennen die Stadt wie Ihre Westentasche: Das Navigationssystem TravelPilot von Blaupunkt.

Zusammenfassung

Visit the **Wie geht's?** iLrn website for more review and practice of the grammar points you have just learned.

🔶 **Q. Hoppla, wo soll das hin? Der Umzug (moving)** You and a friend—your partner— are moving into new apartments right next to each other and are helping each other move. Both apartments are shown on page 169. First, your partner will tell you where to put everything. He/she should be as specific as possible and keep track of his/her instructions. Write the <u>name or abbreviation</u> of each item into the spot where it should go, or draw it in. Then tell your partner where to put your belongings.

🟡 MÖBEL: Stuhl, Schreibtisch, Bücher, Computer, Telefon, Lampe, Regal, Fernseher, Radio, Kühlschrank, Kommode, Nachttisch, Schrank, Sessel, Bild, Tisch, Pflanze (f., plant), Spiegel (m., mirror) usw.

1. **Wohin soll das?**

   BEISPIEL S1 Wohin soll der Teppich?
   S2 Leg den Teppich ins Wohnzimmer vor das Sofa!
   S1 Und die Lampe?
   S2 Stell die Lampe rechts neben das Sofa!

2. **Ist alles da, wo es sein soll?** When you are through with furnishing both apartments, each partner checks with the other whether directions have been followed for each of the respective apartments.

BEISPIEL   S1 Liegt der Teppich im Wohnzimmer vor dem Sofa?
            S2 Ja, ich habe den Teppich vor das Sofa gelegt.
            S1 Steht die Lampe rechts neben dem Sofa?
            S2 Ja, ich habe die Lampe rechts neben das Sofa gestellt.
                (*OR*: Nein, ich habe die Lampe links neben das Sofa gestellt.)

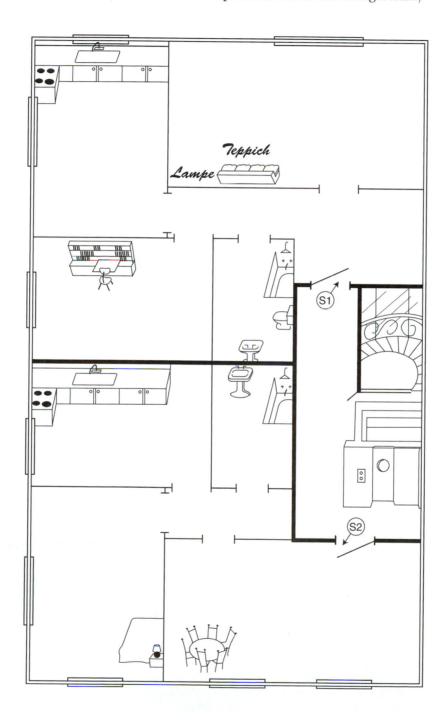

R. Wohnungsanzeigen *(Apartment classified ads)*

Read the rental ads at right, then choose one and pretend you are the landlord. Your partner is looking for an apartment and will inquire about it. Answer his/her questions based on the ad. If some of the information is not given in the ad, make it up. Then reverse roles.

S1 Ich habe gelesen, dass Sie eine Wohnung zu vermieten haben. Wo ist die Wohnung?

S2 . . .

S1 Können Sie mir die Wohnung etwas beschreiben *(describe)*?

S2 Ja, gern. Sie hat . . .

S1 Gibt es auch . . . ?

S2 . . .

S1 Wie weit ist es zu . . . ?

S2 . . .

S1 Und was kostet die Wohnung?

S2 . . .

VERMIETUNGEN
1-Zi-Whg in Uninähe, 25 qm, möbl., schön u. hell, Dusche/WC, 200,— warm. 0941 / 70 63 22
1-Zi-Neubauwhg an Student/in, ca. 29 qm, teilmöbl., zentral, 250,— kalt, ab 1.11.06. 0941 / 4 28 62
2 Zi-Dachgeschoss, Altstadt, ca. 50 qm, 315,— kalt, ab Februar '07. 0941 / 99 06 86
2 1/2 Zi-Whg, Neubau, 60 qm, Balkon, ruhig, 280,—. 0941 / 4 63 61 45
3-ZKB, Balkon, 72 qm, auch an WG 3 Pers., 425,—, zum 1.12.06 frei. 0941 / 5 17 76
3-ZKB, Terrasse, 98 qm, Gäste-WC, Garage, Keller, Kaltmiete 550,—. 0941 / 44 98 69
Bungalow, 120 qm, 4-ZKB, Garten, Terrasse, Sauna, 750,—. 0941 / 4 70 04
2-Zi-Whg auf Bauernhof, 50 qm, Garten, Tiere kein Problem, gegen 10 Stunden Arbeit pro Woche. 0941 / 57 65 98

S. An der Uni: Auf Deutsch bitte!

1. Hello, Hans! Where have you been? 2. I've been in the dorm. 3. Where are you going? —To the library. 4. I'd like to live in a dorm, too. 5. Where do you live now? 6. In an apartment. Unfortunately it's above a disco (**die Disko**) and next to a restaurant. 7. Tell me, are the rooms in the dorm nice? 8. I like my room, but I don't like the furniture. 9. On which floor do you live? —On the third floor. 10. Do you know how much it costs? —180 Euro a month. 11. There's Rico. 12. Who's that? From where am I supposed to know him? (Where am I supposed to know him from?) 13. I didn't know that you don't know him. 14. Let's say hello.

Kaffeepause in der Küche vom Studentenwohnheim

Einblicke

Wortschatz 2

das Reihenhaus, ⁓er	*townhouse, row house*
die Arbeit	*work*
die Eigentumswohnung, -en	*condominium*
am Abend	*in the evening*
am Tag	*during the day*
aufs Land / auf dem Land(e)	*into the country(side) / in the country(side)*
ausgezeichnet	*excellent*
außerdem	*besides* (adverb)
fast	*almost*
leicht	*easy, easily* (lit. *light*)
schwer	*hard, difficult* (lit. *heavy*)
mitten in (+ *acc./dat.*)	*in the middle of*
noch nicht	*not yet*
trotzdem	*nevertheless, in spite of that*
bauen	*to build*
leben	*to live*
lieben	*to love*
sparen	*to save* (money, time)

● Note the difference between **leben** (*to live*, literally: *to be alive*) and **wohnen** (*to reside*): **Dürer lebt nicht mehr. Er hat in dem Haus da drüben gewohnt.**

Vor dem Lesen

A. Fragen

1. Leben die meisten Leute *(most people)* in Ihrer Stadt in Wohnungen oder in Häusern mit Garten? 2. Wo ist Bauland *(building lot[s])* teuer? Wissen Sie, wo es nicht so teuer ist? 3. Was für öffentliche Verkehrsmittel *(public transportation)* gibt es hier? 4. Wie kommen die meisten Leute zur Arbeit? Wie kommen Sie zur Uni? Braucht man hier unbedingt *(necessarily)* ein Auto? 5. Gibt es hier Schlafstädte *(bedroom communities)*, von wo die Leute morgens in die Stadt und abends wieder nach Hause fahren? 6. Wohin gehen oder fahren die Leute hier am Wochenende?

B. Das ist leicht zu verstehen! Welche Silbe ist betont? Was ist das auf Englisch?

der Arbeitsplatz, Biergarten, Clown, Dialekt, Münchner, Musiker, Spielplatz, Stadtpark, Wanderweg; das Boot, Feld; die Energie, Mietwohnung, Wirklichkeit; frei, idyllisch, pünktlich; Ball spielen, eine Pause machen, picknicken

C. Blick auf *(glance at)* den Marktplatz With your partner, form 8 to 10 sentences about the following typical city scene, using the two-way prepositions **in, auf, unter, über, vor, hinter, an, neben,** or **zwischen.**

 ## *Schaffen, sparen, Häuschen bauen*

saying / Swabia
standard German / work hard

little
most / dream of
dream

to the outskirts / move out(side)
commute back and forth
money

sidewalks

with them

goes window-shopping

CD 5,
Track 4

„Schaffe, spare, Häusle baue" ist ein Spruch° aus Schwaben°. Auf Hoch-deutsch° heißt es „Schaffen°, sparen, Häuschen bauen." Der Spruch aus Schwaben ist typisch nicht nur für die Schwaben, sondern für viele Deutsche, Österreicher und Schweizer.

5   In den drei Ländern leben viele Menschen, aber es gibt nur wenig° Land. Die meisten° wohnen in Wohnungen und träumen von° einem Haus mit Garten. Für viele bleibt das aber nur ein Traum°, denn in den Städten ist Bauland sehr teuer. Es gibt auch nicht genug Bauland, weil man nicht überall bauen darf.

Oft muss man an den Stadtrand° oder aufs Land ziehen°, wo mehr Platz ist
10 und wo Land noch nicht so teuer ist. Aber nicht alle möchten so weit draußen° wohnen und stundenlang hin- und herpendeln°. Das kostet Energie, Zeit und Geld°. Abends kommt man auch nicht so leicht ins Kino oder ins Theater. Das Leben auf dem Land ist oft idyllisch, aber nicht immer sehr bequem.

In der Stadt kann man eigentlich sehr gut leben. Die Wohnungen sind oft
15 schön und gemütlich. Man braucht nicht unbedingt ein Auto, weil alles in der Nähe liegt. Fast überall gibt es Bürgersteige° und Fahrradwege, und die öffent-lichen Verkehrsmittel sind ausgezeichnet. Die Busse kommen relativ oft und pünktlich. In Großstädten gibt es auch Straßenbahnen, U-Bahnen und S-Bahnen. Damit° können Sie nicht nur aus der Stadt oder durch die Stadt, sondern auch
20 mitten ins Zentrum, in die Fußgängerzone fahren, wo die Leute am Tag einkaufen und am Abend gern bummeln gehen. Man sieht ein bisschen in die Schaufenster°

Ein Einhorn (unicorn) *beim Umzug* (parade) *in Linz*

und geht vielleicht in eine Bar oder ein Café. Auf den Straßen ist im Sommer fast immer etwas los°. Es gibt Straßenkünstler°, Musiker und Clowns.

there's something going on / sidewalk artists

25   Wenn man in der Stadt wohnt, kann man aber auch leicht aufs Land fahren. Viele tun das gern und oft. Am Wochenende fährt man gern einmal an die See° oder in die Berge. Überall zwischen Wäldern° und Feldern findet man Wanderwege und Fahrradwege. Dort findet man auch leicht ein Restaurant, wo man gemütlich Pause machen kann.

ocean

forests

    Man muss aber nicht unbedingt aufs Land fahren, wenn man ins Grüne° will.
30 Fast alle Städte, ob groß oder klein, haben Stadtparks. Die Münchner z. B. lieben ihren Englischen Garten. Dort gibt es nicht nur Wanderwege, sondern auch Spielplätze und Bänke, Biergärten, Wiesen° zum Picknicken und zum Ballspielen und einen See mit Bootchen.

out into nature

meadows

    Die meisten leben eigentlich gern in der Stadt, entweder in einer Eigentums-
35 wohnung oder einer Mietwohnung. In der Stadt gibt es viel zu sehen und zu tun. Alles ist ziemlich nah, nicht nur der Arbeitsplatz, die Geschäfte und die Schulen, sondern auch die Theater, Kinos, Museen und Parks. Viele träumen trotzdem von einem Haus mit Garten. Sie wissen, dass sie schwer arbeiten und sparen müssen, wenn der Traum Wirklichkeit werden soll. Und das tun auch viele.

Im Münchner Hofgarten

Idyll auf dem Land. Haus mit Strohdach (thatched roof) *in Schleswig-Holstein*

Aktives zum Text

A. Richtig oder falsch?

_____ 1. In Deutschland, in Österreich und in der Schweiz gibt es nicht viel Bauland, besonders nicht in den Städten.

_____ 2. Die meisten Leute dort wohnen in einem Haus mit Garten.

_____ 3. Auf dem Land ist Bauland nicht so teuer wie in der Stadt.

_____ 4. Das Leben auf dem Land ist sehr laut.

_____ 5. In allen Städten gibt es Straßenbahnen, eine U-Bahn und eine S-Bahn.

_____ 6. Mit den öffentlichen Verkehrsmitteln kann man durch die Stadt fahren.

_____ 7. Überall in Wäldern und Feldern gibt es Fahrradwege und Fußgängerzonen.

_____ 8. In der Fußgängerzone kann man am Tag einkaufen, am Abend bummeln gehen und manchmal Musik hören.

_____ 9. Im Englischen Garten darf man nicht picknicken.

_____ 10. Wenn man ein Haus kaufen oder bauen möchte, muss man schwer arbeiten und lange sparen.

B. Haus oder Wohnung? Fill in the appropriate two-way prepositions and articles. Use contractions where possible.

1. Die meisten Deutschen wohnen _____ Wohnung.
2. _____ Städten ist Bauland sehr teuer.
3. Der Traum vom Häuschen mit Garten hat viele _____ Stadtrand (sg. m.) oder _____ Land gebracht.
4. _____ Feldern stehen jetzt Reihenhäuser.
5. Die Reihenhäuser sind manchmal direkt _____ Straße.
6. Morgens fahren viele _____ Stadt.
7. Das Leben _____ Land kann unbequem sein.
8. Viele bleiben _____ Stadt, weil dort alles _____ Nähe ist.
9. _____ Arbeit fahren sie dann noch einmal _____ Zentrum (n.)
10. _____ Zentrum ist fast immer etwas los.

C. In der Großstadt You have never been to Frankfurt/Main before. Ask questions about the city, using **wo** or **wohin.**

> BEISPIEL   In Großstädten gibt es eine U-Bahn.
> *Wo gibt es eine U-Bahn?*

1. Mit der U-Bahn kann man mitten in die Fußgängerzone fahren.
2. Im Zentrum kann man wunderschön bummeln.
3. Abends kann man ins Kino oder ins Theater gehen.
4. Wenn man ins Grüne will, geht man in den Palmengarten.
5. Am Main gibt es überall Wege und Bänke.

D. Kennen oder wissen?

1. _____ Sie den Spruch „Schaffe, spare, Häusle baue"?
2. _____ Sie, wie viele Leute in Deutschland auf dem Land leben?
3. _____ Sie den Englischen Garten?
4. _____ ihr, dass es überall Fahrradwege gibt?
5. Ich habe nicht _____, dass es in der Stadt so viele Fußgängerwege gibt.
6. _____ du Herrn Jakob? Nein, aber Hans _____ ihn.
7. _____ du, dass er mit seinen 80 Jahren immer noch viel wandert?

z. B. Zukunftstechnologie

Wir wissen nicht nur woher, sondern auch wohin der Wind weht.

Sachsen LB
Landesbank Sachsen Girozentrale

Sächsisch als Erfolgsprinzip

E. Was ist typisch auf dem Land und in der Stadt? Work in groups of three. Some groups list the advantages of city life and the disadvantages of country life, while the others do the reverse. Then compare. Which group has the most convincing arguments?

BEISPIEL   *Auf dem Land kann man (nicht) . . . / Auf dem Land gibt es
(kein-) . . .*

In der Stadt kann man (nicht) . . . / In der Stadt gibt es (kein-). . .

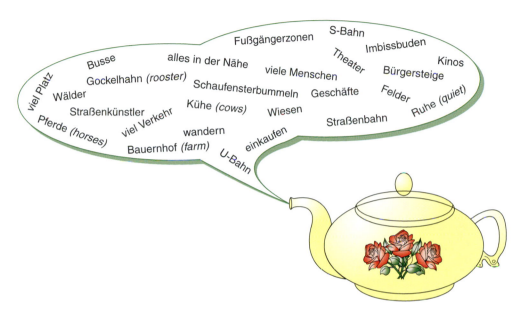

● Optional tongue twister **(der Zungenbrecher):** Wer nichts weiß und weiß, dass er nichts weiß, weiß mehr als der, der *(the one who)* nichts weiß und nicht weiß, dass er nichts weiß.

Fokus   High German and Dialects

The German language has numerous dialects. Generally, these dialects have existed much longer than High German **(Hochdeutsch),** the standard form of German spoken everywhere in Germany and used in schools and businesses. Austria and Switzerland have standard versions and dialects of German as well. The German spoken in Austria is similar to that of Germany for the most part, whereas Swiss German diverges greatly. The differences between regional dialects are often so great, for example, that someone from Münster in the north speaking Westphalian **(Westfälisch)** won't be understood by someone from Munich in the south.

With the European Union's growth in importance, greater interest has developed in local traditions and history and has led to the creation of movements to keep regional dialects alive. North German Radio, for example, broadcasts short daily sermons in Low German **(Plattdeutsch),** while some Bavarian newspapers include regular features in Bavarian **(Bayrisch).**

Some dialects are staging a comeback in song, literature, and theater. In areas where a dialect is spoken, children will learn it automatically at home before starting school. Once in school, however, they will need to master standard German in order to succeed both in their education and, later, professionally.

F. Meinungsumfrage *(Opinion poll)* Ask each other about your lifestyle preferences now and later. Give reasons why. Your instructor then polls the entire class to determine what choices have been made.

BEISPIEL
S1 Wo möchtet ihr jetzt wohnen, in der Stadt oder auf dem Land?
S2 Ich möchte [auf dem Land] wohnen, weil . . .
S3 [Ich auch.]
S1 Und wenn ihr Kinder habt?
S2 Dann möchte ich [auch dort wohnen, weil es ruhig ist.]
S1 Und wenn ihr alt seid?
S3 [Dann vielleicht in der Stadt.]

Schreibtipp

Responding to an Ad

Real estate ads are typically full of abbreviations that people tend to adopt when talking about properties. For example, **2. OG** means that an apartment is upstairs **(Obergeschoss)** on the third floor (the second above ground level). The expression **u.v.m.** means **und viel mehr.** A **2-Zimmer-Wohnung** has two rooms in addition to the kitchen and bathroom. Note that measurements are given in square meters **(qm)**; 91 qm (91 m²) would equal approximately 1000 square feet. In responding to the ad and e-mail from Christian, be sure to ask specific questions. Rephrase any real estate jargon to be sure that you have understood all about the condominium.

 G. Kurzgespräche With a partner, choose one of the situations and prepare a brief dialogue. Then present it to the class.

1. **Einladung zum Mittagessen**

You have been invited to a classmate's house for dinner, but you are quite late. You introduce yourself to his/her mother, who asks you to come in **(herein).** You apologize repeatedly for being so late, while she maintains it doesn't matter. When you hand her the flowers you have brought, she thanks you and says that dinner is ready.

2. **Wo ist das Knochenhauer Amtshaus?**

You are visiting Hildesheim and want to see the well-known Knochenhauer Amtshaus, a 16th-century guild house. You stop a Hildesheimer and ask where the building is. He/She replies that it is at the Marktplatz, across from city hall. Your informant asks whether you see the pedestrian area over there; he/she directs you to walk along that street and turn right at the pharmacy. The Marktplatz is nearby **(ganz in der Nähe).** You thank the stranger and say good-bye.

 **H. Eine E-Mail: Eigentumswohnung in Hildesheim** Pretend you are Ryan or Tiffany and read through the condominium ad and your friend Christian's e-mail. Write a brief response congratulating him on his discovery and ask some more questions about it. Then tell him that you are also looking for a place. Describe what you have in mind and how much something like that costs in your town.

Datum:	Sonntag, 20. September, 20:50
Thema:	Eigentumswohnung
Von:	"Christian Schütz" schuetzchristian@t-online.de
An:	"Ryan Bloxom" ryanbloxom@yahoo.com

Hallo Ryan und Tiffany,

wie geht's euch? Ich glaube, ich habe in Hildesheim eine Eigentumswohnung gefunden: „Wohnen am Kalenberger Graben." Eine Altbauwohnung im 2. Stock, sogar mit Fahrstuhl, 91 qm, total renoviert und möbliert, Parkettfußböden, Wohnzimmer, Schlafzimmer, Einbauküche, Bad und Gäste WC. Das alles mitten im Zentrum gegenüber vom Kalenberger Graben — einem See mit Park und Wanderwegen. Alles ist ganz in der Nähe und man kann von dort überall zu Fuß hingehen. Zur Arbeit laufe ich nur 15 Minuten. Ist das nicht toll? Und der Preis der Wohnung? 158.000 Euro. Wie findet ihr das? Gibt's das bei euch auch?

Christian

■ **EIGENTUMSWOHNUNGEN**

Wohnen am Kalenberger Graben!
Topsanierte 2-Zimmer-Altbauwohnung in einer der bevorzugtesten Lagen von Hildesheim. Die Wohnung liegt im 2. OG (Fahrstuhl im Haus) und verfügt über ca. 91 m² Wohnfl. sowie eine sehr gute Ausstattung wie z. B. hochwert. Parkettfußböden, Komfort-Einbauküche, Gäste-WC u.v.m.

Kaufpreisf.: € 158.000,-

Track 13 **Die Großeltern kommen** Listen to the message that Mrs. Schmidt has left for her children on the answering machine. Then indicate which chores each child has been asked to do; write **S** for Sebastian, **M** for Mareike, and **J** for Julia. Finally, note briefly what the children are *not* supposed to do.

1. **Wer soll was tun?**

____ zum Supermarkt fahren

____ einen Schokoladenpudding machen

____ Bratwurst und Käse kaufen

____ den Großeltern zeigen, wo sie schlafen

____ zum Blumengeschäft fahren

____ Kartoffeln kochen

____ Blumen ins Esszimmer stellen

____ 20 Euro aus dem Schreibtisch nehmen

____ Mineralwasserflaschen zum Supermarkt bringen

____ die Kleidung der *(of the)* Großeltern in den Schrank hängen

____ Wein in den Kühlschrank stellen

2. **Was sollen die Kinder nicht tun?**

a. _____

b. _____

A German house and furniture, Stuttgart and its public transportation: http://wiegehts.heinle.com.

Marktplatz in Quedlinburg

Auf der Bank und im Hotel

Lernziele

In this chapter you will learn about:

Zum Thema

Telling official time, banking, and hotels

Kultur-Fokus

Currency, exchanging money, credit cards, hotels, youth hostels, and Luxembourg

Struktur

Der- and **ein-**words
Separable-prefix verbs
Flavoring particles

Einblicke

Übernachtungsmöglichkeiten

For more information, go to http://iLrn.heinle.com

Hotel Mohrenwirt in Fuschl am See, südöstlich von Salzburg

Vorschau   The History of German Currency

Minidrama: *Ihren Ausweis bitte!*

Although West Germany experienced a postwar economic boom that lasted almost forty years, Germans have always had a fear of inflation. The concern is rooted in the conditions that plagued Germany after World War I, when it experienced what was probably the worst inflation of any modern industrialized country. The German unit of currency, **the Reichsmark (RM),** had so little value at the time that people needed pushcarts to transport the piles of money needed to buy groceries; a single loaf of bread cost billions of marks. In the aftermath of World War II, the Western Allies replaced the **Reichsmark** with the **Deutsche Mark (DM)** to hold inflation in check, to reduce the enormous war debt, and to instill economic confidence. The Soviet Union followed suit with the introduction of the **Mark (M)** in the Soviet-controlled East German zone. Boosted by the Marshall Plan, the West German economy experienced dramatic growth, while the Soviets stripped East German factories of machinery and shipped it east. Nevertheless, the economy of the German Democratic Republic (GDR) became one of the strongest in the East bloc. Yet in spite of that, it always lagged behind the capitalist West. The disparity in economic efficiency widened in the two decades before the collapse of the GDR in 1989.

On July 2, 1990, three months before German reunification, the West German government in Bonn undertook one of the biggest financial bailouts in history by establishing a currency union **(die Währungsunion)** with East Germany. GDR citizens were allowed to exchange up to 6,000 Eastmark (M) for DM at a rate of 1:1; savings above these amounts were converted at a rate of 2:1. This meant that after the exchange **(der Umtausch),** the average savings of a three-member GDR household of 27,000 M became DM 13,500. The introduction of the much-desired, strong West German Mark had a devastating impact on the East German economy by making much of its industry noncompetitive overnight and throwing large numbers of employees out of work. The situation required huge cash infusions from West to East, increasing inflationary pressure in all of Germany. The staunchly independent German Central Bank **(die Bundesbank),** which is charged with ensuring monetary stability, raised interest rates to the highest level in decades. The bank reluctantly lowered them only after the worst recession since World War II hit Germany in the early 1990s.

The introduction in 1999 of the **Euro**—the new all-European currency—for institutional transactions meant the beginning of the end for the **Deutsche Mark,** symbol of German economic power and stability in the second half of the twentieth century. At the beginning of 2002, the euro replaced the DM in everyday transactions, making room for a large, single market with a common currency. (See *Fokus,* Chapter 2.)

Zum Thema

 ## Auf der Bank

CD 5,
Track 6

TOURISTIN	Guten Tag! Können Sie mir sagen, wo ich Geld umtauschen kann?
ANGESTELLTE	Am Schalter 1.
TOURISTIN	Vielen Dank! *(Sie geht zum Schalter 1.)* Guten Tag! Ich möchte Dollar in Euro umtauschen. Hier sind meine Reiseschecks.
ANGESTELLTE	Darf ich bitte Ihren Pass sehen?
TOURISTIN	Hier.
ANGESTELLTE	Unterschreiben Sie bitte hier, dann gehen Sie dort zur Kasse! Da bekommen Sie Ihr Geld.
TOURISTIN	Danke! *(Sie geht zur Kasse.)*
KASSIERER	324 Euro 63: einhundert, zweihundert, dreihundert, zehn, zwanzig vierundzwanzig Euro und dreiundsechzig Cent.
TOURISTIN	Danke! Auf Wiedersehen!

An der Rezeption im Hotel

EMPFANGSDAME	Guten Abend!
GAST	Guten Abend! Haben Sie ein Einzelzimmer frei?
EMPFANGSDAME	Für wie lange?
GAST	Für zwei oder drei Nächte; wenn möglich ruhig und mit Bad.
EMPFANGSDAME	Leider haben wir heute nur noch ein Doppelzimmer, und das nur für eine Nacht. Aber morgen wird ein Einzelzimmer frei. Wollen Sie das Doppelzimmer sehen?
GAST	Ja, gern.
EMPFANGSDAME	Zimmer Nummer 12, im ersten Stock rechts. Hier ist der Schlüssel.
GAST	Sagen Sie, kann ich meinen Koffer einen Moment hier lassen?
EMPFANGSDAME	Ja, natürlich. Stellen Sie ihn da drüben in die Ecke!
GAST	Danke! Noch etwas, wann machen Sie abends zu?
EMPFANGSDAME	Um 24.00 Uhr. Wenn Sie später kommen, müssen Sie klingeln.

A. Fragen

1. Wer möchte Geld umtauschen? 2. Wo ist sie? 3. Wohin muss sie gehen? 4. Was muss die Touristin der Angestellten zeigen? 5. Wo bekommt sie ihr Geld? 6. Wie viele Euros bekommt sie? 7. Was für ein Zimmer möchte der Gast? 8. Für wie lange braucht er es? 9. Was für ein Zimmer nimmt er und wo liegt es? 10. Was gibt die Dame an der Rezeption dem Gast? 11. Wo kann der Gast seinen Koffer lassen? 12. Wann macht das Hotel zu?

 B. Jetzt sind Sie dran! With a partner, create your own dialogue of interaction at a bank counter or the reception desk of a hotel.

Wortschatz 1

Die Uhrzeit *(time of day)*

The formal (official) time system in German-speaking countries is like the one used by the military. The hours are counted from 0 to 24, with 0 to 11 referring to A.M. and 12 to 24 referring to P.M. The system is commonly used in timetables for trains, buses, planes, etc., on radio and television, and to state business hours of stores and banks.

16.05 Uhr = sechzehn Uhr fünf	*4:05 P.M.*
16.15 Uhr = sechzehn Uhr fünfzehn	*4:15 P.M.*
16.30 Uhr = sechzehn Uhr dreißig	*4:30 P.M.*
16.45 Uhr = sechzehn Uhr fünfundvierzig	*4:45 P.M.*
17.00 Uhr = siebzehn Uhr	*5:00 P.M.*
24.00 Uhr = vierundzwanzig Uhr	*midnight*

Die Bank, -en *(bank)*

der Ausweis, -e	*identification card (ID)*	das Geld	*money*
Dollar, -(s)	*dollar*	Bargeld	*cash*
Pass, ⁓e	*passport*	Kleingeld	*change*
Schalter, -	*counter, ticket window*	die Kasse, -n	*cashier's window*
(Reise)scheck, -s	*(traveler's) check*		*(lit. cash register)*

Das Hotel, -s *(hotel)*

der Ausgang, ⁓e	*exit*	das Einzelzimmer, -	*single room*
Eingang, ⁓e	*entrance*	Doppelzimmer, -	*double room*
Gast, ⁓e	*guest*	Gepäck	*baggage, luggage*
Koffer, -	*suitcase*	die Nacht, ⁓e	*night*
Schlüssel, -	*key*	Nummer, -n	*number*
		Tasche, -n	*bag; pocket*

Weiteres

der Blick (in / auf + *acc.*)	*view (of)*
die Lage	*location*
bald	*soon*
frei	*free, available*
auf / zu	*open / closed*
geöffnet / geschlossen	*open / closed*
laut / ruhig	*loud / quiet(ly)*
möglich	*possible*
einen Moment	*(for) just a minute*
Wann machen Sie auf / zu?	*When do you open / close?*
einen Scheck ein·lösen	*to cash a check*
um·tauschen	*to exchange*
wechseln	*to change; to exchange*
lassen (lässt), gelassen	*to leave (behind)*
unterschreiben, unterschrieben	*to sign*

Das glaube ich nicht.	*I don't believe that.*
Das ist doch nicht möglich!	*That's impossible (lit. not possible)!*
Das kann doch nicht wahr sein!	*That can't be true!*
Quatsch!	*Nonsense!*
Vorsicht!	*Careful!*
Pass auf! Passt auf! Passen Sie auf!	*Watch out!*
Warte! Wartet! Warten Sie!	*Wait!*
Halt!	*Stop!*

In newspapers and advertisements, German traditionally separates hours and minutes by a period instead of a colon (**16.05 Uhr** BUT *4:05 P.M.*) However, with the popularity of digital clocks, the use of the colon has also become very common (**16:05 Uhr** AND *4:05 P.M.*). Note that *midnight* can be referred to as **24.00 Uhr** or **0.00 (null) Uhr**.

Zum Erkennen: die Angestellte, -n *(clerk, employee, f.)*; die Empfangsdame, -n *(receptionist)*; klingeln *(here: to ring the doorbell)*; AUCH: der Dienst, -e *(service)*; sparen *(to save [money / time])*

Aktives zum Thema

A. Mustersätze

1. Wo kann ich hier ____?
   Geld wechseln → Wo kann ich hier Geld wechseln?
   Dollar umtauschen, einen Scheck einlösen, Reiseschecks einlösen . . .

2. Darf ich bitte Ihren ____ sehen?
   Pass → Darf ich bitte Ihren Pass sehen?
   Scheck, Reisescheck, Ausweis . . .

3. Können Sie mir das in ____ geben?
   Dollar → Können Sie mir das in Dollar geben?
   Euro, Franken, Kleingeld, Bargeld . . .

4. Wo kann ich ____ lassen?
   mein Auto → Wo kann ich mein Auto lassen?
   meinen Schlüssel, mein Gepäck, meinen Koffer, meine Tasche . . .

5. Wir machen um ____ zu.
   24.00 Uhr → Wir machen um 24.00 Uhr zu.
   22.00 Uhr, 22.15 Uhr, 22.30 Uhr, 22.45 Uhr, 23.00 Uhr . . .

B. Was bedeuten die Wörter und was sind die Artikel?

Ausgangstür, Gästeausweis, Geldwechsel, Gepäckstück, Handtasche, Hoteleingang, Kofferschlüssel, Nachtapotheke, Nachthemd, Nachtmensch, Passnummer, Scheckbuch, Seeblick, Sparbuch, Taschengeld, Taschenlampe, Schlüsselkind

C. Ich brauche Kleingeld. With a partner, practice asking for a place where you can get change. Take turns and vary your responses.

S1 Ich habe kein Kleingeld. Kannst du mir . . . wechseln?
S2 Nein, . . .
S1 Schade!
S2 Aber du kannst . . .
S1 Wo ist . . . ?
S2 . . .
S1 Danke schön!
S2 . . .

Wie viel Kleingeld brauchen Sie?

 D. Im Hotel With a partner, practice inquiring about a hotel room. Take turns and be sure to vary your responses.

S1 Guten . . . ! Haben Sie ein . . . mit . . . frei ?
S2 Wie lange wollen Sie bleiben?
S1 . . .
S2 Ja, wir haben ein Zimmer im . . .
S1 Was kostet es?
S2 . . .
S1 Kann ich es sehen?
S2 . . . Hier ist der Schlüssel. Zimmernummer . . .
S1 Sagen Sie, wo kann ich . . . lassen?
S2 . . .
S1 Und wann machen Sie abends zu?
S2 . . .

 E. Wie spät ist es? Ralf loves his new digital watch. Lea prefers her old-fashioned one with hands. As Ralf says what time it is, Lea confirms it in a more casual way. Work with a classmate. Take turns.

BEISPIEL 14.15

   S1 Auf meiner Uhr ist es vierzehn Uhr fünfzehn.
   S2 Bei mir ist es Viertel nach zwei.

1. 8.05
2. 11.10
3. 12.30
4. 13.25
5. 14.30
6. 17.37
7. 19.40
8. 20.45
9. 22.50
10. 23.59
11. 00.01
12. 02.15

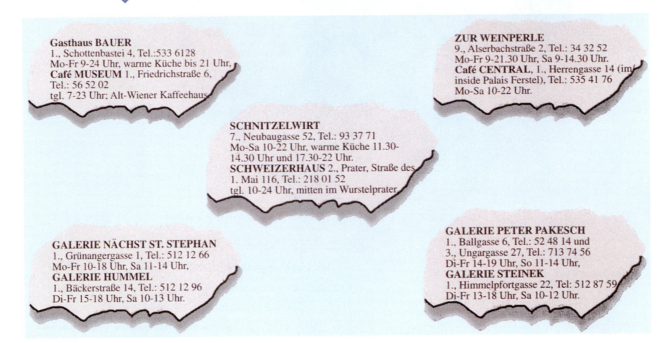

F. Öffnungszeiten Wann sind diese Restaurants und Kunstgalerien geöffnet?

Gasthaus BAUER
1., Schottenbastei 4, Tel.:533 6128
Mo-Fr 9-24 Uhr, warme Küche bis 21 Uhr,
Café MUSEUM 1., Friedrichstraße 6,
Tel.: 56 52 02
tgl. 7-23 Uhr; Alt-Wiener Kaffeehaus

ZUR WEINPERLE
9., Alserbachstraße 2, Tel.: 34 32 52
Mo-Fr 9-21.30 Uhr, Sa 9-14.30 Uhr.
Café CENTRAL, 1., Herrengasse 14 (im
inside Palais Ferstel), Tel.: 535 41 76
Mo-Sa 10-22 Uhr.

SCHNITZELWIRT
7., Neubaugasse 52, Tel.: 93 37 71
Mo-Sa 10-22 Uhr, warme Küche 11.30-
14.30 Uhr und 17.30-22 Uhr.
SCHWEIZERHAUS 2., Prater, Straße des
1. Mai 116, Tel.: 218 01 52
tgl. 10-24 Uhr, mitten im Wurstelprater

GALERIE NÄCHST ST. STEPHAN
1., Grünangergasse 1, Tel.: 512 12 66
Mo-Fr 10-18 Uhr, Sa 11-14 Uhr.
GALERIE HUMMEL
1., Bäckerstraße 14, Tel.: 512 12 96
Di-Fr 15-18 Uhr, Sa 10-13 Uhr.

GALERIE PETER PAKESCH
1., Ballgasse 6, Tel.: 52 48 14 und
3., Ungargasse 27, Tel.: 713 74 56
Di-Fr 14-19 Uhr, So 11-14 Uhr,
GALERIE STEINEK
1., Himmelpfortgasse 22, Tel: 512 87 59
Di-Fr 13-18 Uhr, Sa 10-12 Uhr.

BEISPIEL   *Gasthaus Bauer ist täglich von sieben bis dreiundzwanzig Uhr geöffnet.*

G. Was sagen Sie? Working with a partner, react to the following situations with an appropriate expression, using each expression only once. Take turns.

BEISPIEL   S1 Da kommt ein Auto wie verrückt um die Ecke!
S2 Vorsicht!

1. Hier kostet ein Hotelzimmer 110 Euro.
2. Ich habe ein Zimmer für 240 Euro im Monat gefunden.
3. Du, die Vorlesung beginnt um 14.15 Uhr und es ist schon 14.05 Uhr!
4. Sie bummeln mit einem Freund durch die Stadt. Ihr Freund will bei Rot *(at a red light)* über die Straße laufen.
5. Sie sind auf einer Party und es macht Ihnen viel Spaß. Aber morgen ist eine Prüfung und Sie hören, dass es schon zwei Uhr ist.
6. Sie lernen auf einer Party einen Studenten kennen. Sie hören, dass sein Vater und Ihr Vater zusammen in Heidelberg studiert haben.
7. Sie stehen mit einer Tasse Kaffee an der Tür. Die Tür ist zu. Ein Freund möchte hereinkommen.
8. Ein Freund aus Deutschland will die Kerzen auf seinem Weihnachtsbaum anzünden *(light)*. Sie sind sehr nervös.

H. Interview: Fragen Sie einen Nachbarn/eine Nachbarin, . . . !

1. wo man hier Bargeld oder Kleingeld bekommt
2. wo man hier Franken *(Swiss currency)* oder Euros bekommen kann
3. ob er/sie weiß, wie viele Franken/Euros man für einen Dollar bekommt
4. wie er/sie bezahlt, wenn er/sie einkaufen geht: bar, mit einem Scheck oder mit einer Kreditkarte
5. wie er/sie bezahlt, wenn er/sie reist *(travels)*
6. was er/sie tut, wenn er/sie kein Geld mehr hat
7. ob er/sie schon einmal etwas gewonnen hat; wenn ja, was und wo *(die Lotterie)*

Aussprache: ei, ie

CD 5,
Track 7

A. Laute

1. [ei] **sei**t, **wei**ßt, bl**ei**bst, l**ei**der, fr**ei**, R**ai**ner M**ey**er, B**ay**ern
2. [ie] w**ie**, w**ie** v**ie**l, n**ie**, l**ie**ben, l**ie**gen, m**ie**ten, l**ie**s, s**ie**h, D**ie**nstag
3. v**ie**lleicht, B**ei**spiel, bl**ei**ben / bl**ie**ben, h**ei**ßen / h**ie**ßen, W**ie**n / W**ei**n, W**ie**se / w**ei**ß

B. Wortpaare

1. See / Sie
2. beten / bieten
3. biete / bitte
4. Miete / Mitte
5. leider / Lieder
6. Mais / mies

Hörverständnis

Track 14 **Eine Busfahrt** Listen to the discussion between these American exchange students in Tübingen and their professor before taking a bus trip early in their stay. Then complete the statements below according to the dialogue.

Zum Erkennen: abfahren *(to depart);* das Konto *(account);* die Jugendherberge *(youth hostel);* also *(in other words);* Briefmarken *(stamps)*

1. Der Professor und die Studenten wollen _____ um _____ abfahren.
2. Sie sind von _____ bis _____ in der Schweiz.
3. Sie sind von _____ bis _____ in Österreich.
4. Sie sollen heute noch _____ gehen.
5. Sie brauchen nur etwas Geld, wenn sie _____ oder _____ kaufen wollen.
6. Die Jugendherbergen, _____, _____ und _____ sind schon bezahlt.
7. Manchmal braucht man Kleingeld für _____.

Wer spart, kann große Sprünge machen.

BfG: Die Bank für Gemeinwirtschaft.

Struktur

7.1 Der- and ein-words

1. Der-words

This small but important group of limiting words is called DER-WORDS because their case endings are the same as those of the definite articles **der, das, die.**

alle	*all* (pl.)
der, das, die	*the; that* (when stressed)
dieser, -es, -e	*this; these*
jeder, -es, -e	*each, every* (sg. only)
mancher, -es, -e	*many a* (sg.); *several, some* (usually pl.)
solcher, -es, -e	*such* (usually pl.)
welcher, -es, -e	*which*

● The plural of **jeder** is **alle,** which takes the same endings as the definite article in the plural.

CAUTION: In everyday speech, the singular of **solcher** usually is **so ein,** which is not a **der**-word but an **ein**-word: **so ein Hotel** (*such a hotel*) BUT **solche Hotels** (*such hotels*).

Compare the endings of the definite article and the **der**-words!

	masc.	neut.	fem.	pl.
nom.	der dies**er** welch**er**	das dies**es** welch**es**	die dies**e** welch**e**	die dies**e** welch**e**
acc.	den dies**en** welch**en**			
dat.	dem dies**em** welch**em**	dem dies**em** welch**em**	der dies**er** welch**er**	den dies**en** welch**en**

nom.	Wo ist **der** Schlüssel? —**Welcher** Schlüssel? **Dieser** Schlüssel?
acc.	Hast du **den** Kofferschlüssel gesehen? —Wie soll ich **jeden** Schlüssel kennen?
dat.	Kannst du ihn mit **dem** Schlüssel öffnen? —Mit **welchem** Schlüssel?
plural	Gib mir **die** Schlüssel! —Hier sind **alle** Schlüssel. **Manche** Schlüssel sind vom Haus, **solche** Schlüssel zum Beispiel.
BUT	Der Kofferschlüssel ist **so ein** Schlüssel. Hast du **so einen** Schlüssel?

2. Ein-words

POSSESSIVE ADJECTIVES are called **ein**-words because their case endings are the same as those of the indefinite article **ein** and the negative **kein.**

mein	*my*	**unser**	*our*
dein	*your* (sg. fam.)	**euer**	*your* (pl. fam.)
sein	*his / its*	**ihr**	*their*
ihr	*her / its*	**Ihr**	*your* (sg./pl. formal)

Compare the endings of the indefinite article and the **ein**-words!

	masc.	neut.	fem.	pl.
nom.	ein mein unser	ein mein unser	eine meine unsere	keine meine unsere
acc.	ein**en** mein**en** unser**en**			
dat.	ein**em** mein**em** unser**em**	ein**em** mein**em** unser**em**	ein**er** mein**er** unser**er**	kein**en** mein**en** unser**en**

CAUTION: The **-er** of uns**er** and eu**er** is not an ending!

- **Ein**-words have no endings in the masculine singular nominative and in the neuter singular nominative and accusative.

nom.   Hier ist **ein** Pass. Ist das **mein** Pass oder **dein** Pass?

acc.   Braucht er **keine** Kreditkarte? —Wo hat er **seine** Kreditkarte? Hat sie **einen** Ausweis? —Natürlich hat sie **ihren** Ausweis. Haben Sie **Ihren** Ausweis?

dat.   In welcher Tasche sind die Schlüssel? —Sie sind in **meiner** Tasche. Oder sind die Schlüssel in **einem** Koffer? —Sie sind in **Ihrem** Koffer.

plural   Wo sind die Schecks? —Hier sind **unsere** Schecks und da sind **eu(e)re** Schecks.

● When **unser** and **euer** have an ending, the **-e-** is often dropped (**unsre, eure**), especially in colloquial speech.

Übungen

A. Ersetzen Sie die Artikel!

1. *Der*-Wörter

BEISPIEL   die Tasche *(this)*
diese Tasche

a. das Gepäck *(every, which, this)*
b. der Ausweis *(this, every, which)*
c. die Nummer *(which, every, this)*
d. die Nächte *(some, such, these)*
e. an dem Schalter *(this, which, each)*
f. an der Kasse *(this, every, which)*
g. mit den Schecks *(these, some, all)*

2. *Ein*-Wörter

BEISPIEL   die Gäste *(your/3×)*
deine / eu(e)re / Ihre Gäste

a. der Pass *(my, her, no, his)*
b. das Bargeld *(our, her, their)*
c. die Wohnung *(my, our, your/3×)*
d. neben den Koffer *(your/3×, our, their)*
e. in dem Doppelzimmer *(no, his, your/3×)*
f. mit den Schlüsseln *(your/3×, my, her)*

3. **Der-** und *ein*-Wörter

BEISPIEL   **Das** Bad ist klein. *(our)*
            Unser Bad ist klein.

a. **Das** Zimmer hat einen Fernseher. *(each, my, his, our)*
b. Bitte bringen Sie **den** Koffer zum Auto! *(this, her, our, my)*
c. Ich kann **die** Schlüssel nicht finden. *(your/3×, our, some, my)*
d. Darf ich **das** Gepäck hier lassen? *(her, his, this, our)*
e. Der Ober kennt **den** Gast. *(each, our, this, your/3×)*
f. **Die** Taschen sind schon vor dem Ausgang. *(our, all, some, my)*
g. **Den** Leuten gefällt das Hotel nicht. *(these, some, such)*
h. Du kannst **den** Scheck auf der Bank einlösen. *(this, my, every, such a, your/sg. fam.)*

B. Dias von einer Deutschlandreise *(Slides from a trip to Germany)*

1. Auf _____ Bild seht ihr _____ Freunde aus Holland. 2. Das sind _____
   this   *my*   *their*
Sohn Heiko und _____ Tochter Anke. 3. In _____ Stadt ist _____ Kirche?
                  their   *which*   *this*
4. _____ Kirchen gibt es in Norddeutschland. 5. _____ Haus ist sehr alt,
   Such   *This*

   aber nicht _____ Haus in Neubrandenburg ist so alt. 6. Ich
                 every
finde _____ Häuser sehr schön; Müllers wohnen in _____
         such   *such a*
Haus. 7. Und hier sind _____ Onkel Thomas und _____
                          my   *my*
Tante Hilde. 8. Ist das nicht _____ Auto da vor _____
                                 your (pl. fam.)   *this*
Hotel?

HOTEL VIER TORE
NEUBRANDENBURG

C. Ruck, zuck! Wem gehört das? One person claims to own everything. Quickly correct him/her and tell whose property it is. You may mention the items suggested or think of your own.

BEISPIEL   Das ist mein Buch. *(Heft, Bleistift, Jacke, Tasche, Schlüssel usw.)*
            Quatsch! Das ist nicht dein Buch; das ist mein (ihr, sein) Buch.

7.2 Separable-prefix verbs

1. English has a number of two-part verbs that consist of a verb and a preposition or an adverb.

Watch out! Hurry up! Come back!

In German, such verbs are called SEPARABLE-PREFIX verbs. You are already familiar with two of them:

Passen Sie **auf! Hören** Sie **zu!**

Their infinitives are **aufpassen** and **zuhören.** The prefixes **auf** and **zu** carry the main stress: **auf'·passen, zu'·hören.** From now on, we will identify such separable-prefix verbs with a raised dot (·) between the prefix and the verb in vocabulary lists: **auf·passen, zu·hören.**

- These verbs are separated from the prefixes when the inflected part of the verb is the first or second sentence element: in imperatives, questions, and statements.

Hören Sie bitte **zu!**
Hören Sie jetzt **zu?**
Warum **hören** Sie nicht **zu?**
Wir <u>**hören**</u> immer gut **zu.**
V1   V2

- These verbs <u>are not separated from the prefix</u> when the verb stands at the end of a sentence or clause: with modals, in the present perfect, and in subordinate clauses. Note, however, that in the present perfect the **-ge-** of the past participle is inserted between the stressed prefix and the participle.

Ich soll immer gut **zuhören.**
Ich habe immer gut **zugehört.**
Ich weiß, dass ich immer gut **zuhöre.**
Ich weiß, dass ich immer gut **zuhören** soll.
Ich weiß, dass ich immer gut **zugehört** habe.

2. Knowing the basic meanings of <u>some</u> of the most frequent separable prefixes will help you derive the meanings of <u>some</u> of the separable-prefix verbs.

ab-	*away, off*	**nach-**	*after, behind, later*
an-	*to, up to*	**um-**	*around, over, from*
auf-	*up, open*		*one to the other*
aus-	*out, out of*	**vor-**	*ahead, before*
ein-	*into*	**vorbei-**	*past, by*
her-	*toward (the speaker)*	**zu-**	*closed, shut*
hin-	*away from (the speaker)*	**zurück-**	*back*
mit-	*together with, along with*		

BEISPIEL

an·kommen	*to arrive (come to)*
her·kommen	*to come (toward the speaker)*
herein·kommen	*to come in (toward the speaker)*
heraus·kommen	*to come out (toward the speaker)*
hin·kommen	*to get there (away from the point of reference)*
mit·kommen	*to come along*
nach·kommen	*to follow (come after)*
vorbei·kommen	*to come by*
zurück·kommen	*to come back*

You will need to learn these common separable-prefix verbs:

an·rufen, angerufen	*to call, phone*
auf·machen	*to open*
auf·passen	*to pay attention, watch (out)*
auf·schreiben, aufgeschrieben	*to write down*
auf·stehen, ist aufgestanden	*to get up*
aus·gehen, ist ausgegangen	*to go out*
ein·kaufen	*to shop*
ein·lösen	*to cash (in)*
mit·bringen, mitgebracht	*to bring along*
mit·gehen, ist mitgegangen	*to go along*
mit·kommen, ist mitgekommen	*to come along*
mit·nehmen, mitgenommen	*to take along*
um·tauschen	*to exchange*
vorbei·gehen, ist vorbeigegangen (an, bei)	*to pass (by)*
zu·hören (+ *dat.*)	*to listen*
zu·machen	*to close*
zurück·kommen, ist zurückgekommen	*to come back*

CAUTION: Not all verbs with prefixes are separable, for example, **unterschreiben, wiederholen.** Here the main stress is on the verb, not on the prefix: **unter-schrei'ben, wiederho'len.** Remember also the inseparable prefixes **be-, ent-, er-, ge-, ver-,** and so on. (Chapter 4, *Struktur 4.1*). They never stand alone.

Übungen

D. Was bedeuten diese Verben? Knowing the meanings of the basic verbs and the prefixes, can you tell what these separable-prefix verbs mean?

1. abgeben, abnehmen
2. ansprechen
3. aufbauen, aufgeben, aufstehen, aufstellen
4. ausarbeiten, aushelfen, aus(be)zahlen
5. heraufkommen, herauskommen, herüberkommen, herunterkommen
6. hinaufgehen, hinausgehen, hineingehen, hinuntergehen
7. mitgehen, mitfahren, mitfeiern, mitsingen, mitspielen
8. nachkommen, nachlaufen, nachmachen
9. vorbeibringen, vorbeifahren, vorbeikommen
10. zumachen
11. zurückbekommen, zurückbleiben, zurückbringen, zurückgeben, zurücknehmen, zurücksehen

Mach's nach!

E. Noch einmal Repeat these sentences without a modal.

> BEISPIEL Sie soll ihm zuhören.
> *Sie hört ihm zu.*

1. Wir dürfen am Wochenende ausgehen. 2. Wann musst du morgens aufstehen? 3. Wollt ihr mit mir einkaufen gehen? 4. Ich soll Wein mitbringen. 5. Er will morgen zurückkommen. 6. Ich möchte dich gern mitnehmen. 7. Du kannst das Geld umtauschen. 8. Er will an der Universität vorbeigehen. 9. Können Sie bitte die Fenster aufmachen? 10. Ihr sollt gut aufpassen.

F. Am Telefon Report to a brother what your mother is telling or asking you about tomorrow's family reunion.

> BEISPIEL Sie möchte wissen, ob Rainer und Wolfgang die Kinder mitbringen.
> *Bringen Rainer und Wolfgang die Kinder mit?*
>
> Sie sagt, dass die Tante auch mitkommt.
> *Die Tante kommt auch mit.*

1. Sie sagt, dass wir abends alle zusammen ausgehen.
2. Sie möchte wissen, ob du deine Kamera mitbringst.
3. Sie möchte wissen, wann die Bank aufmacht.
4. Sie sagt, dass sie schnell noch etwas Geld umtauscht.
5. Sie sagt, dass sie dann hier vorbeikommt.

G. Das tut man. Say what things one does before checking out of a hotel.

> BEISPIEL früh aufstehen
> *Man steht früh auf.*

1. die Koffer zumachen 2. das Gepäck zur Rezeption mitnehmen 3. den Schlüssel zurückgeben 4. vielleicht ein Taxi anrufen 5. vielleicht einen Reisescheck einlösen

H. Hoppla, hier fehlt was: Wer hat was getan? Work with a partner to find out whether various family members have finished their tasks. Take turns asking questions until you have both completed your lists. One list is below, the other in Section 11 of the Appendix.

S1:

Wer?	Was tun?	Ja. / Nein.
Vater	bei der Bank vorbeigehen	
Vater	Geld umtauschen	
Mutter	die Kamera mitbringen	Ja, ich glaube.
Mutter	die Nachbarn anrufen	Nein.
Thomas	die Telefonnummer aufschreiben	Ja, ich glaube.
Thomas	die Garagentür zumachen	
Carla	bei der Post vorbeigehen	
Carla	die Fenster zumachen	Nein, noch nicht.
Kinder	den Fernseher ausmachen *(turn off)*	Ja.
Kinder	die Lichter *(lights)* ausmachen	
ich	ein paar Bücher mitnehmen	Ja.

> BEISPIEL S1 Ist Vater bei der Bank vorbeigegangen?
> S2 Ja, er ist gestern bei der Bank vorbeigegangen. Haben die Kinder den Fernseher ausgemacht?
> S1 Ja, sie haben den Fernseher ausgemacht.

I. Nennen Sie alle vier Imperative!

BEISPIEL   die Tür aufmachen
Machen Sie die Tür auf!
Mach die Tür auf!
Macht die Tür auf!
Machen wir die Tür auf!

1. jetzt aufstehen
2. in der Stadt einkaufen
3. den Scheck noch nicht einlösen
4. genug Bargeld mitbringen
5. das Gepäck mitnehmen
6. mit ihnen mitgehen
7. bei der Bank vorbeigehen
8. trotzdem zuhören
9. wieder zurückkommen

J. Nein, das tue ich nicht! Your partner is not very cooperative and makes all sorts of statements that he/she won't do this or that. You plead with him/her not to be so stubborn and do it anyway. Use the verbs listed on page 190 in *Struktur 7.2* of this chapter and follow the example. Take turns.

BEISPIEL   anrufen
S1 Nein, ich rufe sie nicht an!
S2 Ach, ruf(e) sie doch bitte an! Du hast sie doch immer angerufen.

K. Interview: Fragen Sie einen Nachbarn/eine Nachbarin, . . . !

1. wann er/sie heute aufgestanden ist
2. wann er/sie gewöhnlich am Wochenende aufsteht
3. wohin er/sie gern geht, wenn er/sie ausgeht
4. wo er/sie einkauft
5. was er/sie heute mitgebracht hat (drei Beispiele bitte!)

7.3 Flavoring particles

In everyday speech, German speakers use many FLAVORING WORDS (or intensifiers) to convey what English often expresses through gestures or intonation, for example, surprise, admiration, or curiosity. When used in these contexts, flavoring particles have no exact English equivalent. Here are some examples:

aber	*expresses admiration, or intensifies a statement*
denn	*expresses curiosity, interest (usually in a question)*
doch	*expresses concern, impatience, assurance*
ja	*adds emphasis*

Euer Haus gefällt mir **aber!**	*I do like your house.*
Die Möbel sind **aber** schön!	*Isn't this furniture beautiful!*
Was ist **denn** das?	*What (on earth) is that?*
Wie viel kostet **denn** so etwas?	*(Just) how much does something like that cost?*
Das weiß ich **doch** nicht.	*That I don't know.*
Frag **doch** Julia!	*Why don't you ask Julia!*
Du kennst **doch** Julia?	*You do know Julia, don't you?*
Euer Garten ist **ja** super!	*(Wow,) your garden is great!*
Ihr habt **ja** sogar einen Pool!	*(Hey,) you even have a pool!*

Übung

L. Im Hotel: Auf Englisch bitte!

BEISPIEL   Haben Sie denn kein Einzelzimmer frei?
Don't you have any single rooms available?

1. Hier ist ja der Schlüssel!
2. Das Zimmer ist aber schön!
3. Es hat ja sogar einen Balkon!
4. Hat es denn keine Dusche?
5. Wir gehen doch noch aus?
6. Hast du denn keinen Hunger?
7. Komm doch mit!
8. Ich komme ja schon!
9. Lass doch den Mantel hier!
10. Wohin gehen wir denn?

Zusammenfassung

M. Bilden Sie Sätze! Create sentences using the verb forms indicated in parentheses.

BEISPIEL   Eva / gestern / ausgehen / mit Willi *(present perfect)*
Eva ist gestern mit Willi ausgegangen.

1. man / umtauschen / Geld / auf / eine Bank *(present tense)*
2. welch- / Koffer *(sg.)* / du / mitnehmen? *(present tense)*
3. einkaufen / ihr / gern / in / euer / Supermarkt? *(present tense)*
4. unser / Nachbarn *(pl.)* / zurückkommen / vor einer Woche *(present perfect)*
5. wann / ihr / aufstehen / am Sonntag? *(present perfect)*
6. ich / mitbringen / dir / mein / Stadtplan *(present perfect)*
7. vorbeigehen / noch / schnell / bei / Apotheke! *(imperative / sg. fam.)*
8. zumachen / Schalter / um 17.30 Uhr! *(imperative / formal)*
9. umtauschen / alles / in Dollar! *(imperative / pl. fam.)*

Fokus   Accommodations and Tourist Information

Frühstückspension Elisabeth Dalhaus

Berenbrock 51
59348 Lüdinghausen
Tel. 02591/33 38, Fax 70547

Bauernhof

11   TV   ☎   ▦

Auf dem Bauernhof mit alten Linden und Diele mit offenem Kamin, finden Sie Ruhe und können Kraft tanken. Im „besten Zimmer" wird zum Frühstück Selbstgemachtes serviert: Marmeladen, Butter, Honig, Brot, Eier und Milch. Ideal für Familien ist „Mutters Etage" mit 2 Schlafzimmern und eigenem Bad. 8 Betten, Mehrbettzimmer möglich!
In der Nähe: Dortmund-Ems-Kanal, Burg Vischering, Badesee, Hallenbad, Rosengarten, Reitmöglichkeiten

When looking for accommodations in a German city, you can choose from a wide range of prices and comfort levels, from campgrounds to luxury hotels. A **Pension** usually offers a simple room with a sink; shared toilets and showers are sometimes down the hall. Homes offering inexpensive **Fremdenzimmer,** or rooms for tourists, are common in rural areas and can be spotted by a sign saying **Zimmer frei.** Breakfast is usually included in the price of accommodation, regardless of the price category. In the interest of public safety, hotel guests are required by law to fill out a form providing home address, date of birth, and other personal information.

To find accommodations, travelers can rely on a town's tourist information office (**die Touristeninformation** or **das Fremdenverkehrsbüro).** Usually located in the train station or city center, this office will provide tourists with the usual sightseeing information, as well as help them with lodging (**die Zimmervermittlung**) in hotels or private homes.

N. Gedächtnisspiel *(Memory game)* In a small group, one of your classmates starts with a statement using a verb such as **mitbringen** or **umtauschen.** The next student repeats the statement and adds to it, and so on. When your memory fails, or if you forget to add the separable prefix, you're out of the game. Let's see who wins!

BEISPIEL   *Ich bringe Blumen mit.*
Ich bringe Blumen und Wein mit.
Ich bringe Blumen, Wein und Salzstangen mit.

O. An der Rezeption   Auf Deutsch bitte!

1. All (the) hotels are full **(voll).** 2. That can't be true! 3. Wait, there's another hotel. 4. Why don't you *(sg. fam.)* ask at Hotel Marks? 5. Do you *(formal)* still have rooms available? 6. Just a minute. Yes, one room with (a) bath on the second floor. 7. Can we see it? 8. Yes, here is a key. 9. We'll be right back **(zurückkommen).** 10. (Wow,) this is great! 11. I <u>do</u> like this room. 12. Excellent! We'll take it. 13. May I please see your ID? 14. You do take traveler's checks, don't you? —Of course. 15. Did you see our restaurant? —Which restaurant? 16. This restaurant. From every table you have a view of the water. 17. You don't find a restaurant like this (such a restaurant) everywhere. 18. That's true.

Fokus   Youth Hostels

Youth hostels **(Jugendherbergen)** are immensely popular among budget-minded travelers in Germany, Switzerland, and Austria. There are over 780 of them in Germany and over 240 in Austria and Switzerland combined. They are open to individual travelers, groups, and families alike. There is generally no upper age limit, but during peak season, younger members have priority. Accommodation is usually dormitory-style, with several bunk beds in each room and shared bathrooms. Many youth hostels offer laundry facilities, dining halls, and common rooms. Although they are not real hotels—many are closed during the day and have a curfew—youth hostels offer a relatively high level of comfort for the price. Students and backpackers have come to value the hostels as places to meet other young people from around the world. If you plan on hosteling, remember to purchase a membership card **(der Jugendherbergsausweis)** before traveling overseas. For information, contact: www.hiayh.org (USA), www.hihostels.ca (Canada), or www.eurotrip.com/hostels/ (Europe).

Beim Bettenmachen in der Jugendherberge

Einblicke

Wortschatz 2

der Gasthof, ⸚e	small hotel
Wald, ⸚er	forest, woods
die Jugendherberge, -n	youth hostel
Pension, -en	boarding house; hotel
Reise, -n	trip
einfach	simple, simply
meistens	mostly, usually
an·kommen, ist angekommen	to arrive
an·nehmen, angenommen	to accept
kennen lernen	to get to know, meet
packen	to pack
reisen, ist gereist	to travel
reservieren	to reserve
übernachten	to spend the night
Das kommt darauf an.	That depends.

🔸 Two-way prepositions take the dative with **ankommen: Er ist am Bahnhof / in der Stadt angekommen.**

Vor dem Lesen

A. Fragen

1. Wo kann man in den USA / in Kanada gut übernachten? 2. Wie heißen ein paar Hotels oder Motels? 3. Was gibt es in einem Hotelzimmer? 4. Was kostet ein Zimmer in einem Luxushotel in New York oder San Francisco? 5. Wo kann man frühstücken? Kostet das Frühstück extra? 6. Haben Sie schon einmal in einer Jugendherberge übernachtet? Wenn ja, wo? 7. Gehen Sie gern campen? Wenn ja, warum; wenn nein, warum nicht?

Jugendherberge Burg Stahleck in Bacharach am Rhein

Lesetipp
Looking for Conjunctions

Being aware of verb-last word order after subordinating conjunctions can help your reading comprehension. In this reading, note that while some sentences start out with the dependent clause, in others, the dependent clause follows after the main clause and a comma. Pay special attention to the position of the verb in the dependent clauses. How many examples of dependent clauses can you find?

B. Allerlei Hotels: Wo möchten Sie übernachten? With your partner, compare the various hotels listed below and decide which one to recommend to your parents, who are going to visit you in Regensburg.

HOTEL	ADRESSE	TEL.	PREIS					
Am Peterstor	Fröhliche-Türkenstr. 12	5 45 45	50,11	TV		👫 ☕		🅿 🐕
Apollo	Neuprüll 17	91 05-0	81,81	☎ 📻TV		👫 ☕ 〰 🧖		P 🅿 🐕
Bischofshof	Krauterermarkt 3	58 46-0	166,17	☎ MINIBAR 📻TV		♿ 👫 ☽ ☕ DIÄT		🅿 🐕
Courtyard by Marriott	Frankenstr. 28	8 10 10	96,63	☎ MINIBAR 📻TV ✽ 🔌		👫 ☽ ☕ DIÄT	🧖 BAR P	🐕
Münchner Hof	Tändlergasse 9	58 44-0	102,26	☎ MINIBAR TV		👫 ☽ ☕		🅿 🐕
Orphee	Wahlenstr. 1	59 60 20	107,37	☎ MINIBAR 📻TV	🔌	☕ DIÄT	BAR	🐕
Künstlerhaus	Alter Kornmarkt 3	57 13 4	81,81	📻TV				
Spitalgarten	St.-Katharinen-Platz 1	8 47 74	40,90					

SYMBOLE: 📻 = Radio, ✽ = Aircondition, 🔌 = Modemanschluss (…*connection*),

👫 = Fahrstuhl (*elevator*), ☽ = Nachtportier, ☕ = Frühstücksbüfett, 🧖 = Sauna + Solarium

C. Das ist leicht zu verstehen! Welche Silbe ist betont? Markieren Sie sie! Was ist das auf Englisch?

> der Campingplatz, Evangelist; das Formular, Symbol; die Adresse, Attraktion, Bibel, Möglichkeit, Übernachtung, Übernachtungsmöglichkeit; ausfüllen; international, luxuriös, modern, primitiv, privat

Übernachtungsmöglichkeiten

CD 5, Track 9

Wo kann man gut übernachten? Nun°, das kommt darauf an, ob das Hotel elegant oder einfach sein soll, ob es zentral liegen muss oder weiter draußen° sein darf. Wer will, kann auch Gast in einem Schloss oder auf° einer Burg sein.

In Amerika gibt es viele Hotels mit gleichen° Namen, weil sie zu einer
5 Hotelkette° gehören, z. B. Holiday Inn oder Hilton. Bei diesen Hotels weiß man immer, was man hat, wenn man hineingeht. In Deutschland gibt es auch Hotels mit gleichen Namen, z. B. Hotel zur Sonne oder Gasthof Post. Aber das bedeutet nicht, dass solche Hotels innen gleich sind°. Im Gegenteil°! Sie sind meistens sehr verschieden°, weil sie zu keiner Kette gehören. Ihre Namen gehen oft bis ins
10 Mittelalter zurück. Oft sagen sie etwas über° ihre Lage°, z. B. Berghotel, Pension Waldsee. Andere° Namen, wie z. B. Gasthof zum Löwen, zum Adler° oder zum Stier° sind aus der Bibel genommen. Sie sind Symbole für die Evangelisten Markus, Johannes und Lukas.

Manche Hotels sind sehr luxuriös und teuer, andere sind einfach und billig.
15 Sprechen wir von einem normalen Hotel, einem Gasthof oder Gasthaus! Wenn Sie ankommen, gehen Sie zur Rezeption. Dort müssen Sie meistens ein Formular ausfüllen und bekommen dann Ihr Zimmer: ein Einzelzimmer oder Doppelzimmer,

well
farther out
in
same
. . . franchise

are alike inside / on the contrary / different
about / location
other / eagle
bull

ein Zimmer mit oder ohne Bad. Für Zimmer ohne Bad gibt es auf dem Flur eine Toilette und meistens auch eine Dusche. Das Frühstück ist gewöhnlich im Preis
20 inbegriffen°. Übrigens hat jeder Gasthof seinen Ruhetag°. Dann ist das Restaurant geschlossen und man nimmt keine neuen Gäste an. Der Herr oder die Dame an der Rezeption kann Ihnen auch Geschäfte und Attraktionen in der Stadt empfehlen, manchmal auch Geld umtauschen. Aber Vorsicht! Auf der Bank ist der Wechselkurs° fast immer besser°.

included / day off

exchange rate / better

An der Rezeption im Hotel Mohrenwirt

25   Wenn Sie nicht vorher° reservieren können, dann finden Sie auch Übernachtungsmöglichkeiten durch die Touristeninformation am Hauptbahnhof. Hier finden Sie nicht nur Adressen von Hotels, sondern auch von Privatfamilien und Pensionen. So eine Übernachtung ist gewöhnlich nicht sehr teuer, aber sauber und gut.

in advance

Haben Sie schon einmal in einer Jugendherberge oder einem Jugendgästehaus
30 übernachtet? Wenn nicht, tun Sie es einmal! Sie brauchen dafür° einen Jugendherbergsausweis. So einen Ausweis können Sie aber schon vorher in Amerika oder Kanada bekommen. Fast jede Stadt hat eine Jugendherberge, manchmal in einem modernen Haus, manchmal in einer Burg oder in einem Schloss. Jugendherbergen und Jugendgästehäuser sind in den Ferien meistens schnell voll, denn alle Grup-
35 pen reservieren schon vorher. Das Übernachten in einer Jugendherberge kann ein Erlebnis° sein, weil man oft interessante Leute kennen lernt. Jugendherbergen haben nur einen Nachteil°: Sie machen gewöhnlich abends um 23.00 Uhr zu. Wenn Sie später zurückkommen, haben Sie Pech gehabt. In fast allen Großstädten gibt es Jugendgästehäuser. Wenn Sie schon vorher wissen, dass Sie fast jeden
40 Abend ausgehen und spät nach Hause kommen, dann übernachten Sie lieber° in einem Jugendgästehaus, denn diese machen erst° um 24.00 oder 1.00 Uhr zu, und in manchen Gästehäusern kann man sogar einen Hausschlüssel bekommen.

for that

experience
disadvantage

rather
not until

Man kann natürlich auch anders° übernachten, z. B. im Zelt auf einem Campingplatz. Das macht Spaß, wenn man mit dem Fahrrad unterwegs° ist;
45 aber das ist nicht für jeden°. Ob im Hotel oder auf dem Campingplatz, in einer Pension oder Jugendherberge, überall wünschen wir Ihnen viel Spaß auf Ihrer Reise durch Europa.

in other ways
on the road
everybody

Aktives zum Text

A. Was passt? Circle the correct answer.

1. Deutsche Hotels mit gleichen Namen sind ____.
   a. immer alle gleich
   b. innen meistens nicht gleich
   c. alle aus dem Mittelalter
   d. Symbole

2. Wenn man in einem Gasthof ankommt, geht man erst ____.
   a. ins Bad
   b. ins Restaurant
   c. zur Rezeption
   d. ins Zimmer

3. Im Hotel kann man Geld umtauschen, aber ____.
   a. nur morgens
   b. nicht an der Rezeption
   c. der Wechselkurs ist oft super
   d. der Wechselkurs ist meistens nicht sehr gut

4. Das Übernachten in einer Jugendherberge kann sehr interessant sein, weil ____.
   a. man manchmal neue Leute kennen lernt
   b. Jugendherbergen in den Ferien schnell voll sind
   c. sie gewöhnlich um 22.00 Uhr zumachen
   d. sie immer auf einer Burg sind

5. Auf dem Campingplatz ____.
   a. gibt es eine Toilette auf dem Flur
   b. ist das Frühstück im Preis inbegriffen
   c. gibt es Zelte
   d. darf man nicht früh ankommen

B. Wo sollen wir übernachten? Match each lodging with the corresponding description.

a. Campingplatz
b. Gasthof
c. Jugendgästehaus
d. Jugendherberge
e. Luxushotel
f. Pension

_____ 1. Diese Übernachtungsmöglichkeit ist meistens nicht teuer, aber doch gut. Man kann sie z. B. durch die Touristeninformation am Bahnhof finden.

_____ 2. Hier ist es besonders billig, aber wenn es viel regnet, kann es sehr ungemütlich sein.

_____ 3. Wenn man viel Geld hat, ist es hier natürlich wunderbar.

_____ 4. Diese Möglichkeit ist für junge Leute. Sie ist nicht teuer und man kann abends spät zurückkommen oder einen Schlüssel bekommen.

_____ 5. Das Übernachten kann hier sehr bequem und gemütlich sein; das Frühstück kostet nichts extra. Am Ruhetag kann man dort nicht essen.

_____ 6. Hier können Leute mit Ausweis billig übernachten, aber man darf abends nicht nach elf zurückkommen.

C. Übernachtungsmöglichkeiten What's missing?

1. In _____ Hotel kann man gut übernachten, aber das kann man nicht
   von _____ Hotel sagen. *(this, every)*
2. Bei _____ Hotel wissen Sie immer, wie es innen aussieht. *(such a)*
3. _____ Hotels sind sehr luxuriös und teuer, _____ Hotel zum Beispiel.
   (some, this)
4. _____ Hotel ist sehr schön gewesen. *(our)*
5. Hast du schon einmal von _____ Pension gehört? *(this)*
6. Wie gefällt es euch in _____ Jugendherberge? *(your)*
7. _____ Jugendherberge ist in einer Burg. *(our)*
8. In _____ Jugendherberge gibt es noch Platz. *(this)*
9. Wollen wir auf _____ Campingplatz übernachten? *(this)*
10. _____ Campingplatz meinst du *(do you mean)*? *(which)*

D. In der Jugendherberge Repeat these sentences without a modal auxiliary, (a) in the present tense and (b) in the present perfect.

BEISPIEL   Du kannst in den Ferien vorbeikommen.
            Du kommst in den Ferien vorbei.
            Du bist in den Ferien vorbeigekommen.

1. Wann möchtet ihr ankommen?
2. In der Jugendherberge könnt ihr Leute kennen lernen.
3. Du musst natürlich einen Jugendherbergsausweis mitbringen.
4. Wollt ihr abends spät ausgehen?
5. Die Jugendherberge soll um 11 Uhr zumachen.
6. Wer spät zurückkommen möchte, kann Pech haben.

E. Kofferpacken: Was nimmst du mit? Working in groups of three or four students, make a list of what you would take along on vacation to the following destinations. Then compare.

1. ans Meer   2. in die Berge   3. nach Europa

BEISPIEL   *Ich nehme eine Sonnenbrille mit. Und du?*
            Ich nehme eine Sonnenbrille und meine Kamera mit.

● These words are not active vocabulary!

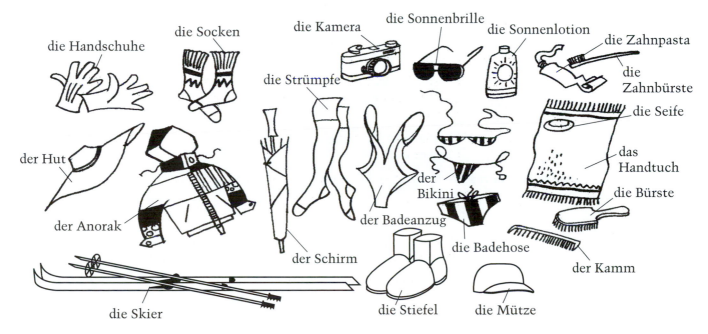

die Handschuhe · die Socken · die Kamera · die Sonnenbrille · die Sonnenlotion · die Zahnpasta · die Zahnbürste · die Strümpfe · die Seife · der Hut · das Handtuch · der Bikini · die Bürste · der Anorak · der Badeanzug · die Badehose · der Kamm · der Schirm · die Skier · die Stiefel · die Mütze

F. Kurzgespräche With a partner, choose one of the situations and prepare a brief dialogue. Then present it to the class.

1. **Überraschung in Heidelberg**

   You are visiting your aunt in Heidelberg. As you tour the castle, you see a German student whom you got to know while you both stayed at a youth hostel in Aachen. Call out to the German student. Both of you express your disbelief that you have met again. Your friend is studying in Heidelberg; you explain why you are there. You ask whether your friend would like to go for a coffee or a soft drink, and he/she agrees.

2. **Hotelsuche in Luxemburg**

   You and a friend are in Stralsund and are looking for a hotel room. You have both inquired in several places. All the hotels you saw had no rooms available at all; in desperation your friend has taken a double room that will cost you 120 euros for one night. You both express your disbelief at your bad luck.

G. Aufsatz: Deutsche reisen in Nordamerika Pretend you are a German who is writing an article for a German travel guide about travel in the United States or Canada. What is it like traveling as a German in North America? What is different about traveling in North America from traveling in Germany?

Fokus   Luxembourg

The Grand Duchy of Luxembourg (**Luxemburg,** pop. 438,000), half the size of Delaware, is one of Europe's oldest and smallest independent countries. It lies between Germany, France, and Belgium. Although it is one of the world's most industrialized nations, its heavy industry—mainly iron and steel production—has not spoiled the natural beauty of the country's rolling hills and dense forests.

Most of the population is Catholic, and there is a high percentage of foreigners—Italians, French, Germans, Belgians, and Portuguese. Almost all Luxembourgers speak **Letzeburgisch,** a German dialect. French, German, and **Letzeburgisch** are all taught in schools and used in public life. Despite close ties to their neighbors, the people of Luxembourg maintain an independent spirit, as expressed in the words of their national anthem: *Mir wölle bleiwe wat mir sin*—**Wir wollen bleiben, was wir sind.** *(We want to stay the way we are.)* The French statesman Robert Schuman (1886–1963) was born in Luxembourg. He was one of the formulators of the cooperative effort, known as the Schuman Plan, by which the coal and steel industries of Germany, Italy, Belgium, Luxembourg, and the Netherlands became economically linked into a Common Market in 1958.

Luxembourg's capital city of the same name (pop. 80,700) is a large financial and banking center and home to several European institutions, including the EURATOM (European Atomic Energy Community). Luxembourg joined the euro currency area in 1999.

Blick auf Luxemburg von der Unterstadt an der Alzette

H. Ein Fax: Hotel Hansablick in Berlin Pretend you are at the front desk of this hotel and write a brief fax answering the following inquiry from a potential hotel guest. Use your imagination.

Jürgen Marmein   den 2. 12. 2006
Bramkoppel 10
22395 Hamburg

An
Hotel Hansablick
Flotowstraße 6
10555 Berlin-Tiergarten

Sehr geehrte Damen und Herren,

meine Frau und ich planen eine Reise nach Berlin. Haben Sie vom 26. 12. bis zum 1. 1. noch Zimmer frei? Wenn ja, was für Zimmer und wie viel kosten sie? Ist das Frühstück inbegriffen? Wo liegt Ihr Hotel? Ist es zentral gelegen und doch ruhig? Haben Sie einen Parkplatz? Wie weit ist es zur U-Bahn oder S-Bahn? Bitte lassen Sie's uns sobald wie möglich wissen!

Mit freundlichem Gruß,

Jürgen Marmein

Hotel Garni ★★★ Hansablick

- ruhige, zentrale Lage am Rande des Tiergartens
- alle Zimmer mit Du/WC, Fön, Telefon, Minibar und Kabel-TV
- großes Frühstücksbüfett
- kostenlose, hoteleigene Parkplätze
- Konferenzräume
- freundlicher Service rund um die Uhr

Flotowstraße 6
10555 Berlin-Tiergarten
Tel. 030-3904800 · Fax 030-3926937
www.hotel-hansablick.de info@hotel-hansablick.de

 # Hörverständnis

Track 15 **Hotel Lindenhof** Mr. Baumann calls the reception of Hotel Lindenhof on Lake Constance. Listen to the conversation. Then complete the sentences with the correct information from the dialogue.

Zum Erkennen: die Person, -en *(person)*; das Frühstücksbüfett *(breakfast buffet)*; das Schwimmbad *(pool)*; Minigolf *(miniature golf)*

1. Herr Baumann und seine Familie fahren im Sommer an den _____.
2. Sie wollen am _____ ankommen und _____ bleiben. 3. Sie brauchen Zimmer für _____ Personen, also _____ Zimmer.
4. Die Zimmer kosten _____ pro Tag. 5. Das Frühstückbüfett kostet _____ extra. 6. Herr Baumannn findet das nicht _____.
7. Die Kinder können dort _____ und in der Nähe auch _____ und _____ spielen. 8. Zum See ist es auch nicht _____.
9. Vom Balkon hat man einen Blick auf den _____ und die _____.
10. Er _____ die Zimmer.

Euros; vacation options; and a visit to Luxembourg: http://wiegehts.heinle.com.

🔸 There is an extensive review section following this chapter in the *Arbeitsbuch.* The accompanying exercises and answer key will help you prepare for the test.

Kapitel 8 Post und Reisen

Lernziele

In this chapter you will learn about:

Zum Thema

Postal service, telephones, and travel

Kultur-Fokus

Phone and postal service, modes of travel, and Switzerland
Hermann Hesse

Struktur

The genitive case
Time expressions
Sentence structure *(continued)*

Einblicke + Literatur

Touristen in der Schweiz
Hermann Hesse: "Im Nebel"

For more information, go to
http://iLrn.heinle.com

Ein ICE kommt aus einem Tunnel.

202

Vorschau Spotlight on Switzerland

Area: Approximately 16,000 square miles, about half the size of Indiana.

Population: About 7.3 million.

Religion: 46% Catholic, 40% Protestant, 14% other.

Geography: This landlocked country is clearly defined by three natural regions: the Alpine ranges that stretch from the French border south of Lake Geneva diagonally across the southern half of Switzerland and include the world-renowned resorts of the Bernese Uplands (**das Berner Oberland**), Zermatt, and St. Moritz in the Inn River valley; the plateaus and valleys of the midland between Lake Geneva and Lake Constance; and the mountains of the Jura in the northernmost section of the Alps.

Currency: Schweizer Franken, 1 sfr = 100 Rappen or Centimes.

Principal cities: Capital Berne (*Bern*, pop. 122,500), Zurich (*Zürich*, pop. 340,900), Geneva (*Genf*, pop. 176,000), Basel (pop. 164,900), Lausanne (pop. 115,600), Winterthur (pop. 91,700).

Isolated and protected by its relative inaccessibility, Switzerland developed as a nation without major hindrance over a span of 700 years. It was founded in 1291, when the cantons of Uri, Schwyz, and Unterwalden formed an alliance against the ruling House of Habsburg. Over time, the original confederation grew into a nation of 26 cantons (states). These cantons maintain considerable autonomy, with their own constitutions and legislatures. The 1848 constitution merged the old confederation into a single federal state by eliminating all commercial barriers and establishing a common postal service, military, legislature, and judiciary.

Despite its small size, few natural resources, and ethnic diversity, Switzerland is one of the most stable nations in the world. Its stability has been attributed to a variety of factors, among them its high standard of living, the conservative character of its people, its geographic isolation, and the country's neutrality in the two world wars. Switzerland has stubbornly adhered to the principle of neutrality—to the extent of staying out of NATO and the European Union; it joined the United Nations (UN) only in 2002, with a narrow margin of 12 cantons voting for and 11 against membership in the international organization. Switzerland's stability and bank-secrecy law continue to attract capital from all over the world, although revelations during the 1990s about the role of Swiss banks in holding gold stolen by the Nazis during World War II have tarnished the image of these renowned financial institutions.

Switzerland is active in the Council of Europe and several specialized agencies of the United Nations. The seat of the League of Nations after World War I, Switzerland is now home to the UN's Economic and Social Council, the International Labor Organization, the World Health Organization, the World Council of Churches, and the International Red Cross. Founded in Geneva in 1864, the Red Cross derived its universally recognized symbol from the inverse of the Swiss flag, which consists of a white cross on a red background. (For pictures and information on practically any Swiss city, visit www.[city name].ch.)

Zum Thema

Auf der Post am Bahnhof

CD 6,
Track 1

HERR   Grüezi!

UTA   Grüezi! Ich möchte dieses Paket nach Amerika schicken.

HERR   Normal oder per Luftpost?

UTA   Per Luftpost. Wie lange dauert das denn?

HERR   Ungefähr eine Woche. Füllen Sie bitte diese Paketkarte aus! . . . Moment, hier fehlt noch Ihr Absender.

UTA   Ach ja! . . . Noch etwas. Ich brauche eine Telefonkarte.

HERR   Für fünf, zehn, zwanzig oder fünfzig Franken?

UTA   Für zwanzig Franken. Vielen Dank!

Am Fahrkartenschalter in Zürich

ANNE   Wann fährt der nächste Zug nach Interlaken?

FRAU   In 5 Minuten. Abfahrt um 11.28 Uhr, Gleis 2.

ANNE   Ach du meine Güte! Und wann kommt er dort an?

FRAU   Ankunft in Interlaken um 14.16 Uhr.

ANNE   Muss ich umsteigen?

FRAU   Ja, in Bern, aber Sie haben Anschluss zum InterCity mit nur 24 Minuten Aufenthalt.

ANNE   Gut. Geben Sie mir bitte eine Hin- und Rückfahrkarte nach Interlaken!

FRAU   Erster oder zweiter Klasse?

ANNE   Zweiter Klasse.

Zug		IC 118	518	1720		IC 120	1520	1822	
		4 ✕	✕			4 ✕	⬦	⬦	4
Zürich HB		10 03	10 28	10 28		11 03	11 07	11 28	
Baden				10 45				11 45	
Brugg (Aargau)				10 53				11 53	
Aarau			10 35	11 07			11 35	12 07	
Olten	24016 ○		10 44	11 15			11 44	12 15	
Olten	24000		10 47				11 47		
Biel/Bienne	○		11 33				12 33		
Lausanne	○						13 48		
Genève	○		13 05						
Zug		IC 721	2521		EC 73		1866		IC 725
					7 ✕		4 ⬦		🛏
Basel SBB		10 00	10 11	10 29	11 00			11 29	12 00
Liestal			10 21	10 46				11 46	
Olten	○	10 26	10 43	11 11	11 26			12 11	12 26
Olten		10 28	10 48	11 17	11 28			12 17	12 28
Langenthal			11 00	11 29				12 29	
Herzogenbuchsee			11 06	11 35				12 35	
Burgdorf			11 18	11 47				12 47	
Bern	○	11 10	11 14	11 35	12 04	12 10	12 14	13 04	13 10
Bern	24004	11 28 ⬅		12 28		12 28		13 28	
Interlaken West	○	12 16		13 16		13 16		14 16	

A. Fragen

1. Wo ist die Post? 2. Wohin will Uta ihr Paket schicken? 3. Wie schickt sie es? 4. Wie lange soll das dauern? 5. Was muss man bei einem Paket ins Ausland *(abroad)* ausfüllen? 6. Was fehlt auf der Paketkarte? 7. Was braucht Uta noch? 8. Was kosten Telefonkarten? 9. Wohin will Anne fahren? 10. Wann fährt der Zug ab und wann kommt er in Interlaken an? 11. Wo muss Anne umsteigen? 12. Was für eine Karte kauft sie?

B. Jetzt sind Sie dran! Diesmal *(this time)* sind Sie an einem Flughafenschalter. Bereiten Sie Ihr eigenes Gespräch mit Ihrem Partner/Ihrer Partnerin vor *(prepare your own dialogue)* und präsentieren Sie es dann vor der Klasse!

S1 Wann gehen Flüge nach . . .?
S2 Zu welcher Tageszeit möchten Sie denn fliegen?
S1 Ich muss um . . . in . . . sein.
S2 Es gibt einen Flug um . . .
S1 Hat er eine Zwischenlandung?
S2 Ja, in . . . Dort haben Sie . . . Aufenthalt.
S1 Muss ich umsteigen?
S2 . . .
S1 . . . Dann geben Sie mir bitte eine Hin- und Rückflugkarte nach . . . !

Auf jeder Reise ist man Ausländer

Wortschatz 1

Die Post *(post office, mail)*

Das Telefon, -e *(telephone)*

der Absender, -	*return address*	die Adresse, -n	*address*
Brief, -e	*letter*	(Ansichts)karte, -n	*(picture) postcard*
Briefkasten, ⸚	*mailbox*	Briefmarke, -n	*stamp*
		E-Mail, -s	*e-mail*
das Fax, -e	*fax*	Postleitzahl, -en	*zip code*
Handy, -s	*cell(ular) phone*	Telefonkarte, -n	*telephone card*
Paket, -e	*package, parcel*	Telefonnummer, -n	*telephone number*
Postfach, ⸚er	*PO box*	Vorwahl, -en	*area code*

● Although Germans say **Briefmarken** for stamps, foreigners will often look in vain for the word in a German post office, where the official word **Postwertzeichen** is more common.

Fokus   Phoning and Postal Services

Telephoning in the German-speaking countries becomes very inexpensive when choosing one of several independent companies and dialing their access number first. Local calls are charged according to minutes spent on the line. The introduction of cell phones **(Handys)** has made a big difference in communication habits. People use cell phones everywhere, a popular version being one with a prepaid card that is especially "handy" for travelers abroad. Motor vehicle operators are not allowed to use cell phones while driving; they can only legally use permanently installed car phones.

Most public phone booths **(Telefonzellen)** require a plastic prepaid phone card **(die Telefonkarte)** to operate. Phone cards can be bought at post offices or newspaper stands. Since hotels usually add a substantial surcharge for phone calls, travelers often find it cheaper to use a long-distance calling card or to place calls from a post office.

Post offices in European countries offer a far greater range of services than in the United States or Canada. For example, it is possible to open a bank account with the post office, wire money, buy traveler's checks, and send a telegram or fax. However, the post office no longer has a monopoly on mail-delivery services; DHL, UPS, and FedEx trucks have become a familiar sight in Europe.

Die Reise, -n *(trip)*

der			das		
	Aufenthalt, -e	*stopover, stay*		Flugzeug, -e	*plane*
	Bahnsteig, -e	*platform*		Gleis, -e	*track*
	Fahrplan, ⸚e	*schedule*	die	Abfahrt, -en	*departure*
	Flug, ⸚e	*flight*		Ankunft, ⸚e	*arrival*
	Flughafen, ⸚	*airport*		Bahn, -en	*railway, train*
	Wagen, -	*car; railroad car*		Fahrkarte, -n	*ticket*
	Zug, ⸚e	*train*		(Hin- und) Rückfahrkarte, -n	*round-trip ticket*
				Fahrt, -en	*trip, drive*

● der **Wagen**, BUT das Auto

Weiteres

ab·fahren (fährt ab), ist abgefahren (von)	*to leave, depart (from)*
ab·fliegen, ist abgeflogen (von)	*to take off, fly (from)*
aus·steigen, ist ausgestiegen	*to get off/out*
ein·steigen, ist eingestiegen	*to get on/in*
um·steigen, ist umgestiegen	*to change (trains, etc.)*
besuchen	*to visit*
einen Satz bilden	*to form a sentence*
erzählen	*to tell*
fehlen	*to be missing / lacking*
fliegen, ist geflogen	*to fly*
landen, ist gelandet	*to land*
schicken	*to send*
telefonieren	*to call up, phone*
in einer Viertelstunde	*in a quarter of an hour*
in einer halben Stunde	*in half an hour*
in einer Dreiviertelstunde	*in three-quarters of an hour*
mit dem Zug / der Bahn fahren, ist gefahren	*to go by train*
Ach du meine Güte!	*My goodness!*
Na und?	*So what?*
Das ist doch egal.	*That doesn't matter. It's all the same to me.*
Das sieht dir (ihm, ihr, ihnen) ähnlich.	*That's typical of you (him, her, them).*
Das freut mich (für dich).	*I'm happy (for you).*
Gott sei Dank!	*Thank God!*

● Like **mit dem Zug fahren**: **mit dem Bus / mit dem Fahrrad / mit der U-Bahn fahren** *to go by bus / bike / subway*

Zum Erkennen: normal *(regular)*; per Luftpost *(by airmail)*; die Paketkarte, -n *(parcel form)*; aus·füllen *(to fill out)*; noch etwas *(one more thing, something else)*; der nächste / letzte Zug nach *(the next / last train to)*; der Anschluss, ⸚e *(connection)*; die Klasse, -n; AUCH: der Anhang *(appendix)*; der Ausdruck, ⸚e *(expression)*; der Genitiv, -e; die Gruppe, -n *(group)*; die Liste, -n; die Tabelle, -n *(chart)*; benutzen *(to use)*; ergänzen *(to add to)*; jemandem eine Frage stellen *(to ask sb. a question)*; heraus·finden *(to find out)*; korrigieren *(to correct)*; präsentieren *(to present)*; überprüfen *(to check)*; Bereiten Sie Ihr eigenes Gespräch vor! *(Prepare your own dialogue!)*; Wechseln Sie sich ab! *(Take turns!)*; diesmal *(this time)*; einer von Ihnen *(one of you)*; der/die andere *(the other one)*; die anderen *(the others)*

Aktives zum Thema

A. Allerlei Fragen

1. Was kostet es, wenn man einen Brief innerhalb von *(within)* Amerika oder Kanada schicken will? Wie lange braucht ein Brief innerhalb der Stadt? nach Europa?

2. Was muss man auf alle Briefe, Ansichtskarten und Pakete schreiben? Schreiben Sie oft Briefe? Wenn ja, wem? Schicken Sie oft E-Mails oder Faxe an Ihre Freunde? Was ist Ihre E-Mail-Adresse?

3. In Deutschland sind Briefkästen gelb. Welche Farbe haben die Briefkästen hier? Wo findet man sie?

4. Wo kann man hier telefonieren? Gibt es Telefonkarten? Wenn ja, wo bekommt man sie?

5. Haben Sie ein Handy? Wenn ja, wann und wo benutzen Sie es besonders viel?

6. In Deutschland darf man beim Autofahren nur mit einem im Auto eingebauten *(built-in)* Handy sprechen. Wie ist das hier? Benutzen Sie Ihr Handy beim Autofahren? Ist es eingebaut? Ist das Telefonieren beim Autofahren gefährlich *(dangerous)*? Warum (nicht)?

7. Wie reisen Sie gern und wie nicht? Warum?

8. Wohin sind Sie zuletzt *(the last time)* gereist? Sind Sie geflogen oder mit dem Wagen gefahren?

B. Was bedeuten diese Wörter und was sind ihre Artikel?

Adressbuch, Abfahrtszeit, Ankunftsfahrplan, Bahnhofseingang, Busbahnhof, Busfahrt, Flugkarte, Flugschalter, Flugsteig, Gepäckkarte, Mietwagen, Nachtzug, Paketschalter, Postfachnummer, Speisewagen, Telefonrechnung

C. Was fehlt?

Finden Sie die Antworten auf dem Fahrplan!

NOTE: 1 km = 0.62 miles. Here is an easy and fairly accurate way to convert kilometers to miles: divide the km figure in half, and add a quarter of that to the half. Thus, 80 km ÷ 2 = 40 + 10 = 50 miles.

km	Zug / Stuttgart–Zürich	E 3504	D 83 R3)	D 381 R3)	D 383			D 85 R4)	D 389 R2)		D 87	D 385 R1)	E 3309 R1)	D 387 R1)
0	Stuttgart Hbf 740		6 48	7 31	9 34			12 44	14 26		17 32	18 26	20 06	
26	Böblingen			7 53	9 56			13 06	14 48		17 55	18 48	20 29	
67	Horb		7 34	8 20	10 24			13 33	15 15		18 21	19 15	21 00	
110	Rottweil		8 05	8 59	10 54			14 02	15 52		18 51	19 45	21 36	
138	Tuttlingen		8 26	9 17	11 13			14 21	16 11		19 09	20 11	21 55	
172	Singen (Hohentwiel)		8 49	9 42	11 37			14 45	16 35		19 32	20 35	22 22	
	Zug					D 2162	✕1)							
192	Singen (Hohentwiel) 730	6 31	8 55	9 49	11 44	12 43	14 51	16 44	19 37	20 44				22 44
	Schaffhausen	6 49	9 10	10 05	12 00	12 58	15 07	17 00	19 52	21 00				23 00
	Zug	1559	(EC 83)				⟨EC 357	(EC 85)		(IC 87)				
238	Schaffhausen 24032	7 02	9 12	10 09	12 09	13 09	15 09	17 09	19 55	21 09				23 09
	Zürich HB	7 47	9 47	10 47	12 47	13 47	15 47	17 47	20 31	21 47				23 47

1. Von Stuttgart nach Zürich sind es _____ Kilometer.
2. Der erste Zug morgens fährt um _____ Uhr und der letzte *(last)* Zug abends um _____ Uhr.
3. Die Reise von Stuttgart nach Zürich geht über _____.
4. Wenn man um 6.48 Uhr von Stuttgart abfährt, ist man um _____ Uhr in Zürich.
5. Die Fahrt dauert ungefähr _____ Stunden.

1. **So geht's!** *(That's the way it goes!)* Lesen Sie die folgenden *(following)* Sätze laut! Was sagen Sie zu Daniels Glück und Pech? Wechseln Sie sich ab *(take turns)*!

1. Daniel hat von seinen Eltern zum Geburtstag ein Auto bekommen.
2. Das Auto ist nicht ganz neu.
3. Aber es fährt so schön ruhig und schnell, dass er gleich am ersten Tag einen Strafzettel *(ticket)* bekommen hat.
4. Am Wochenende ist er in die Berge gefahren, aber es hat immer nur geregnet.
5. Es hat ihm trotzdem viel Spaß gemacht, weil er dort eine Studentin kennen gelernt hat.
6. Auf dem Weg zurück ist ihm jemand in sein Auto gefahren. Totalschaden *(total wreck)*!
7. Daniel hat aber nur ein paar Kratzer *(scratches)* bekommen.
8. Er hat übrigens seit ein paar Tagen eine Wohnung mitten in der Stadt. Sie ist gar nicht teuer.
9. Er möchte das Mädchen aus den Bergen wiedersehen, aber er kann sein Adressbuch mit ihrer Telefonnummer nicht finden.
10. Momentan geht alles schief *(wrong)*. Er kann auch sein Portemonnaie *(wallet)* nicht finden.
11. Noch etwas: Die Katze *(cat)* des Nachbarn hat seine Goldfische gefressen *(ate)*.
12. Sein Bruder hat übrigens eine Operation gehabt. Aber jetzt geht es ihm wieder gut und er ist wieder zu Hause.

Fokus   Car Travel

In Switzerland and Austria, a toll (**die Maut**) is charged for using the express highway (**die Autobahn**). In Germany, a GPS-reliant toll system for large truck travel went into effect in 2005. The 12,000 km of *autobahn* covered is about 1.5 times the 8,000 km of toll roads in the US and approximately the length of all the freeways in California and Texas combined. For enforcement, the system depends on short-range antennas, vehicle profilers, and cameras mounted on 300 gantries over the main line plus a fleet of mobile enforcement vehicles. Large trucks are not allowed on German roads on Sundays or holidays, or on Saturdays during peak vacation times.

Many traffic signs are identical to those in the United States and Canada; some of the different ones are self-explanatory, while others must be learned. Unless otherwise indicated, the driver approaching from the right has the right-of-way. As a rule, right turns at a red light are prohibited, as is passing on the right. The speed limit (**das Tempolimit** or **die Geschwindigkeitsbegrenzung**) in cities and towns is generally 50 km/h (31 mph), and on the open highway 100 km/h (62 mph). Except for certain stretches, there is no official speed limit on the freeway, but drivers are recommended (**die Richtgeschwindigkeit**) not to exceed 130 km/h (81 mph). German drivers are generally more aggressive than those in North America. But watch out! The police in Germany often use radar speed checks to catch drivers who break the speed limit. There are also a number of radar speed boxes installed on some roads. Driving too fast on German roads is expensive and can also mean a temporary loss of driving privileges.

2. **Und wie geht's mir?** Erzählen Sie Ihrer Gruppe, wie es Ihnen geht! Jeder hat mindestens *(at least)* ein Problem. Was sagen die anderen dazu *(the others to that)*?

Aussprache: e, er

For further review, see the Summary of Pronunciation in the front of your *Arbeitsbuch.* Study Part II, subsections 8–10.

CD 6,
Track 2

A. Laute

1. [ə] Adresse, Ecke, Haltestelle, bekommen, besuchen, eine halbe Stunde
2. [ʌ] aber, sauber, schwer, euer, unser, Zimmernummer, Uhr, vor, nur, unter, über, außer, wiederholen

B. Wortpaare

1. Studenten / Studentin
2. Touristen / Touristin
3. diese / dieser
4. arbeiten / Arbeitern
5. lese / Leser
6. mieten / Mietern

Hörverständnis

Track 16 **Weg zur Post** Richtig oder falsch?

Zum Erkennen: Na klar! *(Sure!)*; endlich mal *(finally)*; das Papierwarengeschäft, -e *(office supply store)*; Lass sie wiegen! *(Have them weighed!)*

_____ 1. Bill muss endlich mal an Claudias Eltern schreiben.
_____ 2. Claudia möchte wissen, wo man Ansichtskarten und Briefpapier bekommt.
_____ 3. Bei Schlegel in der Beethovenstraße gibt es Briefpapier.
_____ 4. Postkarten findet man nur in Drogerien.
_____ 5. Gegenüber vom Stadttheater ist die Post.
_____ 6. Bill kauft heute Briefmarken und geht morgen zum Bahnhof.
_____ 7. Er soll zur Post gehen und Claudia Briefmarken mitbringen.

Fokus   Train Travel

Trains are a popular means of transportation in Europe, not only for commuting but also for long-distance travel. The rail network is extensive, and trains are generally clean, comfortable, and on time. Domestic InterCity **(IC)** and international EuroCity **(EC)** trains connect all major western European cities. In Germany, the high-speed InterCityExpress **(der ICE)**, which travels at speeds up to 280 km/h (175 mph), is an attractive alternative to congested highways. Business people can make or receive phone calls on board and even rent conference rooms equipped with fax machines. Non-European residents can benefit from a *Eurailpass,* which permits unlimited train—and some bus and boat—travel in most European countries. Alternatively, the traveler should consider a German *Railpass,* which is less expensive but limited to Germany; both passes must be purchased outside of Europe. Larger train stations provide a wide range of services for the traveler, including coin-operated lockers **(Schließfächer)** or checked luggage rooms **(die Gepäckaufgabe).** The stations in large cities even have a wide range of restaurants and retail establishments.

Im Zug kann man auch schön arbeiten.

Struktur

8.1 The genitive case

The genitive case has two major functions: 1) it expresses possession or another close relationship between two nouns, or 2) it follows certain prepositions.

1. The English phrases *the son's letter* and *the date of the letter* are expressed by the same genitive construction in German.

   Das ist **der Brief des Sohnes.**   *That's the son's letter.*
   Was ist **das Datum des Briefes?**   *What's the date of the letter?*

   a. The genitive form of the INTERROGATIVE PRONOUN **wer** is **wessen** *(whose)*. The chart that follows shows all four cases of the interrogative pronouns.

	Persons	Things and ideas
nom.	wer?	was?
acc.	wen?	was?
dat.	wem?	—
gen.	**wessen?**	—

       Wessen Brief ist das?   *Whose letter is that?*
       Der Brief des Sohnes!   *The son's letter.*

   b. The genitive forms of the DEFINITE and INDEFINITE ARTICLES complete this chart of articles.

Haus des Gastes

DAS KURHAUS IM OSTSEEHEILBAD ZINGST

	SINGULAR			PLURAL
	masc.	**neut.**	**fem.**	
nom.	der ein kein	das ein kein	die eine keine	die — keine
acc.	den einen keinen	das ein kein	die eine keine	die — keine
dat.	dem einem keinem	dem einem keinem	**der einer keiner**	den — keinen
gen.	**des eines keines**	**des eines keines**	**der einer keiner**	**der — keiner**

   c. The genitive case is signaled not only by the forms of the articles, but also by a special ending for MASCULINE and NEUTER nouns in the singular.

   - Most one-syllable nouns and nouns ending in **-s, -ss, -ß, -z, -tz,** or **-zt,** add **-es:**

der Zug	das Geld	der Ausweis	der Pass	der Platz
des Zuges	**des** Geldes	**des** Ausweises	**des** Passes	**des** Platzes

- Nouns with more than one syllable add only an **-s**:

des Flughafen**s**   *of the airport, the airport's*
des Wagen**s**   *of the car, the car's*

NOTE: German uses NO apostrophe for the genitive!

- N-nouns have an **-n** or **-en** ending *in all cases except in the nominative singular.* A very few n-nouns have a genitive **-s** as well.

der Franzose, **-n**, -n	**des** Franzose**n**
Herr, **-n**, -en	Herr**n**
Junge, **-n**, -n	Junge**n**
Mensch, **-en**, -en	Mensch**en**
Nachbar, **-n**, -n	Nachbar**n**
Student, **-en**, -en	Student**en**
Tourist, **-en**, -en	Tourist**en**
Name, **-n(s)**, -n	Name**ns**

Note how n-nouns are listed in vocabularies and dictionaries: the first ending usually refers to the accusative, dative, and genitive singular; the second one to the plural.

d. FEMININE NOUNS and PLURAL NOUNS have no special endings in the genitive.

NOMINATIVE	GENITIVE
die Reise	**der** Reise
die Idee *(idea)*	**der** Idee
die Reisen	**der** Reisen
die Ideen	**der** Ideen

e. Proper names usually add a final **-s**.

Annemarie**s** Flug   *Annemarie's flight*
Frau Strobel**s** Fahrt   *Ms. Strobel's trip*
Wien**s** Flughafen   *Vienna's airport*

Der Planet der Ideen

In colloquial speech, however, **von** is frequently used instead of the genitive of a name: **die Adresse von Hans.**

f. Nouns in the genitive normally follow the nouns they modify, whereas proper names precede them.

Er liest den Brief **der Tante.**
Er liest **Annemaries** Brief.
Er liest **Herrn Müllers** Brief.

CAUTION: Even though the use of the possessive adjectives **mein, dein,** and so on inherently show possession, they still have the genitive case along with the noun.

Das ist **mein** Onkel.	*That's my uncle.*
Das ist der Koffer **meines Onkels.**	*That's my uncle's suitcase (the suitcase of my uncle).*
Er ist der Bruder **meiner Mutter.**	*He's my mother's brother (the brother of my mother).*

2. These prepositions are followed by the genitive case.

(an)statt	*instead of*	Ich nehme oft den Bus **(an)statt der Straßenbahn.**
trotz	*in spite of*	**Trotz des Wetters** bummele ich gern durch die Stadt.
während	*during*	**Während der Mittagspause** gehe ich in den Park.
wegen	*because of*	Heute bleibe ich **wegen des Regens** *(rain)* hier.

Übungen

A. Im Reisebüro *(At the travel agency)* Überprüfen Sie *(check)* noch einmal, ob Ihr Assistent die Reise nach Bern auch gut vorbereitet hat!

> BEISPIEL   Wo ist die Liste der Touristen? (Hotel/*pl.*)
> *Wo ist die Liste der Hotels?*

1. Wie ist der Name des Reiseführers *(tour guide)*? (Schloss, Dom, Museum, Straße, Platz, Tourist, Touristin, Franzose, Französin)

2. Wo ist die Telefonnummer des Hotels? (Gästehaus, Pension, Gasthof, Jugendherberge)

3. Wo ist die Adresse dieser Dame? (Gast, Mädchen, Junge, Herr, Herren, Student, Studenten)

4. Wann ist die Ankunft unserer Gruppe? (Bus, Zug, Flugzeug, Reiseführerin, Gäste)

5. Haben Sie wegen der Reservierung *(reservation)* angerufen? (Zimmer, Schlüssel/*sg.*, Gepäck, Adresse, Theaterkarten)

6. Wir fahren trotz des Gewitters *(thunderstorm)*. (Wetter, Regen/*m.*, Eis, Feiertag, Ferien)

7. Christiane Binder kommt statt ihrer Mutter mit. (Vater, Bruder, Onkel, Nachbar, Nachbarin, Geschwister)

8. Die Lage des Hotels ist sehr zentral. (Bahnhof, Studentenwohnheim, Apotheke, Geschäfte)

Optional English-to-German practice: 1. Is that Eva's train? 2. Do you know the number of the platform? 3. No. Where's the departure schedule [of the trains]? 4. Her train leaves in a few minutes. 5. Take along Kurt's package. 6. Kurt is a student and a friend of a friend *(f.)*. 7. Eva, do you have the student's *(m.)* address? 8. No, but I know the name of the dorm. 9. I'll take (bring) it to him during the holidays. 10. Because of the exams, I don't have time now. 11. I'll send you a postcard instead of a letter. 12. And I'll send you an e-mail instead of a postcard. (See answer key in the Appendix.)

B. Bilden Sie Sätze mit dem Genitiv! Benutzen Sie Wörter von jeder Liste!

> BEISPIEL   *Die Abfahrt des Zuges ist um 19.05 Uhr.*

1	2	3		4	5
die Farbe	d-	Wagen	Gasthof	ist	_____
der Name	dies-	Bus	Ausweis	gefällt	
die Adresse	mein-	Zug	Pass	. . .	
die Nummer	unser-	Bahnsteig	Reisescheck		
das Zimmer	. . .	Koffer	Flug		
das Gepäck		Tasche	Frau		
die Abfahrt		Haus	Herr		
der Preis		Wohnung	Freund(in)		
die Lage *(location)*		Hotel	Tourist(in)		
. . .		Pension	Gäste		
		Berge	. . .		
		Postfach			
		. . .			

C. Wer ist diese Person? Fragen Sie Ihren Partner/Ihre Partnerin!

> BEISPIEL   S1 Wer ist der Vater deiner Mutter?
>   S2 Der Vater meiner Mutter ist mein Großvater.

1. Wer ist der Sohn deines Vaters? 2. Wer ist die Mutter deiner Mutter? 3. Wer ist die Tochter deiner Mutter? 4. Wer sind die Söhne und Töchter deiner Eltern? 5. Wer ist der Sohn deines Urgroßvaters *(great-grandfather)*? 6. Wer ist der Großvater deiner Mutter? 7. Wer ist die Schwester deiner Mutter? 8. Wer ist der Mann deiner Tante? 9. Wer ist die Tochter deines Großvaters?

D. Wem gehört das? Fragen Sie Ihren Partner/Ihre Partnerin!

> BEISPIEL   S1 Gehört die Jacke deinem Freund?
>   S2 Nein, das ist nicht die Jacke meines Freundes.
>   Das ist meine Jacke.

Gehört das Hemd deinem Bruder? Gehört die Uhr deiner Mutter? Gehört das Buch deinem Professor? Gehört die Tasche deiner Freundin? Gehört die Post deinem Nachbarn? Gehört der Kuli Frau . . . *(name a student)*? Gehört das Heft Herrn . . . *(name a student)*? usw.

8.2 Time expressions

1. Adverbs of time

> a. To refer to SPECIFIC TIMES, such as *yesterday evening* or *tomorrow morning*, combine one word from group A with another from group B. The words in group A can be used alone, whereas those in group B must be used in combinations: **gestern Abend, morgen früh.**

A

vorgestern	*the day before yesterday*
gestern	*yesterday*
heute	*today*
morgen	*tomorrow*
übermorgen	*the day after tomorrow*

B

früh, Morgen[1]	*early, morning*
Vormittag[2]	*midmorning (9 A.M.–noon)*[4]
Mittag	*noon (12–2 P.M.)*
Nachmittag	*afternoon (2–6 P.M.)*
Abend[3]	*evening (6–10 P.M.)*
Nacht[3]	*night (after 10 P.M.)*[4]

> ● All boldfaced vocabulary items in these lists are new and must be learned!

> **Morgen früh** bin ich in Frankfurt.
> **Übermorgen** fahre ich nach Bonn.
> **Montagabend** besuche ich Krauses.

---

[1] **Heute früh** is used in southern Germany, **heute Morgen** in northern Germany; both mean *this morning*, BUT *Tomorrow morning* is always **morgen früh.**

[2] The expressions in this column are commonly combined with the days of the week. In that combination—except for **früh**—they combine to make a compound noun: **Montagmorgen, Dienstagvormittag, Donnerstagabend,** BUT: **Montag früh.**

[3] German distinguishes clearly between **Abend** and **Nacht:** Wir sind **gestern Abend** ins Kino gegangen. Ich habe **gestern Nacht** schlecht geschlafen. **Heute Nacht** can mean *last night* or *tonight* (whichever is closer), depending on context.

[4] The times may vary somewhat, but these are close approximations.

b. Adverbs such as **montags** and **morgens** don't refer to specific time (a specific *Monday* or *morning*), but rather imply that events usually occur (more or less regularly), for example, *on Mondays* or *in the mornings, most mornings*. The following new expressions also belong to this group: **täglich** (*daily*), **wöchentlich** (*weekly*), **monatlich** (*monthly*), and **jährlich** (*yearly, annually*).

🟡 Note the difference in spelling: Kommst du **Dienstagabend?** Nein, **dienstagabends** kann ich nicht.

> montags, dienstags, mittwochs, donnerstags, freitags, samstags, sonntags; morgens, vormittags, mittags, nachmittags, abends, nachts, montagmorgens, dienstagabends, **täglich, wöchentlich, monatlich, jährlich**

Sonntags tue ich nichts, aber **montags** arbeite ich schwer.
Morgens und **nachmittags** gehe ich zur Uni. **Mittags** spiele ich Tennis.
Freitagabends gehen wir gern aus und **samstagmorgens** stehen wir dann nicht so früh auf.
Ich muss für die Wohnung **monatlich** 500 Euro zahlen.

2. Other time expressions

a. The accusative of time

To refer to a DEFINITE point in time (**wann?**) or length of time (**wie lange?**), German often uses time phrases in the accusative, without any prepositions. Here are some of the most common expressions.

wann?		wie lange?	
jeden Tag	*each day*	zwei Wochen	*for two weeks*
diese Woche	*this week*	einen Monat	*for one month*

Haben Sie diese Woche Zeit?	*Do you have time this week?*
Die Fahrt dauert zwei Stunden.	*The trip takes two hours.*
Ich bleibe zwei Tage in Zürich.	*I'll be in Zurich for two days.*

b. The genitive of time

To refer to an INDEFINITE point in time (in the past or future), German uses the genitive.

> **eines Tages**   *one day, some day*

Eines Tages ist ein Fax gekommen.	*One day, a fax came.*
Eines Tages fahre ich in die Schweiz.	*Some day, I'll go to Switzerland.*

The following new expressions also belong in this group:

🟡 Anfang / Mitte / Ende **des Monats** BUT: Anfang / Mitte / Ende **Mai**

> **Anfang / Ende der Woche**   *at the beginning / end of the week*
> **Mitte des Monats**   *in the middle of the month*

c. Prepositional time phrases

You are already familiar with the following phrases.

an	am Abend, am Wochenende, am Montag, am 1. April
bis	bis morgen, bis (um) 2.30 Uhr, bis (zum) Freitag, bis (zum) Januar
für	für morgen, für Freitag, für eine Nacht
in	im Juli, im Sommer, in einem Monat; in 10 Minuten, in einer Viertelstunde, in einer Woche, in einem Jahr
nach	nach dem Essen, nach einer Stunde
seit	seit einem Jahr, seit September
um	um fünf (Uhr)
von . . . bis	vom 1. Juni bis (zum) 25. August; von Juli bis August
vor	vor einem Monat, vor ein paar Tagen
während	während des Sommers, während des Tages

- Two-way prepositions usually use the <u>dative</u> in time expressions: Wir fahren **in einer Woche** in die Berge. **Am Freitag** fahren wir ab.
- German uses **seit** plus the present tense to describe an action or condition that began in the past and still continues in the present. English uses the present perfect or present perfect progressive to express the same thing: **Er wohnt seit zwei Jahren hier.** *(He has lived / has been living here for two years.)*

Übungen

E. Ein Besuch *(visit)* Was fehlt?

1. Sven und seine Frau sind _____ bei uns in Luzern angekommen. *(one week ago)*

2. Sie sind _____ abgereist und haben _____ im Zug gesessen. *(Thursday evening at 10 o'clock, for nine hours)*

3. Sven schläft _____ gewöhnlich nicht lange. *(in the morning)*

4. Aber er hat _____ geschlafen. *(this morning until 11 o'clock.)*

5. Die beiden bleiben ungefähr _____ hier. *(for one week)*

6. _____ haben wir einen Bummel *(stroll)* durch die Stadt gemacht. *(The day before yesterday)*

7. _____ gehen wir ins Konzert. *(This evening)*

8. _____ kommen Meike und Thomas vorbei. *(Tomorrow morning)*

9. _____ gehen wir alle essen. *(Tomorrow at noon)*

10. _____ machen wir eine Fahrt auf dem Vierwaldstätter See. *(In the afternoon)*

11. Was wir _____ machen, wissen wir noch nicht. *(the day after tomorrow)*

12. _____ machen wir etwas Besonderes. *(Every day)*

F. Bei mir Erzählen Sie Ihrer Gruppe, wie das bei Ihnen ist! Was tun Sie gewöhnlich? Was haben Sie neulich (*recently*) getan? Benutzen Sie Wörter von den Listen oder ergänzen Sie, was Sie brauchen!

BEISPIEL   *Morgens trinke ich gewöhnlich Kaffee, aber heute Morgen habe ich Tee getrunken.*

1	2	3	4	5	6
morgens	gewöhnlich	ausgehen	aber	letzte Woche	zu Hause bleiben
(nach)mittags	manchmal	in der Bibliothek arbeiten		diese Woche	meine Familie besuchen
(freitag)abends	meistens	die Wohnung putzen		vor ein paar Tagen	ins Konzert gehen
sonntags	oft	fernsehen (*watch TV*)		(vor)gestern	ein Buch lesen
während der Woche	immer	einkaufen gehen		gestern Abend	Tee trinken
am Wochenende	nie	E-Mails schreiben		heute Morgen	Musik hören
jeden Tag		im Internet surfen		(über)morgen	. . .
. . .		Kaffee trinken		. . .	
		. . .			

G. Allerlei Märkte in Bern Finden Sie mit Ihrem Partner/Ihrer Partnerin heraus, wann es welchen Markt wo gibt! Geben Sie die Antwort auf Deutsch und auf Englisch!

BEISPIEL   Weihnachtsmarkt
täglich im Dezember
every day in December

MÄRKTE
MARCHÉS
MARKETS

www.markt-bern.ch

BERN – DIE MÄRITSTADT

① WARENMARKT: AUF DEM WAISENHAUSPLATZ, DAS GANZE JAHR ÜBER JEDEN DIENSTAG UND SAMSTAG. VON ANFANGS APRIL BIS OKTOBER AUCH AM DONNERSTAG MIT ABENDVERKAUF.

② GEMÜSE-, FRÜCHTE- UND BLUMENMARKT: DAS GANZE JAHR AUF DEM BUNDES- UND BÄRENPLATZ UND DEN ANGRENZENDEN GASSEN, JEDEN DIENSTAG UND SAMSTAG VORMITTAGS. AUF DEM BÄRENPLATZ VON APRIL BIS OKTOBER TÄGLICH.

③ FLEISCHMARKT: DIENSTAG UND SAMSTAG VORMITTAGS, MÜNSTERGASSE.

④ HANDWERKMARKT: JEDEN ERSTEN SAMSTAG DES MONATS, MÜNSTERPLATZ.

⑤ FLOHMARKT: AUF DEM MÜHLEPLATZ IN DER MITTE JEDEN DRITTEN SAMSTAG DES MONATS VON MAI BIS OKTOBER.

⑥ GERANIENMARKT: NACH MITTE MAI AUF DEM BUNDESPLATZ, NUR VORMITTAGS.

ZWIEBELMARKT: AM VIERTEN MONTAG DES NOVEMBERS IN DER GANZEN STADT.

⑦ WEIHNACHTSMARKT: DEZEMBER TÄGLICH, MÜNSTER UND WAISENHAUSPLATZ.

Fokus — Switzerland's Mountain World

Not surprisingly, Switzerland has a number of popular and fashionable mountain resorts. The glacier village of **Grindelwald** in the Bernese Uplands is a favorite base for mountain climbers and skiers. **St. Moritz**, south of Davos, is nestled in the Upper Inn Valley next to a lake. Twice host to the Winter Olympics (1928 and 1948), the resort has become a jet-set sports mecca. Another fashionable area is **Saas Fee**, northeast of Zermatt. The village allows no motor vehicles to spoil its magnificent setting facing the great Fee glacier.

Besides the **Matterhorn** (14,692 ft.), the most famous Swiss peaks are the **Jungfrau, Mönch,** and **Eiger** (all ca. 13,000 ft.). A tunnel, almost 4.5 miles long, leads steeply up to the **Jungfraujoch** terminus (11,333 ft.). Its observation deck offers a superb view of the surrounding mountains and the lakes of central Switzerland. From there, on a very clear day, even the Black Forest in southern Germany can be seen.

Blick aufs Matterhorn

8.3 Sentence structure *(continued)*

1. Types of adverbs

   You have already encountered various adverbs and adverbial phrases. They are usually divided into three major groups.

   a. ADVERBS OF TIME, answering the questions **wann? wie lange?**

   am Abend, am 2. April, am 4. Montag, Anfang März, bis Mai, eine Woche, eines Tages, ein paar Minuten, Ende des Monats, heute, im Juni, immer, jetzt, manchmal, meistens, montags, Mitte Juli, morgens, nie, oft, stundenlang, täglich, um zwölf, vor einer Woche, während des Winters usw.

   b. ADVERBS OF MANNER, answering the question **wie?**

   gemütlich, langsam, laut, mit der Bahn, ohne Geld, schnell, zu Fuß, zusammen usw.

   c. ADVERBS OF PLACE, answering the questions **wo? wohin? woher?**

   auf der Post, bei uns, da, dort, hier, im Norden, zu Hause, mitten in der Stadt, überall, nach Berlin, nach Hause, auf die Post, zur Uni, aus Kanada, von Amerika, aus dem Flugzeug usw.

2. Sequence of adverbs

   If two or more adverbs or adverbial phrases occur in one sentence, they usually follow the sequence TIME, MANNER, PLACE.

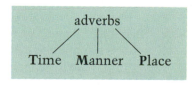

Er kann das Paket **morgen** **mit dem Auto** **zur Post** bringen.
　　　　　　　　　T　　　　　M　　　　　P

- If there is more than one time expression, general time references precede specific time references:

  Er bringt das Paket **morgen** **um zehn Uhr** zur Post.

- Like other sentence elements, adverbs and adverbial phrases may precede the verb.

> **Morgen** kann er das Paket mit dem Auto zur Post bringen.
> **Mit dem Auto** kann er das Paket morgen zur Post bringen.
> **Zur Post** kann er das Paket morgen mit dem Auto bringen.

3. Position of **nicht**

As you already know from Chapter 2, Section 2.3, **nicht** usually comes *after adverbs of definite time* but *before other adverbs, such as adverbs of manner or place.*

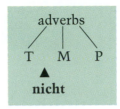

Er bringt das Paket ▲.
Er bringt das Paket ▲ mit.
Er kann das Paket ▲ mitbringen.
Er kann das Paket **morgen** ▲ mitbringen.
Er kann das Paket **morgen** ▲ **mit dem Auto** mitbringen.
Er kann das Paket **morgen** ▲ **mit dem Auto zur Post** bringen.

Übungen

H. Sagen Sie das noch einmal! Benutzen Sie die adverbialen Ausdrücke *(adverbial expressions)* in der richtigen Reihenfolge *(in the proper sequence)!*

> BEISPIEL   Ich kaufe die Briefmarken. (auf der Post, morgen)
> *Ich kaufe die Briefmarken morgen auf der Post.*

1. Er kommt an. (heute Abend, in Wien, mit dem Bus)
2. Sie reist. (nach Deutschland, ohne ihre Familie)
3. Deine Jeans liegen auf dem Sofa. (da drüben, seit drei Tagen)
4. Wir fahren. (zu meiner Tante, am Sonntag, mit der Bahn)
5. Gehst du? (zu Fuß, in die Stadt, heute Nachmittag)
6. Ich kaufe die Eier. (samstags, auf dem Markt, billig)
7. Wir wollen ins Kino gehen. (zusammen, morgen Abend)
8. Ihr müsst umsteigen. (in einer Viertelstunde, in den Zug nach Nürnberg)
9. Sie lässt die Kinder in St. Gallen. (bei den Großeltern, ein paar Tage)

I. So kann man's auch sagen. Beginnen Sie jeden Satz mit dem fettgedruckten *(boldfaced)* Satzteil und sagen Sie es dann auf Englisch!

> BEISPIEL   Wir bleiben **während der Ferien** gewöhnlich zu Hause.
> *Während der Ferien bleiben wir gewöhnlich zu Hause.*
> *During vacations, we usually stay home.*

1. Wir haben gewöhnlich keine Zeit **für Reisen.**
2. Patrick hat **gerade** mit seiner Schwester in Amerika gesprochen.
3. Sie ist **seit einer Woche** bei ihrem Bruder in Florida.
4. Wir wollen sie alle **am Wochenende** besuchen *(visit)*.
5. Das finde ich **schön.**

Fokus

Switzerland and Its Languages

European motor vehicles usually carry a small sticker indicating the country of origin: *D* stands for Germany, *A* for Austria, and *CH* for Switzerland. The abbreviation *CH* stands for the Latin *Confoederatio Helvetica,* a reference to the Celtic tribe of the Helvetii who settled the territory of modern Switzerland when Julius Caesar prevented them from moving to Gaul (today's France). The neutral choice of *CH* is a good example of how the Swiss avoid giving preference to one of their four national languages.

Roughly 70% of the Swiss speak a dialect of Swiss-German (**Schwyzerdütsch**); 20% speak French; 9% Italian; and a tiny minority (1%) speaks Romansh (**Rätoromanisch**). Most Swiss people understand two or three—some even all four—of these languages. This quadrilingualism goes back to the time when the Romans colonized the area. Over time, tribes from present-day Italy, France, and Germany migrated to the region. Romansh is a Romance language that has evolved little from Vulgar Latin and is spoken mainly in the remote valleys of the Grisons (canton *Graubünden*). Although it became one of the four official languages in 1938, Romansh has been under constant pressure from the other major languages in surrounding areas. The fact that Romansh is not one language but a group of dialects (including **Ladin**) makes it even harder to preserve.

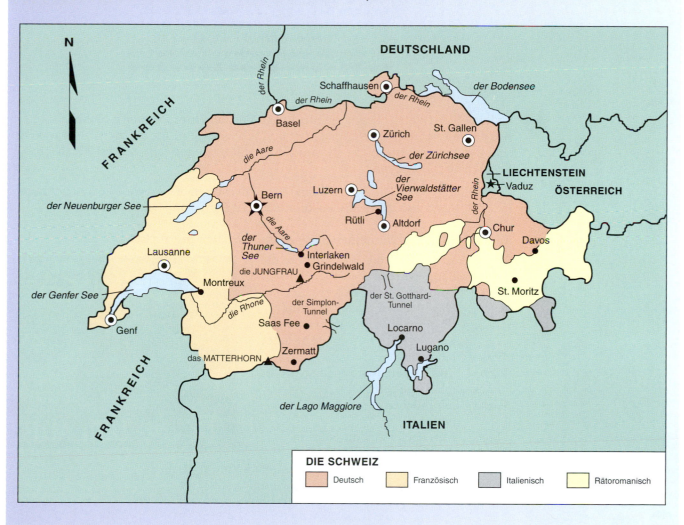

DIE SCHWEIZ
Deutsch — Französisch — Italienisch — Rätoromanisch

J. Das stimmt nicht. Lesen Sie mit Ihrem Partner/Ihrer Partnerin, welche Busreisen es zwischen Weihnachten und Silvester gibt! Ihr Partner/Ihre Partnerin sagt dann etwas, was nicht stimmt, und Sie korrigieren *(correct)* es! Wechseln Sie sich ab *(take turns)*!

BEISPIEL   S1 Die 7-Tage-Busreise zu Silvester in die Schweiz kostet 299 Euro.
S2 Nein, sie kostet nicht 299 Euro, sondern 619 Euro.

K. Ferienwünsche Verneinen Sie *(negate)* die Sätze mit **nicht!**

TANJA	Ich möchte diesen Winter in die Berge fahren.
LARS	Gefallen dir die Berge?
TANJA	Das habe ich gesagt. Warum fliegen wir diesen Winter nach Korsika? 279 Euro ist sehr teuer.
LARS	Ich weiß.
TANJA	Im Flugzeug wird man so müde.
LARS	Ich fliege gern.
TANJA	Ich möchte aber mit dem Auto fahren.
LARS	Mittags kannst du lange in der Sonne liegen.
TANJA	Morgens und nachmittags ist die Sonne so heiß.
LARS	In den Bergen ist es so langweilig.
TANJA	Gut. Wenn wir nach Spanien fliegen, komme ich mit.

Visit the *Wie geht's?* iLrn website for more review and practice of the grammar points you have just learned.

Zusammenfassung

 L. Hoppla, hier fehlt was! Wo sind sie gewesen? Sie und Ihr Partner/Ihre Partnerin erzählen einander *(each other)*, was Ihre Freunde während der Ferien gemacht haben. Finden Sie heraus, was Sie nicht wissen! Einer von Ihnen *(one of you)* sieht auf die Tabelle auf der nächsten Seite, der andere *(the other one)* auf die Tabelle im Anhang *(Appendix)*, Teil 11.

S1:

Wer	Wann / Wie lange	Wie / Obj. + Präposition	Wo und was
Lucian		gemütlich	durch Italien reisen
Christl	ein- Monat		
Steffi	dies- Sommer		zu Hause bleiben
Nina + Kim		mit dem Schiff	
Ben + Michi	jed- Nachmittag	zusammen	
Günther	im August		
Jutta		als Au-Pair	in London arbeiten
Nicole	vor einer Woche		
Yvonne		meistens	im Fitnessstudio trainieren
Jochen			im Restaurant jobben

BEISPIEL   S1 Ich weiß, dass Lucian gemütlich durch Italien gereist ist.
Aber wann?
                 S2 Das weiß ich nicht genau. Ich weiß nur, dass er ein paar
Wochen gereist ist. Und hast du gehört, was Christl gemacht
hat? Sie ist . . .

M. Frau Köchli Bilden Sie Sätze!

BEISPIEL   Hauptstadt / Schweiz / sein / Bern
Die Hauptstadt der Schweiz ist Bern.

1. Tante / unsere Freunde / leben / hier in Bern
2. leider / ich / nicht / wissen / die / Adresse / diese Tante
3. Name / Dame / sein / Köchli
4. wegen / dieser Name / ich / nicht / können / finden / Frau Köchli
5. statt / eine Köchli / da / sein / viele Köchlis
6. du / nicht / wissen / Telefonnummer / euere Freunde?
7. Nummer / stehen / in / Adressbuch / meine Frau
8. ich / nicht / können / finden / Inge / Adressbuch
9. ein Tag / Inge / es / hoffentlich / wieder / finden
10. können / ihr / mir / sagen / Name / ein Hotel?
11. trotz / Preise *(pl.)* / wir / brauchen / Hotelzimmer
12. während / Feiertage / du / haben / Probleme *(pl.)* / wegen / Touristen *(pl.)*

N. Mein Alltag *(My daily life)* Schreiben Sie 8–10 Sätze über *(about)* Ihren Alltag,
zum Beispiel wann Sie aufstehen, wann Sie essen, wann Sie zur Schule / Uni
gehen, welche Vorlesungen Sie wann haben, was Sie abends und am Wochenende
tun usw.! Benutzen Sie so viele Zeitausdrücke wie möglich *(as possible)*!

BEISPIEL   *Ich bin fast jeden Tag an der Uni. Morgens stehe ich um
sechs auf . . .*

Fokus William Tell

William Tell (**Wilhelm Tell**) is a legendary Swiss folk hero and a universal symbol of resistance to oppression. In 1307, he purportedly refused to obey the commands of the tyrannical Austrian bailiff, Gessler, who then forced him to shoot an arrow through an apple on his son's head. Tell did so, but later took revenge by killing Bailiff Gessler. That event was the beginning of a general uprising of the Swiss against the Habsburgs, the ruling dynasty since 1273. In 1439, when the Habsburgs tried to bring Switzerland back under Austrian rule, the Confederation broke free of the Empire. The story of Tell's confrontation with Gessler inspired Friedrich Schiller's drama *Wilhelm Tell* (1804) and Rossini's opera *Guillaume Tell* (1829).

Einblicke

Wortschatz 2

das Dorf, ¨er	*village*
Schnäppchen, -	*bargain*
die Gegend, -en	*area, region*
Geschichte, -n	*history; story*
herrlich	*wonderful, great*
beschreiben, beschrieben	*to describe*
hinauf·fahren (fährt hinauf),	*to go or drive*
ist hinaufgefahren	*up (to)*
weiter·fahren (fährt weiter),	*to drive on, keep*
ist weitergefahren	*on driving*

Jeder Preis ein tolles Schnäppchen!

Vor dem Lesen

A. Etwas Geographie Sehen Sie auf die Landkarte der Schweiz auf Seite 219 und beantworten Sie die Fragen!

1. Wie heißen die Nachbarländer der Schweiz? Wo liegen sie?
2. Wie heißt die Hauptstadt der Schweiz?
3. Nennen Sie ein paar Schweizer Flüsse, Seen und Berge! Welcher Fluss fließt weiter *(flows on)* nach Deutschland / nach Frankreich? Welcher See liegt zwischen der Schweiz und Deutschland / Italien / Frankreich?
4. Wo liegt Bern? Basel? Zürich? Luzern? Genf? Lausanne? Zermatt? Lugano? St. Moritz? Davos? Saas Fee? Grindelwald?
5. Wo spricht man Deutsch? Französisch? Italienisch? Rätoromanisch?
6. Was assoziieren Sie mit der Schweiz?

Im Stadtzentrum von Bern

B. Besuch in Bern Lesen Sie mit Ihrem Partner/Ihrer Partnerin, wie man als Tourist Bern kennen lernen kann: zu Fuß, mit dem Bus oder mit dem Schlauchboot *(inflatable raft)*! Stellen Sie einander *(each other)* Fragen und beantworten Sie sie!

BEISPIEL S1 Wo beginnt die Stadtrundfahrt mit dem Schlauchboot?
S2 Sie beginnt am Schwellenmätteli.

Stadtrundfahrt

Stadtrundfahrt durch Bern unter kundiger lokaler Führung mit Besichtigung des Rosengartens, des Bärengrabens, des Zeitglockenturms, des Münsters sowie des Botschaftsviertels.

1.11.–31. 3.	Sa	**14.00 Uhr**
1. 4.–31.10.	täglich	**14.00 Uhr**
Preis	*Erwachsene*	*CHF 24.—*
	Kinder 6–16 Jahre	*CHF 12.—*
Dauer	*2 Stunden*	
Treffpunkt	**Bahnhof, Tourist Center**	

Stadtrundfahrt im Schlauchboot

Lernen Sie Bern aus einer unbekannten Perspektive kennen. Die Schlauchbootrundfahrt führt Sie vorbei an mächtigen Sandsteinbrücken und blumengeschmückten Häusern. (Rundfahrt in Zusammenarbeit mit Berger Aktiv-Reisen)

2.6.–30.9.	Di, Do, Sa, So	**17.00 Uhr**
Preis	*Erwachsene*	*CHF 30.—*
	Kinder 6–16 Jahre	*CHF 20.—*
Dauer	*1½ Stunden*	
Treffpunkt	**Schwellenmätteli**	

Altstadtbummel

Ein(e) sprachkundige(r) Stadtführer(in) begleitet Sie auf einer Entdeckungsreise durch die Berner Altstadt (UNESCO Welterbe) und führt Sie zu den schönsten Sehenswürdigkeiten der Bundesstadt.

1.6.–30.9.	täglich	**11.00 Uhr**
Preis	*Erwachsene*	*CHF 14.—*
	Kinder 6–16 Jahre	*CHF 7.—*
Dauer	*1½ Stunden*	
Treffpunkt	**Bahnhof, Tourist Center**	

C. Das ist leicht zu verstehen! Welche Silbe ist betont? Markieren Sie sie! Was ist das auf Englisch?

der Film, Besucher, Kanton, Wintersport; das Kurzinterview, Panorama; die Alpenblume, Arkade, Bergbahn, Konferenz, Nation, Rückreise, Schneeszene, Viersprachigkeit; bergsteigen gehen, faszinieren, filmen; autofrei, elegant

Touristen in der Schweiz

CD 6,
Track 4

In Kurzinterviews mit Touristen in Altdorf, Bern und Saas Fee hören wir, was Besuchern in der Schweiz besonders gefällt:

FELIX: Ich finde die Gegend um den Vierwaldstätter See besonders interessant wegen ihrer Geschichte. Gestern bin ich in Luzern gewesen und auch über die
5 Holzbrücke° aus dem Jahr 1408 gelaufen. Heute früh bin ich mit dem Schiff von Luzern zum Rütli gefahren, wo 1291 die drei Kantone Uri, Schwyz und Unterwalden ihren Bund gemacht haben° und die Schweiz als eine Nation begonnen hat. Dann bin ich weitergefahren nach Altdorf zum Wilhelm-Tell-Denkmal und heute Abend gehe ich zu den Wilhelm-Tell-Freilichtspielen°. Dieses Wochenende
10 ist hier auch Bundesfeier° mit Umzügen° und Feuerwerk. Dann geht's wieder zurück mit dem Zug. Die Fahrt durch die Berge ist einfach herrlich.

wooden bridge

created their confederation

outdoor performances
national holiday / parades

Lesetipp
Looking for Genitives

Note the use of genitive constructions in this reading. How many examples of the genitive case can you find? In each case, determine whether the genitive is being used to express a close relationship between two nouns or whether it follows a certain preposition.

fountains

FRAU WEBER: Mir gefällt Bern wegen seiner Arkaden und Brunnen°. Mein Mann und ich fahren fast jedes Jahr im Juni oder Juli in die Schweiz. Auf unserer Fahrt kommen wir gewöhnlich durch Bern und bleiben hier ein paar Tage. Wenn wir

flea market / crafts fair

15 Glück haben, ist gerade Flohmarkt° oder Handwerksmarkt°. Da haben wir schon manches Schnäppchen gemacht. Morgen fahren wir weiter nach Grindelwald ins Berner Oberland. Wir wollen mit der Bergbahn zum Jungfraujoch hinauffahren

enjoy

und von dort oben den Blick auf die Berge genießen°. Trotz der vielen Touristen ist das Berner Oberland immer wieder schön. Haben Sie gewusst, dass man fast 20 alle Schneeszenen der James-Bond-Filme im Berner Oberland gefilmt hat? Auf der Rückreise haben wir Aufenthalt in Zürich, wo mein Mann mit den Banken zu tun hat. Der See mit dem Panorama der Berge ist herrlich. Während der Konferenzen meines Mannes bummle ich gern durch die Stadt. Die Geschäfte in der Bahnhofstraße sind elegant, aber teuer.

Zürich mit Blick auf den Limmat und den Zürichsee

25 FRAU LORENZ: Die Viersprachigkeit der Schweiz fasziniert uns. Unsere Reise hat in Lausanne begonnen, wo wir Französisch gesprochen haben. Jetzt sind wir hier in Saas Fee bei Freunden. Mit uns sprechen sie Hochdeutsch, aber mit der Familie Schwyzerdütsch. Saas Fee ist nur ein Dorf, aber wunderschön. Es ist autofrei und in den Bergen kann man überall wandern und bergsteigen gehen.

altitude / mountain goats
glaciers

30 Wegen der Höhenlage° gibt es viele Alpenblumen und Gämsen° und oben auf den Gletschern° kann man sogar während des Sommers immer noch Ski laufen gehen. Übermorgen fahren wir weiter nach St. Moritz, wo man viel Rätoromanisch hört. Am Ende der Reise wollen wir noch nach Lugano, wo das Wetter fast immer schön sein soll und die Leute Italienisch sprechen. Vier Sprachen in 35 einem Land, das ist schon toll.

Aktives zum Text

A. Richtig oder falsch? Wenn falsch, sagen Sie warum!

_____ 1. Felix findet die Gegend um den Bodensee so interessant wegen ihrer Geschichte.

_____ 2. Die Schweiz hat 1691 als Nation begonnen.

_____ 3. Felix ist wegen des Wilhelm-Tell-Denkmals und der Freilichtspiele in Altdorf.

_____ 4. Frau Weber und ihr Mann fahren jeden Winter ins Berner Oberland.

_____ 5. Während ihrer Reise bleiben sie gewöhnlich ein paar Tage in Bern, weil ihnen die Stadt so gut gefällt.

_____ 6. An Markttagen haben sie dort schon manches Schnäppchen gemacht.

_____ 7. Herr Weber hat in Zürich oft mit der Universität zu tun.

_____ 8. Zürich ist eine Stadt am Genfer See mit dem Panorama der Berge.

_____ 9. Familie Lorenz ist fasziniert von den Sprachen der Schweiz.

_____ 10. Mit ihren Freunden in Saas Fee sprechen sie Rätoromanisch.

_____ 11. Am Ende der Reise fahren sie noch nach Lausanne.

_____ 12. In Lausanne spricht man Italienisch.

B. Etwas Geschichte Lesen Sie laut!

Im Jahr 1291 schlossen Uri, Schwyz und Unterwalden am Rütli einen Bund. Luzern ist 1332 dazu gekommen (here: _joined it_) und Zürich 1351. 1513 hat es 13 Kantone gegeben. Heute, im Jahr 20___ _(add current year)_, sind es 26 Kantone. 1848 ist die Schweiz ein Bundesstaat geworden. Im 1. Weltkrieg (1914–1918) und im 2. Weltkrieg (1939–1945) ist die Schweiz neutral geblieben. Trotz ihrer Tradition von Demokratie können die Frauen der Schweiz erst seit 1971 in allen Kantonen wählen _(vote)_. Seit 1981 gibt es offiziell auch keine Diskriminierung der Frau mehr.

C. Die Eidgenossenschaft _(The Swiss Confederacy)_ Wiederholen Sie die Sätze mit den Ausdrücken in Klammern. Manchmal gibt es mehrere Möglichkeiten.

BEISPIEL   Viele Touristen fahren in die Schweiz. (jedes Jahr)
Viele Touristen fahren jedes Jahr in die Schweiz.
Jedes Jahr fahren viele Touristen in die Schweiz.

1. Felix findet die Gegend um den Vierwaldstätter See interessant. (wegen ihrer Geschichte)
2. Felix ist mit einem Schiff zum Rütli gefahren. (von Luzern)
3. Die drei Kantone Uri, Schwyz und Unterwalden haben ihren Bund am Rütli geschlossen. (1291)
4. Viele Touristen wollen Wilhelm Tells Denkmal sehen. (natürlich)
5. In der Schweiz feiert man die Bundesfeier. (jedes Jahr am 1. August)
6. Felix ist noch einen Tag geblieben. (wegen dieses Festes)

Eine Familie auf dem Bahnsteig (platform) _bekommt Hilfe mit dem Koffer._

D. Kurzgespräche Erzählen Sie den anderen von Ihrer Reise! Was sagen sie dazu *(to that)*?

1. **Die Heimreise** *(trip home)*

   The weather was awful. Your plane arrived two hours late (**mit zwei Stunden Verspätung**) and departed five hours late. You arrived at two o'clock in the morning. Your suitcase wasn't there. There were no buses into town. You didn't have enough cash for a taxi. You phoned your father. You got home at 4 A.M. You were very tired.

2. **Im Schwyzerhüsli**

   Staying overnight: You and your friend arrived in Schaffhausen on the Rhine. You inquired at three hotels, but they had no rooms available. They sent you to the *Schwyzerhüsli*. There they had some rooms. Since you were very tired, you went to bed early **(ins Bett).** There was a party in the hotel until midnight. Then cars kept driving by. It was very loud. At 4 A.M. your neighbors got up, talked in the hallway **(im Gang)** and got into their car. You couldn't sleep anymore, so you got up too, and left. What a night!

E. Wer möchte mit uns tauschen *(trade)*? Lesen Sie die Anzeige und schreiben Sie zurück! Sagen Sie, dass Sie gern einmal tauschen möchten, und beschreiben Sie, was Sie zu bieten haben *(have to offer)*!

Schreibtipp
Choosing Subject Pronouns

Avoid switching back and forth between *one* (**man**) and *you* (**Sie**); try to be consistent. Also, vary your sentence structure, and don't start too many sentences with **ich**. If you are using a compound subject that includes yourself, never name yourself first: Write **Mein Freund und ich . . .** , *not* **Ich und mein Freund . . .** ! Remember: „**Der Esel nennt sich selbst zuerst: Iah!**" (literally: *The donkey names itself first: Hee-haw*)

WOHNUNGSTAUSCH IN DEN FERIEN
ZEIT: 20. JULI BIS 30. AUGUST

Wir bieten:
Unsere Wohnung in der Nähe von Zürich: Wohnzimmer, Küche, Bad, 2 Schlafzimmer, Balkon, Blick auf die Berge, 15 Minuten Fahrt mit der S-Bahn ins Zentrum von Zürich.

Wir suchen:
Wohnung in Amerika oder Kanada, wenn möglich im Zentrum und nicht weit zur Universität.

Wer möchte mit uns tauschen?

Nadine und Martin Hunkeler
Erlenstrasse 10
8134 Adliswil
Schweiz

 Hörverständnis

Track 17 **Im Reisebüro** Was stimmt?

Zum Erkennen: Skilift inbegriffen *(ski lift included)*; die Broschüre, -n *(brochure)*

1. Ulrike und Steffi möchten im _____ reisen.
   a. August
   b. März
   c. Januar

2. Sie wollen _____.
   a. wandern
   b. bergsteigen gehen
   c. Ski laufen gehen

3. Ulrike reserviert ein Zimmer im Hotel _____.
   a. Alpenrose
   b. Alpina
   c. Eiger

4. Ulrike und Steffi fahren mit der Bahn bis _____.
   a. Bern
   b. Interlaken
   c. Grindelwald

5. Sie kommen um _____ Uhr an ihrem Ziel *(destination)* an.
   a. 12.16
   b. 12.30
   c. 13.00

6. Sie fahren am _____ um _____ nach Hause zurück.
   a. 15. / vierzehn
   b. 14. / drei
   c. 16. / sechs

Statistics about Switzerland, a trip to Saas Fee, Swiss export items: http://wiegehts.heinle.com.

Literatur

■ Beginning with this chapter, there will be a brief section with original literature (**die Literatur**) by one or two authors, introduced by a biographical note on the author(s) and accompanied by pre- and post-reading exercises. ■

Biographisches

Hermann Hesse (1899–1962) was awarded the Nobel Prize for literature in 1946. Although born in Germany, he became a Swiss citizen at the outbreak of World War I. The first stage of his writing began with his romantic rendering of the artist as a social outcast. At the beginning of the war, the strain of his pacifist beliefs and domestic crises led him to undergo psychoanalysis, which gave a new dimension to his work. The novels *Demian, Siddhartha,* and *Steppenwolf* were influenced by his readings of Nietzsche, Dostoyevsky, Spengler, and Buddhist mysticism, and are based on his conviction that people must discover their own nature. A third phase began in 1930, balancing the artist's rebellion against the constraints of social behavior. After 1943, when his name was put on the Nazi blacklist, he quit writing novels and concentrated on poems, stories, and essays that articulated a humanistic spirit reminiscent of Goethe's **Weltbürgertum** *(world citizenship)*. Hesse's works also reflect his faith in the spirituality of all mankind, for which he coined the term **Weltglaube.**

Vor dem Lesen

Allgemeine *(general)* Fragen

1. Lesen Sie gern Gedichte *(poems)*? Warum (nicht)?
2. Haben Sie einen Lieblingsdichter *(favorite poet)* oder ein Lieblingsgedicht? Wenn ja, welches Gedicht / welchen Dichter?
3. Warum sind Gedichte oft so zeitlos *(timeless)*?
4. Haben Sie schon mal ein Gedicht auswendig *(by heart)* gelernt? Wenn ja, welches? Können Sie es heute noch auswendig?
5. Dieses Gedicht spricht von Einsamsein *(being lonely)*. Welche Adjektive und Hauptwörter *(nouns)* im Gedicht sind typisch für das Thema?

 Im Nebel

Track 18

Seltsam°, im Nebel° zu wandern!　　　　　　strange / fog
Einsam° ist jeder Busch und Stein,　　　　　　lonely
Kein Baum sieht den andern,
Jeder ist allein.

5　Voll von Freunden war° mir die Welt°,　　　was / world
Als° noch mein Leben licht° war;　　　　　　when / light
Nun, da der Nebel fällt,
Ist keiner mehr sichtbar°.　　　　　　　　　　visible

Wahrlich°, keiner ist weise°,	truly / wise
10 Der nicht das Dunkel kennt,	
Das unentrinnbar° und leise°	inescapably / quietly
Von allen ihn trennt°.	separates

Seltsam, im Nebel zu wandern!
Leben ist Einsamsein.
15 Kein Mensch kennt den andern,
Jeder ist allein.

Hermann Hesse

Nach dem Lesen

A. Fragen zum Gedicht

1. Was ist typisch, wenn es neblig *(foggy)* ist?
2. Wo sind oft die Freunde im Nebel des Lebens?
3. Wie ist das Leben ohne Freunde?
4. Warum ist eine Zeit der Dunkelheit manchmal auch wichtig?
5. Wie ist die Stimmung *(mood)* dieses Gedichts?
6. Wie gefällt Ihnen das Gedicht? Warum?

B. Aufsatz: Ein paar Gedanken *(thoughts)* zum Thema Einsamkeit Tun Sie so, als ob Sie einsam sind und in Ihr Tagebuch *(journal/diary)* schreiben! Warum sind Sie einsam? Was geht Ihnen da alles durch den Kopf? Schreiben Sie sechs bis acht Sätze!

Freizeit und Gesundheit

Lernziele

In this chapter you will learn about:

Zum Thema

Hobbies, leisure activities, and
  physical fitness

Kultur-Fokus

Telephone customs, idioms,
  German pop music, clubs, and
  vacationing
Johann Wolfgang von Goethe,
  Rose Ausländer

Struktur

Endings of preceded adjectives
Reflexive verbs
Infinitives with **zu**

Einblicke + Literatur

Freizeit—Lust oder Frust?
Johann Wolfgang von Goethe:
  "Erinnerung"
Rose Ausländer: "Noch bist du da"

For more information,
go to
http://iLrn.heinle.com

Radtour mit der Familie

Vorschau

Sports and Clubs in the German-Speaking Countries

Minidrama: *Lachen ist die beste Medizin.*

Sports are very popular in Germany, Austria, and Switzerland, not only with spectators—professional sports are big business, as they are anywhere else—but also with amateur athletes. One out of every three people belongs to a sports club **(der Sportverein).** The German Sports Federation **(Deutscher Sportbund)** has more than 75,000 affiliated sports clubs. It sponsors such programs as **Trimm dich** and **Sport für alle** with competitions in running, swimming, cycling, and skiing. Millions of people participate in these events every year. Soccer **(Fußball)** is as important in Europe as football, baseball, and basketball are in North America. Other popular sports are **Handball,** ice hockey, roller skating, and inline skating. Golf and tennis are also becoming more popular, but you usually need to belong to a club in order to play.

High schools and universities are not involved in competitive sports; if they want to play competitively, young people usually join a sports club. Such organizations are basically autonomous, but the government provides some support for those with insufficient funds. This applies particularly to the former East Germany, where an effort has been made to set up independent clubs. In the 1970s and 1980s, these clubs did not exist; instead, the East German government spent a great deal of money on making sports accessible to every citizen, seeking out talented youth early in life and training them in special boarding schools—a practice that led to considerable success in the Olympic Games.

In addition to sports clubs, there are associations promoting all kinds of leisure activities, ranging from dog breeding and pigeon racing to gardening, crafts, music, and dancing. Clubs devoted to regional traditions and dress **(Trachtenvereine)** and centuries-old rifle associations **(Schützenvereine)**—with their own emblems, uniforms, and ceremonial meetings—keep old traditions alive and draw thousands to their annual festivals.

Marathonlauf in Bern

Zum Thema

 Am Telefon

CD 6,
Track 6

FRAU SCHMIDT	Hier Schmidt.
ANNEMARIE	Guten Tag, Frau Schmidt. Ich bin's, Annemarie.
FRAU SCHMIDT	Tag, Annemarie!
ANNEMARIE	Ist Thomas da?
FRAU SCHMIDT	Nein, tut mir Leid. Er ist gerade zur Post gegangen.
ANNEMARIE	Ach so. Können Sie ihm sagen, dass ich heute Abend nicht mit ihm ausgehen kann?
FRAU SCHMIDT	Natürlich. Was ist denn los?
ANNEMARIE	Ich bin krank. Mir tut der Hals weh und ich habe Kopfschmerzen.
FRAU SCHMIDT	Das tut mir Leid. Gute Besserung!
ANNEMARIE	Danke. Auf Wiederhören!
FRAU SCHMIDT	Wiederhören!

Bis gleich!

YVONNE	Bei Mayer.
DANIELA	Hallo, Yvonne! Ich bin's, Daniela.
YVONNE	Tag, Daniela! Was gibt's?
DANIELA	Nichts Besonderes. Hast du Lust, Squash zu spielen oder schwimmen zu gehen?
YVONNE	Squash? Nein, danke. Ich habe noch Muskelkater von vorgestern. Ich kann mich kaum rühren. Mir tut alles weh.
DANIELA	Lahme Ente! Wie wär's mit Schach?
YVONNE	Okay, das klingt gut. Kommst du zu mir?
DANIELA	Ja, bis gleich!

A. Wie geht's weiter?

1. Annemaries Freund heißt . . . 2. Annemarie spricht mit . . . 3. Thomas ist nicht zu Hause, weil . . . 4. Annemarie kann nicht mit ihm . . . 5. Annemaries Hals . . . 6. Sie hat auch . . . 7. Am Ende eines Telefongesprächs sagt man . . . 8. Danielas Freundin heißt . . . 9. Yvonne will nicht Squash spielen, weil . . . 10. Sie hat aber Lust, . . .

 B. Jetzt sind Sie dran! Diesmal sind Sie am Telefon. Sie rufen Ihren Freund/Ihre Freundin an und fragen, ob er/sie Lust hat, etwas zu tun. Aber Sie haben Pech, denn er/sie hat schon Pläne *(plans)* oder ist krank. Wechseln Sie sich ab!

S1 Hier . . .
S2 Tag, . . . ! Ich bin's, . . . Sag mal, hast du Lust, . . . ?
S1 Nein, ich kann nicht . . .
S2 Warum nicht? Was ist los?
S1 Ich bin krank. Mir tut/tun . . . weh.
S2 . . . Wie lange hast du schon . . . schmerzen?
S1 Seit . . .
S2 Hoffentlich . . . Gute Besserung!
S1 . . .

When answering the phone, German-speakers usually identify themselves with their last names. If you were answering your own phone, you would say **Hier . . .** (plus your own name). If you were answering someone else's phone, say Ms. Schmidt's, you would say **(Hier) bei Schmidt.** Only afterwards do you say **Guten Tag!** or **Hallo!** If you are the one making the call, you usually give your own name before asking for the person you are trying to reach: **Guten Abend, hier** spricht . . . (or **Ich bin's, . . .**). **Kann ich bitte mit . . . sprechen?** or **Ich möchte gern . . . sprechen.** The answer might be **Einen Moment bitte!** or **. . . ist nicht da. Kann ich ihm/ihr etwas ausrichten** *(take a message for him/her)?* When ending a phone conversation formally, say **Auf Wiederhören!** (lit. *until we hear each other again*). Friends may simply say **Tschüss!, Mach's gut!, Bis bald!,** or **Bis gleich!**

Wortschatz 1

Das Hobby, -s *(hobby)*

angeln	to fish
backen (bäckt), gebacken	to bake
faulenzen	to be lazy
fern·sehen (sieht fern), ferngesehen	to watch TV
fotografieren	to take pictures
(Freunde) treffen (trifft), getroffen	to meet, get together (with friends)
malen	to paint
<u>sammeln</u>	to collect
schwimmen, ist geschwommen	to swim
Schwimmst du gern?	*Do you like to swim?*
wandern, ist gewandert	to hike

Verb + complement

Dame / Schach spielen	to play checkers / chess
Rad fahren (fährt), ist gefahren	to bicycle, bike
Ich fahre viel Rad.	*I bike a lot.*
Ski laufen (läuft), ist gelaufen	to ski
Lauft ihr gern Ski?	*Do you like to ski?*
Sie läuft gern Ski.	*She loves to ski.*
Sport treiben, getrieben	to engage in sports
Sie treiben nie Sport.	*They never do any sports.*

Verb + gehen

schwimmen gehen, ist gegangen	to go swimming
Ich gehe gern schwimmen.	*I like to go swimming.*
Ski laufen gehen, ist gegangen	to go skiing
Wir gehen gern Ski laufen.	*We like to go skiing.*
spazieren gehen, ist gegangen	to go for a walk (lit.: *walking*)

Die Freizeit *(leisure time)*

der Fußball	soccer
Sport	sport(s), athletics
das Klavier, -e	piano
Spiel, -e	game
die CD, -s	CD
DVD, -s	DVD
Gitarre, -n	guitar
Idee, -n	idea
Karte, -n	card
Kassette, -n	cassette

◉ **sammeln:** ich samm(e)le, du sammelst, er sammelt, wir sammeln, ihr sammelt, sie sammeln. Also like **sammeln:** bummeln, angeln, wechseln, tun

◉ **Verb + complement:** In expressions such as **Rad fahren, Ski laufen, Schach spielen,** and **Sport treiben,** the verb functions as V1, while the other word (the verb complement) functions as V2.

◉ **Verb + gehen:** In these constructions, **gehen** functions as V1 and the other verb or verb + complement as V2. The same holds true for **spazieren gehen,** and could be done with verbs like **angeln, Rad fahren.** Another way of saying **Ich gehe Ski laufen** is **ich gehe zum Skilaufen.** In that case, **Skilaufen** is capitalized and one word, since it is used as a noun.

Skipause oberhalb (above) Innsbruck

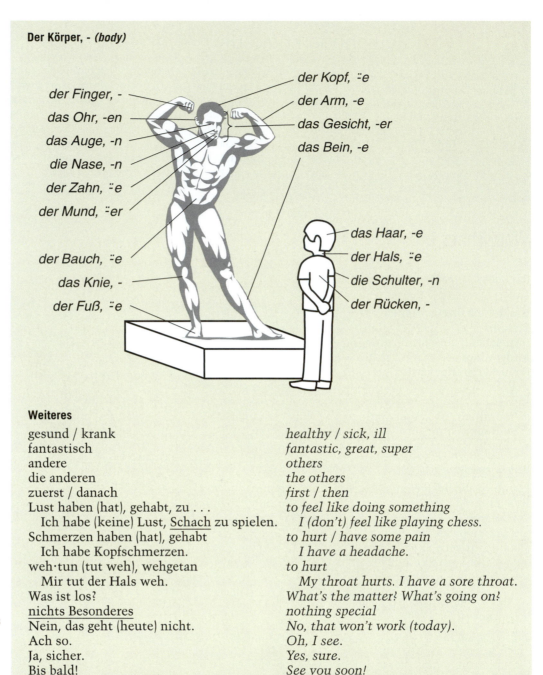

Der Körper, - *(body)*

der Finger, -
das Ohr, -en
das Auge, -n
die Nase, -n
der Zahn, ⸚e
der Mund, ⸚er
der Bauch, ⸚e
das Knie, -
der Fuß, ⸚e

der Kopf, ⸚e
der Arm, -e
das Gesicht, -er
das Bein, -e

das Haar, -e
der Hals, ⸚e
die Schulter, -n
der Rücken, -

Weiteres

gesund / krank	*healthy / sick, ill*
fantastisch	*fantastic, great, super*
andere	*others*
die anderen	*the others*
zuerst / danach	*first / then*
Lust haben (hat), gehabt, zu . . .	*to feel like doing something*
Ich habe (keine) Lust, <u>Schach</u> zu spielen.	*I (don't) feel like playing chess.*
Schmerzen haben (hat), <u>gehabt</u>	*to hurt / have some pain*
Ich habe Kopfschmerzen.	*I have a headache.*
weh·tun (tut weh), wehgetan	*to hurt*
Mir tut der Hals weh.	*My throat hurts. I have a sore throat.*
Was ist los?	*What's the matter? What's going on?*
<u>nichts Besonderes</u>	*nothing special*
Nein, das geht (heute) nicht.	*No, that won't work (today).*
Ach so.	*Oh, I see.*
Ja, sicher.	*Yes, sure.*
Bis bald!	*See you soon!*
Bis gleich!	*See you in a few minutes!*

🔸 Besides **Schach,** the card game **Skat** is also very popular.

🔸 Like **nichts Besonderes:** nichts Neues, nichts Schlechtes OR **etwas Besonderes, etwas Schönes**

Zum Erkennen: Ich bin's. *(It's me.);* Ich habe Muskelkater. *(My muscles are sore.);* Ich kann mich kaum rühren. *(I can hardly move.);* Lahme Ente! *(someone with no pep, lit. lame duck);* Wie wär's mit . . . ? *(How about . . . ?);* zu mir *(to my place);* AUCH: die Aktivität, -en *(activity);* der Dialog, -e; die Beschreibung, -en *(description);* die Endung, -en *(ending);* das reflexive Verb, -en; an·kreuzen *(to mark with an x);* beenden *(to complete, finish)*

Aktives zum Thema

A. Mustersätze

1. Mir tut ____ weh.
   Hals → Mir tut der Hals weh.
   Kopf, Zahn, Bauch, Fuß, Knie, Hand . . .

2. Mir tun die ____ weh.
   Hände → Mir tun die Hände weh.
   Füße, Finger, Ohren, Beine, Augen . . .

3. Ich habe ____schmerzen.
   Kopf → Ich habe Kopfschmerzen.
   Hals, Zahn, Bauch, Ohren . . .

4. Hast du Lust, ____ zu spielen?
   Squash → Hast du Lust, Squash zu spielen?
   Tennis, Fußball, Klavier, CDs, Karten, Schach . . .

B. Was tun Sie dann? Beenden Sie die Sätze mit einer Antwort von der Liste oder mit Ihren eigenen Worten!

____ 1. Wenn ich Kopfschmerzen habe, . . .
____ 2. Wenn mir die Füße wehtun, . . .
____ 3. Wenn mir der Bauch wehtut, . . .
____ 4. Wenn ich Halsschmerzen habe, . . .
____ 5. Wenn ich Augenschmerzen habe, . . .
____ 6. Wenn ich krank bin, . . .
____ 7. Wenn ich gestresst bin, . . .
____ 8. Wenn ich nicht schlafen kann, . . .

a. bleibe ich im Bett.
b. esse ich Nudelsuppe / nichts.
c. gehe ich ins Bett / in die Sauna.
d. gurgele (gargle) ich.
e. gehe ich nicht spazieren.
f. mache ich die Augen zu.
g. meditiere ich.
h. nehme ich Aspirin / Vitamin C.
i. sehe ich nicht fern.
j. rufe ich einen Arzt (doctor) an.
k. trinke ich Tee.
l. trinke ich heiße Milch / Zitrone mit Honig (honey).
m. . . .

C. Was tust du gern in deiner Freizeit? Lesen Sie mit Ihrem Partner/Ihrer Partnerin die drei Listen und kreuzen Sie an *(check)*, was Sie gern in Ihrer Freizeit tun! Fragen Sie danach andere in der Klasse und finden Sie heraus, was sie angekreuzt haben! Welche fünf Aktivitäten sind besonders populär?

BEISPIEL   S1 Ich lese gern. Und du?
            S2 Ich auch. Ich spiele auch gern Videospiele. Und du?
            S1 Ich nicht. Ich spiele lieber *(rather)* Klavier . . .

Ich . . . gern	Ich gehe gern . . .	Ich spiele gern . . .
❏ durch die Geschäfte bummeln	❏ angeln	❏ Basketball
❏ backen	❏ bergsteigen *(mountain climbing)*	❏ Federball *(badminton)*
❏ essen	❏ kegeln *(bowling)*	❏ Fußball
❏ faulenzen	❏ Rollschuh laufen *(roller skating)*	❏ Volleyball
❏ joggen	❏ Schlittschuh laufen *(ice skating)*	❏ Golf
❏ kochen	❏ (Wasser)ski laufen	❏ Minigolf
❏ lesen	❏ segelfliegen *(gliding)*	❏ Tennis
❏ malen	❏ segeln *(sailing)*	❏ Tischtennis
❏ reisen	❏ spazieren	❏ Karten
❏ reiten *(horseback riding)*	❏ wandern	❏ Computerspiele
❏ schwimmen	❏ windsurfen	❏ Videospiele
❏ tanzen	❏ ins Kino	❏ Flöte *(flute)*
❏ im Garten arbeiten	❏ zum Fitnessstudio	❏ Gitarre
❏ im Internet surfen	❏ inlineskaten	❏ Klavier
❏ . . .	❏ . . .	❏ Schach
		❏ Schlagzeug *(the drums)*
		❏ . . .

🔸 Nine-pin bowling **(Kegeln)** without the headpin is very popular in Germany, although US-style bowling is also "in." The **Fußball-Bundesliga** is the "first divison" of German soccer, consisting of the 18 best teams.

🔸 Germans also say **Ping-Pong** instead of **Tischtennis.** The word **Federball** is generally used for recreation and **Badminton** for competitions. **Rollschuhlaufen** is plain *roller skating;* in-line skating is **Inlineskating** or **Rollerblading.** *To rollerblade* = **inlineskaten** *(I like to go rollerblading.* **Ich gehe gern inlineskaten.)**

 D. Interview Fragen Sie einen Nachbarn/eine Nachbarin, . . . !

1. ob er/sie als Kind ein Instrument gelernt hat; wenn ja, welches Instrument und ob er/sie es heute noch spielt
2. ob er/sie gern singt; wenn ja, was und wo (in der Dusche oder Badewanne, im Auto oder Chor)
3. was für Musik er/sie schön findet (klassische oder moderne Musik, Jazz, Hip-Hop-, Rock-, Pop-, Country- oder Volksmusik)
4. ob er/sie viel fernsieht; wenn ja, wann gewöhnlich und was
5. ob er/sie oft lange am Telefon spricht; wenn ja, mit wem
6. wie lange er/sie jeden Tag vor dem Computer sitzt und warum

Aussprache: l, z

CD 6,
Track 7

A. Laute

1. [l] laut, leicht, lustig, leider, Hals, Geld, malen, spielen, fliegen, stellen, schnell, Ball, hell
2. [ts] zählen, zeigen, zwischen, zurück, zuerst, Zug, Zahn, Schmerzen, Kerzen, Einzelzimmer, Pizza, bezahlen, tanzen, jetzt, schmutzig, trotz, kurz, schwarz, Salz, Schweiz, Sitzplatz

B. Wortpaare

1. *felt* / Feld   3. *plots* / Platz   5. seit / Zeit
2. *hotel* / Hotel   4. Schweiß / Schweiz   6. so / Zoo

For further review, see the Summary of Pronunciation in the front of your *Arbeitsbuch*. Study section III, part A.8–10.

Hörverständnis

Track 19

Beim Arzt Hören Sie zu, warum Frau Heller zum Arzt geht und was er ihr sagt! Ergänzen Sie die Aussagen unten!

Zum Erkennen: passieren *(to happen)*; war *(was)*; der Ellbogen, - *(elbow)*; hochlegen *(to put up [high])*; (Schmerz)tabletten *([pain] pills)*

1. Kim geht zum Arzt, weil ihr _____ wehtut. 2. Sie ist mit ihrer Freundin im Harz _____ gegangen. 3. Am letzten Tag ist sie _____. 4. Sie darf ein paar Tage nicht _____. 5. Sie soll das Bein _____. 6. Der Arzt gibt ihr ein paar _____ mit.
7. Wenn Kim in einer Woche immer noch Schmerzen hat, soll sie _____.
8. Kim kann bald wieder _____ oder _____.

Fokus   Some Idiomatic Expressions

As in the case of **Lahme Ente!** in the dialogue, names of animals are frequently used in everyday idiomatic expressions to characterize people—often in a derogatory way: **Ich Esel!** *(donkey)* or **Du Affe!** *(monkey)* for someone who made a mistake or behaves in a silly manner; **Du hast einen Vogel!** or **Bei dir piept's!** *(You're cuckoo.)*; **Fauler Hund!** *(dog)* for someone lazy; **Du Brummbär!** *(grumbling bear)* for someone grumpy; **(Das ist) alles für die Katz'!** if everything is useless or in vain; **Du Schwein!** *(pig)* for someone who is messy or a scoundrel. **Schwein haben,** however, has quite a different meaning: *to be lucky.* In addition, names of food are used in special expressions: **Das ist doch Käse!** *(That's nonsense!)*; **Das ist mir Wurst!** *(I don't care!)*; **Es ist alles in Butter!** *(Everything is O.K.!)*; **Das ist doch Sahne!** *(That's O.K.!)*

Schwein kann man nicht genug haben.

IMMER NUR KÄSE!

IST DOCH WURST!!!

piep piep piep bei dir piept's wohl?

Zum Thema / 237

Struktur

🔸 For a list of **der-** and **ein-** words, see Chapter 7.

9.1 Endings of adjectives preceded by *der-* and *ein-*words

1. PREDICATE ADJECTIVES and ADVERBS do not have endings.

Willi ist schnell.	*Willi is quick.*
Willi fährt schnell.	*Willi drives fast.*

2. However, adjectives preceding a noun (ATTRIBUTIVE ADJECTIVES) do have endings that vary according to the type of article that precedes it and according to the noun's case, gender, and number.

Der schnell**e** Fahrer *(m.)* ist mein Bruder.	*The fast driver is my brother.*
Mein Bruder ist ein schnell**er** Fahrer.	*My brother is a fast driver.*
Er hat ein schnell**es** Auto *(n.)*.	*He has a fast car.*

If you look over the two tables below, you will readily see that there are only four different adjective endings: **-e, -er, -es,** and **-en.** Furthermore, the **-en** ending predominates; it is used in the singular masculine accusative and in all datives, genitives, and plurals.

a. Adjectives preceded by a DEFINITE ARTICLE or **der-**word:

	masculine			neuter			feminine			plural		
nom.	der	neue	Wagen	das	neue	Auto	die	neue	Farbe	alle	neuen	Ideen
acc.	den	neuen	Wagen	das	neue	Auto	die	neue	Farbe	alle	neuen	Ideen
dat.	dem	neuen	Wagen	dem	neuen	Auto	der	neuen	Farbe	allen	neuen	Ideen
gen.	des	neuen	Wagens	des	neuen	Autos	der	neuen	Farbe	aller	neuen	Ideen

b. Adjectives preceded by an INDEFINITE ARTICLE or **ein-**word:

	masculine			neuter			feminine			plural		
nom.	ein	neuer	Wagen	ein	neues	Auto	eine	neue	Farbe	meine	neuen	Ideen
acc.	einen	neuen	Wagen	ein	neues	Auto	eine	neue	Farbe	meine	neuen	Ideen
dat.	einem	neuen	Wagen	einem	neuen	Auto	einer	neuen	Farbe	meinen	neuen	Ideen
gen.	eines	neuen	Wagens	eines	neuen	Autos	einer	neuen	Farbe	meiner	neuen	Ideen

If you compare the two preceding tables, you can see:

- Adjectives preceded by a DEFINITE ARTICLE or any **der-**word have either an **-e** or **-en** ending.

- Adjectives preceded by an INDEFINITE ARTICLE or any **ein-**word are the same as for the definite article/**der-**word in all cases and genders *except three:* in the masculine nominative, neuter nominative, and neuter accusative. In those three exceptions, the **ein-**word itself has no ending. The adjective ending identifies the gender of the noun by adding an **-er** for masculine nouns and an **-es** for neuter nouns.

The following tables show the adjective endings schematically.

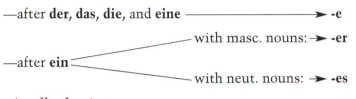

after **der**-words	masc.	neut.	fem.	pl.
nom.		-e		
acc.				
dat.				
gen.		-en		

after **ein**-words	masc.	neut.	fem.	pl.
nom.	-er	-es	-e	
acc.		-es	-e	
dat.				
gen.		-en		

Or, to put it in another way, the endings are as follows:

- in the NOMINATIVE and ACCUSATIVE SINGULAR

—after **der, das, die,** and **eine** ⟶ **-e**

—after **ein** with masc. nouns: ⟶ **-er**
              with neut. nouns: ⟶ **-es**

- in *all other instances* ⟶ **-en**
(incl. masc. accusative sg., all datives and genitives, and all plurals)

Der groß**e** Ball, das schön**e** Spiel und die neu**e** CD sind gut.
Das ist ein gut**er** Preis für so ein fantastisch**es** Geschenk.
Das sind keine teur**en** Geschenke.

NOTE: Adjective endings are not difficult to remember if you understand the basic principle involved: in the nominative and the accusative, one of the words preceding the noun must convey information about its gender, number, and case. If an article does not do so, then the adjective must. For example, **der** is clearly masculine nominative; therefore, the adjective can take the minimal ending **-e.** **Ein,** however, does not show gender or case; therefore, the adjective must do so.

3. If two or more adjectives precede a noun, all have the same ending.

Das sind keine groß**en,** teuer**en** Geschenke.

● When adding an ending, some adjectives such as **teuer** and **dunkel** drop the **-e-** in their stem: **Das Geschenk ist teuer. Das sind teu(e)re Geschenke. Das Zimmer ist dunkel. Das ist ein dunkles Zimmer.** In the case of **teuer,** dropping the **-e-** is optional.

Übungen

A. Familienfotos Inge erzählt, was man auf dem Bild vom 50. Hochzeitstag ihrer Großeltern sieht.

BEISPIEL   Das ist mein Onkel Max mit seinen drei **Kindern.** (wild, klein)
Das ist mein Onkel Max mit seinen drei wilden Kindern.
Das ist mein Onkel Max mit seinen drei kleinen Kindern.

1. Das ist Tante Jutta mit ihrem **Freund** aus London. (verrückt, englisch)
2. Hier sitzen wir alle an einem **Tisch** und spielen Monopoly. (groß, rund)
3. Das ist Oma mit ihrem **Porsche** *(m.).* (teuer, rot)
4. Die Farbe dieses **Autos** gefällt mir. (toll, schnell)
5. Das ist wirklich ein **Geschenk!** (wunderbar, fantastisch)
6. Opa hat ein **Fahrrad** bekommen. (schön, neu)
7. Jetzt kann er mit seinen **Freunden** Fahrrad fahren. (viel, alt)
8. Das hier ist unser **Hund** *(dog, m.).* (klein, braun)
9. Das ist wirklich ein **Hündchen** *(n.).* (lieb, klein)
10. Wegen des **Wetters** haben wir nicht im Garten gefeiert. (schlecht, kalt)

B. Die neue Wohnung Lesen Sie den Dialog mit den Adjektiven!

> BEISPIEL   Ist der Schrank neu? (groß)
> *Ist der große Schrank neu?*

S1   Ist dieser Sessel bequem? (braun)
S2   Ja, und das Sofa auch. (lang)
S1   Die Lampe gefällt mir. (klein)
     Woher hast du diesen Teppich? (fantastisch)
     Und wo hast du dieses Bild gefunden?
     (supermodern)
S2   In einem Geschäft. (alt)
     Wenn du willst, kann ich dir das Geschäft mal zeigen. (interessant)
S1   Ist es in der Müllergasse *(f.)*? (klein)
S2   Ja, auf der Seite. (link-)
S1   Während der Woche habe ich keine Zeit. (nächst-)
     Sind diese Möbel teuer gewesen? (schön)
S2   Natürlich nicht. Für solche Möbel gebe ich nicht viel Geld aus. (alt)

C. Anja zeigt Jens ihr Zimmer. Jens stellt Fragen und kommentiert *(comments)*. Bilden Sie aus zwei Sätzen einen Satz!

> BEISPIEL   Woher kommt dieses Schachspiel? Es ist interessant.
> *Woher kommt dieses interessante Schachspiel?*

1. Weißt du, was so ein Schachspiel kostet? Es ist chinesisch.
2. Bist du Schachspielerin? Spielst du gut? *(add* **ein!***)*
3. Ich bin kein Schachspieler. Ich spiele nicht gut.
4. Woher hast du diese Briefmarkensammlung? Sie ist alt.
5. Mein Vater hat auch eine Sammlung. Sie ist groß.
6. Sammelst du solche Briefmarken auch? Sie sind normal.
7. Was machst du mit so einer Briefmarke? Sie ist doppelt *(double)*.
8. Darf ich diese Briefmarke haben? Sie ist ja doppelt!
9. Hast du diese Bilder gemacht? Sie sind toll.
10. Wer ist der Junge? Er ist klein.
11. Was für ein Gesicht! Es ist fantastisch!
12. Die Augen gefallen mir! Sie sind dunkelbraun.
13. Mit meiner Kamera ist das nicht möglich. Sie ist billig.
14. Und das hier ist ein Tennisspieler, nicht wahr? Er ist bekannt und kommt aus Deutschland.
15. Weißt du, dass wir gestern trotz des Wetters Fußball gespielt haben? Das Wetter ist schlecht gewesen.
16. Leider kann ich wegen meines Knies nicht mehr mitspielen. Das Knie ist kaputt.

 D. Ist das nicht schön?

1. **Das finde ich auch.** Ihr Partner/Ihre Partnerin findet etwas besonders gut. Sagen Sie ihm/ihr, dass Sie das auch finden und reagieren Sie dann wie beim Mustersatz mit einer Frage oder einer Bemerkung *(comment)*!

> BEISPIEL   S1   Ist der Pullover nicht warm?
>   S2   Ja, das ist ein warmer Pullover.
>   Woher hast du den warmen Pullover?

    a.   Ist das Hemd nicht elegant?
    b.   Ist die Uhr nicht herrlich?
    c.   Ist der Hut *(hat)* nicht verrückt?

BEISPIEL   S1 Ist das Hotel nicht gut?
                S2 Ja, das ist ein gutes Hotel.
                    Wo hast du von diesem guten Hotel gehört?

    d. Ist die Pension nicht wunderbar?
    e. Ist der Gasthof nicht billig?
    f. Ist das Restaurant nicht gemütlich?

BEISPIEL   S1 Ist das alte Schloss nicht herrlich?
                S2 Ja, das ist ein altes, herrliches Schloss.
                    Ich gehe gern in alte, herrliche Schlösser.

    g. Ist der große Supermarkt nicht modern?
    h. Ist das neue Geschäft nicht klein?
    i. Ist die alte Kirche nicht interessant?

2. **Und jetzt finden Sie etwas gut (oder nicht so gut).** Was sagt Ihr Partner/Ihre Partnerin dazu *(about it)*? Wechseln Sie sich ab!

BEISPIEL   S1 Ist unser Professor nicht gut?
                S2 Ja, er ist ein guter Professor.
                    Von einem guten Professor kann man viel lernen.

E. Zwei Beschreibungen *(descriptions)*

1. **Brittas Wohnung** Ergänzen Sie die fehlenden *(missing)* Adjektivendungen!

a. Britta wohnt in einem toll___ Haus im neu___ Teil unserer schön___ Stadt. b. Ihre klein___ Wohnung liegt im neunt___ Stock eines modern___ Hochhauses *(high-rise)*. c. Sie hat eine praktisch___ Küche und ein gemüt-lich___ Wohnzimmer. d. Von dem groß___ Wohnzimmerfenster kann sie unsere ganz___ Stadt und die viel___ Brücken über dem breit___ *(wide)* Fluss sehen. e. Britta liebt ihre Wohnung wegen des schön___ Blickes *(view, m.)* und der billig___ Miete. f. In ihrem hell___ Schlafzimmer stehen ein einfach___ Bett und ein klein___ Nachttisch mit einer klein___ Nacht-tischlampe. g. An der Wand steht ein braun___ Schreibtisch und über dem braun___ Schreibtisch hängt ein lang___ Regal mit ihren viel___ Büchern. Britta findet ihre Wohnung schön.

2. **Meine Wohnung** Beschreiben Sie jetzt Ihre Wohnung oder Ihr Zimmer! Schreiben Sie 8–10 Sätze mit ein oder zwei Adjektiven in jedem Satz!

Fokus The German Pop Scene

Just as in other European countries, Anglo-American pop music has domi-nated the charts in Germany. However, German pop music has managed to gain popularity with the German public over the past twenty years. In the 1980s, the so-called **Neue Deutsche Welle** with singer-songwriters like Marius-Müller Westernhagen, Peter Maffay, Herbert Grönemeyer, Udo Lindenberg, and punkrock bands like *Die Ärzte, Die Toten Hosen,* and interna-tionally famous artists like Nina Hagen and Nena proved that songs sung in German could be successful. Since the 1990s, the German pop scene has become more diverse, increasingly reflecting international influences: Rock, Hip-Hop, Rap, Folk, and electronic music with bands and singers singing either in English or German, for example, *Die Fantastischen Vier,* Sabrina Setlur, Xavier Naidoo, *Die Prinzen, Pur, Element of Crime, Fury in the Slaughter-house,* and *Rammstein.* Recently, there has been a movement in favor of re-quiring German radio stations to play a minimum number of German songs in an effort to promote young German artists.

Die Popgruppe „Pur"

9.2 Reflexive verbs

If the subject and one of the objects of a sentence are the same person or thing, a reflexive pronoun must be used for the object. In the English sentence, *I see myself in the picture,* the reflexive pronoun *myself* is the accusative object. *(Whom do I see? —Myself.)* In the sentence, *I am buying myself a CD,* the pronoun *myself* is the dative object. *(For whom am I buying the CD? —For myself.)*

In German, only the third person singular and plural have a special reflexive pronoun: **sich.** *The other persons use the accusative and dative forms of the personal pronouns, which you already know.*

Ich sehe meinen Bruder auf dem Bild.	*I see my brother in the picture.*
Ich sehe **mich** auf dem Bild.	*I see myself in the picture.*
Ich kaufe meinem Bruder eine CD.	*I buy my brother a CD.*
Ich kaufe **mir** eine CD.	*I buy myself a CD.*

nom.	ich	du	er / es / sie	wir	ihr	sie	Sie
acc.	mich	dich					
			sich	uns	euch	sich	sich
dat.	mir	dir					

1. Many verbs you have already learned <u>can be used reflexively</u>, although the English equivalent may not include a reflexive pronoun:

   • The reflexive pronoun used as the DIRECT OBJECT (ACCUSATIVE):

sich fragen	*to wonder*	**sich treffen**	*to meet, gather*
sich legen	*to lie down*	usw.	
sich sehen	*to see oneself*		

Ich frage **mich,** ob das richtig ist.	*I wonder (ask myself) whether that's right.*
Ich lege **mich** aufs Sofa.	*I lie down on the sofa.*
Ich sehe **mich** im Spiegel.	*I see myself in the mirror.*

   • The reflexive pronoun used as the INDIRECT OBJECT (DATIVE):

sich bestellen	*to order for oneself*	**sich nehmen**	*to take for oneself*
sich kaufen	*to buy for oneself*	**sich wünschen**	*to wish (for oneself)*
sich kochen	*to cook for oneself*	usw.	

Ich bestelle **mir** ein Eis.	*I am ordering ice cream (for myself).*
Ich koche **mir** ein Ei.	*I'm cooking myself an egg.*
Ich wünsche **mir** ein Auto.	*I'm wishing for a car (for myself).*

2. Some verbs are <u>always reflexive</u>, or are reflexive when they express a certain meaning. Here are some important verbs that you need to know.

sich an·hören	to listen to
sich an·sehen, angesehen	to look at
sich an·ziehen, angezogen	to put on (clothing), get dressed
sich aus·ziehen, ausgezogen	to take off (clothing), get undressed
sich um·ziehen, umgezogen	to change (clothing), get changed
sich baden	to take a bath
sich beeilen	to hurry
sich duschen	to take a shower
sich erkälten	to catch a cold
sich (wohl) fühlen	to feel (well)
sich (hin·)legen	to lie down
sich kämmen	to comb one's hair
sich konzentrieren	to concentrate
sich (die Zähne / Nase) putzen	to clean (brush one's teeth / blow one's nose)
sich rasieren	to shave
sich (hin·)setzen	to sit down
sich waschen (wäscht), gewaschen	to wash (oneself)

> **Hör dir das an!**

Setz dich (hin)!	*Sit down.*
Warum müsst ihr euch beeilen?	*Why do you have to hurry?*
Ich fühle mich nicht wohl.	*I don't feel well.*
Letzte Woche hat sie sich erkältet.	*Last week she caught a cold.*
Wir treffen uns mit Freunden.	*We're meeting with friends.*

- With some of these verbs, the reflexive pronoun <u>may be either the accusative or the dative object.</u> If there are two objects, then the person (the reflexive pronoun) is in the dative and the thing is in the accusative.

Ich wasche **mich.**	*I wash myself.*
Ich wasche **mir** die Haare.	*I wash my hair.*
Ich ziehe **mich** an.	*I'm getting dressed.*
Ich ziehe **mir** einen Pulli an.	*I'm putting on a sweater.*

3. In English, possessive adjectives are used to refer to parts of the body: *I'm washing my hands.* In German, however, the definite article is usually used together with the reflexive pronoun in the dative.

*I'm washing **my** hands.*	Ich wasche **mir die** Hände.
*She's combing **her** hair.*	Sie kämmt **sich die** Haare.
*Brush **your** teeth.*	Putz **dir die** Zähne!

> Du kannst dir auch mal wieder die Ohren waschen.

REMEMBER: When there are two object pronouns, the accusative pronoun comes before the dative!

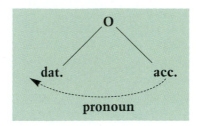

Ich wasche **mir die Hände.**   Du kämmst **dir die Haare.**
Ich wasche **sie mir.**   Du kämmst **sie dir.**

Übungen

Mensch, beeilt euch!

Ich beeil' mich ja schon!

Ich muss mir die Schuhe anziehen.

F. Antworten Sie mit JA!

1. **Singular**

   BEISPIEL   Soll ich mir die Hände waschen?
   Ja, waschen Sie sich die Hände!
   Ja, wasch dir die Hände!

   a. Soll ich mich noch umziehen?   d. Soll ich mich jetzt setzen?
   b. Soll ich mir die Haare kämmen?   e. Soll ich mir die Bilder ansehen?
   c. Soll ich mir ein Auto kaufen?

2. **Plural**

   BEISPIEL   Sollen wir uns die Hände waschen?
   Ja, waschen Sie sich die Hände!
   Ja, wascht euch die Hände!

   a. Sollen wir uns ein Zimmer mieten?   d. Sollen wir uns die CDs
   b. Sollen wir uns ein Haus bauen?   anhören?
   c. Sollen wir uns in den Garten   e. Sollen wir uns die Briefmarken
      setzen?   ansehen?

G. Was fehlt?

1. Kinder, zieht _____ warm an!
2. Einen Moment, ich muss _____ die Nase putzen.
3. Gestern haben wir _____ ein Klavier gekauft.
4. Setzen Sie _____ bitte!
5. Peter, konzentrier _____!
6. Kinder, erkältet _____ nicht!
7. Ich habe _____ zum Geburtstag ein Schachspiel gewünscht.
8. Willst du _____ etwas im Radio anhören?
9. Junge, fühlst du _____ nicht wohl?
10. Möchten Sie _____ die Hände waschen?
11. Bestellst du _____ auch ein Stück Kuchen?
12. Ich setze _____ gemütlich in den Garten.

Park Hotel Blub

blub, blub und sich wohl fühlen, wie ein Fisch im Wasser.

Park Hotel blub und blub Badeparadies.

H. Hoppla, hier fehlt was! Was tun sie morgens? Finden Sie mit Ihrem Partner/Ihrer Partnerin heraus, was die anderen morgens tun! Einer von Ihnen sieht auf die Tabelle unten, der andere auf die Tabelle im Anhang, Teil 11.

S1

	Zuerst	Dann	Danach
BIRTE	s. duschen s. die Haare waschen	s. kämmen s. die Zähne putzen	s. in die Küche setzen s. ein Ei kochen gemütlich frühstücken s. Musik anhören
OLLI			
VERA	zu lange schlafen schnell aufstehen	s. schnell anziehen s. nicht kämmen	ihre Sachen nicht finden etwas zu essen mitnehmen
INGO			

1. **So ist es bei Birte, Olli, Vera und Ingo.**

   BEISPIEL   S1 Was macht Olli morgens?

   S2 Olli zieht sich schnell an und geht joggen. Dann . . .

2. **Und bei Ihnen?**

   BEISPIEL   S1 Ich bin wie *(like)* . . . Zuerst . . . Danach . . .

   S2 Wirklich? Ich bin wie . . . Zuerst . . . Danach . . .

I. Und du, was machst du den ganzen Tag? Fragen Sie Ihren Partner/Ihre Partnerin, was er/sie zu einer gewissen *(certain)* Zeit des Tages tut! Wenn möglich, benutzen Sie in Ihren Fragen und Antworten reflexive Verben! Machen Sie sich Notizen *(take notes)* und erzählen Sie dann der Klasse, was Sie herausgefunden haben!

   BEISPIEL   S1 Was machst du abends um zehn?

   S2 Abends um zehn höre ich mir die Nachrichten an. Und du?

   S1 Um diese Zeit lege ich mich ins Bett . . .

● Optional English-to-German practice: 1. Otto, get dressed. 2. Christian, hurry! 3. Anne und Sabrina, are you putting on a sweater? 4. We still have to brush our teeth. 5. Peter, comb your hair. 6. I don't feel well. 7. Today we're all going jogging. 8. Yes, but I've caught a cold. 9. Then lie down *(sg. fam.)*. (See answer key in the Appendix.)

9.3 Infinitive with *zu*

English and German use infinitives with **zu** *(to)* in much the same way.

Es ist interessant **zu reisen.**   *It's interesting to travel.*
Ich habe keine Zeit gehabt **zu essen.**   *I didn't have time to eat.*

1. In German, if the infinitive is combined with other sentence elements, such as a direct object or an adverbial phrase, a comma usually separates the infinitive phrase from the main clause.

   Haben Sie Zeit, eine Reise **zu** machen?   *Do you have time to take a trip?*

   Note that in German the infinitive comes at the end of the phrase.

2. If a separable-prefix verb is used, the **-zu-** is inserted between the prefix and the base verb.

PREFIX + **zu** + VERB

Es ist Zeit ab**zu**fahren.   *It's time to leave.*

3. Infinitive phrases beginning with **um** explain the purpose of the action described in the main clause.

Wir fahren nach Hessen, **um** unsere   *(in order to visit . . .)*
Oma **zu** besuchen.
Rudi geht ins Badezimmer, **um** sich   *(in order to take a shower)*
zu duschen.

MISEREOR

„Die Menschen haben gelernt, zu schwimmen wie die Fische und zu fliegen wie die Vögel, aber wie Brüder zusammenzuleben haben sie nicht gelernt"
M. L. King

Übungen

J. Wie geht's weiter?

BEISPIEL   Hast du Lust . . . ? (sich CDs anhören)
Hast du Lust, dir CDs anzuhören?

1. Dort gibt es viel . . . (sehen, tun, fotografieren, zeigen, essen)
2. Habt ihr Zeit . . . ? (vorbeikommen, die Nachbarn kennen lernen, faulenzen, euch eine DVD ansehen)
3. Es ist wichtig . . . (aufpassen, sich konzentrieren, Sprachen lernen, Freunde haben, Sport treiben)
4. Es ist interessant . . . (ihm zuhören, Bücher sammeln, mit der Bahn fahren, mit dem Flugzeug fliegen)
5. Es hat Spaß gemacht . . . (reisen, wandern, singen, spazieren gehen, aufs Land fahren, Freunde anrufen)

K. Bilden Sie Sätze!

1. heute / wir / haben / nicht viel / tun
2. es / machen / ihm / Spaß // sich mit Freunden treffen
3. sie *(sg.)* / müssen / noch / einlösen / Scheck
4. ich / haben / keine Zeit // Geschichten / sich anhören *(pres. perf.)*
5. du / haben / keine Lust // mit uns / Ski laufen gehen? *(pres. perf.)*
6. möchten / du / fernsehen / bei uns?
7. wir / möchten / kaufen / neu / Auto
8. es / sein / sehr bequem // hier / sitzen
9. ich / sein / zu müde // Tennis spielen
10. du / sollen / anrufen / dein- / Kusine

L. So bin ich. Sprechen Sie mit den anderen über Ihre Hobbys und Ihre Freizeit!

1. Ich habe keine Lust . . .
2. Ich habe nie Zeit . . .
3. Mir macht es Spaß . . .
4. Ich finde es wichtig . . .
5. Ich finde es langweilig *(boring)* . . .
6. Als *(as)* Kind hat es mir Spaß gemacht . . .
7. Ich brauche das Wochenende gewöhnlich, um . . .
8. Ich lerne Deutsch, um . . .

M. Was tue ich gern? Teilen Sie *(divide)* die Klasse in zwei Mannschaften *(teams)*. Eine Mannschaft denkt an *(of)* ein Hobby. Die andere Mannschaft versucht *(tries)* dann mit bis zu 10 Fragen herauszufinden, was dieses Hobby ist. Nach 10 Fragen wechselt sich die Mannschaft ab!

Drachenflieger (hang-gliders) *vor dem Abflug*

Zusammenfassung

N. Rotkäppchen und der Wolf Was fehlt?

1. Es hat einmal eine gut__ Mutter mit ihrem klein__ Mädchen in einem ruhig__ Dorf gewohnt. 2. Sie hat zu ihrer klein__ Tochter gesagt: „Geh zu deiner alt__ Großmutter und bring ihr diese gut__ Flasche Wein und diesen frisch__ Kuchen! 3. Aber du musst im dunkl__ Wald aufpassen, weil dort der groß__ bös__ *(bad)* Wolf wohnt." 4. Das klein__ Mädchen ist mit seiner groß__ Tasche in den grün__ Wald gegangen. 5. Auf dem dunkl__ Weg ist der bös__ Wolf gekommen und hat das klein__ Mädchen gefragt, wo seine alt__ Großmutter wohnt. 6. Er hat dem gut__ Kind auch die wunderbar__ Blumen am Weg gezeigt. 7. Dann hat der furchtbar__ Wolf die arm__ *(poor)* Großmutter gefressen *(devoured)* und hat sich in das bequem__ Bett der alt__ Frau gelegt. 8. Das müd__ Rotkäppchen ist in das klein__ Haus gekommen und hat gefragt: „Großmutter, warum hast du so groß__ Ohren? Warum hast du so groß__ Augen? Warum hast du so einen groß__ Mund?" 9. Da hat der bös__ Wolf geantwortet: „Dass ich dich besser fressen kann!" 10. Nun *(well)*, Sie kennen ja das Ende dieser bekannt__ Geschichte *(story, f.)*! 11. Der Jäger *(hunter)* hat den dick__ Wolf getötet *(killed)* und dem klein__ Mädchen und seiner alt__ Großmutter aus dem Bauch des tot__ *(dead)* Wolfes geholfen.

Visit the *Wie geht's?* iLrn website for more review and practice of the grammar points you have just learned.

0. Hallo, Max! Auf Deutsch bitte!

1. What have you been doing today? 2. Oh, nothing special. I listened to my old CDs. 3. Do you feel like going swimming (taking a swim)? 4. No, thanks. I don't feel well. I have a headache and my throat hurts. Call Stephan. 5. Hello, Stephan! Do you have time to go swimming? 6. No, I have to go to town **(in die Stadt)** in order to buy (myself) a new pair of slacks and a warm coat. Do you feel like coming along? 7. No, I already went shopping this morning. I bought (myself) a blue sweater and a white shirt. 8. Too bad. I've got to hurry. 9. Okay, I'm going to put on my swim trunks **(die Badehose)** and go swimming. Bye!

Ferien auf dem Bauernhof im Schwarzwald. Das macht Spaß für die ganze Familie.

Fokus   Vacationing

In contrast to North Americans, who often prefer to take their vacation days bit by bit and combine them with holidays or a few long weekends, Germans are more likely to view their annual vacation as the year's major event. With relatively high incomes and a minimum of three to four weeks' paid vacation **(der Urlaub)** each year, Germans are among the world's greatest travelers. Many head north to the beaches of the North Sea **(die Nordsee)** or the Baltic Sea **(die Ostsee)**; others head south to the warm beaches of southern France, Spain, Italy, Greece, Turkey, and North Africa. Still others opt for educational trips, such as language courses abroad or cultural tours. Favorite destinations include North America, Kenya, and Thailand.

Those who wish to stay closer to home may go swimming in a nearby lake, take a bike trip, venture out on a canoe or kayak tour, or spend a week on a farm in the countryside. Feudal manors and vineyards also have guest rooms. With the pressures of everyday living, more and more people also opt for relaxation in one of the many spa hotels where both body and soul receive special attention.

Einblicke

Wortschatz 2

der Urlaub	(paid) vacation
das Leben	life
die Musik	music
ander- (adj.)	other, different
anders (adv.)	different(ly)
beliebt	popular
ganz	whole, entire(ly), all
etwas (ganz) anderes	something (totally) different
(genauso) wie . . .	(just) like . . .
aus·geben (gibt aus), ausgegeben	to spend (money)
sich entspannen	to relax
sich erholen	to recuperate
erleben	to experience
sich fit halten (hält), gehalten	to keep in shape
sich langweilen	to get (or be) bored
vor·ziehen, vorgezogen	to prefer

● In German, **Leben** is normally used only in the singular: Sport ist wichtig **in ihrem Leben** (in her life / in their lives).

● Note the various uses of other: Das Leben auf dem Land ist **anders** (different). Es ist **ein anderes** (a different kind of) **Leben.** In Wortschatz I, you also learned two additional forms of other: Manche Leute leben gern in der Stadt, **andere** (others) gern auf dem Lande. Ich liebe es dort, aber **die anderen** (the others) finden es furchtbar.

Es kommt nicht darauf an, dem Leben mehr Jahre zu geben, sondern den Jahren mehr Leben.

Lesetipp
The Importance of Adjectives

Adjectives make a text come alive by providing additional information about people, places, and things with which the reader can form more vivid images. Note the use of adjectives in the reading passage on page 251. How do they make the reading more interesting? What would the reading be like without them? Give specific examples.

Find all the preceded adjectives in the text. In each case, decide why they have that particular ending. How many can you find?

Vor dem Lesen

A. Allerlei Fragen

1. Wie viele Stunden die Woche (per week) arbeitet man in den USA / in Kanada? 2. Wie viele Wochen Urlaub hat man im Jahr? 3. Was tun die Amerikaner / Kanadier in ihrer Freizeit? 4. Was ist der Nationalsport hier? 5. Was sind andere populäre Sportarten? 6. Wohin fahren Sie gern in den Ferien? 7. Sind Ferien für Sie gewöhnlich Lust oder Frust (frustration)? Warum?

B. Ferientipps Finden Sie mit ihrem Partner/Ihrer Partnerin heraus, wo diese Kurorte (*health resorts*) sind, was sie zu bieten (*offer*) haben und was das kostet! Wenn Sie wollen, besuchen Sie den Kurort im Internet. Was klingt besonders interessant und warum?

Kurort	Wo liegt das?	Was bieten sie dort?	Preis
BAD DRIBURG			
BAD NENNDORF			
BAD REICHENHALL			
BAD TÖLZ			
OBERSTDORF			
ROTTACH-EGERN			

C. Das ist leicht zu verstehen! Welche Silbe ist betont? Markieren Sie sie! Was ist das auf Englisch?

der Arbeiter, Freizeitboom, Freizeitfrust, Musikklub, Trendsport, Urlaubstag; das Fernsehen, Gartenhäuschen, Gartenstück, Industrieland, Musikfestspiel, Privileg, Thermalbad; die Aerobik, Disko, Kulturreise, Massage, Schönheitsfarm; (*pl.*) die Kalorien, Körpermuskeln; mit sich bringen, planen, trainieren; aktiv, deutschsprachig, effektiv, frustriert, überfüllt

Freizeit—Lust oder Frust?

CD 6,
Track 9

Vor hundert Jahren war es° das Privileg der reichen° Leute, nicht arbeiten zu müssen. Die Arbeiter in den deutschsprachigen Ländern haben zu der Zeit aber oft noch 75 Stunden pro Woche gearbeitet. Urlaub für Arbeiter gibt es erst seit 1919: zuerst nur drei Tage im Jahr. Heute ist das anders. Die Deutschen
5 arbeiten nur ungefähr 197 Tage im Jahr, weniger als° die Menschen in fast allen anderen Industrieländern. Außer den vielen Feiertagen haben sehr viele Leute fünf oder sechs Wochen Urlaub im Jahr. So ist die Freizeit ein sehr wichtiger Teil des Lebens und mehr als° nur Zeit, sich vom täglichen Stress zu erholen.

    Was tut man mit der vielen Freizeit? Natürlich ist Fernsehen sehr wichtig.
10 Viele sitzen mehr als zwei Stunden pro Tag vor dem Fernseher. Auch Sport ist sehr populär, nicht nur das Zusehen°, sondern auch das aktive Mitmachen°, um sich fit zu halten. Ein neuer Trendsport ist Nordic Walking, eine besonders effektive Art° des Wanderns mit Stöcken°, wobei° man 90 Prozent° der Körpermuskeln trainiert und viele Kalorien verbrennt°. Aber auch Aerobik, Tai Chi, Squash oder
15 Windsurfen sind „in", genauso wie Tennis und Golf. Fußball ist bei den Deutschen und Österreichern, wie überall in Europa, der Nationalsport. Auch Handball und Volleyball sind in den deutschsprachigen Ländern sehr beliebt.

    Viele Menschen sind gern draußen in der Natur. An Wochenenden fahren sie oft mit dem Zug oder mit dem Auto aufs Land und gehen spazieren, fahren
20 Rad oder wandern. Danach setzt man sich in ein schönes Gartenrestaurant und entspannt sich. Im Sommer gehen sie oft ins öffentliche Schwimm bad oder fahren an einen schönen See. Manche gehen auch angeln oder segeln. Andere sind viel im Garten. Wenn sie in einer Stadtwohnung leben, können sie sich ein kleines Gartenstück pachten° und dort Blumen und Gemüse ziehen°. Viele
25 bauen sich dort ein Gartenhäuschen, wo sie sich duschen, umziehen oder entspannen können.

Im Schrebergarten, für Stadtmenschen eine Oase im Grünen

    Die Deutschen sind reiselustig°. Immer wieder zieht es sie hinaus in die Ferne, z. B. nach Spanien, Griechenland, Frankreich, aber auch nach Nordamerika, China oder Indien. Sie geben fast ein Sechstel° des Touristikumsatzes°
30 der ganzen Welt aus. Manche machen Kulturreisen, um Land und Leute kennen zu lernen, in Museen zu gehen oder sich auf einem der vielen Festspiele Musik anzuhören. Andere reisen, um Sprachen zu lernen oder einmal etwas ganz anderes zu tun, etwas Neues zu erleben. Viele fahren in den warmen Süden, um sich in die Sonne zu legen und schön braun wieder nach Hause zu kommen.
35 Andere ziehen es vor, zu einem Kurort oder einer Schönheitsfarm zu gehen, um sich mit Thermalbädern, Massagen und Hautpflege° verwöhnen zu lassen°.

    Und die jungen Leute? Außer den oben genannten° Aktivitäten macht es ihnen besonders Spaß, sich mit Freunden zu treffen und in Kneipen°, Diskos, Cafés, Musikklubs oder ins Kino zu gehen. Auch gehen sie gern bummeln oder einkaufen.

Margin glosses:

100 years ago, it was / rich

less than

more than

watching / participation

type / poles / where / percent burns

lease / grow

Schrebergärten are small garden colonies on the outskirts of urban areas. The orthopedist Daniel Schreber founded the garden movement in the 19th century as a means for workers to supplement their incomes and defuse urban *angst*. Today, they provide recreation and give city dwellers a chance to grow their own vegetables, fruit, and flowers.

eager to travel

one sixth / *here*: travel dollars

skin care / let themselves be spoiled / above-mentioned

pubs

Inlineskaten und Wandern hält fit.

40   Dieser ganze Freizeitboom bringt aber auch Probleme mit sich. Manche langweilen sich, weil sie nicht wissen, was sie mit ihrer Freizeit machen sollen. Andere sind frustriert, wenn sie auf der Autobahn in lange Staus° kommen oder die Züge überfüllt sind. Manchmal muss man eben° etwas planen. Man muss ja nicht am ersten oder letzten° Urlaubstag unterwegs° sein. Und wenn man seine
45   Ruhe° haben will, darf man nicht in der Hauptsaison° zu den bekannten Ferienplätzen fahren. Sonst° wird Freizeitlust zum Freizeitfrust.

Marginal glosses (left):

traffic jams
just
last / on the road
peace and quiet / high season
otherwise

Aktives zum Text

A. Was passt?

____ 1. Vor hundert Jahren war es das Privileg der reichen Leute, nicht . . .
____ 2. Heute haben sehr viele Leute außer . . . auch noch fünf oder sechs Wochen Urlaub im Jahr.
____ 3. Die Freizeit ist mehr als nur Zeit, sich vom Stress . . .
____ 4. Viele Leute sitzen über zwei Stunden am Tag . . .
____ 5. Andere arbeiten gern . . .
____ 6. Wer keinen Garten hat, hat die Möglichkeit, . . .
____ 7. Wenn das Wetter schön ist, kann man . . .
____ 8. Eine neue Art, . . . , ist Nordic Walking.
____ 9. Eine alte Art, . . . , ist Joga *(Yoga)*.
____ 10. Manche machen Kulturreisen, um sich zum Beispiel auf einem der vielen Musikfeste Musik . . .
____ 11. Andere fahren in den warmen Süden, um . . .
____ 12. Junge Leute gehen gern . . .
____ 13. Am Anfang und am Ende der Ferien sind die Autobahnen oft überfüllt *(overcrowded)* und es gibt . . .
____ 14. Für manche Leute ist Freizeit ein Problem, weil sie nicht wissen, was sie . . . tun sollen.

a. im Garten
b. vor dem Fernseher
c. Staus
d. den vielen Feiertagen
e. mit ihrer Freizeit
f. sich da richtig wohl fühlen
g. sich ein kleines Gartenstück zu pachten

h. zu erholen
i. anzuhören
j. arbeiten zu müssen
k. schön braun zurückzukommen
l. in Diskos
m. Kalorien zu verbrennen *(to burn)*
n. sich zu entspannen

B. Kreativurlaub Lesen Sie die Ferienangebote *(vacation offers)* mit Ihrem Partner/Ihrer Partnerin und finden Sie heraus, ob das etwas für ihn/sie ist! Erzählen Sie dann der Klasse, was ihm/ihr besonders gefällt!

1. Wo gibt es Sprachkurse in Französisch? Wie viele Stunden sind Sie da in der Klasse und wie viele Stunden Praxis *(practice)* bekommen Sie in der Woche?
2. Wo kann man Segelfliegen lernen? Wie lange braucht ein Anfänger *(beginner)*, bevor er/sie allein fliegen kann? Von wann bis wann gibt es Intensivkurse?
3. Wo kann man Husky-Safaris und Rentierschlittenfahrten *(trips with a reindeer sled)* erleben? Wie wär's mit Skilanglauf *(cross-country skiing)*? Haben Sie das schon einmal gemacht? Wenn ja, wo?
4. Wo gibt es noch Skilanglauf? Von wann bis wann sind die Skikurse? Wie wär's mit Kanufahren? Ist das etwas für Sie? Haben Sie das schon einmal gemacht? Wenn ja, wo?
5. Wo gibt es Kunstkurse? Ist das etwas für Sie? Wann gibt es diese Kurse?
6. Wer verkauft Auszeiten *(time-outs)*, wo man die Natur erleben kann? Wo gibt es diese Auszeiten? Ist das etwas für Sie? Warum (nicht)?
7. Wo gibt es Kurse für kreatives Schreiben? Ist das etwas für Sie? Warum (nicht)?
8. Wohin gehen die Skiflüge von Hamburg? Ist das etwas für Sie? Wenn ja, wohin? Was kostet eine solche Woche Skiurlaub? Ist das billig oder teuer?

C. Ich ziehe es vor, . . . Beim Thema Freizeit haben Sie und Ihr Partner/Ihre Partnerin ganz andere Ideen. Folgen Sie *(follow)* dem Beispiel!

> BEISPIEL   Ich habe Lust, . . . (baden gehen, hier bleiben usw.)
> S1   Ich habe Lust, baden zu gehen. Und du?
> S2   Ich ziehe es vor, hier zu bleiben.

1. Nach der Vorlesung habe ich Zeit, . . . (Tennis spielen, mein Buch lesen usw.)
2. Mir gefällt es, . . . (durch Geschäfte bummeln und einkaufen, nichts ausgeben usw.)
3. Ich habe Lust, diesen Sommer . . . (in den Süden fahren, nach Norwegen reisen usw.)
4. Ich finde es schön, abends . . . (tanzen gehen, sich Musik anhören, eine DVD ansehen)

D. Bildbeschreibung: An der Ostsee Beschreiben Sie dieses Bild mit Hilfe der folgenden *(following)* Wörter! Schreiben Sie 8–10 Sätze.

Zum Erkennen: der Adler, - *(eagle)*; Badeanzug, ¨e *(swimsuit)*; Horizont, Rollwagen, -; Sand, Strand *(beach)*; Strandkorb; ¨e *(basket chair)*; Zaun, ¨e *(fence)*; das Gras; Zelt, -e *(tent)*; die Badehose, -n *(swimming trunks)*; Düne, -n *(dune)*; Flagge, -n; Holzterrasse, -n *(wood deck)*; See *(sea, ocean)*; Stange, -n *(pole)*; bunt *(colorful, multicolored)*

Schreibtipp

Describing Pictures

Before starting to write your description, look closely at the picture and think of vocabulary you might need. Look at the vocabulary in *Zum Erkennen* and locate those things in the picture. Consider directional pointers to tell about specific locations in the picture. Such pointers might include phrases like **vorne links** *(in front to the left)*, **hinten rechts** *(in the back to the right)*, **oben, unten, in der Mitte** *(in the middle)*, plus all sorts of prepositions you have learned. Useful verbs might include **sehen** and **sein,** for example: **In der Mitte sieht man . . . , Oben links ist ein . . . ,** and so forth. Make your description more interesting by including adjectives and varying your sentence structure. You can also add some comments to express your personal reaction to the picture.

E. Kurzgespräche Bereiten Sie mit Ihrem Partner/Ihrer Partnerin einen der beiden Dialoge vor und präsentieren Sie ihn danach vor der Klasse!

1. **Ich bin's, Tante Elisabeth!**

   Your aunt Elisabeth, who lives in Zurich, calls. You answer the phone, greet her, and ask how she and Uncle Hans are doing. She says how they are and asks about you. You tell her you've caught a cold and aren't feeling very well. She expresses her sympathy and asks whether you'd like to visit them during . . . (e.g., spring break). Do you want to accept? If so, your aunt says that she's glad, and she reminds you to tell her when you are going to arrive. You both say good-bye.

2. Hier Reisebüro Eckhardt!

You call a travel agency, Reisebüro Eckhardt. An employee answers the phone and connects you with an agent. You ask the agent about trains to Zurich. He/she wants to know when you want to go. You tell him/her on . . . *(give a date)*. He/she says that you need to reserve a seat (**einen Platz reservieren**). He/she says it costs . . . *(give a price)*; you tell him/her to reserve a seat. The agent asks when you want the tickets, and you reply that you'll come by on . . . *(give a day)*. You both say good-bye.

🔴 Since you will be departing for Zurich from Stuttgart, the travel agent will use the schedule in Chapter 8 *(Aktives zum Thema*, Exercise C) to tell you about your options, depending on what time of day you would like to travel. You also ask him/her about the return schedule and the cost of a round-trip ticket.

 ## Hörverständnis

Track 20   **Eine tolle Radtour**   Hören Sie, wo Sabrina mit ihren Freunden gewesen ist! Sind die folgenden *(following)* Aussagen richtig oder falsch?

Zum Erkennen: im Büro *(at the office)*; das Mietfahrrad, ¨er *(rent-a-bike)*; ab·holen *(to pick up)*; die Zahnradbahn *(cog railway)*; das Panorama; die Talfahrt *(descent)*; die Fähre, -n *(ferry)*

_____ 1. Weil Sabrina bei der Post arbeitet, möchte sie in den Ferien etwas ganz anderes tun.
_____ 2. Im Frühling hat sie eine Radtour um den Bodensee gemacht.
_____ 3. Sie hat diese Tour mit ihrer Familie gemacht.
_____ 4. In Lindau haben sie ihre Fahrräder abgeholt.
_____ 5. Am ersten Tag sind sie bis nach Heiden gekommen.
_____ 6. Am zweiten Tag haben sie eine schnelle Talfahrt bis an den See gehabt.
_____ 7. Die zweite Nacht haben sie in Bregenz übernachtet.
_____ 8. Am dritten Tag hat sie eine Fähre zurück nach Friedrichshafen gebracht.
_____ 9. Sie sind in den paar Tagen in drei Ländern gewesen.
_____ 10. Die Tour hat mit Übernachtungen 233 Franken gekostet.
_____ 11. Zum Mittagessen haben sie meistens nichts gegessen.
_____ 12. Mit so einer Radtour hält man sich fit.

🌐 Visit Frankfurt/Main; a train trip to Lindau; leisure activities along Lake Constance: http://wiegehts.heinle.com.

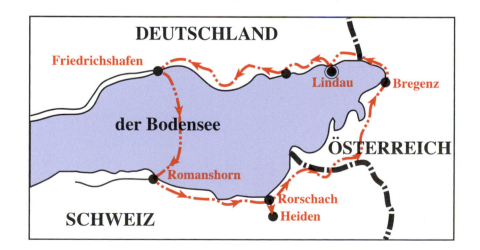

Literatur

Biographisches

Johann Wolfgang von Goethe (1749–1832) was one of Germany's greatest poets, novelists, and playwrights. He was also a leading thinker and scientist. His works include *Faust, Wilhelm Meister,* and *Die Leiden des jungen Werther,* a sensationally successful novel about a sensitive young man alienated from the world around him, which Napoleon is said to have read seven times. Because of his vast scope of knowledge and his comprehensive interest in the world of human experience, Goethe is often referred to as "the last universal man."

Rose Ausländer was one of Germany's most prominent writers of her time. Born into a Jewish family in 1907 in the German-speaking town of Czernowitz, Ukraine, she was transported to a Nazi-guarded ghetto in 1941 and emerged four years later to tell her story. After developing her writing talent during two decades of self-imposed exile in the United States, she returned to Europe in the mid-1960s to settle and publish in Düsseldorf. Themes of persecution, emigration, and loneliness marked her work, which appeared in collections of poetry: *Blinder Sommer* (1956), *Inventar* (1972), and *Ein Stück weiter* (1979), and in her outstanding volume of poetry and prose, *Ohne Visum* (1974). She died in Düsseldorf in 1988.

Vor dem Lesen

Stilfragen *(Questions about style)*

1. Wie viele Strophen *(stanzas)* hat das erste Gedicht und wie viele das zweite?
2. Haben die zwei Gedichte Reime *(rhymes)?* Wenn ja, was reimt sich?
3. Welche Anredeform *(form of address)* benutzen sie?
4. Welche Beispiele von Imperativen gibt es in den beiden Gedichten?
5. Das Gedicht von Rose Ausländer hat kein Komma, keinen Punkt *(period)* und kein Ausrufungszeichen *(exclamation mark).* Ist das typisch für unsere Zeit oder ist das nur ein besonderes Stilmittel *(stylistic device)?*

 ## Erinnerung

Track 21 Willst du immer weiter schweifen°?   continue wandering

Sieh, das Gute liegt so nah.

Lerne nur das Glück ergreifen°,   take hold of

Denn das Glück ist immer da.

Johann Wolfgang von Goethe

Noch bist du da

Track 22

Wirf° deine Angst	Throw
in die Luft°	air
Bald	
ist deine Zeit um°	up
5 bald	
wächst° der Himmel°	grows / sky
unter dem Gras	
fallen deine Träume	
ins Nirgends°	into nowhere
10 Noch	
duftet° die Nelke°	is fragrant / carnation
singt die Drossel°	thrush (bird)
noch darfst du lieben	
Worte verschenken	
15 noch bist du da	
Sei° was du bist	Be
Gib was du hast	

Rose Ausländer

Das Leben ist wie eine Pusteblume. Wenn die Zeit gekommen ist, muss jeder alleine fliegen.

Nach dem Lesen

A. Fragen zu den Gedichten

1. Woran denkt Goethe, wenn er von „weiter schweifen" redet? Was meinen Sie?
2. Was ist der Hauptgedanke *(main idea)* in seinem Gedicht?
3. Glauben Sie, dass er dieses Gedicht früh oder spät in seinem Leben geschrieben hat?
4. Der Titel des Gedichts ist „Erinnerung". Auf Englisch bedeutet Erinnerung entweder *memory* oder *reminder*. Welche Bedeutung von Erinnerung ist hier relevant?
5. Rose Ausländer weiß, dass am Ende des Lebens der Tod *(death)* steht. Was will sie uns mit diesem Gedicht sagen? Was sollen wir tun?
6. Johann Wolfgang von Goethe und Rose Ausländer haben zu ganz verschiedenen *(different)* Zeiten gelebt und ihr Leben war *(was)* ganz anders. Und doch haben diese zwei Gedichte etwas gemeinsam *(in common)*. Was zum Beispiel?
7. Wie gefallen Ihnen die Gedichte? Erklären Sie Ihre Antwort!

B. Lebensqualität Wie bringt man Qualität in sein *(one's)* Leben? Schreiben Sie ein paar Gedanken auf oder, wenn möglich, schreiben Sie ein Gedicht mit vier bis fünf Zeilen!

Lernziele

In this chapter you will learn about:

Zum Thema
Entertainment, media

Kultur-Fokus
German film, theater, music, art, and television
Bertolt Brecht

Struktur
Verbs with prepositional objects
Da- and **wo-**compounds
Endings of unpreceded adjectives

Einblicke + Literatur
Wer die Wahl hat, hat die Qual.
Bertolt Brecht: "Vergnügungen"

For more information, go to http://iLrn.heinle.com

Regisseur (director) *Wolfgang Becker bei Dreharbeiten* (shooting) *für den Film* Good bye Lenin!

Vorschau German Film

Minidrama: *Kino? Ja, bitte!*
Blickpunkt: *Das Hebbel Theater*

During the early days of film, the Ufa studios in the Berlin suburb of Potsdam-Babelsberg were second only to Hollywood in churning out world-class productions, including such classics as *M, Nosferatu, Metropolis,* and *Der blaue Engel.* When the National Socialists came to power, film production continued, although many prominent directors and actors emigrated to the United States and elsewhere. After the war, those studios were taken over by Defa, whose films were subject to the approval of GDR authorities and have subsequently become a bridge to the past. Among Defa's best-known films are Wolfgang Staudte's *Der Untertan* and Frank Beyer's *Jakob der Lügner.* After the fall of the Berlin Wall, Vivendi Universal took over the studios from Germany's Treuhand privatization agency, bringing real change to the studios, which now belong to two German investors.

Beginning in the 1960s, a new wave of young West German filmmakers seized the world's attention. Directors such as Rainer Werner Fassbinder *(Die Ehe der Maria Braun),* Werner Herzog *(Stroszek),* Margarethe von Trotta *(Rosa Luxemburg* and *Das Versprechen),* Doris Dörrie *(Männer* and *Bin ich schön),* Volker Schlöndorff *(Die Stille nach dem Schuss* and *Die Blechtrommel*—based on a Nobel-Prize-winning novel by Günter Grass), and Wolfgang Petersen *(Das Boot)* produced critically acclaimed movies. Many German directors continue to work closely with Hollywood. Examples are Roland Emmerich *(Independence Day)* and Wim Wenders *(Wings of Desire).* While critics lament the domination of American blockbusters (most of which are dubbed), German film has been experiencing a renaissance, characterized by numerous international coproductions, directed by such artists as István Szabó *(Der Fall Furtwängler),* Roman Polanski *(Der Pianist),* and Jean-Jacques Annaud *(Stalingrad).*

Despite internationally renowned achievements such as Tom Tykwer's *Lola rennt* and *Der Krieger und die Kaiserin,* Christian Petzold's *The State I Am In,* Caroline Link's *Jenseits der Stille* and *Nirgendwo in Afrika,* as well as Wolfgang Becker's *Good bye Lenin!* and *Das Leben ist eine Baustelle,* the German film industry is struggling with a relatively small market share. More and more it seems as though film is consumed through the medium of television instead of the big screen. Babelsberg Studio in Potsdam now relies heavily on both television productions and major international movies to make a profit.

• Dates for filmmakers: Staudte (1906–1984), Beyer (1932), Fassbinder (1946–1982), Herzog (1942), v. Trotta (1942), Dörrie (1955), Schlöndorff (1939), Grass (1927), Petersen (1941), Emmerich (1955), Wenders (1945), Szabó (1938), Polanski (1933), Annaud (1943), Tykwer (1965), Petzold (1960), Link (1964), Becker (1954).

M (Eine Stadt sucht einen Mörder), *von Fritz Lang*

Die Blechtrommel *(nach dem Roman von Günther Grass), von Volker Schlöndorff*

Lola rennt, *von Tom Tykwer*

Zum Thema

 ### Blick in die Zeitung

CD 7, Track 1

SONJA   Du, was gibt's denn heute Abend im Fernsehen?

THEO   Keine Ahnung. Sicher nichts Besonderes.

SONJA   Mal sehen! *Gute Zeiten, schlechte Zeiten,* einen Dokumentarfilm und einen Krimi.

THEO   Dazu habe ich keine Lust.

SONJA   Vielleicht gibt's was im Kino?

THEO   Ja, *Good bye Lenin!, Harry Potter* und *Shrek 2.*

SONJA   *Good bye Lenin!* habe ich schon zweimal gesehen, außerdem habe ich ihn auf DVD. Der Film ist klasse! Vielleicht können wir ihn mal bei mir zusammen anschauen, aber nicht heute. Und *Harry Potter* und *Shrek 2* sind für Kinder, oder?

THEO   Stimmt. . . . He, schau mal! Im Theater gibt's *Der kaukasische Kreidekreis* von Brecht.

SONJA   Nicht schlecht. Hast du Lust?

THEO   Ja, das klingt gut. Gehen wir!

> *Good bye Lenin!* tells the tragicomic story of a fatally ill woman in East Berlin who wakes up from a long coma unaware that the GDR no longer exists.

An der Theaterkasse

THEO   Haben Sie noch Karten für heute Abend?

DAME   Ja, erste Reihe erster Rang links und Parkett rechts.

THEO   Zwei Plätze im Parkett! Hier sind unsere Studentenausweise.

DAME   10 Euro bitte!

SONJA   Wann fängt die Vorstellung an?

DAME   Um 20.15 Uhr.

Während der Pause

THEO   Möchtest du eine Cola?

SONJA   Ja, gern. Aber lass mich zahlen! Du hast schon die Programme gekauft.

THEO   Na gut. Wie hat dir der erste Akt gefallen?

SONJA   Prima. Ich habe das Stück schon mal in der Schule gelesen, aber noch nie auf der Bühne gesehen.

THEO   Ich auch nicht.

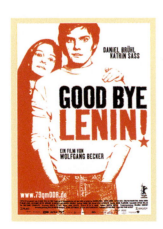

Der kaukasische Kreidekreis, von Bertolt Brecht

A. Fragen

1. Was gibt's im Fernsehen? 2. Gefällt das Theo? 3. Hat Sonja Lust, sich *Good bye Lenin!* im Kino anzuschauen? 4. Warum nicht? 5. Wie soll der Film sein? 6. Was gibt's im Theater? 7. Gibt es noch Karten für dieses Stück? 8. Wo sind Theos und Sonjas Plätze? 9. Wann fängt die Vorstellung an? 10. Was tun Theo und Sonja während der Pause? 11. Wer bezahlt dafür *(for it)*? 12. Woher kennt Sonja das Stück schon?

B. Jetzt sind Sie dran! Sehen Sie sich mit Ihrem Partner/Ihrer Partnerin eine Lokalzeitung an, um herauszufinden, was es im Fernsehen, im Kino und im Theater gibt. Vielleicht machen Sie auch Pläne und gehen zur Kino- oder Theaterkasse oder Sie gehen zur Videothek *(video store)* und holen sich *(get)* ein oder zwei Videos. Wechseln Sie sich ab!

BEISPIEL

S1 Was gibt's im Fernsehen / im Kino / im Theater?
S2 Hast du Lust? / Kennst du den Film . . . ?
S1 Ja. Das klingt gut, gehen wir! / Nein. Dazu habe ich keine Lust.

Fokus   The Magic of the Theater

Theater plays a central role in the cultural life of Germany, Austria, and Switzerland. Germany has more than 400 theaters, the most important ones in metropolises such as Berlin, Hamburg, and Munich. But even medium-sized and small cities have their own repertory theaters as well. Some date back to the 18th century, when—before Germany was united as a country—many local sovereigns founded their own court theaters. By the 19th century, many towns and cities had established theaters as public institutions. Theaters were, after all, a major source of entertainment.

The classic works by Johann Wolfgang von Goethe, Friedrich Schiller, Bertolt Brecht, Max Frisch, Friedrich Dürrenmatt, William Shakespeare, and Molière continue to draw large audiences, as do works by modern playwrights such as Gerlind Reinshagen and the Austrian Elfriede Jelinek, who won the 2004 Nobel Prize for Literature for her controversial novels and plays in which she critiques violence against women and explores sexuality and political extremism in Europe. As in other European countries, the German government has traditionally subsidized the fine arts, but with recent budget cuts, many theater directors are beginning to rely more heavily on corporate sponsorship. States and local governments also subsidize tickets in public venues. Most theaters offer reduced ticket prices for students, seniors, and the unemployed. An active children's theater movement thrives across the country, with marionettes and puppetry drawing delighted crowds.

Municipal theaters in medium-sized cities usually also offer ballet, musicals, and operas. Not only do the traditionally famous German-language operas (for example, Beethoven's *Fidelio,* Mozart's *Die Zauberflöte,* or Richard Strauss's *Der Rosenkavalier*) continue to be popular, but other international and modern operas, such as Puccini's *La Bohème* or Berg's *Wozzeck,* attract large audiences as well. In the summer, many cities entice arts lovers to music, theater, ballet, and open-air film festivals. Broadway musicals have met with notable success in Germany, with special musical theaters being dedicated to the works of British composer Andrew Lloyd Webber, such as *Das Phantom der Oper, Cats, Starlight Express,* or *Die Schöne und das Biest.* Newer musicals popular in Germany include *Mozart* and *Verdi,* a pop adaptation with music and lyrics by Elton John and Tim Rice. Experimental dance has also been well represented in Germany by artists such as Oskar Schlemmer, Gret Palucca, and Pina Bausch with her world-famous Wuppertal Dance Theater.

Dates for celebrities from the German-speaking countries: Goethe (1749–1832), Schiller (1759–1805), Brecht (1898–1956), Frisch (1911–1991), Dürrenmatt (1921–1990), Jelinek (1946), Reinshagen (1926), Beethoven (1770–1827), Mozart (1756–1791), Strauss (1864–1949), Berg (1885–1935), Schlemmer (1888–1943), Palucca (1902–1993), Bausch (1940).

Wortschatz 1

Die Unterhaltung *(entertainment)*

der Anfang, ⸚e	*beginning, start*	die Kunst, ⸚e	*art*
Autor, -en	*author*	Oper, -n	*opera*
Blick (in / auf + acc.)	*glance (at), view (of)*	Pause, -n	*intermission, break*
Chor, ⸚e	*choir*	Vorstellung, -en	*performance*
Film, -e	*film, movie*	Werbung	*advertising*
Komponist, -en, -en	*composer*	Zeitschrift, -en	*magazine*
Krimi, -s	*detective story*	Zeitung, -en	*newspaper*
Maler, -	*painter(artist)*		
Roman, -e	*novel*	dumm	*stupid, silly*
Schauspieler, -	*actor*	komisch	*funny (strange, comical)*
das Ballett, -s	*ballet*		
Ende	*end*	langweilig	*boring*
Gemälde, -	*painting*	nächst- / letzt-	*next / last*
Konzert, -e	*concert*	spannend	*exciting, suspenseful*
Orchester, -	*orchestra*		
Programm, -e	*(general) program; channel*	traurig / lustig	*sad / funny*
Stück, -e	*play, piece (of music or ballet)*	klatschen	*to applaud*
		lachen / weinen	*to laugh / to cry*
		lächeln	*to smile*

Weiteres

am Anfang / am Ende	*in the beginning / at the end*
vor kurzem	*recently*
an·fangen (fängt an), angefangen	*to start, begin*
an·machen / aus·machen	*to turn on / to turn off*
sich an·schauen	*to watch, look at*
sich entscheiden, entschieden	*to decide*
vergessen (vergisst), vergessen	*to forget*
Was gibt's im Fernsehen?	*What's (playing) on television?*
Keine Ahnung!	*No idea!*
Das ist zu . . . (lang, laut).	*That's too . . . (long, loud).*
(Das ist) klasse / spitze!	*(That's) great!*
(Das ist doch) unglaublich!	*(That's) unbelievable! (That's) hard to believe.*
(Das ist) <u>unheimlich interessant!</u>	*(That's) really interesting!*
(Das ist ja) Wahnsinn!	*(That's) crazy / awesome / unbelievable!*
Das ärgert mich.	*That makes me mad.*
Jetzt habe ich aber genug.	*That's enough. I've had it.*
Ich habe die Nase voll.	*I'm fed up (with it).*
Das hängt mir zum Hals(e) heraus.	*I'm fed up (with it).*

🔸 Like **unheimlich interessant**: **unheimlich nett / müde** etc. **Unheimlich** by itself means *tremendous(ly), extreme(ly), uncanny / uncannily*, but it can also mean *frightening, eerie, sinister*.

Zum Erkennen: die Reihe, -n *(row)*; im Rang *(in the balcony)*; im Parkett *(in the orchestra)*; der Akt, -e; AUCH: die Ausstellung, -en *([art] exhibit / show)*; das da-/wo- Kompositum *(da-/wo-compound)*; das Stichwort, ⸚er *(key word)*; die Leseratte, -n *(bookworm)*; der Lieblingsplatz, ⸚e *(favorite place)*; die Rolle, -n *(role, part)*; die Statistik, -en; bewerten *(to rate)*; sich holen *(to get)*; vorausgehend *(preceding)*

Aktives zum Thema

A. Am Frühstückstisch Beenden Sie die Sätze!

1. Auf diesem Bild gehört die . . . zu einem guten Frühstück.
2. Das ist natürlich Werbung für . . .
3. Ich . . . *(know)* diese Zeitung (nicht).
4. Auf dem Frühstückstisch sieht man . . .
5. Ich esse morgens gern . . .
6. Wenn ich Zeit habe, lese ich . . .
7. Diese Woche liest man in den Zeitungen viel über *(about)* . . .
8. Ich interessiere mich besonders für *(am interested in)* . . .
9. Am . . . ist die Zeitung immer sehr dick.

B. Hoppla, hier fehlt was! Was spielt wo und wann? Sehen Sie sich mit Ihrem Partner/Ihrer Partnerin den Spielplan an und finden Sie heraus, was Sie nicht wissen! Einer von Ihnen sieht sich die Tabelle unten an, der andere die Tabelle im Anhang, Teil 11. Entscheiden Sie sich dann, was Sie sehen wollen und warum!

S1:

Wo?	Was?	Wann?
Volksbühne		
Urania-Theater	*Eine Nacht in Venedig*, Operette von Johann Strauss	20.15
Metropol-Theater		
Im Dom	*Jedermann*, Schauspiel von Hugo von Hofmannsthal	15.00
Philharmonie	*Original Wolga-Kosaken*, Lieder und Tänze	15.30
Konzerthaus		
Komödie	*Jahre später, gleiche Zeit*, Komödie von Bernhard Slade	16.00
Kammerspiele	*Carmina Burana*, von Carl Orff	17.30
Filmbühne 1		19.30
Filmbühne 2		22.00

BEISPIEL   S1 Was gibt's heute in der Philharmonie?
         S1 Die Wolga-Kosaken.
         S2 Und wann?
         S1 Um halb vier . . . und im Dom gibt's . . .
         S2 Oh ja, wann denn?
         S1 . . .

BEISPIEL   S1 Hast du . . . schon gesehen / gehört?
              Das ist ein(e) . . . von . . .
         S2 Ja / Nein, . . . aber . . .
         S1 Dann hast du Lust . . . ?
         S2 . . .
         S1 Gut, . . .

C. Allerlei Fragen

1. Lesen Sie gern? Sind Sie eine Leseratte *(bookworm)*? Wenn ja, was für Bücher lesen Sie gern? Wie viele Bücher haben Sie in den letzten drei Monaten gelesen? Welche Autoren finden Sie besonders gut? Welche Zeitungen und Zeitschriften lesen Sie gern? Lesen Sie auch Comics?

2. Wo kann man hier Theaterstücke, Opern oder Musicals sehen? Haben Sie dieses Jahr ein interessantes Stück oder ein gutes Musical / eine gute Oper gesehen? Wenn ja, wo und welche(s)? Wie hat es / sie Ihnen gefallen?

3. Gehen Sie manchmal in ein Rock-, Jazz- oder Popkonzert? Mögen Sie klassische Musik? Country Music? Welche Komponisten oder Musikgruppe hören Sie gern?

4. Wer von Ihnen singt gern? Wer singt im Chor? Wer spielt im Orchester oder in einer Band? Wer von Ihnen spielt ein Instrument?

5. Wer hat schon mal eine Rolle *(role, part)* in einem Theaterstück gespielt? Was für eine Rolle?

6. Wie gefällt Ihnen abstrakte Kunst? Welche Maler finden Sie gut? Gehen Sie manchmal zu Kunstausstellungen *(art shows)*? Wenn ja, wo? Wessen Gemälde gefallen Ihnen (nicht)? Malen Sie auch? Wenn ja, was malen Sie gern?

7. Was kann man hier noch zur *(for)* Unterhaltung tun?

D. Was gibt's Interessantes?

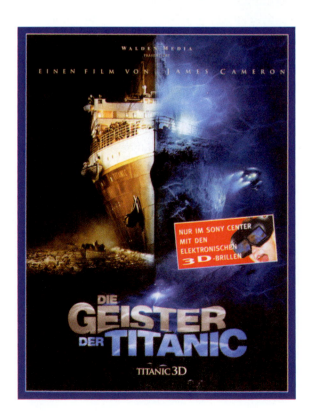

1. **Im CineStar** Sehen Sie sich mit Ihrem Partner/Ihrer Partnerin das Programm vom „CineStar" an und entscheiden Sie sich, was Sie sehen wollen und zu welcher Zeit. Was kosten die Karten? Vergessen Sie nicht, donnerstags gibt's Premieren zum Schnupperpreis *(at bargain prices)*!

2. **Einfach toll / furchtbar!** Sprechen Sie in kleinen Gruppen über einen Film, ein Stück, ein Konzert oder etwas anderes, was Sie vor kurzem gesehen haben, und sagen Sie, wie es Ihnen gefallen hat! Wenn Sie es noch nicht gesehen haben, erzählen Sie, was Sie darüber gehört oder gelesen haben!

E. **Mein Lieblingsplatz** *(favorite place)* Sehen Sie sich mit den anderen die folgende *(following)* Liste an und erzählen Sie den anderen, wo Sie sich besonders wohl fühlen und entspannen können! Warum dort? Vielleicht ist dieser Lieblingsplatz nicht auf dieser Liste.

1. im Billardsalon
2. unter einem Baum im . . .
3. am Strand *(beach)* von . . .
4. in meinem Zimmer
5. in der Badewanne
6. im Fitnessstudio
7. in der Bibliothek
8. in unserer Garage
9. vor dem Computer
10. im Café / Kaffeehaus . . .

▪ Dates for composers from the German-speaking countries: Bach (1685–1750), Händel (1685–1759), Telemann (1681–1767), Mozart (1756–1791), Beethoven (1770–1827), Schubert (1797–1828), Mendelssohn-Bartholdy (1809–1847), Schumann (1810–1856), Weber (1786–1826), Wagner (1813–1883), Brahms (1833–1897), Wieck (1819–1896), Ney (1882–1968), Mutter (1963), Meyer (1960), Mahler (1860–1911), Strauss (1864–1949), Hindemith (1895–1963), Orff (1895–1982), Schönberg (1874–1951), Zimmermann (1918–1970), Henze (1926), Stockhausen (1928).

Fokus Classical Music, Yesterday and Today

Composers from the German-speaking countries have played no small role in shaping the world of music. Johann Sebastian Bach is one of the preeminent German composers and quite prolific: a recent recording of his complete works covers 171 compact discs! His rich work, which includes both religious and secular music, is universally praised for its beauty and perfection. Other important composers of the baroque period are Georg Friedrich Händel and Georg Philipp Telemann.

Wolfgang Amadeus Mozart, another musical genius, dominated the classical period, and Ludwig van Beethoven laid the foundations for the Romantic Movement. The final choral movement of Beethoven's Ninth Symphony, known as the "Ode to Joy" (**"Ode an die Freude"**), was chosen as the European anthem. Composers Franz Schubert, Felix Mendelssohn-Bartholdy, Robert Schumann, Carl Maria von Weber, Richard Wagner, and Johannes Brahms all regarded their works as following in the tradition of Beethoven. Through the interpretation of their music, pianists like Clara Wieck (wife of Robert Schumann) and Elly Ney, violinist Anne-Sophie Mutter, and clarinetist Sabine Meyer have gained international acclaim in a previously male-dominated field.

Great innovators have also influenced the modern era. Gustav Mahler is a link between the lyrical impulse of the Romantic Movement and the more ironic attitudes of the arts in the 20th century. Richard Strauss pioneered musical drama; Paul Hindemith and Carl Orff established new standards in choral music; and Arnold Schönberg introduced the 12-tone system of composition. Contemporary composers Bernd-Alois Zimmermann, Hans Werner Henze, and Karlheinz Stockhausen have all stretched the boundaries of the avant-garde.

Neujahrskonzert in Wien

F. Kurzgespräche Bereiten Sie mit Ihrem Partner/Ihrer Partnerin einen der beiden Dialoge vor und präsentieren Sie ihn danach vor der Klasse!

1. **Im Buchladen**
You are in a bookstore. As the clerk approaches you, tell him/her you need a gift for someone, perhaps a good book about art, music, the theater, or film. He/she shows you several ones that he/she says are very nice, but you don't like any of them. Finally, you find something that's just right, including the price. You take it.

2. **Die Notizen** *(notes)*
You have lent your notebook with class notes to a classmate [give him/her a name] who has failed to return it as promised—again. Not only that, but this classmate has passed the notebook on to a third person who is supposed to return it to you. You have called there and didn't get an answer. You are trying to prepare for a test. Tell your roommate your tale of woe and vent your anger about the situation.

 ## Aussprache: r, er

CD 7,
Track 2

A. Laute

* For further review, see the Summary of Pronunciation in the front of your *Arbeitsbuch*. Study Part II, subsection 9, and Part III, subsection 11.

1. [r] **r**ot, **r**osa, **r**uhig, **r**echts, **R**adio, **R**egal, **R**eihe, **R**oman, P**r**ogramm, Do**r**f, Konze**r**t, Fah**r**t, Gita**rr**e, trau**r**ig, k**r**ank, He**rr**en
2. [ʌ] Orchest**er**, Theat**er**, Mess**er**, Tell**er**, ab**er**, leid**er**, hint**er**, unt**er**, üb**er**, wied**er**, weit**er**
3. [ʌ / r] Uh**r** / Uh**r**en; Oh**r** / Oh**r**en; Tü**r** / Tü**r**en; Cho**r** / Chö**r**e; Auto**r** / Auto**r**en; Klavie**r** / Klavie**r**e

B. Wortpaare

1. *ring* / Ring
2. *Rhine* / Rhein
3. *fry* / frei
4. *brown* / braun
5. *tear* / Tier
6. *tour* / Tour

 ## Hörverständnis

Die Litfasssäule zeigt, was es an Unterhaltung gibt.

Track 23 ***Biedermann und die Brandstifter*** Hören Sie zu, was Daniel und Christian für den Abend planen! Sind die folgenden Aussagen richtig oder falsch?

Zum Erkennen: mal eben *(just for a minute)*; die Inszenierung *(production)*; die Hauptrolle, -n *(leading role)*; die Einladung, -en *(invitation)*

_____ 1. Christians Vater hat ihm zwei Theaterkarten gegeben.
_____ 2. Christian fragt seinen Freund Daniel, ob er mitkommen möchte.
_____ 3. Die Plätze sind in der 2. Reihe vom 1. Rang.
_____ 4. Die Vorstellung beginnt um halb sieben.
_____ 5. Christian muss sich noch die Haare waschen.
_____ 6. Wenn Daniel sich beeilt, können sie noch schnell zusammen essen.
_____ 7. Sie treffen sich an der Straßenbahnhaltestelle in der Breslauer Straße.

Struktur

10.1 Verbs with prepositional objects

In both English and German, a number of verbs are used together with certain PREPOSITIONS. These combinations often have special idiomatic meanings.

I'm thinking of my vacation. I'm waiting for my flight.

Since the German verb + preposition combinations differ from English, they must be memorized.

denken an (+ *acc.*)	*to think of / about*
schreiben an (+ *acc.*)	*to write to*
sich freuen auf (+ *acc.*)	*to look forward to*
sich vor·bereiten auf (+ *acc.*)	*to prepare for*
warten auf (+ *acc.*)	*to wait for*
sich ärgern über (+ *acc.*)	*to get annoyed / upset about*
lächeln über (+ *acc.*)	*to smile about*
sich entscheiden für / gegen (+ *acc.*)	*to decide for / against*
sich informieren über (+ *acc.*)	*to inform oneself / find out about*
sich interessieren für (+ *acc.*)	*to be interested in*
erzählen von (+ *dat.*)	*to tell about*
halten von (+ *dat.*)	*to think of, be of an opinion about*
sprechen von (+ *dat.*) / **über** (+ *acc.*)	*to talk of / about*

CAUTION: The prepositions in these idiomatic combinations (**an, auf, über,** etc.) are not separable prefixes. They function like any other preposition and are followed by nouns or pronouns in the appropriate cases:

Separable-prefix verb	BUT	Verb + preposition
Ich **rufe** dich morgen **an.**		Ich **denke an** dich.
I'll call you tomorrow.		*I'm thinking of you.*

NOTE: In these idiomatic combinations, two-way prepositions most frequently take the accusative.

Er denkt an seine Reise.	*He is thinking about his trip.*
Sie schreibt an ihre Eltern.	*She is writing to her parents.*
Freut ihr euch aufs Wochenende?	*Are you looking forward to the weekend?*
Ich bereite mich auf eine Prüfung vor.	*I'm preparing for an exam.*
Ich warte auf ein Telefongespräch.	*I'm waiting for a phone call.*
Ich ärgere mich über den Brief.	*I'm upset about the letter.*
Über so etwas Dummes kann ich nur lächeln.	*I can only smile about something stupid like that.*
Informier dich über das Programm!	*Find out about the program.*
Interessierst du dich für Sport?	*Are you interested in sports?*
Erzählt uns von eu(e)rem Flug!	*Tell us about your flight.*
Was hältst du denn von dem Film?	*What do you think of the movie?*
Sprecht ihr von *Hotel Ruanda?*	*Are you talking about Hotel Rwanda?*

Changing the case can sometimes dramatically change the meaning. Note these two different uses of **auf:**

Ich warte **auf den** Zug.
I'm waiting for the train.

BUT

Ich warte **auf dem** Zug.
I'm waiting on top of the train.

Übungen

A. Sagen Sie es noch einmal! Ersetzen Sie die Hauptwörter!

BEISPIEL   Sie warten auf den Zug. (Telefongespräch)
                Sie warten auf das Telefongespräch.

1. Wir interessieren uns für Kunst. (Sport, Musik)
2. Er spricht von seinem Urlaub. (Bruder, Hobbys)
3. Sie erzählt von ihrem Flug. (Familie, Geburtstag)
4. Ich denke an seinen Brief. (Ansichtskarte, Name)
5. Wartest du auf deine Familie? (Gäste, Freund)
6. Freut ihr euch auf das Ballett? (Vorstellung, Konzert)
7. Ich habe mich über das Wetter geärgert. (Junge, Leute)
8. Was haltet ihr von der Idee? (Gemälde, Maler)

B. Die Afrikareise   Was fehlt?

1. Meine Tante hat _____ mein__ Vater geschrieben. 2. Sie will uns _____ ihr__ Reise durch Afrika erzählen. 3. Wir freuen uns _____ ihr__ Besuch *(m.)*. 4. Meine Tante interessiert sich sehr _____ Afrika. 5. Sie spricht hier im Museum _____ ihr____ Fahrten. 6. Sie malt auch gern und ist _____ Kunst gut informiert. 7. Ich denke gern _____ sie. 8. Mein Vater ärgert sich _____ sie, wenn sie nicht schreibt. 9. Sie hält einfach nicht viel _____ Briefen und sie hat keinen Computer, aber sie ruft uns manchmal an.

Optional English-to-German practice: 1. I am looking forward to the art show. 2. Have you found out about the tickets? 3. We have talked about the show, but then I didn't think of the date. 4. Please don't wait for me *(pl. fam.)*, but go without me. 5. You *(pl. fam.)* know I'm not interested in art. 6. Why do you get so upset about this painter? 7. I'm not upset, but I know this painter and I don't think much of his paintings. 8. The whole town is talking about him. (See answer key in the Appendix.)

C. Hört euch das an! Erzählen Sie den anderen von drei Situationen, wo Sie sich vor kurzem gefreut oder geärgert haben! Vergessen Sie nicht zu sagen, wie Sie sich fühlen!

BEISPIEL   *Wisst ihr, das Autohaus hat mein Auto schon dreimal repariert (repaired). Ich habe viel Geld dafür (on it) bezahlt und es läuft immer noch nicht richtig. Jetzt habe ich aber die Nase voll!*

As in other parts of Europe, early painting in the German-speaking countries was devoted to religious works, especially altarpieces. In the 16th century, Albrecht Dürer became the first important portrait painter; he also developed landscape painting and is regarded as the inventor of etching. His contemporaries include Lucas Cranach and Hans Holbein. Although painting followed the trends of western European art, it did not reach another zenith until the 19th century. Caspar David Friedrich's landscapes are representative of the Romantic era. Following the Congress of Vienna, the Biedermeier period introduced its idyllic settings. Then, towards the turn of the 20th century, came the Viennese Secession (or **der Jugendstil**) with Gustav Klimt.

Early 20th-century artists conveyed the fears and dangers of their times through

Maske, *von Paul Klee*

the style known as expressionism. Two such artists were Oskar Kokoschka, who reflected the anxious, decadent atmosphere of prewar Vienna, and Paul Klee, who ventured into abstract art. Others, including Käthe Kollwitz, Max Beckmann, and Otto Dix, exercised sharp social criticism through their sculptures and canvasses. The rise of the Nazis, who denounced most modern art as "degenerate," put an abrupt end to this creative period. In the second half of the century, Germany's art scene again came alive, with representatives like Joseph Beuys, who turned visual art into action, Rebecca Horn, who presents sculptures as performances, and Markus Lüpertz, whose representational painting seems to convey a "drunken, rapturous" feeling of life.

D. So beende ich die Sätze. Und du? Beenden Sie die Sätze mit Präpositionen wie **an, auf, für, über** oder **von**! Fragen Sie dann Ihren Partner/Ihre Partnerin, wie er/sie sie beendet hat!

> BEISPIEL   Ich lächele nur . . .
>
> S1 Ich lächele nur über solche komischen Fragen. Und du?
> S2 Ich lächele nur über meine kleine Schwester.

1. Ich denke oft . . .
2. Ich warte . . .
3. Ich schreibe gern . . .
4. Ich interessiere mich . . .
5. Ich freue mich . . .
6. Ich ärgere mich manchmal . . .
7. Ich spreche gern . . .
8. Ich halte nicht viel . . .
9. Ich muss mich . . . vorbereiten.
10. Es ist schwer, sich für . . . zu entscheiden.

• Dates for artists from the German-speaking countries: Dürer (1471–1528), Cranach (1472–1553), Holbein the Younger (1497–1543), Friedrich (1774–1840), Klimt (1910–1962), Kokoschka (1866–1980), Klee (1879–1940), Kollwitz (1867–1945), Beckmann (1884–1950), Dix (1891–1969), Beuys (1921–1986), Horn (1944), Lüpertz (1941).

10.2 *Da-* and *wo-*compounds

1. ***Da*-compounds**

In English, pronouns following prepositions can refer to people, things, or ideas:

> *I'm coming with him.*   *I'm coming with it.*

This is not true for German. Pronouns following prepositions refer only to <u>people</u>:

> Ich komme **mit ihm (mit meinem Freund).**

If you wish to refer to <u>a thing or an idea</u>, you must use what's called a **da**-COMPOUND.

> Ich komme **damit (mit unserem Auto).**

Most accusative and dative prepositions (except **außer, ohne,** and **seit**) can be made into **da**-compounds. If the preposition begins with a vowel (**an, in,** etc.), it is used with **dar-:**

dafür	for it/them	**darauf**	on it/them
dagegen	against it/them	**darin**	in it/them
damit	with it/them	**darüber**	above / about it/them
danach	after it/them	usw.	

Können Sie mir sagen, wo ein Briefkasten ist? —Ja, sehen Sie die Kirche dort? **Daneben** ist eine Apotheke, **dahinter** ist die Post und **davor** ist ein Briefkasten mit einem Posthorn **darauf.**

2. *Wo*-compounds

The interrogative pronouns **wer, wen,** and **wem** refer to <u>people</u>.

Von wem sprichst du?	*About whom are you talking?* *(Who are you talking about?)*
Auf wen wartet ihr?	*For whom are you waiting?* *(Who are you waiting for?)*

In questions about <u>things or ideas</u>, **was** is used. If a preposition is involved, however, a **wo**-COMPOUND is required. Again, if the preposition begins with a vowel, it is combined with **wor-**.

wofür?	*for what?*	**worauf?**	*on what?*
wogegen?	*against what?*	**worüber?**	*above/about what?*
womit?	*with what?*	usw.	

Wovon sprichst du?	*About what are you talking?* *(What are you talking about?)*
Worauf wartet ihr?	*For what are you waiting?* *(What are you waiting for?)*

REMEMBER: To ask where something is located, use the question word **wo**, regardless of the answer expected: **Wo ist Peter?** To ask where someone is going, use **wohin** (NOT <u>wo</u> combined with <u>nach</u> or <u>zu</u>!): **Wohin ist Peter gegangen?** To ask where a person is coming from, use **woher** (NOT <u>wo</u> combined with <u>aus</u> or <u>von</u>!): **Woher kommt Peter?**

Übungen

E. Wo ist nur mein Adressbuch? Helfen Sie Ihrem Partner/Ihrer Partnerin, es zu finden! Benutzen Sie dabei immer ein **da**-Kompositum (*da-compound*)!

BEISPIEL   auf dem Sofa?
                 S1 Liegt es auf dem Sofa?
                 S2 Nein, es liegt nicht darauf.

neben dem Bett?, vor dem Telefon?, hinter der Lampe?, auf dem Esstisch?, in der Tasche?, unter den Fotos?, zwischen den Zeitungen und Zeitschriften? . . .

Wer weiß schon genau, woraus ein Hamburger besteht?

F. Noch einmal bitte! Ersetzen Sie die fettgedruckten *(boldfaced)* Wörter mit einem **da**-Kompositum oder mit einer Präposition + Pronomen!

> BEISPIEL   Hans steht **neben Christa.**   *Hans steht neben ihr.*
> Die Lampe steht **neben dem Klavier.**   *Die Lampe steht daneben.*

1. Was machst du **nach den Ferien?**
2. Bist du auch **mit dem Bus** gefahren?
3. Er hat das Gemälde **für seine Frau** gekauft.
4. Was hast du **gegen Skilaufen?**
5. Das Paket ist **von meinen Eltern** gewesen.
6. Die Karten liegen **auf dem Tisch.**
7. Die Kinder haben **hinter der Garage** gespielt.
8. Anja hat **zwischen Herrn Fiedler und seiner Frau** gesessen.
9. Was halten Sie **von dem Haus?**
10. Ist die Faxnummer **im Adressbuch?**
11. Wir denken oft **an unseren kranken Freund.**
12. Freust du dich auch **auf unsere Fahrt?**

 G. Das Klassentreffen *(class reunion)* Sie erzählen Ihrer Großmutter/Ihrem Großvater (Ihrem Partner/Ihrer Partnerin) von einem Klassentreffen, aber er/sie hört schlecht und möchte, dass Sie alles wiederholen. Tun Sie das und wechseln Sie sich nach jedem Verb ab! Jeder darf einmal schwerhörig *(hard of hearing)* sein.

	Horst	Claire	Max + Eva	Gerd + Elke
sprechen über	Sport	Arbeit	Familie	Schulzeit
denken an	Golf spielen	Mittagspause	Urlaub	Vergangenheit *(past)(f.)*
schreiben an	Golftrainer	Freunde	Reisebüro	Schulfreunde
warten auf	Freundin	Post	Antwort	Klassentreffen *(n.)*
s. freuen auf	jedes Spiel	Besuch	Seereise	Wiedersehen
s. interessieren für	nichts anderes	Kunst	Sprachen	alles
s. informieren über	Wetter	Ausstellungen	Städte in Amerika	Lehrer
s. ärgern über	jeden Fehler	Boss	Kinder	Essen

> BEISPIEL   S1 Claire spricht über die Arbeit.
> S2 Worüber spricht Claire?
> S1 Über die Arbeit!

> BEISPIEL   S2 Claire ärgert sich über ihren Boss.
> S1 Über wen ärgert sie sich?
> S2 Über ihren Boss!

I, eine Maus!

Was hast du gegen Mäuse?

Du hast doch nicht Angst davor, oder?

H. Wie bitte? Ihr Partner/Ihre Partnerin sagt Ihnen etwas, aber Sie hören nicht genau hin und gehen ihm/ihr mit Ihren vielen Fragen etwas auf die Nerven. In den Sätzen benutzt er/sie nur Verben von der Liste im Teil 10.1 der Grammatik *(grammar)*. Wechseln Sie sich ab!

BEISPIEL   S1 Ich freue mich auf die nächste Woche.
S2 Worauf freust du dich?
S1 Auf nächste Woche!
S2 Ach so, darauf!

BEISPIEL   S2 Ich freue mich auf meinen Onkel und meine Tante.
S1 Auf wen freust du dich?
S2 Auf meinen Onkel und meine Tante!
S1 Ach so, auf sie!

Fokus   German Language Broadcasters Abroad

Founded in 1953, **Deutsche Welle (DW)** is Germany's foreign broadcasting network, presenting round-the-clock information from Germany and Europe. **DW-TV**, based in Berlin, broadcasts in German, English, and Spanish. **DW-Radio**, based in Cologne, transmits worldwide in 29 different languages, including Hindi and Swahili. **DW-World** provides a multimedia service that offers analysis and background reports on the Internet (www.dw-world.de).

In 2004, the directors of **Deutsche Welle** and Germany's public TV networks (ARD and ZDF) launched a new German-language premium channel **(German TV)** that targets over a million German-speaking homes in the United States. In 2004, the channel was licensed for Canada as well. Latin America, Australia, and Asia are next on the list. By paying a monthly fee, cable and satellite viewers can receive a mixture of top-quality programs from ARD and ZDF, including films, entertainment series, documentaries, children's programs, and sports.

The majority of German-language foreign broadcasters are based abroad. In the United States and Canada, there are over 120 German-language programs, including San Francisco's **Radio Goethe** (with current pop hits), Ontario's **Radio Herz**, and Ottawa's **German Panorama** television. All these enterprises have been quite successful and provide one more way of promoting greater cultural understanding.

10.3 Endings of unpreceded adjectives

In Chapter 9, you learned how to deal with adjectives preceded by either **der-** or **ein-**words. Occasionally, however, adjectives are preceded by neither; they are then called UNPRECEDED ADJECTIVES. The equivalent in English would be adjectives preceded by neither *the* nor *a(n)*:

We bought fresh fish and fresh eggs.

1. Unpreceded adjectives take the endings that the definite article would have if it were used.

der frische Fisch	**das** frische Obst	**die** frische Wurst	**die** frischen Eier
frisch**er** Fisch	frisch**es** Obst	frische Wurst	frische Eier

	masculine	neuter	feminine	plural
nom.	frisch**er** Fisch	frisch**es** Obst	frische Wurst	frische Eier
acc.	frisch**en** Fisch	frisch**es** Obst	frische Wurst	frische Eier
dat.	frisch**em** Fisch	frisch**em** Obst	frisch**er** Wurst	frisch**en** Eiern
gen.	(frisch**en** Fisches)	(frisch**en** Obstes)	(frisch**er** Wurst)	frisch**er** Eier

Heute Abend gibt es heiß**e** Suppe, holländisch**en** Käse, frisch**e** Brötchen und frisch**es** Obst.

- If there are several unpreceded adjectives, all have the same ending.

Ich wünsche dir schön**e**, interessant**e** Ferien.

> **genitive:** The genitive singular forms are relatively rare. Note also that the masculine and neuter forms of the genitive are irregular and the only two that are different from **der**-word endings. (See *Struktur 8.1, The genitive case* to review **der**-word endings in the genitive.)

2. The following words (sometimes called "quantifiers") are often used as unpreceded adjectives in the plural:

andere	*other*
einige	*some, a few* (pl. only)
mehrere	*several* (pl. only)
viele	*many*
wenige	*few*

Wir haben uns mehrer**e** modern**e** Gemälde angesehen.
Sie haben einig**en** jung**en** Leuten gefallen, aber mir nicht.

- When used in the singular, **viel** *(much, a lot)* and **wenig** *(little, not much)* usually do not have endings in modern German, but they are often used as unpreceded adjectives in the plural.

Viele Studenten haben **wenig** Geld, aber nur **wenige** Studenten haben **viel** Zeit.
Many students have little money, but only a few students have a lot of time.

● The adjectives **prima, klasse, spitze,** and **super** also never have an ending.

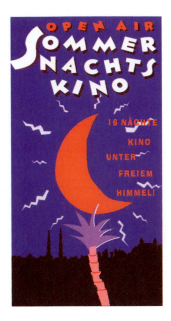

- Numerals, **mehr,** and **ein paar** have no endings. The same holds true for a few of the color words, such as *purple* and *pink* (**lila, rosa**), and adjectives of geographic origin like **Frankfurter, Berliner, Schweizer,** and so on.

Da sind **drei** junge **Wiener** Studenten mit **ein paar** kurzen Fragen.
Haben Sie noch **mehr** graues oder blaues Papier?
Was mache ich mit diesem alten **rosa** Pullover?

Übungen

I. Ersetzen Sie die Adjektive!

BEISPIEL   Das sind nette Leute. (verrückt)
Das sind verrückte Leute.

1. Ich trinke gern schwarzen Kaffee. (heiß, frisch)
2. Sie braucht dünnes Papier. (billig, weiß)
3. Er schreibt tolle Bücher. (spannend, lustig)
4. Heute haben wir wunderbares Wetter. (ausgezeichnet, furchtbar)
5. Dort gibt es gutes Essen. (einfach, gesund)
6. Hier bekommen wir frischen Fisch. (wunderbar, gebacken)
7. Er hat oft verrückte Ideen. (dumm, fantastisch)

J. Sagen Sie es anders! Wiederholen Sie die Sätze, aber diesmal ohne die fettgedruckten Wörter!

BEISPIEL   **Der** holländische Käse ist ausgezeichnet.
Holländischer Käse ist ausgezeichnet.

1. **Die** deutschen Zeitungen haben auch viel Werbung.
2. Der Mann will mit **dem** falschen Geld bezahlen.
3. Sie hat **das** frische Brot gekauft.
4. Er hat **den** schwarzen Kaffee getrunken.
5. Wir haben **die** braunen Eier genommen.
6. Er ist mit **seinen** alten Tennisschuhen auf die Party gegangen.
7. Sie trinken gern **das** dunkle Bier.
8. Auf der Party haben sie **diese** laute Musik gespielt.
9. Er erzählt gern **solche** traurigen Geschichten.
10. Sie hat Bilder **der** bekannten Schauspieler.

Gemütliche Atmosphäre, tolles Ambiente, internationale Küche der Spitzenklasse – das Katzencafé genügt höchsten Ansprüchen!

Restaurant Katzen-Café

Das Café-Restaurant im ♥ des Schnoor

Schnoor 38, 28195 Bremen
Telefon 32 66 21, Fax 32 52 54

Öffnungszeiten:
täglich 12–17 Uhr und 18–0 Uhr
Küche:
täglich 12–15 Uhr und 18–23 Uhr

K. Ein Brief an Freunde Was fehlt?

1. Lieb____ Gudrun, lieb____ Bill! 2. Seit gestern bin ich mit ein paar ander____ Studenten in Dresden. 3. Eine wunderbar____ Stadt mit alt____ Tradition *(f)*! 4. Im Zentrum gibt es viel____ schön____ Gebäude mit barock____ Fassaden *(pl.)*. 5. Die Frauenkirche erinnert an *(reminds of)* furchtbar____ Zeiten. 6. Jetzt hat man sie mit alt____ und neu____ Steinen wieder aufgebaut *(rebuilt)*. 7. Gestern haben wir zwei alt____ Dresdener kennen gelernt. 8. Sie haben uns einige interessant____ Geschichten aus alt____ und neu____ Zeit erzählt. 9. Mit ihnen sind wir abends an der Elbe entlang gelaufen, mit herrlich____ Blick auf *(m.)* die Stadt. 10. Danach haben wir im Ballhaus Watzke gegessen, einer alt____ Brauerei *(brewery)* mit gut____ Atmosphäre *(f.)* und gut____ Bier. 11. Für heute Abend haben wir billig____ Karten für die Oper bekommen. Wie ihr seht, es geht mir gut. Viele Grüße! Eure Anne

L. Das mache ich gern. Und du?

Beenden Sie die folgenden Sätze mit Hauptwörtern und Adjektiven ohne vorausgehenden *(preceding)* Artikel! Fragen Sie dann die anderen in der Gruppe, wie das bei ihnen ist!

BEISPIEL   Ich singe gern . . .
             S1   Ich singe gern alte Lieder. Und du?
             S2   Ich singe gern Rapsongs.
             . . .

1. Ich esse gern . . .
2. Ich trinke gern . . .
3. Ich sammle gern . . .
4. Ich lese gern . . .
5. Ich trage gern . . .
6. Ich sehe gern . . .
7. Ich finde . . . prima.
8. Ich möchte . . .

Fokus   German Television

Both public and commercial television are strong in Germany. After World War II, public corporations were created and given regional broadcasting monopolies, independent of state control. This was to prevent any political party or central government from ever again using the airwaves for propaganda, such as was done during the Nazi era. When television was launched in 1954, the regional broadcasters formed a national network known as **ARD**, commonly known as **Das Erste Programm**. Later, in 1961, a second national channel called **ZDF (Zweites Deutsches Fernsehen)** was founded, based in Mainz. In addition, each of the ARD broadcasters operates a third channel (**Drittes Programm**), which focuses on regional affairs, education, and culture. The public networks also participate in the French/German cultural channel **Arte** and a number of satellite television channels. Mandatory fees paid by each household owning a television set fund this immense bureaucracy. The fees currently amount to some €17 a month per household, a total of around €7 billion per year nationwide. ARD and ZDF are also allowed 20 minutes of advertising per day, restricted to the period before 8 P.M.

It took a constitutional amendment in the mid-1980s to permit private broadcasting in Germany. Now, two major groups dominate what has become a dynamic commercial television market. Market leader **RTL** Group (which operates RTL Television, RTL-2, SuperRTL, Vox and the all-news channel n-tv) is controlled by publishing and music giant Bertelsmann. The largest group, **ProSiebenSat.1** (which operates

SAT 1, Pro 7, Kabel 1, and the news channel N24) was acquired in 2003 by US-Israeli media tycoon Haim Saban. In addition, music channels **MTV** and **Viva**, sports offerings **Eurosport** and **DSF**, and youth-oriented **Tele 5** and **NeunLive** all compete for the remaining viewers. While some of the commercial channels have over-the-air transmitters in some areas, most Germans watch cable television, which serves about 80 percent of Germany's 33 million TV households. Many of the rest have home satellite dishes that receive both public and commercial channels. Supposedly, the average German watches a little more than three hours of television each day.

Zusammenfassung

M. Bilden Sie ganze Sätze!

1. wie lange / du / warten / — / ich? *(pres. perf.)*
2. ich / sich freuen / — / Reise nach Spanien *(pres.)*
3. er / sich ärgern / — / Film *(pres. perf.)*
4. wo- / ihr / sich interessieren? *(pres.)*
5. wollen / sich kaufen / du / einig- / deutsch / Zeitschriften? *(pres.)*
6. in London / wir / sehen / mehrer- / interessant / Stücke *(pres. perf.)*
7. während / Pause / wir / trinken / billig / Sekt *(pres. perf.)*
8. Renate / schon / lesen / ein paar / spannend / Krimi *(pres. perf.)*
9. am Ende / viel / modern / Stücke / Leute / nicht / klatschen / lange *(pres.)*

N. Ein alter Film: *Das Dschungelbuch* Stellen Sie Fragen darüber mit 10 verschiedenen *(different)* Interrogativpronomen, zum Beispiel mit **wer?, wen?, wem?, wessen?, wann?, wo?, wonach?, wogegen?**

Nur wer
kritische Leser hat,
macht eine
gute Zeitung.

Süddeutsche Zeitung

Das Dschungelbuch

 Waldjunge Mowgli, jetzt erwachsen°, rettet° entführte° Offizierstochter —

Abenteuer° mit Jason Scott Lee, frei nach Kiplings Roman

Seit seinem fünften Lebensjahr lebt Mowgli (Jason Scott Lee) im indischen Dschungel°. Menschen kennt er nicht, seine besten Freunde sind Balu, der Bär, und der Panter Baghira. Eines Tages trifft der junge Mann die hübsche Kitty, Tochter des englischen Colonels Brydon (Sam Neill). Die beiden finden heraus, dass sie schon als Kinder zusammen gespielt haben, und sind sich sofort sehr sympathisch°. Aber auch Schurke° Boone (Cary Elwes) ist an Kitty interessiert — fast so sehr wie an den Reichtümern° der Dschungelstadt Monkey City. Er entführt das Mädchen, um Mowgli zu zwingen°, ihn zu dem Schatz° zu bringen. **Fazit°:** Der gute Wilde im Kampf° gegen die böse Zivilisation — Stephen Sommers setzt die simple Story in herrlicher Natur mit viel Herz in Szene.

Der indische Urwald ist sein Zuhause: Mowgli (Jason Scott Lee)

°grown-up, rescues, abducted, adventure, jungle, attractive, crook, richness, force, treasure, result, fight

---

O. Interessanter Besuch Auf Deutsch bitte!

1. Two weeks ago an old friend of my father visited us. 2. He is the author of several plays. 3. I'm very interested in the theater. 4. He knows many important people, even some well-known actresses. 5. Our friend knows many other authors. 6. He spoke about them. 7. He told us some exciting stories. 8. He has just been to (**in**) Vienna. 9. He saw several performances of his new play and bought a few expensive books. 10. He's coming back in the summer. 11. We are looking forward to that. 12. We have also bought him some new novels.

Einblicke

Wortschatz 2

der Bürger, -	citizen
Einfluss, ⸚e	influence
Zuschauer, -	viewer, spectator
das Fernsehen	television (the medium)
die Art, -en (von)	type (of)
Auswahl (an) (+ dat.)	selection / choice (of)
Nachricht, -en	news (on radio and television; usually pl.)
<u>Sendung, -en</u>	(particular) program
also	in other words
etwa	about, approximately
folgend	following
öffentlich / privat	public / private
verschieden	different (kinds of), various
vor allem	mainly, especially, above all
weder . . . noch	neither . . . nor

🟡 Note the difference between **die Sendung** and **das Programm** as they refer to TV: **Die Sendung** refers to *a particular program* (**Diese Kultursendung hat mir gut gefallen.**). **Das Programm** refers to *general programming or a channel.* (Was gibt's **im Abendprogramm / im 1. Programm?**)

Lesetipp
Learning Vocabulary
(continued)

Before reading this text, learn the vocabulary in *Wortschatz 2*. Make a list of the words that have to do with media. Then scan the reading text and see how many additional media words you recognize that are similar to English and add them to the list. Finally, add any other German words relating to the topic of mass media that you already know to complete the list.

Vor dem Lesen

A. Statistiken über junge Deutsche Lesen Sie, was junge Deutsche über den Einfluss der Massenmedien *(mass media)* in ihrem Leben zu sagen haben! Wie ist das bei Ihnen und Ihren Klassenkameraden? (Für % liest man „Prozent".)

Wie viele Stunden sehen Sie jeden Tag fern?	Kein TV	3%
	1–2 Stunden	42%
	2–4 Stunden	28%
	4–6 Stunden	5%
Wie viele Videos sehen Sie pro Woche?	Kein Video	46%
	1–2 Videos	42%
	3–5 Videos	10%
Wie oft sehen Sie die Nachrichten im Fernsehen?	Täglich	39%
	Manchmal	23%
	Nie	4%
Wie oft lesen Sie eine Tageszeitung?	Täglich	42%
	Manchmal	26%
	Nie	7%

Gibt es zu viel Sex im Fernsehen und im Kino oder zu wenig?	Zu viel	38%
	Zu wenig	13%
	Genau richtig	48%
Gibt es zu viel Gewalt *(crime)* im Fernsehen und im Kino?	Zu viel	71%
	Zu wenig	4%
	Genau richtig	25%
Wie viele Bücher haben Sie in den letzten drei Monaten gelesen?	kein Buch	41%
	1–2 Bücher	33%
	3+ Bücher	25%

1. Wie ist das bei Ihnen und Ihrer Familie, bei Ihren Freunden und Mitbürgern *(fellow citizens)*? Kommentieren Sie!
2. Haben Sie einen Computer? Was tun Sie vor allem damit? Wie viele E-Mails pro Tag müssen Sie beantworten? Finden Sie das gut?
3. Können Sie ans Internet? Wenn ja, welche Rolle spielt das Internet in Ihrem Leben? Wie viele Stunden pro Tag sitzen Sie am Computer und surfen Sie im Internet? Was interessiert Sie darin besonders und was nicht? Kaufen oder verkaufen Sie manchmal Sachen im Internet? Wenn ja, wo und was für Sachen?

B. Gehen wir Wörter angeln *(Let's go fishing for words)*! Überfliegen Sie *(scan)* schnell den folgenden Text und finden Sie mit Ihrem Partner/Ihrer Partnerin Beispiele für Adjektive mit und ohne vorausgehenden Artikel! Wovon gibt es mehr *(more)*?

C. Das ist leicht zu verstehen! Welche Silbe ist betont? Markieren Sie sie! Was ist das auf Englisch?

> der Aspekt, Haushalt, Kritiker, Medienmarkt; das Kabarett, Magazin, Satellitenprogramm; die Buchproduktion, Interessengruppe, Kreativität, Society-Publikation, Tageszeitung; finanzieren, registrieren; einflussreich, experimentell, finanziell, informativ, kulturell, politisch, staatlich kontrolliert, unterhaltend

Wer die Wahl hat, hat die Qual°.

Choosing isn't easy (lit. it's a pain).

CD 7, Track 4

Wie überall spielen die Massenmedien, vor allem das Fernsehen, auch in Deutschland eine wichtige Rolle. Fast jeder Haushalt hat heute einen oder zwei Fernseher und kann im Durchschnitt° über 30 Fernsehprogramme empfangen°. Die Auswahl an Sendungen ist groß und wird jedes Jahr größer°.

5 Zu den Hauptprogrammen kommen Programme aus Nachbarländern und auch privates Fernsehen und interessante Kabel- und Satellitenprogramme. Die privaten Sender° sind natürlich auf Werbung angewiesen°. Aber um das öffentliche Fernsehen zu finanzieren, müssen die Deutschen ihre Fernseher und Radios bei der Post registrieren und monatliche Gebühren° zahlen. Werbung gibt es auch im

10 öffentlichen Fernsehen, aber nicht nach acht Uhr abends und nie während Filmsendungen. Sie kommt vor allem vor dem Abendprogramm und dauert fünf bis 10 Minuten. Damit° die Leute den Fernseher dann nicht einfach ausmachen, muss die Werbung natürlich unterhaltend sein.

Das öffentliche Fernsehen ist weder staatlich noch privat kontrolliert, son-

15 dern finanziell und politisch unabhängig°. Darum kann es auch leicht Sendungen für kleine Interessengruppen bringen, z. B. Nachrichten in verschiedenen Sprachen, Sprachunterricht° für Ausländer, experimentelle Musik, politische Diskussionen und lokales Kabarett. Das deutsche Fernsehen präsentiert eigentlich eine gute Mischung aus° aktuellem° Sport und leichter Unterhaltung,

20 von informativen Dokumentarfilmen, internationalen Filmen und kulturellen Sendungen, z. B. Theaterstücken, Opern und Konzerten.

Manche Kritiker halten nicht viel vom Fernsehen. Sie ärgern sich zum Beispiel darüber, dass so viele amerikanische Filme, Serien° und Seifenopern° laufen, obwohl die Statistiken zeigen, dass sich die Zuschauer dafür interes-

25 sieren. Neben guten und informativen Kultursendungen sind auch spannende Filme mit Sex und Gewalt gefragt°. Aber nicht nur darin sehen die Kritiker Probleme, sondern auch in der passiven Rolle der Zuschauer. Manche Menschen, vor allem Kinder, sitzen viel zu lange vor dem Fernseher, oft über drei Stunden täglich. Sie werden dadurch passiv und verlieren an° Kreativität.

30 Trotz der Auswahl an Programmen muss das Fernsehen mit vielen anderen Medien konkurrieren°. Das Radio ist weiterhin° wichtig, denn man hört im Durchschnitt täglich mehr als drei Stunden Radio und liest gern dabei. Viele Deutsche sind Leseratten. Neben den etwa 350 Tageszeitungen gibt es jede Menge° „Special-interest"-Zeitschriften: einflussreiche gesellschaftspolitische°

35 Magazine und Wochenzeitungen wie *Der Spiegel, Focus* oder *Die Zeit* sowie° populäre Society-Publikationen wie *Stern, Bunte* oder *Gala.* Sie alle informieren

on the average
receive / bigger

stations / dependent on

fees

so that

independent

. . . instruction

mixture of / current

series / soap operas

popular

suffer loss of

compete / still

all sorts of / socio-political
as well as

über moderne Aspekte des gesellschaftlichen° Lebens. Man liest auch gern
Bücher. Die Buchproduktion steht international nach den USA auf dem zweiten
Platz. Mehr als° 600 000 Titel sind auf dem Markt und jedes Jahr kommen etwa
40 70 000 Erst- und Neuauflagen° dazu.

　Wie sich das Internet auf die Rolle des Medienmarktes auswirkt°, ist die
große Frage. Denn auch diese moderne Technik konkurriert um° die Zeit der
Bürger. Laut° neuester Statistiken ist Deutsch die fünfthäufigste° Sprache
weltweit im Internet—hinter Englisch, Chinesisch, Japanisch und Spanisch. Die
45 Menschen haben heute eine enorme Auswahl, woher sie ihre Informationen
bekommen und womit sie ihre Freizeit ausfüllen. Diese Wahl ist nicht immer
leicht. Ja, wer die Wahl hat, hat die Qual.

(margin glosses)
social

more than

new editions
affects
competes for
according to / fifth most
　common

Aktives zum Text

A. Richtig oder falsch? Wenn falsch, sagen Sie warum!

____ 1. In Deutschland spielt das Fernsehen keine wichtige Rolle.
____ 2. Nur wenige Haushalte haben einen Fernseher.
____ 3. Die Auswahl an Sendungen ist groß.
____ 4. Weil die Deutschen monatliche Gebühren zahlen, gibt es im
　　　 privaten Fernsehen keine Werbung.
____ 5. Werbung läuft im öffentlichen Fernsehen nie nach sechs Uhr abends.
____ 6. Das öffentliche Fernsehen ist staatlich kontrolliert.
____ 7. Es hat eine gute Mischung aus verschiedenen Sendungen.
____ 8. Manche Kritiker ärgern sich über zu viele deutsche Filme.
____ 9. Sie denken auch, dass zu viel Fernsehen die Leute passiv macht.
____ 10. Wie überall muss das Fernsehen mit anderen Medien konkurrieren.
____ 11. Dazu gehören das Radio, Zeitungen, Zeitschriften und Bücher.
____ 12. Wegen des Internets haben die Deutschen keine Zeit mehr fürs Fernsehen.

B. Was fehlt? Ergänzen Sie die fehlenden Präpositionen, **wo**-Komposita oder **da**-Komposita!

1. Der Lesetext spricht _____ Deutschlands Massenmedien. 2. Wenn wir
in Nordamerika fernsehen, denken wir nur _____ mögliche Kabelgebühren,
aber nicht _____ Fernsehgebühren. Die Deutschen müssen _____
denken. 3. Sie ärgern sich oft _____ diese Gebühren, aber sie können nichts
_____ *(against it)* tun. Sie haben keine Wahl. 4. Viele interessieren sich
nicht nur _____ leichte Unterhaltung, sondern auch _____ informative Dokumentarfilme. 5. Andere warten jeden Abend _____ die
Nachrichten. 6. Sie freuen sich auch hier und da _____ ein Theaterstück
oder ein Konzert. 7. Die großen Nachrichtenmagazine sprechen nicht nur
_____ Politik, sondern auch _____ Kultur und Sport. 8. Manche Leute
sitzen täglich am Computer, um sich _____ alles gut zu informieren. 9. Sie
stellen Fragen _____ andere Leute im Internet und warten dann _____
ihre Antwort. 10. Ich halte nicht viel _____ Fernsehen. 11. Ich bin eine
Leseratte und freue mich _____ mein nächstes *(next)* Buch. 12. _____
interessieren Sie sich mehr: für Fernsehen, Bücher oder das Internet?

(advertisement logo) TELE BINGO
Spannend bis zur letzten Zahl.

● Optional tongue twisters
(Zungenbrecher): 1. Eine
schwarze Swatch 2. Spanier
lieben spannende Spiele.

DAS ERSTE 1 ARD

5.30	**Frühprogramm**
7.30	**Pumuckl TV** Kindermagazin 60-409
8.30	○ **Sesamstraße** Für Kinder 3-138
9.00	**Tagesschau** Nachrichten 64-409
9.03	**Kopfball** Ratespiel 300-004-867
9.30	**Ski alpin: Weltcup Herren** 821-645
live	Riesenslalom, 1. Lauf. Aus Sölden/Öst.
11.00	**Tagesschau** Nachrichten 20-041
11.03	○ Die magische Münze 300-004-003
11.30	☑ **Die Maus** Für Kinder 7-190
12.00	○ **Presseclub** 34-867
live	Polit-Talk mit Journalisten
12.45	**Ski alpin: Weltcup Herren** 2-966-022
live	Riesenslalom, 2. Lauf. Aus Sölden/Öst.
13.45	**Bilderbuch D** Kassel 4-976-119

14

14.03	**Tennis: WTA-Masters** 304-798-108
live	Das Achtelfinale. Aus München
15.55	**Tagesschau** 6-460-924
16.00	○ **Fliege – Die Talkshow** 50-672
	Thema: Vorsicht Bank!
	Ohne Banken läuft in unserem
	Alltag nichts mehr, ihre Macht
	scheint nahezu grenzenlos.

17

17.00	**Tagesschau** Nachrichten 44-643
17.03	○ **ARD-Ratgeber:** 300-003-117
	Bauen & Wohnen Reihe
17.55	**Verbotene Liebe** 60-892
18.25	○ **Marienhof** 58-057
	Nik will Lucy zurückerobern.
18.54	○ **Das Quiz mit Jörg Pilawa**
	Quizshow 408-566-386
19.49	**Das Wetter** 400-104-750
19.51	○ **Lottozahlen** 107-297-556
20.00	☑ **Tagesschau** Nachrichten 86-469

LIEBESKOMÖDIE

20.15 **FILM** **TOP tipp**	○○ ☑ **Während du schliefst** Liebeskomödie, USA 1995 47-573 Mit Sandra Bullock, P. Gallagher Lucy rettet Peter, in den sie schon lange aus der Ferne verliebt ist, das Leben. Während er im Koma liegt, wird Lucy von dessen Verwandten für Peters Verlobte gehalten. Die familiäre Herzlichkeit macht es ihr unmöglich, den Irrtum aufzuklären. **→ S. 122**

22.30	**Tagesthemen** 250
23.00	○ **Friedman** Diskussion 8-637
	mit einem prominenten Gast
23.30	**Das Elend, alt zu werden** 27-328
	Pflege vor dem Kollaps? Von Dörte
	Schipper und Gregor Petersen
	Die Altenpflegerinnen hatten sich
	unter ihrem Beruf ursprünglich et-
	was anderes vorgestellt. Der Film
	zeigt den bedrückenden Alltag in
	der ambulanten und stationären
	Pflege und befragt dazu die
	politisch Verantwortlichen.
0.15	**Nachtmagazin** 457-019

Mi

ZDF

5.30	**Morgenmagazin** 64-053-523
9.00	○ **heute** Nachrichten 17-813
9.05	**Volle Kanne, Susanne** 2-472-078
	Servicemagazin mit Ingo Nommsen
10.00	○ **heute** Nachrichten 88-356
10.03	**Forsthaus Falkenau** 307-615-542
	Familienserie. Zurück nach Falkenau
10.50	**Wie gut, dass es Maria gibt**
	Familienserie. Fan-Post 3-917-144
11.35	**Praxis täglich** Herbst spe- 7-470-250
	zial: Asthma – Aufatmen am Meer
12.00	**Tagesschau** Nachrichten 65-960
12.15	○ **drehscheibe D** 7-295-989
13.00	**Tagesschau** Nachrichten 38-095
13.05	**Mittagsmagazin** 364-502

14

14.00	**heute – in Deutschland** 75-439
14.15	**Discovery** Triumph der 93-675
	Natur – Nationalparks in Amerika
15.00	○ **heute/Sport** 23-052
15.10	**Streit um Drei** 8-745-746
	Alltagskonflikte vor Gericht
16.00	○ **heute – in Europa** 95-255
16.15	○ **Risiko** Quiz 2-447-304

17

17.00	○ **heute/Wetter** 53-521
17.15	○ **hallo Deutschland** 86-453
17.45	**Leute heute** Journal 5-766-057
17.54	○ **NKL-Tagesmillion** 405-796-298
18.00	☑ **Derrick** 8-203-174
	Krimiserie. Familie im Feuer
18.50	○ **Lotto am Mittwoch** 7-882-298
19.00	○ ☑ **heute/Wetter** 65-182
19.25	○ **B** **Die Rettungsflieger (5)**
	10-tlg. Actionserie 5-153-892
	Torstens Entscheidung

UNTERHALTUNG

20.15	○ **30 Jahre „Lustige** 22-683 **Musikanten"** Die große Jubiläumsgala. Gäste u. a.: Patrick Lindner, das Nockalm Quintett Zur Jubiläumsgala in Rotenburg an der Fulda haben Marianne & Michael (Foto) heute, neben den ehemaligen Moderatoren Lolita, Carolin Reiber und Elmar Gunsch, die Comedians Ingolf Lück und Annette Frier eingeladen.

21.45	○ ☑ **heute-journal** 593-618
22.15	○ **Abenteuer Forschung**
	Thema: Die Krise. 141-279
	Energie. Mit Joachim Bublath
	Sonne, Wind, Wasser und Bio-
	masse sollen künftig als Energie-
	quelle an Bedeutung gewinnen.
	Ist dies jedoch wirklich der Beginn
	eines neuen Zeitalters?
22.45	☑ **Der Alte** 5-354-786
	Krimiserie. Alles umsonst …
23.45	○ **heute nacht** 1-859-142
0.00	**nachtstudio** Diskussion 47-632
	Die Zukunft der Religionen

SAT.1

5.30	**Frühstücksfernsehen** 79-364-610
	U. a.: täglich ran – Sport; Morning
	Queen; Superball. Moderation:
	Jessica Winter und Andreas Franke
9.00	Home Shopping Europe 11-821
10.00	**Hallo, Onkel Doc!** 22-937
	Kinderarztserie. Familienkuss
10.15	**Tiny Toon Abenteuer** Trick 2-316-204
10.40	**Familie Feuerstein** Trick 8-956-440
11.10	**Bugs Bunny** Trickserie 4-257-223
11.35	**Police Academy** Trickserie 6-965-759
12.05	**Die Peanuts** Trickserie 405-136
12.35	**Schweine nebenan** Trickserie 72-117
13.00	**The Real Ghostbusters** 2-778
13.30	**Alf** Comedy. Das Kostümfest 5-865

14

14.00	☑ **Der große Diktator** 40-141-889
	Politsatire, USA 1940. Mit Charlie
	Chaplin, Jack Oakie. Buch/
	Regie: Charlie Chaplin **→ S. 24**
15.00	**Allein gegen die Zukunft** 42-117
	Serie. Der Weihnachtsmann
16.00	○ **Star Trek –** 36-487
	Das nächste Jahrhundert
	Science-Fiction-Serie. Déjà vu

17

17.30	**ran – Basketball** BBL, 5. 7-961
	Tag: Avitos Gießen – Opel Sky-
	liners, Brandt Hagen – Leverkusen
18.00	**Einfach Verona! (1)** 1-020
neu	11-tlg. VIP-Magazin
	Mit Verona Feldbusch
18.30	**18:30** Nachrichten mit Sport 76-117
18.45	**ran – Sport** 183-117
19.00	**ran – Bundesliga** 933-594
	U. a.: FC Bayern – Kaiserslautern

ABENTEUERFILM

20.15 **FILM** **TOP tipp**	**Die Maske des Zorro** 49-903-570 Abenteuerfilm, USA 1998 Mit Antonio Banderas Zwanzig Jahre musste Zorro in einer Zelle schmoren, um mit Don Montero abzurechnen, der seine Tochter Elena entführt und groß- gezogen hat. Zwecks Verstärkung trainiert der alternde Kämpfer den Charme und die Degen-Künste des Heißsporns Alejandro. **→ S. 31**

22.55	**Nachrichten** Wahl 2-348-860
	zum Abgeordnetenhaus in Berlin
23.10	○ **Planetopia** 6-216-860
	Magazin. Thema: Lauschangriff –
	You'll never walk alone
	Moderatorin Susanne Kripp be-
	schließt, ein Wochenende in
	Heidelberg zu verbringen. Was sie
	nicht weiß: Seit der Reiseplanung
	sind ihr Spione auf den Fersen.
0.00	**News & Stories** Als 94-938
	Reporter auf allen Kontinenten –
	Ryszard Kapuscinski:
	Die Welt ist mein Notizbuch

C. Das Fernsehprogramm Schauen Sie sich das Programm auf der linken Seite an und beantworten Sie die Fragen darüber!

1. Wann beginnt das Morgenprogramm bei den drei Sendern?
2. Wie heißen die zwei großen Nachrichtensendungen im 1. Programm (ARD) und im 2. Programm (ZDF)?
3. Welche Kinderprogramme gibt es im ARD und bei SAT.1?
4. Was gibt es über Sport, Musik, Gesundheit, Natur und Politik?
5. Wo geht es um Wohnen, die Lotterie, Home Shopping und Banken?
6. Welche amerikanischen Filme finden Sie auf diesem Programm?
7. Aus welchem Jahr ist der Film *Der große Diktator?* Welchen bekannten Schauspieler können wir darin sehen?
8. Was halten Sie von diesen Sendungen im deutschen Fernsehen?

D. Womit? Damit! Stellen Sie Fragen mit einem **wo**-Kompositum oder einer Präposition + **wem** und antworten Sie mit einem **da**-Kompositum oder einer Präposition + Pronomen!

BEISPIEL Das private Fernsehen ist abhängig **von der Werbung.**
Wovon ist es abhängig? —Davon!

Die Werbung ist abhängig **von den Käufern.**
Von wem ist sie abhängig? —Von ihnen!

1. Einige Kritiker halten nicht viel **vom Fernsehen.** 2. Vor allem ärgern sie sich **über die vielen amerikanischen Serien.** 3. Sie sprechen **über die Zuschauer.** 4. Sie warten jede Woche **auf die Fortsetzung** *(continuation).* 5. Diese Kritiker denken auch **an die Kinder.** 6. **Durch zu viel Fernsehen und zu viel Musik** verlieren sie an Kreativität. 7. Manche Leute sitzen jede freie Minute **vor dem Computer.** 8. **Für Familie und Freunde** und auch **fürs Hobby** haben sie oft wenig Zeit.

E. Wofür interessieren Sie sich im Fernsehen? Schauen Sie sich die Auswahl an Programmen an und bewerten Sie *(rate)* sie! Wie sieht das im Vergleich zu *(in comparison to)* den Bewertungen der anderen aus? Benutzen Sie: 1 = sehr interessant, 2 = manchmal interessant, 3 = uninteressant!

❑ Nachrichten	❑ Konzerte	❑ Seifenopern
❑ Politik	❑ Opern	❑ Horrorfilme
❑ Reisen	❑ Krimis	❑ Dokumentarfilme
❑ Hobbys	❑ Western	❑ Geschichtsfilme
❑ Sport	❑ Theaterstücke	❑ Liebesfilme *(love...)*
❑ Sprachen	❑ Fernsehspiele	❑ Science-Fiction-Filme
❑ Ballett	❑ Fernsehquizze	❑ Zeichentrickfilme *(cartoons)*

F. Deutsches Fernsehen Ergänzen Sie die Adjektivendungen, wo nötig *(necessary)*!

1. Das deutsch____ Fernsehen ist eine gut____ Mischung aus kulturell____ Sendungen und leicht____ Unterhaltung. 2. Man bekommt auch viel____ interessant____ Sendungen aus verschieden____ Nachbarländern. 3. Das öffentlich____ Fernsehen finanziert man durch monatlich____ Gebühren. 4. Öffentlich____ Sender *(pl.)* haben natürlich auch öffentlich____ Aufgaben. 5. Sie können leicht verschieden____ Sendungen für klein____ Interessengruppen bringen, z. B. international____ Nachrichten in verschieden____ Sprachen oder auch lokal____ Kabarett *(n.)*. 6. Privat____ Fernsehen gibt es auch. 7. Diese klein____ Sender sind natürlich abhängig von der Werbung. 8. Beim privat____ Fernsehen kann man auch viel____ amerikanisch____ Filme sehen. 9. Kritiker sprechen von schlecht____ Qualität beim privat____ Fernsehen. 10. Viele Deutsche sind groß____ Leseratten. 11. Sie lesen alles, was ihnen in die Hände fällt, von lokal____ Nachrichten und lokal____ Werbung bis zu intellektuell____ *(intellectual)* Nachrichtenmagazinen. 12. Sie hören aber auch gern Radio, von leicht____ bis zu klassisch____ Musik.

G. Aufsatz: Die Funktion von Medien Lesen Sie den *Einblicke-Text* noch einmal und schreiben Sie dann—mit Hilfe der unteren Stichwörter—einen kleinen Aufsatz (10–12 Sätze) über den Einfluss der Medien auf die Menschen in unserer Zeit! Nennen Sie dabei auch Unterschiede *(differences)* zwischen der deutschen und amerikanischen Gesellschaft *(society)*!

Radio	Zeitschriften	Zeitungen	Computer
Fernsehen	Filme	Bücher	Internet

Track 24 **Pläne für den Abend** Wohin will Stefan mit seinen Freunden? Ergänzen Sie die folgenden Aussagen!

Zum Erkennen: ausverkauft *(sold out)*; die Anzeige, -n *(advertisement)*

1. Monika möchte gern ____ gehen.
   a. ins Kino
   b. in die Bibliothek
   c. ins Theater

2. Felix und Stefan finden das ____.
   a. eine gute Idee
   b. furchtbar langweilig
   c. komisch

3. Monika ruft an, um ____.
   a. Karten zu bestellen
   b. zu fragen, ob es noch Karten gibt
   c. zu fragen, wie man zum Theater kommt

4. Sie wollen zur Kabarett-Kneipe KARTOON gehen, weil ____.
   a. das Programm sehr interessant ist
   b. sie dort auch essen können
   c. Monika Gutes darüber gehört hat

5. Sie wollen um ____ Uhr essen.
   a. 18.30
   b. 19.30
   c. 21.00

6. Dorthin kommt man ____ .
   a. zu Fuß
   b. mit der U-Bahn
   c. irgendwie *(somehow),* aber das wissen wir nicht

At the movies, the theater and opera; Karl May, a German in America; music in Germany: http://wiegehts.heinle.com.

Literatur

Biographisches

Bertolt Brecht (1898–1956) is one of Germany's most celebrated 20th-century playwrights. His theory of the "epic theater" (**das epische Theater**) has had a considerable influence on modern theories of drama. By using various visual techniques and artificial acting styles—such as having the actors deliver their lines in a deliberately expressionless way—he tried to minimize the audience's rapport with the action, while increasing its awareness of the play's moral and political message. Brecht fled Berlin in 1933, seeking refuge in Switzerland, Denmark, Finland, and finally the United States (1941–1947). He returned to East Berlin in 1949 and founded the Berlin Ensemble. Brecht's works include *Die Dreigroschenoper* (1928; first film adaptation in 1931), *Mutter Courage und ihre Kinder* (1939), *Der gute Mensch von Sezuan* (1942), *Das Leben des Galilei* (1938/39), and *Der kaukasische Kreidekreis* (1945). Some of his works have been set to music; he worked extensively with composers Kurt Weill, Hanns Eisler, and Paul Dessau.

Vor dem Lesen

Allerlei Fragen

1. Welche kleinen Freuden *(joys)* oder Vergnügungen gehören zum Alltag der Menschen? Machen Sie eine Liste! (z. B. Essen, Trinken, Lesen . . .)
2. Welche Vergnügungen gehören bei Ihnen zum Alltag *(everyday life)*?
3. Überfliegen Sie *(skim through)* dieses Gedicht und finden Sie heraus, was daran ungewöhnlich ist!
   a. Gibt es im Gedicht Sätze? Reime? Kommas, Fragezeichen *(question marks)*, Ausrufungszeichen oder Punkte?
   b. Gibt es darin Adjektive? Wenn ja, welche davon haben Artikel davor und welche nicht?
   c. Welche Verben gibt es darin? Sind sie konjugiert oder stehen sie nur da als Hauptwort?

Vergnügungen

Track 25

Der erste Blick aus dem Fenster am Morgen
Das wiedergefundene alte Buch
Begeisterte° Gesichter   enthusiastic
Schnee, der Wechsel° der Jahreszeiten   change
5 Die Zeitung
Der Hund°   dog
Die Dialektik°   conflicting nature
Duschen, Schwimmen
Alte Musik
10 Bequeme Schuhe
Begreifen°   understanding
Neue Musik
Schreiben, Pflanzen°   planting
Reisen
15 Singen
Freundlich sein.

Bertolt Brecht

Nach dem Lesen

A. Fragen zum Gedicht

1. Welche „Vergnügungen" auf dieser Liste sind Dinge *(things)* und was sind Aktivitäten?

2. Was finden Sie dabei ganz normal und was etwas ungewöhnlich?

3. Ist das, was der Autor listet, in einer bestimmten Reihenfolge *(order)*? Was denken Sie?

4. Ist das wirklich ein Gedicht oder nur eine Liste? Was denken Sie?

5. Glauben Sie, dass der Autor sich beim Schreiben viel Zeit dafür genommen hat?

6. Wie lange brauchen Sie, um so etwas auf Englisch / auf Deutsch zu schreiben?

 B. Jetzt sind Sie dran! Schreiben Sie jetzt Ihr eigenes *(own)* Gedicht—maximal 16 Zeilen wie bei Brecht! Denken Sie zuerst an das, was Ihnen gefällt, und dann an deskriptive Adjektive dafür (6 oder mehr). Passen Sie dabei auch auf die Adjektivendungen auf! In welcher Reihenfolge wollen Sie diese „Vergnügungen" listen: chronologisch oder nach Wichtigkeit? Oder vielleicht willkürlich *(at random)*? Prüfen Sie die Adjektivendungen und machen Sie eventuell Korrekturen *(possibly corrections)*. Lesen Sie es laut vor!

Lernziele

In this chapter you will learn about:

Zum Thema

Relationships, friendship, personal characteristics, and pets

Kultur-Fokus

Love, marriage, equality, pets, and Liechtenstein
The Brothers Grimm, Gotthold Ephraim Lessing, Reinhardt Jung

Struktur

The simple past
Conjunctions: *als, wann, wenn*
The past perfect

Einblicke + Literatur

Rumpelstilzchen
Gotthold Ephraim Lessing: "Der Esel in Begleitung"
Reinhardt Jung: "Reifezeugnis"

For more information, go to http://iLrn.heinle.com.

Zusammen macht das Kartoffelschälen (peeling potatoes) *mehr Spaß.*

Vorschau   Women and Society

Families in Germany—as in other countries—are currently confronted by profound social change. The stereotypical housewife and mother whose life revolves around children, kitchen, and church (**Kinder, Küche, Kirche**) is a thing of the past. The self-confident and highly qualified women of today often want both children and a career. Combining these two goals can become a daunting task within the context of nontraditional lifestyles, new forms of relationships, changes at the workplace, and a variety of obstacles ranging from a shortage of childcare facilities to a lack of financial resources. After all is said and done, most women continue to spend three times as much time as men on housework and child rearing, and men frequently cling to old patterns of behavior while professing to believe in complete gender equality.

Until reunification, West German women—especially those over 30 years of age—were far less likely to have full-time jobs than their counterparts in East Germany. Only half of West German women worked outside the home, compared to more than 90 percent in the East. Women in the GDR were able to combine motherhood with full-time employment because low-cost, state-run day-care centers (**Kinderkrippen**) and other services were readily available. Being able to stay home with a sick child was taken for granted in East Germany, and mothers had the option to take as much as one year of maternity leave with full pay. The loss of these facilities and benefits, coupled with record-high unemployment, caused a drastic decline in the birthrate after reunification.

With the proportion of senior citizens growing in Germany—as it is in all of Europe—a statutory long-term nursing care insurance plan was implemented in the early 1990s to supplement the retirement pensions and the health insurance system. With the social security system built on the principle that the younger generation secures the welfare of the old through its contributions, German laws regarding pregnancy and childbirth now reflect the conviction that women who bear and raise children are performing a task vital to society and therefore are entitled to have their social security contributions at least partially reduced and work-related childcare expenses offset against taxes. Working women are entitled to maternity leave with pay (**der Mutterschaftsurlaub**) six weeks before and eight weeks after childbirth. After that, either the mother or the father is entitled to "parental time" (**die Elternzeit**) for up to three years, or he/she can switch to part-time work up to thirty hours per week. The parents also receive a monthly child-rearing benefit (**das Erziehungsgeld**), which varies based on income during the first two years after the birth of each child. During their "parental time," parents cannot be fired from their jobs. Moreover, every family receives a monthly child benefit (**das Kindergeld**) of 154 euros for each child until the child is financially independent. In addition, time spent on raising a child (as well as time spent caring for a sick family member) is counted when calculating a person's pension later in life. This practice aims for fairness by valuing work within the home as equal to employment outside the home. The problem of the shortage in childcare facilities in Germany has yet to be resolved.

Minidrama: *Der Märchenprinz*

● Two main factors contributed to the high employment rate of women in the former GDR: the need for additional income and the law that required all able-bodied men and women to work.

ZWISCHEN KIND UND KARRIERE

NILS ist jetzt der große Bruder von
Carolin
3. Juli 2004
3.340 g – 50 cm

Es freuen sich mit ihm seine Eltern
Monika und Arnim Thiemann
Adensen, im Juli 2004

Zum Thema

CD 7,
Track 6

Jedem Tierchen sein Pläsierchen!

SONJA Nicole, hör mal! „Gesucht wird: hübsche, dynamische, zärtliche Eva. Belohnung: gut aussehender Adam mit Herz, Ende 20, mag Antiquitäten, alte Häuser, schnelle Wagen, Tiere, Kinder."

> Suche neues Zuhause für unseren kleinen Zoo. Hund, Katze und Vogel gemeinsam abzugeben. 0941/447635.

NICOLE Hmm, nicht schlecht, aber nicht für mich. Ich mag keine Kinder und gegen Tiere bin ich allergisch.

SONJA Dann schau mal hier! „Es gibt, was ich suche. Aber wie finden? Künstler, Anfang 30, charmant, unternehmungslustig, musikalisch, sucht sympathische, gebildete, zuverlässige Frau mit Humor." Ist das was?

NICOLE Ja, vielleicht. Er sucht jemanden mit Humor. Das gefällt mir; und Musik mag ich auch. Aber ob er Jazz mag?

SONJA Vielleicht können wir sie beide kennen lernen?

NICOLE Ich weiß nicht. Mir ist das zu dumm, Leute durch Anzeigen in der Zeitung kennen zu lernen.

SONJA Quatsch! Versuchen wir's doch! Was haben wir zu verlieren?

NICOLE Was meinst du, Frank?

FRANK Ich denke, ihr seid verrückt. Aber naja, jedem Tierchen sein Pläsierchen! . . . Schaut mal hier! Da will jemand einen Hund, eine Katze und einen Vogel gemeinsam abgeben.

NICOLE Das ist alles, was wir brauchen: einen ganzen Zoo! Nein, danke!

FRANK Wie wär's denn mit einem kleinen Hund oder einem Kätzchen?

SONJA Ich liebe Tiere, aber dafür habe ich momentan keinen Platz und auch nicht genug Zeit.

FRANK Aber so ein kleines Kätzchen braucht nicht viel.

SONJA Vielleicht später. Momentan liebe ich meine Freiheit.

FRANK Und ihr wollt euch mit jemandem aus der Zeitung treffen?

NICOLE Ach, davon verstehst du nichts.

> Gesucht wird: hübsche, dynamische, zärtliche EVA. Belohnung: gut aussehender ADAM mit Herz, Ende 20, mag Antiquitäten, alte Häuser, schnelle Wagen, Tiere, Kinder.

> Es gibt, was ich suche. Aber wie finden? Künstler, Anfang 30, charmant, unternehmungslustig, musikalisch, sucht sympathische, gebildete, zuverlässige Frau mit Humor.

A. Fragen

1. Was sehen sich Nicole und Sonja an? 2. Was sucht der erste Mann? 3. Wofür interessiert er sich? 4. Was hält Nicole von dem ersten Mann? 5. Was sucht der zweite Mann? 6. Was hält Nicole von der zweiten Anzeige? 7. Was meint Sonja dazu? 8. Was hält Frank von der Idee, die Männer zu treffen? 9. Was schaut sich Frank an? 10. Was mag Nicole an der ersten Tieranzeige nicht? 11. Wer von den beiden Frauen mag keine Tiere? 12. Was hält Frank von Katzen? 13. Warum will Sonja momentan nichts davon wissen? 14. Wie endet das Gespräch? 15. Meinen Sie, dass die beiden auf die Anzeigen antworten?

B. Jetzt sind Sie dran! Schauen Sie sich mit Ihrem Partner/Ihrer Partnerin Anzeigen in der Zeitung an. Es sind Anzeigen, wo Leute Lebenspartner, Freunde fürs Hobby oder vielleicht auch ein Tier suchen. Reagieren Sie darauf *(react to it)*! Wechseln Sie sich ab!

Ein kleiner süßer Vogel

Fokus   Love and Marriage

The practice of advertising for partners in newspapers and magazines has been commonplace in the German-speaking countries for some time. Television dating shows are not uncommon, and Internet chat rooms that revolve around matchmaking have gained in popularity.

Traditions and laws increasingly reflect the equality of German women and the realities of relationships. Women no longer automatically take the name of their husband when marrying; more and more are using hyphenated last names. Married partners can also keep their own names, and children have the name of either partner. Married women are not addressed with their husband's first name, but with their own—for example, Christiane Binder, not Mrs. Rudolf Binder. Widowed women keep their married name, whereas divorced women are free to use their maiden name (**der Mädchenname**) again.

Same-sex couples in Germany have had the right to marry since 2001, although full equality with traditional marriage—such as tax benefits and survivorship rights—has not yet been realized. Divorce is granted on the basis of irreconcilable differences—not merely infidelity—and all retirement funds accrued during the marriage are distributed in equal shares.

For a marriage to be legally recognized, it must be performed at the office of records (**das Standesamt**), usually located in city hall. A church ceremony afterwards is still popular. Traditionally, both German men and women wear their wedding bands on the left hand during their engagement. The bands are then switched to the right hand after the wedding. Today, the American custom of a separate engagement ring is becoming more common, but the wedding ring is still worn on the right hand.

Wortschatz 1

Die Beziehung, -en (relationship)

der Partner, -	partner	ledig	single
Wunsch, ⁓e	wish	verliebt (in + acc.)	in love (with)
das Vertrauen	trust	verlobt (mit)	engaged (to)
die Anzeige, -n	ad	(un)verheiratet	(un)married
Ehe, -n	marriage	geschieden	divorced
Freundschaft	friendship	sich verlieben (in + acc.)	to fall in love (with)
Hochzeit, -en	wedding	sich verloben (mit)	to get engaged (to)
Liebe	love	heiraten	to marry, get married (to)
Scheidung, -en	divorce		

Die Eigenschaft, -en (attribute, characteristic)

anhänglich	devoted, attached	(un)ehrlich	(dis)honest
attraktiv	attractive	(un)freundlich	(un)friendly
charmant	charming	(un)gebildet	(un)educated
dynamisch	dynamic	(un)geduldig	(im)patient
ernst / lustig	serious / funny	(un)glücklich	(un)happy
fleißig / faul	industrious / lazy	(un)kompliziert	(un)complicated
gut aussehend	good-looking	(un)musikalisch	(un)musical
hübsch / hässlich	pretty / ugly	(un)selbstständig	(dependent)
intelligent / dumm	intelligent / stupid		independent
jung	young	(un)sportlich	(un)athletic
lieb	kind, good	(un)sympathisch	(un)congenial,
liebevoll	loving		(un)likable
nett	nice	(un)talentiert	(un)talented
reich / arm	rich, wealthy / poor	(un)zuverlässig	(un)reliable
schick	chic, neat		
schlank	slim		
schrecklich	awful		
selbstbewusst	self-confident		
seltsam	strange, weird		
süß	sweet, cute		
vielseitig	versatile		
zärtlich	affectionate		

Weiteres

der Hund, -e	dog
Vogel, ⁓	bird
das Pferd, -e	horse
Tier, -e	animal
die Katze, -n	cat
beid- / beide	both / both (of them)
damals	then, in those days
eigen-	own
gemeinsam	together, shared; joint(ly)
jemand	someone, somebody
ein·laden (lädt ein), lud ein, eingeladen	to invite
meinen	to think, be of an opinion
passieren (ist)	to happen
träumen (von)	to dream (of)
vergleichen, verglich, verglichen	to compare
verlieren, verlor, verloren	to lose
versuchen	to try
Ach, wie süß!	Oh, how sweet / cute!
Das gefällt mir aber!	I really like it.
So ein süßes Kätzchen!	Such a cute kitty!
Was für ein hübscher Hund!	What a pretty dog!
Wenn du meinst.	If you think so.

● Note: **der Hund** = **er**; **die Katze** = **sie.**

● Many everyday expressions include an animal **(Tier)**: **Du hast einen Vogel! / Bei dir piept's!** (You're crazy!); **Fauler Hund!** (Lazy bum!); **Alles für die Katz'!** (It's all in vain.) Also, certain animals are associated with certain characteristics: **Schlau wie ein Fuchs** (sly as a fox); **geduldig wie ein Lamm** (very patient); **arbeitsam wie ein Pferd** (hardworking as a horse).

● Note **jemand** in the various cases: **Jemand** ist an der Tür. Er bringt **jemanden** mit. Sie spricht mit **jemandem.**

● **Kätzchen:** As mentioned in Appendix 1, all nouns with the suffix **-chen** are neuter. This suffix makes diminutives of nouns, that is, it denotes them as being small or (as in the case of people or animals) may indicate affection: **das Herrchen, das Frauchen** (loving dog owners). When adding this suffix, other changes might apply: der Hund / **das Hündchen,** der Vogel / **das Vögelchen,** die Katze / **das Kätzchen.**

Zum Erkennen: gesucht wird *(wanted)*; die Belohnung *(reward)*; allergisch gegen *(allergic to)*; mit Humor *(with a sense of humor)*; das Zuhause *(home)*; der Zoo, -s; momentan *(right now, at the moment)*; der Dackel, - *(dachshund)*; das Halsband *(collar)*; die Modepuppe, -n *(fashion doll)*; hassen *(to hate)*; ambitiös *(ambitious)*; herzförmig *(heart-shaped)*; kinderlieb *(loves children)*; schlau *(clever; lit. sly)*; silbern *(silver)*; unternehmungslustig *(enterprising)*; verständnisvoll *(understanding)*; AUCH: das Imperfekt *(simple past)*; die Konjunktion, -en *(conjunction)*; das Perfekt *(present perfect)*; reagieren auf *(+ acc.) (to react to)*; unterstreichen *(to underline)*; Jedem Tierchen sein Pläsierchen! *(To each his own!)*

Fokus   Beloved Pets

There are approximately 22 million pets **(Haustiere)** in Germany, mostly cats, dogs, and small mammals like rabbits or guinea pigs, but also birds and fish. The average German is very fond of animals, and over 30 percent of all households own a pet. Renters must usually have their landlord's permission to keep a pet. Dog owners are required to register with the local tax office **(das Finanzamt)** and pay a dog tax **(die Hundesteuer)**, the amount of which varies from state to state. A personal liability insurance policy is also recommended.

Furthermore, certain breeds of dogs that are considered dangerous (pit bulls, Staffordshire bull terriers, and so forth) must be kept on leashes, muzzled, and neutered.

Dogs are not allowed in grocery stores, but most cafés and restaurants permit them inside. Establishments that don't allow dogs inside have a sign on their windows showing a picture of a dog with the following text: **"Wir müssen leider draußen bleiben."** Dogs and cats can be taken on trains and buses; their tickets cost about half the regular "human" fare.

Aktives zum Thema

A. Was ist das Adjektiv dazu?

der Charme, Ernst, Freund, Reichtum, Sport; das Glück; die Allergie, Attraktion, Bildung, Dynamik, Dummheit, Ehrlichkeit, Faulheit, Geduld, Gemütlichkeit, Intelligenz, Komplikation, Natur, Musik, Scheidung, Selbstständigkeit, Sympathie, Zärtlichkeit, Zuverlässigkeit; sich verlieben, sich verloben, verheiraten

B. Fragen

1. Was machen Sie und Ihre Freunde in der Freizeit? Worüber sprechen Sie?
2. Welche Eigenschaften finden Sie bei Freunden wichtig? Wie dürfen sie nicht sein?
3. Waren Sie schon einmal in einen Schauspieler/eine Schauspielerin oder einen Sänger/eine Sängerin verliebt? Wenn ja, in wen?
4. Was halten Sie vom Zusammenleben vor dem Heiraten? Was halten Sie vom Heiraten? Wie alt sollen Leute mindestens *(at least)* sein, wenn sie heiraten? Finden Sie eine lange Verlobung wichtig? Warum (nicht)?
5. Sind Sie gegen etwas allergisch? Wenn ja, wogegen?

C. Anzeigen über Menschen und Tiere

1. **Adjektivendungen** Ergänzen Sie die fehlenden Adjektivendungen!

In Europe the metric system is standard. Is someone who has a height of 180 cm short or tall? Figure it out yourself. Since one inch equals 2.54 cm, divide the height by 2.54 to get the number of inches. How tall are you in metric terms? Multiply your height in inches by 2.54. People generally state their height informally like this: **Ich bin ein Meter achtzig groß.** *I'm 1 meter 80 cm tall.*

a. Millionär bin ich nicht. Will mein Glück auch nicht kaufen. Ich, 28 / 170, suche keine extravagant____ Modepuppe oder exotisch____ Diskoqueen, sondern ein nett____ , natürlich____ Mädchen, darf auch hübsch____ sein.

b. Tanzen, Segeln und Reisen sind meine groß____ Liebe. Welche sympathisch____ Frau mit Fantasie will mitmachen? Ich bin Journalist, nicht hässlich____ , verständnisvoll____ und mit unkonventionell____ Ideen.

c. Sympatisch____ Klarinettenanfänger sucht humorvoll____ Leute mit Spaß und Freude am gemeinsam____ Musizieren.

d. Man denkt, man arbeitet, man schläft, man lebt? Ist das alles? Temperamentvoll____ Endzwanzigerin, 180, sucht charmant____ , lustig____ ADAM mit vielseitig____ Interessen.

e. Welcher nett____ , intelligent____ Mann, bis 45 Jahre jung, mag Reisen, Tanzen, Schwimmen, Skilaufen und mich? Ich: attraktiv____ , dunkelhaarig____ , unternehmungslustig____ Naturkind. Geschieden____ , Anfang 30, zwei sportlich____ Jungen.

f. Neu in Bonn: Attraktiv____ , dynamisch____ Psychotherapeutin, Mutter und kreativ____ Frau mit Charme und Esprit , natürlich____ und auch lustig____ , sucht Kontakt zu lebensbejahend____ , kultiviert____ , nett____ Leuten für Freizeit, Freundschaft und Aktivitäten.

g. Verloren: Klein____ , braun____ Dackel mit braun____ Halsband und herzförmig____ , silbern____ Schild. Hört auf den Namen „Fiffi".

h. Gefunden: Grauweiß____ Katze, ziemlich alt____ , aber sehr anhänglich____ , hat den Weg nach Hause vergessen. Sind Sie das traurig____ Herrchen oder Frauchen?

i. Zu adoptieren: Klein____ , schwarz____ Pudel, zwei Jahre alt____ , sucht neu____ Familie mit nett____ Kindern, geht gern mit Herrchen oder Frauchen auf lang____ Spaziergänge und ist auch gern bei lang____ Touren mit dem Auto dabei.

2. **Noch einmal!** Lesen Sie die Anzeigen noch einmal und sprechen Sie dann mit den anderen über die folgenden Themen!

a. Welche Qualitäten suchen die Leute in den Anzeigen? Machen Sie eine Liste!

b. Wie sehen die Leute sich selbst *(themselves)*? Was sagen sie und was sagen sie nicht? Machen Sie eine Liste!

D. Freundschaft

1. Welche Qualitäten suchen Sie in einem Freund oder einer Freundin?
2. Sind Freundschaften wichtig? Wenn ja, warum?
3. Was tun Sie gern mit Ihren Freunden?

E. Liebe

Lesen Sie die folgende Liste verschiedener Eigenschaften! Welche fünf davon sind Ihnen beim Lebenspartner besonders wichtig? Vergleichen Sie Ihre Auswahl *(choice)* mit Listen der anderen!

__ häuslich *(domestic)*	__ natürlich	__ zuverlässig	__ schick
__ sparsam *(thrifty)*	__ ehrlich	__ zärtlich	__ tolerant
__ sportlich	__ musikalisch	__ verständnisvoll	__ dynamisch
__ kinderlieb *(loves children)*	__ ernst	__ religiös	__ lustig
__ tierlieb *(loves animals)*	__ schlau	__ ambitiös	__ reich
__ optimistisch	__ ruhig	__ fleißig	__ kreativ

F. So bin ich.

Welche fünf Eigenschaften sind typisch für Sie? Vergleichen Sie Ihre Liste mit der Liste Ihres Nachbarn/Ihrer Nachbarin!

G. Allerlei über Tiere

Lesen Sie die Tieranzeigen noch einmal und stellen Sie dann den anderen die folgenden Fragen! Finden Sie heraus, . . . !

1. wer von den anderen tierlieb ist
2. wer welche Tiere zu Hause hat
3. wer sich welche Tiere wünscht
4. welche Qualitäten ihnen bei Tieren wichtig sind und was sie hassen *(hate)*

H. Eigene Anzeigen

Schreiben Sie Ihre eigene Anzeige auf der Suche nach *(in search of)* Freundschaft, einem Reisepartner/einer Reisepartnerin, nach Liebe oder einem Haustier *(pet)*.

I. Was sagen Sie dazu?

1. Sie haben einen besonders guten Film (Stück, Konzert, Kunstausstellung) gesehen.
2. Sie haben einen sehr netten Mann/eine sehr nette Frau kennen gelernt.
3. Sie sind auf den Turm *(tower)* eines großen Domes gestiegen und haben einen wunderbaren Blick.
4. Ein Freund hat ein sehr schönes, neues Auto.
5. Auf einem Spaziergang treffen Sie Leute mit einem Hund.
6. Sie sind bei Nachbarn eingeladen und finden ihre Tiere toll.
7. Freunde haben Sie zum Essen eingeladen. Sie haben nicht gewusst, dass Ihre Freunde so gut kochen können.
8. Ihre Freunde haben ihre neue Wohnung sehr schick möbliert.
9. Eine junge Frau mit einem süßen Baby sitzt neben Ihnen im Flugzeug.
10. Sie haben Besuch. Sie finden die Leute gut, aber nicht die Kinder.

J. Beschreibung Beschreiben Sie sich selbst *(yourself),* eine andere Person oder ein Tier! Wählen Sie eins der vier Themen und schreiben Sie 8–10 Sätze.

1. So bin ich.
2. Was für ein toller (interessanter, lieber . . .) Mensch!
3. Was für ein seltsamer (langweiliger, schrecklicher . . .) Mensch!
4. Was für ein süßes (interessantes, liebes . . .) Tier!

Aussprache: f, v, ph, w

CD 7, Track 7

A. Laute

1. [f] fast, fertig, freundlich, öffnen, Brief
2. [f] verliebt, verlobt, verheiratet, versucht, vergessen, verloren, Philosophie
3. [v] Video, Klavier, Silvester, Pullover, Universität
4. [v] wer, wen, wem, wessen, warum, schwarz, schwer, zwischen

B. Wortpaare

1. *wine* / Wein	3. *oven* / Ofen	5. Vase / Wasser
2. *when* / wenn	4. *veal* / viel	6. vier / wir

***Der Moderator kocht, wäscht, bügelt –
und kann sogar Babys wickeln***

Johannes B. Kerner: »**Ich bin ein perfekter Hausmann**«

Hörverständnis

Track 26

Leute sind verschieden. Hören Sie, was man Ihnen über vier Leute erzählt! Welche Adjektive sind typisch für Sie? Schreiben Sie den Anfangsbuchstaben ihrer Namen neben die Adjektive, z. B. K = Kirsten, M = Martin, O = Oliver, S = Sabine. Nicht alle Adjektive passen.

Zum Erkennen: das Krankenhaus, ¨er *(hospital)*; während *(while)*; die Katastrophe, -n; nicht einmal *(not even)*

____ arm	____ lustig	____ selbstbewusst
____ attraktiv	____ musikalisch	____ sportlich
____ faul	____ nett	____ temperamentvoll
____ fleißig	____ populär	____ unsportlich
____ freundlich	____ reich	____ unternehmungslustig
____ intelligent	____ ruhig	____ verständnisvoll

Struktur

11.1 The simple past *(imperfect, narrative past)*

The past tense is often referred to as the SIMPLE PAST because it is a single verb form in contrast to the perfect tenses (or "compound past tenses"), which consist of two parts: an auxiliary and a past participle.

We spoke German.   Wir **sprachen** Deutsch.

The present perfect is the preferred tense in spoken German—especially in southern Germany, Austria, and Switzerland. Only the simple past of **haben, sein,** and the modals is common everywhere. The simple past is used primarily in continuous narratives such as novels, short stories, newspaper reports, and letters relating a sequence of events. Therefore, it is often also called the NARRATIVE PAST.

As with other tenses, one German verb form corresponds to several in English.

Sie **sprachen** Deutsch.

$\begin{cases} \textit{They } \textbf{spoke}\textit{ German.} \\ \textit{They } \textbf{were speaking}\textit{ German.} \\ \textit{They } \textbf{did speak}\textit{ German.} \\ \textit{They } \textbf{used to speak}\textit{ German.} \end{cases}$

1. T-verbs *(weak verbs)*

   T-verbs can be compared to regular English verbs such as *love / loved* and *work / worked*, which form the past tense by adding *-d* or *-ed* to the stem. To form the simple past of t-verbs, add **-te, -test, -te, -ten, -tet, -ten** to the STEM of the verb.

ich	lern**te**	wir	lern**ten**
du	lern**test**	ihr	lern**tet**
er	lern**te**	sie	lern**ten**

   Familiar verbs that follow this pattern include: angeln, anschauen, ärgern, benutzen, danken, diskutieren, entspannen, ergänzen, erholen, erleben, erzählen, faulenzen, fehlen, fragen, freuen, glauben, gratulieren, hören, interessieren, kochen, lächeln, lachen, legen, machen, malen, meinen, passieren, reisen, sagen, sammeln, schmecken, setzen, spielen, suchen, stellen, stimmen, träumen, wandern, weinen, wohnen, wünschen.

   a. Verbs with stems ending in **-d, -t,** or certain consonant combinations add an **-e-** before the simple past ending.

ich	arbeit**e**te	wir	arbeit**e**ten
du	arbeit**e**test	ihr	arbeit**e**tet
er	arbeit**e**te	sie	arbeit**e**ten

   Familiar verbs that follow this pattern include: antworten, baden, bedeuten, beenden, bilden, heiraten, kosten, landen, mieten, öffnen, übernachten, vorbereiten, warten.

b. Irregular t-verbs—sometimes called *mixed verbs*—usually have a stem change. Compare the English *bring / brought* with the German **bringen / brachte.**

ich brachte	wir brachten
du brachtest	ihr brachtet
er brachte	sie brachten

Here is a list of the PRINCIPAL PARTS of all the irregular t-verbs that you have used thus far. Irregular present-tense forms are also noted. You already know all the forms of these verbs except their simple past. Verbs with prefixes have the same forms as the corresponding simple verbs **(brachte mit).** If you know the principal parts of a verb, you can derive all the verb forms you need!

Infinitive	Present	Simple Past	Past Participle
bringen		**brachte**	gebracht
denken		**dachte**	gedacht
haben	hat	**hatte**	gehabt
kennen		**kannte**	gekannt
nennen		**nannte**	genannt
wissen	weiß	**wusste**	gewusst

Modals also belong to this group. (The past participles of these verbs are rarely used.)

dürfen	darf	**durfte**	(gedurft)
können	kann	**konnte**	(gekonnt)
müssen	muss	**musste**	(gemusst)
sollen	soll	**sollte**	(gesollt)
wollen	will	**wollte**	(gewollt)

NOTE: The simple past of irregular t-verbs has the same stem change as the past participle.

2. N-verbs *(strong verbs)*

N-verbs correspond to such English verbs as *write / wrote / written* and *speak / spoke / spoken.* They usually have a stem change in the simple past that is difficult to predict and must therefore be memorized. (Overall they fall into a number of groups with the same changes. For a listing by group, see the Appendix.) To form the simple past, add **-, -st, -, -en, -t, -en** to the IRREGULAR STEM of the verb.

ich sprach	wir sprachen
du sprachst	ihr spracht
er sprach	sie sprachen

Here is a list of the PRINCIPAL PARTS of n-verbs that you have used up to now. You already know all the forms except the simple past. Irregular present-tense forms and the auxiliary **sein** are also noted.

Infinitive	Present	Simple Past	Past Participle
an·fangen	fängt an	**fing an**	angefangen
an·ziehen		**zog an**	angezogen
beginnen		**begann**	begonnen
bleiben		**blieb**	ist geblieben
ein·laden	lädt ein	**lud ein**	eingeladen
empfehlen	empfiehlt	**empfahl**	empfohlen
entscheiden		**entschied**	entschieden
essen	isst	**aß**	gegessen
fahren	fährt	**fuhr**	ist gefahren
fallen	fällt	**fiel**	ist gefallen
finden		**fand**	gefunden
fliegen		**flog**	ist geflogen
geben	gibt	**gab**	gegeben
gefallen	gefällt	**gefiel**	gefallen
gehen		**ging**	ist gegangen
halten	hält	**hielt**	gehalten
hängen		**hing**	gehangen
heißen		**hieß**	geheißen
helfen	hilft	**half**	geholfen
kommen		**kam**	ist gekommen
lassen	lässt	**ließ**	gelassen
laufen	läuft	**lief**	ist gelaufen
lesen	liest	**las**	gelesen
liegen		**lag**	gelegen
nehmen	nimmt	**nahm**	genommen
rufen		**rief**	gerufen
schlafen	schläft	**schlief**	geschlafen
schreiben		**schrieb**	geschrieben
schwimmen		**schwamm**	ist geschwommen
sehen	sieht	**sah**	gesehen
sein	ist	**war**	ist gewesen
singen		**sang**	gesungen
sitzen		**saß**	gesessen
sprechen	spricht	**sprach**	gesprochen
stehen		**stand**	gestanden
steigen		**stieg**	ist gestiegen
tragen	trägt	**trug**	getragen
treffen	trifft	**traf**	getroffen
treiben		**trieb**	getrieben
trinken		**trank**	getrunken
tun	tut	**tat**	getan
vergessen	vergisst	**vergaß**	vergessen
vergleichen		**verglich**	verglichen
verlieren		**verlor**	verloren
waschen	wäscht	**wusch**	gewaschen
werden	wird	**wurde**	ist geworden

3. Sentences in the simple past follow familiar word-order patterns.

Der Zug **kam** um acht.
Der Zug **kam** um acht **an**.
Der Zug <u>sollte</u> um acht <u>ankommen</u>.
      V1   V2

               Er wusste, dass der Zug um acht **kam.**
               Er wusste, dass der Zug um acht **ankam.**
               Er wusste, dass der Zug um acht <u>ankommen sollte.</u>
                                      V2   V1

Übungen

A. Nennen Sie das Imperfekt *(simple past)!*

BEISPIEL   feiern   *feierte*

1. fragen, erzählen, klatschen, lächeln, legen, bummeln, ersetzen, wechseln, fotografieren, passieren, erleben, schicken, putzen, benutzen, versuchen, sich kämmen, sich rasieren, sich entspannen, sich ärgern, sich erholen
2. arbeiten, baden, bilden, beenden, bedeuten, kosten, antworten, übernachten, warten, vorbereiten, öffnen
3. haben, müssen, denken, wissen, können, kennen, nennen
4. nehmen, essen, vergessen, sehen, lesen, ausgeben, herausfinden, singen, sitzen, liegen, kommen, wehtun, sein, hängen *(n-verb)*, beschreiben, treiben, heißen, entscheiden, einsteigen, vergleichen, schlafen, fallen, lassen, fahren, tragen, waschen, werden, einladen

B. Ersetzen Sie die Verben!

BEISPIEL   Sie schickte das Paket. (mitbringen)
                    Sie brachte das Paket mit.

1. Sie schickten ein Taxi. (suchen, bestellen, mieten, warten auf)
2. Das hatte ich damals nicht. (wissen, kennen, denken, mitbringen)
3. Wann solltet ihr zurückkommen? (müssen, wollen, dürfen, können)
4. Wir fanden es dort. (sehen, lassen, verlieren, vergessen)
5. Er dankte seiner Mutter. (antworten, zuhören, helfen, schreiben)
6. Du empfahlst den Sauerbraten. (bestellen, nehmen, wollen, bringen)

C. Wiederholen Sie die Texte im Imperfekt!

1. **Weißt du noch?** Ein Bruder und eine Schwester—Sie und Ihr Partner/Ihre Partnerin—erinnern sich *(remember).*

BEISPIEL   Großvater erzählt stundenlang von seiner Kindheit *(child-hood).*—Wir setzen uns aufs Sofa.
                  S1 Großvater erzählte stundenlang von seiner Kindheit.
                  S2 Wir setzten uns aufs Sofa.

  a. Ich höre ihm gern zu.—Seine Geschichten interessieren mich auch.
  b. Vater arbeitet viel im Garten.—Du telefonierst oder besuchst gern die Nachbarn.
  c. Marita und Finn spielen stundenlang Karten.—Mutter kauft ein oder bezahlt Rechnungen.
  d. Großmutter legt sich nachmittags ein Stündchen hin.—Sie freut sich danach auf ihre Tasse Kaffee. Richtig?

2. **Haben Sie das nicht gewusst?** Ein paar Nachbarn klatschen *(gossip)* über Lothar und Ute.

BEISPIEL   Hat Ute ihren Mann schon lange gekannt?
Kannte Ute ihren Mann schon lange?

a. Wie hat sie ihn kennen gelernt?
b. Hast du nichts von ihrer Anzeige gewusst? Sie hat Lothar durch die Zeitung kennen gelernt.
c. Der Briefträger *(mail carrier)* hat ihr einen Brief von dem jungen Herrn gebracht.
d. Gestern haben sie Hochzeit gefeiert. Sie hat Glück gehabt.
e. Das habe ich mir auch gedacht.

3. **Schade!** Anna erzählt ihrer Freundin, warum sie traurig ist.

BEISPIEL   Was willst du denn machen?
Was wolltest du denn machen?

a. Ich will mit Thomas ins Kino gehen, aber ich kann nicht.
b. Warum? Darfst du nicht?
c. Doch, aber meine Kopfschmerzen wollen einfach nicht weggehen.
d. Musst du im Bett bleiben?
e. Nein, aber ich darf nicht schon wieder krank werden. Leider kann ich nicht mit Thomas sprechen. Seine Mutter will es ihm sagen. Er soll mich anrufen.

4. **Wo wart ihr?** Caroline erzählt von ihrer kurzen Reise in die Schweiz.

BEISPIEL   Wir sind eine Woche in Saas Fee gewesen.
Wir waren eine Woche in Saas Fee.

a. Von unserem Zimmer haben wir einen Blick auf die Alpen gehabt. b. Die Pension hat natürlich Alpenblick geheißen. c. Morgens haben wir lange geschlafen, dann haben wir gemütlich gefrühstückt. d. Später bin ich mit dem Sessellift auf einen Berg gefahren und bin den ganzen Nachmittag Ski laufen gegangen. e. Wolfgang ist unten geblieben, hat Bücher gelesen und Briefe geschrieben.

D. Eine vielseitige Persönlichkeit Nennen Sie die fehlenden Verbformen im Imperfekt!

1. Else Lasker-Schüler ist eine vielseitige Persönlichkeit aus der deutschen Kunstszene. 2. Geboren 1868 in Wuppertal, _____ (gehören) sie zu einer jüdischen Familie, wo man ihr damals viel Freiheit _____ (lassen). 3. 1894 _____ (heiraten) sie einen Berliner Arzt, _____ (beginnen) zu zeichnen *(draw)* und ihre ersten Gedichte *(poems)* zu schreiben. 4. In Berlin _____ (bringen) sie 1899 ihren Sohn Paul zur Welt. 5. Bald danach _____ sie aus dem bürgerlichen *(bourgeois)* Leben _____ (aus·steigen), _____ (lassen) sich scheiden und _____ (heiraten) 1903 Herwarth Walden, den Herausgeber *(editor)* der Zeitschrift *Der Sturm,* mit Kontakt zu allen Künstlern Berlins. 6. Zwischen 1910 und 1930 _____ (werden) sie selbst sehr bekannt. 7. Sie _____ (leben) nicht nur von ihren Gedichten und ihrer Prosa, sondern auch als Grafikerin. 8. 1933 _____ die Nazis ihre Zeichnungen *(drawings)* _____ (weg·nehmen) und sie _____ (gehen) ins Exil in die Schweiz, später nach Palästina. 9. Als sie 1939 in Palästina _____ (an·kommen), _____ (sein) sie schockiert. 10. Ihr ganzes Leben lang _____ (träumen) sie von einem Land, wo verschiedene Kulturen und Religionen harmonisch _____ (zusammen·leben). 11. Dieses Palästina _____ (haben) nichts mit dem Land ihrer Träume zu tun. 12. Sie _____ (fühlen) sich dort wie im Exil. 13. So _____ (schreiben) sie 1942: „Ich bin keine Zionistin, keine Jüdin, keine Christin, ich glaube aber, ein tieftrauriger Mensch." 14. Lasker-Schüler starb *(died)* 1945 im Alter von 77 Jahren in Jerusalem.

Lasker-Schülers Porträts einiger bekannter Freunde:

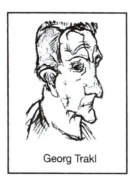
Georg Trakl

George Grosz

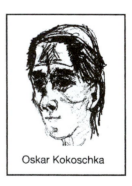
Oskar Kokoschka

E. So war das damals. Stellen Sie Ihrem Partner/Ihrer Partnerin Fragen über frühere *(earlier)* Zeiten! Wechseln Sie sich ab! Fragen Sie, . . . !

1. wo er/sie früher wohnte
2. wo er/sie zur Schule ging
3. wie viele Leute zu Hause wohnten
4. was die Familie gewöhnlich am Wochenende machte
5. was sie in den Ferien machten
6. wie eine typische Woche aussah
7. ob er/sie Tiere zu Hause hatte; wenn ja, welche, wie sie waren und wie sie hießen
8. was ihm/ihr damals gefiel und was nicht
9. . . .

> 1. The Austrian poet **Georg Trakl** (1887–1914) was acutely aware that his world, both personal and external, was breaking apart. The outbreak of World War I and his experience with the wounded at the front overtaxed his resources. He died from an overdose of drugs while serving as a pharmacist in the army. 2. **George Grosz** (1893–1959) was a painter, caricaturist, and graphic artist who satirized the military, industrialists, and bourgeois life and got into trouble with the Nazis because of it. Between 1932 and 1959, he lived in the United States; he died shortly after his return to Germany. 3. **Oskar Kokoschka** (1886–1980) was an Austrian painter and playwright, best known for his expressionist portraiture and the expressionist magazine *Der Sturm,* edited by Herwarth Walden. In 1938 he emigrated to England and in 1954 to Switzerland.

> Optional tongue twisters **(Zungenbrecher):** 1. Fischers Fritze fischte frische Fische. Frische Fische fischte Fischers Fritze. 2. Blaukraut bleibt Blaukraut und Brautkleid *(wedding dress)* bleibt Brautkleid.

The Principality of Liechtenstein (**das Fürstentum Liechtenstein**) lies between Austria and Switzerland. Its territory is about the size of Washington, D.C., and it has around 34,000 inhabitants.

Die fürstliche Familie: Prinz Maximilian, Prinzessin Tatjana, Prinz Constantin, Fürstin Marie, Fürst Hans-Adam II., Prinz Alois von und zu Liechtenstein

The country maintains close relations with Switzerland, sharing customs, currency, postal service, and management of foreign affairs. While many Liechtensteiners speak Alemannish, a German dialect, standard German is the official language of the country. Thanks to favorable tax policies, a large number of foreign businesses and banks have established nominal headquarters in Liechtenstein.

The castle in Vaduz, the capital serves as the residence of Liechtenstein's royal family. According to the 1921 constitution, the country is a constitutional monarchy, hereditary in the male line. In 1989, Prince Hans Adam II succeeded to the throne. When his son Prince Alois married Princess Sophie in 1993, the royal family invited all its subjects to the wedding celebrations.

11.2 Conjunctions: *als, wann, wenn*

Care must be taken to distinguish among the conjunctions **als, wann,** and **wenn,** all of which correspond to the English *when.*

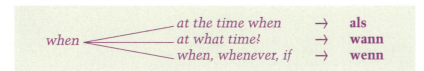

> *when* ─┬─ *at the time when* → **als**
> ├─ *at what time?* → **wann**
> └─ *when, whenever, if* → **wenn**

- **Als** refers to *a single (or particular) event in the past.*

    Als ich gestern Abend nach Hause kam, war er noch nicht zurück.
    When I came home last night, he wasn't back yet.

- **Wann** introduces direct or indirect *questions referring to time.*

    Ich frage mich, **wann** er nach Hause kommt.
    I wonder when (or at what time) he'll come home.

- **Wenn** covers all other situations.

    Wenn du ankommst, ruf mich an!
    When you arrive, call me! (referring to a present or future event)

    Wenn er kam, brachte er immer Blumen mit.
    Whenever he came, he brought flowers. (repeated event in the past)

Remember that **wenn** *(if)* can also introduce a conditional clause:

    Wenn es nicht regnet, gehen wir spazieren.
    If it doesn't rain, we'll take a walk.

Übungen

F. *Als, wann* oder *wenn?*

1. _____ ihr kommt, zeigen wir euch die Bilder von unserer Reise.
2. Können Sie mir sagen, _____ der Zug aus Köln ankommt?
3. _____ wir letzte Woche im Theater waren, sahen wir Stefan und Sonja.
4. Sie freute sich immer sehr, _____ wir sie besuchten.
5. Sie bekommen diese Möbel, _____ sie heiraten; aber wer weiß, _____ sie heiraten.
6. _____ ich klein war, habe ich nur Deutsch gesprochen.

G. Verbinden Sie die Sätze mit *als, wann* oder *wenn!*

BEISPIEL   Sie riefen an. Ich duschte mich. *(when)*
Sie riefen an, als ich mich duschte.

(when) Ich duschte mich. Sie riefen an.
Als ich mich duschte, riefen sie an.

1. Wir sahen Frau Loth heute früh. Wir gingen einkaufen. *(when)*
2. *(when)* Sie spricht von Liebe. Er hört nicht zu.
3. Sie möchte (es) wissen. Die Weihnachtsferien fangen an. *(when)*
4. *(when)* Ich stand gestern auf. Es regnete.
5. *(when)* Das Wetter war schön. Die Kinder spielten immer im Park.
6. Er hat mir nicht geschrieben. Er kommt. *(when)*

 H. Was dann? Stellen Sie den anderen Fragen mit den Konjunktionen **als, wann** oder **wenn!** Benutzen Sie dabei das Präsens *(present tense)*, Perfekt *(present perfect)* oder Imperfekt! Wechseln Sie sich ab!

1. **Wo warst du, als . . . ?**

    BEISPIEL   S1 Wo warst du, als am 11. September 2001 die Flugzeuge ins World Trade Center flogen?
                   S2 Als das passierte, war ich . . .

2. **Wann warst du . . . ?**

    BEISPIEL   S1 Wann warst du in New York?
                   S2 Ich war letzten Sommer in New York.

3. **Was tust du gewöhnlich, wenn . . . ?**

    BEISPIEL   S1 Was siehst du dir gewöhnlich an, wenn du in New York bist?
                   S2 Ich sehe mir die Kunst und Architektur an.

 I. Ein Bericht *(report)* oder eine Beschreibung: Damals Schreiben Sie acht bis zehn Sätze über eins der folgenden Themen. Benutzen Sie dabei möglichst viele Verben im Imperfekt und die Konjunktionen **als, wann** oder **wenn!**

1. **Eine schöne Reise** Sagen Sie, wo Sie waren und mit wem, was Sie sahen und erlebten!

2. **Als ich klein war . . .** Beschreiben Sie etwas aus Ihrer Kindheit *(childhood)* oder Jugend *(youth)*!

    BEISPIEL   *Als ich klein war, musste / wollte ich zu Fuß zur Schule gehen . . .*

Women in Germany have had equal rights under the law (**die Gleichberechtigung**) only since 1976. Until that time, the constitution stipulated that women could work outside the home only if the job was compatible with their family obligations. Subsequently, women have used equal access to schools, universities, and other training facilities to take advantage of new opportunities. Yet, while they have had the right to vote since 1918, women still play a relatively limited role—albeit a gradually more important one—in the upper echelons of business, government, and academia. Interestingly, women in the former East Germany have maintained some of their earlier independence: one-third of east German businesses are now owned by women, compared to less than one-fourth in the west.

Discrimination in hiring, firing, working conditions, or advancement, as well as any kind of sexual harassment, are forbidden by law. Even though equal pay for equal work is legally guaranteed, women's incomes are generally lower than men's, partly because women tend to interrupt their careers to rear children, enter the labor force later, and/or work in lower paying positions. While women in western Germany earn about 75 percent as much as men, women in eastern Germany earn about 90 percent of what men earn. In all of Germany, however, the unemployment rate for women is higher than for men.

Today, a great deal of attention is paid to the idea of "gender mainstreaming," a systematic strategy to promote equal opportunity for women *and* men and to break down traditional role patterns. As such, all activities and career options in the German Armed Forces are now open to women. The number of women in politics has also increased continuously. In 2005, 32 percent of the members of parliament were women. While considerable progress has been made, there is still much room for improvement.

11.3 The past perfect

1. Like the present perfect, the PAST PERFECT in both English and German is a compound form consisting of an auxiliary and a past participle, with the auxiliary itself in the simple past.

Ich **hatte** das gut **gelernt.**	*I had learned that well.*
Er **war** um 10 Uhr nach Hause **gekommen.**	*He had come home at 10 o'clock.*

ich	**hatte** . . . gelernt	**war** . . . gekommen
du	**hattest** . . . gelernt	**warst** . . . gekommen
er	**hatte** . . . gelernt	**war** . . . gekommen
wir	**hatten** . . . gelernt	**waren** . . . gekommen
ihr	**hattet** . . . gelernt	**wart** . . . gekommen
sie	**hatten** . . . gelernt	**waren** . . . gekommen

2. The past perfect is used to refer to events *preceding other events* in the past.

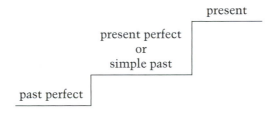

Er hat mich gestern angerufen. ⎫ Er rief mich gestern an. ⎬	*He called me yesterday.*
Ich **hatte** ihm gerade **geschrieben.**	*I had just written to him.*
Wir sind zu spät am Bahnhof angekommen. ⎫ Wir kamen zu spät am Bahnhof an. ⎬	*We arrived at the station too late.*
Der Zug **war** schon **abgefahren.**	*The train had already left.*

3. The conjunction **nachdem** *(after)* is usually followed by the past perfect in the subordinate clause, whereas the main clause is in the simple past or present perfect.

| nachdem | *after* |

Nachdem er mich **angerufen hatte,** schickte ich den Brief nicht mehr ab.
Nachdem der Zug **abgefahren war,** gingen wir ins Bahnhofsrestaurant.

Übungen

● Optional English-to-German practice: 1. We got **(kommen)** to the airport after the plane had landed. 2. When I arrived, they had already picked up **(holen)** their luggage. 3. After we had found them, we drove home. 4. My mother had been looking forward to this day. 5. After she had shown them the house, we sat down in the living room and talked about the family. (See answer key in the Appendix.)

J. Ersetzen Sie das Subjekt!

BEISPIEL   Sie hatten uns besucht. (du)
               Du hattest uns besucht.

1. Du hattest den Schlüssel gesucht. (ihr, Sie, sie/*sg.*)
2. Sie hatten das nicht gewusst. (wir, du, ich)
3. Ich war nach Dresden gereist. (sie/*pl.,* ihr, er)
4. Sie waren auch in der Dresdner Oper gewesen. (du, ich, wir)

K. Nicht schon wieder! Auf Englisch bitte!

1. Meine Schwester wollte den Film sehen. 2. Er war ein großer Erfolg. 3. Ich hatte ihn schon zweimal gesehen. 4. Ich hatte schon lange nicht mehr so gelacht. 5. Aber meine Schwester war nicht mit mir gegangen. 6. Sie hatte keine Zeit gehabt. 7. So sind wir später noch einmal zusammen / gemeinsam gegangen.

L. Und dann?

1. **Bei Schneiders** Frau/Herr Schneider—Ihr Partner/Ihre Partnerin—erzählt von einem typischen Tag bei sich zu Hause. Fragen Sie immer wieder **Und dann?,** um herauszufinden, was dann passierte! Sehen Sie, wie Frau/Herr Schneider vom Perfekt *(present perfect)* zum Plusquamperfekt *(past perfect)* wechselt? Wechseln Sie sich nach den ersten fünf Sätzen ab!

   BEISPIEL   S1   Ich bin aufgestanden.
                 S2   Und dann?
                 S1   Nachdem ich aufgestanden war, habe ich mir die Zähne geputzt.

   a. Ich bin aufgestanden.
   b. Ich habe mir die Zähne geputzt.
   c. Ich habe mich angezogen.
   d. Ich habe Frühstück gemacht.
   e. Alle haben sich an den Tisch gesetzt.
   f. Das Telefon hat geklingelt *(rang).*
   g. Ich habe mit Helmut gesprochen.
   h. Er hat die Zeitung gelesen.
   i. Er ist zur Arbeit gegangen.
   j. Ich habe mich an den Computer gesetzt . . .

2. **Letztes Wochenende** Fragen Sie Ihren Partner/Ihre Partnerin, was er/sie am Wochenende gemacht hat! Benutzen Sie auch andere Verben als *(than)* in Übung L.1!

   BEISPIEL   S1   Was hast du am Wochenende gemacht?
                 S2   Ich bin um zehn Uhr aufgestanden.
                 S1   Und dann?
                 S2   . . .

The Brothers Grimm and Their Fairy Tales

The brothers Grimm, Jacob (1785–1863) and Wilhelm (1786–1859), are well remembered for their collection of fairy tales (**Märchen**), including **Hänsel und Gretel**, **Schneewittchen** (Snow White), **Rotkäppchen** (Little Red Riding Hood), **Aschenputtel** (Cinderella), **Dornröschen** (Sleeping Beauty), **Rumpelstilzchen**, **Rapunzel**, **König Drosselbart** (King Thrushbeard), **Die Bremer Stadtmusikanten**, and many others. Such stories had been transmitted orally from generation to generation and were long considered typically German. Modern research has shown, however, that some of these tales originated in other countries. The story of Rapunzel, for example, had already appeared in an Italian collection in 1634; there the heroine is named "Petrosinella." The next traceable reference is from France, where the girl's name is "Persinette." Researchers assume that the story traveled to Germany and Switzerland with the Huguenots (French Protestants) who left France after Louis XIV lifted the edict that granted them religious freedom. Jacob and Wilhelm Grimm heard many of the stories from women living in and around Kassel in northern Hesse, among them the 16-year-old Dorothea Wild, who later became Wilhelm's wife.

Jacob Grimm also wrote the first historical German grammar (**Deutsche Grammatik**), in which he compared fifteen different Germanic languages and analyzed their stages of development. The brothers' work on the *Deutsches Wörterbuch* was a pioneering effort that served as a model for later lexicographers. In 1840, the brothers became members of the German Academy of Sciences in Berlin.

 Visit the **Wie geht's?** iLrn website for more review and practice of the grammar points you have just learned.

 M. So war's! Beschreiben Sie Ihr Wochenende oder Ihre Ferien. Benutzen Sie dabei die Konjunktion **nachdem**! Schreiben Sie 8–10 Sätze.

Zusammenfassung

N. Wiederholen Sie die Sätze im Imperfekt!

1. Lothar denkt an Sabine. 2. Er will ein paar Wochen segeln gehen. 3. Aber sie hat keine Lust dazu. 4. Er spricht mit Holger. 5. Die beiden setzen eine Anzeige in die Zeitung. 6. Ute liest die Anzeige und antwortet darauf. 7. Durch die Anzeige finden sie sich. 8. Danach hat Lothar für Sabine keine Zeit mehr. 9. Er träumt nur noch von Ute. 10. Am 24. Mai heiraten die beiden. 11. Sie laden Holger zur Hochzeit ein. 12. Die Trauung *(ceremony)* ist in der lutherischen Kirche. 13. Ute heißt vorher *(before)* Kaiser. 14. Jetzt wird sie Ute Müller. 15. Die Hochzeitsreise verbringen *(spend)* sie auf einem Segelboot.

Das Brautpaar schneidet den Hochzeitskuchen an (cuts the wedding cake).

Verliebt...
...Verlobt...
...Verheiratet

Lothar Müller
Ute Müller
geb. Kaiser

Vahrenwalder Str. 93
Hannover 1

Kirchliche Trauung am 24. Mai 2007, 15ºº Uhr in der Ev.-luth. Vahrenwalder Kirche

O. Hoppla, hier fehlt was: Unser Kätzchen! Thomas und sein Zimmerkollege haben ein Kätzchen durch eine Zeitungsanzeige gefunden, aber es ging nicht alles so wie geplant. Finden Sie mit Ihrem Partner/Ihrer Partnerin heraus, was passierte! Einer von Ihnen schaut auf die Tabelle unten, der andere auf die Tabelle im Anhang, Teil 11. Benutzen Sie dabei das Perfekt und das Plusquamperfekt!

S1:

	Nachdem . . .	Dann . . .
Thomas	die Anzeige lesen	
Besitzer	über die Katze erzählen	Thomas seine Adresse geben
Thomas	dorthin fahren und s. die Katze ansehen	
Thomas	die Katze mit nach Hause nehmen	sie Ingo zeigen
Die beiden	ihr etwas Milch geben	
Die Katze	s. einleben *(get used to the place)*	oft auf Ingos Bett schlafen
Die beiden	die Katze eine Woche haben	
Ingo	die Katze zwei Wochen auf seinem Bett haben	richtig krank davon werden
Die beiden	eine lange Diskussion haben	
Besitzer	zwei Wochen ohne die Katze sein	sie sehr vermissen *(miss)*
Besitzer	auf die Anzeige antworten	

BEISPIEL   S1   Was passierte, nachdem Thomas die Anzeige gelesen hatte?
S2   Nachdem Thomas die Anzeige gelesen hatte, rief er den Besitzer *(owner)* an. Der Besitzer erzählte über die Katze—und dann?
S1   Nachdem der Besitzer von der Katze erzählt hatte, . . .

P. Die Hochzeit   Auf Deutsch bitte! Benutzen Sie das Imperfekt, wenn nicht anders gefragt!

1. Arthur had been thinking of his daughter's wedding. 2. When we saw Maren in December, she was in love with a charming, wealthy man. 3. They were supposed to get married in April. 4. I had already bought a beautiful present. 5. Two weeks ago, on July 9, she got engaged to another man. 6. Stephan is a poor student at **(an)** her university. 7. They didn't say when they wanted to get married. 8. On the weekend, she called her parents. 9. She and Stephan had just gotten married. 10. They hadn't invited the parents to **(zu)** their wedding. 11. Arthur gets annoyed when he thinks about it. 12. He just can't believe it.

Wir haben uns am 9. Juli 2004 in Niendorf/Ostsee verlobt
Maren
Lütje
Harsum
Stephan
Grosser

Einblicke

Wortschatz 2

der König, -e	*king*
das Gold	*gold*
die Königin, -nen	*queen*
Welt	*world*
das erste (zweite . . .) Mal	*the first (second . . .) time*
zum ersten (dritten . . .) Mal	*for the first (third . . .) time*
allein	*alone*
froh	*glad, happy*
<u>niemand</u>	*nobody, no one*
nun	*now*
plötzlich	*sudden(ly)*
sofort	*right away, immediately*
voll	*full*
geschehen (geschieht), geschah, ist geschehen	*to happen*
herein·kommen, kam herein, ist hereingekommen	*to enter, come in*
spinnen, spann, gesponnen	*to spin*
springen, sprang, ist gesprungen	*to jump*
sterben (stirbt), starb, ist gestorben	*to die*
versprechen (verspricht), versprach, versprochen	*to promise*

🔸 Just like with **jemand**, note the use of **niemand** in the various cases: Da ist **niemand** an der Tür. Er hat **niemanden** mitgebracht. Sie sprach mit **niemandem**. Das sind **niemandes** Schlüssel.

Vor dem Lesen

A. Allerlei Fragen

1. Wie beginnen viele Märchen auf Englisch? 2. Wo spielen sie? 3. Welche Personen sind typisch in einem Märchen? 4. Welche Märchen kennen Sie? 5. Haben Sie als Kind gern Märchen gelesen? Warum (nicht)?

 B. Gehen wir Wörter angeln! Lesen Sie das Märchen mit Ihrem Partner/Ihrer Partnerin still *(quietly)* durch. Wenn Sie einen Imperfekt finden, lesen Sie diesen laut und nennen Sie den passenden Infinitiv dazu! Das gleiche Verb in der gleichen Verbform brauchen Sie nicht zu wiederholen. Wechseln Sie sich ab!

BEISPIEL	S1	war	*sein*
	S2	hatte	*haben*
	S1	geschah	*geschehen*

C. Das ist leicht zu verstehen! Welche Silbe ist betont? Markieren Sie sie! Was ist das auf Englisch?

der Müller, Ring, Rückweg, Sonnenaufgang; das Feuer, Männchen, Spinnrad; die Nachbarschaft; testen; golden

Lesetipp
Recognizing Elements in Fairy Tales

A fairy tale is a story in which strange or unusual events take place. The figures are often out-of-the-ordinary characters, such as kings, princesses, or even nonhuman beings. Magical transformations often play a significant role. The number three is also a recurrent feature of many fairy tales: events often occur three times and things appear in groups of three. As you work with this reading, look for examples of such elements.

Rumpelstilzchen

once upon a time
there was

straw

chamber

locked

necklace

expected
more / ordered

Es war einmal° ein Müller. Er war arm, aber er hatte eine schöne Tochter. Eines Tages geschah es, dass er mit dem König sprach. Weil er dem König gefallen wollte, sagte er ihm: „Ich habe eine hübsche und intelligente Tochter. Sie kann Stroh° zu Gold spinnen." Da sprach der König zum Müller: „Das gefällt mir.
5 Wenn deine Tochter so gut ist, wie du sagst, bring sie morgen in mein Schloss! Ich will sie testen." Am nächsten Tag brachte der Müller seine Tochter aufs Schloss. Der König brachte sie in eine Kammer° mit viel Stroh und sagte: „Jetzt fang an zu arbeiten! Wenn du bis morgen früh nicht das ganze Stroh zu Gold gesponnen hast, musst du sterben." Dann schloss er die Kammer zu° und die
10 Müllerstochter blieb allein darin.

Da saß nun das arme Mädchen und weinte, denn sie wusste nicht, wie man Stroh zu Gold spinnt. Da öffnete sich plötzlich die Tür. Ein kleines Männchen kam herein und sagte: „Guten Abend, schöne Müllerstochter! Warum weinst du denn?" „Ach", antwortete das Mädchen, „weil ich Stroh zu Gold spinnen soll,
15 und ich weiß nicht wie." „Was gibst du mir, wenn ich dir helfe?", fragte das Männchen. „Meine goldene Kette°", antwortete das Mädchen. Das Männchen nahm die Goldkette, setzte sich an das Spinnrad und spann bis zum Morgen das ganze Stroh zu Gold. Bei Sonnenaufgang kam der König. Er freute sich, als er das viele Gold sah, denn das hatte er nicht erwartet°. Dann brachte er sie sofort in
20 eine andere Kammer, wo noch viel mehr° Stroh lag. Er befahl° ihr, auch das Stroh in einer Nacht zu Gold zu spinnen, wenn ihr das Leben lieb war.

Wieder weinte das Mädchen; und wieder öffnete sich die Tür und das Männchen kam herein. „Was gibst du mir, wenn ich dir das Stroh zu Gold spinne?", fragte es. „Meinen Ring vom Finger", antwortete das Mädchen. Wieder setzte
25 sich das Männchen ans Spinnrad und spann das Stroh zu Gold. Der König freute sich sehr, aber er hatte immer noch nicht genug. Nun brachte er die Müllerstochter in eine dritte Kammer, wo noch sehr viel mehr Stroh lag und sprach: „Wenn du mir dieses Stroh auch noch zu Gold spinnst, heirate ich dich morgen." Dabei dachte er sich: Wenn es auch nur eine Müllerstochter ist, so eine reiche
30 Frau finde ich in der ganzen Welt nicht. Als das Mädchen allein war, kam das Männchen zum dritten Mal. Es sagte wieder: „Was gibst du mir, wenn ich dir noch einmal das Stroh spinne?" Die Müllerstochter aber hatte nichts mehr, was sie ihm geben konnte. „Dann versprich mir dein erstes Kind, wenn du Königin bist", sagte das Männchen. Die Müllerstochter wusste nicht, was sie tun sollte,
35 und sagte ja. Am nächsten Morgen heiratete sie den König und wurde Königin.

became afraid / kingdom
living
more important than
pity
keep

messenger

borders

Nach einem Jahr brachte sie ein schönes Kind zur Welt. Sie hatte aber das Männchen schon lange vergessen. Da stand es aber plötzlich in ihrer Kammer und sagte: „Gib mir das Kind, wie du es mir versprochen hast!" Die Königin bekam Angst° und versprach dem Männchen das ganze Gold im Königreich°, wenn es ihr
40 das Kind lassen wollte. Aber das Männchen sagte: „Nein, etwas Lebendes° ist mir wichtiger als° alles Gold in der Welt." Da fing die Königin an zu weinen, dass das Männchen Mitleid° bekam. „Na gut", sagte es, „du hast drei Tage Zeit. Wenn du bis dann meinen Namen weißt, darfst du das Kind behalten°."

Nun dachte die Königin die ganze Nacht an Namen und sie schickte einen
45 Boten° über Land. Er sollte fragen, was es sonst noch für Namen gab. Am ersten Abend, als das Männchen kam, fing die Königin an mit „Kaspar, Melchior, Balthasar . . . ", aber bei jedem Namen lachte das Männchen und sagte: „Nein, so heiß' ich nicht." Am nächsten Tag fragte man die Leute in der Nachbarschaft nach Namen. Am Abend sagte die Königin dem Männchen viele komische Na-
50 men wie „Rippenbiest" und „Hammelbein", aber es antwortete immer: „Nein, so heiß' ich nicht." Am dritten Tag kam der Bote zurück und erzählte: „Ich bin bis an die Grenzen° des Königreichs gegangen und niemand konnte mir neue Namen nennen. Aber auf dem Rückweg kam ich in einen Wald. Da sah ich ein

CD 7,
Track 9

kleines Häuschen mit einem Feuer davor. Um das Feuer sprang ein komisches
55 Männchen. Es hüpfte° auf einem Bein und schrie°:

> Heute back ich, morgen brau° ich,
> übermorgen hol ich der Königin ihr Kind;
> ach, wie gut, dass niemand weiß,
> dass ich Rumpelstilzchen heiß!

60   Die Königin war natürlich sehr froh, als sie das hörte. Am Abend fragte sie
das Männchen zuerst: „Heißt du vielleicht Kunz?" „Nein!" „Heißt du vielleicht
Heinz?" „Nein!" Heißt du vielleicht Rumpelstilzchen?" „Das hat dir der Teufel°
gesagt, das hat dir der Teufel gesagt!", schrie das Männchen und stampfte° mit
dem rechten Fuß so auf den Boden°, dass es bis zum Körper darin versank°. Dann
65 packte° es den linken Fuß mit beiden Händen und riss° sich selbst in Stücke°.

hopped / screamed

brew

devil

stomped

ground / sank in
grabbed / ripped / to pieces

Märchen der Brüder Grimm (nacherzählt°)   retold

Aktives zum Text

A. Rumpelstilzchen Erzählen Sie die Geschichte noch einmal mit eigenen
Worten *(in your own words)*! Benutzen Sie das Imperfekt und die folgenden
Stichwörter!

> Müller, Tochter, König, Stroh zu Gold spinnen, Kammer, sterben, weinen,
> Männchen, Goldkette, Spinnrad, noch mehr, heiraten, Ring, Kind, Königin,
> nach einem Jahr, Angst, Mitleid, behalten, einen Boten schicken, Häuschen,
> Feuer, springen, Teufel, auf den Boden stampfen, im Boden versinken (ver-
> sank), sich selbst in Stücke reißen (riss)

● Fairy tales are a great way to show the use of the past tense. That's why we chose *Rumpelstilzchen* for this chapter. They also lend themselves to retelling and for discussion.

B. *Als, wenn* oder *wann*?

1. _____ die Müllerstochter das hörte, fing sie an zu weinen.
2. Immer, _____ die Königin nicht wusste, was sie tun sollte, weinte sie.
3. _____ du mir das Stroh zu Gold spinnst, heirate ich dich morgen.
4. Das Männchen lachte nur, _____ die Königin fragte, ob es Melchior hieß.
5. _____ die Königin den Namen Rumpelstilzchen nannte, ärgerte sich das
   Männchen furchtbar.
6. Wir wissen nicht genau, _____ sie geheiratet haben, aber _____ sie
   nicht gestorben sind, dann leben sie noch heute.

C. Gespräch zwischen Mutter und Sohn

1. **Wusstest du das?** Lesen Sie, was die Königin ihrem Sohn nach dem Tod *(death)* des Vaters erzählt! Unterstreichen Sie *(underline)* das Plusquamperfekt!

Jetzt, wo dein Vater gestorben ist, kann ich dir erzählen, wie es dazu kam, dass dein Vater und ich heirateten. Er wollte nie, dass du weißt, dass dein Großvater nur Müller war. Mein Vater brachte mich eines Tages hier aufs Schloss, weil er am Tag davor dem König gesagt hatte, dass ich Stroh zu Gold spinnen kann. Der König brachte mich damals in eine Kammer voll Stroh und ich sollte es zu Gold spinnen. Ich wusste natürlich nicht, wie man das macht. Weil der König gesagt hatte, dass ich sterben sollte, wenn das Stroh nicht am nächsten Morgen Gold geworden war, hatte ich große Angst und fing an zu weinen. Da kam plötzlich ein Männchen in die Kammer. Für meine Halskette wollte es mir helfen. Bevor es Morgen war, hatte es das ganze Stroh zu Gold gesponnen. Aber dein Vater brachte mich in eine andere Kammer voll Stroh. Wieder kam das Männchen und half mir, nachdem ich ihm meinen Ring gegeben hatte. Aber in der dritten Nacht hatte ich nichts mehr, was ich schenken konnte. Da musste ich ihm mein erstes Kind versprechen. Am nächsten Tag heirateten wir und ich wurde Königin. Nach einem Jahr kamst du auf die Welt und plötzlich stand das Männchen vor mir und wollte dich mitnehmen. Ich hatte es aber schon lange vergessen. Als ich weinte, sagte es, dass ich dich behalten dürfte, wenn ich in drei Tagen seinen Namen wüsste *(knew)*. Am letzten Tag kam mein Bote zurück und sagte mir, dass er ein Männchen gesehen hatte, wie es um ein Feuer tanzte und schrie: „Ach, wie gut, dass niemand weiß, dass ich Rumpelstilzchen heiß'." Nachdem ich dem Männchen seinen Namen gesagte hatte, riss es sich selbst in Stücke und du durftest bei mir bleiben.

2. **Ich muss dir was erzählen!** Spielen Sie jetzt mit Ihrem Partner/Ihrer Partnerin die Rolle von Mutter und Sohn. Die Mutter erzählt die Geschichte noch einmal, aber nach jedem Satz hat der Sohn etwas zu sagen.

BEISPIEL   S1   Jetzt, wo dein Vater gestorben ist, kann ich dir erzählen, wie es dazu kam, dass dein Vater und ich heirateten.
                    S2   Dann erzähl mal!

D. Mensch, du glaubst nicht, was . . . !
Erzählen Sie Ihrem Partner/Ihrer Partnerin, was Ihnen . . . (an der Uni, bei der Arbeit, in den Ferien und so weiter) passiert ist! Ihr Partner/Ihre Partnerin hat zu jedem Satz etwas zu sagen.

E. Allerlei Fragen

1. Aus welcher Zeit kommen solche Märchen wie *Rumpelstilzchen*?
2. Warum ist *Rumpelstilzchen* ein typisches Märchen? Was ist charakteristisch für Märchen?
3. Was ist die Rolle der Frau in diesem Märchen? Sieht man die Frau auch heute noch so?
4. Was für Frauen findet man oft in Märchen? In welchen Märchen findet man starke *(strong)* Frauen? Welche Rollen spielen sie meistens?
5. Warum heiratet der König die Müllerstochter? Gibt es das heute auch noch?
6. Wie endet die Geschichte in der englischen Version? Warum? Was für Geschichten hören (oder sehen) Kinder heute? Sind sie anders? Wenn ja, wie?

Erzähltipp
Beginning a Story and Encouraging the Storyteller

As you just saw, many fairy tales start with the phrase **Es war einmal . . .** Here are some common expressions to catch a listener's attention when beginning to relate a story: **Weißt du, was mir passiert ist?/Mensch du glaubst nicht, was . . . !/ Ich muss dir was erzählen./Ich vergesse nie . . ./Hast du gewusst, dass . . . ?/ Hast du schon gehört, dass . . . ?**

And this is how a listener might reply in order to show interest: **Wirklich? Natürlich! Klar! Und (dann)? Was hast du dann gemacht? Und wo warst du, als . . . ? Und wie geht's weiter?**

Schloss Neuschwanstein von Ludwig II. stammt aus (dates back to) dem 19. Jahrhundert.

● Situated near the city of Füssen in southern Germany, the extravagant Neuschwanstein Castle was built between 1869 and 1886 by King Ludwig II of Bavaria. It has come to represent the ultimate fairy-tale castle in the minds of many.

● There is an extensive review section following this chapter in the *Arbeitsbuch (Rückblick: Kapitel 8–11)*. The accompanying exercises and answer key will help you prepare for the test.

 ## Hörverständnis

Track 27 **Vier berühmte Märchen** Welcher Text gehört zu welchem Märchen? Schreiben Sie die Nummer daneben!

Zum Erkennen: brachen ab *(broke off)*; schütteten *(dumped)*; die Linsen *(lentils)*; die Asche; auslesen *(to pick out)*; der Turm *(tower)*; das Spinnrad *(spinning wheel)*; die Spindel *(spindle)*; kaum *(hardly)*; erfüllte sich *(was fulfilled)*; der Zauberspruch *(magic spell)*; stach *(pricked)*; schlief ein *(fell asleep)*

_____ *Aschenputtel*

_____ *Dornröschen*

_____ *Hänsel und Gretel*

_____ *Rapunzel*

_____ *Rotkäppchen*

_____ *Schneewittchen*

Personal ads, one couple's wedding preparations, a visit to Liechtenstein: http://wiegehts.heinle.com.

Literatur

Biographisches

Gotthold Ephraim Lessing (1729–1781) was one of the most influential figures of the German Enlightenment. After studying theology and medicine, he began his writing career in Leipzig, where two of his early comedies, *Der Freigeist* and *Die Juden* (both written in 1740), were performed. The first exposes a freethinker's intolerance; the second is a plea for racial and religious tolerance. Representing a break with the French style of his day, Lessing's domestic tragedy *Miß Sara Sampson* (1755) exemplifies English literary concepts. His comedy *Minna von Barnhelm* (1767) was published after the Seven Years' War (1756–1763). As an art and theater critic, Lessing made his mark with *Laokoon* (1766) and the *Hamburgische Dramaturgie* (1767–1768). *Emilia Galotti* (1722) exerted a strong influence on the **Sturm und Drang** movement, whose chief exponents were Goethe and Schiller. Lessing's final years were dominated by polemics against the influential clergyman Johann Melchior Goeze. Silenced by a ban on publishing further articles, he wrote his parable about religious tolerance, *Nathan der Weise* (1799), and his moral testament, *Die Erziehung des Menschengeschlechts* (1780).

Reinhardt Jung (1949–1999) was a writer of books and radio plays for young people and heavily involved with the children's support organization International Federation *terre des hommes* (IFTDH). After starting out his career as a journalist and advertising copyeditor in Berlin, he became head of children's broadcasting at SWR (**Südwestrundfunk**) in Stuttgart in 1992. His approach to storytelling is contemporary and creative. In *Auszeit oder der Löwe von Kaúba* (1996), for instance, he presents the story of a disabled boy who in a series of connected nightmares conceives the course his life might have taken if he had lived in the time of the Third Reich. The boy realizes that there are indeed virtuous people in his life who attempt to stand up for him; but out of fear, no one commits wholeheartedly to his cause. As his dreams end, he reflects on present-day attitudes and whether we are still making judgments about what kind of life is "worth living." *Bamberts Buch der verschollenen Geschichten* (1998) is a multilayered, poetic story about another young disabled man who finds solace in writing. One day, he decides to send his stories out into the world attached to balloons, with a letter asking that they be rewritten and returned to him. The result is a collection of heartwarming stories on friendship, the universality of human experience, and the human spirit's triumph over adversity. Jung felt it important that young minds be challenged. His motto was: "Für die Kleinsten nur von dem Feinsten." He received numerous awards for his work, including the Austrian Children's Book Prize (1995, 1997) and the renowned Janusz-Korczak Prize (1998).

Vor dem Lesen

Etwas über Fabeln und ein paar Fragen zu Reinhardt Jungs Gedicht

1.
   a. Was verstehen Sie unter einer Fabel?
   b. Warum liest man sie immer noch gern?
   c. Sind Fabeln gewöhnlich kurz oder lang?
   d. Welche Tiere sprechen manchmal in Fabeln?
   e. Kennen Sie andere Fabeln? andere Autoren von Fabeln?

2.
   a. Mit welchem Pronomen beginnt jeder Satz in Reinhardt Jungs Gedicht?
   b. Welche zwei Verben wiederholen sich in jeder Strophe *(stanza)*?
   c. Hat das Gedicht Reime?
   d. Hat es Adjektive? Wenn ja, welche(s)?
   e. Was ist besonders am letzten Satz?

Der Esel in Begleitung

lion / once allowed / donkey / accompany / encountered

who / walked proudly / threw up high / trumpeted reluctantly / impertinent / shouted at

related / better than accompaniment

Track 28

Ein Löwe° erlaubte einst° einem Esel°, ihn zu begleiten°. Eines Tages begegnete° ihnen ein anderer Esel. „Guten Tag, Bruder!", sagte dieser Esel freundlich. Der Esel, der° neben dem Löwen einherstolzierte°, warf den Kopf in die Höhe° und trompetete unwillig°. „Unverschämt°!", fuhr er seinen Verwandten an°. „Warum
5 soll ich unverschämt sein, wenn ich dich grüße?", fragte der andere Esel. „Sind wir nicht verwandt°? Bist du etwa, weil du mit einem Löwen gehst, besser als° ich? Du bleibst auch in Begleitung° eines Löwen das, was du bist, ein Esel wie ich!"

Gotthold Ephraim Lessing

Reifezeugnis

Ich wollte Nähe—und bekam die Flasche.
Ich wollte Eltern—und bekam Spielzeug°.   toys

Ich wollte reden—und bekam ein Buch.
Ich wollte lernen—und bekam Zeugnisse°.   report cards

5   Ich wollte denken—und bekam Wissen.
Ich wollte einen Überblick°—und bekam einen Einblick°.   overview / insight

Ich wollte frei sein—und bekam Disziplin.
Ich wollte Liebe—und bekam Moral.

Ich wollte einen Beruf—und bekam einen Job.
10   Ich wollte Glück—und bekam Geld.

Ich wollte Freiheit—und bekam ein Auto.
Ich wollte einen Sinn°—und bekam eine Karriere.   purpose

Ich wollte Hoffnung—und bekam Angst.
Ich wollte ändern°—und erhielt Mitleid°.   change things / received pity
15   Ich wollte leben

Reinhardt Jung

Nach dem Lesen

A. Inhaltsfragen *(Questions about content)* zur Fabel und zum Gedicht

1. a. Warum ist der Esel in Lessings Fabel so unheimlich stolz *(proud)*?
   b. Mit wem will er plötzlich nichts mehr zu tun haben? Warum nicht?
   c. Was symbolisiert der Esel und was symbolisiert der Löwe?
   d. Was will Lessing uns mit der Fabel sagen?

2. a. Über welche Stadien *(stages)* des Lebens spricht Jung in den verschiedenen Strophen seines Gedichts?
   b. Was wiederholt sich in seinem ganzen Leben?
   c. Reife bedeutet *maturity* und Zeugnis *report card*. Warum hat er diesen Titel gewählt *(chosen)*? Was denken Sie?
   d. Was meint Jung, wenn er sagt „Ich wollte leben"? Was denken Sie?

B. So, wie ich es sehe

1. a. Warum hat Lessings Fabel etwas mit dem Thema Beziehungen zu tun? Was denken Sie?
   b. Wie gefällt Ihnen diese Fabel?
   c. Erzählen Sie sie noch einmal mit eigenen Worten *(in your own words)*!

2. a. Was halten Sie von Jungs Gedicht?
   b. Statt das Gedicht noch einmal zu lesen, erzählen Sie es jetzt mit eigenem Kommentar *(commentary)*!

   BEISPIEL   *Als er klein war, also nur ein Baby, suchte er vor allem die Wärme der Mutter. Stattdessen aber steckte man ihm eine Babyflasche in den Mund . . .*

 C. So war's bei mir. Schreiben Sie selbst ein ähnliches Gedicht oder einen kleinen Aufsatz über Ihr eigenes Leben!

Wege zum Beruf

Lernziele

In this chapter you will learn about:

Zum Thema

Professions, education, and employment

Kultur-Fokus

German school system, vocational training, gender bias in employment, women in business, foreign workers, and social policy
Aysel Özakin

Struktur

Comparison of adjectives and adverbs
The future tense
Predicate nouns and adjectival nouns

Einblicke + Literatur

Die Berufswahl
Aysel Özakin: "Die dunkelhaarigen Kinder von Berlin"

For more information, go to http://iLrn.heinle.com

Die Wissenschaftlerin Christiane Nüsslein-Vollhard vom Max-Planck-Institut in Tübingen erhielt für ihre Forschung (research) in Embryologie den Nobelpreis für Medizin.

Vorschau   German Schools and Vocational Training

In Germany, education falls under the authority of the individual states (**Länder**). Every child attends the elementary school (**die Grundschule**) for the first four years of schooling (six years in Berlin and Brandenburg). After that, teachers, parents, and students choose one of three possible educational tracks, dependent upon which track best suits a child's interests and abilities. About one-third of German students go to a college preparatory school (**das Gymnasium, die Oberschule, or höhere Schule**), which in most of the states now runs from grades 5 through 12. During their final two years, students must pass a series of rigorous exams to earn their diploma (**das Abitur or Reifezeugnis**), a prerequisite for university admission. Students who do not aim to go to a university attend either a **Hauptschule** or **Realschule**. The **Hauptschule** runs through grade 9 and leads to some form of vocational training. The **Realschule**, a six-year intermediate school covering grades 5 through 10, offers business subjects in addition to a regular academic curriculum, but one less demanding than that of a **Gymnasium**. Its diploma (**die Mittlere Reife**) qualifies students to enter a business or technical college (**die Fachschule** or **Fachoberschule**).

This three-tiered school system has often been criticized for forcing decisions about a child's future too early. As a result, an orientation phase (**die Orientierungsstufe**) was introduced for grades 5 and 6 that gives parents more time to decide which type of school their child should attend. In another effort to increase flexibility, comprehensive schools (**Gesamtschulen**) have been established that combine the three different types of schools into one and offer a wide range of courses at various degrees of difficulty. At the same time, the federal government is promoting all-day schools (**Ganztagsschulen**) to help improve the quality of education as well as to help parents combine family and employment. Educational reforms have been one of the main topics of discussion in Germany in recent years.

Since school attendance is compulsory for ages 6 to 18, most of those who end their general schooling at age 15 or 16 must continue in a three-year program of practical, on-the-job training that combines an apprenticeship (**die Lehre**) with 8 to 10 hours per week of theoretical instruction in a vocational school (**die Berufsschule**). Apprentices are called **Lehrlinge** or **Auszubildende** (shortened to **der/die Azubi, -s**). At the end of their training (**die Ausbildung**) and after passing exams at school and at the training site, they become journeymen/journeywomen (**Gesellen/Gesellinnen**). Five years later, after further practical and theoretical training and after passing another rigorous exam (**die Meisterprüfung**), qualified professionals can attain the status of masters (**Meister/Meisterinnen**), a certification that allows them to become independent and train the new generation of apprentices, who are considered invaluable by German business and industry.

Apprenticeships date back to the Middle Ages, when apprentices served for approximately three years under one or several masters in order to learn a trade. This principle extends today to all nonacademic job training. Very few young Germans enter the job market (**der Arbeitsmarkt**) without such preparation. Apprenticeship training is carefully regulated in order to ensure a highly skilled workforce.

Minidrama: *Anwälte gibt es wie Sand am Meer.*
Blickpunkt: *Frauen im Beruf*

● The **Orientierungsstufe** was not introduced everywhere; in fact, it has been abolished in some states.

● To be precise, the term **Lehrling** is still used strictly for the trades (**das Handwerk**) while the term **Azubi** refers to young people being trained for nonacademic professions in general.

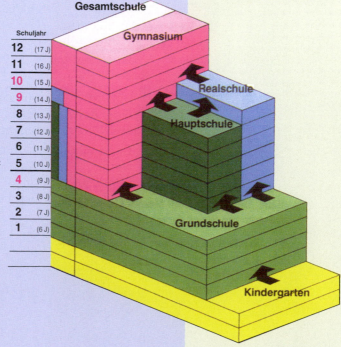

Zum Thema

 Weißt du, was du einmal werden willst?

CD 8,
Track 1

TRUDI	Sag mal, Elke, weißt du schon, was du einmal werden willst?
ELKE	Ja, ich will Tischlerin werden.
TRUDI	Ist das nicht viel Schwerarbeit?
ELKE	Ach, daran gewöhnt man sich. Ich möchte mich vielleicht mal selbstständig machen.
TRUDI	Das sind aber große Pläne!
ELKE	Warum nicht? Ich habe keine Lust, immer nur im Büro zu sitzen und für andere Leute zu arbeiten.
TRUDI	Und wo willst du dich um eine Lehrstelle bewerben?
ELKE	Überhaupt kein Problem. Meine Tante hat ihre eigene Firma und hat mir schon einen Platz angeboten.
TRUDI	Da hast du aber Glück.
ELKE	Und wie ist es denn mit dir? Weißt du, was du machen willst?
TRUDI	Vielleicht werde ich Zahnärztin. Gute Zahnärzte braucht man immer und außerdem verdient man sehr gut.
ELKE	Das stimmt, aber das dauert doch so lange.
TRUDI	Ich weiß, aber ich freue mich trotzdem schon darauf.

A. Was stimmt?

🟡 The most popular jobs requiring apprenticeships are auto mechanic, painter, electrician, carpenter, hairdresser, administrative assistant, physician's assistant, and dental assistant.

1. Elke will _____ werden.
   a. Lehrerin   b. Sekretärin   c. Tischlerin
2. Sie möchte später gern _____.
   a. selbstständig sein   b. im Büro sitzen   c. für andere Leute arbeiten
3. Elkes Tante hat _____ für sie.
   a. eine Lehrerstelle   b. eine Lehrstelle   c. ein Möbelgeschäft
4. Trudi will _____ werden.
   a. Augenärztin   b. Kinderärztin   c. Zahnärztin
5. Zahnärzte sollen gut _____.
   a. dienen   b. verdienen   c. bedienen

 B. Jetzt sind Sie dran! Sprechen Sie mit Ihrem Partner/Ihrer Partnerin über Ihre Berufspläne. Bereiten Sie ein kleines Gespräch vor; es darf auch länger *(longer)* sein. Präsentieren Sie es dann vor der Klasse!

S1 Weißt du schon, was du mal werden willst?
S2 Ich werde . . .
S1 Und warum?
S2 . . . Und wie ist es denn mit dir? Weißt du, was du machen willst?
S1 . . .
S2 Ist das nicht sehr . . . ?
S1 . . .

Wortschatz 1

The feminine form of a noun can usually be derived by adding **-in** to the masculine form: **Architekt/Architektin**. Some also require an umlaut in the feminine form (**Arzt/Ärztin**) and/or other minor spelling changes (**Franzose/Französin**). In help wanted ads, forms are often listed with slashes, with the feminine ending in parentheses, or with the **I** of **-in** capitalized: **Journalist/Journalistin, Journalist/in, Journalist(in),** or **JournalistIn.** To save space, this book lists only the masculine forms, unless irregular changes are required for the feminine version.

Der Beruf, -e *(profession, career)*

der Architekt, -en, -en	*architect*
Arzt, ̈e	*physician, doctor*
Betriebswirt, -e	*graduate in business management*
Geschäftsmann, ̈er	*businessman*
Hausmann, ̈er	*househusband*
Ingenieur, -e	*engineer*
Journalist, -en, -en	*journalist*
Krankenpfleger, -	*(male) nurse*
Künstler, -	*artist*
Lehrer, -	*teacher*
Polizist, -en, -en	*policeman*

der Rechtsanwalt, ̈e	*lawyer*
Reiseleiter, -	*travel agent*
Sekretär, -e	*secretary*
Wissenschaftler, -	*scientist*
Zahnarzt, ̈e	*dentist*
die Geschäftsfrau, -en	*business-woman*
Hausfrau, -en	*housewife*
Krankenschwester, -n	*(female) nurse*

Die Ausbildung *(training, education)*
Die Schule, -n *(school)*

der Kurs, -e	*course*
Plan, ̈e	*plan*
das Büro, -s	*office*
Einkommen, -	*income*
Geschäft, -e	*business*

die Erfahrung, -en	*experience*
Firma, Firmen	*company; business*
Klasse, -n	*class*
Sicherheit	*safety, security*
Stelle, -n	*position, job*
Stunde, -n	*hour*
Verantwortung	*responsibility*
Zukunft	*future; also: future tense auxiliary*

● Note, **Geschäftsmann / Geschäftsfrau, Hausmann / Hausfrau.** When referring to *business people,* the plural **Geschäftsleute** is common.

● When talking about elementary or secondary school, German refers to **die Schule.** At the postsecondary level, it becomes **die Hochschule** or **die Universität.** To indicate what university you attend, you can say: **Ich studiere an der Uni** [*or actual institution name*] **in** [*city, location, etc.*], for example: **Ich studiere an der Uni in Tübingen.**

● The word **Kurs** is a rather general term for *class,* e.g., **Sie sind in meinem Deutschkurs.** The word **Klasse** is commonly used for a group of students or classmates, but also for a specific grade (level): **Sabine ist in der fünften Klasse.** *Sabine is in the fifth grade.*

● When talking about an instructional period in elementary or secondary school, German refers to **die Stunde.** At the university level, terminology becomes more specific, e.g., **die Vorlesung** *(lecture)* versus **das Seminar.** Stunde also refers to work hours at a job: **Wie viele Stunden arbeitest du?**

Weiteres

anstrengend	*strenuous*
arbeitslos	*unemployed*
früher	*earlier; once, former(ly)*
gleich	*equal, same*
hoch (hoh-)	*high*
(un)sicher	*(un)safe, (in)secure*
(an·)bieten, bot (an), (an)geboten	*to offer*
sich bewerben (bewirbt), bewarb, beworben (um)	*to apply (for)*
erklären	*to explain*
sich gewöhnen an (+ *acc.*)	*to get used to*
glauben (an + *acc.*)	*to believe (in)*
Recht haben (hat), hatte, gehabt	*to be right*
Du hast Recht.	*You're right.*
verdienen	*to earn, make money*
werden (wird), wurde, ist geworden	*to become, be*
Was willst du ([ein]mal) werden?	*What do you want to be (one day)?*
Ich will . . . werden.	*I want to be a(n) . . .*
Ach was!	*Oh, come on!*
Das ist doch lächerlich.	*That's ridiculous.*
einerseits / andererseits	*on the one hand / on the other hand*
Genau!	*Exactly! Precisely!*
Im Gegenteil!	*On the contrary!*
Nun / also / na ja / tja, . . .	*Well, . . .*
Unsinn!	*Nonsense!*

● **hoch** is the predicate adjective and adverb; **hoh-** is the attributive adjective: **Die Berge sind hoch.** BUT: **die hohen Berge.**

Zum Erkennen: der Tischler, - *(cabinetmaker)*; die Schwerarbeit *(hard / menial work)*; Überhaupt kein Problem! *(No problem at all!)*; AUCH: das Adverb, -ien; die Aussage, -n *(statement)*; die Form, -en; der Komparativ, -e *(comparative)*; das substantivierte Adjektiv, -e *(adjectival noun)*; der Superlativ, -e *(superlative)*; der Vergleich, -e *(comparison)*; besprechen *(to discuss, talk about)*; sowie *(as well as)*

Aktives zum Thema

A. Kurze Fragen

1. Was ist die weibliche *(fem.)* Form von Ingenieur? Betriebswirt? Reiseleiter? Künstler? Arzt? Rechtsanwalt?
2. Was ist die männliche *(masc.)* Form von Architektin? Lehrerin? Krankenschwester? Geschäftsfrau? Hausfrau?
3. Wo arbeitet die Apothekerin? der Bäcker? der Fleischer? die Sekretärin? die Hausfrau? der Pfarrer *(pastor)*? der Lehrer? die Professorin? der Verkäufer?

Fokus   Gender Bias and Language

The traditional use of the masculine German plural to refer collectively to both men and women serves to reinforce outmoded notions that certain professions are only for men (for example, **Ärzte, Wissenschaftler,** and so on). Women appear to be left out of the picture and out of speech. In current-day usage, official documents and journalistic writing often use both masculine and feminine forms in an effort to break out of this pattern of gender exclusivity and be overtly gender inclusive, for example, **Ärzte und Ärztinnen, Wissenschaftler und Wissenschaftlerinnen.** Some publications have opted for a new formation that combines the masculine and feminine into one word: **ÄrztInnen, WissenschaftlerInnen.**

B. Was sind das für Berufe? Sagen Sie die Berufe auf Englisch und erklären Sie dann auf Deutsch, was die Leute tun!

Zahntechniker/in
Uhrmacher (Meister)
Gebrauchtwagenverkäufer Putzfrau
Fernfahrer Koch
Bankangestellter **Chemie-Laboranten(innen)**
Damen- und Herrenfriseur Telefonistin Sozialpädagogin
Fonotypistinnen Arztsekretärin
Industriekaufmann
Rechtsanwaltsgehilfin
Diplom-Ingenieur Krankengymnast(in)
REISELEITER/-INNEN **Systemberater(in)** Repräsentanten Bäcker
Haushälterin Zahnarzthelferin
Buchhalter/in PSYCHOLOGE/IN
Kassiererin Fremdsprachenkorrespondentin Hausmeister

C. Zu welchem Arzt/welcher Ärztin geht man?

1. Wenn man Zahnschmerzen hat, geht man zum . . .
2. Wenn man schlechte Augen hat, geht man zum . . .
3. Mit einem kranken Kind geht man zum . . .
4. Wenn man Hals-, Nasen- oder Ohrenprobleme hat, geht man zum . . .
5. Frauen gehen zum . . .

D. Früher und heute Was waren früher typische Männer- und Frauenberufe? Machen Sie mit den anderen eine Liste und besprechen Sie dann, wie das heute ist!

E. Ein interessanter Beruf

1. **Das ist mir wichtig.** Fragen Sie Ihren Partner/Ihre Partnerin, was ihm/ihr am Beruf wichtig ist und in welcher Reihenfolge *(sequence)!* Vergleichen Sie dann Ihre Antworten mit den Resultaten der anderen!

   - ❑ Reisen
   - ❑ freies Wochenende
   - ❑ lange Sommerferien
   - ❑ saubere Arbeit
   - ❑ interessante Arbeit
   - ❑ Kreativität
   - ❑ elegante Kleidung
   - ❑ flexible Arbeitszeit
   - ❑ Prestige
   - ❑ Sicherheit
   - ❑ Erfahrung

   - ❑ wenig Stress
   - ❑ wenig Papierkrieg *(paperwork)*
   - ❑ Arbeit in der freien Natur
   - ❑ Abenteuer *(adventure)*
   - ❑ Abwechslung *(variety)*
   - ❑ Aussichten *(prospects)* für die Zukunft
   - ❑ eigener Firmenwagen
   - ❑ Verantwortung
   - ❑ Kontakt zu Menschen
   - ❑ Selbstständigkeit
   - ❑ hohes Einkommen

2. **In welchen Berufen findet man das?** Schauen Sie sich mit Ihrem Partner/Ihrer Partnerin Ihre Listen noch einmal an und sagen Sie dann, in welchen Berufen man diese Kriterien *(criteria)* findet!

Aussprache: b, d, g

CD 8,
Track 2 **Laute**

• For further review, see the
Summary of Pronunciation in the
front of your *Arbeitsbuch*. Study
Part III, subsection 3.

1. [p] **Ob**st, Her**b**st, Er**b**se, hü**b**sch, o**b**, hal**b**, gel**b**
BUT [p / b] verlie**b**t / verlie**b**en; blei**b**t / blei**b**en; ha**b**t / ha**b**en
2. [t] un**d**, gesun**d**, anstrengen**d**, Gel**d**, Han**d**, sin**d**
BUT [t / d] Freun**d** / Freun**d**e; Ba**d** / Bä**d**er; Kin**d** / Kin**d**er; wir**d** / wer**d**en
3. [k] Ta**g**, Zu**g**, We**g**, Bahnstei**g**, Flu**g**zeug, Ber**g**
BUT [k / g] fra**g**st / fra**g**en; flie**g**st / flie**g**en; trä**g**st / tra**g**en; le**g**st / le**g**en

Hörverständnis

Track 30 **Was bin ich?** Welcher Sprecher ist was auf dieser Liste? Schreiben Sie die Nummer des Sprechers links neben den richtigen Beruf!

Zum Erkennen: unterwegs *(on the go)*; die Katastrophe; Politiker *(politicians)*; weg *(gone)*; Klienten *(clients)*; ein Testament machen *(to set up a will)*

_____ Architekt/in	_____ Journalist/in	_____ Rechtsanwalt/-anwältin
_____ Reiseleiter/in	_____ Künstler/in	_____ Sekretär/in
_____ Hausmann/-frau	_____ Lehrer/in	_____ Zahnarzt/-ärztin
_____ Ingenieur/in	_____ Polizist/in	_____ Zeitungsverkäufer/in

---

Fokus   Women in Business and Industry

In Germany as in North America, many jobs used to be considered exclusively "men's work." Over the years, there has been a considerable shift in attitude, and more professions are now open to both sexes. In 1970, 37 percent of all apprentices were women; in 2000, this figure rose to nearly 50 percent. Likewise, the proportion of professionally trained working women increased from 38 percent in 1970 to 48 percent in 2005. In technical and scientific professions, however, women still have a rather low showing in the statistics.

At the university level, women account for only 20 percent of those studying technical and engineering subjects—courses leading to fast-track professions. They are, however, well represented in the arts and humanities, where career potential is more limited. More recently, an increasing number of female students are pursuing degrees in economics, law, and business administration. As this trend is relatively new, it is not yet reflected by the composition of leadership positions at the top of the professional ladder. Only 8 percent of senior consultants and around 10 percent of all full professors are women; in business and industry, 20 percent of the top positions are occupied by women; only 2 percent of women have jobs in engineering. However, this situation should improve as more highly trained women enter the workforce.

Wir sind noch in der Lehre.

Struktur

12.1 Comparison of adjectives and adverbs

In English and German, adjectives have three degrees:

POSITIVE	COMPARATIVE	SUPERLATIVE
cheap	*cheaper*	*cheapest*
expensive	*more expensive*	*most expensive*

Whereas there are two ways to form the comparative and the superlative in English, there is only *one way* in German; it corresponds to the forms of *cheap* above. In German there is no equivalent to such forms as *more expensive* and *most expensive*.

1. To form the COMPARATIVE, add **-er;** to form the SUPERLATIVE, add **-(e)st.**

billig	billig**er**	billig**st-**

a. Many one-syllable adjectives with the stem vowel **a, o,** or **u** have an umlaut in the comparative and superlative, which is shown in the end vocabulary as follows: warm **(ä),** groß **(ö),** jung **(ü).**

warm	wärmer	wärmst-
groß	größer	größt-
jung	jünger	jüngst-

Other adjectives that take an umlaut include: alt, arm, dumm, gesund, kalt, krank, kurz, lang, nah, rot, schwarz.

b. Most adjectives ending in **-d** or **-t,** in an **s**-sound, or in vowels add **-est** in the superlative.

> ● A few adjectives ending in **-el** or **-er** (e.g., **dunkel, teuer**) drop the **-e-** in the comparative: **dunkler, teurer.**

gesund	gesünder	gesünd**est-**
kalt	kälter	kält**est-**
heiß	heißer	heiß**est-**
kurz	kürzer	kürz**est-**
neu	neuer	neu**est-**

Adjectives and adverbs that follow this pattern include: alt (ä), bekannt, beliebt, charmant, ernst, intelligent, interessant, kompliziert, laut, leicht, nett, oft (ö), rot (ö), schlecht, talentiert, verrückt; hübsch, weiß, süß, schwarz (ä), stolz; frei, schlau.

c. A few adjectives and adverbs have irregular forms in the comparative and/or superlative.

gern	**lieber**	**liebst-**
groß	**größer**	**größt-**
gut	**besser**	**best-**
hoch (hoh-)	**höher**	**höchst-**
nah	**näher**	**nächst-**
viel	**mehr**	**meist-**

2. The comparative of PREDICATE ADJECTIVES (after **sein**, **werden**, and **bleiben**) and of ADVERBS is formed as described above. The superlative, however, is preceded by **am** and ends in **-sten**.

billig	billig**er**	**am** billig**sten**

Die Wurst ist billig.	*The sausage is cheap.*
Der Käse ist billig**er**.	*The cheese is cheaper.*
Das Brot ist **am** billig**sten**.	*The bread is cheapest.*

Ich fahre **gern** mit dem Bus.	*I like to go by bus.*
Ich fahre **lieber** mit dem Fahrrad.	*I prefer to (I'd rather) go by bike.*
Ich gehe **am liebsten** zu Fuß.	*Best of all I like (I like best) to walk.*

Ich laufe **viel**.	*I walk a lot.*
Theo läuft **mehr**.	*Theo walks more.*
Katrin läuft **am meisten**.	*Katrin walks the most (i.e., more than Theo and I).*

CAUTION: **Meisten** in **die meisten Leute** is an adjective; **am meisten** is an adverb of manner; and **meistens** is an adverb of time.

Die **meisten** Leute gehen gern spazieren.	*Most people love to walk.*
Mein Vater geht **am meisten** spazieren.	*My father walks the most.*
Mein Vater geht **meistens** in den Park.	*My father goes mostly to the park.*

3. Adjectives preceding nouns are called ATTRIBUTIVE ADJECTIVES. In the comparative and superlative, attributive adjectives have not only the appropriate comparative or superlative markers, but also the adjective endings just as in the positive degree (see Chapters 9 and 10).

der gut**e** Käse	der besser**e** Käse	der best**e** Käse
Ihr gut**er** Käse	Ihr besser**er** Käse	Ihr best**er** Käse
gut**er** Käse	besser**er** Käse	best**er** Käse

Haben Sie keinen besser**en** Käse? Doch, aber besser**er** Käse ist teu(e)**rer**.

4. There are four special phrases frequently used in comparisons:

a. When you want to say that one thing is like another or not quite like another, use the following:

(genau)so . . . wie	or	**nicht so . . . wie**

Ich bin **(genau)so alt wie** er.	*I'm (just) as old as he is.*
Sie ist **nicht so fit wie** ich.	*She is not as fit as I am.*

NOTE: Ich bin **so alt wie** er (nominative). Ich bin **älter als** er (nominative).

b. If you want to express a difference, use the following:

comparative + als

Ich bin **älter als** Helga.	*I'm older than Helga.*
Sie ist **jünger als** er.	*She is younger than he (is).*

Lieber ⚠ **als** 🛣

c. If you want to express the idea that something is increasingly more so, use the following:

immer + comparative

Die Tage werden **immer länger**.	*The days are getting longer and longer.*
Ich gehe **immer später** ins Bett.	*I'm going to bed later and later.*
Autos werden **immer teu(e)rer**.	*Cars are getting more and more expensive.*

d. If you are dealing with a pair of comparatives, use the following:

> **je** + comparative . . . **desto** + comparative

Je länger, **desto** besser.	*The longer, the better.*
Je länger ich arbeite,	*The longer I work,*
desto müder bin ich.	*the more tired I am.*
Je früher ich ins Bett gehe, **desto**	*The earlier I go to bed, the earlier*
früher stehe ich morgens auf.	*I get up in the morning.*

Note that **je** introduces a dependent clause. The **desto** + comparative phrase is followed by a main clause in inverted word order.

Übungen

A. Komparativ und Superlativ Nennen Sie den Komparativ und den Superlativ, und dann die Formen des Gegenteils!

> BEISPIEL   schnell   *schneller, am schnellsten*
>   langsam   *langsamer, am langsamsten*

billig, gesund, groß, gut, hübsch, intelligent, jung, kalt, kurz, laut, nah, sauber, schwer, viel

B. Ersetzen Sie die Adjektive!

> BEISPIEL   Diese Zeitung ist so langweilig wie die andere Zeitung. (interessant)
>   *Diese Zeitung ist so interessant wie die andere Zeitung.*

1. Axel ist so groß wie Horst. (alt, nett)
2. Hier ist es kühler als bei euch. (kalt, heiß)
3. Fernsehsendungen werden immer langweiliger. (verrückt, dumm)
4. Je länger das Buch ist, desto besser. (spannend / interessant; komisch / populär)

C. Antworten Sie mit NEIN! Benutzen Sie das Adjektiv oder Adverb in Klammern für den Komparativ!

> BEISPIEL   Ist dein Großvater auch so alt? (jung)
>   *Nein, er ist jünger.*

1. Waren eu(e)re Schuhe auch so schmutzig? (sauber)
2. Verdient Jutta auch so wenig? (viel)
3. Ist seine Wohnung auch so toll? (einfach)
4. Sind die Verkäufer dort auch so unfreundlich? (freundlich)
5. Ist es bei Ihnen auch so laut? (ruhig)
6. Ist die Schule auch so weit weg? (nah)
7. Ist Ihre Arbeit auch so anstrengend? (leicht)

D. Wie geht's weiter? Beenden Sie die Sätze mit einem Superlativ! Seien Sie kreativ!

> BEISPIEL   Inge spricht schnell, Lars spricht schneller, aber . . .
>   *Inge spricht schnell, Lars spricht schneller, aber Peter spricht am*
>   *schnellsten.*

1. Willi hat lange geschlafen, Boris hat länger geschlafen, aber . . .
2. Brot zum Frühstück schmeckt gut, Müsli schmeckt besser, aber . . .
3. Ich trinke morgens gern Tee, ich trinke lieber Kaffee, aber . . .
4. Die Montagszeitung ist dick, die Donnerstagszeitung ist dicker, aber . . .
5. Ich telefoniere viel, ich schreibe mehr, aber . . .
6. Türkisch ist schwer, Swahili ist schwerer, aber . . .
7. Hier ist es schön, in Hawaii ist es schöner, aber . . .

E. Ersetzen Sie die Adjektive!

BEISPIEL Peter ist der sportlichste Junge. (talentiert)
Peter ist der talentierteste Junge.

1. Da drüben ist ein moderneres Geschäft. (gut)
2. Mein jüngster Bruder ist nicht verheiratet. (alt)
3. Das ist die interessanteste Nachricht. (neu)
4. Zieh dir einen wärmeren Pullover an! (dick)
5. Die besten Autos sind sehr teuer. (viel)

F. Eine bessere Stelle Was fehlt?

1. Möchtest du nicht _____ Beamtin *(civil servant)* werden? *(rather)*
2. Der Staat bezahlt _____ deine Firma. *(better than)*
3. Da hast du _____ Sicherheit. *(the greatest)*
4. Beim Staat hast du _____ Freizeit _____ bei deiner Firma. *(just as much . . . as)*
5. Vielleicht hast du _____ Zeit _____ jetzt. *(more . . . than)*
6. Es ist auch nicht _____ anstrengend _____ jetzt. *(as . . . as)*
7. _____ Leute arbeiten für den Staat. *(more and more)*
8. Den _____ Leuten gefällt es. *(most)*
9. Ich finde es beim Staat _____ und _____ *(the most interesting, the most secure)*
10. Eine _____ Stelle gibt es nicht. *(nicer)*
11. _____ du wirst, _____ ist es zu wechseln. *(the older . . . the harder)*
12. Vielleicht verdienst du etwas _____, aber dafür hast du _____ keine Probleme. *(less, mostly)*

G. Was ist am wichtigsten im Leben?

1. **Umfrage *(survey)* bei jungen Deutschen** Die folgende Tabelle zeigt, was ihnen am wichtigsten im Leben ist. Sehen Sie sich die Tabelle an und machen Sie so viele Vergleiche wie möglich!

Freizeit	93%	Beruf und Karriere	59%
Liebe	83%	Materielle Sicherheit	58%
Freundschaft	82%	Musik und Kultur	40%
Familie	78%	Sport	40%
Gesundheit	65%	Idealismus	19%

BEISPIEL *Sport ist wichtiger als Idealismus und genauso wichtig wie Musik und Kultur.*

2. **Was ist dir am wichtigsten?** Wie sehen die eigenen Prioritäten *(own priorities)* aus im Vergleich zu den Prioritäten der anderen? Fragen Sie Ihren Partner/Ihre Partnerin!

BEISPIEL S1 Was ist dir am wichtigsten? am unwichtigsten?
S2 Die Familie ist mir am wichtigsten. Geld ist mir am unwichtigsten.

H. Interview Fragen Sie einen Nachbarn/eine Nachbarin, . . . !

1. ob er/sie jüngere Geschwister hat; wer am jüngsten und am ältesten ist
2. welche Fernsehsendung ihm/ihr am besten gefällt; was er/sie am meisten sieht
3. was er/sie am liebsten in der Freizeit macht; was er/sie am nächsten Wochenende tut
4. welche amerikanische / kanadische Stadt er/sie am schönsten und am hässlichsten findet und warum
5. welche drei Eigenschaften ihm/ihr bei einem Freund/einer Freundin oder Partner/Partnerin am wichtigsten sind

> **Die größten Ereignisse, das sind nicht unsere lautesten, sondern unsere stillsten Stunden.**
>
> *Friedrich Wilhelm Nietzsche*

● Friedrich Nietzsche (1844–1900)

12.2 The future tense

Future events are often referred to using the PRESENT TENSE in both English and German, particularly when a time expression points to the future.

Wir **sehen** heute Abend eine DVD.   *We're watching a DVD tonight.*
We will watch a DVD tonight.

In German conversation, the present tense is the preferred form. German does have a FUTURE TENSE, however. It is used when there is no time expression and the circumstances are somewhat more formal.

werden . . . + infinitive	
ich **werde** . . . gehen	wir **werden** . . . gehen
du **wirst** . . . gehen	ihr **werdet** . . . gehen
er **wird** . . . gehen	sie **werden** . . . gehen

1. The future tense consists of **werden** as the auxiliary and the infinitive of the main verb.

Ich **werde** ins Büro **gehen.**   *I'll go to the office.*
Wirst du mich **anrufen?**   *Will you call me?*

2. If the future tense sentence also contains a modal, the modal appears as an infinitive at the very end.

werden . . . + verb infinitive + modal infinitive

Ich **werde** ins Büro **gehen müssen.**   *I'll have to go to the office.*
Wirst du mich **anrufen können?**   *Will you be able to call me?*

3. Sentences in the future follow familiar word order rules.

Er **wird** auch **kommen.**
Er **wird** auch **mitkommen.**
Er <u>**wird**</u> auch <u>**mitkommen wollen.**</u>
  V1   V2

Ich weiß, dass er auch **kommen wird.**
Ich weiß, dass er auch <u>**mitkommen wird**</u>.
            V2   V1

4. The future form can also express PRESENT PROBABILITY, especially when used with the word **wohl.**

Er wird **wohl** auf dem Weg sein.   *He is probably on the way (now).*

5. Remember that **werden** is also a full verb meaning *to get, to become.*

present tense: Wir **werden** müde.   *We're getting tired.*
future tense: Wir **werden** müde **werden.**   *We will get tired.*

Fokus — Foreign Workers in Germany

In the 1950s, the West German and Turkish governments signed a contract that allowed Turkish workers to be recruited to work in Germany as guest workers (**Gastarbeiter**). In 1961, 2,500 Turks were living in Germany; today there are 2.3 million, many of them second- and third-generation residents. In the 1960s and 1970s, Turks were employed mainly in mining and in the steel and auto industries; today more and more are working in the service sector. Turks are by far the largest ethnic group in Germany, and they are becoming more involved in domestic politics and service organizations. In addition to foreign guest workers from around the Mediterranean and asylum-seekers (**Asylanten**) from all over the world, Germany also has taken in a great number of resettlers (**Aussiedler**), most of them ethnic Germans from the successor states to the Soviet Union who have chosen to resettle in Germany.

Since the year 2000, children born in Germany of non-German parents automatically have German citizenship as long as one of the parents has been a resident for at least eight years or in possession of an unrestricted residence permit for at least three years. As of January 2005, the new Immigration Act (**das Einwanderungsgesetz**) regulates immigration and the integration of foreigners in Germany. This law simplifies the granting of residence permits, prompts the integration of non-EU foreigners through compulsory language courses, and speeds up the procedures for asylum seekers. Another important aspect of the law is the opening of the employment market to highly skilled foreigners and foreign graduates of German universities. This law is designed to take into account the new challenges that modern Germany is facing, such as an aging population and a shortage of skilled information-technology workers.

Deutschunterricht in der Grundschule

Übungen

I. Sagen Sie die Sätze in der Zukunft!

BEISPIEL   Gute Zahnärzte braucht man immer.
            Gute Zahnärzte wird man immer brauchen.

1. Dabei verdiene ich auch gut. 2. Aber du studierst einige Jahre auf der Universität. 3. Ich gehe nicht zur Uni. 4. Meine Tischlerarbeit ist anstrengend. 5. Aber daran gewöhnst du dich. 6. Dieser Beruf hat bestimmt Zukunft. 7. Ihr seht das schon. 8. Eines Tages mache ich mich selbstständig. 9. Als Chefin *(boss)* in einem Männerberuf muss ich besonders gut sein.

J. Beginnen Sie jeden Satz mit „Wissen Sie, ob . . . ?"

BEISPIEL   Er wird bald zurückkommen.
            Wissen Sie, ob er bald zurückkommen wird?

1. Wir werden in Frankfurt umsteigen. 2. Sie wird sich die Sendung ansehen. 3. Zimmermanns werden die Wohnung mieten. 4. Willi und Eva werden bald heiraten. 5. Müllers werden in Zürich bleiben. 6. Er wird fahren oder fliegen.

K. Wie heißt das auf Englisch?

BEISPIEL   Martina wird Journalistin.
            Martina is becoming a journalist.

1. Walter will Polizist werden. 2. Die Kinder werden zu laut. 3. Ich werde am Bahnhof auf Sie warten. 4. Petra wird wohl nicht kommen. 5. Wir werden Sie gern mitnehmen. 6. Sie wird Informatik *(computer science)* studieren wollen. 7. Oskar wird wohl noch im Büro sein. 8. Wirst du wirklich Lehrer?

L. Was hältst du davon?

1. **Verschiedene Aussagen** Reagieren Sie ganz kurz darauf wie im Beispiel! Wechseln Sie sich ab!

BEISPIEL Eltern sind verantwortlich für alles, was ihre Kinder tun.
Das stimmt. / Quatsch! / Unmöglich! . . .

a. Die Schweiz ist keine Reise wert.
b. Wir haben heute viel zu viel Freizeit.
c. Wir leben heute gesünder als unsere Eltern und Großeltern.
d. Es ist heute noch wichtiger als früher, Fremdsprachen zu lernen.
e. Wir sitzen alle zu viel vor dem Fernseher.
f. Fernsehen macht dumm.
g. Kinder interessieren sich heute nicht mehr für Märchen.
h. Die meisten Menschen verdienen lieber weniger Geld und haben mehr Freizeit.
i. Wenn mehr Menschen weniger arbeiten, können mehr Menschen arbeiten.
j. Je länger man im Ausland arbeitet, desto besser sind die Berufschancen.
k. Weil Deutschland eines der größten Industrie- und Handelsländer der Welt ist, wird es für Amerikaner und Kanadier immer interessanter, Deutsch zu lernen.
l. Ich stelle mir vor, dass es in den nächsten Jahren in der Wirtschaft viel besser aussehen wird.
m. Kriminalität in den Schulen hat oft mit Langeweile *(boredom)* zu tun.

2. **Na ja!** Bilden Sie verschiedene Aussagen in der Zukunft! Die anderen reagieren darauf.

BEISPIEL S1 Morgen haben wir eine Prüfung.
S2 Wirklich? / Ach was! / Schrecklich!
S1 Je billiger das Benzin *(gasoline)*, desto größer werden die Autos.
S2 Ja, das ist verrückt.

M. Kein Hundeleben mehr!
Sicher haben auch Sie schon einmal schwer für eine Prüfung lernen müssen. Da fühlt man sich müde wie ein Hund. Schauen Sie sich die Zeichnung *(drawing)* an und schreiben Sie dazu acht Sätze im Präsens oder in der Zukunft!

1. Im Präsens: Wenn die nächste Prüfung vorbei ist, …
2. In der Zukunft: Wenn ich mit meinem Studium *(course of studies)* fertig bin, …

12.3 Predicate nouns and adjectival nouns

1. Certain predicate nouns

As you already know, German—unlike English—does *not* use the indefinite article before PREDICATE NOUNS denoting professions, nationalities, religious affiliation, or political adherence (see Chapter 1, *Aktives zum Thema*).

Er ist **Amerikaner.**   *He is an American.*
Sie ist **Ingenieurin.**   *She's an engineer.*

However, when a predicate noun is used in the singular and preceded by an adjective, the definite article **ein** is used. In the plural, that does not apply.

Er ist **ein** typischer Amerikaner.   *He's a typical American.*
Sie ist **eine** gute Ingenieurin.   *She's a good engineer.*
Das sind interessante Leute.   *They are interesting people.*

• Optional English-to-German practice: 1. Children, I want to tell you something. 2. Your mother is going to be a lawyer. 3. I'll have to stay home. 4. I'll (do the) cook(ing). 5. Lena, you will do the laundry **(die Wäsche waschen)**. 6. Jan and Maria, you will (do the) clean(ing). 7. We'll (do the) shop(ping) together. 8. We'll have to work hard. 9. But we'll get used to it. 10. When we get tired, we'll take a break **(eine Pause machen)**. 11. Your mother will make a lot of money (earn well). 12. And we will help her. (See answer key in the Appendix.)

• M *(drawing):* **Das ist nun einerlei.** *That doesn't matter any more.* **Es ist mir einerlei.** *I don't care.*

2. Adjectival nouns

ADJECTIVAL NOUNS are nouns derived from adjectives, that is, the original noun is dropped and the adjective itself becomes the noun. Adjectival nouns are used in English, but not very often. Plural forms usually refer to people, singular nouns to abstract concepts.

> Give me your **tired** (people), your **poor.**
> The **best** is yet to come.

German uses adjectival nouns quite frequently. They are capitalized to show that they are nouns, and they have the endings they would have had as attributive adjectives, depending on the preceding article, case, number, and gender. Use the same system you have already learned for adjectives to put the correct endings on adjectival nouns (see below and Chapters 9 and 10). Masculine forms refer to males, feminine forms to females, and neuter forms to abstract concepts.

der Alte	*the old man*	mein Alter	*my old man, my husband*
die Alte	*the old woman*	meine Alte	*my old woman, my wife*
die Alten	*the old people*	meine Alten	*my old people, my parents*

das Alte	*the old, that which is old, old things*
das Beste	*the best thing(s)*

After **etwas** and **nichts, viel** and **wenig,** the adjectival noun will always be NEUTER.

etwas Interessantes	*something interesting*
nichts Neues	*nothing new*
viel Hässliches	*a lot of ugly things*
wenig Schönes	*not much that's beautiful*

Examples of common adjectival nouns are:

der/die Angestellte	*employee*	**der/die Kranke**	*sick person*
der/die Bekannte	*acquaintance*	**der/die Verlobte**	*fiancé / fiancée*
der/die Deutsche	*German person*	Also: **der Beamte**	*civil servant*

> These adjectival nouns are sometimes listed as follows: **der Angestellte (ein Angestellter), der Deutsche (ein Deutscher),** assuming that the rest of the forms can be deduced.

> der <u>Beamte</u>, BUT: die Beam**tin**!

> Also: **der/die Arbeitslose** (*unemployed person*), **Schwerbehinderte** (*handicapped person*), **Verwandte** (*relative*)

	SINGULAR		PLURAL
	masc.	**fem.**	
nom.	der Deutsche ein Deutscher	die Deutsche eine Deutsche	die Deutschen keine Deutschen
acc.	den Deutschen einen Deutschen		
dat.	dem Deutschen einem Deutschen	der Deutschen einer Deutschen	den Deutschen keinen Deutschen
gen.	des Deutschen eines Deutschen	der Deutschen einer Deutschen	der Deutschen keiner Deutschen

Karl ist Angestellt**er** bei uns und seine Frau Angestellt**e** bei VW.
Ein Angestellt**er** wollte dich sprechen. Wie heißt der Angestellt**e?**
Siehst du den Angestellt**en** da drüben? Nein, ich sehe keinen Angestellt**en.**

Übungen

N. Artikel oder nicht? Entscheiden Sie in den folgenden Sätzen, ob man da einen Artikel braucht oder nicht! Wenn ja, welchen Artikel? Wiederholen Sie dann den Satz auf Englisch!

> BEISPIEL   er / sein / Komponist
> *Er ist Komponist. He is a composer.*

1. sie / sein / Wissenschaftlerin 2. sie / sein / sehr gut / Biologin 3. er / werden / Hausmann 4. er / sein *(simple past)* / dynamisch / Lehrer / und / er / sein *(future)* / liebevoll / Vater 5. sie / sein / ledig / Österreicherin 6. er / sein / bekannt / Schweizer 7. sie / sein / interessant / Nachbarn

O. Substantivierte Adjektive Welches substantivierte Adjektiv passt dazu?

> BEISPIEL   Bist du mit diesem Herrn **verwandt** *(related to)*?
> *Nein, das ist kein* **Verwandter** (relative) *von mir.*

1. Herr Schneider war lange bei uns **angestellt.** Geben Sie dem ＿＿＿＿＿＿ die Papiere!

2. Er ist uns allen gut **bekannt.** Er ist ein guter ＿＿＿＿＿＿ von uns allen.

3. Jetzt hat er seine Arbeit verloren und sucht, wie viele **deutsche** Kollegen, eine andere Stelle. Wie ihm geht es vielen ＿＿＿＿＿＿.

4. Besonders in den östlichen Ländern Deutschlands sind viele **arbeitslos.** Manche ＿＿＿＿＿＿ versuchen ihr Glück im Westen.

5. Herr Schneider ist noch jung, aber **schwerbehindert** *(handicapped)*. Als ＿＿＿＿＿＿ wird er sicher Hilfe vom Arbeitsamt *(unemployment agency)* bekommen.

6. Er ist mit einer Schweizerin **verlobt.** Seine ＿＿＿＿＿＿ ist Krankenpflegerin.

7. Sie pflegt *(takes care of)* **kranke** Menschen. Alle ihre ＿＿＿＿＿＿ lieben sie.

8. Herr Schneider träumt von einer **Beamten**stelle. Als ＿＿＿＿＿＿ verdient man ganz gut.

9. Wenn er damit kein Glück hat, will er sich **selbstständig** machen. ＿＿＿＿＿＿ müssen schwer arbeiten.

10. Das wird für ihn kein Problem sein, denn er ist sehr **fleißig.** Er ist wirklich ein ＿＿＿＿＿＿.

11. Er ist auch **unternehmungslustig.** ＿＿＿＿＿＿ finden immer einen Weg.

12. Seine Verlobte weiß, dass er nicht **faul** ist. Mit ＿＿＿＿＿＿ hat sie nichts zu tun.

50 000 Jobs für Schwerbehinderte

P. Das ist nichts Neues. Lesen Sie die folgende Adjektivliste und reagieren Sie dann auf die Aussagen Ihres Partners/Ihrer Partnerin mit einem substantivierten Adjektiv!

Wer sagt, dass der Beruf Pilot nur für Männer ist?

BEISPIEL   S1 Er hat wieder mal kein Geld.
      S2 Das ist nichts Neues!

besonder-, besser, billig, dumm, furchtbar, interessant, schön, toll, traurig, verrückt . . .

S1 In diesem Geschäft ist nichts, was mir gefällt.
S2 Ich finde auch nichts . . .
S1 Gehen wir zu dem Laden da drüben!
S2 Wenn du meinst. Vielleicht gibt's da etwas . . .
S1 Carlos sagt, dass sein Vater ihm einen Porsche kaufen wird.
S2 Und so etwas . . . soll ich glauben?
S1 Hast du von der Katastrophe in Spanien gehört?
S2 Ja, es gibt doch viel . . . auf dieser Welt.
S1 Und doch gibt es auch viel . . . , worüber man sich freuen kann.
S2 . . .

Q. Kurzgespräch mit den Eltern Bereiten Sie ein Gespräch mit dem Vater oder der Mutter (Ihrem Partner/Ihrer Partnerin) vor und präsentieren Sie den Dialog danach vor der Klasse!

You are discussing your career choice (**Autoverkäufer, Beamter, Krankenpfleger/in,** etc.) with your parents. They are not happy with your decision and express their disagreement. You agree or disagree with their objections.

Fokus — Hard Times and Social Policy

The worldwide trend toward greater industrial efficiency, higher productivity, and lower labor costs, coupled with the enormous expenses of reunification, has led to high unemployment (**die Arbeitslosigkeit**), uncommon in Germany before 1990. Rebuilding and privatizing the uncompetitive, formerly state-run industries in the former East Germany during an era of increased international competition and slow growth in Europe turned out to be much more difficult than anticipated. The extensive modernization required costly, federally financed training and retraining programs, and resulted in large-scale early retirements (**die Frührente**).

To address the challenges in Germany today, such as a longer life expectancy, low birthrates, and high unemployment, the government passed a series of social reforms. Private pensions are encouraged and long-term employment benefits and public welfare have been merged. Plans are underway for changes in the health insurance system as well. But despite some cutbacks in social benefits, the fundamental principles of a social policy aimed at achieving a high degree of social justice have not changed. All sorts of government assistance continues to be provided to those in need, including social security (**die Rentenversicherung**), public welfare (**die Sozialhilfe**), and health insurance (**die Krankenversicherung**). With people living ever longer, an important addition to this tightly knit net is long-term care insurance (**die Pflegeversicherung**), which was put into law in the early 1990s.

Labor unions (**Gewerkschaften**) have always been very important in Germany. However, with the onset of a recessionary economy since reunification, they have been forced to compromise on their long-standing goals of job security with ever higher pay and more benefits. Nevertheless, labor unions remain quite strong and were instrumental in reducing the 40-hour work week in some industries to 36 hours, or even less in some large industrial companies, in order to save jobs. As unions participate in the decision-making process (**das Mitbestimmungsrecht**), their relationship with management has—with a few exceptions, especially since the year 2000—been a flexible, cooperative, nonconfrontational partnership, a partnership that has contributed to industrial peace and to one of the highest standards of living in the world.

Besuch bei der Ärztin

Zusammenfassung

R. Die zehn beliebtesten Lehrberufe (*professions based on apprenticeship programs*) Vergleichen Sie mit den anderen die Situation in Ost und West.

 Visit the **Wie geht's?** iLrn website for more review and practice of the grammar points you have just learned.

NEUE BUNDESLÄNDER

Beruf	
Bankkaufmann/-frau	6 980
Gas- und Wasserinstallateur/-in	7 040
Maler/Lackierer/-in	7 372
Koch/Köchin	7 557
Elektroinstallateur/-in	7 829
Bürokaufmann/-frau	10 116
Kfz-Mechaniker/-in	10 162
Industriemechaniker/-in	10 626
Einzelhandelskaufmann/-frau	15 240
Maurer/-in	19 864

ALTE BUNDESLÄNDER

Beruf	
Zahnarzthelfer/-in	34 695
Friseur/-in	39 119
Elektroinstallateur/-in	42 251
Arzthelfer/-in	47 716
Groß- und Außenhandelskaufmann/-frau	47 994
Bankkaufmann/-frau	58 105
Bürokaufmann/-frau	58 847
Industriekaufmann/-frau	59 693
Einzelhandelskaufmann/-frau	61 304
Kfz-Mechaniker/-in	74 846

DIE BELIEBTESTEN LEHRBERUFE

Lehrlinge zur Zeit in Ausbildung

Quelle: Statistisches Bundesamt

Graphik: Christoph Blumrich

1. Welche Berufe sind in beiden Teilen Deutschlands besonders beliebt? Nennen Sie fünf!
2. In den neuen Bundesländern ist die Lehre für . . .
   a. . . . beliebter als . . .
   b. . . . fast genauso beliebt wie . . .
   c. . . . weniger beliebt als . . .
3. In den alten Bundesländern ist die Lehre für . . .
   a. . . . beliebter als . . .
   b. . . . fast genauso beliebt wie . . .
   c. . . . weniger beliebt als . . .
4. In beiden Teilen stehen . . . und . . . an 8. und 9. Stelle der zehn beliebtesten Lehrberufe.

S. Zukunftspläne Auf Deutsch bitte!

1. Did you (*pl. fam.*) know that Alex wants to become a journalist? 2. He doesn't want to be a teacher. 3. There are only a few positions. 4. I've gotten used to it. 5. Nina is as enterprising as he is. 6. She was my most talented student. 7. If she wants to become a dentist, she will become a dentist. 8. She's smarter, more independent, and nicer than her brother. 9. She says that she will work hard. 10. I know that she'll be self-employed one day. 11. I'll go to her rather than to another dentist (I'll rather go to her than . . .). 12. The more I think of it, the better I like the idea.

Einblicke

Wortschatz 2

der Arbeiter, -	(blue-collar) worker
Bereich, -e	area, field
Handel	trade
Ort, -e	place, location; town
Rat	advice, counsel
das Praktikum, Praktika	internship
Unternehmen, -	large company
die Arbeitslosigkeit	unemployment
Berufswahl	choice of profession
Entscheidung, -en	decision
(Fach)kenntnis, -se	(special) knowledge, skill
darum	therefore
(gut) ausgebildet	(well-)trained
ins / im Ausland	abroad
jedoch	however
unbedingt	definitely
unter (+ *dat.*)	among
aus·sehen (sieht aus), sah aus, ausgesehen (wie + *nom.*)	to look (like)
bitten, bat, gebeten (um)	to ask (for), request
erwarten	to expect
genießen, genoss, genossen	to enjoy
hoffen	to hope
sich (*dat.*) Sorgen machen (um)	to be concerned / worried (about)
sich (*dat.*) vor·stellen	to imagine
Ich stelle mir vor, dass . . .	I imagine that . . .

Vor dem Lesen

A. Was denken Sie?

1. Ist es schwer, in den USA, in Kanada oder in Ihrem Land Arbeit zu finden?
2. Was für Stellen findet man leicht? 3. Welche Jobs sind schwerer zu finden?
4. Wie ist es für Leute mit einer Universitätsausbildung, für so genannte Akademiker? 5. Welche Berufe haben eine gute Zukunft? 6. Welche Probleme gibt es mit vielen Stellen?

 B. Gehen wir Wörter angeln! Lesen Sie mit Ihrem Partner/Ihrer Partnerin den Text gemeinsam durch. Welche Berufe sowie *(as well as)* Komparative und Superlative finden Sie darin?

C. Das ist leicht zu verstehen! Welche Silbe ist betont? Markieren Sie sie! Was ist das auf Englisch?

der Akademiker, Auslandsaufenthalt, Briefsortierer, Computerkünstler, Experte, Job, Telekommunikationsspezialist, Tourismus; das Filmstudio, Industrieunternehmen, Risiko, Studium, Team; die Arbeitszeit, Berufsmöglichkeit, Flexibilität, Lebenskrise, Mobilität, Perspektive, Suche (nach); Handelsbeziehungen, Informatikkenntnisse; in der Zwischenzeit; absolut, beruflich, intensiv, kreativ, optimal, praktisch, qualifiziert; jobben, organisieren, reduzieren

Mobil telefonieren, wo Deutschland am schönsten ist. Zu Hause.

Lesetipp
Identifying a Speaker's Main Point

Just as speakers typically introduce the topic of their discourse in the first sentence of a paragraph, they often encapsulate the main idea in the final sentence. Find examples in this reading where speakers summarize their ideas in their last sentence.

Die Berufswahl

CD 8, Track 4

(Eine öffentliche Diskussion an der Universität Göttingen)

Wie viele andere Studenten und Studentinnen macht Lore Weber sich Sorgen um ihre berufliche Zukunft. Sie hat darum eine Diskussionsgruppe organisiert und eine Professorin und andere Studenten gebeten, Ideen beizutragen°.   *to contribute*

LORE WEBER: Eine der wichtigsten Entscheidungen heute ist die Frage der Berufs-
5 wahl. Obwohl es besser wird, ist die Arbeitslosigkeit immer noch° hoch, nicht   *still*
nur unter den Arbeitern, sondern auch unter uns Akademikern. Viele Industrieunternehmen werden in den nächsten Jahren weitere° Arbeitsplätze abbauen° und   *additional / cut back*
im öffentlichen Dienst° wird es nicht besser aussehen. Einige meiner Freunde mit   *civil service*
abgeschlossener° Ausbildung suchen seit Monaten Arbeit und jobben in der Zwi-   *completed*
10 schenzeit als Bedienung oder als Verkäufer, Taxifahrer oder Briefsortierer bei der
Post. Wir fragen uns alle, wie unsere Zukunft aussehen wird, und hoffen, dass wir
durch unsere Diskussion eine bessere Vorstellung° davon bekommen. Ich möchte   *idea*
jetzt Frau Professor Weigel bitten, ihre Perspektive über das Problem zusammen-
zufassen. Frau Professor Weigel!

15 PROFESSOR WEIGEL: Vielen Dank, Frau Weber! Auf die Frage nach sicheren
Berufen kann man nur schwer eine Antwort geben. Ich stelle mir vor, dass die
Berufswahl immer komplizierter wird. Zu den Berufen mit Zukunft zählen aber
bestimmt Umweltexperten° und Biochemiker, Telekommunikations- und   *environmental . . .*
Computerspezialisten, Betriebswirte und Mathematiker. Selbstständige in den

demand
need / humanities scholars
outside of
publishing houses

ability
radical changes
One thing is for sure
broad

direct
workers
counseling

more health-conscious
well-being
himself, herself
field, subject

freelance

tied to / just as well

20 verschiedenen Bereichen, vor allem auch im Tourismus, werden sicher genug
Arbeit finden. Auch für Lehrer wird es eine größere Nachfrage° geben. Jedoch sinkt
der Bedarf° für Rechtsanwälte und Architekten. Den Geisteswissenschaftlern°
unter Ihnen empfehle ich, flexibel zu bleiben und auch außerhalb° Ihres Studiums
praktische Erfahrungen zu sammeln, zum Beispiel bei Verlagen° und anderen Fir-
25 men und auch durch Auslandsaufenthalte. Was Sie unbedingt brauchen, sind
Computerkenntnisse. Neben guten Sprach- und Fachkenntnissen wird man besondere Eigenschaften suchen, wie zum Beispiel Flexibilität, Mobilität und die
Fähigkeit°, immer wieder Neues zu lernen und kreativ zu denken, im Team zu arbeiten und Umbrüche° als Chance statt als Risiko zu sehen. Es ist heute keine
30 Lebenskrise mehr, wenn man den Job wechselt. Eins ist jedoch klar°: Eine gute
und breite° Ausbildung ist und bleibt die beste Sicherheit.

CHRISTL MEININGER: Ich leite° seit drei Jahren ein Wellness-Hotel. Ich liebe meine
Arbeit, aber die Suche nach qualifizierten Arbeitskräften° habe ich mir leichter
vorgestellt. Ich glaube, dass Bereiche wie Wellness, Freizeit und Beratung° immer
35 beliebter werden. Wir leben heute unter größerem Stress als früher und sind viel
gesundheitsbewusster° geworden. Man wird also mehr und mehr Geld für sein
eigenes Wohlbefinden° ausgeben. Mein Rat: Lernen Sie das, was Ihnen Spaß
macht, und lernen Sie viel! Fit machen für den Job muss sich jeder selbst°. Je mehr
man in seinem Fach° weiß, desto besser.

40 REINHOLD HOLTKAMP: Ich bin Grafik-Designer und arbeite freiberuflich°, oft
natürlich auch nachts. Als Familienvater genieße ich es, jeden Tag mit meiner
Frau und den Kindern zusammen zu sein. Das finde ich optimal. Kreativität ist
für mich nicht an Ort oder Arbeitszeit gebunden°; darum kann ich genauso gut°
zu Hause arbeiten. Mein Rat: Arbeiten Sie intensiv, bleiben Sie flexibel und
45 erwarten Sie keine absolute Sicherheit!

Dieser Grafik-Designer arbeitet lieber freiberuflich zu Hause als irgendwo (somewhere) *in einem Büro.*

BRIGITTE SCHINDLER: Ich studiere Kunst und Informatik. Ich hoffe, dass ich eines Tages als Computerkünstlerin für ein Filmstudio oder beim Fernsehen arbeiten werde. Ich finde es wichtig, dass die Arbeit Spaß macht. Nur wenn man etwas gern tut, wird man wirklich gut sein. Und weil die Arbeitslosigkeit unter uns
50 Frauen größer ist als unter Männern, müssen wir einfach besser sein. Ich versuche gerade, einen Platz für ein Praktikum in Amerika zu finden. Je mehr man gemacht hat, desto besser die Chancen. Auslandserfahrung ist wichtig. Mit der wachsenden Bedeutung° der EU—wo wir mit unserer Ausbildung überall arbeiten können—und Deutschlands Handelsbeziehungen mit der ganzen Welt
55 werden unsere Berufsmöglichkeiten immer interessanter. Die Konkurrenz° wird natürlich auch größer. Ich stelle mir vor, dass jedes bisschen Erfahrung hilft. Die besten Jobs werden immer die Besten bekommen.

growing importance

competition

Es ist nicht gut genug, klug zu sein. Es ist besser, gut zu sein

Aktives zum Text

A. Was stimmt?

1. Viele Industrieunternehmen werden in den nächsten Jahren ____.
   a. Arbeitsplätze reduzieren
   b. die billigsten Arbeiter haben
   c. ihre Probleme zusammenfassen
2. Frau Professor Weigel glaubt, dass Studenten vor allem ____ brauchen.
   a. Auslandsaufenthalte
   b. Rechtsanwälte
   c. Flexibilität, Mobilität und Kreativität
3. Christl Meininger ____.
   a. möchte am liebsten in einem Wellness-Zentrum arbeiten
   b. hatte es sich leichter vorgestellt, qualifizierte Arbeitskräfte für ihr Hotel zu finden
   c. meint, dass die Menschen heute weniger gesundheitsbewusst sind als früher
4. Reinhold Holtkamp ____.
   a. ist Angestellter bei einer Grafik-Design-Firma
   b. hasst seine Arbeit, weil er wenig Zeit für seine Familie hat
   c. genießt es, zu Hause arbeiten zu können
5. Brigitte Schindler meint, dass ____.
   a. Informatik für sie sehr schwer sein wird
   b. Frauen beruflich besser sein müssen als Männer
   c. praktische Erfahrungen in der Berufswelt nicht immer helfen

B. Blick auf den Arbeitsmarkt Wiederholen Sie die Sätze in der Zukunft!

1. Die Berufswahl bleibt eine der wichtigsten Entscheidungen. 2. So fragen wir uns alle, wie unsere Zukunft aussieht. 3. Habe ich mit meiner Ausbildung gute Berufsmöglichkeiten oder sitze ich eines Tages auf der Straße? 4. Absolute Sicherheit gibt es in keinem Beruf. 5. Man muss flexibel bleiben. 6. Praktische Erfahrung im Ausland und Sprachkenntnisse helfen auch. 7. Die Konkurrenz wird immer größer. 8. Mit einer guten Ausbildung können die Deutschen in Zukunft überall in der EU arbeiten.

C. Wunschprofil von Arbeitgebern *(employers)* Sehen Sie sich mit den anderen die folgende Tabelle an! Wie viele Aussagen mit Komparativen und Superlativen können Sie darüber machen?

BEISPIEL *Flexibilität ist den Arbeitgebern am wichtigsten.*

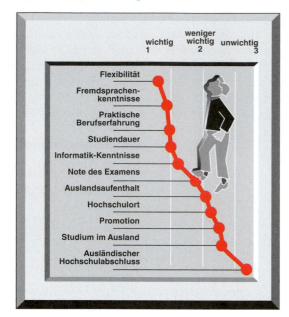

D. So wird's werden. Was fehlt?

1. _____ Leute müssen mindestens *(at least)* einmal ihren Beruf wechseln. *(most)*
2. Gute theoretische Kenntnisse werden _____ wichtig sein _____ praktische Erfahrungen. *(just as . . . as)*
3. _____ praktische Erfahrung man hat, _____ sind die Berufschancen. *(the more . . . the better)*
4. Man wird auch _____ Zusatzqualifikationen suchen. *(more and more)*
5. _____ man seine Prüfungen hinter sich hat, muss man bereit *(willing)* sein, dorthin zu ziehen, wo es Arbeit gibt. *(as soon as)*
6. Wer nicht flexibel ist, wird _____ Chancen auf dem Arbeitsmarkt haben und vielleicht auch _____ verdienen. *(fewer; less)*

E. Was bin ich? Nehmen Sie als Muster *(model)* die *Hörverständnis*-Übung am Ende von *Aktives zum Thema* und schreiben Sie ein paar Sätze! Lesen Sie laut, was Sie geschrieben haben! Die anderen versuchen dann zu raten *(guess)*, was Sie sind.

BEISPIEL *Viele Leute kommen zu mir nur, wenn ihnen etwas wehtut. Sie kommen mit Schmerzen, setzen sich in meinen gemütlichen Stuhl und bald sind die Schmerzen weg. Was bin ich?*

F. Zwanzig Fragen: An wen denke ich? Jemand in Ihrer Gruppe von vier oder fünf Studenten denkt an eine bekannte Person. Die anderen dürfen bis zu 20 Fragen stellen, um herauszufinden, woran dieser Jemand denkt.

G. Aufsatz: Etwas über mich Schreiben Sie acht bis zehn Sätze über eins der folgenden Themen!

1. Was ich einmal werden möchte/wollte und warum
2. Mein Leben in . . . Jahren. So stelle ich mir mein Leben in zehn, zwanzig oder dreißig Jahren vor.

H. Mein Lebenslauf *(résumé)* Lesen Sie das folgende Resümee und schreiben Sie dann Ihren eigenen Lebenslauf! Vergleichen Sie ihn zu dem der *(that of)* anderen!

Susan Gerber
512 Rainer Blvd.
Maple Valley, Washington 98038
Tel. 001 (425) 555-5583
E-mail sgerber@nnnnnn.com

Persönliche Daten: geboren am 21. 12. 1983 in Palo Alto, Kalifornien; U.S. Amerikanerin

Ausbildung:
20. Mai 1999   Nathan Hale High School, Seattle, Washington
                                High School Abschluss

09/99 – 05/03   University of Washington, Seattle, Washington
                                Studienfächer: Betriebswirtschaft und Deutsch
                                Studienschwerpunkte: Buchhaltung, Finanzwesen,
                                Deutsche Kultur und Sprache
16. Mai 2003   BA in Business Administration
                                Studienabschluss: Betriebswirtschaft

Arbeitserfahrung:
Seit 07/03   Boeing Company, Seattle, Washington
                                Buchhaltungsassistentin, Mitarbeit im Export-Team

Besondere Kenntnisse und Interessen:
                                Computer Microsoft Office, Account Geek, SAP
                                Präsidentin des Businessclubs meiner Universität

Sprachen: Englisch (Muttersprache)
                                Deutsch (fließend)

Susan Gerber   13. März 2005

Schreibtipp
Writing a Résumé

A résumé provides general information about your life and describes the development of your professional career beginning with your education. While the traditional **Lebenslauf** was handwritten and in narrative form, the modern version is typed, brief, and to the point. Limit yourself to just one page. **In der Kürze liegt die Würze** *(Clarity is in brevity,* lit. *In brevity lies the spiciness).* The sample shown here shows just one way to prepare a German-style résumé. A photograph is common and usually required in the job application process. Don't forget to sign your résumé at the bottom. Do remember to provide a professional-sounding e-mail address.

Hörverständnis

Track 31   **Drei Lebensläufe**   Hören Sie sich an, was die drei jungen Deutschen über sich zu erzählen haben! Bevor Sie aber die folgenden Fragen beantworten, lesen Sie noch einmal kurz die *Vorschau* am Anfang des Kapitels!

Zum Erkennen: halbtags *(part-time)*; verlassen *(to leave)*; Schwerpunktfächer *(majors)*; der Vorarbeiter *(foreman)*; zum Militär *(to the army)*; der Autounfall *(accident)*

Richtig oder falsch?

_____ 1. Die Schmidts haben zwei Kinder: eine Tochter und einen Sohn.
_____ 2. Claudias Vater ist Ingenieur, ihre Mutter Sekretärin.
_____ 3. In ihrer Freizeit ist Claudia stinkfaul.
_____ 4. Wolf Wicke ist am 23.11.1990 geboren.
_____ 5. Wolf macht eine Lehre und geht zur Hauptschule.
_____ 6. Wolf war schon beim Militär.
_____ 7. Kristinas Mutter lebt nicht mehr.
_____ 8. Kristinas Bruder ist fünf Jahre älter als sie.
_____ 9. Nach dem Abitur hat sie zuerst ein Jahr gearbeitet.
_____ 10. Jetzt ist sie Medizinstudentin in Heidelberg.

Realschule vs. Gymnasium; statistics about national income; Turkish people and culture in Germany; http://wiegehts.heinle.com.

Literatur

Biographisches

Aysel Özakin was born in Turkey in 1942 and came to Germany in 1981, where she studied French and won several German literary prizes, including the City Writer Award in Hamburg and a fellowship at the Günter Grass House. She moved to England, where she married a British painter (the late Bryan Ingham) and where she continues today to write poetry, short prose, and novels, mostly in English. Because she was a successful and recognized author in Turkey before she went to live in Germany, she does not identify herself as an author of **Ausländer-** or **Gastarbeiterliteratur**. As a cosmopolitan, she aligns herself with other artists and writers who transgress boundaries, and argues against limiting individuals by their nationalities.

Part of her work describes her experiences in Germany and addresses foreigners and Germans alike. This story, "Die dunkelhaarigen Kinder von Berlin," taken from a larger collection called *Soll ich hier alt werden? Türkin in Deutschland,* takes place during the 1980s in Kreuzberg, a district in Berlin that was and still is home to many foreigners, especially of Turkish origin. It has also become associated with young Germans from the counterculture scene who, in their protest against materialism, occupied old houses slated to be torn down or modernized. They opposed the city's renovation program largely because it would force them out of their low-cost housing and prevent them from continuing the alternative lifestyle they preferred.

Vor dem Lesen

Allgemeine Fragen

1. Welche Ausländergruppen gibt es in Ihrer Stadt und Ihrem Land?
2. Welche Probleme haben manche dieser Ausländer?
3. Wer von ihnen hat gewöhnlich größere Probleme, die Jüngeren oder die Älteren? Warum?
4. Wie kann man helfen?
5. Haben Sie schon einmal Heimweh *(homesickness)* gehabt? Wenn ja, wie haben Sie sich gefühlt und was haben Sie vermisst?

Die dunkelhaarigen Kinder von Berlin

Track 32

Ich bemühe mich°, sie nicht aus den Augen zu verlieren. Auf dem Platz hinter der Kirche spielt ein junger Deutscher Gitarre und singt dazu. Leute stehen dabei, die° trinken Bier und essen Kuchen. Man hört laute Stimmen°, es wird geküsst°, gespielt. Die Gesichter sind rot, grün, blau oder gelb angemalt. Alle bewegen sich° im Rhythmus der Musik. Ich bemühe mich, sie nicht aus den Augen zu verlieren: dieses kleine Mädchen, diesen kleinen Körper mit dem Kopftuch°.—Der Sänger mit den dreckigen Jeans . . . brüllt° in das Mikrofon. Er protestiert gegen die Kleinbürgerlichkeit°, gegen die Polizei, gegen den Konservatismus.

Das kleine Mädchen ist angezogen wie eine arme, ältere Frau . . . Ich möchte wissen, wie sie sich Jahre später sehen wird.—Die Fete° der jungen Hausbesetzer° geht weiter. Das Mädchen läuft mit anderen dunklen Kindern zu dem Stand, der° für Kinder aufgebaut wurde° . . . Die blonden Kinder sitzen auf den Schultern der Erwachsenen°. Deren° Gesichter sind genauso bunt wie die° ihrer Kinder . . . Das kleine Mädchen mit dem Kopftuch nimmt einen Pinsel° . . . und tupft sich° einen roten Punkt auf die Nase. Sie schaut in den Spiegel und lächelt . . . Ein verkrampftes° Lächeln. Ein altes, ein einsames° Kind.

Ich stehe unmittelbar° hinter ihr . . . Wie sie, bin ich kein Teil dieser blonden Welt und werde es nie sein. Ich komme daher, wo° sie auch hergekommen ist. Ich hatte Gelegenheit°, mich zu entwickeln°, frei zu werden. Ich könnte hier tanzen, singen. Aber etwas in mir hält mich gefangen° . . .—Das Licht der Straßenlaterne° erhellt die Gesichter der fröhlichen jungen Leute. Das sind

<!-- glossary -->
try

they / voices
they're kissing
move

head scarf / screams
narrow-mindedness

party
squatters
that / was put up
adults / their / those
paintbrush
dabs
tense / lonely
directly
from where
opportunity / develop
keeps me prisoner
. . . lantern

Menschen, die° ihre Jugend°, ihre Freiheit in ganzer Fülle° erleben wollen. Sie machen sich lustig über° allen Besitz° und über alle, die auch das Leben wie einen Besitz behandeln°. Sie sind mir sympathisch°, aber ich weiß, dass ich nie eine von ihnen sein kann.

> who / youth / to the fullest
> make fun of / possessions
> treat like / I like them.

Jetzt halte ich die Hand des kleinen Mädchens. Sie wird rot°, geniert sich° vielleicht, weil ich Türkisch spreche; vielleicht auch, weil sie sich angemalt hat . . . Was wird sie denken, wenn sie an ihre Kindheit hier zurückdenkt? . . . Ich frage sie, was ihr Vater macht.

> blushes / is embarrassed

„Er arbeitet in einer Schokoladenfabrik°.“

> . . . factory

„Und deine Mutter?“

„Spült°“ . . .

> washes dishes

„Würdest du lieber in der Türkei leben?“

„Ja.“

„Warum?“

„Wir besuchen da meinen Opa.“ . . .

„Was möchtest du später werden?“

„Weiß nicht.“

„Möchtest du so werden wie deine Mutter?“

„Nein.“

„Wovon träumst du am meisten?“

„Von unseren Hühnern°.“

> chickens

Die anderen Kinder rufen°. Sie geht.

> are calling

Der Sänger trägt jetzt ein Lied über seine Festnahme° vor° . . . Der Schmerz der Unterdrückung° einigt° uns . . . Die Leute auf dem Platz tanzen—jeder so, wie er will. Nur mir gelingt es nicht, meinen Körper vom Druck der Gedanken zu lösen°. Mein Land hat . . . andere Sorgen. Es hat eine Art der Unterdrückung. Das hält mich zurück . . . Das kleine Mädchen mit dem Kopftuch tanzt auch . . . Plötzlich erfriert° ihre ganze Freude, die Freiheit. Sie schämt sich° der Bewegungen° ihres kleinen Körpers und verlässt° die Menge°. Ich schaue ihr nach, bis ich sie aus den Augen° verliere. Der Himmel fängt an, Schnee zu streuen°. Das diesige° Grau des Abends senkt sich° auf den Platz.

> arrest / sings
> oppression / unites
> I can't free myself from my oppressive thoughts.
> freezes / is embarrassed
> movement / leaves / crowd
> out of sight
> It starts to snow / misty / descends

Aysel Özakin

Nach dem Lesen

A. Inhaltsfragen

1. Was für Leute sind zu diesem Straßenfest gekommen?
2. Woran kann man die Hausbesetzer erkennen und woran die ausländischen Kinder?
3. Was hält die Autorin von den Hausbesetzern? Was hat sie mit ihnen gemeinsam?
4. Wen findet sie besonders interessant und warum?
5. Welchen Vorteil (advantage) hat Deutschland der Autorin gebracht?
6. Warum fühlt sie sich trotzdem nicht ganz wohl dort und kann sich nicht so richtig freuen?
7. Warum ist das kleine Mädchen so schüchtern (shy)? Was meinen Sie?
8. Wo arbeiten die Eltern der Kleinen? Wovon träumt sie?
9. Möchte sie einmal so wie ihre Mutter werden? Warum (nicht)?

B. Leben in einem anderen Land

1. Welche Ausländergruppen gibt es in Deutschland, in Österreich und in der Schweiz?
2. Warum gibt es manchmal Ausländerhass (xenophobia)? Was kann man dagegen tun?
3. Welche Ausländer dürfen in Deutschland arbeiten. Wer hat es schwerer, Arbeit zu finden? (See *Fokus* note on "Foreign Workers in Germany.")
4. Möchten Sie dort gern einmal arbeiten? Wenn ja, als was und wo? Wenn nein, warum nicht?

Lernziele

In this chapter you will learn about:

Zum Thema

University studies and student life

Kultur-Fokus

The German university system, studying in Germany, German bureaucracy, US and German companies abroad
Christine Nöstlinger

Struktur

The subjunctive mood
The present-time general subjunctive (Subjunctive II)
The past-time general subjunctive

Einblicke + Literatur

Ein Jahr drüben wäre super!
Christine Nöstlinger: "Ohne Vorurteile"

For more information, go to http://iLrn.heinle.com.

Im Hörsaal an der Uni

Vorschau German Universities

Minidrama: *Amerika ist anders.*

The first German universities were founded in the Middle Ages: Heidelberg in 1386, Cologne in 1388, Erfurt in 1392, Leipzig in 1409, and Rostock in 1419. At the beginning of the 19th century, Wilhelm von Humboldt—a renowned professor of the time—redefined the purpose and mission of universities, viewing them as institutions for pure research and independent study by the nation's preeminent minds. In time, however, it became obvious that this ideal conflicted with the needs of modern education. While the universities continue their academic orientation, other institutions of higher learning, such as the **Fachhochschulen** (first established in the 1960s), prepare students for specific careers in such fields as business and engineering. Courses of study are shorter, although curriculum choices are more limited.

There is no tradition of private universities in Germany. Practically all universities are state supported and charge only minimal tuition **(Studiengebühren)** and fees that cover expenses such as public transportation and health insurance. Under the Federal Education Promotion Act **(Bundesausbildungsförderungsgesetz = BAföG),** needy students can obtain financial assistance, partly in the form of a grant and partly as a loan to be repaid in relatively small installments over several years after the student has finished his or her education (see www.das-neue-bafoeg.de).

Generally speaking, a student may enter a degree program at the university of his or her choice after graduating from the **Gymnasium** (college-preparatory high school) and passing the **Abitur** (a state comprehensive exam). (See *Vorschau* in Chapter 12 for more information on the school system.) Openings in certain academic programs **(Studienplätze),** however, are limited and are filled on the basis of the average grade received in the **Abitur.** The admissions quotas—known by the Latin term **Numerus clausus**—are the norm for certain fields of study, such as medicine. The spots are allocated by a central office in Dortmund, with a certain percentage of places reserved for foreign applicants. In the past, young Germans took it for granted that they could study at minimal cost for as long as they wanted. In recent years, however, as record numbers of young people have chosen the academic track, universities have come under pressure to keep up with the influx of students. In some states, special tuition fees have been introduced for students who study longer than the normative time for a given degree program **(die Regelstudienzeit).**

Overall, there is a push for greater competitiveness among universities and their faculties. It is hoped that this will make German universities more attractive internationally. The recently introduced and internationally recognized bachelor's and master's degrees are becoming more popular, as they reduce the time periods of study and, thus, make possible an earlier start in the job market while being recognized everywhere in the EU. In addition to these new opportunities in the public universities, a few private institutions of higher learning have begun competing for students, most of them with a strong business orientation. Although these small universities are "private," almost all of them also receive some public funds which, however, are proving insufficient to meet institutional needs. Small universities are part of the changing landscape in higher education, which continues to be a national topic of intense debate.

Wir nutzen nur 10% unseres geistigen Potentials
A. Einstein

Zum Thema

 Bei der Immatrikulation

CD 8,
Track 6

PETRA   Hallo, John! Wie geht's?

JOHN   Ganz gut. Und dir?

PETRA   Ach, ich kann nicht klagen. Was machst du denn da?

JOHN   Ich muss noch Immatrikulationsformulare ausfüllen.

PETRA   Soll ich dir helfen?

JOHN   Wenn du Zeit hast. Ich kämpfe immer mit der Bürokratie.

PETRA   Hast du deinen Pass dabei?

JOHN   Nein, wieso?

PETRA   Darin ist deine Aufenthaltserlaubnis; die brauchst du unbedingt.

JOHN   Ich kann ihn ja schnell holen.

PETRA   Tu das! Ich warte hier so lange auf dich.

Etwas später

JOHN   Hier ist mein Pass. Ich muss mich jetzt auch bald entscheiden, welche Seminare ich belegen will. Kannst du mir da auch helfen?

PETRA   Na klar. Was studierst du denn?

JOHN   Mein Hauptfach ist moderne Geschichte. Ich möchte Seminare über deutsche Geschichte und Literatur belegen.

PETRA   Hier ist mein Vorlesungsverzeichnis. Mal sehen, was sie dieses Semester anbieten.

A. Was fehlt?

1. John füllt gerade ein . . . aus. 2. Leider hat er seinen . . . nicht dabei. 3. Er muss ihn erst . . . 4. Im Pass ist seine . . . 5. John weiß noch nicht, was er . . . will. 6. Petra fragt ihn, was . . . ist. 7. Sein Hauptfach ist . . . 8. Petra kann ihm helfen, weil sie ihr . . . dabei hat.

 B. Jetzt sind Sie dran! Sie sind bei einem Studienberater *(academic advisor)*, weil Sie nicht so richtig wissen, was Sie studieren sollen. Dabei können Sie auch auf die Liste der Studienfächer unter Übung B in *Aktives zum Thema* sehen. Wechseln Sie sich ab!

Fokus   German Bureaucracy

Everyone living in Germany must register with the local registration office (**das Einwohnermeldeamt**) within 7 to 14 days of changing address. Likewise, when moving again, residents give the registration office notice with an **Abmeldung.** Non-Germans who wish to stay in Germany longer than three months must go to the **Ausländeramt** and request a residence permit (**die Aufenthaltserlaubnis**). They will need to prove that they can support themselves financially. Non-EU citizens who wish to work in Germany have to show an employment contract before obtaining a work permit (**die Arbeitserlaubnis**). Exceptions are made for students and participants in training programs.

Wortschatz 1

Das Studium *([course of] study)*

der	Abschluss, ¨e	*degree; diploma*	das	Semester, -	*semester*
	Hörsaal, Hörsäle	*lecture hall*		Seminar, -e	*seminar*
	Mitbewohner, -	*housemate*		Stipendium,	*scholarship*
	Professor, -en	*professor*		Stipendien	
	Student, -en, -en	*(college) student*		System, -e	*system*
	Zimmerkollege, -n, -n	*roommate*	die	Fachrichtung, -en	*field of*
das	Fach, ¨er	*subject*			*study*
	Hauptfach, ¨er	*major (field)*		(Natur)wissen-	*(natural)*
	Nebenfach, ¨er	*minor (field)*		schaft, -en	*science*
	Labor, -s	*lab(oratory)*		Note, -n	*grade*
	Quartal, -e	*quarter*		(Seminar)arbeit, -en	here: *term*
	Referat, -e	*oral presentation*			*paper*

aus·füllen	*to fill out*
belegen	*to sign up for, take (a course)*
etwas dagegen haben	*to mind sth., lit. to have sth. against sth.*
Hast du etwas dagegen, wenn . . . ?	*Do you mind, if . . . ?*
holen	*to get (fetch)*
lehren	*to teach*
das Studium ab·schließen, schloss ab, abgeschlossen	*to finish one's degree, graduate*
eine Prüfung machen	*to take an exam*
(eine Prüfung) bestehen, bestand, bestanden	*to pass (a test)*
(bei einer Prüfung) durch·fallen (fällt durch), fiel durch, ist durchgefallen	*to flunk, fail (a test)*
ein Referat halten (hält), hielt, gehalten	*to give an oral presentation*
teil·nehmen (nimmt teil), nahm teil, teilgenommen (an + *dat.*)	*to participate (in)*

Weiteres

Na klar.	*Of course.*
schwierig	*difficult*
Wieso?	*Why? How come?*

Zum Erkennen: klagen *(to complain)*; das Immatrikulationsformular, -e *(enrollment form)*; kämpfen *(to struggle, fight)*; die Bürokratie (here: *red tape*); dabei haben *(to bring along)*; das Vorlesungsverzeichnis, -se *(course catalog)*; AUCH: die Bewerbung, -en (um + *acc.*) *application (for)*; die Fremdsprache, -n *(foreign language)*; der Indikativ; der Konjunktiv *(subjunctive)*, analysieren; sich beziehen auf (+ *acc.*) *(to refer to)*; erwähnen *(to mention)*; herum·fragen *(to ask around)*; hinzu·fügen *(to add)*; einander *(each other)*

● The German word **Studenten** generally refers to university students or students at other institutions of higher learning, but not to high school students (**Schüler**).

● **der Zimmerkollege** BUT **die Zimmerkollegin, -nen.**

Aktives zum Thema

 A. Deutsch als Fremdsprache *(foreign language)* Stellen Sie Ihrem Partner/Ihrer Partnerin Fragen über diesen Schein *(certificate).* Wechseln Sie sich dabei ab! Erzählen Sie dann den anderen in etwa fünf Sätzen, was Sie über Theresa Rumery herausgefunden haben!

🔸 German university students receive a grade card or **Schein** for each course taken. Grading is based on a six-level scale, with conventions and approximate US equivalents as follows: **sehr gut (1)** = A; **gut (2)** = B; **befriedigend** *(satisfactory)* **(3)** = B–/C+; **ausreichend** *(sufficient)* **(4)** = C/C–; **mangelhaft** *(lacking)* **(5)** = D; **ungenügend** *(unsatisfactory)* **(6)** = F

Universität Regensburg
        Lehrgebiet
Deutsch als Fremdsprache

Frau/Herrn   **Theresa R u m e r y**

Aus   U S A

wird hiermit bescheinigt, dass sie/er an dem DEUTSCHKURS
        Konversation - studienbegleitende Oberstufe I (2 SWS)
                mit Referat zum Thema:

                „Die Frauenbewegung in Deutschland"

im Winter-Semester 2005/06 regelmäßig teilgenommen hat.

Sie/Er hat den Kurs mit „sehr gut" (Note 1) bestanden/nicht bestanden.

Regensburg, den 09.02.2006

                                (Dr. Armin Wolff)
                                Akademischer Direktor

Bewertung:
Bestanden: Sehr gut (1); gut (2); befriedigend (3); ausreichend (4); *Nicht bestanden:* mangelhaft (5); ungenügend

---

B. Sag mal, was studierst du? Finden Sie Ihr Hauptfach auf der Liste; wenn es nicht dabei ist, fügen Sie es hinzu *(add)*! Fragen Sie dann herum *(around),* wer das auch noch studiert!

🔸 Accounting is part of **Betriebswirtschaft;** *the accountant =* **der Wirtschaftsprüfer, -.**

BEISPIEL   S1 Sag mal, was studierst du?
                S2 Ich studiere Psychologie. Und du?
                S1 Ich studiere Wirtschaftswissenschaft.

English studies	Anglistik°	Gesundheitswissenschaft	Naturwissenschaft
home economics	Archäologie	Hauswirtschaft°	Pädagogik
computer science	Architektur	Informatik°	Pharmazie
law	Astronomie	Jura°	Philosophie
mining	Bergbau°	Kommunikationswissenschaft	Physik
business administration / nursing / political science	Betriebswirtschaft°	Krankenpflege°	Politologie°
	Biochemie	Kunst	Psychologie
agriculture / Romance languages	Biologie	Landwirtschaft°	Romanistik°
	Chemie	Lebensmittelchemie	Soziologie
education	Elektrotechnik	Lehramt°	Sport
forestry / mechanical engineering	Forstwirtschaft°	Maschinenbau°	Theologie
civil engineering	Chemie	Linguistik	Tiefbau°
veterinary science	Geographie	Mathematik	Tiermedizin°
economics	Geologie	Medizin	Wirtschaftswissenschaft°
dentistry	Germanistik	Mineralogie	Zahnmedizin°
	Geschichte	Musik	

C. Fragen zum Studium   Fragen Sie einen Nachbarn/eine Nachbarin, . . . !

1. wie viele Kurse er/sie dieses Semester / Quartal belegt hat und welche
2. welche Kurse er/sie besonders gut findet, und worin er/sie die besten Noten hat
3. ob er/sie viele Arbeiten schreiben muss; wenn ja, in welchen Fächern
4. ob er/sie schon Referate gehalten hat; wenn ja, in welchen Fächern und worüber
5. ob er/sie außer Deutsch noch andere Sprachen spricht oder lernt
6. wie lange er/sie noch studieren muss
7. was er/sie danach macht
8. wie die Chancen sind, in seinem/ihrem Beruf eine gute Stelle zu bekommen
9. in welchen Berufen es momentan schwierig ist, Arbeit zu finden
10. wo es noch bessere Möglichkeiten gibt

Aussprache: s, ss, ß, st, sp

CD 8,
Track 7   **Laute**

1. [z]   **s**auber, **s**icher, **S**eme**s**ter, **S**eminar, Pau**s**e
2. [s]   Au**s**wei**s**, Kur**s**, Profe**ss**or, wi**ss**en, la**ss**en, flei**ß**ig, Fu**ß**, Grü**ß**e
3. [št] **St**udium, **St**ipendium, **St**elle, **st**udieren, be**st**ehen, an**st**rengend
4. [st] zuer**st**, mei**st**ens, de**st**o, Komponi**st**, Kün**st**ler
5. [šp] **Sp**iel, **Sp**ort, **Sp**aß, **Sp**rache, Bei**sp**iel, **sp**ät

Hörverständnis

Track 33 **Ein guter Start**   Hören Sie, warum und wo verschiedene Studenten in Deutschland an ihrem MBA arbeiten. Ergänzen Sie die folgenden Aussagen!

Zum Erkennen: das Privileg; wissenschaftlich *(scientific)*; verbessern *(to improve)*; Vollzeitstudenten; die Abschlussarbeit *(thesis)*; die Karriere *(career)*

1. Den MBA ____.
   a. gibt es nur in Amerika   b. wird es bald auch in Deutschland geben   c. gibt es jetzt auch in Deutschland

2. Die Studenten am Europa-Institut kommen ____.
   a. nur aus Deutschland   b. aus vielen verschiedenen Ländern   c. alle aus Europa

3. Dieses Europa-Institut ist in ____.
   a. Saarbrücken   b. Heidelberg   c. Worms

4. Terry Furman war in Deutschland auf dem Gymnasium und hat dann in ____ Jura studiert.
   a. Frankreich   b. Spanien   c. England

5. Der Franzose Dominique Laurent ist ____ und verspricht sich vom MBA bessere Berufschancen.
   a. Rechtsanwalt   b. Ingenieur   c. Geschäftsmann

6. Am Ende des MBAs steht ____ mit einer Abschlussarbeit.
   a. ein Praktikum   b. eine Lehre   c. eine Auslandsreise

7. Die Wissenschaftliche Hochschule in Koblenz ist ____.
   a. schon alt   b. privat   c. öffentlich

8. Dort kostet der MBA ____.
   a. nichts   b. nicht sehr viel   c. viel Geld

● For further review, see the Summary of Pronunciation in the front of your *Arbeitsbuch*. Study Part III, subsections 6 and 12.

Struktur

13.1 The subjunctive mood

Until now, almost all sentences in this book have been in the INDICATIVE MOOD. Sentences in the indicative mood generally reflect a direct, factual reality. Sometimes, however, we want to speculate on matters that are unreal, uncertain, or unlikely; or we wish for something that cannot be; or we want to approach other people less directly, more discretely and politely. For that purpose we use the SUBJUNCTIVE MOOD.

1. Polite requests or questions

    Would you like a cup of coffee?
    Could you help me for a moment?

2. Hypothetical statements and questions

    What would you do?
    You should have been there.

3. Wishes

    If only I had more time.
    I wish you would hurry up.

4. Unreal conditions

    If I had time, I'd go to the movies. (But since I don't have time, I'm not going.)
    If the weather were good, we'd go for a walk. (But since it's raining, we won't go.)
    If you had told me, I could have helped you. (But since you didn't tell me, I couldn't help you.)

    Contrast the sentences above with real conditions:

    If I have time, I'll go to the movies.
    If the weather is good, we'll go for a walk.

    In real conditions, the possibility exists that the events will take place. In unreal conditions, this possibility does not exist or is highly unlikely.

    • The forms of the PRESENT-TIME SUBJUNCTIVE are derived from the simple past: *If I told you (now)* . . .
    • Those of the PAST-TIME SUBJUNCTIVE are derived from the past perfect: *If you had told me (earlier)* . . .
    • Another very common way to express the subjunctive mood is with the form *would*: *I'd go; I would not stay home.*

Übung

A. Indikativ oder Konjunktiv (subjunctive)? Analysieren Sie die Sätze und sagen Sie, ob sie im Indikativ oder Konjunktiv sind. Entscheiden Sie auch, ob sie sich auf jetzt, früher oder später beziehen *(refer to)!*

BEISPIEL   If you don't ask, you won't know.   *indicative: now or later*
               What would you have done?   *subjunctive: earlier*

1. If she can, she'll write. 2. If only I had known that. 3. They could be here any minute. 4. Will you take the bike along? 5. Would you please hold this? 6. I had known that a long time. 7. We should really be going. 8. I wish he had told me. 9. If you could stay until Sunday, you could fly for a lower fare. 10. What would he have done if you hadn't come along?

13.2 The present-time general subjunctive

German has two subjunctives. The one most commonly used is often referred to in grammar books as the GENERAL SUBJUNCTIVE or SUBJUNCTIVE II. (The SPECIAL SUBJUNCTIVE or SUBJUNCTIVE I is explained in Chapter 15.)

1. Forms

The PRESENT-TIME SUBJUNCTIVE refers to the present *(now)* or the future *(later)*. As in English, its forms are derived from the forms of the <u>simple past</u>. You already know the verb endings from having used the **möchte**-forms of **mögen,** which are actually subjunctive forms. All verbs in the subjunctive have these endings:

Infinitive	Simple Past, Indicative	Present-time Subjunctive
mögen	ich mochte	möchte
	du mochtest	möcht**est**
	er mochte	möchte
	wir mochten	möcht**en**
	ihr mochtet	möcht**et**
	sie mochten	möcht**en**

a. T-verbs *(weak verbs)*

The present-time subjunctive forms of regular t-verbs are identical to those of the simple past. Their use usually becomes clear from context.

Infinitive	Simple Past, Indicative	Present-time Subjunctive
glauben	glaubte	**glaubte**
antworten	antwortete	**antwortete**

Wenn Sie mir nur **glaubten!**	*If only you believed me!*
Wenn er mir nur **antwortete!**	*If only he would answer me!*

b. Irregular t-verbs *(mixed verbs)*

Most of the irregular t-verbs, which include the modals, have an umlaut in the present-time subjunctive. Exceptions are **sollen** and **wollen.**

Infinitive	Simple Past, Indicative	Present-time Subjunctive
haben	hatte	**hätte**
bringen	brachte	**brächte**
denken	dachte	**dächte**
wissen	wusste	**wüsste**
dürfen	durfte	**dürfte**
müssen	musste	**müsste**
können	konnte	**könnte**
mögen	mochte	**möchte**
sollen	sollte	**sollte**
wollen	wollte	**wollte**

haben		wissen	
ich hätte	wir hätt**en**	ich wüsste	wir wüsst**en**
du hätt**est**	ihr hätt**et**	du wüsst**est**	ihr wüsst**et**
er hätte	sie hätt**en**	er wüsste	sie wüsst**en**

Hättest du Zeit?	*Would you have time?*
Könntest du kommen?	*Could you come?*

c. N-verbs *(strong verbs)*

The present-time subjunctive forms of n-verbs add subjunctive endings to the past stem. If the past stem vowel is an **a**, **o**, or **u**, the subjunctive forms have an umlaut.

Infinitive	Simple Past, Indicative	Present-time Subjunctive
sein	war	**wäre**
werden	wurde	**würde**
bleiben	blieb	**bliebe**
fahren	fuhr	**führe**
finden	fand	**fände**
fliegen	flog	**flöge**
geben	gab	**gäbe**
gehen	ging	**ginge**
laufen	lief	**liefe**
sehen	sah	**sähe**
tun	tat	**täte**

sein	
ich wäre	wir wär**en**
du wär**est**	ihr wär**et**
er wäre	sie wär**en**

gehen	
ich ging**e**	wir ging**en**
du ging**est**	ihr ging**et**
er ging**e**	sie ging**en**

Wenn ich du **wäre, ginge** ich nicht.	*If I were you, I wouldn't go.*
Wenn er **flöge, könnte** er morgen hier sein.	*If he were to fly, he could be here tomorrow.*

d. The **würde**-form

In conversation, speakers of German commonly use the subjunctive forms of **haben, sein, werden, wissen,** and the modals.

Hättest du Zeit?	*Would you have time?*
Das **wäre** schön.	*That would be nice.*
Was **möchtest** du tun?	*What would you like to do?*
Wenn ich das nur **wüsste!**	*If only I knew that!*

For the subjunctive forms of other verbs, however, German speakers frequently substitute a simpler verb phrase that closely corresponds to the English *would + infinitive*. It is preferred when the subjunctive form is identical to the indicative form, as is the case with t-verbs and with the plural forms of n-verbs whose subjunctive forms don't have an umlaut (e.g., **gingen**). It is also frequently used in the conclusion clause of contrary-to-fact conditions.

Das täte ich nicht. Das **würde** ich nicht **tun.**	*I wouldn't do that.*
Wenn er mir nur glaubte! Wenn er mir nur **glauben würde!**	*If only he would believe me!*
Wir gingen lieber ins Kino. Wir **würden** lieber ins Kino **gehen.**	*We would rather go to the movies.*
Wenn sie Zeit hätte, käme sie mit. Wenn sie Zeit hätte, **würde** sie **mitkommen.**	*If she had time, she would come along.*

2. Uses

You are already familiar with the most common uses of the subjunctive in English. Here are examples of these uses in German.

a. Polite requests or questions

Möchtest du eine Tasse Kaffee?	*Would you like a cup of coffee?*
Würdest du mir die Butter geben?	*Would you pass me the butter?*
Dürfte ich etwas Käse haben?	*Could I have some cheese?*
Könntest du mir einen Moment helfen?	*Could you help me for a minute?*

b. Hypothetical statements and questions

Er sollte jeden Moment hier sein.	*He should be here any minute.*
Das wäre schön.	*That would be nice.*
Es wäre mir lieber, wenn er hier wäre.	*I'd rather he be here.* (lit. *I'd prefer it if he would be here.*)
Was würdest du tun?	*What would you do?*
Ich würde ihm alles erzählen.	*I'd tell him everything.*

c. Wishes

- Wishes starting with **Wenn . . .** usually add **nur** after the subject or any pronoun object.

Wenn ich nur mehr Zeit hätte!	*If only I had more time!*
Wenn er mir nur glauben würde!	*If only he'd believe me!*

- Wishes starting with **Ich wünschte, . . .** have both clauses in the subjunctive.

Ich wünschte, ich hätte mehr Zeit.	*I wish I had more time.*
Ich wünschte, du würdest dich beeilen.	*I wish you'd hurry.*

d. Unreal conditions

Wenn ich morgen Zeit hätte, würde ich mit dir ins Kino gehen.	*If I had time tomorrow, I'd go to the movies with you.*
Wenn das Wetter schöner wäre, würden wir draußen essen.	*If the weather were nicer, we'd eat outside.*
Wenn wir euch helfen könnten, würden wir das tun.	*If we could help you, we would do it.*

Contrast the preceding sentences with real conditions.

Wenn ich morgen Zeit habe, gehe ich mit dir ins Kino.	*If I have time tomorrow, I'll go to the movies with you.*
Wenn das Wetter schön ist, essen wir draußen.	*If the weather is nice, we'll eat outside.*
Wenn wir euch helfen können, tun wir es.	*If we can help you, we'll do it.*

Wenn ich ein Vöglein° wär'
und auch zwei Flügel° hätt',
flög' ich zu dir.
Weil's aber nicht kann sein,
weil's aber nicht kann sein,
bleib' ich allhier°.

little bird
wings

right here

Mein Hut°, der hat drei Ecken.
Drei Ecken hat mein Hut.
Und hätt' er nicht drei Ecken,
dann wär' es nicht mein Hut.

hat

Übungen

B. Was tun? Auf Englisch bitte!

1. Wohin möchtest du gehen?
2. Wir könnten uns einen Film ansehen.
3. Wir sollten uns eine Zeitung holen.
4. Ich würde gern ins Kino gehen.
5. Ich wünschte, ich wäre nicht so müde.
6. Ich würde lieber zu Hause bleiben.
7. Hättest du etwas dagegen, wenn ich ein paar Freunde mitbringen würde?
8. Es wäre mir lieber, wenn wir allein gehen würden.
9. Hättest du morgen Abend Zeit?
10. Ich ginge heute lieber früh ins Bett.
11. Morgen könnte ich länger schlafen.
12. Dann wäre ich nicht so müde.
13. Du könntest dann auch deine Freunde mitbringen.
14. Wäre das nicht eine bessere Idee?

C. Nennen Sie das Imperfekt und die Konjunktivform!

BEISPIEL   ich hole   *ich holte*   *ich holte*
               du bringst   *du brachtest*   *du brächtest*
               er kommt   *er kam*   *er käme*

1. ich frage, mache, hoffe, belege, lächele, studiere, versuche
2. du arbeitest, antwortest, beendest, erwartest, öffnest, heiratest
3. er muss, kann, darf, soll, mag
4. wir bringen, denken, wissen, haben
5. ihr bleibt, schlaft, fliegt, seid, gebt, esst, singt, sitzt, tut, seht, versprecht, werdet, fahrt

D. Reisepläne

1. **In Wien** Was fehlt? Ergänzen Sie die richtige Form von **würde!**

   BEISPIEL   Bauers _würden_ nach Wien fahren.

   a. Dort _____ wir erst eine Stadtrundfahrt machen.
   b. Dann _____ Dieter sicher den Stephansdom ansehen. Und du _____ dann durch die Kärntner Straße bummeln. Natürlich _____ ihr auch in die Hofburg gehen.
   c. Ja, und einen Abend _____ wir in Grinzing feiern.
   d. Das _____ euch gefallen.

2. **In der Schweiz** Ergänzen Sie die richtige Form vom Konjunktiv II!

   BEISPIEL   Ute _führe_ in die Schweiz. (fahren)

   a. Ich _____ mit ein paar Freunden in die Schweiz fahren. (können)
   b. Erst _____ wir an den Bodensee. (fahren)
   c. Von dort _____ es weiter nach Zürich und Bern. (gehen)
   d. In Zürich _____ ich mir gern das Thomas-Mann-Archiv (*archives*) _____. (ansehen)
   e. Ihr _____ auch nach Genf fahren. (sollen)
   f. Dort _____ du Französisch sprechen. (müssen)
   g. Das _____ keine schlechte Idee! (sein)

E. Sagen Sie's höflicher (more politely)!

BEISPIEL Können Sie uns die Mensa zeigen?
Könnten Sie uns die Mensa zeigen?

1. Darf ich kurz mit Ihnen sprechen? 2. Haben Sie Lust mitzukommen?
3. Können wir uns an einen Tisch setzen? 4. Haben Sie etwas Zeit?

BEISPIEL Rufen Sie mich morgen an!
Würden / Könnten Sie mich morgen anrufen?

5. Erzählen Sie uns von der Reise! 6. Bringen Sie die Fotos mit! 7. Machen Sie mir eine Tasse Kaffee! 8. Geben Sie mir die Milch!

F. Und noch einmal ganz höflich! Was ist richtig?

1. Der Student sagt:
   a. „Hättest du vielleicht ein Stück Papier?"
   b. „Wenn ich doch nur ein Stück Papier hätte!"
   c. „Ein Stück Papier, aber schnell bitte!"

2. Die Studentin sagt:
   a. „Ich brauche unbedingt ein Vorlesungsverzeichnis."
   b. „Würdest du mir bitte mal das Vorlesungsverzeichnis geben?"
   c. „Gibst du mir jetzt das Vorlesungsverzeichnis oder nicht?"

3. Der Beamte sagt:
   a. „Geben Sie mir Ihr Immatrikulationsformular!"
   b. „Ich will jetzt aber Ihr Immatrikulationsformular sehen."
   c. „Dürfte ich bitte Ihr Immatrikulationsformular sehen?"

4. Die Studenten sagen:
   a. „Wären Sie wohl so nett, uns die Noten zu sagen?"
   b. „Unsere Noten!"
   c. „Wenn Sie uns nicht die Noten sagen, dann gehen wir."

G. Allerlei Wünsche

BEISPIEL Das Seminar ist schwer.
Ich wünschte, das Seminar wäre nicht so schwer.

1. Ich muss viel lesen. 2. Das kostet viel Zeit. 3. Ich bin müde. 4. Ihr seid faul.

BEISPIEL Ich wünschte, ich könnte schlafen.
Wenn ich nur schlafen könnte!

5. Ich wünschte, wir hätten keine Referate.
6. Ich wünschte, ich wüsste mehr über das Thema Wirtschaft.
7. Ich wünschte, du könntest mir helfen.
8. Ich wünschte, diese Woche wäre schon vorbei.

H. Wiederholen Sie die Sätze im Konjunktiv!

BEISPIEL Wenn das Wetter schön ist, kann man die Berge sehen.
Wenn das Wetter schön wäre, könnte man die Berge sehen.

1. Wenn es möglich ist, zeige ich euch das Schloss.
2. Wenn du das Schloss sehen willst, musst du dich beeilen.
3. Wenn ihr zu spät kommt, ärgert ihr euch.
4. Wenn das Schloss zu ist, können wir in den Schlosspark gehen.
5. Wenn ihr mehr sehen wollt, müsst ihr länger hier bleiben.

I. Eine besondere Art von Studium Was fehlt?

Studium mit staatlichen britischen Abschlüssen (auch ohne Abitur ab 25 Jahre).
2 Jahre EURO-AKADEMIE Köln + Praktikum + 1 Jahr Uni in Großbritannien:
B.A. (Hons.) in European Business Management
- Management + Wirtschaft + Sprachen
MBA - Master of Business Administration
- 2 Jahre Köln + 2 Jahre Uni in GB
Beginn: Jährlich August und Februar. Prospekt anfordern! Tel. 02 21/ 73 60 74
EURO AKADEMIE, Elsa-Brändström-Straße 8 · 50668 Köln

1. Kevin, ich habe gerade von einer Euro-Akademie gelesen, wo man seinen B.A. in Management, Wirtschaft und Sprachen _____. *(could make)* 2. Dafür _____ man zwei Jahre an dieser Akademie in Köln und dann ein Jahr in England _____. *(would have to study)* 3. Dazu _____ noch ein Praktikum. *(would come)* 4. Wenn du _____, _____ du dort auch deinen Magister (M.A.) _____. *(wanted, could make)* 5. Dazu _____ du außer in Köln noch zwei Jahre an der Uni in England _____. *(would have to study)* 6. Weil du über 25 Jahre alt bist, _____ du kein Abitur. *(would need)* 7. Mensch, _____ das nicht was für dich? *(would be)* 8. Das ganze Studium _____ nicht länger als vier Jahre _____. *(ought to take)* 9. Dann _____ du deinen Abschluss in der Tasche. *(would have)* 10. Du _____ entweder im August oder im Februar _____. *(could start)* 11. Ich _____, ich _____ noch einmal so jung wie du! *(wish, were)* 12. Ich _____ das _____. *(would do)*

⬤ Optional English-to-German practice: 1. Can you *(pl. fam.)* stay? 2. We could go for a walk. 3. I was supposed to visit my grandfather last week. 4. Now we have to do it on Saturday. 5. I wish I knew why he has not called. 6. I know he would call me if he needed anything. 7. Would you *(pl. fam.)* feel like going to a restaurant? 8. That would be nice. 9. We wish we had time. 10. If Walter didn't have to work, we could stay. (See answer key in the Appendix.)

J. Zwei wichtige Fragen für junge Deutsche und für Sie

1. **Das würden junge Deutsche tun.** Schauen Sie sich die folgenden Tabellen an und stellen Sie den anderen in Ihrer Gruppe Fragen dazu!

BEISPIEL S1 Was würden 20 Prozent der jungen Deutschen tun?
S2 20 Prozent würden als Single in einer Penthouse-Wohnung wohnen.

Was wäre, wenn Sie so leben könnten, wie Sie wollten?	
als Globetrotter um die Welt ziehen	25%
als Single in einer Penthouse-Wohnung wohnen	20%
als Handwerker/in in einer Kleinstadt leben	14%
als Chirurg/in mit Familie in einer Villa wohnen	13%
als Künstler/in in einem alten Haus leben	12%
als Playboy / Model immer da sein, wo etwas los ist	8%
Aktivist/in für Greenpeace sein	4%
als Bundespräsident/in im Schloss Bellevue wohnen	4%

Was wäre, wenn Ihre Oma Ihnen 5 000 Euro hinterlassen würde?	
das Geld zur Bank bringen	25%
verreisen	22%
sich Kleidung kaufen	18%
etwas Größeres kaufen	13%
sich fragen, wo die restlichen 45 000 Euro sind	8%
mit Freunden feiern und alles zahlen	6%
Aktien *(stocks)* kaufen	5%
den Armen etwas geben	3%

2. **Das würde ich tun.** Beschreiben Sie nun, wie das bei Ihnen aussähe, was Ihnen wichtig und weniger wichtig wäre! Wenn Sie wollen, können Sie auch eigene Aussagen hinzufügen.

BEISPIEL S1 Wie wäre es, wenn du so leben könntest, wie du wolltest?
S2 Wenn ich leben könnte, wie ich wollte, zöge ich . . .

K. Wie geht's weiter?

BEISPIEL   Ich wäre glücklich, wenn . . .
Ich wäre glücklich, wenn ich gut Deutsch sprechen könnte.
Und du?

1. Ich wäre froh, wenn . . .
2. Ich fände es prima, wenn . . .
3. Es wäre furchtbar, wenn . . .
4. Ich würde mich ärgern, wenn . . .
5. Ich würde sparen, wenn . . .
6. Ich wüsste, was ich täte, wenn . . .

L. Dürfte ich . . . ? Fragen Sie Ihren Partner/Ihre Partnerin um Erlaubnis *(for permission)* und hören Sie, was er/sie dazu zu sagen hat! Wechseln Sie sich ab!

1. mal kurz dein Buch haben
2. deine Hausaufgaben sehen / abschreiben *(copy)*
3. mein Radio anmachen / eine neue CD spielen
4. deinen Kuli / deinen Pullover / . . . borgen *(borrow)*
5. für dich zahlen / dir die Rechnung geben
6. deine Kreditkarte / dein Handy / dein Auto / . . . borgen

Fokus US and German Companies Doing Business Abroad

Germany is an essential trade partner of the United States and vice versa. The European Union is the second-largest trading partner of the United States, and Germany alone ranks number five. German companies account for approximately 850,000 jobs in the United States and American companies account for about 800,000 jobs in Germany. Many major American companies have a strong presence in Germany, including UPS, FedEx, Compaq, Hewlett Packard, Proctor & Gamble, and GE—some of them in part through acquisition of German firms or through mergers with German firms. For instance, the German car maker Opel is a division of General Motors. Daimler-Chrysler Corporation (of which Mercedes-Benz is a division) was formed as the result of a US-German merger. The international cell phone giant T-Mobile is part of Deutsche Telekom. In turn, the names of many German companies are familiar in the United States: car makers Volkswagen, Audi, BMW, and Porsche; shoe and sporting goods companies Birkenstock, Adidas, and Puma; the electronic innovator Siemens; the software company SAP; and the chemical giant BASF. BMG Music and Entertainment is part of Germany's Bertelsmann multimedia empire.

13.3 The past-time general subjunctive

You already know that a simple-past form in English can express the present-time subjunctive (referring to _now_ or _later_). The past-perfect form, or _would have_ + participle, expresses the same thought in the PAST-TIME SUBJUNCTIVE (referring to an _earlier_ point of time).

NOW OR LATER: If I _had_ time, I _would go_ with you.
EARLIER: If I _had had_ time, I _would have gone_ with you.

1. Forms

   a. In German, the forms of the past-time subjunctive are based on the forms of the <u>past perfect</u>. The past-time subjunctive is very easy to learn because it simply consists of a form of **hätte** or **wäre** plus the past participle:

   $$\left.\begin{array}{l} \textbf{hätte} \ldots \\ \textbf{wäre} \ldots \end{array}\right\} + \text{participle}$$

Hättest du das **getan?**	_Would you have done that?_
Das **hätte** ich nicht **getan.**	_I wouldn't have done that._
Wärest du nicht lieber ins Kino **gegangen?**	_Wouldn't you have rather gone to the movies?_
Ich wünschte, du **hättest** mir das **gesagt!**	_I wish you had told me that!_
Wenn ich das **gewusst hätte, wären** wir ins Kino **gegangen.**	_If I had known that, we would have gone to the movies._

   b. All modals follow this pattern in the past-time subjunctive:

   hätte . . . + verb infinitive + modal infinitive

Du **hättest** mir das **sagen sollen.**	_You should have told me that._
Wir **hätten** noch ins Kino **gehen können.**	_We still could have gone to the movies._

   For now, avoid using these forms in dependent clauses.

2. Uses

   The past-time subjunctive is used for the same purposes as the present-time subjunctive. Note that there are no polite requests in the past.

   a. Hypothetical statements and questions

Ich wäre zu Hause geblieben.	_I would have stayed home._
Was hättet ihr gemacht?	_What would you have done?_

   b. Wishes

Wenn ich das nur gewusst hätte!	_If only I had known that!_
Ich wünschte, du wärest da gewesen.	_I wish you had been there._

   c. Unreal conditions

Wenn du mich gefragt hättest, hätte ich es dir gesagt.	_If you had asked me, I would have told you._
Wenn du da gewesen wärest, hättest du alles gehört.	_If you had been there, you would have heard everything._

Übungen

M. Sagen Sie die Sätze in der Vergangenheit!

BEISPIEL   Sie würde das tun.
Sie hätte das getan.

1. Sie würde euch anrufen. 2. Ihr würdet ihr helfen. 3. Ihr würdet schnell kommen. 4. Du würdest alles für sie tun.

BEISPIEL   Hannes sollte nicht so viel Schokolade essen.
Hannes hätte nicht so viel Schokolade essen sollen.

5. Wir dürften ihm keine Schokolade geben. 6. Das sollten wir wissen.
7. Er könnte auch Obst essen. 8. Wir müssten besser aufpassen.

N. Was wäre gewesen, wenn . . . ?

1. **Wiederholen Sie die Sätze in der Vergangenheit!**

BEISPIEL   Wenn ich es wüsste, würde ich nicht fragen.
Wenn ich es gewusst hätte, hätte ich nicht gefragt.

a. Wenn wir eine Theatergruppe hätten, würde ich mitmachen.
b. Wenn der Computer billiger wäre, würden wir ihn kaufen.
c. Wenn ich Hunger hätte, würde ich mir etwas kochen.
d. Wenn sie mehr arbeitete, würde es ihr besser gehen.

2. **Und dann?** Was würden Sie tun oder hätten Sie getan? Wechseln Sie sich ab!

BEISPIEL   Ich hatte keinen Hunger. Wenn ich Hunger gehabt hätte, . . .
        S1 Ich hatte keinen Hunger. Wenn ich Hunger gehabt hätte,
            wäre ich in die Küche gegangen.
        S2 Und dann?
        S1 Dann hätte ich mir ein Wurstbrot gemacht.

a. Gestern hat es geregnet. Wenn das Wetter schön gewesen wäre, . . .
b. Ich bin nicht lange auf der Party geblieben. Wenn ich zu lange gefeiert hätte, . . .
c. Natürlich hatten wir letzte Woche Vorlesungen. Wenn wir keine Vorlesungen gehabt hätten, . . .

Studenten an der Universität in Erfurt

Optional English-to-German practice: 1. Too bad, we should have stayed at home. 2. If the weather had been better, we could have gone swimming in the lake. 3. But it rained all day. 4. I wish they hadn't invited us. 5. If we had stayed home, we could have watched / seen the detective story. 6. You *(sg. fam.)* should have gone out with her. 7. If I had had time, I would have called her. 8. If I have time, I'll call her tomorrow. 9. I had no time to call her yesterday. 10. I should have called the day before yesterday, but I forgot (it). (See answer key in the Appendix.)

1. **Imaginäre *(imaginary)* Großeltern** Hören Sie, was Ihnen Ihr Partner/Ihre Partnerin mit Hilfe der Information im Anhang über seinen/ihren imaginären Großvater vorliest *(reads to you)*! Schauen Sie dabei auf die Tabelle unten und machen Sie ein Kreuz *(check mark)* unter **Ja** oder **Nein,** je nachdem *(depending on)*, was der Großvater getan oder nicht getan hat. Wechseln Sie sich dann ab! Während Sie den unteren Text (S1) über Ihre imaginäre Großmutter vorlesen, macht Ihr Partner/Ihre Partnerin Kreuze in seine/ihre Tabelle im Anhang. Vergleichen Sie am Ende, ob die Tabellen stimmen!

Und was sagt Ihnen Ihr Partner/Ihre Partnerin?

	Ja	Nein
Der Opa ist aus Deutschland gekommen.	x	
Die Familie ist mit dem Schiff gefahren.		
Der Opa ist gern nach Amerika gekommen.		
Die Familie hat in New York gewohnt.		
Er ist Polizist geworden.		
Er konnte gut singen.		
Er hat gelernt, Klavier zu spielen.		
Er ist dieses Jahr nach Deutschland gefahren.		

 **Mathe = Mathematik**

S1: Meine Oma ist gern zur Schule gegangen. Sie war besonders gut in <u>Mathe</u>. Wenn ihre Familie Geld gehabt hätte, hätte sie gern studiert. Sie wäre furchtbar gern Lehrerin geworden. Aber sie musste als Kindermädchen *(nanny)* bei einer reichen Familie arbeiten. Dann hat sie meinen Großvater kennen ge-lernt und geheiratet. Meine Oma liebt Kinder und sie hätte gern eine große Familie gehabt. Sie hatten aber nur ein Kind. Sie ist immer gern gereist. Wenn mein Großvater länger gelebt hätte, hätten sie zusammen eine große Weltreise gemacht.

2. **Meine Großeltern** Erzählen Sie einander *(each other)* von Ihren wirklichen Großeltern!

Zusammenfassung

P. Indikativ oder Konjunktiv? Was bedeutet das auf Englisch?

1. Wenn er uns besuchte, brachte er immer Blumen mit.
2. Können Sie mir Dominiks Telefonnummer geben?
3. Wenn du früher ins Bett gegangen wärest, wärest du jetzt nicht so müde.
4. Gestern konnten sie nicht kommen, aber sie könnten uns morgen besuchen.
5. Er sollte gestern anrufen.
6. Ich möchte Architektur studieren.
7. Sie waren schon um 6 Uhr aufgestanden.

 Q. Guter Rat ist teuer *(hard to come by)*.

1. **Was soll ich tun?** Jemand in Ihrer Gruppe erwähnt *(mentions)* ein Problem, echt *(real)* oder nicht echt (zum Beispiel: er/sie hat kein Geld oder keine Energie / Hunger oder Durst / etwas verloren . . .), und die anderen geben Rat.

BEISPIEL   S1 Ich bin immer so müde.
                  S2 Wenn ich du wäre, würde ich früher ins Bett gehen.

2. **Was hätte ich tun sollen?** Geben Sie Rat, was man hätte (nicht) tun sollen!

BEISPIEL   S1 Ich habe meine Schlüssel verloren.
                  S2 Du hättest besser aufpassen sollen.

Studying in Germany

Studying in Germany is considerably different from studying in North America. Students enter the university with a broad general education, received during their years at the **Gymnasium**, and can therefore immediately focus on their major (**das Hauptfach**) with few courses required in unrelated fields.

All academic syllabi are divided into so-called basic and main studies (**das Grundstudium** and **das Hauptstudium**). Depending on the particular major, students have to attend a certain number of required classes, but they are still free to choose their own emphasis of studies by selecting from a variety of optional classes. Lecture courses (**Vorlesungen**) have little discussion and, at times, a written exam at the end of the term; seminars (**Seminare**) require research papers and class presentations leading to discussions, daily assignments, and a test (**die Klausur**) at the end. Students have to collect certificates (**Scheine**) for each attended course; today, the partial introduction of the international credit-point system at many institutions is changing that.

Ultimately, students are responsible for their own progress and for acquiring the necessary knowledge to pass the qualifying intermediate exam (**die Zwischenprüfung**) and eventually the comprehensive final exam (**die Abschlussprüfung**). The basic degree in the arts and humanities is equivalent to the

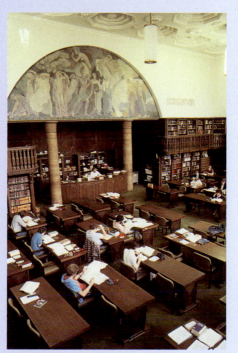

In der Universitätsbibliothek in Tübingen

American M.A. (**der Magister**); in the natural sciences and in engineering, students acquire an M.Sc. or M.Eng. degree (**das Diplom**). Some graduates choose to continue their studies to obtain a doctorate. Those who wish to become teachers, medical doctors, or lawyers must pass a comprehensive state exam (**das 1. Staatsexamen**) in their field, followed by a second exam (**das 2. Staatsexamen**) after an internship of several years.

The academic calendar is officially divided into a winter semester (from mid-October to mid-February) and a summer semester (from about mid-April to mid-July, varying somewhat from state to state). The vacation period (**die vorlesungsfreie Zeit**; literally: a period without classes)—two months in spring and three months in late summer—is intended to allow students to catch up on work, to take a job, or to go on vacation. German universities are academically self-governing and are headed by a president (**der Rektor**), elected for several years. Purely administrative matters are handled by a permanent staff of civil servants under the direction of a chancellor (**der Kanzler**).

Foreigners can study one or two semesters in Germany through one of the many partnerships with other universities abroad. In addition to this, there are more than 150 European study programs that stipulate that at least two semesters must be completed abroad (see www.studieren-in-deutschland.de).

R. Der Weg ist frei. Auf Deutsch bitte!

1. My friends told me that Germany has a new immigration law (**das Zuwanderungsgesetz**). 2. That would make Germany more interesting for foreign experts (**der ausländische Experte**). 3. Sibi is from India and just graduated from the University of Tübingen. 4. As a computer expert, he would not have to return to India. 5. He could stay here and work. 6. Thang is from Vietnam and an engineer. 7. He would like to apply for (**sich bewerben um**) a job at Siemens. 8. He thinks that would be great. 9. Irina Burlakov is becoming a doctor. 10. She is from Russia and speaks German very well. 11. Without the language, everything would have been much more difficult. 12. She also would not have found friends so quickly. 13. Irina will stay in Germany. 14. Sibi and Thang would like to stay for another year, maybe longer.

Visit the **Wie geht's?** iLrn website for more review and practice of the grammar points you have just learned.

Einblicke

Wortschatz 2

an deiner/seiner Stelle	*in your/his shoes; if I were you/he*
auf diese Weise	*(in) this way*
ausländisch	*foreign*
bestimmt	*surely, for sure; certain(ly)*
deshalb	*therefore*
jedenfalls	*in any case*
so dass	*so that*
sowieso	*anyhow*
wahrscheinlich	*probably*
Angst haben (vor + *dat.*)	*to fear, be afraid (of)*
an·nehmen (nimmt an), nahm an, angenommen	*to suppose; to accept*
auf·hören	*to end; to stop doing something*
teilen	*to share; also: to divide*

Lesetipp
Brainstorming Contextual Knowledge

You have learned quite a bit about the German university system in this chapter. With a partner, make a list of at least five ways in which the system in your country is different from the German system. With these differences in mind, you will be more prepared to read the text, which deals with this subject.

Vor dem Lesen

A. Allerlei Fragen

1. Würden Sie gern in Europa studieren? Wo, wann und wie lange?
2. Worauf würden Sie sich freuen?
3. Denken Sie, es würde mehr oder weniger kosten, drüben zu studieren?
4. Was würden Sie in den Ferien tun?
5. Hat Ihre Uni ein Austauschprogramm? Wenn ja, mit welcher Universität?
6. Haben Sie Freunde, die *(who)* drüben studiert haben? Wenn ja, wo; und wie hat es ihnen gefallen?

 B. Gehen wir Wörter angeln! Lesen Sie den folgenden Text mit Ihrem Partner/Ihrer Partnerin still durch! Welche Konjunktive finden Sie darin? Wie würde man das auf Englisch sagen?

C. Das ist leicht zu verstehen! Welche Silbe ist betont? Markieren Sie sie! Was ist das auf Englisch?

> der Grammatikkurs, Intensivkurs, Lesesaal; das Archiv, Auslandsprogramm; die Sprachprüfung; teilmöbliert

 ## Ein Jahr drüben wäre super!

CD 8, Track 9 (Gespräch an einer amerikanischen Universität)

	TINA	Hallo, Margaret!
	MARGARET	Tag, Tina! Kennst du Bernd? Er ist aus Heidelberg und studiert ein Jahr bei uns.
well	TINA	Guten Tag! Na°, wie gefällt's dir hier?
5	BERND	Sehr gut. Meine Vorlesungen und die Professoren sind ausgezeichnet. Ich wünschte nur, es gäbe nicht so viele Prüfungen!
	TINA	Habt ihr keine Prüfungen?
instead	BERND	Doch, aber weniger. Dafür° haben wir nach ungefähr vier Semestern eine große Zwischenprüfung und dann am Ende des Studiums
10		das Examen.

TINA	Ich würde gern einmal in Europa studieren.	
MARGARET	Ja, das solltest du unbedingt.	
TINA	Es ist bestimmt sehr teuer.	
MARGARET	Ach was, so teuer ist es gar nicht. Mein Jahr in München hat auch	
15	nicht mehr gekostet als ein Jahr hier.	
TINA	Wirklich?	
BERND	Ja, unsere Studentenwohnheime und die Mensa sind billiger als bei	
	euch und wir haben nur geringe° Studiengebühren°. Ohne mein	minimal / tuition
	Stipendium könnte ich nicht in Amerika studieren.	
20 TINA	Ist es schwer, dort drüben einen Studienplatz zu bekommen?	
BERND	Wenn du Deutsche wärest, wäre es wahrscheinlich nicht so	
	einfach—je nachdem°, was du studieren willst. Aber als Ausländerin	depending on
	in einem Auslandsprogramm hättest du gar kein Problem.	
TINA	Ich muss noch mal mit meinen Eltern sprechen. Sie haben Angst,	
25	dass ich ein Jahr verlieren würde.	
MARGARET	Wieso denn? Wenn du mit einem Auslandsprogramm nach	
	Deutschland gingest, würde das doch wie ein Jahr hier zählen.	
TINA	Ich weiß nicht, ob ich genug Deutsch kann.	
MARGARET	Keine Angst! Viele Studenten können weniger Deutsch als du.	
30	Du lernst es ja schon seit vier Jahren. Außerdem bieten die meisten	
	Programme vor Semesteranfang einen Intensivkurs für ausländische	
	Studenten an. Du kannst auch Kurse in „Deutsch als Fremdsprache"	
	belegen.	
TINA	Das geht? Vielleicht kann ich dann doch im Herbst ein Semester	
35	nach Deutschland.	
MARGARET	Im Herbst ginge ich nicht, weil das Wintersemester in Deutschland	
	erst Mitte Februar aufhört.	
TINA	Mitte Februar? Und wann ist das Frühjahrssemester°?	spring . . .
BERND	Bei uns gibt es ein Wintersemester und ein Sommersemester. Das	
40	Wintersemester geht von Mitte Oktober bis Mitte Februar, das Som-	
	mersemester von Mitte April bis Mitte Juli. Du müsstest deshalb	
	ein ganzes Jahr bleiben oder nur für das Sommersemester kommen.	
	Ein ganzes Jahr wäre sowieso besser, denn dann hättest du zwischen	
	den Semestern Zeit zu reisen.	
45 MARGARET	Stimmt. In der Zeit bin ich auch viel gereist. Ich war in Frankreich,	
	Spanien, Italien, Griechenland und danach noch in Ungarn.	
TINA	Super! Was für Vorlesungen sollte ich belegen?	
BERND	Im ersten Semester würde ich nur Vorlesungen belegen. Da hört	
	man nur zu und schreibt mit°. Im zweiten Semester solltest du dann	takes notes
50	aber auch ein Seminar belegen. Bis dann ist dein Deutsch jedenfalls	
	gut genug, so dass du auch eine längere Seminararbeit schreiben	
	oder ein Referat halten könntest.	
TINA	Seminararbeiten und Referate auf Deutsch?	
MARGARET	Am Anfang geht's langsam, aber man lernt's.	
55 BERND	Ich mach's ja auch auf Englisch.	
TINA	Und wie ist das mit Studentenwohnheimen?	
MARGARET	Wenn du an einem Auslandsprogramm teilnimmst, hast du keine	
	Probleme.	
BERND	An deiner Stelle würde ich versuchen, ein Zimmer im Studenten-	
60	wohnheim zu bekommen. Auf diese Weise könntest du leichter	
	andere Studenten kennen lernen. Die Zimmer sind nicht schlecht,	
	teilmöbliert und mit Bad. Die Küche auf einem Flur müsstest du	
	aber mit fünf oder sechs anderen Studenten teilen.	
TINA	Da habe ich nichts dagegen. Findet ihr, Heidelberg wäre besser als	
65	Berlin oder München?	

BERND	Ach, das ist schwer zu sagen.
MARGARET	Ich glaube, wenn ich Berlin gekannt hätte, hätte ich bestimmt dort studiert. Mir hat es da sehr gut gefallen. Aber erst musst du wissen, ob du wirklich nach Deutschland willst. Wenn du das weißt, dann kann ich dir weiterhelfen.
TINA	Danke! Macht's gut! Ich muss zur Vorlesung.

70

Heidelberg am Neckar mit Blick auf die Altstadt und das Schloss

Aktives zum Text

A. Ein Jahr im Ausland Was fehlt?

a. haben Angst b. Europa c. ein Jahr d. die Küche e. München f. Prüfungen
g. Sommersemester h. Intensivkurs i. andere Studenten j. Vorlesungen
k. Heidelberg l. Wintersemester

1. Bernd ist aus ____ und studiert ____ in Amerika.
2. Ihm gefallen nur die vielen ____ nicht.
3. Tina möchte gern in ____ studieren.
4. Margarets Jahr in ____ hat nicht viel mehr gekostet als ein Jahr zu Hause.
5. Tinas Eltern ____, dass ihre Tochter drüben ein Jahr verliert.
6. Ausländische Studenten können vor Semesteranfang an einem ____ teilnehmen.
7. Das ____ geht von Mitte Oktober bis Mitte Februar, das ____ von Mitte April bis Mitte Juli.
8. Im ersten Semester sollte Tina nur ____ belegen.
9. In einem Studentenwohnheim kann man leichter ____ kennen lernen.
10. In einem deutschen Studentenwohnheim muss man ____ mit anderen Studenten teilen.

 B. Das Studium hier und dort Vergleichen Sie als Gruppe die beiden Systeme! Machen Sie Listen!

1. Prüfungen 2. Studiengebühren 3. Semesterkalender 4. Kurse
5. Bibliotheken

C. An der Uni Was fehlt?

1. Bernd _____, es _____ nicht so viele Prüfungen. *(wished, [there] were)*

2. Wenn Bernd kein Stipendium _____ , _____ er hier nicht _____. *(had gotten, could have studied)*

3. Wenn Tina mit einem Austauschprogramm nach Deutschland _____, _____ das wie ein Jahr hier _____. *(would go, would count)*

4. Tina _____ ein ganzes Jahr _____, oder sie _____ nur für das Sommersemester _____. *(would have to stay, could go)*

5. Ein ganzes Jahr drüben _____ besser. *(would be)*

6. Dann _____ Tina Zeit, zwischen den Semestern zu reisen. *(would have)*

7. In einem Studentenwohnheim _____ Tina leichter deutsche Studenten _____. *(would get to know)*

8. Wenn Margaret Berlin _____, _____ sie dort _____. *(had known, would have studied)*

9. Wenn sie nicht an einer deutschen Uni _____, _____ sie nicht so gut Deutsch _____. *(had studied, could speak)*

10. Tina _____, dass ihr Deutsch nicht gut genug _____. Aber das _____ kein Problem _____. *(is afraid, would be, shouldn't be)*

D. Das Vorlesungsverzeichnis Lesen Sie das Verzeichnis und beenden Sie die Sätze mit Ihrem Partner/Ihrer Parnerin!

1. In allen Vorlesungen geht es um *(it's about)* . . .
2. Mich würde besonders die Vorlesung über . . . interessieren. Sie wäre . . . von . . . bis . . .
3. Außerdem dürfte die Vorlesung von Professor . . . über . . . interessant sein.
4. . . . würde mich nicht / weniger interessieren, weil . . .

Geschichte der Stadt Rom in der Zeit der römischen Republik 3st., Mo 11 - 13, Mi 12 - 13	Lippold
Die sozialen und wirtschaftlichen Verhältnisse in der griechischen Welt von der Archaischen Zeit bis zum Beginn des Hellenismus 2st., Mo 14 - 15.30	Hennig
Kirche und Gesellschaft im früheren Mittelalter (5.-12. Jahrhundert) 3st., Do 12-13, Fr 11 - 13	Hartmann
Deutschland und Frankreich im 15. und 16. Jahrhundert. Der Beginn eines europäischen Gegensatzes 2st., Di, Mi 9 - 10	Schmid
Politik und Geschichte in Deutschland nach 1945 2st., Do 13 - 15	Haan
Demokratie oder Volksherrschaft? Zur Geschichte der Demokratie seit dem späten 18. Jahrhundert II 2st., Do 16 - 18	Lottes
Deutschland in der Industrialisierung 2st., Di 10 - 11, Mi 11 - 12	Bauer
Bayerische Geschichte zwischen 1800 und 1866 2st., Mi, Do 11 - 12	Volkert
Wirtschaft und Gesellschaft Bayerns im Industriezeitalter 2st., Mo, Di 11 - 12	Götschmann
Das Ostjudentum (19./20. Jahrhundert) 2st., Mi, Fr 8 - 9	Völkl
Europa zwischen den Weltkriegen (1919-1939) 2st., Mo 10 -12	Möller

E. Am liebsten würde ich . . . Beenden Sie die Sätze und vergleichen Sie sie dann mit den Sätzen der anderen!

1. Wenn ich könnte, würde ich einmal in . . . studieren.
2. Am liebsten würde ich in . . . wohnen, weil . . .
3. Am Anfang des Semesters . . .
4. Am Ende des Semesters
5. Während der Semesterferien . . .
6. Wenn ich in Deutschland arbeiten könnte, würde ich bei . . . arbeiten.
7. Ein Praktikum bei . . . wäre auch interessant.
8. Man könnte ja mal an . . . schreiben.

 F. Ein Kurzgespräch mit Margaret Bereiten Sie mit Ihrem Partner/Ihrer Partnerin den folgenden Dialog vor und präsentieren Sie ihn danach vor der Klasse!

You call Margaret, who has been to Germany. You introduce yourself and inquire whether you might ask her some questions. She says to go ahead, and you ask whether you should study in Germany. She replies that she would do so if she were you. You ask her for how long you should go. She suggests that you go for a year. You would learn more German and see more of Europe. You ask whether you could have lunch together the next day. She says she would prefer it if you could have dinner. You agree and say good-bye.

 G. Das wäre schön! Schreiben Sie sechs bis acht Sätze über eines der folgenden Themen! Benutzen Sie dabei mindestens *(at least)* fünf Konjunktivformen!

1. Ein Jahr drüben wäre super!
2. Mein Traumhaus
3. Meine Traumfamilie
4. Das würde mir gefallen.
5. Das hätte mir gefallen.
6. Das wäre schrecklich!

Schreibtipp
Applying for a Job

When applying for a job, introduce yourself briefly, state why that position is of interest to you, and state why your particular background should be of interest to the employer. Note that here the use of the subjunctive comes in handy and adds politeness to your letter. Even though your letter should be typed, be sure to sign it by hand. Note that in Germany it is customary, even expected, that you include a photo with your job application. (See application on p. 363.)

Ein Student aus Nigerien im Gespräch mit einem deutschen Studenten in der Cafeteria der Humboldt-Universität

H. Bewerbung *(application)*: Meine Antwort

Lesen Sie die folgende Anzeige und Bewerbung und schreiben Sie dann Ihre eigene Bewerbung! Vergleichen Sie sie mit der *(one of)* der anderen!

TRAUMSCHIFF VERDI sucht: Reiselustige Studenten

Alter:	18–30
Sprachen:	Deutch und Englisch oder Spanisch
Sport:	Segeln, Tennis oder Volleyball
Unterhaltung:	Musik, Tanzen
Service:	Restaurant, Boutique, Rezeption

Bewerbung mit Foto an: Traumreisen GmbH
Leopoldstraße 65 • D-81925 München 81
Tel.: (089) 348 55 52 • E-Mail: traumreisen@verdi-web.de

Ben Bode
Mainstraße 26
64625 Bensheim
Tel.: 06251/692 22

Bensheim, den 11. 4. 2006

An die Traumreisen GmbH
Leopoldstraße 65
D-81925 München 81

Betr.: Bewerbung für das Traumschiff Verdi

Sehr geehrte Damen und Herren,

mein Name ist Ben Bode. Ich bin 23 und Student an der Universität Tübingen. Ich studiere Psychologie und würde gern einmal etwas ganz anderes tun. Die Arbeit an der Rezeption Ihres Schiffes würde mich sehr interessieren. In meiner Schulzeit war ich ein Jahr in Amerika und spreche fließend Englisch. Auch Spanisch verstehe ich sehr gut. Über eine Antwort wäre ich Ihnen sehr dankbar.

Mit freundlichem Gruß,

Ben Bode

Hörverständnis

Track 34 Zwei Briefe Hören Sie zu, an wen Dagmar Schröder und Joe Jackson einen Brief schreiben und warum! Sind die folgenden Aussagen richtig oder falsch?

Zum Erkennen: das Stellenangebot *(job opening)*; erfüllen *(to fulfill)*; der ADAC *(AAA)*; beigelegt *(enclosed)*; sich vorstellen *(to introduce or present oneself)*; absolvieren *(to complete)*; vermitteln *(to help find)*

_____ 1. a. Dagmar Schröder hat Touristik studiert.
_____   b. Sie würde gern als Reiseleiterin arbeiten.
_____   c. Sie spricht gut Italienisch.
_____   d. Das Reisebüro hätte aber gern jemanden mit Russischkenntnissen.
_____   e. Frau Schröder hofft, dass ihre Auslandsaufenthalte für sie sprechen.
_____   f. Dem Brief ist ein Lebenslauf beigelegt.
_____ 2. a. Joe Jackson studiert Betriebswirtschaft in Seattle, Washington.
_____   b. Er würde gern ein Praktikum in Österreich absolvieren.
_____   c. Davor würde er aber gern noch etwas mehr Geschäftsdeutsch lernen.
_____   d. Er würde sich freuen, wenn ihm die Carl-Duisburg-Gesellschaft in Köln Informationen und Formulare dazu schicken könnte.

Some universities; a visit to the Goethe Institute in Dresden: http://wiegehts.heinle.com.

Literatur

Biographisches

Christine Nöstlinger (born in Vienna in 1936) is one of Austria's most eminent authors writing for children and young adults. Since her first success in 1970 *(Die feuerrote Friederike)*, she has written more than a hundred books and won numerous prizes. Highly individualistic, humorous, and witty in style, her stories give a realistic description of social backgrounds, often siding with the weak (e.g., *Das Austauschkind*) and criticizing traditional patterns of society. Her humane views are reflected in books dealing with Austria's recent past (e.g., *Rosa Riedl Schutzgespenst,*

Der geheime Großvater). In addition to writing children's literature, she also writes stories and verse for adults in Viennese dialect, contributes to a variety of magazines and newspapers, and works for Austrian broadcasting. In 1996, Nöstlinger joined *SOS Mitmensch,* a social organization concentrating on the integration of refugees and foreigners and fighting xenophobia. "Ohne Vorurteile" is taken from her best-seller *Mein Tagebuch* (1989), a collection of short sketches dealing with contemporary family life in a changing society.

Vor dem Lesen

Allgemeine Fragen

1. Was verstehen Sie unter Vorurteilen *(prejudices)*?
2. Wo gibt es sie und warum?
3. Welche Vorurteile gibt es gegen Frauen in der Berufswelt?
4. Gibt es auch Vorurteile gegen Männer? Wenn ja, welche?
5. Wie sieht der typische Alltag *(everyday life)* einer Frau mit Familie aus? Stellen Sie eine Liste auf!
6. Wie war das bei Ihnen zu Hause? Wer hat was im Haushalt getan? Haben Sie auch geholfen?
7. Was würden Sie anders tun, wenn Sie Kinder hätten?

Ohne Vorurteile

Track 35

Der Chef von Frau M. ist ein Mann, der° keine Vorurteile kennt. Und schon gar keine gegen Frauen! Frauen, sagt er immer, seien° genauso tüchtig° und strebsam° im Beruf wie Männer. Im Grunde genommen°, sagt er, hätte er nichts dagegen, alle „höheren" Posten° in seiner Firma mit Frauen zu besetzen°.

5 Darum war er auch schon vor zwanzig Jahren ehrlich bekümmert°, als er der damals noch sehr jungen Frau M. „den besseren" Posten nicht geben konnte und ihr einen sehr jungen Mann vorziehen musste.

„Schauen Sie", erklärte er damals der Frau M., „Sie sind jung verheiratet. Sie werden sicher demnächst° ein Kind bekommen. Dann fallen Sie für ein Jahr aus°.
10 Aber auf diesem Posten brauche ich eine Person, mit der ich rechnen kann°. So eine verantwortungsvolle Stellung kann ich nicht ein Karenzjahr lang° mit einer Aushilfskraft° besetzen!"

Frau M. sah das ein°, wurde—ganz wie der Chef vorausgesehen° hatte—schwanger°, bekam Zwillinge°, war ein Jahr daheim° und arbeitete dann bei
15 ihrem lieben Chef brav° weiter. Die Zwillinge versorgte° die Oma. Als nach

Glosses (left margin):
- who
- are / capable
- ambitious / basically
- positions / fill
- sad
- before long / are gone
- that I can count on
- for a year's leave
- temporary help
- understood / foreseen
- pregnant / twins / at home
- quietly / babysat

etlichen° Jahren wieder ein „besserer" Posten frei wurde, bewarb sich Frau M. *many*
wieder, denn mit den Zwillingen war ihr Bedarf an Nachwuchs gedeckt° und sie *she had enough kids*
konnte ihrem Chef versichern°, dass kein Karenzjahr mehr drohte°. Aber der *assure / would be coming*
arme Chef konnte ihr den Posten wieder nicht geben.

20   „Schauen Sie", erklärte er ihr, „diese Stellung bedarf ganzen Einsatzes°! Eine *requires total commitment*
Mutter, das weiß man, hat keine Freude mit Überstunden°. Und wenn die Kinder *overtime*
krank werden, gibt es auch immer Zores°. Ja, ja, die Oma hütet° die Kinder! Aber *trouble / takes care of*
seien Sie doch ehrlich, eine Mutter ist mit ihrem halben Hirn° immer daheim *half a brain*
bei den Kindern und nicht im Büro!"

25   Also arbeitete Frau M. weiter in ihrer alten Position. In achtzehn Jahren
nahm sie insgesamt° vier Tage Pflegeurlaub°. Ob sie „mit halbem Hirn" nicht im *altogether / child-care leave*
Büro war, lässt sich schwer entscheiden°, jedenfalls war ihre Arbeitsleistung° *is hard to tell / . . . performance*
nicht geringer° als die° ihrer männlichen Kollegen. *less / that*
    Nun sind Frau M.s Zwillinge erwachsen° und in Frau M.s Firma ist wieder *grown-up*
30 einmal ein „höherer" Posten zu besetzen. Den musste ihr der Chef—leider,
leider—wieder verweigern°. *refuse*
    Gewiss°, nun muss Frau M. auch nicht mehr mit dem „halben Hirn" bei den *for sure*
Kindern sein, auch Überstunden würden sie nicht mehr stören°, aber nun erklärt *bother*
ihr der Chef: „Ja doch! Eine Frau wäre mir sehr willkommen° für diesen Posten. *I'd welcome*
35 Eine vitale°, dynamische Person. Aber in Ihrem Alter, liebe Frau M., schafft man *energetic*
das doch nicht° mehr!" *can't do*

Christine Nöstlinger

Nach dem Lesen

A. Allerlei Fragen

1. Wie ist Frau M.? Beschreiben Sie sie bei der Arbeit!
2. Was hätte sie gern gehabt?
3. Warum bekam sie die bessere Stelle nicht, als sie das erste Mal frei wurde?
   Was sagte Frau M. dazu?
4. Welche Personen spielen heutzutage *(nowadays)* bei Familien mit Kindern
   eine große Rolle? Wie helfen sie zum Beispiel?
5. Welche Ausrede *(excuse)* hatte der Chef das zweite Mal, als eine bessere
   Stelle frei wurde? Warum ist das unfair?
6. Welche Ausrede hatte der Chef das dritte Mal? Wie reagierte Frau M. darauf?
7. Was wäre Ihre Reaktion gewesen?
8. Finden Sie, dass Frau M.s Erfahrung typisch ist für viele Frauen in der Berufswelt? Wenn ja, können Sie andere Beispiele nennen?
9. Glauben Sie, dass das eines Tages besser wird? Warum (nicht)?

 B. Nacherzählung: Noch einmal bitte! Erzählen Sie den anderen die Geschichte
noch einmal mit eigenen Worten!

Berlin: Damals und heute

Lernziele

In this chapter you will learn about:

Zum Thema

Life in Berlin

Kultur-Fokus

German history since WW II, history of Berlin, multiculturalism
Wolfgang Borchert

Struktur

Relative clauses
Indirect speech

Einblicke + Literatur

Berlin, ein Tor zur Welt
Wolfgang Borchert: "Das Brot"

Berlins Brandenburger Tor mit Feuerwerk zur Jahrtausendwende (turn of the millennium) im Jahr 1999

Vorschau

Chronicle of German History since World War II

Minidrama: *Eine Stadt mit vielen Gesichtern*
Blickpunkt: *Mein Berlin*

1945   Unconditional surrender of Germany (May 9) marks the end of World War II on the European front. The Allies assume supreme power, dividing Germany into four zones and Berlin (in the middle of the Russian zone) into four sectors. Potsdam Conference determines Germany's new borders.

1947   American Marshall Plan provides comprehensive aid for the rebuilding of Europe, including West Germany. Plan is rejected by the Soviet Union and its Eastern European satellites.

1948   Introduction of the D-Mark *(Deutsche Mark)* in the Western Zone leads to the Soviet blockade of West Berlin. Allies respond with Berlin Airlift (June 1948–May 1949).

1949   Founding of the Federal Republic of Germany in the West (May 23) and the German Democratic Republic (October 7) in the East.

1952   East Germany begins to seal the border with West Germany (May 27).

1953   Workers' uprising in East Berlin (June 17) is crushed by Soviet tanks.

1954   West Germany becomes a NATO member.

1955   East Germany joins the Warsaw Pact. West Germany becomes a sovereign nation; the occupation ends.

1961   East Germany constructs the Berlin Wall and extensive fortifications along the border with West Germany to prevent East Germans from fleeing to the West.

1970   As an important step in his new *Ostpolitik*, West German Chancellor Willy Brandt meets with East German Premier Willi Stoph in Erfurt, East Germany.

1971   Four-Power Agreement on Berlin guarantees unhindered traffic between West Berlin and West Germany. De facto recognition of East Germany.

1973   Bundestag approves treaty of mutual recognition with East Germany. Brandt's opponents accuse him of forsaking the goal of unification.

1989   Opening of Hungarian border to Austria (September 10) brings streams of refugees from East to West Germany. Protest rallies take place all across East Germany. Berlin Wall opens on November 9.

1990   Economic union of both German states (July 2) is followed by German reunification (October 3). First all-German elections are held (December 2).

1994   Last Allied troops withdraw from Berlin.

1999   Reopening of the renovated Reichstag building.

2000   Relocation of the federal government to Berlin complete.

2002   After 54 years, Germans say good-bye to the *Deutsche Mark* with the introduction of the euro.

2005   Introduction of a new immigration law speeding up the procedures for asylum seekers, simplifying the granting of residence permits, and opening the employment market to highly skilled foreigners and foreign graduates of German universities.

2005   Angela Merkel succeeds Gerhard Schröder as first woman chancellor of Germany.

Zum Thema

CD 9,
Track 1

In Berlin ist immer etwas los.

(Heike zeigt Martin Berlin.)

HEIKE	Und das hier ist die Gedächtniskirche mit ihren drei Gebäuden. Wir nennen sie den „Hohlen Zahn", den „Lippenstift" und die „Puderdose".
MARTIN	Berliner haben doch für alles einen Spitznamen.
HEIKE	Der alte Turm der Gedächtniskirche soll als Mahnmal so bleiben, wie er ist; die neue Gedächtniskirche mit dem neuen Turm ist aber modern—wie so manches in Berlin: jede Menge Altes und jede Menge Neues.
MARTIN	Sag mal, wohnst du gern hier in Berlin?
HEIKE	Na klar! Berlin ist unheimlich lebendig und hat so viel zu bieten, nicht nur historisch, sondern auch kulturell. Hier ist immer was los. Außerdem ist die Umgebung wunderschön.
MARTIN	Ich hab' irgendwo gelesen, dass 24 Prozent der Stadtfläche Wälder und Seen sind, mit 800 Kilometern Fahrradwegen.
HEIKE	Ist doch toll, oder?
MARTIN	Wahnsinn! Sag mal, warst du dabei, als sie die Mauer durchbrochen haben?
HEIKE	Und ob! Meine Eltern und ich, wir haben die ganze Nacht gewartet, obwohl es ganz schön kalt war. Als das erste Stück Mauer kippte, haben wir alle laut gesungen: „So ein Tag, so wunderschön wie heute, so ein Tag, der dürfte nie vergeh'n."
MARTIN	Ja, das war schon einmalig. Und jetzt ist das alles schon wieder so lange her.
HEIKE	Seitdem hat sich in Berlin enorm viel verändert. Die Spuren der Mauer sind fast verschwunden.
MARTIN	Wer hätte das je gedacht!
HEIKE	Hier gibt's heute wirklich alles, ein buntes Gemisch an Leuten und Sprachen.
MARTIN	Bist du froh, dass Berlin wieder Hauptstadt ist?
HEIKE	Nun, ich könnte mir's gar nicht mehr anders vorstellen.
MARTIN	Du, hättest du Lust, heute Abend etwas durch die Stadt zu bummeln?
HEIKE	Okay, was würde dich interessieren?
MARTIN	Eigentlich alles, vielleicht auch ein Klub oder eine Kneipe.
HEIKE	Gehen wir doch zum Prenzlauer Berg! Das dürfte interessant sein.

A. Richtig oder falsch?

____ 1. Martin ist Berliner.

____ 2. Der „Hohle Zahn" ist ein Teil der Gedächtniskirche.

____ 3. Er soll die Berliner an den Zahnarzt erinnern.

____ 4. Martin hat verschiedene Spitznamen für die Berliner.

____ 5. Heike gefällt's unheimlich gut in Berlin.

____ 6. Heike war dabei, als sie die Mauer durchbrochen haben.

____ 7. Martin hat dort auch mitgefeiert.

____ 8. Das Ganze geschah an einem schönen, warmen Nachmittag.

____ 9. Als das erste Stück Mauer kippte, haben die Leute die Polizei gerufen.

____ 10. Manche haben laut gesungen.

____ 11. Seitdem hat sich in Berlin nicht viel verändert.

____ 12. Berlin ist heute international und dort gibt es ein buntes Gemisch an Menschen.

B. Jetzt sind Sie dran! Was würden Sie einem ausländischen Besucher (Ihrem Partner/Ihrer Partnerin) sagen, dem *(to whom)* Sie Ihre eigene Stadt zeigen? Machen Sie es so interessant wie möglich!

S1 Und das ist . . .
S2 . . .
S1 Ja, wir finden das auch . . .
S2 Wie ist das Leben . . . ?
S1 . . .
S2 Ist hier kulturell viel los?
S1 . . .
S2 Die Umgebung ist . . .
S1 Wie findest du/finden Sie . . . ?
S2 . . .

Wortschatz 1

● These stamps are no longer valid as they are denominated in **Deutsche Mark,** but they are of interest historically.

Damals und heute *(then and today)*

der Frieden	peace	die Grenze,-n	border
Krieg, -e	war	Mauer, -n	wall
Spitzname, -ns, -n	nickname	Umgebung	surrounding(s)
Turm, ̈e	tower		
das Gebäude, -	building		
Volk, ̈er	people (as a whole or nation)		

● Note the difference between **Wand** and **Mauer:** A Wand is usually thinner and part of the inside of a house. A **Mauer** is much thicker—like an outside wall of a fortress—and usually freestanding.

Weiteres

einmalig	unique, incredible
historisch	historical(ly)
wunderschön	very beautiful
berichten	to report
erinnern (an + *acc.*)	to remind (of)
sich erinnern (an + *acc.*)	to remember
führen	to lead
(sich) verändern	to change
verschwinden, verschwand, ist verschwunden	to disappear
vorbei·führen (an + *dat.*)	to pass by, guide along
irgendwo	somewhere
jede Menge (+ *nom.*)	all sorts of
kaum	hardly, barely, scarcely
oder?	isn't it? don't you think so?
Und ob!	You bet! / You better believe it!
seitdem	since then

● **(sich) erinnern:** Ich werde dich **an** die Karten **erinnern.** *(I'll remind you of the tickets.)* BUT: Ich kann **mich an** nichts **erinnern.** *(I can't remember anything.)*

● Like **irgendwo: irgendwann, irgendwie, irgendwer,** etc.

Zum Erkennen: hohl *(hollow);* der Lippenstift, -e *(lipstick);* die Puderdose, -n *(compact);* als Mahnmal *(as a memorial of admonishment);* lebendig *(lively);* bieten *(to offer);* die Stadtfläche *(. . . area);* durchbrochen *(broken through);* (um)kippen *(to tip over);* vergehen *(to pass);* das ist schon lange her *(that's a long time ago);* die Spur, -en *(trace, track);* je *(ever);* ein buntes Gemisch an (+ *dat.*) *(a diverse [lit. colorful] mixture of);* AUCH: das Relativpronomen, - *(relative pronoun);* der Relativsatz, ̈e *(relative clause);* das vorhergehende Wort, ̈er *(antecedent);* die indirekte Rede *(indirect speech);* bestätigen *(to confirm);* definieren; unterstreichen *(to underline)*

Berliners are known for their self-assured manner, their humor, and their "big mouth" (**die Berliner Schnauze**). They always manage to find the right words at the right time, especially when it comes to choosing amusing names for places around their city. Besides the nicknames for parts of the Memorial Church (**Hohler Zahn, Lippenstift,** and **Puderdose**), places already mentioned in the dialogue, Berliners talk about the **Schwangere Auster** (*pregnant oyster*), a cultural center; the **Hungerkralle** (*hunger claw*), the monument to the Berlin Airlift; the **Telespargel** (*television-asparagus*), the television tower; the old **Palazzo Prozzo** (*Braggarts' Palace*) or **Honeckers Lampenladen** (*[East German leader Erich] Honecker's lamp store*), the former parliament building of East Germany; the **Mauerspechte** (*wall woodpeckers*), the souvenir hunters who chipped away at the Berlin Wall after it was opened; and for the new chancellor's office, the **Waschmaschine** (*washing machine*), a reference to its architectural style.

Die Gedächtniskirche bei Nacht

Aktives zum Thema

A. Wie geht's weiter? Lesen Sie die Satzfragmente und bilden Sie damit Ihre eigenen Sätze! Benutzen Sie Ihre Fantasie!

> BEISPIEL   . . . sieht gut aus.
> *Mein Auto sieht gut aus.*

1. . . . sieht aus wie ein(e) . . .
2. . . . hat viel zu bieten.
3. Ich erinnere mich gern an . . .
4. . . . war immer etwas los.
5. . . . gibt es eine Menge . . .
6. Ich kann mich noch gut an die Zeit erinnern, als . . .
7. Bitte erinnere mich nicht an . . . !
8. . . . hat sich . . . verändert.
9. Seitdem . . .

B. Stadtplan von Berlin Sehen Sie auf den Stadtplan und beenden Sie dann die Sätze mit einem Wort aus der Liste!

a. Brandenburger
b. Dom
c. Fernsehturm
d. Gedächtniskirche
e. Juni
f. Kulturen der Welt
g. Philharmonie
h. Reichstagsgebäude
i. Spree
j. Stadtplan
k. Unter den Linden
l. Zoo(logische Garten)

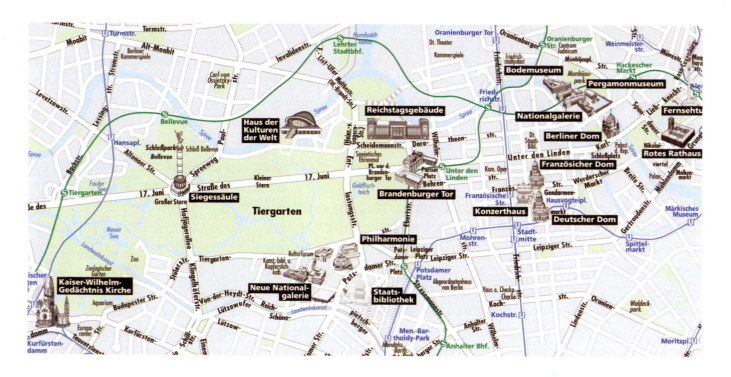

1. Dieser _____ von Berlin zeigt Ihnen, wo die verschiedenen Straßen und wichtigsten Gebäude sind. 2. Im Südwesten ist der Kurfürstendamm oder Ku'damm. Er führt zur _____ 3. In der Nähe ist auch der _____. 4. Quer durch den großen Park läuft eine lange Straße. Sie erinnert an den 17. _____ 1953, als die Ostberliner und die Deutschen in Ostdeutschland gegen die Sowjetunion rebellierten. 5. Sie führt vorbei am Großen Stern mit der Siegessäule (Victory Column) und weiter bis zum _____ Tor (gate). 6. Die Straße hat verschiedene Namen. Östlich vom Brandenburger Tor heißt sie _____. 7. Südlich vom Brandenburger Tor ist der Potsdamer Platz und an der Potsdamer Straße die Staatsbibliothek und die _____. 8. Ganz in der Nähe vom Brandenburger Tor ist auch das für den Bundestag (federal parliament) renovierte _____ mit der neuen Glaskuppel, die (which) nachts den Himmel von Berlin erhellt (brightens up). 9. Nicht weit davon ist das Haus der _____, die frühere Kongresshalle mit dem Spitznamen „Schwangere Auster". 10. Unter den Linden führt ins alte Zentrum von Berlin und auf eine Insel mit dem Pergamonmuseum und dem Berliner _____. 11. Auf beiden Seiten der Insel fließt (flows) die _____. 12. Beim Dom bekommt die Straße wieder einen neuen Namen und geht weiter bis zum Alexanderplatz mit dem modernen _____, dem „Telespargel".

 ## Aussprache: qu, pf, ps

CD 9, Track 2 **Laute**

1. [kv] **Qu**atsch, **Qu**alität, **Qu**antität, **Qu**artal, be**qu**em
2. [pf] **Pf**arrer, **Pf**effer, **Pf**lanze, **Pf**und, A**pf**el, Ko**pf**, em**pf**ehlen
3. [ps] **Ps**ychologe, **Ps**ychologie, **ps**ychologisch, **Ps**alm, **Ps**eudonym, Ka**ps**el

● For further review, see the Summary of Pronunciation in the front of your *Arbeitsbuch*. Study Part III, subsections 19, 21–22.

Track 36 **Mit dem Fahrrad durch Berlin** Hören Sie zu, wie man Berlin auch kennen lernen kann! Was fehlt in den folgenden Aussagen?

Zum Erkennen: der Doppeldeckerbus, -se *(double-decker bus)*; in Ruhe *(quietly, without being rushed)*; der Stadtbummel *(stroll through the city)*; völlig *(totally)*; radeln (ist) *(to bike)*; der Zauber *(magic)*

<table>
<tr><td>

Afternoon-Clubtour

Berliner DJ's tauschen die Plattenteller gegen das Zweirad und präsentieren die Clubkultur der Hauptstadt. Die Route führt an knapp 20 Tanztempeln vorbei. Auf einem Partyschiff ist Zeit für einen Drink.

Mi 18 Uhr, Sa 15 Uhr

</td><td>

Nightseeing - Tour

Wenn es Nacht wird, hat Berlin eine ganz besondere Atmosphäre. Wir gleiten vorbei an illuminierten Gebäuden, stillen Gewässern und quirligen Szenetreffpunkten und erleben den Zauber einer Stadt, die nie schläft.

Fr und Sa 20 Uhr

</td></tr>
</table>

1. Der Sprecher erzählt von Möglichkeiten, Berlin _____. 2. Man könnte zum Beispiel eine _____ mit dem Tourbus machen. 3. Von oben im Doppeldeckerbus hätte man einen guten _____. 4. Eine ganz andere Perspektive gäbe eine kleine Fahrt mit dem _____. 5. Dem Erzähler würde aber der Stadtbummel _____ und mit der U-Bahn besser gefallen. 6. Da wäre man wenigstens _____. 7. Was ihm das letzte Mal besonders gut gefallen hat, war eine Stadttour mit dem _____. 8. Die Gruppe wäre ungefähr _____ Stunden unterwegs *(on the go)* gewesen. 9. Das nächste Mal hätte er Lust, an einer Afternoon-_____ teilzunehmen. 10. Auch eine Nightseeing-Tour fände er interessant, denn nachts hätte Berlin eine ganz andere _____.

Berlin mit dem Fahrrad zu erleben macht Spaß.

Struktur

14.1 Relative clauses

RELATIVE CLAUSES supply additional information about a noun in a sentence.

> There's the professor **who** teaches the course.
> He taught the course **(that)** I enjoyed so much.
> He teaches a subject **in which** I'm very interested (. . . **which/that** I'm very interested **in**).
> He's the professor **whose** course I took last semester.

English relative clauses may be introduced by the RELATIVE PRONOUNS *who, whom, whose, which,* or *that.* The noun to which the relative pronoun "relates" is called the ANTECEDENT. The choice of the relative pronoun depends on the antecedent (is it a person or a thing?) <u>and</u> on its function in the relative clause. The relative pronoun may be the subject *(who, which, that),* an object, or an object of a preposition *(whom, which, that),* or it may indicate possession *(whose).* German relative clauses work essentially the same way. However, whereas in English the relative pronouns are frequently omitted (especially in conversation), <u>in German they must always be used.</u>

> Ist das der Roman, **den** ihr gelesen habt?   *Is that the novel you read?*

1. Forms and use

The German relative pronouns have the same forms as the definite article, except for the genitive forms and the dative plural.

	masc.	neut.	fem.	pl.
nom.	der	das	die	die
acc.	den	das	die	die
dat.	dem	dem	der	denen
gen.	dessen	dessen	deren	deren

The form of the relative pronoun is determined by two factors:

- Its ANTECEDENT: is the antecedent masculine, neuter, feminine, or in the plural?

> Das ist **der Fluss, der** auf der Karte ist.
> Das ist **das Gebäude, das** auf der Karte ist.
> Das ist **die Kirche, die** auf der Karte ist.
> Das sind **die Plätze, die** auf der Karte sind.

- Its FUNCTION in the relative clause: is the relative pronoun the subject, an accusative or dative object, an object of a preposition, or does it indicate possession?

> Ist das der Mann, **der** in Berlin wohnt?   = SUBJECT
> Ist das der Mann, **den** du meinst?   = ACCUSATIVE OBJECT
> Ist das der Mann, **dem** du geschrieben hast?   = DATIVE OBJECT
> Ist das der Mann, **mit dem** du gesprochen hast? = OBJECT OF A PREPOSITION
> Ist das der Mann, **dessen** Tochter hier studiert? = GENITIVE

The following examples indicate the antecedent and state the function of the relative pronoun (RP) in each relative clause.

> . . . ANTECEDENT, (preposition +) RP _____ V1.

Das ist der Professor. Er lehrt an meiner Universität.
Das ist der Professor, der an meiner Universität lehrt.
*That's **the professor who** teaches at my university.*

ANTECEDENT: der Professor = sg. / masc.
PRONOUN FUNCTION: subject → nom.

Wie heißt der Kurs? Du findest ihn so interessant.
Wie heißt **der Kurs, den** du so interessant findest?
*What's the name of **the course (that)** you find so interesting?*

ANTECEDENT: der Kurs = sg. / masc.
PRONOUN FUNCTION: object of **finden** → acc.

Da ist der Student. Ich habe ihm mein Buch gegeben.
Da ist **der Student, dem** ich mein Buch gegeben habe.
*There's **the student to whom** I gave my book (. . . I gave my book to).*

ANTECEDENT: der Student = sg. / masc.
PRONOUN FUNCTION: object of **geben** → dat.

Kennst du die Professorin? Erik hat ihr Seminar belegt.
Kennst du **die Professorin, deren Seminar** Erik belegt hat?
*Do you know **the professor whose seminar** Erik took?*

ANTECEDENT: die Professorin = sg. / fem.
PRONOUN FUNCTION: related possessively to **Seminar** → gen.

Das Buch ist von einem Autor. Ich interessiere mich sehr für ihn.
Das Buch ist von **einem Autor, für den** ich mich sehr interessiere.
*The book is by **an author in whom** I'm very interested.*

ANTECEDENT: der Autor = sg. / masc.
PRONOUN FUNCTION: object of **für** → acc.

Die Autoren sind aus Leipzig. Der Professor hat von ihnen gesprochen.
Die Autoren, von denen der Professor gesprochen hat, sind aus Leipzig.
***The authors of whom** the professor spoke are from Leipzig.*

ANTECEDENT: die Autoren = pl.
PRONOUN FUNCTION: object of **von** → dat.

CAUTION: Don't use the interrogative pronoun in place of the relative pronoun!

Wer hat das Seminar gegeben?
Das ist der Professor, **der** das Seminar gegeben hat.

***Who** gave the seminar?*
*That's the professor **who** gave the seminar.*

2. Word order
   a. Relative pronouns can be the objects of prepositions. If that is the case, the preposition will always precede the relative pronoun.

   Das Buch ist von einem Autor, **für den** ich mich sehr interessiere.
   *The book is by an author **in whom** I'm very interested.*

b. The word order in the RELATIVE CLAUSE is like that of all subordinate clauses: the inflected part of the verb (V1) comes last. Always separate the relative clause from the main clause by a comma. If the relative clause is imbedded in the main clause, then place a comma before and after the relative clause.

> . . . , RP _____ V1, . . .

Der Professor, **der** den Prosakurs **lehrt,** ist sehr nett.
          RP   V1

*The professor **who teaches** the prose course is very nice.*

c. Relative clauses immediately follow the antecedent unless the antecedent is followed by a prepositional phrase that modifies it, by a genitive, or by a verb complement (V2).

Das Buch von Dürrenmatt, **das wir lesen sollen,** ist leider ausverkauft.
Das Buch des Autors, **das wir lesen sollen,** ist teuer.
Ich kann **das Buch** nicht bekommen, **das wir lesen sollen.**

Kinder
die man liebt, werden
Erwachsene, die lieben.

Übungen

A. Analysieren Sie die Sätze! Finden Sie das vorhergehende Wort *(antecedent)*, beschreiben Sie es und nennen Sie die Funktion des Relativpronomens im Relativsatz!

BEISPIEL   Renate Berger ist eine Frau, die für gleiche Arbeit gleiches Einkommen möchte.
ANTECEDENT: *eine Frau = sg. / fem.*
PRONOUN FUNCTION: *subject → nom.*

1. Der Mann, der neben ihr arbeitet, verdient pro Stunde einen Euro mehr.
2. Es gibt leider noch viele Frauen, deren Kollegen ein höheres Gehalt *(salary)* bekommen.
3. Und es gibt Frauen, denen schlecht bezahlte Arbeit lieber ist als keine Arbeit.
4. Was denken die Männer, deren Frauen weniger Geld bekommen als ihre Kollegen?
5. Der Mann, mit dem Renate Berger verheiratet ist, findet das nicht so schlecht.
6. Aber die Frauen, die bei der gleichen Firma arbeiten, ärgern sich sehr darüber.
7. Frau M. in Christine Nöstlingers Geschichte war so eine Frau, die sich ärgerte, aber sich nicht beklagte.
8. Sie war eine Frau, die bei der Arbeit fleißig und zuverlässig war.
9. Den besseren Job, von dem sie träumte, bekamen aber immer andere.
10. Der Chef, den sie hatte, war ein Mensch mit großen Vorurteilen gegen Frauen.
11. Chefs, die so denken wie Frau M.s Chef, gibt es überall.
12. Das ist ein Problem, das andere Firmen auch haben.
13. Die Berufe, in denen fast nur Frauen arbeiten, sind am schlechtesten bezahlt.
14. Wir leben in einer Welt, in der Gleichberechtigung noch nicht überall Realität ist.

B. Stadtrundfahrt Während Sepp ein paar Bilder von seinem Besuch in Berlin zeigt, stellen seine österreichischen Freunde Fragen dazu. Antworten Sie wie im Beispiel und benutzen Sie dabei Relativpronomen!

> BEISPIEL   Ist das der Alexanderplatz?
> *Ja, das ist der Alexanderplatz, der so bekannt ist.*

1. Ist das der Fernsehturm? 2. Ist das das Rote Rathaus? 3. Ist das der Berliner Dom? 4. Ist das das Hotel Adlon? 5. Sind das die Museen?

> BEISPIEL   Ist das der Potsdamer Platz?
> *Ja, das ist der Potsdamer Platz, den du da siehst.*

6. Ist das die Konzerthalle? 7. Ist das das Nikolaiviertel? 8. Ist das der Gendarmenmarkt? 9. Ist das die Spree? 10. Ist das der Berliner Antikmarkt?

> BEISPIEL   Ist das die Hochschule für Musik?
> *Ja, das ist die Hochschule für Musik, zu der wir jetzt kommen.*

11. Ist das der Zoo? 12. Ist das die Siegessäule? 13. Ist das die alte Kongresshalle? 14. Ist das das Reichstagsgebäude? 15. Sind das die Universitätsgebäude?

> BEISPIEL   Wo ist der Student? Sein Vater lehrt an der Universität.
> *Da ist der Student, dessen Vater an der Universität lehrt.*

16. Wo ist die Studentin? Ihre Eltern wohnten früher *(formerly)* in Berlin. 17. Wo ist das Mädchen? Ihr Bruder war so lustig. 18. Wo ist der Herr? Seine Frau sprach so gut Englisch. 19. Wo sind die alten Leute? Ihr Sohn ist jetzt in Amerika.

C. Wer oder was ist das genau? Lesen Sie mit den anderen durch die folgenden Kategorien und nennen Sie dann eigene Beispiele dazu mit Relativpronomen!

> BEISPIEL   ein Restaurant   *Taj Mahal ist ein Restaurant, das mir gefällt.*
> ein Film   *Der Film, über den wir sprachen, heißt Good bye Lenin!*

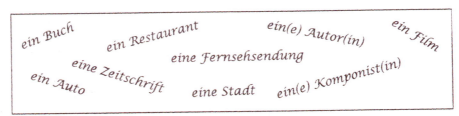

ein Buch   ein Restaurant   ein(e) Autor(in)   ein Film
eine Fernsehsendung
eine Zeitschrift   eine Stadt   ein(e) Komponist(in)
ein Auto

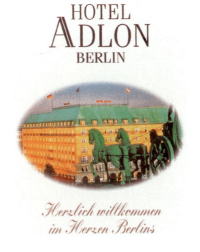

HOTEL
ADLON
BERLIN

*Herzlich willkommen
im Herzen Berlins*

D. Kein Wiedersehen Ergänzen Sie die fehlenden Relativpronomen!

1. Der junge Mann, _____ da steht, heißt David.
2. Das Mädchen, mit _____ er spricht, heißt Tina.
3. Das andere Mädchen, _____ daneben steht, heißt Margaret.
4. Sie sprechen über einen Film, _____ früher einmal im Kino gelaufen ist.
5. Der Film, über _____ sie sprechen, spielte in Berlin.
6. Die Geschichte spielte kurz vor dem Bau der Mauer, _____ Berlin von 1961 bis 1989 geteilt hat.
7. In den fünfziger Jahren sind viele mit der S-Bahn, _____ ja quer durch *(right through)* die Stadt fuhr, geflohen.
8. Ein junger Mann, _____ Freundin nicht wusste, ob sie in den Westen wollte, fuhr mit der S-Bahn nach West-Berlin und blieb dort.
9. Die Freundin, _____ Arbeit in Halle war, ging in den Osten zurück.
10. Das war kurz vor dem Tag, an _____ man die Mauer baute.
11. Es war ein Ereignis *(m., event)*, _____ ihr Leben total verändern sollte.
12. Den Freund, _____ sie in West-Berlin zurückgelassen hatte und _____ dort auf sie wartete, würde sie nie wiedersehen.
13. Am Ende des Filmes, _____ in der damaligen *(then)* DDR gedreht wurde *(was filmed)*, blieb nur die Erinnerung an den Freund.
14. So wie ihnen ging es vielen Menschen, durch _____ Privatleben plötzlich diese schreckliche Mauer ging.
15. Heute ist von der Mauer, _____ so viel Leid brachte, fast nichts mehr zu sehen.

E. Verbinden Sie die Sätze! Verbinden Sie sie mit Hilfe von Relativpronomen! Wenn nötig, übersetzen Sie *(translate)* den Satz zuerst!

BEISPIEL   Der Ku'damm ist eine bekannte Berliner Straße. Jeder kennt sie.
(The Ku'damm is a famous Berlin street [that] everyone knows.)
Der Ku'damm ist eine bekannte Berliner Straße, die jeder kennt.

1. Die Gedächtniskirche gefällt mir. Ihr habt schon von der Gedächtniskirche gehört.
2. Der alte Turm soll kaputt bleiben. Die Berliner nennen ihn den „Hohlen Zahn".
3. Der Ku'damm beginnt bei der Gedächtniskirche. Am Ku'damm gibt es viele schöne Geschäfte.
4. Mittags gingen wir ins Nikolaiviertel. Es hat schöne alte Gebäude und die älteste Kirche Berlins.
5. Da gibt's auch kleine Restaurants. Man kann in den Restaurants gemütlich sitzen.
6. Wir waren ins „Wirtshaus *(n.)* zum Nußbaum" gegangen. Seine Alt-Berliner Küche ist bekannt.
7. Mein Freund hat mir wirklich alles gezeigt. Seine Familie wohnt in Berlin-Mitte.
8. Seine Schwester war auch sehr nett. Ich bin mit ihr am Abend in eine Disko in den Hackeschen Höfen gegangen.
9. Diese Disko war in der Nähe der neuen Synagoge. Die Atmosphäre der Disko war einmalig.
10. Die Synagoge ist im maurischen Stil *(Moorish style)* gebaut. In dieser Synagoge hatte Albert Einstein am 29.1.1930 ein Violinkonzert gegeben.

● Optional English-to-German practice: 1. Where is the lecture hall in which Prof. Kunert is lecturing (reading)? 2. The course he teaches is Modern German History. 3. The students who take his courses must work hard. 4. History is a subject that I find very interesting. 5. But I have a roommate *(m.)* who finds nothing interesting. 6. He is a person **(Mensch)** I don't understand. 7. He studies subjects he doesn't like. 8. The friends he goes out with (with whom he goes out) are boring. 9. He laughs at his father, whose money he gets every month. 10. But the woman he's engaged to (to whom he is engaged) is very nice. (See answer key in the Appendix.)

18 Biere vom Faß
Gastlichkeit auf
Wirtshaus zum **Nußbaum**
Alt-Berliner Art
Bundesplatz 5 • 10715 Berlin (Wilmersdorf)
Tel./Fax (030) 854 50 20
Reservierungen erbeten
täglich geöffnet von 11.30 Uhr bis ?
Alt-Berliner Küche nach Mutters Original-Rezepten
Besonders preiswert: wechselnde Mittagsgerichte Menüs für Reisegruppen

In Berlins Hackeschen Höfen kann man sich gemütlich mit Freunden treffen.

 F. Woran denke ich? Definieren Sie Ihrem Partner/Ihrer Partnerin verschiedene Wörter mit Relativsätzen, die er/sie dann versucht zu erkennen. Wechseln Sie sich ab!

BEISPIEL S1 Ich denke an ein Tier mit zwei Beinen, das klein ist und fliegen kann.
S2 Ist es ein Vogel? . . .
S2 Ich denke an jemanden in der Klasse, der immer zu spät kommt.
S1 Ist es . . . ?

> **„Berlin ist mehr ein Weltteil als eine Stadt."**
>
> **Jean Paul**
> *Deutscher Dichter*
> *(1763–1825)*

Fokus A Multicultural Melting Pot

Berlin is one of Europe's most cosmopolitan urban centers, with more than 400,000 foreign nationals from more than 180 countries living within the city limits. In addition to the influx of Jews from the former Soviet Union since the fall of the Berlin Wall in 1989, the country's liberal asylum laws and the need for manual laborers have drawn people to Berlin from around the globe. Despite signs of cultural tensions in some neighborhoods, the presence and continuing influx of foreigners adds to the cosmopolitan flair of Berlin. The traditionally homogeneous German society is thus changing rapidly in the capital of a reunited Germany. The annual **Karneval der Kulturen,** a three-day music and dance festival with a street parade organized by the various cultural and ethnic associations of Berlin, is testament to an active multicultural scene in the city.

Diese Synagoge ist heute ein jüdisches Museum.

14.2 Indirect speech

When reporting what someone else has said, you can use DIRECT SPEECH with quotation marks, or INDIRECT SPEECH without quotation marks.

> *Heike said, "Berlin has a lot to offer."*
> *Heike said (that) Berlin has a lot to offer.*

An utterance in indirect speech may well require different personal pronouns and possessive adjectives than are in the direct speech sentence, depending on who reports the conversation.

- If Heike says to Martin "I'll bring my map," and she reports the conversation to someone else later, she will say: *I told him I would bring my map.*

- If Martin reported the conversation, he would say: *She told me she would bring her map.*

- If a third person reported the same conversation, he or she would say: *She told him she would bring her map.*

In spoken German such indirect speech is generally in the INDICATIVE when the opening verb is in the PRESENT (**Sie sagt, . . .**). However, when the opening verb is in the PAST (**Sie sagte, . . .**), the SUBJUNCTIVE usually follows. This section focuses on the latter.

Direct speech:	„Ich **bringe** meinen Stadtplan mit."
Indirect speech:	
Indicative	Sie sagt, sie **bringt** ihren Stadtplan mit.
Subjunctive	Sie sagte, sie **würde** ihren Stadtplan **mitbringen.**

NOTE: In German, opening quotation marks are placed at the bottom of the line, especially in handwriting. Many publishers use an alternative form of quotation mark: »Ich bringe meinen Stadtplan mit.« With the advent of the Internet, English style quotation marks are becoming more common.

1. Statements

   The tense of the indirect statement is determined by the tense of the direct statement.

   a. Direct statements in the present or future are reported indirectly in the present-time subjunctive or the **würde**-form.

present tense future tense	present-time subjunctive or **würde**-form

   | „Ich komme später." | Sie sagte, sie käme später. |
   | „Ich werde später kommen." | Sie sagte, sie würde später kommen. |

b. Direct statements in *any past tense* are reported indirectly in the past-time subjunctive.

simple past tense	
present perfect tense }	past-time subjunctive
past perfect tense	

„Ich hatte keine Zeit."
„Ich habe keine Zeit gehabt." } Sie sagte, sie hätte keine Zeit gehabt.
„Ich hatte keine Zeit gehabt."

c. The conjunction **dass** may or may not be used. If it is not used, the clause retains the original word order. If **dass** is used, the inflected part of the verb comes last.

> Sie sagte, sie käme morgen.
> Sie sagte, **dass** sie morgen **käme.**
>
> Sie sagte, sie hätte andere Pläne gehabt.
> Sie sagte, **dass** sie andere Pläne gehabt **hätte.**

2. Questions

The tense of the indirect question is also determined by the tense of the direct question. Indirect YES/NO QUESTIONS are introduced by **ob,** and indirect INFORMATION QUESTIONS by a question word.

Er fragte: „Hast du jetzt Zeit?"	*He asked, "Do you have time now?"*
Er fragte, **ob** sie jetzt Zeit hätte.	*He asked whether she had time now.*
Er fragte: „Wo warst du?"	*He asked, "Where were you?"*
Er fragte, **wo** sie gewesen wäre.	*He asked where she had been.*

3. Imperatives

Direct requests in the imperative are expressed indirectly with the auxiliary **sollen.**

Sie sagte: „Frag nicht so viel!"	*She said, "Don't ask so many questions."*
Sie sagte, er **sollte** nicht so viel **fragen.**	*She said he shouldn't ask so many questions.*

Übungen

G. Wie war das noch mal? Bestätigen Sie *(confirm),* dass die Leute in Phillips Familie das wirklich gesagt haben! Beginnen Sie die indirekte Rede mit **dass!**

BEISPIEL   Hat Phillip Sanders gesagt, er hätte vorher in Bonn gewohnt?
Ja, er hat gesagt, dass er vorher in Bonn gewohnt hätte.

1. Hat Phillip gesagt, seine Familie wäre nicht gern nach Berlin gezogen *(moved)*?
2. Hat seine Mutter gesagt, sie wäre lieber in Bonn geblieben?
3. Hat seine Mutter gesagt, sie hätten dort ein wunderschönes Haus mit Garten gehabt?
4. Hat sein Bruder gesagt, er wollte nicht die Schule wechseln?
5. Hat sein Bruder gesagt, er würde lieber in Bonn sein Abitur machen?
6. Hat Phillip gesagt, er könnte auch hier Freunde finden?
7. Hat Phillip gesagt, er würde Berlin eine Chance geben?

Fokus   Berlin Today

Since becoming the capital of the reunified Germany, Berlin has seen tremendous changes, especially as a new government and business district was constructed where the wall once stood. The historic Reichstag building has been transformed by the British architect Sir Norman Foster into a modern seat of parliament, with a glass dome atop the roof to represent a link between past and present. Numerous embassies and organizations are located in Berlin, and several prominent German and foreign firms have chosen Berlin as their headquarters.

Berlin now boasts some thirty art museums, two important symphony orchestras, three opera houses, numerous theaters and cabarets, and three major universities. Young people from all over Europe have come to appreciate Berlin's groundbreaking film, theater, art, and music scenes. Tourism has experienced a major boom since reunification.

More than any other city in Europe, Berlin embodies both the confrontational division of the Cold War and the subsequent coming together of the continent's nations. Germany's unique modern history enhances its role as a mediator between East and West. The eastward expansion of the EU will profit Berlin politically as well as economically, making it the new center of Europe.

Besucher in der Kuppel (dome) *des Reichstagsgebäudes*

H. Verschiedene Leute im Gespräch Wiederholen Sie auf Englisch die Beispiele von indirekter Rede!

1. **Elke erzählt über Trudi.**

   Trudi sagte, . . .

   a. sie wollte Zahnärztin werden. b. gute Zahnärzte würde man immer brauchen. c. sie könnte leicht weniger arbeiten, wenn sie mal Kinder hätte. d. als Zahnarzt würde man gut verdienen. e. man müsste natürlich lange studieren, aber darauf würde sie sich schon freuen.

2. **Bernd erzählt über Carolyn.**

   Carolyn sagte, . . .

   a. sie hätte letztes Jahr in Deutschland studiert. b. es hätte ihr unheimlich gut gefallen. c. sie hätte „Deutsch als Fremdsprache" belegt. d. während der Semesterferien wäre sie in die Schweiz gefahren. e. sie wäre erst vor drei Wochen zurückgekommen.

3. **Martin und Heike**

   Er hat sie gefragt, . . .

   a. ob ihr Berlin jetzt besser gefallen würde. b. ob sie beim Mauerdurchbruch *(opening of the Wall)* dabei gewesen wäre. c. wie lange sie schon in Berlin wäre. d. wo das Brandenburger Tor wäre. e. wie man dorthin käme. f. was es hier noch zu sehen gäbe.

   Sie hat ihm gesagt, . . .

   g. er sollte sich die Museen ansehen. h. er sollte in ein Konzert gehen. i. er sollte die Filmfestspiele besuchen.

4. **Leonie und Simone**

a. Leonie erzählte, dass sie letzten Sommer in Berlin gewesen wäre. b. Sie hätte dort ein Praktikum an einem Krankenhaus gemacht. c. Sie hätte viel gearbeitet, aber auch unheimlich viel gesehen. d. Sie hätte viele nette Leute kennen gelernt. e. Natürlich wäre sie auch in Potsdam gewesen. f. Das hätte ihr besonders gut gefallen. g. Auch hätte sie die Filmstudios in Babelsberg besucht, wo Marlene Dietrich die Hauptrolle in dem Film *Der blaue Engel* gespielt hatte. h. Als Leonie sagte, dass sie diesen Sommer wahrscheinlich wieder nach Berlin gehen würde, wollte ihre Schwester Simone wissen, ob sie mitkommen könnte. i. Leonie meinte, dass das keine schlechte Idee wäre. j. Die Wohnung wäre groß genug für beide.

I. Der Berliner Antik- und Flohmarkt Wiederholen Sie in indirekter Rede, was Ihnen Freunde darüber erzählt haben!

BEISPIEL   Erika: „Der Antikmarkt liegt mitten in Berlins historischem Zentrum.“
Erika sagte, dass der Antikmarkt mitten in Berlins historischem Zentrum läge.

1. Claire: „In den 13 ausgebauten S-Bahnbögen (*. . . arches*) am Bahnhof Friedrichstraße gibt es etwa 40 Antikhändler (*merchants*). Da findet man vieles. Man muss nur Zeit haben. Ich habe mir einen Ring gekauft.“
2. Tom: „Ich interessiere mich für alte Bücher und Bilder von Berlin. Da kann man wirklich gut herumschnuppern (*snoop around*). Das hat mir Spaß gemacht. Ich habe aber nichts gekauft.“

J. Was hat er/sie gesagt? Stellen Sie Ihrem Nachbarn/Ihrer Nachbarin ein paar persönliche Fragen. Berichten Sie dann den anderen in indirekter Rede!

BEISPIEL   *Er/sie hat mir erzählt, er/sie wäre aus Chicago, er/sie hätte zwei Brüder . . .*

iLrn

Visit the *Wie geht's?* iLrn website for more review and practice of the grammar points you have just learned.

Zusammenfassung

K. Ein toller Tag! Ergänzen Sie das fehlende Relativpronomen!

● This is the official text of Germany's national anthem and the third stanza of the original hymn written by Hoffmann von Fallersleben in 1841.

> Einigkeit und Recht und Freiheit für das deutsche Vaterland.
> Danach lasst uns alle streben, brüderlich mit Herz und Hand.
> Einigkeit und Recht und Freiheit sind des Glückes Unterpfand.
> Blüh im Glanze dieses Glückes, blühe deutsches Vaterland.
>
> *Hoffmann von Fallersleben (1798–1874)*

1. Christa Grauer ist eine Frau, _____ mit einem Computer die Anzeigetafeln (*scoreboards*) in einem Kölner Fußballstadion bedient (*operates*). 2. Sie erzählt von einem Tag, _____ sie nie vergessen wird. 3. Eine Woche nach dem 9. November 1989, einem Tag, _____ Geschichte gemacht hat, spielte die deutsche Fußballnationalmannschaft (*. . . team*) gegen Wales. 4. Vor dem Spiel, zu _____ 60 000 Menschen gekommen waren, schrieb Christa wie immer die dritte Strophe (*stanza*) des Deutschlandliedes auf die Anzeigetafeln. 5. Das hatte sie schon Jahre lang getan. Aber es gab wenige Spiele, bei _____ die Leute wirklich mitsangen. 6. Aber diesmal sangen Tausende mit, denn die Strophe, _____ Text ihnen bisher nicht viel bedeutet hatte, bewegte sie (*moved them*) plötzlich sehr.

Berlin's Past

Today it is nearly impossible to pass through Berlin without uncovering reminders of the city's long history. Founded more than 750 years ago, Berlin became the seat of the Prussian kings in 1701. The Brandenburg Gate, constructed at the end of the 18th century, was intended as a "Gate of Peace." Instead, it would witness two centuries of war and revolution.

Unter den Linden, the city's most prominent boulevard, led up to the famous gate. Here Napoleon's victorious army paraded through Berlin; revolutionaries erected barricades in 1848 and 1918; and the Nazis staged their book burnings in 1933. After World War II, the devastated capital was divided into Allied and Soviet sectors. At first it was relatively easy to cross from one zone to the other, but Berlin soon became the first battlefield in the Cold War. The Soviet blockade of the Allied zones in 1948–1949 triggered the Berlin Airlift, a humanitarian effort that won over the hearts of West Berliners. Later, as increasing numbers of East Berliners fled to the West, the East German regime constructed the Berlin Wall in 1961. The Wall, which cut through the heart of the city, was reinforced with minefields, self-firing machine guns, and steel fences to prevent East Germans from escaping. The Brandenburg Gate stood right next to the Wall, just inside East Berlin.

For almost 30 years, West Berlin remained an island of capitalism in Communist East Germany—until Mikhail Gorbachev's spirit of reform in the Soviet Union swept across Eastern Europe. Again, thousands of East Germans tried to flee to West Germany, and in the confusion that ensued, a Communist Party official mistakenly announced an easing of travel restrictions. Almost by accident, the Wall was opened on November 9, 1989. Reunification followed a year later on October 3, 1990, and the Brandenburg Gate once more became the focal point of the city. (For a chronicle of the Berlin Wall, see www.chronik-der-mauer.de.)

L. Stimmen der Zeit Berichten Sie in direkter Rede, was die zwei Sprecher gesagt haben!

1. **Hiroko Hashimoto, Journalistin**

   a. Hiroko sagte, sie wäre Journalistin und arbeitete freiberuflich *(freelance)* für eine japanische Firma. b. Ihr Mann wäre Deutscher und Wissenschaftler an der Technischen Universität. c. Ihr hätte Berlin schon immer gefallen, aber jetzt wäre es noch viel interessanter geworden. d. Hier gäbe es alles und auch Leute aus der ganzen Welt. e. Am Wochenende nähmen sie oft ihre Fahrräder und führen in die Umgebung. f. Keine andere Stadt hätte so viel zu bieten. g. Sie hätte nie gedacht, dass sie so lange hier bleiben würde. h. Aber sie fühlten sich hier unheimlich wohl.

2. **Moha Rezaian, Schüler**

   a. Moha sagte, er wäre Schüler an einem Gymnasium. b. Seine Eltern wären vor Jahren aus dem Iran gekommen, weil sein Onkel in Kreuzberg einen Teppichladen gehabt hätte. c. Seine Schwester und er wären aber in Berlin geboren und hier groß geworden. d. Sie wären noch nie im Iran gewesen und würden den Rest der Familie nur von Besuchen kennen. e. Sein Vater hätte jetzt ein Autogeschäft und verdiente gut. f. Das würde ihn aber nicht interessieren. g. Er wollte Arzt werden. h. So könnte er vielen Menschen helfen.

M. Hoppla, hier fehlt was: Reaktionen auf den Durchbruch der Mauer Hier sind Aussagen, die verschiedene Leute damals über den Mauerdurchbruch gemacht haben. Manche Aussagen zeigen, von wem sie sind, und andere nicht. Lesen Sie durch die Liste von Leuten und fragen Sie dann Ihren Partner/Ihre Partnerin, dessen/deren Tabelle und Liste im Anhang ist, wer die verschiedenen Aussagen gemacht haben könnte! Wechseln Sie sich ab!

Liste von Leuten:

ein Major der DDR-Grenztruppe	ein afrikanischer Diplomat	Michail Gorbatschow
ein Ostberliner Taxifahrer	die Autorin Christa Wolf	der Autor Stephan Heym
ein kanadischer Fußballspieler	der Autor Günter Grass	Ronald Reagan

BEISPIEL S1 Wer hat gesagt, es wäre eine verrückte Zeit? War das Ronald Reagan?
S2 Nein, das war nicht Ronald Reagan, sondern ein Major der DDR-Grenztruppe. Und wer hat gesagt, vor seinen Augen hätte die Freiheit getanzt? War das . . .?

S1:

WER?	AUSSAGEN
	„Es ist eine verrückte Zeit."
NBC-Korrespondent:	„Vor meinen Augen tanzte die Freiheit."
	„So viel Fernsehen habe ich noch nie gesehen."
Westberliner Polizist über seinen Kollegen in Ost-Berlin:	„Wir haben uns jeden Tag gesehen. Jetzt will ich ihm mal die Hand schütteln *(shake)*."
	„Ich dachte, die Deutschen können nur Fußball spielen oder im Stechschritt *(goose-step)* marschieren, aber jetzt können sie sogar Revolutionen machen."
Autor Wolf Biermann:	„Ich muss weinen vor Freude, dass es so schnell und einfach ging. Und ich muss weinen vor Zorn *(anger)*, dass es so elend *(terribly)* lange dauerte."
	„Jetzt wird sich zeigen, ob der jahrzehntelangen Rhetorik von den ‚Brüdern und Schwestern' auch entsprechendes *(corresponding)* politisches Handeln *(action)* folgen wird."
	„Die einzige Chance, die wir haben, den Sozialismus zu retten *(save)*, ist richtiger Sozialismus."
Ex-Bundeskanzler Willy Brandt:	„Ich bin Gott dankbar, dass ich das noch erleben darf."
	„Auf beiden Seiten sind Deutsche. Der Kommunismus hat seine Chance gehabt. Er funktioniert nicht."
Tschechischer Reformpräsident Alexander Dubček:	„Wir haben zu lange im Dunkeln gelebt. Treten wir *(let's step)* ins Licht!"

N. Eine bekannte Berlinerin: Käthe Kollwitz Auf Deutsch bitte!

1. Käthe Kollwitz was an artist who was at home in Berlin. 2. Her pictures and sculptures (**Skulpturen**) were full of compassion (**voller Mitgefühl**) for poor people, whose suffering (**das Leid**) she wanted to show. 3. They remind us of hunger and war, which make the life of people terrible. 4. Kaiser Wilhelm II was no friend of her art, which for him was "gutter art" (**Kunst der Gosse**). 5. In 1918 she became a professor at the Art Academy (**die Kunstakademie**) in Berlin, at which she taught until 1933. 6. Then came the Nazis, who also didn't like / care for her art, and she lost her position. 7. She died (**starb**) in 1945, shortly before the end of the war.

„Mutter und toter Sohn", eine Skulptur von Käthe Kollwitz (1867–1945) in der Berliner Neuen Wache, einer Gedenkstätte (memorial) *gegen Krieg und Gewalt*

Einblicke

Wortschatz 2

der Gedanke, -ns, -n	*thought*
das Tor, -e	*gate; gateway*
die Grenze, -n	*border*
Heimat	*homeland, home*
Insel, -n	*island*
Jugend	*youth*
Luft	*air*
Macht, ⸚e	*power*
Mitte	*middle*
(Wieder)vereinigung	*(re)unification*
berühmt	*famous*
einst	*once*
leer	*empty*
vereint	*united*
aus·tauschen	*to exchange*
erkennen, erkannte, erkannt	*to recognize*
verlassen (verlässt), verließ, verlassen	*to leave (a place)*

Lesetipp

Anticipating Content

You have learned a lot about Berlin and its people. This reading also deals with the city. Look at the title of the reading and at the sub-headings in the reading. Based on them and your knowledge thus far about the city, what sorts of topics and themes do you expect might come up? Anticipating content of a reading helps you prepare the vocabulary and think about the ideas you will need to understand the reading successfully.

Vor dem Lesen

A. Allerlei Fragen

1. Wo liegt Berlin? 2. An welchem Fluss liegt es? 3. Was sind die Daten des Zweiten Weltkrieges? 4. In wie viele Teile war Berlin geteilt? 5. Wann endete die Teilung *(division)* von Berlin? 6. Was war Ost-Berlin bis dahin *(then)*? 7. Seit wann ist Berlin wieder die Hauptstadt / der Regierungssitz *(seat of parliament)* von Deutschland? 8. Was wissen Sie noch über Berlin?

B. Gehen wir Wörter angeln! Unterstreichen Sie zusammen mit Ihrem Partner/Ihrer Partnerin alle Relativpronomen und vorhergehenden Wörter im Lesetext! Wie viele Beispiele haben Sie gefunden?

C. Das ist leicht zu verstehen! Welche Silbe ist betont? Markieren Sie sie! Was ist das auf Englisch?

der Bomber, Einmarsch, Ökologe, Sonderstatus, Städteplaner; das Angebot, Turmcafé; die Blockade, Demokratie, Funktion, Luftbrücke, Metropole, Olympiade, Orientierung, Passkontrolle, Rampe, Rote Armee; *(pl.)* die Medikamente, Westmächte; aus aller Welt, zwanziger Jahre; grenzenlos, kapitalistisch, sowjetisch, sozialistisch, symbolisch, teils, total blockiert, ummauert, unfreiwillig

Berlin, ein Tor zur Welt

CD 9, Track 4

Antje Dirks, eine Amerikanerin, erinnert sich an den Besuch mit ihrem Vater in Berlin und berichtet über ihren Eindruck° von Berlin heute.

impression

Besuch im Jahre 1985

Da saßen wir nun, Vater und Tochter, im Flugzeug auf dem Weg zu der Stadt,
5 die er eigentlich nie vergessen konnte: Berlin. „Ich bin schon lange in Amerika,
aber Berlin . . . Nun, Berlin ist eben meine Heimat. Da bin ich geboren und
aufgewachsen°." Und dann wanderten seine Gedanken zurück zu den zwanziger   *have grown up*
bis vierziger Jahren, zu der Zeit, als er dort gelebt hatte. Die Viereinhalbmillio-
nenstadt, von deren Charme und Esprit er immer noch schwärmte°, hatte seine   *raved*
10 Jugend geprägt°. Und er erzählte mir von dem, was er dort so geliebt hatte: von   *shaped*
den Wäldern und Seen in der Umgebung und von der berühmten Berliner Luft;
von den Museen, der Oper und den Theatern, deren Angebot damals einmalig
gewesen wäre; vom Kabarett mit seiner typischen „Berliner Schnauze" und
den Kaffeehäusern, in denen immer etwas los war. „In Berlin liefen alle Fäden°   *threads*
15 zusammen, nicht nur kulturell, sondern auch politisch und wirtschaftlich. Es war
einst die größte Industriestadt Europas. Die Zentralverwaltung° fast aller wichti-   *headquarters*
gen Industriefirmen war in Berlin. Und man kannte sich, tauschte Gedanken aus,
auch mit Wissenschaftlern an der Universität. Einfach fantastisch!"
 „Und dann kam 1933. Viele verließen Berlin, teils freiwillig, teils unfreiwillig.
20 Die Nazis beherrschten° das Straßenbild°. Bei der Olympiade 1936 sah die ganze   *dominated / . . . scene*
Welt nicht nur Berlins moderne S-Bahn und schöne Straßen, sondern auch Hitler.
Und drei Jahre später war Krieg!" Nun sprach er von den schweren Luftangriffen°   *air raids*
und den Trümmern°, die diese hinterlassen° hatten, vom Einmarsch der Roten   *rubble / left behind*
Armee, der Teilung Deutschlands unter den vier Siegermächten° (1945) und auch   *victorious Allies*
25 von der Luftbrücke, mit der die Westmächte auf die sowjetische Blockade reagiert
hatten. „Plötzlich waren wir total blockiert, eine Insel. Es gab nichts zu essen,
keine Kleidung, kein Heizmaterial°, keine Medikamente, kaum° Wasser und   *heating fuel / hardly any*
Strom°. An guten Tagen landeten in den nächsten 10 Monaten alle paar Minuten   *electricity*
britische und amerikanische Transportflugzeuge—wir nannten sie die Rosinen-
30 bomber°—und brachten uns, was wir brauchten. Ohne die Westmächte hätten   *raisin bombers*
wir es nie geschafft°!" . . .   *accomplished*

Ein „Rosinenbomber" während der Blockade

 Dann kamen wir in West-Berlin an. Erst machten wir eine Stadtrundfahrt.
„Es ist wieder schön hier; und doch, die Weite° ist weg. Berlin schien früher gren-   *wide-open space*
zenlos, und jetzt . . . überall diese Grenze." Immer wieder stand man vor der
35 Mauer, die seit 1961 mitten durch Berlin lief. Besonders traurig machte ihn der
Blick auf das Brandenburger Tor, das auf der anderen Seite der Mauer stand. Und
doch gefiel mir diese ummauerte Insel. West-Berlin war wieder eine lebendige
Metropole, die unheimlich viel zu bieten hatte.

experience	Der Besuch in Ost-Berlin, der damaligen Hauptstadt von Ostdeutschland,
GDR police (Volkspolizei)	40 war wirklich ein Erlebnis°, wie eine Reise in eine andere Welt. Allein schon die Gesichter der Vopos° am Checkpoint Charlie und das komische Gefühl, das man bei der Passkontrolle hatte! Berlin-Mitte war für meinen Vater schwer wieder-zuerkennen. Der Potsdamer Platz, der früher voller Leben gewesen war, war leer. Leichter zu erkennen waren die historischen Gebäude entlang Unter den Linden:
	45 die Staatsbibliothek, die Humboldt-Universität und die Staatsoper. Interessant waren auch das Pergamonmuseum, der Dom und gegenüber davon der Palast der Republik, den die Berliner „Palazzo Prozzo" nannten und in dem die Volkskam-
GDR house of representatives	mer° saß. Dann über allem der Fernsehturm, dessen Turmcafé sich dreht°. Wir
turns / patrolled	sahen auch einen britischen Jeep, der Unter den Linden Streife fuhr°, was uns an
came together	50 den Sonderstatus Berlins erinnerte. Hier trafen die kapitalistische und die sozia-listische Welt aufeinander°; und für beide Welten waren Ost- und West-Berlin
display windows / opposing	Schaufenster° zweier gegensätzlicher° Systeme.

Heute

Heute ist das alles Geschichte. Die Berliner können wieder reisen, wohin sie wollen. Berlin ist keine Insel mehr. Ich erinnere mich noch gut an die Reaktion
55 meines Vaters, als wir den Mauerdurchbruch im amerikanischen Fernsehen sa-hen. Immer wieder sagte er „Wahnsinn! Dass ich das noch erleben durfte!" und

tears	ihm standen Tränen° in den Augen. Unsere Gedanken gingen damals zurück zu Präsident Kennedys Worten 1963 an der Mauer: „Alle freien Menschen sind Bürger Berlins . . . Ich bin ein Berliner!"

John F. Kennedy in Berlin am 26.6.1963

	60 Seit der Wiedervereinigung hat sich in Berlin sehr viel verändert. Politiker,
achieved	Städteplaner, Architekten und Ökologen haben enorme Arbeit geleistet°. Da, wo einst die Mauer stand, stehen jetzt moderne Gebäude und die alte Mitte Berlins ist wieder Stadtmitte geworden. Hier findet man Menschen aus aller Welt, die
leave their traces / dome	überall ihre Spuren hinterlassen°. Die moderne Kuppel° des Reichstagsgebäudes
on the one hand / shines	65 hat eine neue, symbolische Funktion. Einerseits° strahlt° sie in der Nacht wie
lantern / enlightenment / on the other hand / observation deck / look down	eine Laterne°, wie eine Art Erhellung der Vernunft°. Andererseits° haben die Leute, die auf der Rampe nach oben zur Aussichtsplattform° laufen, die Möglichkeit, auf ihre Politiker herabzuschauen°. Hier diskutiert man nicht mehr
closed	hinter verschlossenen° Türen, sondern die Demokratie ist offener geworden. Als
expanded	70 Hauptstadt des vereinten Deutschlands in einem neuen, erweiterten° Europa hat Berlin neue Aufgaben bekommen und durch seine Lage—nur knapp 100 km von
barely away	Polen entfernt°—erlebt es jetzt auch eine größere Orientierung zum Osten. Berlin ist wieder ein Tor zur Welt.

Aktives zum Text

A. Richtig oder falsch?

_____ 1. Der Vater und die Tochter fliegen nach Amerika.
_____ 2. Der Vater hat lange in Berlin gelebt.
_____ 3. Er hat Berlin sehr geliebt.
_____ 4. In Berlin war aber damals nicht viel los.
_____ 5. 1939 hat der Krieg begonnen.
_____ 6. 1945 teilten die Siegermächte Deutschland und Berlin.
_____ 7. Die Luftbrücke brachte den Berlinern nur Rosinen.
_____ 8. Von 1961 bis 1989 teilte die Mauer Berlin.
_____ 9. Ein Vopo war ein ostdeutsches Auto.
_____ 10. Der Potsdamer Platz war der „Palazzo Prozzo" Ost-Berlins.
_____ 11. Unter den Linden ist eine berühmte alte Straße in Berlin.
_____ 12. Ost-Berlin war ein Schaufenster des Kapitalismus.
_____ 13. Der Vater ist beim Mauerfall in Berlin gewesen.
_____ 14. Präsident Nixon sagte 1963: „Ich bin ein Berliner."
_____ 15. Seit dem Jahr 2000 ist Berlin wieder die Hauptstadt Deutschlands.

B. Was fehlt?

1. Mir gefällt diese Stadt, in _____ mehr als drei Millionen Menschen wohnen. 2. Es ist ein Kulturzentrum (n.), _____ unheimlich viel zu bieten hat. 3. Die Filmfestspiele, _____ Filme meistens sehr gut sind, muss man mal gesehen haben. 4. Morgen Abend gehe ich mit Heike, _____ Vater Extrakarten hat, ins Hebbel Theater. 5. Es ist ein kleines Theater, _____ 1998 unter die Leitung (leadership) der Intendantin (artistic director) Neele Härtling kam und kein eigenes Ensemble hat. 6. Sie machen international zeitgenössisches (contemporary) Theater, _____ Künstler aus aller Welt anzieht (attracts). 7. Zu dem Stammpublikum (regular clients) gehören Leute, _____ sich für Neues und Experimentelles interessieren. 8. Oft präsentieren sie auch junge Künstler aus Mittel- und Osteuropa, _____ dort, wo sie herkommen, renommiert (well-known) sind, aber hier unbekannt sind.

● Optional tongue twister **(der Zungenbrecher):** Der Mondschein (moonlight) schien schon schön.

C. Gespräch zwischen Vater und Tochter
Lesen Sie das Gespräch und berichten Sie indirekt zusammen mit einem Partner/einer Partnerin, was die beiden gesagt haben!

BEISPIEL   S1   Die Tochter fragte, wie lange er dort gewohnt hätte.
S2   Er sagte, dass er ungefähr 25 Jahre dort gewohnt hätte.

TOCHTER   Wie lange hast du dort gewohnt?
VATER   Ungefähr 25 Jahre.
TOCHTER   Wohnten deine Eltern damals auch in Berlin?
VATER   Nein, aber sie sind 1938 nachgekommen.
TOCHTER   Hast du dort studiert?
VATER   Ja, an der Humboldt-Universität.
TOCHTER   Hast du dort Mutti kennen gelernt?
VATER   Ja, das waren schöne Jahre.
TOCHTER   Und wann seid ihr von dort weggegangen?
VATER   Ach, das ist eine lange Geschichte. Setzen wir uns in ein Café! Dann werde ich dir davon erzählen.

D. Interview: Menschen in Berlin Interviewen Sie jemanden (Ihren Partner/Ihre Partnerin), den Sie in Berlin kennen gelernt haben! Vielleicht ist dieser Jemand jung oder alt, Student/in oder Geschäftsmann/frau, Künstler/in oder Politiker/in, Berliner oder Ausländer. Entscheiden Sie zuerst gemeinsam, welche Rolle dieser Jemand spielt und bereiten Sie dann zehn Fragen vor! Danach schreiben Sie einen kleinen Absatz *(paragraph)* über ihn/sie!

> **BEISPIEL** *Er/sie sagt, er wäre Student an der Humboldt Universität. Dort studierte er …*

Hörverständnis

Track 37 **Realität und Hoffnung** Hören Sie zu, was der Sprecher über die Situation in den neuen Bundesländern zu sagen hat! Sind die folgenden Aussagen richtig oder falsch?

Zum Erkennen: blühende Landschaften *(flourishing areas)*; restaurieren *(to restore)*; die Sächsische Schweiz *(part of the **Elbsandsteingebirge** south of Dresden)*; sind neu entstanden *(have reemerged)*; liefern *(to distribute)*; die Fabrik, -en *(factory)*; konkurrieren *(to compete)*; die Werft, -en *(shipyard)*; der Erfolg, -e *(success)*; erfolgreich *(successful)*; die Marke, -n *(brand)*; der Verlag, -e *(publisher)*; die Entwicklung *(development)*; der Zusammenbruch *(collapse)*; verschwand *(disappeared)*; die Personalkosten (pl., *staffing costs)*; vermeiden *(to avoid)*; die Forschung *(research)*

_____ 1. Helmut Kohl meinte, dass sich die neuen Bundesländer nach dem Mauerfall in blühende Landschaften verwandeln *(transform)* würden.

_____ 2. Er hat nur teilweise *(partially)* Recht gehabt.

_____ 3. Nur wenige Touristen fahren in den Ferien an die Ostsee.

_____ 4. In der Sächsischen Schweiz gibt es schöne Schlösser.

_____ 5. In Bitterfeld produziert Nestlé Schokolade für ganz Europa.

_____ 6. In Dresden macht die amerikanische Firma AMD *(Advanced Micro Devices)* Computerchips.

_____ 7. BMW hat jetzt eine Fabrik in Mecklenburg-Vorpommern.

_____ 8. Wismar und Rostock haben moderne Werften.

_____ 9. Rotkäppchen ist ein erfolgreicher Wein aus dem Osten.

_____ 10. Die Firma Zeiss (Optik) ist heute nicht mehr geteilt in Ost und West.

_____ 11. Die neuen Bundesländer haben viel Geld in die alten Bundesländer gepumpt.

_____ 12. Im Osten sind viele Menschen arbeitslos.

_____ 13. Viele junge Menschen sind wegen der Arbeitslosigkeit in den Osten gezogen.

_____ 14. Um für junge qualifizierte Leute attraktiv zu bleiben, investiert man im Osten viel Geld für Forschung und Wissenschaft.

_____ 15. Diese wissenschaftlichen Zentren, oder Clusters, kooperieren mit den Hochschulen und der Geschäftswelt.

_____ 16. Sie dürften ein Magnet für Wissenschaftler aus aller Welt und aus Osteuropa sein.

A divided country and city; Berlin today; and a visit to Potsdam: http://wiegehts.heinle.com.

Literatur

Biographisches

Wolfgang Borchert (1921–1947) started out his career as an actor, until he was drafted into the army in 1941 and sent to the Russian front. Wounded and seriouly ill, he was sent home for a hospital stay. His critical attitude toward the Third Reich led him into conflict with the regime and eventually earned him a death sentence. That, however, was reduced to nine months of solitary confinement and brought him back to the front in a "punishment battalion." His failing health left him ill fit for such rigors. After receiving a medical discharge, he was promptly retried for defeatist statements and sent to prison. Set free by American troops at the end of the war, he walked home some 500 miles to his beloved Hamburg, a city in ruins. Physically broken, Borchert survived the war by barely two years. It was during this brief time that he turned to writing in order to come to terms with the horrors of war and his own personal experiences. His most successful work was the drama *Draußen vor der Tür,* performed originally as a radio play and aired for the first time in Hamburg one day after his death. Borchert's stories are mostly short, bleak vignettes of life in wartime or its aftermath. There are no elaborate descriptions or memorable characters. His figures remain anonymous, suffering and questioning. Plots are reduced to series of abrupt images, repetitions of phrases or key words, metaphors, and brief dialogues.

Vor dem Lesen

Allgemeine Fragen

1. Was wissen Sie über die Nachkriegszeit in Deutschland? Wie zum Beispiel sah das tägliche Leben im Jahre 1945 aus?
2. Wofür ist „Brot" ein Symbol, besonders wenn man es nicht hat?
3. Wie sind oder werden Menschen oft, wenn sie hungrig sind?
4. Können Sie sich an eine Zeit erinnern, wo Sie nicht genug zu essen gehabt haben? Kennen Sie persönlich jemanden, der nicht genug zu essen gehabt hatte? Wenn ja, erzählen Sie!
5. Wo hungern heute Menschen auf dieser Welt?

Das Brot

Track 38

Plötzlich wachte sie auf°. Es war halb drei. Sie überlegte°, warum sie aufgewacht war. Ach so! In der Küche hatte jemand gegen einen Stuhl gestoßen°. Sie horchte° nach der Küche. Es war still. Es war zu still und als sie mit der Hand über das Bett neben sich fuhr, fand sie es leer. Das war es, was es so
5 besonders still gemacht hatte: sein Atem° fehlte. Sie stand auf und tappte° durch die dunkle Wohnung zur Küche. In der Küche trafen sie sich. Die Uhr war halb drei. Sie sah etwas Weißes am Küchenschrank stehen. Sie machte Licht°. Sie standen sich im Hemd gegenüber. Nachts. Um halb drei. In der Küche.

Auf dem Küchentisch stand der Brotteller. Sie sah, dass er sich Brot
10 abgeschnitten° hatte. Das Messer lag noch neben dem Teller. Und auf der Decke° lagen Brotkrümel°. Wenn sie abends zu Bett gingen, machte sie immer das Tischtuch° sauber. Jeden Abend. Aber nun lagen Krümel auf dem Tuch. Und das Messer lag da. Sie fühlte, wie die Kälte der Fliesen° langsam an ihr hochkroch°. Und sie sah von dem Teller weg.
15   „Ich dachte, hier wäre was", sagte er und sah in der Küche umher°. „Ich habe auch was gehört", antwortete sie, und dabei fand sie, dass er nachts im Hemd doch schon recht alt aussah. So alt wie er war. Dreiundsechzig. Tagsüber sah er manchmal jünger aus. Sie sieht doch schon alt aus, dachte er, im Hemd sieht sie doch ziemlich alt aus. Aber das liegt vielleicht an den Haaren. Bei den Frauen

	woke up / wondered
	bumped / listened
	breath / tiptoed
	turned on the light
	cut off / tablecloth
	bread crumbs
	tiles / crept up
	around

barefoot
stand it / was lying

light switch

rain gutter / bangs
rattles

naked / pattered

noticed / fake / voice
yawned / crawl / blanket

chewed / breathed /
  intentionally / regular /
  fell asleep
slices
Before

tolerate
bent over

shortened

20 liegt das nachts immer an den Haaren. Die machen dann auf einmal so alt. „Du
hättest Schuhe anziehen sollen. So barfuß° auf den kalten Fliesen. Du erkältest
dich noch." Sie sah ihn nicht an, weil sie nicht ertragen° konnte, dass er log°.
Dass er log, nachdem sie neununddreißig Jahre verheiratet waren . . .

Sie hob die Hand zum Lichtschalter°. Ich muss das Licht jetzt ausmachen,
25 sonst muss ich nach dem Teller sehen, dachte sie. Ich darf doch nicht nach dem
Teller sehen. „Komm man", sagte sie und machte das Licht aus, „das war wohl
draußen. Die Dachrinne° schlägt° immer bei Wind gegen die Wand. Es war sicher
die Dachrinne. Bei Wind klappert° sie immer."

Sie tappten sich beide über den dunklen Korridor zum Schlafzimmer. Ihre
30 nackten° Füße platschten° auf den Fußboden. „Wind ist ja", meinte er. „Wind
war schon die ganze Nacht." Als sie im Bett lagen, sagte sie: „Ja, Wind war schon
die ganze Nacht. Es war wohl die Dachrinne." „Ja, ich dachte, es wäre in der
Küche. Es war wohl die Dachrinne." Er sagte das, als ob er schon halb im Schlaf
wäre. Aber sie merkte°, wie unecht° seine Stimme° klang, wenn er log. „Es ist
35 kalt", sagte sie und gähnte° leise, „ich krieche° unter die Decke°. Gute Nacht."
„Nacht", antwortete er noch: „ja, kalt ist es schon ganz schön."

Dann war es still. Nach vielen Minuten hörte sie, dass er leise und vorsichtig
kaute°. Sie atmete° absichtlich° tief und gleichmäßig°, damit er nicht merken
sollte, dass sie noch wach war. Aber sein Kauen war so regelmäßig°, dass sie
40 davon langsam einschlief°.

Als er am nächsten Abend nach Hause kam, schob sie ihm vier Scheiben°
Brot hin. Sonst° hatte er immer nur drei essen können. „Du kannst ruhig vier essen", sagte sie und ging von der Lampe weg. „Ich kann dieses Brot nicht so recht
vertragen°. Iss du man eine mehr. Ich vertrag es nicht so gut." Sie sah, wie er
45 sich tief über den Teller beugte°. Er sah nicht auf. In diesem Augenblick tat er ihr
Leid. „Du kannst doch nicht nur zwei Scheiben essen", sagte er auf seinen
Teller. „Doch. Abends vertrag ich das Brot nicht gut. Iss man. Iss man." Erst
nach einer Weile setzte sie sich unter die Lampe an den Tisch.

Wolfgang Borchert (etwas gekürzt°)

Nach dem Lesen

A. inhaltsfragen

1. Warum geht *sie* in die Küche und wen findet sie dort?
2. Was bemerkt *(notices)* sie und wie reagiert sie darauf?
3. Wie reagiert der Mann auf ihr Kommen?
4. Glauben Sie, dass er weiß, dass sie weiß, was er getan hat? Erklären Sie!
5. Was tut er, statt sich zu entschuldigen?
6. Was tut sie, statt ihn zu beschuldigen *(accuse)*?
7. Was hört sie, als sie und ihr Mann wieder im Bett sind? Warum sagt sie nichts?
8. Was gibt sie ihm am nächsten Tag nach der Arbeit? Wie reagiert er darauf?
9. Welche Ausrede *(excuse)* hat sie für sich?
10. Woher wissen wir, dass er sich schämt *(is embarrassed)*?
11. Warum sind sie nicht ehrlicher miteinander *(with each other)*?
12. Glauben Sie, dass die beiden sich noch lieben? Erklären Sie!
13. Wie hätten Sie in so einer Situation reagiert?
14. Warum gibt der Autor den beiden keinen Namen? Was meinen Sie?
15. Der Autor wiederholt öfter die Wörter „kalt" und „still" im Text. Sagt das vielleicht etwas über einen Mangel an *(lack of)* Kommunikation zwischen Mann und Frau? Was meinen Sie?

B. Von direkter zu indirekter Rede
Finden Sie mit Ihrem Partner/Ihrer Partnerin Beispiele von direkter Rede im Text und ändern Sie diese zu indirekter Rede!

BEISPIEL   Er sagte: „Ich dachte, hier wäre was."
Er sagte, er hätte gedacht, hier wäre was.

Sie antwortete: „Ich habe auch was gehört."
Sie antwortete, sie hätte auch was gehört.

C. Wenn das später passiert wäre!
Bereiten Sie mit Ihrem Partner/Ihrer Partnerin einen kleinen Dialog über eins der beiden Themen vor!

1. So hätte sich das Gespräch zwischen zwei Menschen zwanzig Jahre später angehört.
2. So würde sich das Gespräch heute bei mir [zu Hause . . .] anhören.

Deutschland, Europa und die Umwelt

Lernziele

In this chapter you will learn about:

Zum Thema

Landscape and the environment

Kultur-Fokus

A united Europe, European
  cultural capital Weimar,
  German identity
Franz Kafka, Erich Kästner

Struktur

The passive voice
Review of the uses of **werden**
The special subjunctive (Subjunctive I)

Einblicke + Literatur

Der Wind kennt keine Grenzen.
Franz Kafka: "Der Aufbruch"
Erich Kästner: "Das Eisenbahn-
  gleichnis"

For more information,
go to
http://iLrn.heinle.com

Deutsche und polnische Kinder des Eurokindergartens in Frankfurt an der Oder und Slubice feiern auf der gemeinsamen Stadtbrücke die Erweiterung (expansion) *der EU. Sie werden zweispraching aufwachsen.*

Vorschau   The Path to a United Europe

Minidrama: *Der Wind, der Wind, das himmlische Kind*

1945   World War II leaves Europe devastated and its inhabitants hungry.

1949   The North Atlantic Treaty Organization (NATO) and the Council of Europe are established.

1950   France launches the Schuman Plan, which proposes putting French and West German coal and steel production under a single authority.

1951   Italy, Belgium, the Netherlands, and Luxembourg found the European Coal and Steel Community (ECSC), known as *Montanunion*.

1957   France, Germany, Italy, Belgium, the Netherlands, and Luxembourg establish the European Economic Community (EEC) and the European Atomic Energy Commission (EURATOM), known collectively as the Treaties of Rome. The EEC, EURATOM, and ECSC are called the "European Communities," or EC.

1960   Great Britain, Austria, Switzerland, Portugal, and the Scandinavian countries form the European Free Trade Association (EFTA), an alternative to the EC.

1973   Denmark, Ireland, and Great Britain join the EC.

1979   First direct elections to the European Parliament are held.

1981   Greece joins the EC.

1986   Spain and Portugal become members of the EC.

1989   With the fall of the Berlin Wall, the division of Europe comes to an end.

1990   German unification extends EC membership to the former East Germany.

1993   Signed in 1991, the Maastricht Treaty now goes into effect, paving the way to economic and monetary union and increasing political unity. The "European Communities" are now called the European Union (EU).

1995   The entry of Austria, Finland, and Sweden into the EU brings the number of member states to 15. The Schengen Agreement, an EU treaty that makes passport-free travel possible between signatory states, goes into effect.

1997   The heads of the member states draw up the Amsterdam Treaty, which lays out internal reform and expansion eastward.

1999   The euro is introduced as common currency for financial transactions in 11 member states, marking the beginning of the end of the deutsche mark and the various national EU currencies.

2002   The euro replaces national currencies such as the deutsche mark and schilling for all daily transactions in 12 EU nations.

2004   Expansion of the EU to 25 member countries with the accession of Poland, Hungary, the Czech Republic, Slovenia, Slovakia, Latvia, Lithuania, Estonia, Cyprus (represented by the Greek Cypriot government), and Malta.

2005   A proposal for a European Constitution is voted down by several member nations and, thus, cannot be ratified.

Zum Thema

 Zu Besuch in Weimar

CD 9,
Track 6

TOM   Komisch, dieses Denkmal von Goethe und Schiller kenne ich doch! Ich glaube, ich habe es schon irgendwo gesehen.

DANIELA   Warst du schon mal in San Francisco?

TOM   Na klar!

DANIELA   Warst du auch im Golden Gate Park?

TOM   Ach ja, da steht genau das gleiche Denkmal! Das haben, glaub' ich, die Deutsch-Amerikaner in Kalifornien einmal bauen lassen.

DANIELA   Richtig! Übrigens, weißt du, dass Weimar 1999 Kulturhauptstadt Europas war?

TOM   Nein, das ist mir neu. Wieso denn?

DANIELA   Im 18. Jahrhundert haben hier doch viele berühmte Leute gelebt und die Weimarer Republik ist auch danach benannt.

TOM   Ja ja, aber heute früh, als ich am Mahnmal vom Konzentrationslager Buchenwald auf die Stadt herabblickte, hatte ich sehr gemischte Gefühle.

DANIELA   Ja, da hast du natürlich Recht.

Das Goethe-Schiller-Denkmal vor dem Nationaltheater in Weimar

In der Altstadt

DANIELA   Schau mal, die alten Häuser hier sind doch echt schön.

TOM   Ja, sie sind gut restauriert worden. Ich finde es vor allem schön, dass hier keine Autos fahren dürfen.

DANIELA   Gott sei Dank! Die Fassaden hätten die Abgase der Trabbis nicht lange überlebt.

TOM   Bei uns gibt es jetzt auch eine Bürgerinitiative, alle Autos in der Altstadt zu verbieten, um die alten Gebäude zu retten.

DANIELA   Das finde ich gut.

TOM   Sind die Container da drüben für die Mülltrennung?

DANIELA   Ja, habt ihr auch Mülltrennung?

TOM   Ja, freiwillig. Da könnte man ganz bestimmt noch viel mehr tun. Zum Beispiel weiß ich nie, wohin mit alten Batterien oder Medikamenten.

DANIELA   Die alten Batterien kann man in jedem Supermarkt in spezielle Sammelbehälter werfen und die alten Medikamente, die bringst du zur Apotheke.

TOM   Das geht bei uns nicht und so landet schließlich vieles in der Mülltonne.

DANIELA   Das ist bei uns verboten.

TOM   Das sollte es auch sein. Ihr seid da eben weiter als wir.

The Trabant, or **Trabbi** (see drawing), was an East German car with a two-stroke engine that emitted roughly nine times more hydrocarbons and five times more carbon dioxide than cars with four-stroke engines. Nicknamed **Plastikbomber, Asphaltblase** (. . . Bubble), or **Rennpappe** (Racing Cardboard), it was nevertheless expensive by GDR standards. People had to save the equivalent of 10 to 27 months' salary; credit did not exist. Delivery of the 26 HP car normally took at least 10 years; its spare parts were one of the underground currencies of the former GDR.

Fokus — Weimar, a European Cultural Capital

In 1985, the European Community selected Athens to be the first cultural capital of Europe: Luxembourg, Thessaloniki, Stockholm, and other cities followed in the years to come, with a different city being chosen each year. Weimar received this honor in the year 1999. It is not only the smallest of the European cultural capitals to date; it is also the first city from one of the former communist countries to bear this title.

Weimar boasts a proud cultural history. Johann Sebastian Bach was court organist there in the early 18th century. Goethe, who lived and worked in Weimar from 1775 until his death in 1832, drew Schiller, Gottfried Herder, and many others to the town, which, nourished by genius, gave birth to "Weimar Classicism." Franz Liszt was musical director in Weimar in the mid-19th century, and the philosopher and author Friedrich Nietzsche lived there during his final years as well. In 1919, following World War I,

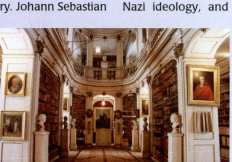

Die Anna Amalia Bibliothek in Weimar vor dem Brand (fire) *im Jahre 2004.*

the National Assembly met in Weimar to draft a constitution for the new republic—henceforth known as the Weimar Republic. The assembly chose this site because of its popular associations with Germany's classical tradition. The new republic lasted only 14 years, dissolved by Hitler soon after he was appointed chancellor in 1933. During the Nazi period, Weimar and its traditions were used selectively to promote Nazi ideology, and some of Goethe's works were even banned from schools. On the Ettersberg, a hill above the town, a memorial recalls the nearby Nazi concentration camp of Buchenwald. Since the fall of East Germany, tourists from across Europe are again flocking to Weimar's historical and cultural landmarks. In September 2004, a fire swept through the 17th-century Anna Amalia Library, which housed around one million books. Many were damaged, including the world's largest collection of works on Goethe's *Faust*.

A. Richtig oder falsch?

_____ 1. Tom und Daniela sind in Weimar.

_____ 2. Sie sehen ein Denkmal von Goethe und Nietzsche.

_____ 3. Eine Kopie dieses Denkmals steht in New York.

_____ 4. Die Gebäude in der Innenstadt sind schön restauriert.

_____ 5. Im Zentrum gibt es auch eine Fußgängerzone.

_____ 6. Tom kommt aus einer Stadt, in deren Altstadt bis jetzt noch Autos fahren dürfen.

_____ 7. Für die Mülltrennung gibt es in Weimar besondere Container.

_____ 8. Tom meint, dass es das bei ihm zu Hause nicht gibt.

_____ 9. Tom weiß zum Beispiel nie, wohin mit alten Batterien.

_____ 10. Daniela sagt, dass jeder Supermarkt Sammelbehälter dafür hätte.

B. Jetzt sind Sie dran! Sprechen Sie mit Ihrem Partner/Ihrer Partnerin über das Thema „Autos in der Altstadt". Finden Sie heraus, was er/sie davon hält, dort alle Autos zu verbieten! Welche Konsequenzen hätte das?

Wortschatz 1

Die Landschaft *(landscape, scenery)*
Die Umwelt *(environment)*

der Abfall, ⸚e	*trash*	die Erhaltung	*preservation*
Bau, -ten	*building; structure*	Küste, -n	*coast*
Behälter, -Behälter	*container*	Mülltonne, -n	*garbage can*
Müll	*garbage; waste*	Natur	*nature*
(Umwelt)schutz	*(environmental) protection*	Rede, -n	*speech*
das Denkmal, ⸚er	*monument*	Sammelstelle, -n	*collection site*
Gebiet, -e	*area, region*	Verschmutzung	*pollution*
Naturschutzgebiet,- e	*nature preserve*		

Weiteres

allerdings	*however*
schließlich	*after all, in the end*
übrigens	*by the way*
umweltbewusst	*environmentally aware*
ab·reißen, riss ab, abgerissen	*to tear down*
(wieder) auf·bauen	*to (re)build*
finanzieren	*to finance*
garantieren	*to guarantee*
planen	*to plan*
reden (mit +*dat.* / über + *acc.*)	*to talk (to/about)*
renovieren	*to renovate*
restaurieren	*to restore*
<u>retten</u>	*to save, rescue*
schaden	*to hurt; to damage*
schonen	*to go easy on, protect*
schützen	*to protect*
trennen	*to separate*
verbieten, verbot, verboten	*to forbid*
verwenden	*to use, utilize*
werfen (wirft), warf, geworfen	*to throw*
<u>weg·werfen</u> (wirft weg), warf weg, weggeworfen	*to throw away, discard*
zerstören	*to destroy*

Wirf Altglas nicht fort. Container stehn an jedem Ort!

🔸 Don't confuse **retten** *(to save in the sense of to rescue)* with **sparen** *(to save in the sense of saving money or time).*

🔸 Note, **wegwerfen** means the same as **fortwerfen** (used in the illustration), but in everyday speech, **wegwerfen** might be more common.

Zum Erkennen: bauen lassen *(to have built)*; benennen nach *(to name after)*; das Konzentrationslager, - *(concentration camp)*; herab·blicken auf (+ *acc.*)*(to look down on)*; gemischte Gefühle *(mixed feelings)*; die Fassade, -n; die Abgase *(exhaust fumes)*; überleben *(to survive)*; die Bürgerinitiative, -n *(citizens' initiative)*; der Container, -; die Mülltrennung *(waste separation)*; freiwillig *(voluntary)*; die Batterie, -n; die Medikamente *(pl., medicine)*; ihr seid da eben weiter *(in that regard, you are just more progressive)*; AUCH: das Aktiv *(active voice)*; das Passiv *(passive voice)*; die Zeitform, -en *(tense)*; die Konsequenz, -en; erfahren *(to find out)*

Aktives zum Thema

A. Im Rathaus Als Radioreporter hören Sie sich die Rede eines Städteplaners an. Berichten Sie Ihren Zuhörern *(listeners)*, was Sie gehört haben!

> BEISPIEL   *Der Städteplaner hat gesagt, wir sollten nicht auf die Bürger hören, die immer . . .*

„Hören Sie nicht auf die Bürger, die immer wieder alles, ja die ganze Altstadt, retten wollen. Viele alte Innenhöfe *(inner courts)* sind dunkel und hässlich. Abreißen ist viel billiger und einfacher als zu renovieren. Wenn man die alten Gebäude abreißt und die Innenstadt schön modern aufbaut, dann kommt bestimmt wieder Leben in unser Zentrum. Auf diese Weise kann man auch die Straßen verbreitern *(widen)* und alles besser planen. Fußgängerzonen sind sicher schön und gut, aber nicht im Zentrum, denn alle wollen ihr Auto in der Nähe haben. Das ist doch klar, weil's viel bequemer und sicherer ist! Ich kann Ihnen garantieren, wenn Sie aus dem Zentrum eine Einkaufszone machen, zu deren Geschäften man nur zu Fuß hinkommt *(gets to)*, dann verlieren Sie alle, meine Damen und Herren, viel Geld!"

B. Altbau oder Neubau? Wo würden Sie lieber wohnen? Was spricht dafür und was dagegen? Stellen Sie mit Ihrem Partner/Ihrer Partnerin eine Liste auf und machen Sie eine Meinungsumfrage *(opinion poll)!*

C. Schützt unsere Umwelt! Fragen Sie einen Nachbarn/eine Nachbarin, . . . !

1. was er/sie mit Altglas, Altpapier, alten Batterien, alten Farben, altem Öl, alten Medikamenten, alten Dosen *(cans),* Plastikflaschen und Plastiktüten *(. . . bags)* macht
2. was er/sie mit alter Kleidung, alten CDs, DVDs oder alten Büchern macht
3. ob er/sie eine Waschmaschine oder Spülmaschine *(dishwasher)* benutzt; wenn ja, wie viel Waschmittel oder Spülmittel er/sie dafür benutzt
4. wofür er/sie Chemikalien *(chemicals)* benutzt und wie oft
5. ob er/sie manchmal ein Umweltverschmutzer ist; wieso (nicht)
6. ob er/sie gern Musik hört; wenn ja, ob er/sie sie auf laut oder leise *(quiet)* stellt und ob andere darüber manchmal auch böse sind
7. ob er/sie einen Hund hat; wenn ja, was für einen Hund und ob er/sie beim „Gassi gehen" seine „Geschäfte" aufsammelt
8. was er/sie und seine/ihre Freunde für die Umwelt tun

> ● If you are curious: **s. erbauen an** *to enjoy;* **der Abfall-Wurf** *littering;* **das Waschmittel, -** *laundry detergent;* **in kleinen Gaben** *in small amounts;* **üblich** *customary;* **entgegen•nehmen** *to accept;* **der Verstand** *common sense;* **der Ölwechsel** *oil change;* **sei helle** *be smart;* **Gassi gehen** *to walk the doggie.*

Aussprache

CD 9, Track 7

Knacklaute *(glottal stops)*

1. +Erich +arbeitet +am +alten Schloss.
2. Die +Abgase der +Autos machen +einfach +überall +alles kaputt.
3. +Ulf +erinnert sich +an +ein +einmaliges +Abendkonzert +im +Ulmer Dom.
4. +Otto sieht +aus wie +ein +alter +Opa.
5. +Anneliese +ist +attraktiv +und +elegant.

> ● For further review, see the Summary of Pronunciation in the front of your *Arbeitsbuch.* Study Part II, subsection F.

Mit dem Pferdewagen durchs Wattenmeer oder Watt

 Hörverständnis

Track 39 **Habitat Wattenmeer** Hören Sie zu, was man Ihnen über das Wattenmeer erzählt! Sind die folgenden Aussagen richtig oder falsch?

Zum Erkennen: das flache Vorland *(tidal flats)*; grenzen an *(to border on)*; die Ebbe *(low tide)*; die Flut *(high tide)*; die Muschel, -n *(clam)*; das Paradies; die Krabbe, -n *(crab)*; knabbern *(to nibble)*; der Seehund, -e *(seal)*; das empfindliche Ökosystem *(delicate ecosystem)*; das Düngemittel, - *(fertilizer)*; der Kompromiss, -e; das Reservat, -e *(reservation)*; der Fischfang *(fishing)*; begrenzt *(limited)*

____ 1. Das Wattenmeer liegt vor der Ostseeküste.
____ 2. Alle 12 Stunden wechselt es von Ebbe zu Flut.
____ 3. Bei Ebbe kann man weit ins Watt hinauslaufen.
____ 4. Dabei kann man alle möglichen *(all sorts of)* Tiere beobachten.
____ 5. Gehfaule können auch mit dem Pferdewagen ins Watt fahren.
____ 6. Wegen seines empfindlichen Ökosystems haben die Deutschen dieses Gebiet zum Naturschutzgebiet erklärt.
____ 7. Auch die Dänen und Niederländer sind am Schutz dieser Landschaft interessiert.
____ 8. Die Dänen dürfen noch im Wattenmeer fischen, aber nicht die Deutschen.

Struktur

15.1 The passive voice

English and German sentences are in one of two voices: the active or the passive. In the ACTIVE VOICE, the subject of the sentence is doing something; it's "active."

> *The students ask the professor.*

In the PASSIVE VOICE, the subject is not doing anything; rather, something is being done to it; it's "passive."

> *The professor is asked by the students.*

Note what happens when a sentence in the active voice is changed into the passive voice: The direct object of the active becomes the subject of the passive.

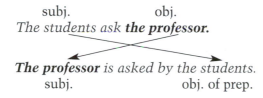

In both languages, the active voice is used much more frequently than the passive voice, especially in everyday speech. The passive voice is used when the focus is on the action itself or on the person or thing at whom the action is directed, rather than on the agent who is acting.

Active Voice	**Die Studenten** fragen den Professor.
Passive Voice	**Der Professor** wird von den Studenten gefragt.

1. Forms

   a. In English, the passive voice is formed with the auxiliary *to be* and the past participle of the verb. In German, it is formed with the auxiliary **werden** and the past participle of the verb.

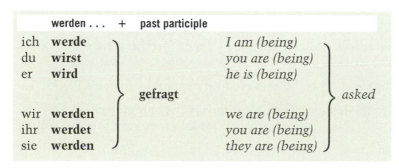

Der Professor **wird** von den Studenten **gefragt.**
Die Professoren **werden** von den Studenten **gefragt.**

b. The passive voice has the same tenses as the active voice. They are formed with the various tenses of **werden** + the past participle of the verb. Note, however, that in the perfect tenses of the passive voice, the past participle of **werden** is **worden!** When you see or hear **worden,** you know immediately that you are dealing with a sentence in the passive voice.

PRESENT	Er **wird** . . . gefragt.	*He is being asked . . .*
SIMPLE PAST	Er **wurde** . . . gefragt.	*He was asked . . .*
FUTURE	Er **wird** . . . gefragt **werden.**	*He will be asked . . .*
PRES. PERF.	Er **ist** . . . gefragt **worden.**	*He has been asked . . .*
PAST PERF.	Er **war** . . . gefragt **worden.**	*He had been asked . . .*

Die Altstadt wird renoviert.	*The old part of town is being renovated.*
Die Pläne wurden letztes Jahr gemacht.	*The plans were made last year.*
Alles wird finanziert werden.	*Everything will be financed.*
Das ist entschieden worden.	*That has been decided.*
Manche Gebäude waren im Krieg zerstört worden.	*Some buildings had been destroyed during the war.*

In subordinate clauses, the pattern is:

Ich weiß, dass die Altstadt renoviert wird.
         , dass die Pläne letztes Jahr gemacht wurden.
         , dass alles finanziert werden wird.
         , dass das schon entschieden worden ist.
         , dass manche Gebäude im Krieg zerstört worden waren.

c. Modals themselves are not put into the passive voice. Rather, they follow this pattern:

modal . . . + past participle + **werden**

In this book, only the present and simple past tense of the modals will be used in the passive.

PRESENT	Er **muss** . . . gefragt **werden.**	*He must (has to) be asked.*
SIMPLE PAST	Er **musste** . . . gefragt **werden.**	*He had to be asked*

Das Gebäude muss renoviert werden.	*The building must be renovated.*
Das Gebäude sollte letztes Jahr renoviert werden.	*The building was supposed to be renovated last year.*

In subordinate clauses the inflected verb stands at the end.

Ich weiß, dass das Gebäude renoviert werden **muss.**
         , dass das Gebäude letztes Jahr renoviert werden **sollte.**

2. Expression of the agent

If the agent who performs the act is expressed, the preposition **von** is used.

Der Professor wird **von den Studenten** gefragt.	*The professor is asked by the students.*
Alles ist **vom Staat** finanziert worden.	*Everything was financed by the state.*

3. Impersonal use

In German, the passive voice is frequently used without a subject or with **es** functioning as the subject.

> Hier darf nicht gebaut werden. } *You can't build here.*
> **Es** darf hier nicht gebaut werden. } *Building is not permitted here.*

4. Alternative to the passive voice

One common substitute for the passive voice is a sentence in the active voice with **man** as the subject.

> Hier darf nicht gebaut werden.
> Es darf hier nicht gebaut werden.
> **Man darf hier nicht bauen.**

Übungen

A. Trier Aktiv oder Passiv?

1. Trier was founded by the Romans in 15 B.C.
2. Its original name was *Augusta Treverorum.*
3. Under Roman occupation, Germania along the Rhine and Danube had been transformed into a series of Roman provinces.
4. The names of many towns are derived from Latin.
5. Remnants from Roman times can still be seen today.
6. New discoveries are made from time to time.
7. Beautiful Roman museums have been built.
8. One of them is located in the former *Colonia Agrippina* (Cologne).

B. Köln Was bedeutet das auf Englisch?

1. a. Köln wurde während des Krieges schwer zerbombt *(destroyed by bombs).*
   b. Achtzig Prozent der Häuser in der Innenstadt waren zerbombt worden.
   c. Inzwischen *(in the meantime)* ist Köln wieder schön aufgebaut und restauriert worden.
   d. Zur Karnevalszeit wird hier schwer gefeiert.
   e. Es ist eine Stadt, in der jedes Jahr verschiedene Messen *(fairs)* gehalten werden.
   f. Die Popkomm, Kölns Messe für Popmusik und Unterhaltung, wird von einem großen Musikfestival begleitet *(accompanied),* das in der ganzen Stadt gefeiert wird.

2. a. Erst mussten neue Wohnungen gebaut werden.
   b. Manche alten Gebäude konnten gerettet werden.
   c. Der Dom musste restauriert werden.
   d. Die alten Kirchen aus dem 12. Jahrhundert dürfen auch nicht vergessen werden.
   e. Das kann natürlich nicht ohne Geld gemacht werden.
   f. Durch Bürgerinitiativen wurde genug Geld für die Restaurierung gesammelt.

3. a. In der Altstadt wird in Parkgaragen geparkt.
   b. Es wird viel mit dem Bus gefahren.
   c. In der „Hohen Straße" wird nicht Auto gefahren.
   d. Dort wird zu Fuß gegangen.
   e. Dort wird gern eingekauft.
   f. In der Vorweihnachtszeit wird die Fußgängerzone mit vielen Lichtern dekoriert.

C. Ein schönes Haus Sagen Sie die Sätze im Aktiv!

BEISPIEL   Nicht alle Gebäude waren vom Krieg zerstört worden.
Der Krieg hatte nicht alle Gebäude zerstört.

1. Viele Gebäude sind von Planierraupen *(bulldozers)* zerstört worden.
2. Dieses Haus wurde von den Bürgern gerettet.
3. Viele Unterschriften *(signatures)* wurden von Studenten gesammelt.
4. Das Haus ist von der Uni gekauft worden.
5. Die Fassade wird von Spezialisten renoviert werden.
6. Die Hauspläne werden von Architekten gemacht.

BEISPIEL   Der Hausplan darf von den Architekten nicht sehr verändert werden.
Die Architekten dürfen den Hausplan nicht sehr verändern.

7. Ein Teil soll von der Stadt finanziert werden.
8. Der Rest muss von der Universität bezahlt werden.
9. Das Haus konnte von der Uni als Gästehaus ausgebaut werden.
10. Der große Raum im Parterre darf von den Studenten als Treffpunkt *(meeting place)* benutzt werden.

BEISPIEL   Das Gästehaus wird viel besucht.
Man besucht das Gästehaus viel.

11. Dort werden Gedanken ausgetauscht.
12. Es wird auch Englisch und Italienisch gesprochen.
13. Heute Abend wird ein Jazzkonzert gegeben.
14. Letzte Woche wurde ein Film gezeigt.
15. Hier werden auch Seminare gehalten werden.

D. Ein alter Film Wiederholen Sie die Sätze im Passiv, aber in einer anderen Zeitform!

BEISPIEL   Ein alter Film wird gespielt. *(simple past)*
Ein alter Film wurde gespielt.

1. Er wird von den Studenten sehr empfohlen. *(present perfect)*
2. Zu DDR-Zeiten wird er nicht gezeigt. *(simple past)*
3. Er wird verboten. *(past perfect)*
4. Es wird viel darüber geredet. *(future)*
5. Daraus kann viel gelernt werden. *(simple past)*
6. Er soll übrigens wiederholt werden. *(simple past)*

E. Post und Geld Wiederholen Sie die Sätze im Passiv, aber mit einem Modalverb! Wie heißt das auf Englisch?

BEISPIEL   Das Paket wird zur Post gebracht. (sollen)
Das Paket soll zur Post gebracht werden.
The package is supposed to be taken to the post office.

1. Ein Formular wird noch ausgefüllt. (müssen)
2. Dann wird es am ersten Schalter abgegeben. (können)
3. Auf der Post werden auch Telefongespräche gemacht. (dürfen)
4. Dollar werden auf der Bank umgetauscht. (sollen)
5. Nicht überall wird mit Reiseschecks bezahlt. (können)
6. Taxifahrer werden mit Bargeld oder Kreditkarte bezahlt. (wollen)

F. Im Restaurant Sagen Sie die Sätze im Passiv!

BEISPIEL   Hier spricht man Deutsch.
            Hier wird Deutsch gesprochen.

1. Am anderen Tisch spricht man Französisch.
2. Mittags isst man warm.
3. Dabei redet man gemütlich.
4. Natürlich redet man nicht mit vollem Mund.
5. Übrigens hält man die Gabel normalerweise *(normally)* in der linken Hand.
6. Und vor dem Essen sagt man „Guten Appetit!"

G. Schont die Parkanlagen! Sie und ein Freund (Ihr Partner/Ihre Partnerin) sind in einem deutschen Park und sehen dieses Schild. Sie lesen es, sind aber nicht ganz sicher, ob Sie es richtig verstanden haben. Sagen Sie, was Sie darunter verstehen! Wechseln Sie sich nach jedem Satz ab!

BEISPIEL   S1 Es wird gebeten, auf den Wegen zu bleiben.
            S2 Ich glaube, das bedeutet, dass man auf den Wegen bleiben soll.

SCHONT DIE PARKANLAGEN!

Es wird gebeten°:   please; lit. it is requested
Auf den Wegen zu bleiben
Blumen nicht abzupflücken°   pick
Hunde an der Leine zu führen°   lead on a leash
Denkmäler   sauber zu halten
Im Park nicht Fußball zu spielen
Fahrräder nicht in den Park mitzunehmen

H. Die Party: Was muss noch gemacht werden? Sagen Sie im Passiv, dass alles schon gemacht (worden) ist!

BEISPIEL   Fritz und Lisa müssen noch angerufen werden.
            Fritz und Lisa sind schon angerufen worden.

1. Die Wohnung muss noch geputzt werden. 2. Der Tisch muss noch in die Ecke gestellt werden. 3. Die Gläser müssen noch gewaschen werden. 4. Das Bier muss noch kalt gestellt werden. 5. Die Kartoffelchips müssen noch in die Schüssel *(bowl)* getan werden.

I. Wohin damit? Fragen Sie Ihren Partner/Ihre Partnerin, was bei Ihnen zu Hause mit Dingen wie alten Blumen, alten Telefons und Handys, Computern und Haushaltsmaschinen gemacht wird! Benutzen Sie dabei das Passiv!

BEISPIEL   S1 Was macht ihr mit alten Blumen?
            S2 Alte Blumen werden bei uns auf den Kompost geworfen.
            S1 Bei uns auch. / Bei uns nicht. Bei uns . . .

15.2 Review of the uses of *werden*

Distinguish carefully among the various uses of **werden.**

1. **werden** + predicate noun / adjective = a FULL VERB

Er wird Arzt.	*He's going to be a doctor.*
Es wird dunkel.	*It's getting dark.*

2. **werden** + infinitive = auxiliary of the FUTURE TENSE

Ich werde ihn fragen.	*I'll ask him.*

3. **würde** + infinitive = auxiliary in the PRESENT-TIME SUBJUNCTIVE

Ich würde ihn fragen.	*I would ask him.*

4. **werden** + past participle = auxiliary in the PASSIVE VOICE

Er wird von uns gefragt.	*He's (being) asked by us.*
Goethe wurde 1749 geboren.	*Goethe was born in 1749.*

● *NOTE:* To express *I was born* . . . , either **ich bin . . . geboren** or **ich wurde . . . geboren** are used. The simple past of the passive form must be used for people who are no longer living.

Übungen

J. Was ist was? Lesen Sie die folgenden Sätze und analysieren Sie sie mit Ihrem Partner/Ihrer Partnerin! Sagen Sie, wie **werden** benutzt wird und wie Sie das auf Englisch sagen würden! Wechseln Sie sich ab!

> BEISPIEL Leonie ist nach Amerika eingeladen worden.
> *werden + past participle = passive voice*
> *Leonie was invited to America.*

1. Leonie möchte Englischlehrerin werden.
2. Das Studium dort musste von ihr bezahlt werden.
3. Es ist allerdings teurer geworden, als sie dachte.
4. Das wurde ihr nie erklärt.
5. Was würdest du an ihrer Stelle tun?
6. Ich würde ein Semester arbeiten.
7. Das wird nicht erlaubt werden.
8. Übrigens wird ihr Englisch schon viel besser.
9. Der Amerikaaufenthalt wird ihr später helfen.

K. Der Strom *(electricity)* der Zukunft Lesen Sie den folgenden Text und entscheiden Sie, wie **werden** benutzt wird! Wie würde man das auf Englisch sagen?

> BEISPIEL Über die Umwelt <u>wird</u> viel <u>geschrieben</u>.
> *passive, present; is (being) written*
>
> Die Frage ist, <u>wird</u> man etwas dafür <u>tun</u>?
> *indicative, future; will do*

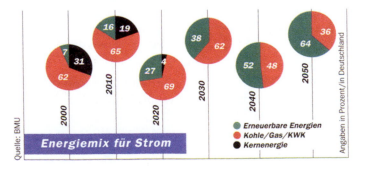

1. Seit der Ölkrise 1973 <u>wurde</u> in Deutschland viel Geld in die Forschung von alternativen Energien <u>investiert</u>. 2. Ein Resultat sind moderne „Windmühlen", durch die Strom <u>gewonnen wird</u>. 3. Investoren wissen, dass sie damit gut <u>verdienen werden</u>. 4. Die Windräder <u>werden</u> vom Staat <u>subventioniert</u> (*subsidized*). 5. Die Pachtverträge (*lease contracts*) <u>werden</u> oft auf zwanzig Jahre <u>gemacht</u>. 6. Wenn man heute durch Deutschlands Norden fährt, <u>wird</u> man immer wieder Windparks <u>sehen</u>, die mitten in die Felder <u>gestellt worden sind</u>. 7. Ihre Gegner (*opponents*) sprechen von einer „brutalen Zerstörung" der Landschaft. Häuser, die in der Nähe von solchen „Monstern" stehen, <u>werden</u> schlecht <u>zu verkaufen sein</u>. 8. Viele Leute protestieren dagegen, weil ihre Lebensqualität dadurch <u>beeinflusst wird</u>. 9. Sie sagen, man könnte diese „Windtürme" hören, sie <u>würden</u> Schatten (*shadows*) <u>werfen</u> und ihre roten Warnlichter <u>würden</u> nachts einen Disko-Effekt <u>geben</u>. 10. Ein Politikwissenschaftler, der dagegen ist, <u>wurde</u> von der Windlobby als „Don Quichotte" <u>verlacht</u> (*made fun of*). 11. In Deutschland <u>wird</u> heute schon so viel Windenergie <u>gewonnen</u> wie in Dänemark, Spanien und den USA zusammen. 12. Die Reparatur- und Wartungskosten (*repair and maintenance costs*) <u>werden</u> hoch <u>sein</u>. 13. Das, was sie produzieren, <u>wird</u> nicht genug <u>sein</u>. 14. So wie es aussieht, <u>wird</u> der Strom der Zukunft von einem Mix aus erneuerbaren (*renewable*) Energien, Kohle- (*coal*), Gas- und Kernenergie (*nuclear . . .*) <u>kommen müssen</u>. 15. Dabei <u>werden</u> die erneuerbaren Energien eine immer größere Rolle <u>spielen</u>.

15.3 The special subjunctive

German has another type of subjunctive, often called the SPECIAL SUBJUNCTIVE or SUBJUNCTIVE I. English only has a few remnants of this subjunctive.

Thanks be to God! / Long live Freedom! / Be that as it may.

In German, the special subjunctive is used in similar expressions.

Gott sei Dank! / Es lebe die Freiheit! / Wie dem auch sei.

Other than in such phrases, the Subjunctive I is rarely heard in conversation. It is primarily used in formal writing and indirect speech, often to summarize another person's findings or opinion. It is most frequently encountered in critical literary or scientific essays, in literature, and in news articles, where it distances the author from his or her report and preserves a sense of objectivity.

In general, the forms of the third person singular are the ones used most often because they clearly differ from those of the indicative. When the forms of the special subjunctive are identical with those of the indicative, the general subjunctive is used instead. At this point, you need only to be able to recognize the forms of the special subjunctive and know why they are used.

1. PRESENT-TIME forms

The PRESENT-TIME forms of the special subjunctive have the same endings as the general subjunctive and are added to the stem of the infinitive:

glauben	
ich glaube	wir glauben
du glaubest	ihr glaubet
er glaube	sie glauben

Note, however, that verbs having a vowel change in the second and third person singular of the indicative *do not* have that vowel change in the special subjunctive. Note also that the first and third person singular forms of **sein** are irregular in that they do not have an **-e** ending.

Infinitive	Special Subj. er / es / sie	Indicative er / es / sie
haben	**habe**	hat
sein	**sei**	ist
tun	**tue**	tut
denken	**denke**	denkt
fahren	**fahre**	fährt
sehen	**sehe**	sieht
werden	**werde**	wird
wissen	**wisse**	weiß
dürfen	**dürfe**	darf
können	**könne**	kann
mögen	**möge**	mag
müssen	**müsse**	muss
wollen	**wolle**	will

ich habe	wir haben
du habest	ihr habet
er habe	sie haben

ich müsse	wir müssen
du müssest	ihr müsset
er müsse	sie müssen

ich sei	wir seien
du seiest	ihr seiet
er sei	sie seien

Er sagte, er **habe** keine Zeit.   *He said he had no time.*
Er sagte, sie **sei** nicht zu Hause.   *He said she wasn't home.*

2. To refer to the FUTURE *(to later)*, combine the special subjunctive of **werden** with an infinitive.

werde . . . + infinitive

Er sagte, er **werde** bald fertig **sein.**   *He said he'd be finished soon.*

3. To form the PAST-TIME special subjunctive, use the special subjunctive of **haben** or **sein** with a past participle.

habe . . .
sei . . .   } + past participle

Er sagt, er **habe** keine Zeit **gehabt.**   *He says he didn't have time.*
Er sagte, sie **sei** nicht zu Hause **gewesen.**   *He said she hadn't been home.*

Fokus   In Search of an Identity

The unification of Germany and the progressive emergence of an ever more integrated Europe have contributed to a new assessment of what it means to be German. This search for a national identity goes back to a time well before Bismarck united the country in 1871. For centuries, Germany had been divided into numerous small, autocratically ruled principalities. This fragmentation contributed to the significant diversity among various parts of Germany, yet also inhibited the development of a broadly based democratic consciousness. While most Germans continue to reject nationalism and embrace the idea of a united Europe enthusiastically, a new pride in their own localities is noticeable at the same time. A new interest in local dialects, history, and the restoration and rebuilding of destroyed historical sites is symptomatic of this trend. As more people of other ethnic and religious heritages become German citizens, and the corresponding new customs and ways of living make for an increasingly diverse culture, the question of what it means to be German takes on new dimensions and continues to be as relevant as ever.

Übungen

L. Finden Sie den Konjunktiv und unterstreichen Sie ihn!

1. Städte deutscher Kultur

Mein Onkel sagte, dass Weimar, Leipzig, Halle, Wittenberg und Eisenach wichtige deutsche Kulturstädte seien. In Weimar sei Johann Wolfgang von Goethe Theaterdirektor und Staatsminister gewesen und dort habe Friedrich von Schiller seine wichtigsten Dramen geschrieben. In Leipzig habe Johann Sebastian Bach 27 Jahre lang Kantaten und Oratorien für den Thomanerchor komponiert. Dieser Knabenchor *(boys choir)* sei heute noch sehr berühmt. Nicht weit von Leipzig liege Halle, wo Georg Friedrich Händel geboren worden sei. In Wittenberg, das man heute die Lutherstadt nenne, habe Martin Luther mit seinen 95 Thesen die Reformation begonnen. Sein Zimmer auf der Wartburg bei Eisenach, wo er die Bibel ins Deutsche übersetzt hat, sei heute noch zu besichtigen. Man könne auch heute noch sehen, wo er dem Teufel ein Tintenfass nachgeworfen habe *(had thrown an inkwell at the devil)*. Er wisse allerdings nicht, woher diese Geschichte komme. Er glaube sie nicht.

● Goethe (1749–1832), Schiller (1759–1805), Bach (1685–1750), Händel (1685–1759), Luther (1483–1546)

Die Wartburg bei Eisenach

2. Gedanken zur Umwelt

Die Wissenschaftler sagten, dass man mit mehr Wohlstand *(affluence)* mehr Energie brauchen werde. Mehr Energie bedeute aber mehr Kohlendioxid-Emissionen *(carbon dioxide . . .)*. Kohlendioxid sei mitverantwortlich für den so genannten Treibhauseffekt *(greenhouse effect)*. Damit man die Umwelt nicht noch mehr verschmutze und ihr auf diese Weise noch mehr schade, müsse man alles tun, um sie zu schützen. Es müsse mehr in die Umwelttechnologie investiert werden. Die Nordamerikaner und Europäer tragen dabei eine besondere Verantwortung, denn sie, mit nur 10 Prozent der Weltbevölkerung, verbrauchen *(consume)* fast die Hälfte der Energie. In Asien liege der Verbrauch bei etwa einem Viertel der Weltenergie, obwohl allein in China 20 Prozent der Menschheit *(mankind)* lebe. Darüber solle man sich echt einmal Gedanken machen. Die Gefahr *(danger)* der Klimaveränderung und seiner Konsequenzen sei für viele Wissenschaftler die wichtigste Herausforderung *(challenge)* des 21. Jahrhunderts.

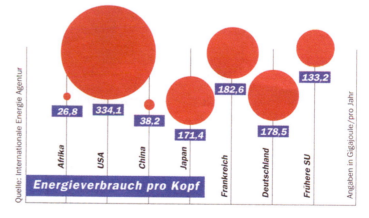

Quelle: Internationale Energie Agentur

26,8 | 334,1 | 38,2 | 171,4 | 182,6 | 178,5 | 133,2

Afrika | USA | China | Japan | Frankreich | Deutschland | Frühere SU

Energieverbrauch pro Kopf

Angaben in Gigajoule/pro Jahr

KLIMA UND UMWELT

Zusammenfassung

M. Der Leipziger Hauptbahnhof Übersetzen Sie die verschiedenen unterstrichenen Verbformen!

1. Der Leipziger Hauptbahnhof ist zu einem modernen Einkaufszentrum <u>umgebaut worden</u>. 2. Auf den drei neuen Ebenen *(levels)*, die durch große Freitreppen verbunden sind *(are connected)*, gibt es viele schöne Geschäfte und es <u>wird</u> viel <u>gebummelt</u>. 3. Wer auf der Durchreise ist und etwas Zeit hat, <u>wird</u> es hier interessant <u>finden</u>. 4. Eberhard Roll hat in der Nähe von Bahnsteig 13 / 14 seinen Juwelierladen *(jewelry store)*. Er hat als Schüler erlebt, wie am 7. Juli 1944 der Bahnhof <u>zerbombt wurde</u>. 5. Er sagt, dass er den Tag nie <u>vergessen werde</u>. 6. Heute ist er stolz, einer der ersten Mieter des neuen Hauptbahnhofs <u>gewesen zu sein</u>. 7. In den ersten sieben Tagen nach der Eröffnung <u>wurden</u> fast eine Million Besucher <u>gezählt</u>. 8. Die Innenstadt <u>ist</u> mit dem neuen Bahnhof um eine Attraktion reicher <u>geworden</u>. 9. Übrigens <u>werden</u> die meisten Geschäfte im Bahnhof auch sonntags nicht <u>geschlossen</u>. 10. Andere Städte <u>werden</u> dem Beispiel <u>folgen</u>.

Der neue Bahnhof in Leipzig

N. Dresdens Frauenkirche Lesen Sie durch den folgenden Text und übersetzen Sie die verschiedenen Verbformen; nur eine davon ist im Passiv! Welche Zeitformen werden dabei benutzt?

BEISPIEL Die Frauenkirche <u>zeigt sich</u> wieder in voller Pracht *(full splendor)*.
presents itself (present)

. . . crane / copper hood
dome / cross
direction / silversmith / made
air raid
died / Duke of Kent
enemies
appealed / building

landmark

Im Juni 2004 <u>setzte</u> ein Spezialkran° die kupferne Turmhaube° wieder auf die Kuppel° der Dresdner Frauenkirche. Das neue goldene Kreuz° <u>wurde</u> in England unter Leitung° eines Silberschmiedes° <u>hergestellt</u>°, dessen Vater 1945 als Pilot den Luftangriff° auf Dresden <u>mitgeflogen hatte</u>. Rund 35,000 Menschen <u>waren</u> dabei <u>ums Leben gekommen</u>°. Der Herzog von Kent°, Präsident des „Dresden Trust", <u>sagte</u> bei der Feier im Juni, dass das Projekt Menschen, die einst Feinde° <u>waren</u>, in Freundschaft <u>zusammengebracht</u> hätte. Er <u>appellierte</u>°, beim Aufbau° eines vereinten Europas die traurige Vergangenheit nicht <u>zu vergessen</u>. Seit Oktober 2004 <u>ist</u> der Wiederaufbau der Frauenkirche abgeschlossen. In der Festwoche <u>haben</u> die New Yorker Philharmoniker in dem wieder aufgebauten Wahrzeichen° Dresdens <u>gespielt</u>.

Dresdens Frauenkirche im Juni 2004. Die kupferne Turmhaube wird wieder auf die Kuppel des Gebäudes gesetzt.

Möge diese Welt mit Gottes Hilfe eine Wiedergeburt der Freiheit erleben!

● This is the text of the Liberty Bell in Berlin's Schöneberger Rathaus, a present of the US after the Berlin Blockade.

0. Wo ist mein Pass? Auf Deutsch bitte!

1. Yesterday was a bad day. 2. First I lost my passport. 3. Then my handbag and my money were stolen **(gestohlen).** 4. I tried to pay with traveler's checks. 5. But without my passport, my checks weren't accepted. 6. It was good that Anne was there. 7. The bill was paid by Anne. 8. This morning, I was called by the police **(die Polizei).** 9. They had found my handbag. 10. But my passport hasn't been found yet. 11. I wish I knew what I did with it. 12. I hope it will be found soon.

Einblicke

Wortschatz 2

die Bevölkerung	*population*
einzeln	*individual(ly)*
endlich	*finally*
gefährlich	*dangerous*
gemeinsam	*(in) common*
inzwischen	*in the meantime*
stolz (auf + *acc.*)	*proud (of)*
typisch	*typical(ly)*
verbinden, verband, verbunden	*to connect, tie together, link*
wachsen (wächst), wuchs, ist gewachsen	*to grow*
zusammen·wachsen (wächst zusammen), wuchs zusammen, ist zusammengewachsen	*to grow together*

Vor dem Lesen

A. Diagnose Identitätsschwund *(loss of identity)* Fragen Sie die anderen, . . . !

1. wer diese Leute im Bett sind
2. was das Bett symbolisiert
3. welche Leute sie an ihrem Hut / ihrer Mütze *(cap)* erkennen können
4. wer die Diagnose macht und wer auch zuschaut
5. was sie von der Zeichnung halten

Lesetipp

Anticipating Content (continued)

Anticipating the content of a text can help you prepare not only the vocabulary you need to understand the reading, but also the ideas that will be explored in the reading. This reading deals with issues of loss of national identity associated with the European Union. Brainstorm with a small group what you think the word **Europäisierung** could mean. What do you think some member states might be fearful of giving up? Make a list.

B. Fragen zum eigenen Land

1. Wie lange ist dieses Land (z. B. Amerika, Kanada usw.) schon ein Bundesstaat?
2. Wird Ihre Ausbildung im ganzen Land anerkannt *(recognized)* oder müssen Prüfungen wiederholt werden? Können Sie überall arbeiten?
3. Gibt es etwas, was typisch ist für die Bewohner *(residents)* mancher Staaten? Gibt es Spitznamen für sie?
4. Gibt es regionale Dialekte? Wenn ja, wo?

C. Das ist leicht zu verstehen! Welche Silbe ist betont? Markieren Sie sie! Was ist das auf Englisch?

der Dialekt, Kontakt, Lebensstandard; das Ausländische, Parlament; die Armee, Globalisierung, Identität, Kooperation, Lebensqualität, Luftverschmutzung, Meinung, Solidarität, Souveränität, Zusammengehörigkeit; aufwachsen; arrogant, europaweit, geteilt, kritisch, offiziell, regional, weltoffen; im Prinzip, teilweise, zu Beginn

Der Wind kennt keine Grenzen.

CD 9,
Track 9

Europa ist größer geworden. Seine 25 Mitgliedstaaten° haben zum Beispiel einen gemeinsamen Pass, ein gemeinsames Parlament, einen gemeinsamen Gerichtshof° und sogar eine kleine gemeinsame Armee. Allerdings haben sie nicht in allem eine gemeinsame Meinung, wie zum Beispiel in der Außenpolitik°.
5 Und doch macht man Fortschritte°; Europa scheint enger° zusammenzuwachsen. Jeder Europäer kann jetzt in jedem europäischen Land arbeiten; seine Ausbildung soll europaweit anerkannt° werden. Durch persönliche Kontakte wird sich allmählich° ein Gefühl der Zusammengehörigkeit und Solidarität entwickeln°. Das heißt aber nicht, dass Europa ein einziger° Bundesstaat wird, sondern es soll
10 ein loser Staatenbund° sein, in dem die einzelnen Staaten ihre Souveränität, ihre eigene Sprache und Kultur behalten° wollen. Auf eine europäische Hauptsprache hat man sich nicht einigen° können.

Was bedeutet es für Deutschland, dass es jetzt nicht mehr am Rande°, sondern in der Mitte Europas liegt? Natürlich fühlen sich die Deutschen als
15 Europäer, aber sie wollen auch Deutsche bleiben. Vor allem aber muss Deutschland selbst erst einmal° zusammenwachsen, denn es war ja bis 1990 offiziell ein geteiltes Land. Als die Mauer dann endlich fiel, existierte sie weiter in den Köpfen: Plötzlich gab es „Ossis" und „Wessis"°. Viele Westdeutsche meinten, dass die „Ossis" unselbstständige und ehrgeizlose arme Teufel° seien. Auf der
20 anderen Seite meinten viele Ostdeutsche, dass die „Wessis" arrogant seien und dächten, ihnen gehöre die Welt. Sie würden immer alles besser wissen—daher° der Spitzname „Besserwessis".

Was verbindet nun eigentlich alle Deutschen? Natürlich die Sprache, Kultur und Geschichte, aber im Prinzip gibt es eigentlich wenig, was typisch für alle
25 Deutschen wäre. Vielleicht sind es die kleineren Dinge im Leben. So könnte man zum Beispiel sagen, dass die meisten gesellig° sind und gern in Straßencafés oder Gartenrestaurants sitzen, dass sie Fußball lieben und sich in Vereinen organisieren. Die Familie und die Freizeit bedeutet ihnen oft mehr als der Staat. Sicherlich sind viele Deutsche reiselustig°, aber sie lieben auch ihre Heimat: die
30 Landschaft, in der sie aufgewachsen sind, die Stadt oder das Dorf. Viele sind wieder stolz auf ihre Herkunft°; regionale Dialekte werden wieder mehr gesprochen und auch im Radio und im Theater gepflegt°. Das mag teilweise historische Gründe° haben, denn die Bevölkerung bestand schon immer aus° verschiedenen Volksstämmen° und sie waren nur kurze Zeit *ein* Staat, nämlich
35 von Bismarcks Reichsgründung° 1871 bis zum Ende des 2. Weltkrieges 1945. Mit der zunehmenden° Europäisierung möchten viele gerade heute ihre regionale Identität nicht verlieren.

Wenn es schon schwer zu sagen ist, wie die Deutschen sind, so kann man doch sehen, dass sie europäischer geworden sind, das heißt weltoffener und
40 informierter. Auch ist die Bevölkerung mit einem größeren Anteil° von Ausländern multikultureller geworden. Die Deutschen sind heute kritischer und nicht mehr so autoritätsgläubig° wie zu Beginn des 20. Jahrhunderts. Das so genannte Typisch-Deutsche ist nicht mehr so wichtig; das Ausländische ist interessanter geworden. Es werden Jeans statt Lederhosen° getragen. Die Musik in Deutschland

member . . .	
court	
foreign policy	
progress / closer	
recognized	
gradually / develop	
just one	
loose confederation	
keep	
agree on	
at the outskirts	
first of all	
East and West Germans (*derogatory*) / poor devils without ambition	
hence	
sociable	
love to travel	
origin	
cultivated	
reasons / consisted of	
ethnic groups	
founding of the empire	
increasing	
share	
believing in authority	
leather pants	

45 ist international. Man isst besonders gern Italienisch, und französischer Wein wird genauso gern getrunken wie deutsches Bier. Ja, und man engagiert sich° wieder.

Der Kampf um° Umweltschutz und um eine bessere Lebensqualität ist auch sehr wichtig geworden. Man weiß, wie notwendig° die Kooperation der Nachbarländer ist, wenn es darum geht°, Probleme wie Kriminalität und Terrorismus zu
50 bekämpfen°. Natürlich wollen die Deutschen ihren hohen Lebensstandard erhalten, aber sie glauben, das dürfte auch mit weniger Energieverbrauch° und weniger Chemie möglich sein. Mülltrennung wird zum Beispiel in weiten Kreisen der Bevölkerung sehr ernst genommen°. Auch wissen sie, dass zum Beispiel die Luftverschmutzung nur europaweit bewältigt° werden kann, denn der Wind
55 kennt keine Grenzen.

Aktives zum Text

A. Was passt?

1. Die EU-Mitgliedstaaten haben _____ .
   - a. eine gemeinsame Bank
   - b. eine gemeinsame Sprache
   - c. ein gemeinsames Parlament
2. Die Ausbildung in verschiedenen europäischen Staaten soll in Zukunft in ganz _____ anerkannt werden.
   - a. Amerika
   - b. Deutschland
   - c. Europa
3. Damit können die Deutschen _____ überall in Europa studieren oder arbeiten.
   - a. fast
   - b. gemeinsam
   - c. leider
4. Als die Mauer 1989 fiel, existierte sie weiter in manchen _____.
   - a. Bäuchen
   - b. Gesichtern
   - c. Köpfen
5. Manche Westdeutschen dachten, dass „Ossis" _____ seien.
   - a. unselbstständig
   - b. arrogant
   - c. gefährlich
6. Manche Ostdeutschen dachten, dass „Wessis" _____.
   - a. arme Teufel seien
   - b. alle arm wären
   - c. immer alles besser wüssten
7. Vielleicht kann man allgemein von vielen Deutschen sagen, dass sie _____.
   - a. keine Fragen stellen
   - b. reiselustig sind
   - c. alle Dialekt sprechen
8. Sie lieben ihre _____.
   - a. Heimat
   - b. Spitznamen
   - c. Geschichte
9. Die Deutschen sollen _____ geworden sein.
   - a. autoritätsgläubiger
   - b. weltfremder
   - c. weltoffener
10. Auch sind sie umweltbewusster geworden und nehmen _____ ernst.
    - a. die ganze Bevölkerung
    - b. alles Ausländische
    - c. den Umweltschutz
11. Sie wissen, dass Kriminalität und _____ gemeinsam mit den Nachbarländern bekämpft werden müssen.
    - a. Umweltschutz
    - b. Terrorismus
    - c. ein hoher Lebensstandard
12. Auch die Luftverschmutzung ist etwas, was nicht _____ bewältigt werden kann.
    - a. allein
    - b. zusammen
    - c. gemeinsam

 B. Typisch Deutsch! Machen Sie mit den anderen eine Liste mit all den Eigenschaften, die der Autor im Text über die Deutschen erwähnt! Wie sehen diese (these) im Vergleich zu dem Bild aus, das Sie von den Deutschen haben?

C. Meinungsumfrage unter Deutschen Was erfahren Sie *(learn)* durch die Umfrage unter Deutschen im Alter von 18–25 Jahren? Wie hätten Sie darauf reagiert? Machen Sie eine Umfrage in Ihrer Klasse!

Wovor haben Sie am meisten Angst?	
Umweltkatastrophen	24%
Terrorismus	21%
Arbeitslosigkeit	17%
Einsamkeit *(loneliness)*	15%
Kriminalität	12%
Scheidung *(divorce)* der Eltern	5%
Prüfungen	4%
Ausländer	2%

Beim Wort „Europa" denke ich an . . .	
Kultur	29%
Zukunft	28%
Frieden	26%
Bürokratie	23%
Zahlmeister *(paymaster)* Deutschland	22%
Heimat	16%
nichts Besonderes	16%

Ich fühle mich vor allem als . . .	
Deutscher	31%
Kölner, Leipziger, Münchner . . .	16%
Europäer	14%
Weltbürger	13%
Hesse, Sachse, Thüringer . . .	10%
Ostdeutscher oder Westdeutscher	6%

 D. Hoppla, hier fehlt was: So sind sie. Schauen Sie sich die folgende Collage mit den verschiedenen nationalen Eigenschaften an! Eine zweite Collage ist im Anhang. Finden Sie mit Ihrem Nachbarn/Ihrer Nachbarin heraus, was die Leute aus diesen 12 Ländern charakterisiert. Sie brauchen nicht alles über sie aufzuschreiben, nur ein paar Wörter.

> Die Iren: sehr sportlich, . . .   Die Italiener: . . .
> Die Luxemburger: . . .   Die Holländer: . . .
> Die Portugiesen: . . .   Die Spanier: . . .

S1:
BEISPIEL   S1 Wie sind die Iren?
            S2 Die Iren lieben den Sport. Jeder zweite . . . Und wie sind die Belgier?
            S1 Sie haben . . .

Versorgte Belgier

Belgien ist mit Medikamenten super versorgt, hat die meisten Apotheken je Einwohner.

Patente Deutsche

Die Deutschen sind in Europa die größten Erfinder – sie melden jährlich über 260 000 Patente an.

Gesunde Griechen

Die Griechen essen die meisten Vitamine. Je Einwohner und Jahr 195 Kilo Gemüse und 76 Kilo Obst.

Gesellige Dänen

Die Dänen sind die geselligsten Europäer. 83 Prozent der Bevölkerung sind Mitglieder in Vereinen.

Lebensfrohe Franzosen

In Frankreich leben die Europäer am längsten, besonders Frauen. Sie werden im Schnitt älter als 80.

Belesene Briten

Die Briten sind zeitungsgierig. Auf jeden kommen 3 Zeitungen – Europa-Rekord im Zeitungslesen.

A visit to Weimar; the European University in Frankfurt/Oder; and concerns about the climate change:
http://wiegehts.heinle.com.

● There is an extensive review section following this chapter in the *Arbeitsbuch (Rückblick: Kapitel 12–15)*. The accompanying exercises and answer key will help you prepare for the test.

E. Was wäre, wenn . . . ? Stellen Sie sich vor, Sie hätten in ein anderes Land geheiratet! Was würde Ihnen als typisch amerikanisch (kanadisch usw.) dort fehlen? Oder meinen Sie, dass Sie überall gleich (equally) zu Hause sein könnten? Besprechen Sie das Thema mit Ihrem Partner/Ihrer Partnerin! Berichten Sie danach den anderen, was Sie herausgefunden haben!

F. Bericht: Die Deutschen Schreiben Sie, was der Lesetext—Absatz (paragraph) 3 bis 5—über die Deutschen zu sagen hat. Benutzen Sie dabei die indirekte Rede und den Konjunktiv I!

BEISPIEL   *Der Autor fragte sich, was alle Deutschen **verbinde**. Natürlich die Sprache, Kultur und Geschichte, aber im Prinzip **gebe** es eigentlich wenig, was typisch für alle Deutschen **sei**.*

Hörverständnis

Track 40

Europa-Schulen Hören Sie, was an diesen Schulen so besonders ist! Ergänzen Sie dann die folgenden Aussagen!

Zum Erkennen: erziehen (to educate, raise); die Klassenkameradin (classmate); das Lehrbuch, ¨er (textbook); chauvinistisch; die Flotte (fleet); sich konzentrieren auf (to concentrate on); der Rektor, -en (vice chancellor)

1. Europa-Schulen gibt es _____.
   a. in jedem Land der EU
   b. in mehreren europäischen Ländern
   c. auf der ganzen Welt

2. Die Schüler haben _____.
   a. keine Fächer in ihrer Muttersprache
   b. manche Fächer in ihrer Muttersprache
   c. nicht mehr als zwei Sprachen

3. Sie lernen Geschichte _____.
   a. immer in ihrer Muttersprache
   b. aus internationalen Lehrbüchern
   c. nie in ihrer Muttersprache

4. In französischen Lehrbüchern liest man _____.
   a. nicht viel über solche Länder wie Belgien oder Luxemburg
   b. interessante Informationen über englische Kultur
   c. stolz, wie Nelson die spanische Flotte bei Trafalgar zerstört hat

5. Die Schüler lernen im Geschichtsunterricht, _____.
   a. chauvinistischer zu werden
   b. die Geschichte ihres eigenen Landes objektiver zu sehen
   c. gutes Deutsch

Literatur

Biographisches

Franz Kafka (1883–1924) was a German-speaking Jewish writer, born in Prague, who gained international fame after World War II. His works, most of which were published posthumously, depict modern man's anxiety and alienation in a hostile and indifferent world. Typical for his work are characters who are frustrated in their attempts to gain knowledge, social acceptance, or salvation; their alienation is rooted in a feeling of personal guilt and an inescapable destiny. In his novel *Der Prozeß* (1925), a man is arrested, convicted, and executed by a mysterious court without ever learning the nature of his crime. *Das Schloß* (1930) portrays the futile struggle of a newcomer to gain acceptance in a village that is ruled by an unknown authority in the castle. *Amerika* (1927) describes the inconclusive struggle of a young immigrant trying to gain a foothold in an alien, incomprehensible country. Kafka's best-known short stories include: "Das Urteil," the story of a rebellious son condemned to suicide by his father; "Die Verwandlung," a detailed description of a son who suffers the literal and symbolic transformation into an ugly, fatally wounded insect; and "Ein Hungerkünstler," an exploration of the community where Kafka was born and the solitary life of an artist. For financial support Kafka worked most of his life as an insurance lawyer. He died of tuberculosis.

Erich Kästner (1899–1974) was a German writer known for his sarcastic poems—often directed against narrow-mindedness and militarism—and his witty novels and children's books. In 1933, the Nazis burned those books by Kästner that they considered disrespectful. Yet when officials noticed how well received his books were abroad, they relaxed their prohibition and allowed him to write apolitical and humorous stories and publish them through a Swiss publishing house. Kästner's works include the poetry anthology *Bei Durchsicht meiner Bücher* (1946) and the stories *Emil und die Detektive* (1929), *Das fliegende Klassenzimmer* (1933), *Das doppelte Lottchen* (1949), and *Konferenz der Tiere* (1949) in which he denounced the madness of armament. All his best-known works have been filmed. His satirical comedy *Die Schule der Diktatoren* appeared in 1957, the year in which he was awarded the renowned Büchner Prize.

Vor dem Lesen

Stilfragen zu Kafkas Parabel *(parable)* und Kästners Gedicht

1. a. In welcher Zeitform *(tense)* erzählt Kafka seine Parabel? Finden Sie verschiedene Beispiele davon im Text!
   b. Sind die Sätze kurz oder lang? einfach oder kompliziert *(complicated)*?
   c. Welches Pronomen benutzt der Erzähler immer wieder für sich?
   d. Wie spricht der Diener *(servant)* seinen Herrn an *(addresses)*, mit **Sie** oder mit **du**?
   e. Haben der Diener oder der Herr einen Namen?

2. a. In welcher Zeitform sind fast alle Verben in Kästners Gedicht?
   b. Gibt es Reime in diesem Gedicht? Wenn ja, folgen sie einem bestimmten Muster *(pattern)*, z. B. ababa, abbab oder abaab?
   c. Welches Pronomen wird immer wieder wiederholt?
   d. In der ersten und letzten Strophe erscheint *(appears)* ein Satz zweimal in der Vergangenheit. Wie heißt dieser Satz?
   e. In der zweiten Strophe benutzt ein Satz das Passiv. Finden Sie ihn! Was bedeutet er auf Englisch?

Der Aufbruch°

Track 41 Ich befahl° mein Pferd aus dem Stall° zu holen. Der Diener° verstand mich nicht. Ich ging selbst in den Stall, sattelte° mein Pferd und bestieg° es. In der Ferne° hörte ich eine Trompete blasen°, ich fragte ihn, was das bedeute. Er wusste nichts und hatte nichts gehört. Beim Tore hielt er mich auf und fragte:
5 „Wohin reitest du, Herr?" „Ich weiß es nicht", sagte ich, „nur weg von hier, nur

departure

ordered / stable / servant
saddled / climbed on
In the distance / sound of a trumpet

weg von hier. Immerfort° weg von hier, nur so kann ich mein Ziel° erreichen°."
„Du kennst also dein Ziel?" fragte er. „Ja" antwortete ich, „ich sagte es doch:
‚Weg-von-hier', das ist mein Ziel." „Du hast keinen Essvorrat° mit", sagte er.
„Ich brauche keinen", sagte ich, „die Reise ist so lang, dass ich verhungern°
10 muss, wenn ich auf dem Weg nichts bekomme. Kein Essvorrat kann mich retten.
Es ist ja zum Glück° eine wahrhaft ungeheuere° Reise."

Franz Kafka

Eisenbahngleichnis°

Track 42

Wir sitzen alle im gleichen Zug
und reisen quer durch° die Zeit.
Wir sehen hinaus. Wir sahen genug.
Wir fahren alle im gleichen Zug
5 und keiner weiß wie weit.

Ein Nachbar schläft, ein anderer klagt°,
ein dritter redet viel.
Stationen° werden angesagt°.
Der Zug, der durch die Jahre jagt,°
10 kommt niemals an sein Ziel.

Wir packen aus. Wir packen ein.
Wir finden keinen Sinn°.
Wo werden wir wohl morgen sein?
Der Schaffner° schaut zur Tür herein
15 und lächelt vor sich hin°.

Auch er weiß nicht, wohin er will.
Er schweigt° und geht hinaus.
Da heult° die Zugsirene schrill!
Der Zug fährt langsam und hält still.
20 Die Toten° steigen aus.

Ein Kind steigt aus. Die Mutter schreit.
Die Toten stehen stumm°
am Bahnsteig der Vergangenheit.
Der Zug fährt, er jagt durch die Zeit,
25 und niemand weiß, warum.

Die 1. Klasse ist fast leer.
Ein feister° Herr sitzt stolz
im roten Plüsch° und atmet° schwer.
Er ist allein und spürt° das sehr.
30 Die Mehrheit° sitzt auf Holz°.

Wir reisen alle im gleichen Zug
zur Gegenwart in spe°.
Wir sehen hinaus. Wir sahen genug.
Wir sitzen alle im gleichen Zug
35 und viele im falschen Coupé°.

Erich Kästner

. . . parable

all across

complains

stops / announced
races

purpose

conductor
to himself

keeps quiet
howls

dead

silently

fat

plush upholstery / breathes
feels
majority / wood(en benches)

full of hope

compartment

Nach dem Lesen

A. Inhaltsfragen zu Kafkas Parabel und Kästners Gedicht

1. a Was befiehlt *(orders)* der Herr dem Diener in Kafkas Parabel?
   b. Tut der Diener das? Warum (nicht)?
   c. Was hört der Herr in der Ferne und wie reagiert der Diener darauf?
   d. Warum will der Herr weg?
   e. Wohin reist er und was nimmt er mit?

2. a Wohin fährt der Zug in Kästners Gedicht?
   b. Fährt er langsam oder schnell?
   c. Wohin fahren die Leute und was tun sie während der Fahrt?
   d. Wer sitzt allein und wie fühlt er sich da? Wo sitzen die meisten Leute?
   e. Was meint Kästner damit, wenn er sagt, dass viele „im falschen Coupé" sitzen?

B. Ein Vergleich der beiden Parabeln

1. In Kafkas Geschichte beginnt die Reise gerade erst *(only just)*. Der Herr geht allein auf diese Reise. Er ergreift *(takes)* selbst die Initiative und sattelt sein Pferd. Was motiviert ihn? Wie bereitet er sich vor? Warum kann ihm niemand dabei helfen? Warum nimmt er nichts mit? Was ist sein Ziel? Wie interpretieren Sie das? Was will Kafka uns über den Sinn *(purpose)* des Lebens sagen?

2. In Kästners Gedicht hat die Reise schon begonnen. Die Menschen sitzen gemeinsam im Zug. Gibt es Zeichen *(indications)* von Initiative oder Resignation? Was ist das Ziel der Leute? Warum lächelt der Schaffner? Wer könnte das sein? Was will Kästner uns über den Sinn des Lebens sagen?

3. Was halten Sie von den beiden Parabeln? Ist eine der Parabeln positiver als die andere? Warum (nicht)? Bitte erklären Sie und begründen *(support)* Sie Ihre Antwort mit Beispielen aus den Texten!

Appendix

1. Predicting the gender of certain nouns

As a rule, nouns must be learned with their articles because their genders are not readily predictable. However, here are a few hints to help you determine the gender of some nouns in order to eliminate unnecessary memorizing.

a. Most nouns referring to males are MASCULINE.

der Vater, der Bruder, der Junge

- Days, months, and seasons are masculine.

    der Montag, der Juni, der Winter

b. Most nouns referring to females are FEMININE.

die Mutter, die Schwester, die Frau BUT das Mädchen, das Fräulein (*Miss*, seldom used today)

- Many feminine nouns can be derived from masculine nouns by adding **-in.** Their plurals always end in **-nen.**

    sg.: der Schweizer/die Schweizerin; der Österreicher/die Österreicherin

    pl.: die Schweizerinnen, Österreicherinnen

- Most nouns ending in **-heit, -keit, -ie, -ik, -ion, -schaft, -tät,** and **-ung** are feminine. Their plurals end in **-en.**

    sg.: die Schönheit, Richtigkeit, Geographie, Musik, Religion, Nachbarschaft, Qualität, Rechnung

    pl.: die Qualitäten, Rechnungen usw.

- Most nouns ending in **-e** are feminine. Their plurals end in **-n.**

    sg.: die Sprache, Woche, Hose, Kreide, Farbe, Seite

    pl.: die Sprachen, Wochen usw.

c. All nouns ending in **-chen** or **-lein** are NEUTER. These two suffixes make diminutives of nouns, that is, they denote them as being small. In the case of people, the diminutive may indicate affection, or even belittlement. Such nouns often have an umlaut, but there is no plural ending.

sg.: der Bruder → das Brüderchen; die Schwester → das Schwesterlein

pl.: die Brüderchen, Schwesterlein

- Because of these suffixes, two nouns referring to females are neuter.

    das Mädchen, das Fräulein (*see b. above*)

- Most cities and countries are neuter.

    (das) Berlin, (das) Deutschland BUT die Schweiz, die Türkei, der Irak

2. Summary chart of the four cases

	use	follows . . .	masc.	neut.	fem.	pl.
nom.	Subject, predicate noun **wer? was?**	**heißen, sein, werden**	der dieser[1] ein mein[2]	das dieses ein mein	die diese eine meine	die diese keine meine
acc.	Direct object **wen? was?**	**durch, für, gegen, ohne, um**	den diesen einen meinen			
		an, auf, hinter, in, neben, über, unter, vor, zwischen				
dat.	Indirect object **wem?**	**aus, außer, bei, mit, nach, seit, von, zu** **antworten, danken, gefallen, gehören, glauben,**[3] **helfen, zuhören** usw.	dem diesem einem meinem	dem diesem einem meinem	der dieser einer meiner	den diesen keinen meinen
gen.	Possessive **wessen?**	**(an)statt, trotz, während, wegen**	des dieses eines meines	des dieses eines meines	der dieser keiner meiner	der dieser keiner meiner

---

NOTE: [1] The **der**-words are **dieser, jeder, welcher, alle, manche, solche.**

[2] The **ein**-words are **kein, mein, dein, sein, ihr, unser, euer, ihr, Ihr.**

[3] Ich glaube **ihm.** BUT Ich glaube **es.**

3. Adjective endings

a. Preceded adjectives

	masculine	neuter	feminine	plural
nom.	der neue Krimi	das neue Stück	die neue Oper	die neuen Filme
acc.	den neuen Krimi	das neue Stück	die neue Oper	die neuen Filme
dat.	dem neuen Krimi	dem neuen Stück	der neuen Oper	den neuen Filmen
gen.	des neuen Krimis	des neuen Stückes	der neuen Oper	der neuen Filme

	masculine	neuter	feminine	plural
nom.	ein neuer Krimi	ein neues Stück	eine neue Oper	keine neuen Filme
acc.	einen neuen Krimi	ein neues Stück	eine neue Oper	keine neuen Filme
dat.	einem neuen Krimi	einem neuen Stück	einer neuen Oper	keinen neuen Filmen
gen.	eines neuen Krimis	eines neuen Stückes	einer neuen Oper	keiner neuen Filme

Comparing the two tables above, you can see:

- Adjectives preceded by the definite article or any **der**-word have either an **-e** or **-en** ending.
- Adjectives preceded by the indefinite article or any **ein**-word have two different adjective endings WHENEVER **ein** HAS NO ENDING: **-er** for masculine nouns and **-es** for neuter nouns. Otherwise the **-en** ending predominates and is used in the masculine accusative singular, all datives and genitives, and in all plurals.

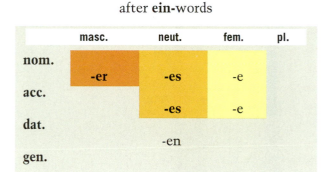

after **der**-words	masc.	neut.	fem.	pl.
nom.				
acc.		-e		
dat.				
gen.		-en		

after **ein**-words	masc.	neut.	fem.	pl.
nom.	-er	-es	-e	
acc.		-es	-e	
dat.				
gen.		-en		

Or, to put it in another way, the endings are:

- in the NOMINATIVE AND ACCUSATIVE SINGULAR

    –after **der, das, die,** and **eine** → **-e**

    –after **ein**   with masc. nouns → **-er**

          with neut. nouns → **-es**

- in ALL OTHER CASES   → **-en**

b. **Unpreceded adjectives**

Unpreceded adjectives take the endings that the definite article would have, if it were used.

der frische Fisch	**das** frische Obst	**die** frische Wurst	**die** frischen Eier
frisch**er** Fisch	frisch**es** Obst	frische Wurst	frische Eier

	masculine	neuter	feminine	plural
nom.	frisch**er** Fisch	frisch**es** Obst	frische Wurst	frische Eier
acc.	frisch**en** Fisch	frisch**es** Obst	frische Wurst	frische Eier
dat.	frisch**em** Fisch	frisch**em** Obst	frisch**er** Wurst	frisch**en** Eiern
gen.	(frisch**en** Fisches)	(frisch**en** Obstes)	(frisch**er** Wurst)	frisch**er** Eier

Several important words are often used as unpreceded adjectives in the plural: **andere, einige, mehrere, viele, wenige.**

4. Endings of nouns

a. **N-nouns**

	singular	plural
nom.	der Student	die Studenten
acc.	den Student**en**	die Studenten
dat.	dem Student**en**	den Studenten
gen.	des Student**en**	der Studenten

Other n-nouns are: **Herr (-n, -en), Franzose, Gedanke (-ns, -n), Journalist, Junge, Komponist, Mensch, Nachbar, Name (-ns, -n), Polizist, Tourist, Zimmerkollege.**

b. **Adjectival nouns**

	SINGULAR		PLURAL
	masc.	**fem.**	
nom.	der Deutsche ein Deutscher	die Deutsche eine Deutsche	die Deutschen keine Deutschen
acc.	den Deutschen einen Deutschen		
dat.	dem Deutschen einem Deutschen	der Deutschen einer Deutschen	den Deutschen keinen Deutschen
gen.	des Deutschen eines Deutschen	der Deutschen einer Deutschen	der Deutschen keiner Deutschen

Other adjectival nouns are: **der/die Angestellte, Bekannte, Kranke, Verlobte, der Beamte** (BUT **die Beamtin**).

5. Pronouns

a. **Personal pronouns**

nom.	ich	du	er	es	sie	wir	ihr	sie	Sie
acc.	mich	dich	ihn	es	sie	uns	euch	sie	Sie
dat.	mir	dir	ihm	ihm	ihr	uns	euch	ihnen	Ihnen

b. **Reflexive pronouns**

nom.	ich	du	er / es / sie	wir	ihr	sie	Sie
acc.	mich	dich					
dat.	mir	dir	sich	uns	euch	sich	sich

c. **Relative pronouns**

	masc.	neut.	fem.	pl.
nom.	der	das	die	die
acc.	den	das	die	die
dat.	dem	dem	der	denen
gen.	dessen	dessen	deren	deren

6. Comparison of irregular adverbs and adjectives

	gern	groß	gut	hoch	nah	viel
comparative	lieber	größer	besser	höher	näher	mehr
superlative	liebst-	größt-	best-	höchst-	nächst-	meist-

7. N-verbs ("strong verbs") and irregular t-verbs ("weak verbs")

a. Principal parts listed alphabetically

This list is limited to the active n-verbs and irregular t-verbs used in this text. Compound verbs like **ankommen** or **abfliegen** are not included, since their principal parts are the same as those of the basic verbs **kommen** and **fliegen**.

infinitive	present	simple past	past participle	meaning
anfangen	fängt an	fing an	angefangen	*to begin*
backen	bäckt	buk (backte)	gebacken	*to bake*
beginnen		begann	begonnen	*to begin*
bekommen		bekam	bekommen	*to receive, get*
bewerben	bewirbt	bewarb	beworben	*to apply*
bieten		bot	geboten	*to offer*
binden		band	gebunden	*to bind, tie*
bitten		bat	gebeten	*to ask, request*
bleiben		blieb	ist geblieben	*to remain*
bringen		brachte	gebracht	*to bring*
denken		dachte	gedacht	*to think*
einladen	lädt ein	lud ein	eingeladen	*to invite*
empfehlen	empfiehlt	empfahl	empfohlen	*to recommend*
entscheiden		entschied	entschieden	*to decide*
essen	isst	aß	gegessen	*to eat*
fahren	fährt	fuhr	ist gefahren	*to drive, go*
fallen	fällt	fiel	ist gefallen	*to fall*
finden		fand	gefunden	*to find*
fliegen		flog	ist geflogen	*to fly*
geben	gibt	gab	gegeben	*to give*
gefallen	gefällt	gefiel	gefallen	*to please*
gehen		ging	ist gegangen	*to go*
genießen	genießt	genoss	genossen	*to enjoy*
geschehen	geschieht	geschah	ist geschehen	*to happen*
haben	hat	hatte	gehabt	*to have*
halten	hält	hielt	gehalten	*to hold; stop*
hängen		hing	gehangen	*to be hanging*
heißen	heißt	hieß	geheißen	*to be called / named*
helfen	hilft	half	geholfen	*to help*
kennen		kannte	gekannt	*to know*
klingen		klang	geklungen	*to sound*
kommen		kam	ist gekommen	*to come*
lassen	lässt	ließ	gelassen	*to let; leave (behind)*
laufen	läuft	lief	ist gelaufen	*to run; walk*
lesen	liest	las	gelesen	*to read*
liegen		lag	gelegen	*to lie*
nehmen	nimmt	nahm	genommen	*to take*
nennen		nannte	genannt	*to name, call*
reißen	reißt	riss	gerissen	*to tear*
rufen		rief	gerufen	*to call*
scheinen		schien	geschienen	*to shine; seem*
schlafen	schläft	schlief	geschlafen	*to sleep*
schreiben		schrieb	geschrieben	*to write*
schwimmen		schwamm	ist geschwommen	*to swim*
sehen	sieht	sah	gesehen	*to see*
sein	ist	war	ist gewesen	*to be*

infinitive	present	simple past	past participle	meaning
singen		sang	gesungen	*to sing*
sitzen		saß	gesessen	*to sit*
spinnen		spann	gesponnen	*to spin*
sprechen	spricht	sprach	gesprochen	*to speak*
springen		sprang	ist gesprungen	*to jump*
stehen		stand	gestanden	*to stand*
steigen		stieg	ist gestiegen	*to climb*
sterben	stirbt	starb	ist gestorben	*to die*
tragen	trägt	trug	getragen	*to carry; wear*
treffen	trifft	traf	getroffen	*to meet*
treiben		trieb	getrieben	*to engage in (sports)*
trinken		trank	getrunken	*to drink*
tun	tut	tat	getan	*to do*
vergessen	vergisst	vergaß	vergessen	*to forget*
vergleichen		verglich	verglichen	*to compare*
verlieren		verlor	verloren	*to lose*
verschwinden		verschwand	ist verschwunden	*to disappear*
wachsen	wächst	wuchs	ist gewachsen	*to grow*
waschen	wäscht	wusch	gewaschen	*to wash*
werden	wird	wurde	ist geworden	*to become; get*
werfen	wirft	warf	geworfen	*to throw*
wissen	weiß	wusste	gewusst	*to know*
ziehen		zog	(ist) gezogen	*to pull; (move)*

b. **Principal parts listed by stem-changing groups**

This is the same list as the previous one, but this time it is divided into groups with the same stem changes.

I. essen	(isst)	aß	gegessen
vergessen	(vergisst)	vergaß	vergessen
geben	(gibt)	gab	gegeben
geschehen	(geschieht)	geschah	ist geschehen
sehen	(sieht)	sah	gesehen
lesen	(liest)	las	gelesen
bitten		bat	gebeten
liegen		lag	gelegen
sitzen		saß	gesessen
II. bewerben	(bewirbt)	bewarb	beworben
empfehlen	(empfiehlt)	empfahl	empfohlen
helfen	(hilft)	half	geholfen
nehmen	(nimmt)	nahm	genommen
sprechen	(spricht)	sprach	gesprochen
sterben	(stirbt)	starb	ist gestorben
treffen	(trifft)	traf	getroffen
werfen	(wirft)	warf	geworfen
beginnen		begann	begonnen
schwimmen		schwamm	ist geschwommen
spinnen		spann	gesponnen
bekommen		bekam	bekommen
kommen		kam	ist gekommen

III.	binden		band	gebunden
	finden		fand	gefunden
	klingen		klang	geklungen
	singen		sang	gesungen
	springen		sprang	ist gesprungen
	trinken		trank	getrunken
	verschwinden		verschwand	ist verschwunden
IV.	bleiben		blieb	ist geblieben
	entscheiden		entschied	entschieden
	scheinen		schien	geschienen
	schreiben		schrieb	geschrieben
	steigen		stieg	ist gestiegen
	treiben		trieb	getrieben
	reißen	(reißt)	riss	gerissen
V.	bieten		bot	geboten
	fliegen		flog	ist geflogen
	genießen	(genießt)	genoss	genossen
	verlieren		verlor	verloren
	ziehen		zog	ist gezogen
VI.	einladen	(lädt ein)	lud ein	eingeladen
	fahren	(fährt)	fuhr	ist gefahren
	tragen	(trägt)	trug	getragen
	wachsen	(wächst)	wuchs	ist gewachsen
	waschen	(wäscht)	wusch	gewaschen
VII.	fallen	(fällt)	fiel	ist gefallen
	gefallen	(gefällt)	gefiel	gefallen
	halten	(hält)	hielt	gehalten
	lassen	(lässt)	ließ	gelassen
	schlafen	(schläft)	schlief	geschlafen
	laufen	(läuft)	lief	ist gelaufen
	heißen	(heißt)	hieß	geheißen
	rufen		rief	gerufen

VIII. N-verbs that do not belong to any of the groups above:

anfangen	(fängt an)	fing an	angefangen
backen	(bäckt)	buk (backte)	gebacken
gehen		ging	ist gegangen
hängen		hing	gehangen
sein	(ist)	war	ist gewesen
stehen		stand	gestanden
tun	(tut)	tat	getan
werden	(wird)	wurde	ist geworden

IX. Irregular t-verbs:

bringen		brachte	gebracht
denken		dachte	gedacht
haben	(hat)	hatte	gehabt
kennen		kannte	gekannt
nennen		nannte	genannt
wissen	(weiß)	wusste	gewusst

8. Sample forms of the subjunctive

a. General subjunctive (Subjunctive II)

	können	haben	sein	werden	lernen	bringen	gehen
ich	könnte	hätte	wäre	würde	lernte	brächte	ginge
du	könntest	hättest	wärest	würdest	lerntest	brächtest	gingest
er	könnte	hätte	wäre	würde	lernte	brächte	ginge
wir	könnten	hätten	wären	würden	lernten	brächten	gingen
ihr	könntet	hättet	wäret	würdet	lerntet	brächtet	ginget
sie	könnten	hätten	wären	würden	lernten	brächten	gingen

b. Special subjunctive (Subjunctive I)

	können	haben	sein	werden	lernen	bringen	gehen
ich	könne	habe	sei	werde	lerne	bringe	gehe
du	könnest	habest	seiest	werdest	lernest	bringest	gehest
er	könne	habe	seie	werde	lerne	bringe	gehe
wir	können	haben	seien	werden	lernen	bringen	gehen
ihr	könnet	habet	seiet	werdet	lernet	bringet	gehet
sie	können	haben	seien	werden	lernen	bringen	gehen

9. Verb forms in different tenses

a. Indicative

	present		simple past		future	
ich	frage	fahre	fragte	fuhr	werde	
du	fragst	fährst	fragtest	fuhrst	wirst	
er	fragt	fährt	fragte	fuhr	wird	fragen / fahren
wir	fragen	fahren	fragten	fuhren	werden	
ihr	fragt	fahrt	fragtet	fuhrt	werdet	
sie	fragen	fahren	fragten	fuhren	werden	

	pres. perf.				past perf.			
ich	habe		bin		hatte		war	
du	hast		bist		hattest		warst	
er	hat	gefragt	ist	gefahren	hatte	gefragt	war	gefahren
wir	haben		sind		hatten		waren	
ihr	habt		seid		hattet		wart	
sie	haben		sind		hatten		waren	

b. Subjunctive

PRESENT-TIME

	general subj.				special subj.	
ich	fragte	führe	würde		frage	fahre
du	fragtest	führest	würdest		fragest	fahrest
er	fragte	führe	würde	fragen / fahren	frage	fahre
wir	fragten	führen	würden		fragen	fahren
ihr	fragtet	führet	würdet		fraget	fahret
sie	fragten	führen	würden		fragen	fahren

PAST-TIME

	general subj.				special subj.		
ich	hätte			habe			
du	hättest		wäre	habe			sei
du	hättest		wärest	habest			seiest
er	hätte	gefragt	wäre	gefahren	habe	gefragt	sei	gefahren
wir	hätten		wären	haben		seien
ihr	hättet		wäret	habet		seiet
sie	hätten		wären	haben		seien

c. **Passive voice**

	present		simple past		future	
ich	werde		wurde		werde	
du	wirst		wurdest		wirst	
er	wird	gefragt	wurde	gefragt	wird	gefragt werden
wir	werden		wurden		werden	
ihr	werdet		wurdet		werdet	
sie	werden		wurden		werden	

	pres. perf.		past perf.	
ich	bin		war	
du	bist		warst	
er	ist	gefragt worden	war	gefragt worden
wir	sind		waren	
ihr	seid		wart	
sie	sind		waren	

10. Translation of the Gespräche

Schritt 1

p. 4

How are you?   MR. SANDERS: Hello. MS. LEHMANN: Hello. MR. SANDERS: My name is Sanders, Willi Sanders. And what's your name? MS. LEHMANN: My name is Erika Lehmann. MR. SANDERS: Pleased to meet you.

MR. MEIER: Good morning, Mrs. Fiedler. How are you? MRS. FIEDLER: Fine, thank you. And you? MR. MEIER: I'm fine, too. Thank you.

HEIDI: Hi, Ute! How are you? UTE: Hi, Heidi! Oh, I'm tired. HEIDI: So am I. Too much stress. See you later! UTE: Bye! Take care!

Schritt 2

p. 7

What's that?   GERMAN PROFESSOR: Listen carefully and answer in German. What is that? JIM MILLER: That's the pencil. GERMAN PROFESSOR: What color is the pencil? SUSAN SMITH: Yellow. GERMAN PROFESSOR: Make a sentence, please. SUSAN SMITH: The pencil is yellow. GERMAN PROFESSOR: Is the notebook yellow, too? DAVID JENKINS: No, the notebook isn't yellow. The notebook is light blue. GERMAN PROFESSOR:

Good. SUSAN SMITH: What does *hellblau* mean? GERMAN PROFESSOR: *Hellblau* means *light blue* in English. SUSAN SMITH: And how does one say *dark blue*? GERMAN PROFESSOR: *Dunkelblau*. SUSAN SMITH: Oh, the pen is dark blue. GERMAN PROFESSOR: Correct. That's all for today. For tomorrow please read the dialogue again and learn the vocabulary, too.

p. 11   ### Schritt 3

In the department store   SALESCLERK: Well, how are the pants? CHRISTIAN: Too big and too long. SALESCLERK: And the sweater? MEIKE: Too expensive. CHRISTIAN: But the colors are great. Too bad!

SALESCLERK: Hello. May I help you? SILVIA: I need some pencils and paper. How much are the pencils? SALESCLERK: 55 cents. SILVIA: And the paper? SALESCLERK: 2 euros 40 cents. SILVIA: Fine. I'll take six pencils and the paper. SALESCLERK: Is that all? SILVIA: Yes, thank you. SALESCLERK: 5 euros 70 cents.

p. 16   ### Schritt 4

The weather in April NORBERT: It's nice today, isn't it? JULIA: Yes, that's for sure. The sun is shining again. RUDI: Only the wind is cool. JULIA: Oh, that doesn't matter. NORBERT: I think it's great.

HANNES: Man, what lousy weather! It's already snowing again. MARTIN: So what? HANNES: In Mallorca it's nice and beautiful. MARTIN: But we're here, and not in Mallorca. HANNES: Too bad.

LEA: The weather is awful, isn't it? HEIKO: I think so, too. It's raining and raining. SARA: And it's so cold again. Only 7 degrees! HEIKO: Yes, typical April.

p. 20   ### Schritt 5

What time is it? RITA: Hi, Axel! What time is it? AXEL: Hi, Rita! It's ten to eight. RITA: Oh no, in ten minutes I have philosophy. AXEL: Take care, then. Bye! RITA: Yes, bye!

PHILLIP: Hi, Steffi! What time is it? STEFFI: Hi, Phillip! It's eleven thirty. PHILLIP: Shall we eat now? STEFFI: OK, the lecture doesn't start till a quarter past one.

MR. RICHTER: When are you finished today? MR. HEROLD: At two o'clock. Why? MR. RICHTER: Are we going to play tennis today? MR. HEROLD: Yes, great! It's now twelve thirty. How about at quarter to three? MR. RICHTER: Fine! See you later!

p. 28   ### Kapitel 1

At the Goethe Institute SHARON: Roberto, where are you from? ROBERTO: I'm from Rome. And you? SHARON: I'm from Sacramento, but now my family lives in Seattle. ROBERTO: Do you have (any) brothers or sisters? SHARON: Yes, I have two sisters and two brothers. How about you? ROBERTO: I have only one sister. She lives in Montreal, in Canada. SHARON: Really? What a coincidence! My uncle lives there, too.

Later ROBERTO: Sharon, when is the test? SHARON: In ten minutes. Say, what are the names of some rivers in Germany? ROBERTO: In the north is the Elbe, in the east the Oder, in the south . . . SHARON: . . . the Danube? ROBERTO: Right! And in the west the Rhine. Where is Düsseldorf? SHARON: Düsseldorf? Hm. Where's a map? ROBERTO: Oh, here. In the west of Germany, north of Bonn, on the Rhine. SHARON: Oh yes, right! Well, good luck!

Kapitel 2

p. 50

At the grocery store CLERK: Hello. May I help you? OLIVER: I'd like some fruit. Don't you have any bananas? CLERK: Yes, over there. OLIVER: How much are they? CLERK: 90 cents a pound. OLIVER: And the oranges? CLERK: 45 cents each. OLIVER: Fine, two pounds of bananas and six oranges, please. CLERK: Anything else? OLIVER: Yes, two kilos of apples, please. CLERK: 8 euros 10 cents, please. Thank you. Good-bye.

In the bakery CLERK: Good morning. May I help you? SIMONE: Good morning. One rye bread and six rolls, please. CLERK: Anything else? SIMONE: Yes, I need some cake. Is the apple strudel fresh? CLERK: Of course, very fresh. SIMONE: Fine, then I'll take four pieces. CLERK: Is that all? SIMONE: I'd also like some cookies. What kind of cookies do you have today? CLERK: Lemon cookies, chocolate cookies, butter cookies . . . SIMONE: Hm . . . I'll take 300 grams of chocolate cookies. CLERK: Anything else? SIMONE: No, thank you. That's all. CLERK: Then that comes to 9 euros 55 cents, please.

Kapitel 3

p. 74

In the restaurant AXEL: Waiter, the menu, please. WAITER: Here you are. AXEL: What do you recommend today? WAITER: All of today's specials are very good. AXEL: Gabi, what are you having? GABI: I don't know. What are you going to have? AXEL: I think I'll take menu number one: veal cutlet and potato salad. GABI: And I will take menu number two: stuffed beef rolls with potato dumplings. WAITER: Would you like something to drink? GABI: A glass of apple juice. And what about you? AXEL: Mineral water. *(The waiter comes with the food.)* Enjoy your meal! GABI: Thanks, you too . . . Mm, that tastes good. AXEL: The veal cutlet, too.

Later GABI: We'd like to pay, please. WAITER: All right. All together? GABI: Yes. Please give me the bill. AXEL: No, no, no. GABI: Yes, Axel. Today I'm paying. WAITER: Well, one menu number one, one menu number two, one apple juice, one mineral water, two cups of coffee. Anything else? AXEL: Yes, one roll. WAITER: That comes to 30 euros 30 cents, please. GABI: *(She gives the waiter 40 euros)* Make it 32 euros, please. WAITER: And eight euros change (back). Thank you very much.

Kapitel 4

p. 100

On the telephone NADJA: Hi, Simon! SIMON: Hi, Nadja! How are you? NADJA: Not bad, thanks. What are you doing on the weekend? SIMON: Nothing special. Why? NADJA: It's Erik's birthday the day after tomorrow, and we're giving a party. SIMON: Great! But are you sure that Erik's birthday is the day after tomorrow? I think his birthday is on May 7. NADJA: Nonsense. Erik's birthday is on May 3. And Saturday is the third. SIMON: OK. When and where is the party? NADJA: Saturday at seven at my place. But don't say anything. It's a surprise. SIMON: OK. Well, see you then. NADJA: Bye. Take care!

Klaus rings Christa's doorbell NADJA: Hi, Erik! Happy birthday! ERIK: What? SIMON: All the best on your birthday! ERIK: Hello, Simon! . . . Hello, Silke! Tobias and Sabine, you too? ALL: We wish you a happy birthday! ERIK: Thanks! What a surprise! But my birthday isn't today; my birthday is on the seventh. NADJA: Really?—Well, then Simon was right. Oh well, it doesn't matter. We'll celebrate today.

p. 128 **Kapitel 5**

Excuse me! Where is . . . ? TOURIST: Excuse me! Can you tell me where the Hotel Sacher is? VIENNESE PASSERBY: First street on the left behind the opera. TOURIST: And how do I get from there to St. Stephen's Cathedral? VIENNESE PASSERBY: Straight ahead along Kärtner Straße. TOURIST: How far is it to the cathedral? VIENNESE PASSERBY: Not far. You can walk (there). TOURIST: Thank you. VIENNESE PASSERBY: You're welcome.

Over there TOURIST: Excuse me. Where is the Burgtheater? GENTLEMAN: I'm sorry. I'm not from Vienna. TOURIST: Pardon me. Is that the Burgtheater? LADY: No, that's not the Burgtheater, but the opera house. Take the streetcar to city hall. The Burgtheater is across from city hall. TOURIST: And where does the streetcar stop? LADY: Over there on your left. TOURIST: Thank you very much. LADY: You're most welcome.

p. 154 **Kapitel 6**

Apartment for rent ANNA: Hello, my name is Anna Moser. I've heard that you have a two-room apartment for rent. Is that right? LANDLORD: Yes, near the cathedral, with a view of the market square. ANNA: How old is the apartment? LANDLORD: Fairly old, but it's been renovated and it's quite big and light. It even has a balcony. ANNA: A balcony? That's super. I have a lot of plants. What floor is it on? LANDLORD: On the fourth floor. ANNA: Is it furnished or unfurnished? LANDLORD: Unfurnished. ANNA: And how much is the rent? LANDLORD: €550. ANNA: Is that without or with heat? LANDLORD: Without heat. ANNA: Oh, that's a little too expensive. Well, thank you very much. Good-bye! LANDLORD: Good-bye!

In the co-op ANNA: I like your house. JÖRG: We still have room for you. Come, I'll show you everything . . . Here on the left is our kitchen. It's small, but practical. ANNA: Who does the cooking? JÖRG: We all (do): Benno, Verena, and I. ANNA: And that's the living room? JÖRG: Yes. It's a bit dark, but that's all right. ANNA: I like your chairs. JÖRG: They're old, but really comfortable . . . Well, and up here are four bedrooms and the bathroom. ANNA: Mm, the bedroom is very cozy, but only one bath? JÖRG: Yes, unfortunately! But downstairs is another toilet. ANNA: How much do you pay per month? JÖRG: 200 euros each. ANNA: Not bad. And how do you get to the university? JÖRG: No problem. I walk. ANNA: (That) sounds good!

p. 180 **Kapitel 7**

At the bank TOURIST: Hello. Can you tell me where I can exchange money? TELLER: At counter 1. TOURIST: Thank you very much. *(She goes to counter 1.)* Hello. I'd like to exchange (some) dollars into euros. Here are my traveler's checks. TELLER: May I please see your passport? TOURIST: Here you are. TELLER: Sign here, please, then go to the cashier over there. There you'll get your money. TOURIST: Thank you. *(She goes to the cashier.)* CASHIER: 324 euros 63 cents: one hundred, two hundred, three hundred, ten, twenty, twenty-four euros and sixty-three cents. TOURIST: Thank you. Good-bye.

At the hotel reception desk RECEPTIONIST: Good evening. GUEST: Good evening. Do you have a single room available? RECEPTIONIST: For how long? GUEST: For two or three nights; if possible, quiet and with a bath. RECEPTIONIST: Unfortunately today we have only one double room, and that for only one night. But tomorrow there will be a single room available. Would you like to see the double room? GUEST: Yes, I would. RECEPTIONIST: Room number 12, on the second floor to the right. Here's the key. GUEST: Say, can I leave my suitcase here for a minute? RECEPTIONIST: Yes, of course. Put it over there in the corner. GUEST:

Thank you. One more thing, when do you close at night? RECEPTIONIST: At midnight. If you come later, you'll have to ring the bell.

Kapitel 8

p. 204

At the post office in the train station CLERK: Hi! UTA: Hi! UTA: I'd like to send this package to the United States. CLERK: By surface mail or by airmail? UTA: By airmail. How long will it take? CLERK: About one week. Please fill out this parcel form! . . . Just a minute. Your return address is missing here. UTA: Oh yes . . . One more thing. I need a telephone card. CLERK: For five, ten, twenty, or fifty francs? UTA: For twenty francs. Thank you!

At the ticket counter in Zurich ANNE: When does the next train for Interlaken leave? CLERK: In five minutes. Departure at 11:28 A.M., track 2. ANNE: Good grief! And when will it arrive there? CLERK: Arrival in Interlaken at 2:16 P.M. ANNE: Do I have to change trains? CLERK: Yes, in Bern, but you have a connection to the InterCity Express with only a 24-minute stopover. ANNE: Fine. Give me a round-trip ticket to Interlaken, please. CLERK: First or second class? ANNE: Second class.

Kapitel 9

p. 232

On the telephone MRS. SCHMIDT: This is Mrs. Schmidt. ANNEMARIE: Hello, Mrs. Schmidt. It's me, Annemarie. MRS. SCHMIDT: Hi, Annemarie! ANNEMARIE: Is Thomas there? MRS. SCHMIDT: No, I'm sorry. He just went to the post office. ANNEMARIE: I see. Can you tell him that I can't go out with him tonight? MRS. SCHMIDT: Naturally. What's the matter? ANNEMARIE: I'm sick. My throat hurts and I have a headache. MRS. SCHMIDT: I'm sorry. I hope you get better soon. ANNEMARIE: Thank you. Good-bye. MRS. SCHMIDT: Good-bye.

See you in a few minutes! YVONNE: Mayer residence. DANIELA: Hi, Yvonne! It's me, Daniela. YVONNE: Hi, Daniela! What's up? DANIELA: Nothing special. Do you feel like playing squash or going swimming? YVONNE: Squash? No thanks. I'm still sore from the day before yesterday. I can hardly move. I am hurting all over. DANIELA: Poor baby (*lit.* lame duck)! How about chess? YVONNE: OK, that sounds fine. Are you coming to my place? DANIELA: Yes, see you in a few minutes.

Kapitel 10

p. 260

A glance at the newspaper SONJA: Hey, what's on TV tonight? THEO: I have no idea. Nothing special for sure. SONJA: Let me see. *Good Times, Bad Times*, a documentary, and a detective story. THEO: I don't feel like (watching) that. SONJA: Maybe there's something at the movies? THEO: Yes, *Good bye Lenin!*, *Harry Potter*, and *Shrek 2*. SONJA: *Good bye Lenin* I've seen twice already, besides, I also have it on DVD. The movie is great! Maybe one day we can watch it together at my place, but not today. And *Harry Potter* and *Shrek 2* are for kids, aren't they? THEO: That's right. Hey, look! At the theater, they're playing *The Caucasian Chalk Circle*, by Brecht. SONJA: Not bad. Do you feel like going? THEO: Yes, that sounds good. Let's go.

At the ticket window THEO: Do you still have tickets for tonight? LADY: Yes, in the first row of the first balcony on the left, and on the right in the orchestra. THEO: Two seats in the orchestra. Here are our student ID's. LADY: 10 euros, please. SONJA: When does the performance start? LADY: At 8:15 P.M.

During the intermission THEO: Would you like a cola (drink)? SONJA: Yes, I'd love one. But let me pay. You've already bought the programs. THEO: OK. How did you like the first act? SONJA: Great. I once read the piece in school, but I've never seen it on stage. THEO: I haven't either.

p. 288 **Kapitel 11**

To each his own. SONJA: Hey, Nicole, listen! "Wanted: pretty, dynamic, affectionate EVA. Reward: good-looking ADAM with a big heart, end 20s, likes antiques, old houses, fast cars, animals, (and) kids. NICOLE: Hmm, not bad, but not for me. I don't like children and I'm allergic to animals. SONJA: Then have a look at this! "What I'm looking for exists. But how to find it? Artist, beginning 30s, charming, enterprising, musical is looking for a congenial, well-educated, reliable woman with a sense of humor." Does that sound interesting? NICOLE: Yes, perhaps. SONJA: He's looking for someone with a sense of humor. I like that, and I also like music. But whether he likes jazz? SONJA: Perhaps we could meet them both. NICOLE: I don't know. I think it's sort of stupid to meet people through ads in the newspaper. SONJA: Nonsense! Let's try it! What do we have to lose? NICOLE: What do you think, Frank? FRANK: I think you're crazy. But so what, to each his own! . . . Take a look at this! Somebody wants to give away a dog, a cat, and a bird, all together. NICOLE: That's all we need: a whole zoo! No thanks! FRANK: How about a little puppy or a little cat? SONJA: I love animals, but right now I don't have the space and also not enough time for that. FRANK: But such a little kitty doesn't need much. SONJA: Perhaps later. Right now I love my freedom. FRANK: And you want to meet with someone from the newspaper? NICOLE: Oh, you wouldn't understand.

p. 316 **Kapitel 12**

Do you know what you want to be? TRUDI: Say, Elke, do you already know what you want to be? ELKE: Yes, I'd like to become a cabinet-maker. TRUDI: Isn't that very strenuous? ELKE: Oh, you get used to it. Perhaps someday I'll open my own business. TRUDI: Those are big plans. ELKE: Why not? I don't feel like always sitting in an office and working for other people. TRUDI: And where do you want to apply for an apprenticeship? ELKE: No problem at all. My aunt has her own business and has already offered me a position. TRUDI: You're lucky. ELKE: And how about you? Do you know what you want to do? TRUDI: Perhaps I'll be a dentist. Good dentists are always needed and besides, it pays very well. ELKE: That's true, but that takes so long. TRUDI: I know, but I'm looking forward to it anyway.

p. 342 **Kapitel 13**

During registration PETRA: Hi, John. How are you? JOHN: Pretty good, and you? PETRA: Well, I can't complain. What are you doing there? JOHN: I've still got to fill out these registration forms. PETRA: Shall I help you? JOHN: If you have time. I'm always struggling with red tape. PETRA: Do you have your passport with you? JOHN: No, why? PETRA: Your residence permit is in it; you really need it. JOHN: I can get it quickly. PETRA: Do that. I'll wait for you here.

A little later JOHN: Here's my passport. I'll also have to decide soon what seminars I want to take. Can you help me with that, too? PETRA: Sure. What's your major? JOHN: My major is modern history. I'd like to take some seminars in German history and literature. PETRA: Here's my course catalog. Let's see what they're offering this semester.

p. 368 **Kapitel 14**

There's always something going on in Berlin. HEIKE: And that's the Memorial Church with its three buildings. We call them the "Hollow Tooth," the "Lipstick," and the "Compact." MARTIN: Berliners have nicknames for everything, you know. HEIKE: The old tower of the Memorial Church is to stay the way it is, as a memorial (to the war). The new Memorial Church with the new tower, however, is modern. Like so many things in Berlin: a lot of old things and a lot of new things. MARTIN: Tell me, do you like living here in Berlin? HEIKE: Of course! Berlin is really alive and has so much to offer, not only historically but also culturally. There's always something going on here. Besides, the surroundings are beautiful. MARTIN: Somewhere I read that 24 percent of Berlin's total area consists of forests and lakes, with 800 kilometers of biking trails. HEIKE: That's great, isn't it? MARTIN: Awesome! Say, were you there when they broke through the Wall? HEIKE: You bet! My parents and I waited all night, even though it was really cold. When the first piece of Wall tipped over, we all sang loudly: "A beautiful day like today, a day like this should never end." MARTIN: Yes, that was really incredible (*lit.* a unique experience). And now that's already a long time ago. HEIKE: Since then, a lot of things have changed in Berlin. The traces of the Wall are almost gone. MARTIN: Who would have ever thought that! HEIKE: Today, you really find everything here, a diverse (*lit.* colorful) mix of people and languages. MARTIN: Are you glad that Berlin is again the capital (of Germany)? HEIKE: Well, I couldn't imagine it any other way. MARTIN: Hey, would you like to take a little stroll through town this evening? HEIKE: OK, what would you be interested in? MARTIN: Actually in everything, maybe also a club or a pub. HEIKE: Let's go to the Prenzlauer Berg (district)! That ought to be interesting.

Kapitel 15 p. 396

A visit to Weimar TOM: It's funny, but this monument of Goethe and Schiller seems so familiar to me. I think I've seen it somewhere before. DANIELA: Have you (ever) been to San Francisco? TOM: Of course! DANIELA: Were you in Golden Gate Park, too? TOM: I see, there's exactly the same monument! I think the German-Americans in California had it built. DANIELA: Right! By the way, did you know that Weimar was the cultural capital of Europe for the year 1999? TOM: No, that's new to me. How come? DANIELA: In the 18th century, a lot of famous people lived here, and the Weimar Republic is also named for it. TOM: Yes, that's true. But this morning, when I looked down at the town from the memorial of the Buchenwald concentration camp, I had very mixed feelings. DANIELA: Yes, there you have a point (*lit.* you're right).

In the old part of town DANIELA: Look, the old houses here are really pretty, aren't they? TOM: Yes, they've been wonderfully restored. I find it especially nice that no cars are allowed here. DANIELA: Thank God! The façades wouldn't have survived the exhaust fumes of the Trabbis for long. TOM: In our city, there's now also a citizens' initiative to ban all cars from the old part of town in order to save the old buildings. DANIELA: I think that's good. TOM: Are the containers over there for recycling (*lit.* waste separation)? DANIELA: Yes, do you also have recycling? TOM: Yes, on a voluntary basis. In that respect, certainly much more could be done. For example, I never know how to get rid of my old batteries or medicine. DANIELA: Old batteries you can throw into special containers at every supermarket, and the old medications you bring to the pharmacy. TOM: We can't do that, and therefore a lot of things finally end up in the garbage can. DANIELA: With us [in Germany], that's forbidden. TOM: And that's the way it should be. In that regard, you're just more progressive than we are.

11. Supplementary charts for *Hoppla, hier fehlt was!*

p. 41 **Kapitel 1**

S2:

Name	Nationalität	Wohnort	Alter
Toni	Schweizer		32
Katja		Ulm	
	Österreicherin		61
	Französin	Lyon	
Pierre	Franzose		
	Italiener		25
Maria		Madrid	
	Kanadier		28
Amy		Miami	

p. 87 **Kapitel 3**

S2:

	Bruder	Schwester	Mutter	Vater	Großeltern
Bild					
Bücher					x
Tennishose					
Hausschuhe				x	
Pulli					
Ringe *(pl.)*					
T-Shirts		x			
Mantel			x		
Messer *(sg.)*	x				
Gläser					

p. 113 **Kapitel 4**

S2:

	Kai	Eva	Max	Sven	ich	Partner/in
an alles denken						
mit dem Essen helfen	x					
Getränke bringen			x		x	
den Sekt öffnen						
viel essen			x		x	
viel trinken			x			
schön singen						
etwas tanzen	x					
mit allen sprechen						
nichts tun						
nicht lange bleiben					x	

S2:

WER?	WAS?	WARUM?	WANN?	INFORMATION?
Dieter	bei den Wiener Festwochen in Wien sein	Er sieht nicht genug Opern und Theaterstücke. (können)		
	Silvester in Wien feiern		31.12–1.1.	www.wien-event.at
Sonja	das Museum moderner Kunst besichtigen	Es hat alles, von Pablo Picasso bis Andy Warhol. (sollen)		
	zum Christkindlmarkt am Rathausplatz		17.11–24.12.	www.christkindlmarkt.at
Karen + Charlie	zum Wiener Eistraum gehen	Da tanzen die Leute auf dem Eis vor dem Rathaus. (dürfen)		

Kapitel 6 p. 169

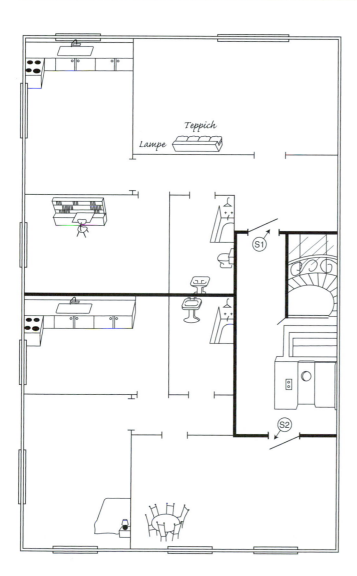

Kapitel 7

S2:

Wer?	Was tun?	Ja. / Nein.
Vater	bei der Bank vorbeigehen	Ja, gestern.
Vater	Geld umtauschen	Ja.
Mutter	die Kamera mitnehmen	
Mutter	die Nachbarn anrufen	
Thomas	die Telefonnummer aufschreiben	
Thomas	die Garagentür zumachen	Nein, noch nicht.
Carla	bei der Post vorbeigehen	Ja, gestern.
Carla	die Fenster zumachen	
Kinder	den Fernseher ausmachen (*turn off*)	
Kinder	die Lichter (*lights*) ausmachen	Nein, noch nicht.
Du	ein paar Bücher mitnehmen	

Kapitel 8

S2:

Wer	Wann / Wie lange	Wie / Obj. + Präposition	Wo und was
Lucian	ein paar Wochen		
Christl		bei ein- Gastfamilie	in Amerika sein
Steffi		wegen ihr- Prüfung	
Nina + Kim	während d- Ferien		von Passau bis Wien fahren
Ben + Michi			in ein- Pizzeria arbeiten
Günther		trotz d- Wetter	auf der Insel Rügen campen
Jutta	vom 1. bis 31. Juli		
Nicole		wieder	von Griechenland zurückkommen
Yvonne	morgens		
Jochen	mittags	gewöhnlich	

Kapitel 9

S2:

	Zuerst	Dann	Danach
BIRTE			
OLLI	s. schnell anziehen joggen gehen	s. duschen s. umziehen s. vor den Spiegel stellen	s. die Haare kämmen s. rasieren Joghurt und Müsli essen
VERA			
INGO	s. das Gesicht waschen s. eine Tasse Kaffee machen s. anziehen	s. an den Computer setzen s. die E-Mails ansehen	s. wieder hinlegen s. nicht beeilen

S2:

Wo?	Was?	Wann?
Volksbühne	*Macbeth*, Schauspiel von William Shakespeare	19.30
Urania-Theater		
Metropol-Theater	*West Side Story*, Musical von Leonard Bernstein	19.00
Im Dom		
Philharmonie		
Konzerthaus	*Flamenco-Festival*, mit Montse Salazar	20.00
Komödie		
Kammerspiele		
Filmbühne 1	*Das Leben ist eine Baustelle*, von Wolfgang Becker	
Filmbühne 2	*Nirgendwo in Afrika*, von Caroline Link	

Kapitel 11

p. 306

S2:

	Nachdem . . .	Dann . . .
Thomas	die Anzeige lesen	den Besitzer *(owner)* anrufen
Besitzer	über die Katze erzählen	
Thomas	dorthin fahren und s. die Katze ansehen	s. in die Katze verlieben
Thomas	die Katze mit nach Hause nehmen	
die beiden	ihr etwas Milch geben	mit ihr spielen
die Katze	s. einleben *(get used to the place)*	
die beiden	die Katze eine Woche haben	wässrige *(watery)* Augen und eine verstopfte *(stuffed-up)* Nase bekommen
Ingo	die Katze zwei Wochen auf seinem Bett haben	
die beiden	eine lange Diskussion haben	eine Anzeige in die Zeitung setzen
Besitzer	zwei Wochen ohne die Katze sein	
Besitzer	auf die Anzeige antworten	die Katze zurücknehmen

Kapitel 13

p. 356

Und was sagt Ihnen Ihr Partner/Ihre Partnerin?

	Ja	Nein
Die Oma ist gern zur Schule gegangen.	x	
Sie war gut in Mathe.		
Sie hat an der Uni studiert.		
Sie ist Lehrerin geworden.		
Sie hat bei einer reichen Familie gearbeitet.		
Sie hat geheiratet.		
Sie hatte viele Kinder.		
Sie hat mit ihrem Mann eine große Weltreise gemacht.		

S2:

Erzählen Sie Ihrem Partner/Ihrer Partnerin:

Mein Opa ist aus Deutschland gekommen. Seine Familie ist mit dem Schiff nach Amerika gefahren. Opa konnte kein Englisch und er wäre lieber in Deutschland geblieben. Seine Familie hat in New York gewohnt. Er ist Polizist geworden. Er hat sich immer für Musik interessiert. Er konnte gut singen, und ich habe viele deutsche Lieder von ihm gelernt. Wenn er Zeit gehabt hätte, hätte er gelernt, Klavier zu spielen. Er hat seine Verwandten in Deutschland oft besucht. Dieses Jahr wäre er auch nach Deutschland gefahren, wenn er nicht krank geworden wäre.

p. 384   **Kapitel 14**

Liste von Leuten:

ein NBC-Korrespondent	Ronald Reagan	Willy Brandt
Lyndon Johnson	der Sänger Wolf Biermann	Alexander Dubček
ein Westberliner Polizist	eine amerikanische Studentin	Leonard Bernstein

S2:

Wer?	Aussagen
Major der DDR-Grenztruppe:	„Es ist eine verrückte Zeit."
	„Vor meinen Augen tanzte die Freiheit."
Ostberliner Taxifahrer:	„So viel Fernsehen habe ich noch nie gesehen."
	„Wir haben uns jeden Tag gesehen. Jetzt will ich ihm mal die Hand schütteln *(shake)*."
Afrikanischer Diplomat:	„Ich dachte, die Deutschen können nur Fußball spielen oder im Stechschritt *(goose-step)* marschieren, aber jetzt können sie sogar Revolutionen machen."
	„Ich muss weinen vor Freude, dass es so schnell und einfach ging. Und ich muss weinen vor Zorn *(anger)*, dass es so elend *(terribly)* lange dauerte."
Autor Günter Grass:	„Jetzt wird sich zeigen, ob der jahrzehntelangen Rhetorik von den ‚Brüdern und Schwestern' auch entsprechendes *(corresponding)* politisches Handeln *(action)* folgen wird."
Autor Stephan Heym:	„Die einzige Chance, die wir haben, den Sozialismus zu retten *(save)*, ist richtiger Sozialismus."
	„Ich bin Gott dankbar, dass ich das noch erleben *(experience)* darf."
Amerikanischer Präsident Ronald Reagan:	„Auf beiden Seiten sind Deutsche. Der Kommunismus hat seine Chance gehabt. Er funktioniert nicht."
	„Wir haben zu lange im Dunkeln gelebt. Treten wir *(let's step)* ins Licht!"

> Die Belgier: . . .   Die Dänen: . . .
> Die Deutschen: . . . Die Franzosen: . . .
> Die Griechen: . . .   Die Briten: . . .

S2:

Sportliche Iren

Die Iren lieben den Sport mehr als alle anderen Europäer. Jeder zweite ist verrückt danach.

Offene Luxemburger

Luxemburg hat europaweit die meisten Ausläder—29%. Die meisten Beamte der EU.

Fleißige Portugiesen

Die Portugiesen sind das fleißigste Völkchen Europas, höchste Jahresarbeitszeit—2025 Stunden.

Schnelle Italiener

Jedes Jahr kommen die Hälfte aller europäischen Telegramme allein aus ihrem Land.

Maritime Holländer

Die Holländer sind die größten Seefahrer Europas. Das Land besitzt fast 4000 Schiffe.

Sehfreudige Spanier

Die Spanier sitzen am häufigsten unter den Europäern vor dem Fernseher—vier Stunden am Tag.

12. Answers for the optional English-to-German practice in the exercises

Kapitel 1   p. 35

1. Wir lernen Deutsch. 2. Ich zähle langsam. 3. Woher kommt ihr? 4. Sie kommen aus Kanada. 5. Ich komme / bin aus Amerika. 6. Antwortest du auf Englisch? 7. Nein, ich spreche Deutsch. 8. Sie öffnet das Buch. 9. Ich brauche das Buch. 10. Was sagt sie? 11. Verstehst du das? 12. Wiederholt sie das? 13. Sie heißt Sabrina. 14. Sie wohnen in Wittenberg.

Kapitel 4   p. 110

1. Sie hat noch geschlafen. 2. Sie haben auch geholfen. 3. Hast du (habt ihr, haben Sie) schon gegessen? 4. Haben Sie es gefunden? 5. Ich habe das nicht verstanden. 6. Hast du das gelesen? 7. Ich habe die Frage wiederholt. 8. Wer hat es genommen? 9. Sie haben Wintermäntel gekauft. 10. Meine Tante hat das Geschäft empfohlen. 11. Habt ihr die Bücher verkauft? 12. Ich habe die Rechnungen bezahlt.

Kapitel 5

1. Hast du (habt ihr, haben Sie) ihm gedankt? 2. Wir haben ihr gratuliert. 3. Ich habe sie überrascht. 4. Wir zeigen dir (euch, Ihnen) das Schloss. 5. Haben sie euch geantwortet? 6. Ich habe dir geschrieben. 7. Gibst du ihm das Geschenk? 8. Sie glaubt mir nicht.   p. 135

1. Er will den Dom sehen. 2. Sie müssen zur Post (gehen). 3. Ich kann das nicht lesen. 4. Ihr sollt Deutsch sprechen. 5. Du darfst ein Stück Kuchen bestellen. 6. Sie soll lernen. 7. Wir müssen den Weg finden. 8. Kannst du (könnt ihr, können Sie) mir nicht helfen? 9. Wir möchten nach Wien (fahren). 10. Dürfen wir das Schloss sehen?   p. 140

p. 192 **Kapitel 7**

1. Du hast dein Buch nicht zugemacht. 2. Hören Sie zu! 3. Sie sind am Wochenende zurückgekommen. 4. Geht ihr bald aus (weg)? 5. Ich weiß nicht, ob sie mitkommt. 6. Weißt du, wann sie ausgegangen (weggegangen) ist? 7. Ich habe unser Geld umgetauscht. 8. Wen haben Sie mitgebracht?

p. 212 **Kapitel 8**

1. Ist das Evas Zug? 2. Weißt du die Bahnsteignummer / die Nummer des Bahnsteigs? 3. Nein, wo ist der Abfahrtsplan (der Züge)? 4. Ihr Zug fährt in ein paar Minuten ab. 5. Nimm Kurts Paket mit! 6. Kurt ist Student und ein Freund einer Freundin. 7. Eva, hast du die Adresse des Studenten? 8. Nein, aber ich weiß den Namen des Studentenwohnheims. 9. Ich bringe es ihm während der Feiertage / Ferien. 10. Wegen der Prüfungen / Examen habe ich jetzt keine Zeit. 11. Ich schicke dir eine Ansichtskarte / Postkarte statt eines Briefes. 12. Und ich schicke dir eine E-Mail statt einer Ansichtskarte / Postkarte.

p. 245 **Kapitel 9**

1. Otto, zieh dich an! 2. Christian, beeil dich! 3. Anne und Sabrina, zieht ihr euch einen Pullover an? 4. Wir müssen uns noch die Zähne putzen. 5. Peter, kämm dir die Haare! 6. Ich fühle mich nicht wohl. 7. Heute gehen wir alle joggen. 8. Ja, aber ich habe mich erkältet. 9. Dann leg dich hin!

Kapitel 10

p. 268 1. Ich freue mich auf die Kunstausstellung. 2. Hast du dich über die Karten informiert / Hast du etwas über die Karten herausgefunden? 3. Wir haben über die / von der Ausstellung gesprochen, aber dann habe ich nicht ans Datum gedacht. 4. Bitte wartet nicht auf mich, sondern geht ohne mich! 5. Ihr wisst, ich interessiere mich nicht für Kunst. 6. Warum ärgerst du dich so über diesen Maler? 7. Ich ärgere mich nicht, aber ich kenne diesen Maler und ich halte nicht viel von seinen Gemälden. 8. Die ganze Stadt spricht von ihm / über ihn.

p. 272 1. a. Sie sitzt neben ihnen. b. Sie haben zwei Geschenke, eins für sie und eins für ihn. c. Siehst du den Stuhl? Die Geschenke liegen darauf. d. Was ist d(a)rin? e. Ist das für mich? f. Was tut / macht man damit? g. Was hältst du davon? h. Setz dich nicht d(a)rauf! 2. a. Mit wem kommt er? b. Wovon / worüber sprechen sie? c. Woran denkst du? d. Auf wen wartet er? e. Worüber ärgert ihr euch? f. Wofür interessiert sie sich? g. Wem / an wen schreibst du? h. Für wen ist dieses Geschenk?

p. 304 **Kapitel 11**

1. Wir kamen zum Flughafen, nachdem das Flugzeug gelandet war. 2. Als ich ankam, hatten sie schon ihr Gepäck geholt. 3. Nachdem wir sie gefunden hatten, fuhren wir nach Hause. 4. Meine Mutter hatte sich auf diesen Tag gefreut. 5. Nachdem sie ihnen das Haus gezeigt hatte, setzten wir uns ins Wohnzimmer und sprachen von der / über die Familie.

Kapitel 12

p. 327

1. Kinder, ich möchte / will euch (et)was sagen. 2. Eure Mutter wird Rechtsanwältin. 3. Ich werde zu Hause bleiben müssen. 4. Ich werde kochen. 5. Lena, du wirst die Wäsche waschen. 6. Jan und Maria, ihr werdet putzen. 7. Wir werden zusammen einkaufen (gehen). 8. Wir werden schwer arbeiten müssen. 9. Aber wir werden uns daran gewöhnen. 10. Wenn wir müde werden, machen wir eine Pause (werden . . . machen). 11. Eure Mutter wird viel Geld / gut verdienen. 12. Und wir werden ihr helfen.

Kapitel 13

p. 352

1. Könnt ihr bleiben? 2. Wir könnten spazieren gehen (einen Spaziergang machen). 3. Ich sollte meinen Großvater letzte Woche besuchen. 4. Jetzt müssen wir es (am) Samstag tun. 5. Ich wünschte, ich wüsste, warum er nicht angerufen hat. 6. Ich weiß, er würde mich anrufen, wenn er etwas bräuchte/brauchte (brauchen würde). 7. Hättet ihr Lust, in ein Restaurant zu gehen? 8. Das wäre schön. 9. Wir wünschten, wir hätten Zeit. 10. Wenn Walter nicht arbeiten müsste, könnten wir bleiben.

p. 356

1. Schade, wir hätten zu Hause bleiben sollen. 2. Wenn das Wetter besser gewesen wäre, hätten wir im See baden / schwimmen (gehen) können. 3. Aber es hat den ganzen Tag geregnet. 4. Ich wünschte, sie hätten uns nicht eingeladen. 5. Wenn wir zu Hause geblieben wären, hätten wir den Krimi sehen können. 6. Du hättest mit ihr ausgehen sollen. 7. Wenn ich Zeit gehabt hätte, hätte ich sie angerufen. 8. Wenn ich Zeit habe, rufe ich sie morgen an. 9. Ich hatte (gestern) keine Zeit, sie (gestern) anzurufen. 10. Ich hätte vorgestern anrufen sollen, aber ich habe es vergessen.

Kapitel 14

p. 377

1. Wo ist der Hörsaal, in dem Professor Kunert liest/lehrt? 2. Der Kurs, den er lehrt, ist Moderne Deutsche Geschichte. 3. Die Studenten, die seine Kurse belegen, müssen schwer / fleißig arbeiten. 4. Geschichte ist ein Fach, das ich sehr interessant finde. 5. Aber ich habe einen Zimmerkollegen, der nichts interessant findet / den nichts interessiert. 6. Er ist ein Mensch, den ich nicht verstehe. 7. Er studiert Fächer, die ihm nicht gefallen / die er nicht mag. 8. Die Freunde, mit denen er ausgeht, sind langweilig. 9. Er lacht / macht sich lustig über seinen Vater, dessen Geld er jeden Monat bekommt. 10. Aber die Frau, mit der er verlobt ist, ist sehr nett.

German–English Vocabulary

The German–English Vocabulary includes all the ACTIVE AND PASSIVE vocabulary used in *Wie geht's?* The English definitions of the words are limited to their use in the text. Each active vocabulary item is followed by a number and a letter indicating the chapter and section where it first occurs.

Nouns Nouns are followed by their plural endings unless the plural is rare or nonexistent. In the case of n-nouns, the singular genitive ending is also given: **der Herr, -n, -en.** Nouns that require adjective endings appear with two endings: **der Angestellte (ein Angestellter).** Female forms of masculine nouns are usually not listed if only **-in** needs to be added: **der Apotheker.**

Verbs For regular t-verbs ("weak verbs"), only the infinitive is listed. All irregular t-verbs ("irregular weak verbs") and basic n-verbs ("strong verbs") are given with their principal parts: **bringen, brachte, gebracht; schreiben, schrieb, geschrieben.** Separable-prefix verbs are identified by a dot between the prefix and the verb: **mit·bringen.** Compound mixed and n-verbs are printed with an asterisk to indicate that the principal parts can be found under the listing of the basic verb: **mit·bringen*, beschreiben*.** When **sein** is used as the auxiliary of the perfect tenses, the form **ist** is given: **wandern (ist); kommen, kam, ist gekommen.**

Adjectives and Adverbs Adjectives and adverbs that have an umlaut in the comparative and superlative are identified by an umlauted vowel in parentheses: **arm (ä) = arm, ärmer, am ärmsten.**

Accentuation Stress marks are provided for all words that do not follow the typical stress pattern. The accent follows the stressed syllable: **Balkon', Amerika'ner, wiederho'len.** The stress is not indicated when the word begins with an unstressed prefix, such as **be-, er-, ge-.**

Abbreviations

~	repetition of the key word	*nom.*	nominative
abbrev.	abbreviation	*o.s.*	oneself
acc.	accusative	*pl.*	plural
adj.	adjective	*refl. pron.*	reflexive pronoun
adv.	adverb	*rel. pron.*	relative pronoun
coll.	colloquial	*sb.*	somebody
comp.	comparative	*sg.*	singular
conj.	subordinate conjunction	*s.th.*	something
dat.	dative		
fam.	familiar	*S*	Schritt
gen.	genitive	*W*	Wortschatz 1
inf.	infinitive	*G*	Grammatik, Struktur
lit.	literally	*E*	Einblicke (Wortschatz 2)

A

der **Aal, -e** eel

ab- away, off (7G)

ab starting, as of

ab·bauen to reduce, cut back

ab·brechen* to break off

ab·brennen* to burn down

der **Abend, -e** evening; **(Guten) ~!** (Good) evening. (S1); **am ~** in the evening (6E); **gestern ~** yesterday evening (8G); **heute ~** this evening (8G)

das **Abendbrot** evening meal

das **Abendessen, -** supper, evening meal (3W); **zum ~** for supper (3W)

abends in the evening, every evening (S5); **donnerstag~** Thursday evenings (8G)

das **Abenteuer, -** adventure

aber but, however (S3, 2G, 5G); *flavoring particle expressing admiration* (7G)

ab·fahren* (von) to depart, leave (from) (8W)

die **Abfahrt, -en** departure (8W); descent

der **Abfall, ⸚e** waste, garbage (15W)

ab·fliegen* (von) to take off, fly (from) (8W)

die **Abgase** (*pl.*) exhaust fumes

ab·geben* to give away, hand in

abhängig (von) dependent (on)

die **Abhängigkeit** dependence

ab·holen to pick up

das **Abitur, -e = Abi** (*coll.*) final comprehensive exam at the end of the *Gymnasium*

die **Abmeldung** report that one is leaving or moving

ab·nehmen* to take s.th. from, take away

abonnie'ren to subscribe

ab·pflücken to pick, break off

ab·reißen* to tear down (15W)

der **Absatz, ⸚e** paragraph

ab·schließen, schloss ab, abgeschlossen to conclude, finish; **das Studium / die Ausbildung ~** to graduate, finish one's degree / education (13W)

der **Abschluss, ⸚e** degree, diploma (13W)

die **Abschlussparty, -s** graduation party

die **Abschlussprüfung, -en** final exam

ab·schneiden* to cut off

der **Absender, - (Abs.)** return address (8W)

absichtlich intentional(ly)

absolut' absolute(ly)

absolvie'ren to complete

sich **ab·wechseln** to take turns

die **Abwechslung, -en** distraction, variety

ach oh; **~ so!** Oh, I see! (9W); **~ was!** Oh, come on! (12W)

die **Achtung** respect; **~!** Watch out! Be careful!

der **ADAC = Allgemeiner Deutscher Automobil-Club** a German automobile association

ade (*or* **adé**) good-bye, farewell

addie'ren to add

das **Adjektiv, -e** adjective; **substantivier'te ~** adjectival noun

der **Adler, -** eagle

die **Adres'se, -n** address (8W)

der **Advents'kranz, ⸚e** Advent wreath

die **Advents'zeit** Advent season

das **Adverb', -ien** adverb

die **Aero'bik** aerobics

der **Affe, -n, -n** monkey; **Du ~!** You nut!

(das) **Ägy'pten** Egypt

der **Ägy'pter, -** the Egyptian

ägy'ptisch Egyptian

Aha'! There, you see. Oh, I see.

ähnlich similar; **Das sieht dir ~.** That's typical of you. (8W)

die **Ahnung: Keine ~!** (I have) no idea. (10W)

die **Akademie', -n** academy

der **Akade'miker, -** (university) graduate

akade'misch academic

der **Akkusativ, -e** accusative

der **Akt, -e** act (play)

das **Aktiv** active voice

aktiv' active; **~es zum Thema** topical activities; **Video ~** *here:* Video Manual

die **Aktivität', -en** activity

aktuell' up-to-date, current

der **Akzent', -e** accent

akzeptie'ren to accept

all- all (7G); **vor ~em** above all, mainly (10E); **~e drei Jahre** every three years

allein' alone (11E)

allerdings however (15W)

die **Allergie', -n** allergy

aller'gisch gegen allergic to

allerlei all sorts of (2W)

alles everything, all (2W); **Das ist ~.** That's all. (2W)

allgemein' (in) general; **im ~en** in general

allmäh'lich gradual(ly)

der **Alltag** everyday life

die **Alpen** (*pl.*) Alps

die **Alpenblume, -n** Alpine flower

das **Alphabet'** alphabet

als as; (*conj.*) (at the time) when (11G); (*after comp.*) than (12G)

also therefore, thus, so; in other words (10E); well (12W)

alt (ä) old (S3); **stein~** very old; **ur~** ancient

der **Alte (ein Alter)** old man (12G); **die ~, -n, -n** old lady (12G); **das ~** old things (12G)

das **Alter** age

die **Altstadt, ¨e** old part of town

der **Amateur', -e** amateur

ambitiös' ambitious

die **Ameise, -n** ant

(das) **Ame'rika** America (1W)

der **Amerika'ner, -** the American (1W)

amerika'nisch American (1W)

die **Ampel, -n** traffic light

an- to, up to (7G)

an (+ *acc.* / *dat.*) to, at (the side of), on (vertical surface) (6G)

die **Analy'se, -n** analysis

analysie'ren to analyze

die **Ananas, -** pineapple

an·bieten* to offer (12W)

ander- other (9E; **~e** others (9W); **der / die ~e** the other one; **die ~en** the others (9W); **etwas (ganz) ~es** s.th. (quite) different (9E)

andererseits on the other hand

ändern to change

anders different(ly), in other ways (9E); **Sagen Sie es ~!** Say it differently!

anerkannt recognized, accredited

an·erkennen* to recognize; acknowledge

die **Anerkennung, -en** recognition

der **Anfang, ¨e** beginning, start (10W); **~ der Woche** at the beginning of the week (8G); **am ~** in the beginning (10W)

an·fangen* to begin, start (10W)

der **Anfänger, -** beginner

die **Angabe, -n** information

das **Angebot, -e** offering, offer

angeln to fish (9W); **~ gehen*** to go fishing (9W)

angepasst geared / adjusted to

angeschlagen posted

der **Angestellte (ein Angestell- ter) / die Angestellte, -n, -n** employee, clerk (12G)

angewiesen sein* auf (+ acc.) to be dependent on

die **Anglis'tik** English studies

der **Angriff, -e** attack; raid

die **Angst, ¨e** fear, anxiety; **~ haben*** (**vor** +*dat.*) to fear, be afraid (of) (13E); **~ bekommen*** to become afraid, get scared

an·halten* to continue

der **Anhang** appendix

anhänglich devoted, attached (11W)

sich **an·hören** to listen to (9G); **Hör dir das an!** Listen to that.; to sound

an·kommen* (**in** + *dat.*) to arrive (in) (7E); **Das kommt darauf an.** That depends. (7E)

an·kreuzen to mark with an X

die **Ankunft** arrival (8W)

an·machen to turn on (a radio, etc.) (10W)

die **Anmeldung** reception desk; registration

die **Annahme, -n** hypothetical statement or question; supposition

an·nehmen* to accept (7E); to suppose (13E)

der **Anorak, -s** parka

anpassungsfähig adaptable

die **Anrede** address; **~form** form of address

an·reden to address

an·richten to do (damage)

der **Anruf, -e** (phone) call

der **Anrufbeantworter, -** answering machine

an·rufen* to call up, phone (7G)

an·sagen to announce

sich **an·schauen** to look at; to watch (10W)

an·schlagen* to post

der **Anschluss, ¨e** connection

die **Anschrift, -en** address

(sich) **an·sehen*** to look at (9G); to watch

die **Ansicht, -en** opinion, attitude; view

die **Ansichtskarte, -n** (picture) postcard (8W)

an·sprechen* to address, speak to

(an)statt (+ *gen.*) instead of (8G)

anstrengend strenuous (12W)

der **Anteil, -e** share; proportion

der **Antikmarkt, ¨e** antique mall

die **Antiquität', -en** antique

der **Antrag, ¨e** application

die **Antwort, -en** answer

antworten to answer (S2)

an·wachsen* to increase

die **Anwaltsfirma, -firmen** law firm

die **Anzahl** number, amount

die **Anzeige, -n** ad (11W)

die **Anzeigetafel, -n** scoreboard

(sich) **an·ziehen*** to put on (clothing), get dressed (9G)

der **Anzug, ¨e** men's suit

an·zünden to light

der **Apfel, ¨** apple (2W)

der **Apfelstrudel, -** apple strudel

die **Apothe'ke, -n** pharmacy (2E)

der **Apothe'ker, -** pharmacist

appellie'ren to appeal

der **Appetit'** appetite; **Guten ~!** Enjoy your meal. (3W)

die **Apriko'se, -n** apricot

der **April'** April (S4); **im ~** in April (S4)

der **Äqua'tor** equator

das **Äquivalent'** equivalent

der **Araber, -** Arab

ara'bisch Arabic

die **Arbeit, -en** work (6E); (term) paper (13W); **bei der ~** at work; **Tag der ~** Labor Day

arbeiten to work (1E)

der **Arbeiter, -** (blue-collar) worker (12W); **Vor~** foreman

der **Arbeitgeber, -** employer

der **Arbeitnehmer, -** employee

arbeitsam hard-working; **~ wie ein Pferd** extremely hard-working

das **Arbeitsbuch, ¨er** workbook

die **Arbeitserlaubnis** work permit

das **Arbeitsheft, -e** workbook

das **Arbeitsklima** work climate

die **Arbeitskraft, ¨e** worker

die **Arbeitsleistung** output; performance

arbeitslos unemployed (12W)

der **Arbeitslose (ein Arbeitsloser) / die Arbeitslose, -n, -n** unemployed person

die **Arbeitslosigkeit** unemployment (12E)

der **Arbeitsmarkt, ¨e** job market

der **Arbeitsplatz, ¨e** job; place of employment

das **Arbeitszimmer, -** study (6W)

archa'isch archaic

die **Archäologie'** archeology

der **Architekt', -en, -en** architect (12W)

die **Architektur'** architecture

das **Archiv', -e** archive

ärgerlich annoying

sich **ärgern über** (+ *acc.*) to get annoyed/upset about (10G); **Das ärgert mich.** That makes me angry / mad. (10W)

die **Arka'de, -n** arcade

arm (ä) poor (11W)

der **Arm, -e** arm (9W)

die **Armbanduhr, -en** wristwatch

die **Armee', -n** army

die **Armut** poverty

arrogant' arrogant

die **Art, -en (von)** kind, type (of) (10E)

der **Arti'kel, - (von)** article (of)

der **Arzt, ¨e / die Ärztin, -nen** physician, doctor (12W)

die **Asche** ashes

assoziie'ren to associate

ästhe'tisch aesthetic

die **Astronomie'** astronomy

der **Asylant', -en, -en** asylum seeker

der **Atem** breath

atmen to breathe

die **Atmosphä're** atmosphere

die **Attraktion', -en** attraction

attraktiv' attractive (11W)

auch also, too (S1); **ich ~** me too

auf (+ *acc. / dat.*) on (top of) (6G); open (7W)

auf- up, open (7G)

auf·atmen to breathe a sigh of relief

auf·bauen to build, put up (15W); **wieder ~** to rebuild (15W)

aufeinan'der treffen* (ist) to come together

der **Aufenthalt, -e** stay, stopover (8W); **Auslands~** stay abroad

die **Aufenthaltserlaubnis** residence permit

auf·essen* to eat up

auf·fassen to consider (to be)

die **Aufgabe, -n** assignment; task, challenge

auf·geben* to give up

auf·halten* to hold open; to stay

auf·hören (zu + *inf.*) to stop (doing s.th.) (13E)

die **Aufklärung** enlightenment

der **Aufkleber, -** sticker

die **Auflage, -n** edition

auf·machen to open (7G)

die **Aufnahme** acceptance, reception

auf·nehmen* to take (a picture)

auf·passen to pay attention, watch out (7W)

der **Aufsatz, ¨e** essay, composition, paper

der **Aufschnitt** (*sg.*) assorted meats / cheeses, cold cuts

auf·schreiben* to write down (7G)

auf·stehen* to get up (7G)

auf·stellen to put up, set up

auf·wachen (ist) to wake up

auf·wachsen* to grow up

der **Aufzug, ¨e** elevator

das **Auge, -n** eye (9W)

der **Augenblick, -e** moment; **(Einen) ~!** Just a minute!

die **Augenbraue, -n** eyebrow

der **August'** August (S4); **im ~** in August (S4)

aus (+ *dat.*) out of, from (a place of origin) (3G); **Ich bin ~ . . .** I'm from (a native of) . . . (1W); **aus sein*** to be over

aus- out, out of (7G)

aus·arbeiten to work out

aus·(be)zahlen to pay out

aus·bilden to train, educate

die **Ausbildung** training, education (12W)

der **Ausdruck, ¨e** expression

sich **auseinan'der entwickeln** to develop apart

die **Ausfuhr** export

aus·füllen to fill out (13W)

der **Ausgang, ¨e** exit (7W)

aus·geben* to spend (money) (9E)

aus·bilden to train, educate

ausgebildet (als) trained (as); **gut~** well-trained (12E) aus·gehen* to go out (7G)

ausgezeichnet excellent (6E)

aus·helfen* to help out

die Aushilfskraft, ⁻e temporary help

das Ausland foreign country; im/ins ~ abroad (12E)

der Ausländer, - foreigner (1E); ~hass xenophobia

ausländisch foreign (13E)

der Auslandsaufenthalt, -e stay abroad

das Auslandsprogramm, -e foreign-study program

aus·leihen* to loan, lend out

aus·lesen* to pick out

aus·machen turn off (a radio etc.) (10W)

aus·packen to unpack

die Ausrede, -n excuse

ausreichend sufficient; approx. grade D

aus·richten to tell; Kann ich etwas ~? Can I take a message?

das Ausrufungszeichen, - exclamation mark

die Aussage, -n statement

aus·sehen* (wie + nom.) to look (like) (12E)

außer (+ dat.) besides, except for (3G)

äußer- outer

außerdem (adv.) besides (6E)

außerhalb (+ gen.) outside (of)

die Aussicht, -en (auf + acc.) prospect (for); view (of)

die Aussichtsplattform, -en observation deck

der Aussiedler, - emigrant; ethnic immigrant

die Aussprache pronunciation

aus·steigen* to get off (8W)

aus·stellen to issue; to exhibit

die Ausstellung, -en exhibition, show

aus·sterben* to become extinct

der Austausch exchange; das ~programm, -e exchange program

aus·tauschen to exchange (14E)

die Auster, -n oyster

ausverkauft sold out

die Auswahl (an + dat.) choice, selection (of) (10E)

der Ausweis, -e ID, identification (7W)

auswendig by heart

aus·werten to evaluate, assess

sich aus·wirken auf (+ acc.) to affect

aus·zahlen to pay out

die Auszeit, -en time-out

(sich) aus·ziehen* to get undressed (9G)

der Auszubildende (ein Auszubildender) / die Auszubildende, -n, -n = Azubi, -s (coll.) trainee

authen'tisch authentic

das Auto, -s car (5W)

die Autobahn, -en freeway

autofrei free of cars

der Automat', -en, -en machine

automatisiert' automated

die Automobil'branche car industry

der Autor', -en author (10W)

autoritäts'gläubig believing in authority

B

die Backe, -n cheek

backen (bäckt), buk (backte), gebacken to bake (9W)

der Bäcker, - baker

die Bäckerei', -en bakery (2W)

das Bad, ⁻er bath(room) (6W)

der Badeanzug, ⁻e swimsuit

die Badehose, -n swimming trunks

baden to bathe, swim (6W); sich ~ to take a bath (9G)

die Badewanne, -n bathtub

das Badezimmer, - bathroom

die Bahn, -en railway, train (8W); ~übergang, ⁻e railroad crossing

der Bahnhof, ⁻e train station (5W)

der Bahnsteig, -e platform (8W)

bald soon (7W); Bis ~! See you soon! (9W); so~' (conj.) as soon as (12E)

baldig soon-to-come

der Balkon', -s / -e balcony (6W)

der Ball, ⁻e ball

das Ballett' ballet (10W)

der Ballett'tänzer, - ballet dancer

die Bana'ne, -n banana (2W)

bange worried

die Bank, -en bank (7W)

die Bank, ⁻e bench

der Bankier', -s banker

der Bann ban

die Bar, -s bar, pub

der Bär, -en, -en bear; Du bist ein Brumm~. You're a grouch.

barfuß barefoot

das Bargeld cash (7W)

der Bart, ⁻e beard

basteln to do crafts

die Batterie', -n battery

der Bau, -ten building construction (15W)

der Bauch, ⁻e stomach, belly (9W)

bauen to build (6E); ~ lassen* to have built

der Bauer, -n, -n farmer

der Bauernhof, ⁻e farm

das Baugesetz, -e building code

der Bauingenieur, -e structural engineer

das Bauland building lots

der Baum, ⁻e tree (6W)

die Baumwolle cotton

die Baustelle, -n construction site

der Baustoff, -e building material

der Bayer, -n, -n the Bavarian

(das) **Bayern** Bavaria (in south-east Germany)

bay(e)risch Bavarian

der **Beamte (ein Beamter) / die Beamtin, -nen** civil servant (12G)

beantworten to answer

der **Bedarf (für)** need (for)

bedeuten to mean, signify (S2)

die **Bedeutung, -en** meaning; significance, importance

bedienen to take care of, serve

die **Bedienung** server, service (3W); **~!** *Waiter! / Waitress!* (3W); service charge

bedroht threatened; **sich ~ fühlen** to feel threatened

sich **beeilen** to hurry (9G)

beeindrucken to impress

beeinflussen to influence

beenden to finish, complete

der **Befehl, -e** instruction, request, command

befehlen (befiehlt), befahl, befohlen to order, command

befriedigend satisfactory; approx. grade C

befürchten to fear

begegnen (ist) to encounter

begehrt desired

begeistert enthusiastic(ally)

der **Beginn** beginning; **zu ~** in the beginning

beginnen, begann, begonnen to begin (S5)

begleiten to accompany

die **Begleitung** accompaniment

begreifen* to understand, grasp

begrenzt limited

die **Begrenzung, -en** limit(ation), restriction

begrüßen to greet, welcome

die **Begrüßung, -en** greeting;

zur ~ as a greeting

behalten* to keep

der **Behälter, -** container (15W)

behandeln (wie) to treat like

die **Behandlung, -en** treatment

beherrschen to dominate, rule

bei (+ *dat.*) at, near, at the home of (3G); **Hier ~ ___.** This is ___'s office / residence.

beide both (11W)

beige beige

bei·legen to enclose

das **Bein, -e** leg (9W); **auf den ~en** on the go

das **Beispiel, -e** example; **zum ~ (z. B.)** for example (e.g.)

bei·tragen* (zu) to contribute (to)

bekämpfen to combat

bekannt well-known (5E); **Das kommt mir ~ vor.** That seems familiar to me.

der **Bekannte (ein Bekannter) / die Bekannte, -n, -n** acquaintance (12G)

bekommen* (hat) to get, receive (4W)

bekümmert sad

belasten to burden; pollute

belegen to sign up for, take (a course) (13W)

belgisch Belgian

beliebt popular (9E)

die **Belohnung, -en** reward

bemerken to notice

sich **bemühen** to try (hard)

benennen* nach to name after

benutzen to use

das **Benzin'** gas(oline)

der **Benzin'schlucker, -** gas guzzler

beo'bachten to watch, observe

die **Beo'bachtung, -en** observation

bequem' comfortable, convenient (6W)

der **Berater, -** counselor, adviser, consultant

die **Beratung** counseling

berauben to rob

der **Bereich, -e** area, field (12E)

der **Berg, -e** mountain (1W)

bergab' downhill

bergauf' uphill

die **Bergbahn, -en** mountain train

der **Bergbau** mining

berghoch' uphill

bergsteigen gehen* to go mountain climbing

der **Bericht, -e** report

berichten to report (14W)

berieseln *here:* to shower with

der **Beruf, -e** profession (12W)

beruflich professional(ly); **~ engagiert'** professionally active

die **Berufsschule, -n** vocational school

der **Berufstätige (ein Berufstätiger) / die Berufstätige, -n, -n** someone working in a profession

die **Berufswahl** choice of profession (12E)

berühmt famous (14E)

die **Beschäftigung** activity; occupation

beschämend embarrassing

bescheinigen to verify, document

beschreiben* to describe (8E)

die **Beschreibung, -en** description

beschriftet labeled

beschuldigen to accuse

besetzen to fill, occupy

besichtigen to visit (an attraction), tour (5W)

der **Besitz** property, possession

besitzen* to own

der **Besitzer, -** owner

besonders especially (3E); **nichts Besonderes** nothing special (9W)

besprechen* to discuss, talk about
besser better (12G)
die **Besserung** improvement; **Gute ~!** Get well soon. (4W)
best- best (12G); **am ~en** it's best (12G)
bestätigen to confirm
bestehen* to pass (an exam) (13W); **~ aus** (+ *dat.*) to consist of; **es besteht** there is; **~ auf** (+ *dat.*) to insist on
besteigen* to climb on
bestellen to order (3W)
die **Bestellung, -en** order
bestimmt surely, for sure, certain(ly) (13E)
der **Besuch, -e** visit; visitor(s)
besuchen to visit (8W); attend
der **Besucher, -** visitor
beten to pray
der **Beton'** concrcte
betonen to stress, emphasize
Betr(eff) concerning
betreffen* to concern
betreten* to enter, step on
der **Betriebswirt, -e** graduate in business management (12W)
die **Betriebswirtschaft** business administration
das **Bett, -en** bed (6W); **ins ~** to bed
sich **beugen über** (+ *acc.*) to bend over
die **Bevölkerung** population (15E)
bevor (*conj.*) before (4G)
bewachen to guard, watch over
bewältigen to overcome, cope with; finish
sich **bewegen** to move
die **Bewegung, -en** movement
sich **bewerben (um)** to apply (for) (12W)
die **Bewerbung, -en (um +** *acc.***)** application (for)

bewerten to rate
die **Bewertung, -en** evaluation, grading
der **Bewohner, -** inhabitant; resident
bewölkt cloudy
bewusst conscious(ly)
bezahlen to pay (for) (3W)
sich **beziehen* auf** (+ *acc.*) to refer to
die **Beziehung, -en** relationship (11W)
der **Bezirk, -e** district
die **Bibel, -n** Bible
die **Bibliothek', -en** library (5W)
die **Biene, -n** bee
das **Bier, -e** beer (2W); **~ vom Fass** draught beer
der **Biergarten, ⸗** beer garden
der **Bierkrug, ⸗e** stein
bieten, bot, geboten to offer
der **Biki'ni, -s** bikini
die **Bilanz', -en: eine ~ auf·stellen** to make an evaluation
das **Bild, -er** picture (S2)
bilden to form; **~ Sie einen Satz!** Make / form a sentence. (8W)
die **Bildung** education
das **Billard** billiards
billig cheap(ly), inexpensive(ly) (S3)
binden, band, gebunden to bind
die **Biochemie'** biochemistry
der **Bioche'miker, -** biochemist
Biogra'phisches biographical data
der **Bio-Laden, ⸗** health-food store
der **Biolo'ge, -n, -n / die Biolo'gin, -nen** biologist
die **Biologie'** biology
die **Birne, -n** pear
bis to, until; **~ später!** See you later! So long! (S1); **~ bald!** See you soon! (9W); **~ gleich!** See you in a few minutes (9W)
bisher' until now

bishe'rig previous
bisschen: ein ~ some, a little bit (of) (4E); **Ach du liebes ~!** Good grief!, My goodness!, Oh dear! (2E)
bitte please (S1); **~! / ~ bitte!** You're welcome. (S5, 2E); **~ schön!** You're welcome. (4W); **Hier ~!** Here you are.; **~ schön?** May I help you?; **Wie ~?** What did you say? Could you say that again? (S5)
die **Bitte, -n** request
bitten, bat, gebeten (um) to ask (for), request (12E)
das **Blatt, ⸗er** leaf; sheet
blau blue (S2)
der **Blazer, -** blazer
das **Blei** lead
bleiben, blieb, ist geblieben to stay, remain (3W)
der **Bleistift, -e** pencil (S2)
der **Blick (in / auf +** *acc.***)** view (of) (7W); glance at (10W)
der **Blickpunkt, -e** focus
blind blind
der **Blitz, -e** flash of lightning
blitzen to sparkle; **es blitzt** there's lightning
die **Blitzreaktion', -en** quick reaction
der **Block, ⸗e** block
die **Blocka'de, -n** blockade
die **Blockflöte, -n** recorder (*musical instrument*)
blockie'ren to block
der **Blödsinn** nonsense; **So ein ~!** What nonsense!
blond blond
bloß only; **was . . . ~?** what on earth . . . ?; **wie . . . ~?** how on earth . . . ?
blühen to flourish; to bloom; **~d** flourishing
die **Blume, -n** flower (2E)
der **Blumenkohl** cauliflower
die **Bluse, -n** blouse (S3)
der **Boden** ground, floor
der **Bogen, ⸗** bow; arch

die **Bohne, -n** bean (2W)
der **Bomber, -** bomber
das **Bonbon, -s** (piece of) candy
der **Bonus, -se** bonus
das **Boot, -e** boat
borgen to borrow
die **Börse, -n** stockmarket
der **Börsenmakler, -** stock-broker
böse angry, mad, upset
der **Bote, -n, -n / die Botin, -nen** messenger
die **Bouti'que, -n** boutique
die **Bowle, -n** alcoholic punch
boxen to box
die **Branche, -n** branch
der **Brasilia'ner, -** Brasilian
brasilia'nisch Brasilian
der **Braten, -** roast; **Schweine~** pork roast; **Rinder~** beef roast; **Sauer~** marinated pot roast
die **Bratkartoffeln** (*pl.*) fried potatoes
die **Bratwurst, ̈e** fried sausage
der **Brauch, ̈e** custom
brauchen to need (S3)
brauen to brew
die **Brauerei, -en** brewery
braun brown (S2); **~ge-brannt** tanned
die **Braut, ̈e** bride
der **Bräutigam, -e** bridegroom
das **Brautkleid, -er** wedding dress
die **BRD (Bundesrepublik Deutschland)** FRG (Federal Republic of Germany)
brechen (bricht), brach, gebrochen to break
der **Brei, -e** porridge; **Kartof-fel~** (*sg.*) mashed potatoes
breit broad, wide
das **Brett, -er** board; das **Schwarze ~** bulletin board
die **Brezel, -n** pretzel
der **Brief, -e** letter (8W)

der **Briefkasten, ̈** mailbox (8W)
brieflich by letter
die **Briefmarke, -n** stamp (8W)
der **Briefsortierer, -** mail sorter
der **Briefträger, -** mailman
die **Brille, -n** glasses
bringen, brachte, gebracht to bring (3W); **mit sich ~** to bring with itself / o.s.
die **Brokkoli** (*pl.*) broccoli
die **Broschü're, -n** brochure
das **Brot, -e** bread (2W); **Toast~** piece of toast; **Grau~** bread with wheat and rye; **Vollkorn~** bread with cracked rye and wheat grains; **Lein-samen~** bread with lin-seed; **Sonnenblumen-kern~** bread with sunflower seeds
das **Brötchen, -** roll (2W); **belegte ~** sandwich
der **Brotkrümel, -** bread crumb
der **Brotwürfel, -** small piece of bread, cube
die **Brücke, -n** bridge (5W)
der **Bruder, ̈** brother (1W)
das **Brüderchen, -** little brother
brüderlich brotherly
brüllen to scream
brummig grouchy
der **Brunnen, -** fountain
die **Brust, ̈e** chest, breast
das **Buch, ̈er** book (S2); **Arbeits~** workbook
der **Bücherwurm, ̈er** book-worm
die **Buchführung** bookkeep-ing
der **Buchhalter, -** bookkeeper
die **Buchhandlung, -en** book-store (2W)
das **Büchlein, -** booklet, little book
der **Buchstabe, -n, -n** letter (of the alphabet)
buchstabie'ren to spell; **~ Sie auf Deutsch!** Spell in German!

die **Bude, -n** booth, stand; **Schieß~** shooting gallery
das **Büfett', -s** dining room cabinet; buffet
das **Bügeleisen, -** (clothing) iron
die **Bühne, -n** stage; **auf der ~** on stage
der **Bummel** stroll
bummeln (ist) to stroll (5E)
der **Bund, ̈e** confederation; federal government
die **Bundesbank** central bank
der **Bundesbürger, -** citizen of the Federal Republic
die **Bundesfeier, -n** Swiss national holiday
das **Bundesland, ̈er** state, province
die **Bundespost** federal postal service
die **Bundesrepublik (BRD)** Federal Republic of Germany (FRG)
der **Bundesstaat, -en** federal state
der **Bundestag** German federal parliament
bunt colorful; multi-colored
die **Burg, -en** castle, fortress
der **Bürger, -** citizen (10E); **Mit~** fellow citizen
bürgerlich bourgeois, middle-class
der **Bürgersteig, -e** sidewalk
das **Bürgertum** citizenry
das **Büro', -s** office (12W)
die **Bürokratie'** bureaucracy, red tape
die **Bürste, -n** brush
der **Bus, -se** bus (5W); **mit dem ~ fahren*** to take the bus (5W)
der **Busbahnhof, ̈e** bus depot
der **Busch, ̈e** bush
der **Busen, -** bosom
die **Butter** butter (2W); **(Es ist) alles in ~.** Every-thing is all right.

C

das **Café', -s** café (3W)

die **Cafeteri'a, -s=Cafe'te** (coll.) cafeteria

campen to camp; ~ **gehen*** to go camping

der **Campingplatz, ¨e** campground

der **Cappucci'no, -s** cappuccino

die **CD, -s** CD, compact disc (9W)

der **Cellist', -en, -en** cello player

das **Cello, -s** cello

der **Cent, -s** cent (S3); **fünf ~** five cents (S3)

CH = Confoederatio Helvetica Helvetic Confederation (Switzerland)

das **Chaos** chaos

chao'tisch chaotic

die **Charakterisie'rung, -en** characterization

charakteris'tisch characteristic

charmant' charming (11W)

der **Charme** charm

der **Chauffeur', -e** chauffeur

chauvinis'tisch chauvinist

der **Chef, -s** boss

die **Chemie'** chemistry

die **Chemika'lie, -n** chemical

chemisch chemical(ly)

der **Chine'se, -n, -n / die Chine'sin, -nen** Chinese

chine'sisch Chinese

der **Chor, ¨e** choir (10W)

der **Christbaum, ¨e** Christmas tree

der **Christkindlmarkt, ¨e** Christmas fair

chronolo'gisch chronological

Ciao! (coll.) Bye!

der **Clown, -s** clown

der **Cockerspaniel, -** Cocker spaniel

die **Cola** cola drink, soft drink (2W)

das **College, -s** college

der **Collie, -s** Collie; Sheltie

die **Combo, -s** (musical) band

der **Compu'ter, -** computer; **~künstler, -** graphic designer

computerisiert' computerized

der **Contai'ner, -** container

die **Cornflakes** (pl.) cornflakes, cereal

das **Coupé, -s** compartment

der **Cousin', -s / Cousi'ne, -n** cousin

cremig creamy, smooth

D

da there (S2); **~ drüben** over there (5W)

dabei' along; there; yet; **~ haben*** to have with o.s.

das **Dach, ¨er** roof

der **Dachboden, ¨** attic

der **Dachdecker, -** roofer

das **Dachgeschoss** attic floor; **im ~** on the attic floor

die **Dachrinne, -n** gutter

der **Dackel, -** dachshund

dage'gen against it (10G); **Hast du etwas ~, wenn . . . ?** Do you mind if . . . ? (13W)

daheim' at home

daher therefore, hence; from there

dahin: bis ~ until then

die **Dahlie, -n** dahlia

das **da-Kompo'situm, Kompo'sita** da-compound

damalig (adj.) then

damals then, in those days (11W)

die **Dame, -n** lady (5W); **Sehr geehrte ~n und Herren!** Ladies and gentlemen!; **~ spielen** to play checkers (9W)

danach' later, after that (9W)

der **Däne, -n, -n / die Dänin, -nen** the Dane

(das) **Dänemark** Denmark

dänisch Danish

der **Dank: Vielen / Herzlichen ~!** Thank you very much. (4W); **Gott sei ~!** Thank God! (8W)

dankbar grateful, thankful

danke thank you (S1); **~ schön!** Thank you very much (4W); **~ gleichfalls!** Thanks, the same to you. (3W)

danken (+ dat.) to thank (3G); **Nichts zu ~!** You're welcome. My pleasure. (4W)

dann then (2W)

dar·stellen to portray

der **Darsteller, -** actor

darum therefore (12E); **eben ~** that's why

das that (S2)

dass (conj.) that (4G); **so~** (conj.) so that (13E)

der **Dativ, -e** dative

das **Datum, Daten** (calendar) date (4W); **Welches ~ ist heute?** What date is today? (4W)

die **Dauer** length, duration

dauern to last (duration) (4W); **Wie lange dauert das?** How long does that take? (4W)

der **Daumen, -** thumb

die **DDR (Deutsche Demokratische Republik)** German Democratic Republic (GDR)

die **Decke, -n** blanket; tablecloth

definie'ren to define

dein (sg. fam.) your (1W)

die **Dekoration', -en** decoration

dekorie'ren to decorate

demnächst before long

der **Demokrat', -en, -en** democrat

die **Demokratie'** democracy

demokra'tisch democratic

der **Demonstrant', -en, -en** demonstrator

die **Demonstration', -en** demonstration

demonstrie'ren to demonstrate

denken, dachte, gedacht to think (4W); ~ **an** (+ *acc.*) to think of / about (10G)

der **Denker, -** thinker

das **Denkmal, ¨er** monument (15W)

denn because, for (2G); *flavoring particle expressing curiosity, interest* (7G)

der **Deo-Stift, -e** deodorant stick

die **Depression', -en** (mental) depression

deshalb therefore (13E)

deskriptiv' descriptive

deswegen therefore

deutsch German

(das) **Deutsch: auf ~** in German (S2); **Sprechen Sie ~?** Do you speak German? (1W); **Hoch~** (standard) High German; **Platt~** Low German (*northern German dialect*)

der **Deutsche (ein Deutscher) / die Deutsche, -n, -n** the German (1W, 12G)

die **Deutsche Demokratische Republik (DDR)** German Democratic Republic (GDR)

(das) **Deutschland** Germany (1W)

deutschsprachig German-speaking

der **Dezem'ber** December (S4); **im ~** in December (S4)

sich **drehen** to turn

d. h. (das heißt) that is (i.e.)

das **Dia, -s** slide (photograph)

der **Dialekt', -e** dialect

die **Dialek'tik** conflicting nature, dialectics

der **Dialog', -e** dialogue

dick thick, fat (S3); ~ **machen** to be fattening (3E)

dickköpfig stubborn

die **Diele, -n** foyer

dienen to serve

der **Diener, -** servant

der **Dienst, -e** service; **öffentliche ~** civil service

der **Dienstag** Tuesday (S4); **am ~** on Tuesday (S4)

dienstags on Tuesdays (2E)

dies- this, these (7G)

diesig misty

diesmal this time (10W)

das **Diktat', -e** dictation

die **Dimension', -en** dimension

das **Ding, -e** thing

das **Diplom', -e** diploma (*e.g., in natural and social sciences, engineering*), M.A

der **Diplomat', -en, -en** diplomat

direkt' direct(ly)

der **Direk'tor, -en, -en** (school) principal, manager

der **Dirigent', -en, -en** (music) conductor

die **Diskothek', -en = Disko, -s** discotheque

die **Diskussion', -en** discussion

diskutie'ren to discuss

sich **distanzie'ren** to keep apart

die **Disziplin'** discipline

die **DM (Deutsche Mark)** German mark

der **Dobermann, ¨er** Doberman

doch yes (I do), indeed, sure (2W); yet, however, but; on the contrary; *flavoring particle expressing concern, impatience, assurance* (7G)

der **Dokumentar'film, -e** documentary

der **Dollar, -(s)** dollar (7W)

der **Dolmetscher, -** interpreter

der **Dom, -e** cathedral (5W)

dominie'ren to dominate

donnern to thunder; **es donnert** it's thundering

donnernd rumbling

der **Donnerstag** Thursday (S4); **am ~** on Thursday (S4)

donnerstags on Thursdays (2E)

der **Doppeldeckerbus, -se** double-decker bus

der **Doppelpunkt, -e** colon

doppelt double

das **Doppelzimmer, -** double room (7W)

das **Dorf, ¨er** village (8E)

dort (over) there (4E)

dorthin to there (5W)

die **Dose, -n** can; **~npfand** deposit on a can

der **Drachenflieger, -** hang-glider

dran at it; **Jetzt sind Sie ~!** Now it's your turn.

draußen outside, outdoors; **hier ~** out here; **weit ~** far out

die **Dreißigerin, -nen** woman in her 30s

die **Droge, -n** drug

die **Drogerie', -n** drugstore (2E)

der **Drogist', -en, -en** druggist

drohen to threaten

der **Dschungel** jungle

duften to smell good

dumm (ü) stupid, silly (10W, 11W); **Das ist (wirklich) zu ~.** That's (really) too bad.

die **Dummheit, -en** stupidity

der **Dummkopf, ¨e** dummy

die **Düne, -n** dune

das **Düngemittel, -** fertilizer

dunkel dark (6W); **~haarig** dark-haired; **im Dunkeln** in the dark(ness)

die **Dunkelheit** darkness

dünn thin, skinny (S3)

durch (+ *acc.*) through (2G); **mitten~** right through; by (*agent*)

durchbre'chen* to break through, penetrate

der **Durchbruch** breakthrough

durcheinander mixed up, confused

durch·fallen* to flunk (an exam) (13W)

der **Durchschnitt** average; **im ~** on the average

dürfen (darf), durfte, gedurft to be allowed to, may (5W); **Was darf's sein?** May I help you?

der **Durst** thirst (2E); **Ich habe ~.** I'm thirsty. (2E)

die **Dusche, -n** shower

(sich) **duschen** to take a shower (6W; 9G)

der **Duschvorhang, ¨e** shower curtain

das **Dutzend, -e** dozen

sich **duzen** to call each other *"du"*

die **DVD, -s** DVD (9W)

die **Dyna'mik** dynamics

dyna'misch dynamic

E

die **Ebbe** ebb tide, low tide

eben after all, just (*flavoring particle*); **mal ~** just for a minute

die **Ebene, -n** plain, level

ebenfalls also, likewise

ebenso just as, just the same

der **EC, -s** EuroCity (train)

echt real, authentic, genuine; **~?** Really? (4W); **un~** fake

die **Ecke, -n** corner (6W)

der **Effekt', -e** effect

egal' the same; **Das ist doch ~.** That doesn't matter. (8W); **Es ist mir ~.** It's all the same to me. I don't care.; **~ wie/wo** no matter how/where

die **Ehe, -n** marriage (11W)

ehemalig former

das **Ehepaar, -e** married couple

eher rather

die **Ehre, -n** honor

ehrgeizig ambitious

ehrgeizlos without ambition

ehrlich honest (11W)

die **Ehrlichkeit** honesty

das **Ei, -er** egg (2W); **ein gekochtes ~** boiled egg; **Rühr~** scrambled egg; **Spiegel~** fried egg; **verlorene ~er** poached eggs

die **Eidgenossenschaft** Swiss Confederation

das **Eigelb** egg yolk

eigen- own (11W)

die **Eigenschaft, -en** characteristic (11W)

eigentlich actual(ly) (4E); **~ schon** actually, yes

der **Eigentümer, -** owner

die **Eigentumswohnung, -en** condo(minium) (6E)

eilig hurried; **es ~ haben*** to be in a hurry

ein a, an (16G,7G); **die ~en** the ones

einan'der each other

die **Einbahnstraße, -n** one-way street

der **Einbau** installation

der **Einblick, -e** insight

der **Eindruck, ¨e** impression

eine(r) von Ihnen one of you

einerlei: Das ist nun ~. That doesn't matter anymore; **Es ist mir ~.** I don't care.

einerseits . . . andererseits on the one hand . . . on the other hand

einfach simple, simply (7E)

die **Einfahrt, -en** driveway; **Keine ~!** Do not enter.

einfarbig all one color

der **Einfluss, ¨e** influence (10E)

die **Einfuhr** import

ein·führen to introduce

die **Einführung, -en** introduction

sich **engagie'ren** to engage, commit o.s.

der **Eingang, ¨e** entrance (7W)

einher'·stolzieren (ist) to strut around

das **Einhorn, ¨er** unicorn

einig- (*pl. only*) some, a few (10G); **so ~es** all sorts of things

einigen to unite; **sich ~** (+ *acc.*) to agree (on)

die **Einigkeit** unity

ein·kaufen to shop; **~ gehen*** to go shopping (2E, 7G)

die **Einkaufsliste, -n** shopping list

die **Einkaufstasche, -n** shopping bag

das **Einkaufszentrum, -zentren** shopping center

das **Einkommen, -** income (12W)

ein·laden (lädt ein), lud ein, eingeladen (zu) to invite (to) (11W)

die **Einladung, -en** invitation

sich **ein·leben** to settle down

ein·lösen to cash (in) (7G); **einen Scheck ~** to cash a check (7W)

(ein)mal once, (at) one time / day (5E); **noch ~** once more, again (S3); one order of; **auch ~** for once; **erst ~** first of all; **nicht ~** not even; **es war ~** once upon a time

einmalig unique, incredible (14W)

der **Einmarsch, ¨e** entry, invasion

ein·packen to pack (in a suitcase)

ein·richten to furnish

die **Einrichtung, -en** furnishings and appliances

einsam lonely

die **Einsamkeit** loneliness

ein·schlafen* (ist) to fall asleep

ein·schließen* to lock up

sich **ein·schreiben*** to register

das **Einschreibungsformular', -e** application for university registration sich **ein·setzen (für)** to support actively

einst once (14E)

ein·steigen * to get on / in (8W)

der **Eintritt** entrance fee

die **Einwanderung** immigration

der **Einwohner, -** inhabitant

das **Einwohnermeldeamt, ̈er** resident registration office

einzeln individual(ly) (15E)

das **Einzelzimmer, -** single room (7W)

einzig- only; **ein ~er** just one

das **Eis** ice, ice cream (3W)

eisern (made of) iron

eisig icy

eiskalt ice-cold

eitel vain

ekelhaft disgusting

sich **ekeln** to be digusted

der **Elefant', -en, -en** elephant

elegant' elegant

der **Elek'triker, -** electrician

elek'trisch electric

die **Elektrizität'** electricity

der **Elek'tromecha'niker, -** electrical mechanic / technician

elektro'nisch electronic

die **Elek'trotech'nik** electrical engineering

das **Element', -e** element

der **Ell(en)bogen, -** elbow

die **Eltern** (*pl.*) parents (1W); **Groß~** grandparents (1 W); **Schwieger~** parents-in-law; **Stief~** stepparents; **Urgroß~** great-grandparents

die **E-Mail, -s** e-mail (8W); **~-Adresse, -n** e-mail address

die **Emanzipation'** emancipation

emanzipiert' emancipated

emotional' emotional(ly)

empfangen * to receive

die **Empfangsdame, -n** receptionist

empfehlen (empfiehlt), empfahl, empfohlen to recommend (3W)

die **Empfehlung, -en** recommendation

empfindlich delicate; sensitive

das **Ende** end (10W); **~ der Woche** at the end of the week (8G); **am ~** in the end (10W); **zu ~ sein** * to be finished

enden to end

endlich finally (15E)

die **Endung, -en** ending

die **Energie', -n** energy

eng narrow

sich **engagie'ren (in** + *dat.*) to get involved (in)

der **Engel, -** angel

(das) **England** England (1W)

der **Engländer, -** the Englishman (1W)

englisch English

(das) **Englisch: auf ~** in English (S2); **Sprechen Sie ~?** Do you speak English? (1W)

der **Enkel, -** grandchild

das **Enkelkind, -er** grandchild

die **Enkeltochter, ̈** granddaughter

der **Enkelsohn, ̈e** grandson

enorm' enormous; **~ viel** an awful lot

die **Ente, -n** duck; **Lahme ~!** Poor baby! Lame duck!

entfernt' away

entgegen·nehmen * to accept

enthalten * to contain

der **Enthusias'mus** enthusiasm

entlang' along (5W)

sich **entscheiden, entschied, entschieden** to decide (10W); **~ (für / gegen)** to decide for / against (10G)

die **Entscheidung, -en** decision (12E); **eine ~ treffen** * to make a decision

entschuldigen to excuse; **~ Sie bitte!** Excuse me, please. (5W)

die **Entschuldigung, -en** excuse; **~!** Excuse me! Pardon me! (5W)

sich **entspannen** to relax (9E)

entsprechen * to correspond to; **~d** corresponding

entstehen * **(ist)** to develop, emerge, be built; **neu ~** to reemerge

entwerten to cancel (ticket); devalue (currency)

(sich) **entwickeln** to develop; **sich auseinan'der·~** to develop apart

die **Entwicklung, -en** development

entzwei'·brechen * to break apart

(sich) **entzwei'·reißen** * to tear (o.s.) apart

sich **erbauen an** (+ *dat.*) to be delighted about, enjoy

die **Erbse, -n** pea (2W)

das **Erdbeben, -** earthquake

die **Erdbeere, -n** strawberry (2W)

die **Erde** earth (12E); **unter der ~** underground; **zur ~ fallen** * to fall down

das **Erdgeschoss, -e** ground level; **im ~** on the ground level

die **Erdnuss, ̈e** peanut; **~ butter** peanut butter

das **Ereignis, -se** event

erfahren * to find out, learn

die **Erfahrung, -en** experience (12W); **Lebens~** life experience

erfinden * to invent

der **Erfolg, -e** success

erfolgreich successful

erfrieren * **(ist)** to freeze to death

erfüllen to fulfill; **sich ~** to be fulfilled, come true

die **Erfüllung** fulfillment

ergänzen to supply, add to

ergreifen* to take (hold of)

erhalten* to keep up, preserve, maintain

die **Erhaltung** preservation (15W)

die **Erhellung** illumination

sich **erholen** to recuperate (9E)

die **Erholung** recuperation, relaxation

erinnern (an + *acc.*) to remind (of) (14W); **sich ~ (an** + *acc.*) to remember (14W)

die **Erinnerung, -en (an** + *acc.*) reminder, memory (of)

erkalten (ist) to grow cold; (*poetic*) to become insensitive

sich **erkälten** to catch a cold (9G)

die **Erkältung, -en** cold

erkennen* to recognize (14E); **Zum Erkennen** for recognition

erklären to explain (12W)

die **Erklärung, -en** explanation

erlauben to permit, allow

die **Erlaubnis** permit, permission; **Arbeits~** work permit; **Aufenthalts~** residence permit

erleben to experience (9E)

das **Erlebnis, -se** experience

erlesen exquisite, high-quality

die **Ermäßigung, -en** discount

die **Ernährung** nutrition

erneuerbar renewable

ernst serious(ly)

die **Ernte, -n** harvest

das **Erntedank'fest** (Harvest) Thanksgiving

eröffnen to open up, establish

erreichen to reach

erscheinen* (ist) to appear, seem (4G)

erschrecken (erschrickt), erschrak, ist erschrocken to be frightened

ersetzen to replace

erst- first

erst only, not until

ertragen* to tolerate, stand

erwachsen grown-up, adult

der **Erwachsene (ein Erwachsener) / die Erwachsene, -n, -n** adult

erwähnen to mention

erwärmen to heat (up)

erwarten to expect (12E)

erweitern to expand; **erweitert** expanded

erzählen to tell (8W); **~ (von** + *dat.*) to tell (about) (10G); **nach·~** to retell

erziehen* to educate, raise

die **Erziehung** education

das **Erziehungsgeld** monthly child-raising benefit

der **Esel, -** donkey, ass; **Du ~!** You dummy!

der **Espres'so, -s** espresso

der **Esprit'** esprit

essbar edible

essen (isst), aß, gegessen to eat (S5)

das **Essen, -** food, meal (2W); **beim ~** while eating

der **Essig** vinegar

der **Essvorrat, ¨e** provision

das **Esszimmer, -** dining room (5W)

der **Este, -n, -n / die Estin, -nen** Estonian

(das) **Estland** Estonia

estnisch Estonian

die **Eta'ge, -n** floor

ethnisch ethnic

etliche many

etwa about, approximately (10E)

etwas some, a little (2W); something (3W); **so ~ wie** s.th. like; **noch ~** one more thing, s.th. else; **Sonst noch ~?** Anything else?

euer (*pl. fam.*) your (7G)

der **Euro, -s** euro (S3); **zehn ~** ten euros

(das) **Euro'pa** Europe

der **Europä'er, -** the European

europä'isch European

die **Europäische Union (EU)** European Union (1W); **in der ~** in the EU (1E)

das **Euroland** euro region

die **Europäisie'rung** Europeanization

euro'paweit all over Europe

der **Evangelist', -en, -en** evangelist

eventuell' perhaps, possibly

ewig eternal(ly); **für ~** forever

exakt' exact(ly)

das **Exa'men, -** exam; **Staats~** comprehensive state exam

das **Exemplar', -e** sample, copy

das **Exil', -e** exile

existie'ren to exist

experimentell' experimental(ly)

der **Exper'te, -n, -n / die Expertin, -nen** expert

extra extra

das **Extrablatt, ¨er** special publication

exzen'trisch excentric

F

die **Fabel, -n** fable

fabelhaft fabulous

die **Fabrik', -en** factory

das **Fach, ¨er** subject (13W); **Haupt~** major (field) (13W); **Neben~** minor (field) (13W); **Schwerpunkt~** major (field)

das **Fach, ¨er** special field

der **Fachbereich, -e** field (of study)

die **Fachkenntnis, -se** special skill

die **Fach(ober)schule, -n** business or technical school

die **Fachhochschule, -n** university of applied sciences

die **Fachrichtung, -en** field of study, specialization (13W)

das **Fachwerkhaus, ⸚er** half-timbered house

der **Faden, ⸚** thread

die **Fähigkeit, -en** ability

die **Fähre, -n** ferry

fahren (fährt), fuhr, ist gefahren to drive, go (by car, etc.) (3G)

die **Fahrerei'** (incessant) driving

die **Fahrkarte, -n** ticket (8W)

der **Fahrplan, ⸚e** schedule (of trains, etc.) (8W)

das **(Fahr)rad, ⸚er** bicycle (5W); **mit dem ~ fahren*** to bicycle

der **(Fahr)radweg, -e** bike path

der **Fahrstuhl, ⸚e** elevator

die **Fahrt, -en** trip, drive (8W)

fair fair(ly)

der **Fall, ⸚e** case; **auf jeden ~** in any case

fallen (fällt), fiel, ist gefallen to fall (4E); **~ lassen*** to drop

falsch wrong, false (S2)

die **Fami'lie, -n** family (1W)

der **Fami'lienstand** marital status

fangen (fängt), fing, gefangen to catch

die **Fantasie', -n** fantasy, imagination

fantas'tisch fantastic(ally) (9W)

die **Farbe, -n** color (S2); **Welche ~ hat . . . ?** What color is . . . ? (S2)

der **Farbstoff, -e** dye, (artificial) color

der **Fasching** carnival; **zum ~** for carnival (Mardi Gras)

das **Fass, ⸚er** barrel; **Bier vom ~** beer on tap

die **Fassa'de, -n** façade

fast almost (6E)

die **Fastenzeit** Lent

die **Faszination'** fascination

faszinie'ren to fascinate

faul lazy (11W)

faulenzen to be lazy (9W)

die **Faulheit** laziness

das **Fax, -e** fax (8W)

das **Faxgerät, ⸚e** fax machine

der **Februar** February (S4); **im ~** in February (S4)

fechten (ficht), focht, gefochten to fence

der **Federball, ⸚e** badminton (ball)

fehlen to be missing, lacking (8W); **hier fehlt was** s.th. is missing (here); **was fehlt?** what's missing?

fehlend missing

der **Fehler, -** mistake

die **Feier, -n** celebration, party (4W)

feierlich festive

feiern to celebrate (4W)

der **Feiertag, -e** holiday (4W)

feige cowardly; **er ist ~** he's a coward

fein fine

die **Feind, -e** enemy

feindlich hostile

das **Feld, -er** field

das **Fenster, -** window (S2)

die **Ferien** (pl.) vacation (4W)

der **Ferienplatz, ⸚e** vacation spot

fern far, distant

die **Ferne** distance

der **Fernfahrer, -** truck driver

das **Ferngespräch, -e** long-distance call

fern·sehen* to watch TV (9W)

das **Fernsehen** TV (the medium) (10E); **im ~** on TV (10W)

der **Fernseher, -** TV set (6W)

fertig finished, done (S5); **~·machen** to finish

das **Fest, -e** celebration (4W)

festgesetzt fixed

festlich festive(ly)

das **Festspiel, -e** festival

die **Fete, -n** (coll.) party

das **Feuer, -** fire

das **Feuerwerk, -e** firework(s)

die **Figur', -en** figure

der **Film, -e** film (10W)

filmen to shoot a film

die **Finan'zen** (pl.) finances

finanziell' financial(ly)

finanzie'ren to finance (15W)

die **Finanzie'rung** financing

finden, fand, gefunden to find (S4); **Ich finde es . . .** I think it's . . . (S4); **Das finde ich auch.** I think so, too. (S4)

der **Finger, -** finger (9W); **Zeige~** index finger

der **Fingernagel, ⸚** fingernail

der **Finne, -n, -n / die Finnin, -nen** the Finn

finnisch Finnish

(das) Finnland Finland

die **Firma, Firmen** company, business (12W)

der **Fisch, -e** fish (2W); Pisces; **ein kalter ~** a cold-hearted person

der **Fischfang** fishing

fit in shape; **sich ~ halten*** to keep in shape (9E)

flach flat

die **Fläche, -n** area

der **Flachs** flax

die **Flagge, -n** flag

die **Flamme, -n** flame

die **Flasche, -n** bottle (3E); **eine ~ Wein** a bottle of wine (3E); **Mehrweg~** bottle with a deposit

das **Fleisch** (sg.) meat (2W)

der **Fleischer, -** butcher

die **Fleischerei', -en** butcher shop

fleißig industrious(ly), hard-working (11W)

flexi'bel flexible, flexibly

die **Flexibilität'** flexibility

flieder lavender

die **Fliege, -n** fly

fliegen, flog, ist geflogen to fly (8W); **mit dem Flugzeug ~** to go by plane (8W)

fliehen, floh, ist geflohen to flee, escape

die **Fliese, -n** tile

fließen, floss, ist geflossen to flow

fließend   fluent(ly)

die **Flitterwochen** (*pl.*)
 honeymoon

flitzen (ist)   to dash

der **Flohmarkt, ̈e**   flea market

das **Floß, ̈e**   raft

die **Flöte, -n**   flute; **(Block)~**
 recorder, wooden
 flute

die **Flotte, -n**   fleet

die **Flucht**   escape

der **Flüchtling, -e**   refugee

der **Flug, ̈e**   flight (8W)

der **Flügel, -**   wing

der **Flughafen, ̈**   airport (8W)

die **Flugkarte, -n**   plane ticket

der **Flugsteig, -e**   gate

das **Flugzeug, -e**   airplane
 (8W)

der **Flur**   hallway, entrance
 foyer (6W)

der **Fluss, ̈e**   river (1W)

die **Flut**   high tide

folgen (ist) (+ *dat.*)   to
 follow

folgend   following (10E)

der **Fokus**   focus

der **Fön, -e**   hair dryer

das **Fondue', -s**   fondue

die **Fonotypist', -en, -en**
 audio/dictaphone-typist

fördern   to encourage

die **Forel'le, -n**   trout

die **Form, -en**   form, shape

das **Formular', -e**   form

formulie'ren   to formulate

die **Forschung**   research; **der
 ~szweig, -e**   field of
 research

der **Förster,-**   forest ranger

die **Forstwirtschaft**   forestry

fort-   away

fort·fahren*   to drive
 away; to continue

der **Fortschritt, -e**   progress

fort·werfen*   to throw
 away

die **Fotografie'**   photo(graph);
 photography

fotografie'ren   to take pictures (9W)

die **Frage, -n**   question (1W);
 Ich habe eine ~. I have
 a question. (S5);

jemandem eine ~ stellen
 to ask sb. a question

fragen   to ask (S2); **sich ~**
 to wonder (9G)

das **Fragezeichen, -**   question
 mark

fraglich   questionable

der **(Schweizer) Franken, -**
 (Swiss) franc

(der) **Frankfurter Kranz**   rich
 cake ring with whipped
 cream and nuts

fränkisch   Franconian

(das) **Frankreich**   France (1W)

der **Franzo'se, -n, -n / die
 Franzö'sin, -nen**
 French person (1W, 2G)

franzö'sisch   French (1W)

(das) **Franzö'sisch; auf ~**   in
 French (1W); **Ich
 spreche ~.** I speak
 French. (1W)

die **Frau, -en**   Mrs., Ms. (S1);
 woman; wife (1W)

das **Frauchen, -** (*coll.*)   (female)
 owner of a pet

die **Frauenbewegung**
 women's movement

das **Fräulein, -** (*old fash-
 ioned*) Miss; young lady

frech   impudent(ly), sassy,
 fresh

die **Frechheit**   impertinence

frei   free, available (7W)

freiberuf'lich   self-employed, freelance

freigiebig   generous(ly)

die **Freiheit**   freedom

das **Freilichtspiel, -e**   outdoor
 performance

frei·nehmen*   to take
 time off

der **Freitag**   Friday (S4);
 am ~ on Friday (S4);
 Kar~ Good Friday

freitags   on Fridays (2E)

freiwillig   voluntary;
 voluntarily

die **Freizeit**   leisure time (9W)

fremd   foreign, strange

das **Fremdenzimmer, -**   guest-
 room

die **Fremdsprache, -n**   foreign
 language

der **Fremdsprachenkorrespon-
 dent', -en, -en**
 bilingual secretary

**fressen (frisst), fraß,
 gefressen**   to eat (like a
 glutton or an animal);
 auf·~ to devour

das **Frettchen, -**   ferret

die **Freude, -n**   joy

sich **freuen auf** (+ *acc.*)   to look
 forward to (10G); **Freut
 mich.**   I'm pleased to
 meet you. (S1); **(Es) freut
 mich auch.**   Likewise,
 pleased to meet you,
 too; **Das freut mich für
 dich.**   I'm happy for you.
 (8W)

der **Freund, -e**   (boy)friend (3E)

die **Freundin, -nen**
 (girl)friend (3E)

freundlich   friendly (11W)

die **Freundlichkeit**   friendliness

die **Freundschaft, -en**   friendship (11W)

der **Frieden**   peace (14W)

friedlich   peaceful(ly)

frieren, fror, gefroren   to
 freeze

frisch   fresh(ly) (2W)

der **Friseur', -e**   barber,
 hairdresser

die **Friseu'se, -n = Friseu'rin,
 -nen**   beautician, hairdresser

friesisch   Frisian

froh   glad(ly), happy, hap-
 pily (11E); **Frohe
 Weihnachten!** Merry
 Christmas (4W)

fröhlich   cheerful(ly),
 merry, merrily; **Fröh-
 liche Weihnachten!**
 Merry Christmas! (4W)

der **Fronleich'nam(stag)**
 Corpus Christi (holiday)

der **Frosch, ̈e**   frog

früh   early, morning (8G)

früher   earlier, once, for-
 mer(ly) (12E)

der **Frühling, -e**   spring (S4)

das **Frühjahrssemester, -**
 spring semester

das **Frühstück** breakfast (3W);
Was gibt's zum ~? What's
for breakfast? (3W)
frühstücken to eat breakfast (3W)

der **Frust** frustration
frustriert' frustrated

die **Frustrie'rung** frustration

der **Fuchs, ̈-e** fox; **schlau wie
ein ~** clever as a fox; **ein
alter ~** a sly person

sich **fühlen** to feel (a certain
way) (9W)
führen to lead (14W)

der **Führerschein, -e** driver's
license

die **Führung, -en** guided tour

die **Fülle** abundance; **in
ganzer ~** to the fullest
füllen to fill

die **Funktion', -en** function
für (+ *acc.*) for (S2,2G);
was ~ ein . . . ? what
kind of a . . . ? (2W)

die **Furcht** fear, awe
furchtbar terrible, terribly, awful(ly) (S4)

sich **fürchten** (**vor** + *dat.*) to be
afraid (of)

der **Fürst, -en, -en** sovereign,
prince

das **Fürstentum, ̈-er** principality

der **Fuß, ̈-e** foot (9W); **zu ~
gehen*** to walk (5W)

der **Fußball, ̈-e** soccer (ball)
(9W)

der **Fußgänger, -** pedestrian;
~weg, -e pedestrian sidewalk; **~überweg, -e**
pedestrian crossing;
~zone, -n pedestrian
area

der **Fußnagel, ̈-** toenail

G

die **Gabe, -n** gift; **in kleinen
~n** in small doses

die **Gabel, -n** fork (3W)
gähnen to yawn

die **Galerie', -n** gallery

die **Gans, ̈-e** goose; **eine
dumme ~** a silly person
(fem.)

ganz whole, entire(ly), all
(9E); very; **~ meinerseits.**
The pleasure is all mine;
~ schön quite (nice);
~tags full-time

das **Ganze** the whole thing;
im Großen und ~n on
the whole

die **Gara'ge, -n** garage (6W)
garantie'ren to guarantee
(15W)

die **Gardi'ne, -n** curtain
gar nicht not at all (13E)

der **Garten, ̈-** garden (6W);
Bier~ beer garden

das **Gartenstück, -e** garden
plot

die **Gasse, -n** narrow street
Gassi gehen* to take a
dog on a walk

der **Gast, ̈-e** guest (7W)

der **Gastarbeiter, -** foreign
(guest) worker

das **Gästezimmer, -** guest
room

das **Gasthaus, ̈-er** restaurant,
inn

der **Gasthof, ̈-e** small hotel
(7E)

die **Gaststätte, -n** restaurant,
inn

die **Gastwirtschaft, -en**
restaurant, inn

das **Gebäck** pastry

das **Gebäude, -** building (14W)
geben (gibt), gab, gegeben
to give (3G); **es gibt**
there is, there are (2W);
Was gibt's? What's
up?; **Was gibt's Neues?**
What's new? (9W); **Was
gibt's im . . . ?** What's
(playing) on . . . ? (10W);
Das gibt's doch nicht! I
don't believe it! That's
impossible! (4W)

das **Gebiet, -e** area, region
(15W)
gebildet well educated
(11W)
geboren: Ich bin . . . ~. I
was born . . . (S4); **Wann
sind Sie ~?** When were
you born? (S4); **Wann**

wurde . . . ~? When was
. . . born?

die **Geborgenheit** security
gebrauchen to use,
utilize

der **Gebrauchtwagen, -** used
car

die **Gebühr, -en** fee
gebunden tied down;
orts~ tied to a certain
town or place

die **Geburt, -en** birth; **Wieder~**
rebirth

der **Geburtstag, -e** birthday
(4W); **Wann haben Sie ~?**
When is your birthday?
(4W); **Ich habe am . . .-
(s)ten ~.** My birthday is
on the . . . (date) (4W);
Ich habe im . . . ~. My
birthday is in . . .
(month). (4W); **Alles
Gute / Herzlichen
Glückwunsch zum ~!**
Happy birthday! (4W);
zum ~ at the / for the
birthday (4W)

der **Geburtsort, -e** place of
birth

das **Gedächtnis** memory

der **Gedanke, -ns, -n** thought
(14E)

das **Gedeck, -e** complete dinner

das **Gedicht, -e** poem

die **Geduld** patience
geduldig patient (11W);
~ wie ein Lamm really
patient

die **Gefahr, -en** danger (12E)
gefährlich dangerous
(15E)

das **Gefälle, -** decline
**gefallen (gefällt), gefiel,
gefallen** (+ *dat.*) to like,
be pleasing to (3G); **Es
gefällt mir.** I like it.
(3G); **Das gefällt mir
aber!** I really like it.
(11W)
gefangen halten* to keep
prisoner

das **Gefängnis, -se** prison
gefettet greased

der **Gefrierschrank, ¨e**
freezer

das **Gefühl, -e** feeling; **Mit~**
compassion

gegen (+ *acc.*) against
(2G); toward (time),
around

die **Gegend, -en** area, region
(8E)

der **Gegensatz, ¨e** contrast,
opposite

gegensätzlich opposing

das **Gegenteil, -e** opposite
(S3); **im ~** on the con-
trary(12W)

gegenüber (von + *dat.*)
across (from) (5W)

die **Gegenwart** present
(tense)

der **Gegner, -** opponent

das **Gehalt, ¨er** salary

gehen, ging, ist gegangen
to go, walk (S5); **Es geht
mir . . .** I am (feeling) . . .
(S1); **Wie geht's? Wie
geht es Ihnen?** How are
you? (S1); **zu Fuß ~** to
walk (5W); **Das geht.**
That's OK. (13E); **Das
geht (heute) nicht.** That
won't work (today).
(9W); **So geht's.** That's
the way it goes.; **wenn
es darum geht** when it's
a matter of

gehorchen to obey

gehören (+ *dat.*) to belong
to (3G)

die **Geige, -n** violin

der **Geisteswissenschaftler, -**
humanities scholar

geistig mental(ly), intel-
lectual(ly)

geizig stingy

das **Geländer, -** railing,
banister

gelaunt: gut / schlecht ~ in
a good / bad mood

gelb yellow (S2)

das **Geld** money (7W); **Bar~**
cash (7W); **Klein~**
change (7W); **Erzie-
hungs~** government
stipend for child care;

~ aus·geben* to spend
money (9E)

der **Geldautomat', -en, -en**
ATM machine

der **Geldschein, -e** banknote
(15E)

die **Gelegenheit, -en** opportunity, chance

**gelingen, gelang, ist gelun-
gen** to succeed; **Es
gelingt mir nicht.** I
can't.

gelten (gilt), galt, gegolten
to apply to, be valid for,
be true

das **Gemälde, -** painting
(10W)

die **Gemeinde, -n** community

gemeinsam together,
shared, joint(ly) (11W);
(in) common (15E)

die **Gemeinschaft, -en**
community

das **Gemisch** mixture; **ein
buntes ~ an (+ dat.)** a
great diversity in

gemischt mixed

die **Gemse, -n** mountain goat

das **Gemüse, -** vegetable(s)
(2W)

gemütlich cozy, pleasant,
comfortable, convivial
(5E)

die **Gemütlichkeit** nice atmosphere, coziness

genau exact(ly); **~!** Exactly! Precisely! (12W);
~so the same; **~so ___
wie** just as ___ as; **~ wie**
(+ *nom.*) just like (9E)

die **Generation', -en** generation

generös' generous(ly)

sich **genieren** to be embarrassed

genießen, genoss, genossen
to enjoy (12E)

der **Genitiv, -e** genitive

genug enough (5E); **Jetzt
habe ich aber ~.** That's
enough. I've had it.
(10W)

geöffnet open (7W)

die **Geographie'** geography

geolo'gisch geological

die **Geologie'** geology

das **Gepäck** baggage, luggage
(7W)

die **Gepäckaufgabe, -n**
checked luggage room

gepunktet dotted

gerade just, right now
(4W); **~ als** just when;
(immer) ~aus' (keep)
straight ahead (5W)

die **Gerechtigkeit** justice

das **Gericht, -e** dish; **Haupt~**
main dish

der **Gerichtshof, ¨e** court

gering' little, small; **~er**
less

germa'nisch Germanic

die **Germanis'tik** study of
German language and
literature

gern (lieber, liebst-)
gladly (2W); **furchtbar ~**
very much;**~ geschehen!**
Glad to . . . ; **Ich hätte ~.**
I'd like to have . . . (2W)

die **Gesamtschule, -n** comprehensive high school

das **Geschäft, -e** store (2W);
business (12W)

geschäftlich concerning
business

die **Geschäftsfrau, -en** businesswoman / **Geschäfts-
mann, ¨er** businessman /
Geschäftsleute (*pl.*)
business people (12W)

**geschehen (geschieht),
geschah, ist geschehen**
to happen (11E); **Das
geschieht dir recht.** That
serves you right.

das **Geschenk, -e** present
(4W)

die **Geschichte, -n** story,
history (8E)

geschickt talented,
skillful

geschieden divorced
(11W)

das **Geschlecht, -er** gender,
sex

geschlossen closed (7W)

der **Geschmack, ¨-er** taste
geschmacklos tacky
das **Geschrei** screaming
die **Geschwindigkeit, -en** speed; **~sbegrenzung** speed limit; **Richt~** recommended speed
die **Geschwister** (*pl.*) brothers and/or sisters, siblings (1W)
der **Geselle, -n, -n / die Gesellin, -nen** journeyman / journeywoman
gesellig sociable
die **Gesell'schaft, -en** society
gesellschaftlich' societal, social(ly)
gesell'schaftspoli'tisch socio-political
das **Gesetz, -e** law
gesetzlich legal(ly)
gesichert secure
das **Gesicht, -er** face (9W)
das **Gespräch, -e** conversation, dialogue
das **Geständnis, -se** confession
gestern yesterday (4W,8G); **vor~** the day before yesterday (4W)
gestreift striped
gesucht wird wanted
gesund (ü) healthy (9W)
die **Gesundheit** health
das **Gesundheitsamt** health department
gesundheitsbewusst health conscious
der **Gesundheitsfana'tiker, -** health nut
geteilt divided; shared
das **Getränk, -e** beverage
getrennt separated, separate(ly)
die **Gewalt** violence
die **Gewerkschaft, -en** trade / labor union
der **Gewinn, -e** profit, benefit
gewinnen, gewann, gewonnen to win (12E)
gewiss for sure
das **Gewitter, -** thunderstorm
sich **gewöhnen an** (+ *acc.*) to get used to (12W)

gewöhnlich usual(ly) (3E)
gierig greedy
gießen, goss, gegossen to pour; **es gießt** it's pouring
das **Gift, -e** poison
der **Giftstoff, -e** toxic waste (15W)
die **Giraf'fe, -n** giraffe
die **Gitar're, -n** guitar (9W)
die **Gladio'le, -n** gladiola
der **Glanz** brilliance, splendor
das **Glas, ¨-er** glass (2E); **ein ~** a glass of (2E)
glauben to believe, think (2W;3G); **Ich glaube es / ihr.** I believe it / her.; **~ an** (+ *acc.*) to believe in (12W)
glaubhaft convincing(ly)
gleich equal(ly), same (12W); right away; **Bis ~!** See you in a few minutes! (9W)
gleichberechtigt with equal rights
die **Gleichberechtigung** equality, equal rights
gleichfalls: Danke ~! Thank you, the same to you. (3W)
gleichgeschlechtlich same-sex
gleichmäßig regularl(ly)
das **Gleichnis, -se** parable
das **Gleis, -e** track (8W)
der **Gletscher, -** glacier
die **Glocke, -n** bell
glorreich glorious
das **Glück** luck, happiness; **~ haben*** to be lucky (4E); **~ gehabt!** I was (you were, etc.) lucky! (4E); **Viel ~!** Good luck! (4W); **Du ~spilz!** You lucky thing!; **zum ~** luckily
glücklich happy, happily (11W)
der **Glückwunsch, ¨-e** congratulation; **Herzlichen ~ (zum Geburtstag)!** Congratulations (on your birthday)! (4W); **Herzliche Glück-**

wünsche! Congratulations! Best wishes! (4W)
der **Glühwein** mulled wine
der **Gnom, -e** gnome, goblin
das **Gold** gold (11E)
golden golden
der **Goldfisch, -e** goldfish
(das) **Golf** golf; **Mini~** miniature golf
der **Gott** God; **~ sei Dank!** Thank God! (8W); **Um ~es willen!** For Heaven's sake! My goodness!
der **Gott, ¨-er** god
der **Grad, -e** degree
die **Gramma'tik** grammar
gramma'tisch grammatical(ly)
die **Grapefruit, -s** grapefruit
das **Gras** grass
gratulie'ren (+ *dat.*) to congratulate (4W); **Wir ~! / Ich gratuliere!** Congratulations!
grau gray (S2)
greifen, griff, gegriffen to grab, seize
die **Grenze, -n** border (14E)
grenzen (**an** + *acc.*) to border
grenzenlos unlimited, endless(ly)
der **Grieche, -n, -n / die Griechin, -nen** the Greek
(das) **Griechenland** Greece
griechisch Greek
die **Grippe** flu, influenza
groß (größer, größt-) large, big, tall (S3); **im Großen und Ganzen** on the whole, by and large
die **Größe, -n** size, height
die **Großeltern** (*pl.*) grandparents (1W); **Ur~** great-grandparents
das **Großmaul, ¨-er** big mouth
die **Großmutter, ¨-** grandmother (1W); **Ur~** great-grandmother
der **Großteil** major part / portion

der **Großvater, ⁻** grandfather (1W); **Ur~** greatgrandfather

Grüezi! Hi! (*in Switzerland*)

grün green (S2); **ins Grüne / im Grünen** out in(to) nature

der **Grund, ⁻e** reason; **aus diesem ~** for that reason; **im ~e genommen** basically

gründen to found

das **Grundgesetz** Constitution, Basic Law

die **Grundschule, -n** elementary school, grades 1–4

das **Grundstück, -e** building lot

der **Grundstücksmakler, -** real estate broker

die **Gründung, -en** founding

die **Grünfläche, -n** green area

die **Gruppe, -n** group

der **Gruß, ⁻e** greeting; **Viele Grüße** (**an** [+ *acc.*] . . .)! Greetings (to . . .)!

grüßen to greet; **Grüß dich!** Hi!; **Grüß Gott!** Hello! Hi! (*in southern Germany*)

der **Gummi** rubber

gurgeln to gargle

die **Gurke, -n** cucumber (2W); **saure ~** pickle

der **Gürtel, -** belt

gut (besser, best-) good, fine, well (S1); **~ aussehend** good-looking (11W); **Das ist noch mal ~ gegangen.** Things worked out all right (again); **na ~** well, all right; **Mach's ~!** Take care. (S1); **~** approx. grade B; **sehr ~** approx. grade A

das **Gute: Alles ~!** All the best! (4W); **Alles ~ zum Geburtstag!** Happy birthday! (4W)

die **Güte** goodness; **Ach du meine ~!** My goodness! (8W)

gütig kind(ly)

das **Gymna'sium, Gymna'sien** academic high school (grades 5–12/13)

H

das **Haar, -e** hair (9W)

haben (hat), hatte, gehabt to have (S5,2G); **Ich hätte gern . . .** I'd like (to have) . . . (2W)

das **Habitat, -e** habitat

der **Hafen, ⁻** port

die **Haferflocken** (*pl.*) oatmeal

das **Hähnchen, -** grilled chicken

der **Haken, -** hook

halb half (to the next hour) (S5); **~tags** part-time; **in einer ~en Stunde** in half an hour (8W)

die **Hälfte, -n** half

die **Halle, -n** large room for work, recreation, or assembly

Hallo! Hello! Hi!

der **Hals, ⁻e** neck, throat (9W); **Das hängt mir zum ~ heraus.** I'm fed up (with it). (10W)

das **Halsband, ⁻er** collar

Halt! Stop! (7W)

halten (hält), hielt, gehalten to hold; stop (a vehicle) (5W); **~ von** to think of, be of an opinion about (10G)

die **Haltestelle, -n** (bus, etc.) stop (5W)

das **Halteverbot, -e** no stopping or parking

der **Hamburger Matjestopf** pickled herring with sliced apples and onion rings in a sour-cream sauce

der **Hamster, -** hamster

die **Hand, ⁻e** hand (3E,9W)

die **Handarbeit, -en** needlework

der **Handball, ⁻e** handball

der **Handel** trade (12E)

das **Handeln** action

die **Handelsbeziehung, -en** trade relation(s)

die **Handelsnation', -en** trading nation

der **Handelspartner, -** trading partner

der **Händler, -** merchant, dealer

der **Handschuh, -e** glove

das **Handtuch, ⁻er** towel

der **Handwerker, -** craftsman

das **Handy, -s** cellular phone (8W)

hängen to hang (up) (6W)

hängen, hing, gehangen to hang (be hanging) (6W)

harmo'nisch harmonious

hart (ä) hard; tough

das **Häschen, -** rabbit, bunny

der **Hass** hate

hassen to hate

hässlich ugly (11W)

die **Haube, -n** hood

das **Hauptfach, ⁻er** major (field of study) (13W)

der **Hauptmann, ⁻er** captain

die **Hauptrolle, -n** leading role

die **Hauptsache, -n** main thing

hauptsächlich mainly

die **Hauptsaison** (high) season

die **Hauptschule, -n** basic high school (grades 5–9)

die **Hauptstadt, ⁻e** capital (1W)

das **Hauptwort, ⁻er** noun

das **Haus, ⁻er** house (6W); **nach ~e** (toward) home (3W); **zu ~e** at home (3W)

der **Hausbesetzer, -** squatter

das **Häuschen, -** little house

die **Hausfrau, -en** housewife (12W)

der **Haushalt, -e** household

der **Haushälter, -** housekeeper

häuslich home-loving, domestic

das **Haustier, -e** pet

die **Hauswirtschaft** home economics

die **Haut** skin

die **Hautpflege** skin care

das **Heft, -e** notebook (S2)

heilig holy; **Aller ~en** All Saints' Day; **~e Drei Könige** Epiphany

der **Heiligabend** Christmas Eve; **am ~** on Christmas Eve

die **Heimat** homeland, home (14E)

der **Heimcompu'ter, -** home computer

die **Heimreise, -n** trip home

Heimweh haben* to be homesick

heiraten to marry, get married (11W)

heiratslustig eager to marry

heiß hot(ly) (S4)

heißen, hieß, geheißen to be called; **Ich heiße . . .** My name is . . . (S1); **Wie ~ Sie?** What's your name? (S1)

die **Heizung** heating (system)

das **Heizmaterial'** heating material, fuel

helfen (hilft), half, geholfen (+ *dat.*) to help (3G)

hell light, bright (6W); **Sei ~e!** Be smart!

das **Hemd, -en** shirt (S3); **Nacht~** nightgown

die **Henne, -n** hen

her- toward (the speaker) (7G)

herab'·blicken (auf + *acc.*) to look down (on)

herab'·schauen (auf + *acc.*) to look down (on)

heran'- up to

heraus'·finden* to find out

die **Heraus'forderung, -en** challenge

der **Herbst, -e** fall, autumn (S4)

der **Herd, -e** (kitchen) range

herein'- in(to)

herein'·kommen* to come in, enter (11E)

herein'·lassen* to let in

der **Hering, -e** herring

die **Herkunft** origin

der **Herr, -n, -en** Mr., gentleman (S1,2G); Lord; **Sehr geehrte Damen und ~en!** Ladies and gentlemen!

das **Herrchen, -** (*coll.*) (male) owner of a pet

herrlich wonderful(ly), great(ly), splendid(ly) (8E)

her'·stellen to manufacture, produce

herum'- around

herum'·fragen to ask around

herum'·laufen* to run around

herum'·reisen (ist) to travel around

herum'·schnuppern to snoop around

hervor'·bringen* to produce

das **Herz, -ens, -en** heart; **mit ~** with feelings

herzförmig heart-shaped

der **Herzog, ¨e** duke

heulen to cry; howl

der **Heurige, -n** (*sg.*) new wine

die **Heurigenschänke, -n** Viennese wine-tasting inn

heute today (S4); **für ~** for today (S2)

heutig- of today

heutzutage nowadays

hier here (S2)

die **Hilfe, -n** help (15E)

hilfsbereit helpful

das **Hilfsverb, -en** auxiliary verb

der **Himmel** sky; heaven; **~fahrt(stag)** Ascension (Day)

himmlisch heavenly

der **Himmlische (ein Himmlischer) / die Himmlische, -n, -n** Heavenly one

hin- toward (the speaker) (7G)

hin und her back and forth

hinauf'·fahren* to go or drive up (to) (8E)

hinein'·gehen* to go in(to), enter

hin·kommen* to get / come to

hin·legen to lay or put down; **sich ~** to lie down (9G)

hin·nehmen* to accept

sich **(hin·)setzen** to sit down (9G)

hinter (+ *acc. / dat.*) behind (6G)

hinterlas'sen* to leave behind

der **Hintern, -** behind

die **(Hin- und) Rückfahrkarte, -n** round-trip ticket (8W)

hinun'ter·fahren* to drive down

hinzu'- added to

hinzu'·fügen to add

das **Hirn** brain

der **Hirsch, -e** red deer

histo'risch historical(ly) (14W)

das **Hobby, -s** hobby (9W)

hoch (hoh-) (höher, höchst-) high(ly) (12W)

das **Hochdeutsch** standard High German

das **Hochhaus, ¨er** high-rise building

hoch·kriechen* (an + *dat.*) to creep up (on)

hoch·legen to put up (high)

die **Hochschule, -n** university, college; **Fach~** university of applied sciences

die **Hochzeit, -en** wedding (11W); **der ~stag, -e** wedding day / anniversary

(das) **Hockey** hockey

der **Hof, ¨e** court, courtyard

hoffen to hope (12E)

hoffentlich hopefully, I hope (5E)

die **Hoffnung, -en** hope

höflich polite(ly)

die **Höhe, -n** height, altitude; **in die ~** up high; **Das ist doch die ~!** That's the limit!

der **Höhepunkt, -e** climax

hohl hollow

die **Höhle, -n** cave

(sich) **holen** to (go and) get, pick up, fetch (13W)

der **Holländer, -** the Dutchman

holländisch Dutch

die **Hölle** hell

das **Holz** wood; **die ~terrasse, -n** wooden terrace

hölzern wooden

der **Honig** honey

hoppla oops, whoops

hörbar audible, audibly

horchen (nach) to listen (for)

hören to hear (S2)

der **Hörer, -** listener; receiver

der **Hörsaal, -säle** lecture hall (13W)

das **Hörspiel, -e** radio play

das **Hörverständnis** listening comprehension (activity)

die **Hose, -n** slacks, pants (S3); **Latz~** overall

der **Hosenanzug, ̈e** pant suit

das **Hotel', -s** hotel (5W,7W)

hübsch pretty (11W)

der **Hügel, -** hill

das **Huhn, ̈er** chicken

das **Hühnchen, -** little chicken

der **Humor'** (sense of) humor

der **Hund, -e** dog (11W); **Fauler ~!** Lazy bum!

hundert hundred; **Hunderte von** hundreds of

der **Hunger** hunger (2E); **Ich habe ~.** I'm hungry. (2E)

hungrig hungry, hungrily

hüpfen (ist) to hop

der **Hut, ̈e** hat

hüten to watch (over)

die **Hütte, -n** hut, cottage

die **Hymne, -n** hymn, anthem

I

der **ICE, -s** InterCityExpress (train)

ideal' ideal(ly)

das **Ideal', -e** ideal

der **Idealis'mus** idealism

die **Idee', -n** idea (9W); **Gute ~!** That's a good idea!

sich **identifizie'ren** to identify o.s.

iden'tisch identical(ly)

die **Identität', -en** identity; **der ~sschwund** loss of identity

idyl'lisch idyllic(ally)

ignorie'ren to ignore

ihr her, its, their (7G) **Ihr** (formal) your (1W,7G)

imaginär' imaginary

die **Imbissbude, -n** snack bar, fast-food stand

die **Immatrikulation'** enrollment (at university)

immer always (4E); **~ geradeaus** always straight ahead (5W); **~ länger** longer and longer (12G); **~ noch** still; **~ wieder** again and again (12G)

der **Imperativ, -e** imperative

das **Imperfekt** imperfect, simple past

in (+ acc. / dat.) in, into, inside of (6G)

inbegriffen (in + dat.) included (in)

der **India'ner, -** the Native American

der **In'dikativ** indicative

in'direkt indirect(ly)

die **Individualität'** individuality

individuell' individual(ly)

die **Industrie', -n** industry

der **Industrie'kaufmann / die ~kauffrau / die ~leute** industrial manager

industriell' industrial

das **Industrie'unternehmen, -** large industrial company

der **Infinitiv, -e** infinitive

die **Informa'tik** computer science

die **Information', -en** information

die **Informations'suche** search for information

informativ' informative

(sich) **informie'ren (über** + acc.) to inform o.s., find out (about) (10G)

der **Ingenieur', -e** engineer (12W)

die **Initiati've, -n** initiative

inlineskaten to rollerblade; **~ gehen*** to go rollerblading

innen (adv.) inside

der **Innenhof, ̈e** inner court

die **Innenstadt, ̈e** center (of town), downtown

inner- inner

innerhalb within

die **Insel, -n** island (14E)

insgesamt' altogether

das **Institut', -e** institute

das **Instrument', -e** instrument; **Musik'~** musical instrument

die **Inszenie'rung, -en** production

intellektuell' intellectual(ly)

intelligent' intelligent(ly) (11W)

die **Intelligenz'** intelligence

der **Intendant', -en, -en** artistic director

intensiv' intensive(ly)

interessant' interesting (5E); **etwas Interessantes** s.th. interesting; **unheimlich ~** really interesting (10W)

das **Interes'se, -n (an** + dat.) interest (in)

sich **interessie'ren für** to be interested in (10G)

international' international(ly)

das **Internet** Internet

interpretie'ren to interpret

das **Interview, -s** interview

interviewen to interview

in'tolerant intolerant

das **Inventar', -e** inventory

investie'ren to invest

der **Inves'tor, Investo'ren**
    investor
inzwi'schen in the mean-
    time
irden (*poet.*) earthen
irgend: ~wie somehow;
    ~wo somewhere (14W)
(das) **Ita'lien** Italy (1W)
der **Italie'ner, -** the Italian
    (1W)
italie'nisch Italian (1W)
Iwrith the official He-
    brew language in Israel

J

ja yes (S1); *flavoring par-
    ticle expressing empha-
    sis* (7G)
die **Jacke, -n** jacket (S3);
    Strick~ cardigan
jagen (ist) to race
der **Jäger, -** hunter
das **Jahr, -e** year (S4); **Ein
    gutes neues ~!** Have a
    good New Year! (4W)
jahrelang for years
die **Jahreszeit, -en** season
das **Jahrhun'dert, -e** century
-jährig years old; years
    long
jährlich yearly
das **Jahrtau'send, -e** millen-
    nium (15E); **die ~wende**
    turn of the millennium
jammern to complain,
    grieve
der **Januar** January (S4); **im ~**
    in January (S4)
der **Japa'ner, -** Japanese
japa'nisch Japanese
je (+ *comp.*) **. . . desto**
    (+ *comp.*) **. . .** the . . .
    the . . . (12G); **~ nach-
    dem'** depending on
die **Jeans** (*pl.*) jeans (S3)
jed- (*sg.*) each, every (7G)
jedenfalls in any case (13E)
jeder each one, everyone,
    everybody
jederzeit any time
jedoch' however (12E)
der **Jeep, -s** jeep
jemand someone, some-
    body (11W)

jetzt now (S5)
der **Job, -s** job
jobben to have a job that
    is not one's career
joggen to jog; **~ gehen*** to
    go jogging
der **Jog(h)urt** yogurt (*frequent-
    ly also used with* **das**)
der **Journalist', -en, -en** jour-
    nalist (12W)
das **Jubilä'um, Jubilä'en**
    anniversary
der **Jude, -n, -n / die Jüdin,
    -nen** Jew
das **Judentum** Jewry
jüdisch Jewish
(das) **Judo: ~ kämpfen** to do
    judo
die **Jugend** youth (14E)
die **Jugendherberge, -n** youth
    hostel (7E)
der **Juli** July (S4); **im ~** in July
    (S4)
jung (**ü**) young (11W)
der **Junge, -n, -n** boy (1W,2G)
die **Jungfrau, -en** virgin;
    Virgo
der **Junggeselle, -n, -n**
    bachelor
der **Juni** June (S4); **im ~** in
    June (S4)
Jura: Er studiert ~. He's
    studying law.
der **Juwelier'laden, ⸚** jewelry
    store

K

das **Kabarett', -e** (*or* **-s**)
    cabaret
das **Kabelfernsehen** cable TV
der **Kaffee** coffee (2W); **~ mit
    Schlag** coffee with
    whipped cream
der **Kaffeeklatsch** coffee
    klatsch, chatting over
    coffee (and cake)
der **Kaiser, -** emperor
der **Kaiserschmarren** pan-
    cakes pulled to pieces
    and sprinkled with pow-
    dered sugar and raisins
der **Kaka'o** hot chocolate
das **Kalb, ⸚er** calf; **die ~sleber**
    calves' liver

der **Kalen'der, -** calendar
kalt (**ä**) cold (S4); **~ oder
    warm?** with or without
    heat?
die **Kälte** cold(ness)
die **Kamera, -s** camera
der **Kamin', -e** fireplace
der **Kamm, ⸚e** comb
(sich) **kämmen** to comb (o.s.)
    (9G)
die **Kammer, -n** chamber
der **Kampf, ⸚e (um)** fight,
    struggle (for)
kämpfen (um + *acc.***)** to
    fight, struggle (for)
(das) **Kanada** Canada (1W)
der **Kana'dier, -** the Canadian
    (1W)
kana'disch Canadian
    (1W)
der **Kanal', ⸚e** channel
das **Känguru, -s** kangaroo
die **Kanti'ne, -n** cafeteria (at
    a workplace)
der **Kanton', -e** canton
das **Kanu, -s** canoe
der **Kanzler, -** chancellor
kapitalis'tisch capitalist
das **Kapi'tel, -** chapter
das **Käppi, -s** (*coll.*) cap
kaputt' broken
kaputt·gehen* to get bro-
    ken, break
das **Karenz'jahr, -e** year's leave
der **Karfreitag** Good Friday
kariert' checkered
der **Karneval** carnival
die **Karot'te, -n** carrot (2W)
die **Karrie're, -n** career
die **Karte, -n** ticket (8W);
    card (9W); **~n spielen** to
    play cards (9W)
die **Kartof'fel, -n** potato (3W);
    der ~brei (*sg.*) mashed
    potatoes; **die ~chips** (*pl.*)
    potato chips; **das ~mehl**
    potato flour, starch; **der
    ~salat** potato salad
der **Käse** cheese (2W); **Das ist
    (doch) ~!** That's non-
    sense; **Kräuter~** herbed
    cheese
die **Kasse, -n** cash register,
    cashier's window (7W)

das **Kasseler Rippchen, -** smoked loin of pork

die **Kasset'te, -n** cassette (9W)

die **Kassie'rer, -** cashier; clerk, teller

die **Katastro'phe, -n** catastrophe

die **Katze, -n** cat (11W); **(Das ist) alles für die Katz'!** (That's) all for nothing!; **So ein süßes Kätzchen!** Such a cute kitty. (11W)

kauen to chew

der **Kauf** purchase; **der ~mann / die ~frau / die ~leute** trained employee in some branch of business

kaufen to buy (2W)

das **Kaufhaus, ̈er** department store (2W)

kaum hardly, barely, scarcely (14W)

kegeln to bowl

kein no, not a, not any (1G)

der **Keller, -** basement, cellar (6W)

der **Kellner, -** waiter / die **Kellnerin, -nen** waitress (3W)

kennen, kannte, gekannt to know, be acquainted with (6G)

kennen lernen to get to know, meet (7E)

der **Kenner, -** connoisseur

die **Kenntnis, -se** knowledge, skill (12E)

der **Kerl, -e** guy

der **Kern, -e** core

die **Kern'energie'** nuclear energy

kernlos seedless

die **Kerze, -n** candle (4E)

die **Kette, -n** chain, necklace

die **Ket'tenreaktion', -en** chain reaction

khaki khaki

das **Kilo, -s (kg)** kilogram

der **Kilome'ter, - (km)** kilometer

das **Kind, -er** child (1W)

der **Kindergarten, ̈** kindergarten

der **Kindergärtner, -** kindergarten teacher

kinderlieb fond of children; **sie ist ~** she loves children

das **Kinn, -e** chin

das **Kino, -s** movie theater (5W)

die **Kirche, -n** church (5W)

die **Kirsche, -n** cherry

kitschig cheesy, kitschy

die **Kiwi, -s** kiwi

klagen (über + acc.) to complain (about) (14W)

die **Klammer, -n** parenthesis

klappen to work out

klappern to rattle

klar clear; **(na) ~!** Sure! Of course! (13W); **eins ist ~** one thing is for sure

klasse (adj.) great, superb (10W)

die **Klasse, -n** class (12W)

der **Klas'senkamerad', -en, -en** classmate

das **Klassentreffen, -** class reunion

das **Klassenzimmer, -** classroom

klassisch classical(ly)

die **Klausur', -en** big test

klatschen to clap (10W); to gossip

das **Klavier', -e** piano (9W)

das **Kleid, -er** dress (S3)

der **(Kleider)bügel, -** clothes hanger

der **Kleiderschrank, ̈e** closet

die **Kleidung** clothing (S3)

der **Kleidungsarti'kel, -** article of clothing

klein small, little, short (S3)

die **Kleinbürgerlichkeit** narrow-mindedness

das **Kleingeld** change (7W)

der **Klempner, -** plumber

der **Klient', -en, -en [Kli:ent']** client

das **Klima, -s** climate

die **Klimaanlage, -n** air conditioning

klingeln to ring a (door) bell

klingen, klang, geklungen to sound; **(Das) klingt gut.** (That) sounds good. (6W)

das **Klo, -s (coll.)** toilet

klopfen to knock

der **Klops, -e** meat ball

der **Kloß, ̈e** dumpling

das **Kloster, ̈** monastery; convent

der **Klub, -s** club

klug (ü) smart, clever(ly)

knabbern to nibble

der **Knabe, -n, -n** boy

die **Knappheit** shortage

die **Kneipe, -n** pub (14W)

das **Knie, -** knee (9W)

der **Knirps, -e** little fellow, dwarf

der **Knoblauch** garlic

der **Knöd(e)l, -** dumpling (in southern Germany)

der **Knopf, ̈e** button

der **Knoten, -** knot

knuspern to nibble

k.o. knocked-out; **ich bin ~** I am exhausted

der **Koch, ̈e / die Köchin, -nen** cook

kochen to cook (6W)

der **Koffer, -** suitcase (7W)

die **Kohle** coal

das **Kohlendioxid', -e** carbon dioxide

der **Kolle'ge, -n, -n / die Kolle'gin, -nen** colleague; **Zimmer~** roommate (13W)

die **Kolonialisie'rung** colonization

kombinie'ren to combine

der **Komfort'** comfort

komisch funny, strange(ly), comical(ly) (10W)

das **Komitee, -s** committee

das **Komma, -s** comma

kommen, kam, ist gekommen to come (1W); **Komm rüber!** Come on over!

der **Kommentar', -e** commentary

kommentie'ren to comment

kommerziell' commercial(ly)

die **Kommo'de, -n** dresser (6W)

kommunis'tisch communist

der **Kom'parativ, -e** comparative

die **Komplikation', -en** complication

kompliziert' complicated (11W)

komponie'ren to compose

der **Komponist', -en, -en** composer (10W)

das **Kompott', -e** stewed fruit

der **Kompromiss', -e** compromise

die **Konditorei', -en** pastry shop

die **Konferenz', -en** conference

der **Konflikt', -e** conflict

der **Kongress', -e** conference

der **König, -e** king (11E); **Heilige Drei ~e** Epiphany (Jan. 6)

die **Königin, -nen** queen (11E)

das **Königreich, -e** kingdom

konjugie'ren to conjugate

die **Konjunktion', -en** conjunction

der **Kon'junktiv** subjunctive

die **Konkurrenz'** competition

konkurrie'ren to compete

können (kann), konnte, gekonnt to be able to, can (5G)

die **Konsequenz', -en** consequence

konservativ conservative

das **Konservie'rungsmittel, -** preservative

das **Konsulat', -e** consulate

die **Kontakt'linse, -n** contact lense

das **Konto, -s (or Konten)** account

der **Kontrast', -e** contrast

die **Kontrol'le, -n** control

kontrollie'ren to control, check

die **Konversation', -en** conversation; **~sstunde, -n** conversation lesson

das **Konzentrations'lager, -** concentration camp

sich **konzentrie'ren (auf** + *acc.*) to concentrate (on)

das **Konzert', -e** concert (10W)

die **Kooperation'** cooperation

der **Kopf, ̈e** head (9W); **pro ~** per person; **~ stehen*** to stand on one's head

das **Kopftuch, ̈er** head scarf

die **Kopie', -n** copy

der **Kopie'rer, -** copy machine

der **Korb, ̈e** basket

der **Korbball, ̈e** basketball

der **Körper, -** body (9W)

körperlich physical(ly)

die **Korrektur', -en** correction

der **Korrespondent', -en, -en** correspondent

korrigie'ren to correct

kosten to cost; **Was ~. . . ?** How much are . . . ? (S3); **Das kostet (zusammen) . . .** That comes to . . . (S3)

die **Kosten** *(pl.)* cost

kostenlos free (of charge)

das **Kostüm', -e** costume; lady's suit

die **Krabbe, -n** crab

der **Kracher, -** firecracker

die **Kraft, ̈e** strength, power

die **Kralle, -n** claw

der **Kran, ̈e** crane

krank (ä) sick, ill (9W)

der **Kranke (ein Kranker) / die Kranke, -n, -n** sick person (12G)

der **Krankenbesuch, -e** sick visit

die **Krankengymnast', -en, -en** physical therapist

das **Krankenhaus, ̈er** hospital

die **Krankenkasse, -n** health insurance agency

die **Krankenpflege** nursing

der **Krankenpfleger, -** male nurse (12W)

die **Krankenschwester, -n** female nurse (12W)

die **Krankenversicherung, -en** health insurance

die **Krankheit, -en** sickness, illness, disease

der **Kranz, ̈e** wreath; **Advents'~** Advent wreath

der **Krapfen, -** doughnut

der **Kratzer, -** scratch

das **Kraut** cabbage

die **Krawat'te, -n** tie

kreativ' creative(ly)

die **Kreativität'** creativity

der **Krebs, -e** crab; cancer; Cancer

die **Kredit'karte, -n** credit card

die **Kreide** chalk (S2)

der **Kreis, -e** circle; county

das **Kreuz, -e** cross, mark

die **Kreuzung, -en** intersection

das **Kreuzworträtsel, -** crossword puzzle

kriechen, kroch, ist gekrochen to creep, crawl

der **Krieg, -e** war (14W); **die Nach~szeit** postwar period

der **Krimi, -s** detective story (10W)

die **Kriminalität'** crime

der **Krimskrams** old junk

das **Krite'rium, Krite'rien** criterion

der **Kritiker, -** critic

kritisch critical(ly)

kritisie'ren to criticize

die **Krone, -n** crown

krönen to crown

die **Küche, -n** kitchen (6W); cuisine

der **Kuchen, -** cake (2W)

der **Küchenschrank, ̈e** kitchen cabinet

die **Kugel, -n** ball

kühl cool (S4)

der **Kühlschrank, ̈e** refrigerator (6W)

der **Kuli, -s** pen (S2)

die **Kultur'**, **-en** culture
kulturell' cultural(ly) (14W)

sich **kümmern (um)** to take care (of)

die **Kunst, -̈e** art (10W)

der **Künstler, -** artist (12W); **Compu'ter~** graphic designer

das **Kupfer** copper
kupfern (*adj.*) (made of) copper

die **Kuppel, -n** cupola, dome

der **Kurfürst, -en, -en** elector (prince)

der **Kurort, -e** health resort, spa

der **Kurs, -e** course (S5)
kurz (ü) short(ly), brief(ly) (S3); **~ vor** shortly before; **vor ~em** recently (10W)

die **Kürze** shortness, brevity; **In der ~ liegt die Würze.** Brevity is the soul of wit. (*lit.*, In brevity lies the seasoning).

das **Kurzgespräch, -e** brief conversation

die **Kusi'ne, -n** (*fem.*) cousin (1W)
küssen to kiss

die **Küste, -n** coast (15W)

L

das **Labor', -s** (*or* **-e**) lab(oratory) (13W)

der **Laboran't, -en, -en** lab assistant

der **Labrador, -s** Labrador (dog)
lachen to laugh (10W)
lächeln to smile (10W); **~ über (+ acc.)** to smile about (10G)
lächerlich ridiculous (12W)
laden (lädt), lud, geladen to load

der **Laden, -̈** store; **Bio-~/ grüne ~** environmental store; **Tante-Emma-~** small grocery store

die **Lage, -n** location (7W)

lahm lame; lacking enthusiasm; **~e Ente!** Poor baby!

das **Lamm, -̈er** lamb; **geduldig wie ein ~** really patient

die **Lampe, -n** lamp (6W); **Hänge~** hanging lamp; **Steh~** floor lamp

das **Land, -̈er** country, state (1W); **auf dem ~(e)** in the country (6E); **aufs ~in(to)** the country(side) (6E)
landen (ist) to land (8W)

die **Landeskunde** cultural and geographical study of a country

die **Landkarte, -n** map (1W)

die **Landschaft, -en** landscape, scenery (15W)

die **Landung, -en** landing

der **Landwirt, -e** farmer

die **Landwirtschaft** agriculture
landwirtschaftlich agricultural
lang (ä) (*adj.*) long (S3)
lange long, for a long time; **noch ~ nicht** not by far; **schon ~ (nicht mehr)** (not) for a long time; **wie ~?** how long? (4W)
langsam slow(ly) (S3)

sich **langweilen** to get / be bored (9E)
langweilig boring, dull (10W)
lassen (lässt), ließ, gelassen to leave (behind) (7W)
lässig casual(ly)

die **Last, -en** burden

(das) **Latein'** Latin

die **Later'ne, -n** lantern

die **Latzhose, -n** overall
laufen (läuft), lief, ist gelaufen to run, walk (3G)

der **Laut, -e** sound
laut loud(ly), noisy (4E;7W); **Lesen Sie ~!** Read aloud.; **Sprechen Sie ~er!** Speak up. (S3)
läuten to ring

der **Lautsprecher, -** loudspeaker
leben to live (6E)

das **Leben** life (9E); **ums ~ kommen*** to die, perish
lebend living; **etwas Lebendes** s.th. living
leben'dig alive; lively

die **Lebensfreude** zest for life
lebensfroh cheerful, full of life

der **Lebenslauf, -̈e** résumé

die **Lebensmittel** (*pl.*) groceries (2W)

der **Lebensstandard** standard of living

die **Leber, -n** liver; **Kalbs~** calves' liver

der **Leberkäs(e)** (Bavarian) meatloaf made from minced pork

die **Leberwurst** liver sausage

der **Lebkuchen, -** gingerbread

das **Leder** leather

die **Lederhose, -n** leather pants
ledig single (11W)
leer empty (14E)
legen to lay, put (flat) (6W); **sich (hin·)~** to lie down (9G

das **Lehrbuch, -̈er** textbook

die **Lehre, -n** apprenticeship
lehren to teach (13W)

der **Lehrer, -** teacher (12W)

der **Lehrling, -e** apprentice

die **Lehrstelle, -n** apprenticeship (position)
leicht light, easy, easily (6E); **Das ist ~ zu verstehen!** That's easy to understand.

das **Leid** misery; **Es tut mir ~.** I'm sorry. (5W)

die **Leidenschaft, -en** passion
leider unfortunately (5E)
leihen, lieh, geliehen to lend

die **Leine, -n** leash
leise quiet(ly), soft(ly)
leisten to achieve
leiten to direct

der **Leiter, -** director

die **Leiter, -n** ladder

die **Leitung** leadership, direction

das **Leitungswasser** tap water

lernen to learn, study (S2)

der **Lerntipp, -s** study tip

das **Lernziel, -e** learning objective

lesbar legible, legibly

lesen (liest), las, gelesen to read (S2); ~ **Sie laut!** / ~ **Sie es vor!** Read it aloud.

der **Leser, -** reader

die **Leseratte, -n** bookworm

der **Lesesaal, -säle** reading room

(das) **Lettland** Latvia

der **Lette, -n, -n** / die **Lettin, -nen** Latvian

lettisch Latvian

letzt- last (10W)

(das) **Letzeburgisch** Luxembourg dialect

die **Leute** (*pl.*) people (1W)

licht (*poetic*) light

das **Licht, -er** light; **ins ~ treten*** to step out into the light

die **Lichterkette, -n** candlelight march

der **Lichtschalter, -** light switch

lieb- dear (5E, 11W)

die **Liebe** love (11W)

lieben to love (6E)

lieber rather (12G); **Es wäre mir ~, wenn . . .** I would prefer it, if . . .

liebevoll loving (11W)

der **Liebling, -e** darling, favorite; **~sdichter** favorite poet; **~sfach** favorite subject; **~splatz** favorite place

liebst-: am ~en best of all (12G)

das **Lied, -er** song (4E); **Volks~** folk song

liefern to distribute, deliver

liegen, lag, gelegen to lie, be (located) (1W); be lying (flat) (6W)

der **Liegestuhl, ⸚e** lounge chair

lila purple

die **Lilie, -n** lily, iris

die **Limona'de, -n = Limo, -s** soft drink (2W); **die Zitro'nen~** carbonated lemonade

die **Linguis'tik** linguistics

die **Linie, -n** line

link- left; **auf der ~en Seite** on the left

links left (5W); **erste Straße ~** first street on the left (5W)

die **Linse, -n** lentil; lense

die **Lippe, -n** lip

der **Lippenstift, -e** lipstick

die **Liste, -n** list; **eine ~ auf·stellen** to make a list

der **Litaue, -n, -n** / die **Litauin, -nen** Lithuanian

(das) **Litauen** Lithuania

litauisch Lithuanian

der **Liter, -** liter

die **Literatur'** literature

das **Loch, ⸚er** hole

locken to lure, attract

der **Löffel, -** spoon (3W); **Ess~** tablespoon (of); **Tee~** teaspoon (of)

logisch logical(ly)

lokal' local(ly)

los: ~·werden* to get rid of; **etwas ~ sein*** to be happening, going on; **Was ist ~?** What's the matter? (9W)

lose loose

lösen to solve; **sich ~ von** to free o.s. of

die **Lösung, -en** solution

die **Lotterie'** ?lottery

der **Löwe, -n, -n** / die **Löwin, -nen** lion; Leo

die **Luft** air (14E)

der **Luftangriff, -e** air raid

die **Luftbrücke** airlift

die **Luftpost** airmail; **per ~** by airmail

die **Luftverschmutzung** air pollution

die **Lüge, -n** lie

lügen to lie

die **Lust** inclination, desire, fun; **Ich habe (keine) ~ (zu) . . .** I (don't) feel like (doing s.th.) . . . (9W)

lustig funny (4E); **reise~ sein*** to love to travel; **sich ~ machen (über +** *acc.*) to make fun of (14W)

luxemburgisch Luxembourgish

luxuriös' luxurious(ly)

der **Luxus** luxury

M

machen to make, do (2W); **Spaß ~** to be fun (4E); **Mach's gut!** Take care! (S1); **Was machst du Schönes?** What are you doing?; **(Das) macht nichts.** (That) doesn't matter. That's okay. (5E); **Das macht zusammen . . .** That comes to . . .

die **Macht, ⸚e** power (14E); **die Westmächte** (*pl.*) western Allies

das **Mädchen, -** girl (1W); **der ~name** maiden name

das **Magazin', -e** magazine; feature (e.g., on TV)

die **Magd, ⸚e** (*archaic*) maid

der **Magen, ⸚ / -** stomach

der **Magis'ter, -** master's degree, M.A.

die **Mahlzeit, -en** meal; **~!** Enjoy your meal (food)!

das **Mahnmal, -e** memorial (of admonishment)

der **Mai** May (S4); **im ~** in May (S4)

der **Mais** corn

mal times, multiplied by; **~ sehen!** Let's see.

das **Mal, -e: das erste ~** the first time (11E); **zum ersten ~** for the first time (11E)

malen to paint (9W)

der **Maler, -** painter(-artist) (10W); house painter

man one (they, people, you) (3E)

man (*adv.; north German coll.*): **Komm ~!** Come on!; **Lass ~ gut sein!** Forget it!

das **Management** management

manch- many a, several, some (7G)

manchmal sometimes (3E)

der **Mangel (an +** *dat.***)** lack (of)

mangelhaft poor; approx. grade D

die **Mango, -s** mango

manipuliert' manipulated

der **Mann, ⁇er** man; husband (1W)

das **Männchen, -** little guy

männlich masculine, male

die **Mannschaft, -en** team

der **Mantel, ⁇** coat (S3)

das **Manuskript', -e** manuscript

das **Märchen, -** fairy tale

die **Margari'ne, -n** margarine

die **Mari'ne, -n** navy

die **Marke, -n** brand

markie'ren to mark

der **Markt, ⁇e** market (2W); **Super~** supermarket (2W); **Wachstums~** growth market

die **Marmela'de, -n** marmalade, jam (2W)

der **März** March (S4); **im ~** in March (S4)

die **Maschi'ne, -n** machine

der **Maschi'nenbau** mechanical engineering

die **Maske, -n** mask

die **Massa'ge, -n** massage

die **Maß** large glass holding about 1 liter of beer

die **Masse, -n** mass

die **Massenmedien** (*pl.*) mass media

die **Maßnahme, -n** step, measure

das **Material'** material

die **Mathematik'** mathematics

die **Mauer, -n** (thick) wall (14W)

das **Maul, ⁇er** big mouth (of animal)

der **Maurer, -** bricklayer

maurisch Moorish

die **Maus, ⁇e** mouse; **~efalle, -n** mousetrap

der **Mecha'niker, -** mechanic

die **Medien** (*pl.*) media

das **Medikament', -e** medicine, medication

die **Medizin'** (the field of) medicine

das **Meer, -e** ocean, sea

das **Meerschweinchen, -** guinea pig

das **Mehl** flour

mehr more (12G); **immer ~** more and more (12G); **~ als** more than

mehrer- (*pl.*) several (10G)

die **Mehrheit** majority

die **Mehrwertsteuer, -n** value-added tax

meiden, mied, gemieden to avoid

mein my (1W,7G)

meinen to mean, think (be of an opinion) (11W); **Wenn du meinst.** If you think so. (11W)

die **Meinung, -en** opinion; **meiner ~ nach** in my opinion

die **Meinungsumfrage, -n** opinion poll

meist-: am ~en most (12G)

meistens mostly, usually (7E)

der **Meister, -** master

die **Melo'ne, -n** melon

die **Menge, -n** crowd; **jede ~** all sorts of (14W)

die **Mensa** student cafeteria (3W)

der **Mensch, -en, -en** human being, person; people (*pl.*) (1E,2G); **~!** Man! Boy! Hey!; **Mit~** fellow human being

die **Menschheit** humankind

das **Menü', -s** complete meal (usually including soup and dessert); **Tages~** daily special

merken to notice, find out

die **Messe, -n** (trade) fair

das **Messegelände, -** fairgrounds

das **Messer, -** knife (3E); **Taschen~** pocket knife

das **Metall', -e** metal

der **Meter, -** meter

die **Metropo'le, -n** metropolis

der **Metzger, -** butcher

die **Metzgerei', -en** butcher shop

mies miserable

die **Miete, -n** rent

mieten to rent (6W)

der **Mieter, -** renter, tenant

die **Mietwohnung, -en** apartment

der **Mikrowellenherd, -e = die Mikrowelle, -n** microwave oven

die **Milch** milk (2W)

das **Militär'** military, army

militä'risch military

der **Million', -en** million

der **Millionär', -e** millionaire

der **Mindestbestellwert** minimum order

mindestens at least

die **Mineralogie'** mineralogy

das **Mineral'wasser** mineral water

der **Minimumbestellwert** minimum order

minus minus

die **Minu'te, -n** minute (S5)

mischen to mix; **darun'ter·~** to blend in

der **Mischmasch** mishmash, hodgepodge

die **Mischung, -en (aus +** *dat.***)** mixture (of)

misera'bel miserable, miserably

die **Mission', -en** mission

mit- together, with, along (7G)

mit (+ *dat.*) with (3G); along

das **Mitbestimmungsrecht** right to participate in

the decision-making
process

der **Mitbewoh'ner, -** housemate (13W)

mit·bringen* to bring
along (7G)

mit·fahren* to drive
along

mit·feiern to join in the
celebration

das **Mitgefühl** compassion

mit·gehen* to go along
(7G)

das **Mitglied, -er** member

mit·kommen* to come
along (7G)

das **Mitleid** pity

mit·machen to participate

mit·nehmen* to take
along (7G)

mit·schicken to send
along

mit·singen* to sing along

der **Mittag, -e** noon; **heute ~**
at noon today (8G)

das **Mittagessen, -** lunch,
mid-day meal (3W);
beim ~ at lunch; **zum ~**
for lunch (3W)

mittags at noon (S5);
dienstag~ Tuesdays at
noon (8G)

die **Mitte** middle, center
(14E); **~ des Monats** in
the middle of the month
(8G); mid

das **Mittel, -** means (of)

das **Mittelalter** Middle Ages;
im ~ in the Middle Ages
(14W)

mittelalterlich medieval

(das) **Mitteleuro'pa** Central
Europe

mittelgroß average size

mitten: ~durch right
through the middle of
(6E); **~drin** right in the
middle of it

die **Mitternacht: um ~** at
midnight

der **Mittwoch** Wednesday
(S4); **am ~** on Wednes-
day (S4); **Ascher~** Ash
Wednesday

mittwochs on Wednes-
days (2E)

der **Mix** mixture

die **Möbel** (*pl.*) furniture (6W)

die **Mobilität'** mobility

möbliert' furnished

möchten (*subj. of* **mögen**)
would like (2W;5G); **Ich
möchte . . .** I would like
(to have) . . . (2W)

das **Modal'verb, -en** modal
auxiliary

die **Mode** fashion; custom;
in ~ in(to) vogue

die **Modepuppe, -n** fashion doll

modern' modern

mögen (**mag**), **mochte**,
gemocht to like (5G);
Ich mag kein(e/en) . . .
I don't like (any) . . .
(*+ acc. noun*) (3W)

möglich possible (7W);
Das ist doch nicht ~!
That's impossible. (7W);
alle ~en all sorts of

die **Möglichkeit, -en** possibil-
ity

der **Mohnkuchen** poppy-seed
cake

der **Moment', -e** moment;
(Einen) ~! One moment!
Just a minute! (2W,7W)

momentan' at the mo-
ment, right now

der **Monat, -e** month (S4);
im ~ a month, per
month (6W); **einen ~** for
one month (8G)

monatelang for months

monatlich monthly (8G)

der **Mond, -e** moon

der **Mondschein** moonlight

das **Monster, -** monster

der **Montag** Monday (S4);
am ~ on Monday (S4)

montags on Mondays
(2E)

die **Moral'** moral

der **Mörder, -** murderer

morgen tomorrow
(S4,4W); **Bis ~!** See you
tomorrow; **für ~** for tomorrow (S2); **über~** the
day after tomorrow (4W)

der **Morgen** morning: **Guten
~!** Good morning. (S1);
heute ~ this morning
(8G)

morgens in the morning
(S5), every morning;
montag~ Monday morn-
ings (8G)

das **Mosaik', -e** mosaic

der **Moslem, -s / die Moslime,
-n** Moslem man /
woman

mosle'misch Moslem

der **MP3-Spieler,-** MP3 player

müde tired (S1); **tod~**
dead tired

die **Müdigkeit** fatigue

der **Müll** garbage, waste
(15W)

der **Müller, -** miller

der **Müllschlucker, -** garbage
disposal

die **Mülltonne, -n** garbage
can (15W)

die **Mülltrennung** garbage
sorting (15W)

der **Mund, ¨er** mouth (9W)

die **Mundharmonika, -s** har-
monica

mündlich oral(ly)

die **Münze, -n** coin

die **Muschel, -n** clam; shell

das **Muse'um, Muse'en** museum (5W)

die **Musik'** music (9E)

musika'lisch musical(ly)
(11W)

der **Musiker, -** musician

die **Musik'wissenschaft** mu-
sicology

(der) **Muskat'** nutmeg

der **Muskelkater** sore mus-
cle(s); **Ich habe ~.** My
muscles are sore.

das **Müsli** whole-grain granola

müssen (**muss**), **musste**,
gemusst to have to,
must (5G)

das **Muster, -** example,
model; pattern

der **Mustersatz, ¨e** sample
sentence

die **Mutter, ¨** mother (1W);
Groß~ grandmother

(1W); **Schwieger~** mother-in-law; **Urgroß~** great-grandmother

mütterlich motherly

der **Mutterschaftsurlaub** maternity leave

die **Muttersprache** mother tongue

die **Mutti, -s** Mom

N

na well; ~ **also** well; ~ **gut** well, all right; ~ **ja** well (12W); ~ **klar** of course (13W); ~ **und?** So what? (8W)

nach- after, behind (7G)

nach (+ *dat.*) after (time), to (cities, countries, continents) (3G); **je** ~ depending on

der **Nachbar, -n, -n** neighbor (1E,2G)

die **Nachbarschaft, -en** neighborhood; neighborly relations

nachdem' *(conj.)* after (11G); **je** ~ depending on

nacherzählt retold, adapted

die **Nachfrage** demand

nachher afterwards

nach·kommen* to follow

nach·laufen* to run after

nach·machen to imitate

der **Nachmittag, -e** afternoon; **am** ~ in the afternoon; **heute** ~ this afternoon (8G)

nachmittags in the afternoon (S5), every afternoon

der **Nachname, -ns, -n** last name

die **Nachricht, -en** news (10E)

nächst- next (11E)

die **Nacht, ̈e** night (7W); **Gute ~!** Good night!; **heute** ~ tonight; last night (8G)

der **Nachteil, -e** disadvantage

die **Nachteule, -n** night owl

das **Nachthemd, -en** nightgown

der **Nachtisch** dessert (3W); **zum** ~ for dessert (3W)

der **Nachtmensch, -en, -en** night person

nachts during the night, every night (8G); **sonntag~** Sunday nights (8G)

der **Nachttisch, -e** nightstand

der **Nachtwächter, -** night watchman

nach·werfen* to throw after

nackt naked

die **Nadel, -n** needle

nah (näher, nächst-) near (5W,12G)

die **Nähe** nearness, vicinity; **in der ~** nearby; **in der ~ von** (+ *dat.*) near (5W)

nähen to sew

der **Name, -ns, -n** name (8G); **Mein ~ ist . . .** My name is . . . (S1); **Mädchen~** maiden name; **Vor~** first name; **Nach~** last name; **Spitz~** nickname (14W)

nämlich namely, you know

die **Nase, -n** nose (9W); **Ich habe die ~ voll.** I'm fed up (with it). (10W)

nass wet

die **Nation', -en** nation, state

national' national(ly)

der **Nationalis'mus** nationalism

die **Nationalität', -en** nationality

die **Natur'** nature (15W)

das **Natur'kind, -er** child of nature

natür'lich natural(ly), of course (2W)

das **Natur'schutzgebiet, -e** nature preserve (15W)

die **Natur'wissenschaft, -en** natural science (13W)

natur'wissenschaftlich scientific(ally)

der **Nebel** fog

neben (+ *acc. / dat.*) beside, next to (6G)

nebeneinander next to each other

das **Nebenfach, ̈er** minor (field of study) (14W)

der **Nebensatz, ̈e** subordinate clause

neblig foggy

der **Neffe, -n, -n** nephew

negativ negative(ly)

nehmen (nimmt), nahm, genommen to take (S3); to have (food) (3G)

nein no (S1)

die **Nelke, -n** carnation

nennen, nannte, genannt to name, call (4W, 11G); **Ich nenne das . . .** That's what I call . . .

nett nice (11W)

neu new(ly) (S3); **Was gibt's Neues . . . ?** What's new? (9W)

neugierig curious(ly)

der **Neujahrstag** New Year's Day

nicht not (S1); ~ **wahr?** isn't it? (S4); **gar** ~ not at all (13E); ~ **nur . . . sondern auch** not only . . . but also (3E)

die **Nichte, -n** niece

nichts nothing (3W); ~ **Besonderes / Neues** nothing special / new (9W)

nicken to nod

nie never (4E); **noch** ~ never before, not ever (4E)

sich **nieder·legen** to lie down

niedrig low

niemand nobody, no one (11E)

das **Niemandsland** no man's land

nimmermehr *(poetic)* nevermore, never again

nirgends nowhere; **ins Nirgends** into nowhere

nobel noble, nobly

noch still (4W); ~ **(ein)mal** once more, again (S2); ~ **ein** another (3W); ~ **kein(e)** still no;

~ **etwas** s.th. else; ~ **lange nicht** not by far; ~ **nie** never (before), not ever (4E); ~ **nicht** not yet (6E); **Sonst ~ etwas?** Anything else?; **was ~?** what else?; **weder . . . ~** neither . . . nor (10E); **immer ~** still

der **Nominativ, -e** nominative

die **Nonne, -n** nun

der **Norden: im ~** in the north (1W)

nördlich (von) to the north, north (of) (1W)

normal' normal; by regular (surface) mail

(das) **Nor'wegen** Norway

der **Nor'weger, -** the Norwegian

nor'wegisch Norwegian

die **Note, -n** grade (13W)

nötig necessary, needed

die **Notiz', -en** note; **~en machen** to take notes

notwendig necessary

der **Novem'ber** November (S4); **im ~** in November (S4)

nüchtern sober

die **Nudel, -n** noodle (3W)

null zero (S3)

der **Numerus clausus** admissions restriction at a university

die **Nummer, -n** number (7W)

nun now (11E); **~, . . .** well, . . . (12W)

nur only (S4)

die **Nuss, ̈e** nut

der **Nussknacker, -** nutcracker

nutzen to use

O

ob (*conj.*) if, whether (4G); **Und ~!** You bet. You better believe it. (14W)

oben upstairs (6W); up; **~ genannt** above mentioned

der **Ober, -** waiter (3W); **Herr ~!** Waiter! (3W)

die **Oberin, -nen** mother superior

die **Oberschule, -n** college preparatory school (*see* **Gymnasium**)

die **Oberstufe, -n** upper level

das **Objekt', -e** object

objektiv' objective(ly)

das **Obst** (*sg.*) fruit (2W)

obwohl (*conj.*) although (4G)

oder or (S3,2G); **~?** Isn't it? Don't you think so? (14W)

der **Ofen, ̈** oven

offen open (2E)

offiziell' official(ly)

öffnen to open; **~ Sie das Buch auf Seite . . .!** (S5) Open the book on / to page . . .!

öffentlich public(ly) (10E)

oft often (2E)

ohne (+ *acc.*) without (2G)

das **Ohr, -en** ear (9W)

Oje'! Oops! Oh no!

der **Ökolo'ge, -n, -n / die Ökolo'gin, -nen** ecologist

die **Ökologie'** ecology

ökolo'gisch ecological(ly)

das **Ökosystem', -e** ecological system

der **Okto'ber** October (S4); **im ~** in October (S4)

das **Öl, -e** oil; lotion

oliv' olive-colored

der **Ölwechsel** oil change

die **Olympia'de, -n** Olympics

die **Oma, -s** grandma

das **Omelett', -s** omelet(te)

der **Onkel, -** uncle (1W)

der **Opa, -s** grandpa

die **Oper, -n** opera (10W); **Seifen~** soap opera

die **Operet'te, -n** operetta

das **Opfer, -** victim

optimal' optimal(ly)

optimis'tisch optimistic(ally)

oran'ge (color) orange (S2)

die **Oran'ge, -n** orange (2W)

das **Orches'ter, -** orchestra (10W)

ordentlich orderly; regular(ly)

die **Ordinal'zahl, -en** ordinal number (4W)

die **Ordnungszahl, -en** ordinal number

die **Organisation', -en** organization

(sich) **organisie'ren** to organize

die **Orgel, -n** organ

die **Orientie'rung** orientation

das **Original', -e** original

der **Ort, -e** place, location; town (12E)

der **Ossi, -s** (*derogatory nickname*) East German

der **Osten: im ~** in the east (1W)

(das) **Ostern: zu ~** at/for Easter (4W); **Frohe ~!** Happy Easter!

(das) **Österreich** Austria (1W)

der **Österreicher, -** the Austrian (1W)

österreichisch Austrian

östlich (von) east (of), to the east (of) (1W)

der **Ozean, -e** ocean

P

paar: ein ~ a couple of, some (2E)

das **Paar, -e** couple, pair

die **Pacht** lease; **der ~vertrag, ̈e** lease agreement / contract

pachten to lease

packen to pack (7E); to grab

die **Pädago'gik** education

das **Paddelboot, -e** canoe

paddeln to paddle

das **Paket', -e** package, parcel (8W)

die **Paket'karte, -n** parcel form

die **Palatschinken** (*pl.*) crêpes

das **Panora'ma** panorama

die **Panne, -n** mishap

der **Panzer, -** tank

der **Papagei'**, **-en** parrot

das **Papier'**, **-e** paper (S2)

der **Papier'krieg** paper work, red tape

das **Papier'warengeschäft, -e** office supply store

die **Pappe** cardboard

die **Para'bel, -n** parable

das **Paradies'** paradise

der **Paragraph', -en, -en** paragraph

das **Parfüm', -s** perfume

der **Park, -s** park (5W)

die **Parkanlage, -n** park

parken to park (15W)

das **Parkett': im ~** (seating) in the orchestra

der **Parkplatz, ̈e** parking lot (7W)

parlamenta'risch parliamentary

die **Partei', -en** (political) party

das **Parter're: im ~** on the first / ground floor (6W)

das **Partizip', -ien** participle

der **Partner, -** partner (11W)

die **Partnerschaft, -en** partnership

die **Party, -s** party (4W)

der **Pass, ̈e** passport (7W)

passen to fit; **Was passt? What fits?; Das passt mir nicht.** That doesn't suit me.

passend appropriate(ly), suitable, suitably

passie'ren (ist) to happen (11W)

passiv passive(ly)

das **Passiv** passive voice

pauken to cram

die **Pause, -n** intermission, break (10W); **eine ~ machen** to take a break

das **Pech** tough luck; **~ haben*** to be unlucky (4E); **~ gehabt!** Tough luck!; **Du ~vogel!** You unlucky thing!

der **Pekine'se, -n, -n** Pekinese

pendeln (ist) to commute; **hin- und her·~** to commute back and forth

die **Pension', -en** boarding house; hotel (7E)

die **Pensionie'rung** retirement

das **Perfekt** present perfect

permanent' permanent(ly)

perplex' baffled

die **Person', -en** person; **pro ~** per person

das **Personal'** personnel, staff; **die ~kosten** *(pl.)* staffing cost

persön'lich personal(ly)

der **persön'liche digita'le Assistent', -en, -en (PDA)** personal digital assistant

die **Persön'lichkeit, -en** personality

die **Perspekti've, -n** perspective

pessimis'tisch pessimistic(ally)

das **Pfand, ̈er** deposit; security

der **Pfannkuchen, -** pancake

der **Pfarrer, -** (Protestant) minister; cleric

der **Pfeffer** pepper (3W)

die **Pfeffermin'ze** peppermint

die **Pfeife, -n** pipe

pfeifen, pfiff, gepfiffen to whistle; boo

der **Pfeil, -e** arrow

das **Pferd, -e** horse (11W); **arbeitsam wie ein ~** really hard-working

der **Pferdewagen, -** horse-drawn wagon

(das) **Pfingsten** Pentecost

der **Pfirsich, -e** peach

die **Pflanze, -n** plant

das **Pflaster, -** adhesive bandage

pflaume plum-colored

die **Pflaume, -n** plum

die **Pflegemutter, ̈** foster mother

pflegen to take care of, cultivate; **er pflegt, das zu tun** he usually does that

die **Pflegeversicherung, -en** long-term care insurance

die **Pflicht, -en** duty, obligation

das **Pflichtfach, ̈er** required subject

das **Pfund, -e** pound (2W); **zwei ~** two pounds (of) (2W)

die **Pharmazie'** pharmaceutics; pharmacy

die **Philologie'** philology

der **Philosoph', -en, -en** philosopher

die **Philosophie'** philosophy

die **Physik'** physics

der **Physiker, -** physicist

physisch physical(ly)

das **Picknick, -s** picnic

picknicken to (have a) picnic; **~ gehen*** to go picnicing

piepen to peep, chirp; **Bei dir piept's!** You're cuckoo. You must be kidding.

der **Pilot', -en, -en** pilot

der **Pinsel, -** paintbrush

die **Pizza, -s** pizza (3W)

der **Plan, ̈e** plan (12W); **Spiel~** schedule of performances

planen to plan (15W)

die **Planier'raupe, -n** bulldozer

das **Plastik** plastic

die **Plastiktüte, -n** plastic bag

platschen to patter

das **Plattdeutsch** Low German (dialect)

die **Platte, -n** record; platter

der **Plattenspieler, -** record player

der **Platz, ̈e** (town) square, place (5W); seat

die **Platzanweiser, -** usher

das **Plätzchen, -** cookie (2W)

plötzlich sudden(ly) (11E)

der **Plural, -e (von)** plural (of)

plus plus

der **Plüsch** plush

das **Plusquamperfekt** past perfect

der **Pole, -n, -n / die Polin, -nen** native of Poland

(das) **Polen** Poland

polnisch Polish

die **Politik'** politics

der **Poli'tiker, -** politician
die **Politik'(wissenschaft)** political science, politics
poli'tisch political(ly)
die **Polizei'** (*sg.*) police
der **Polizist', -en, -en** policeman (12W)
die **Pommes frites** (*pl.*) French fries (3W)
der **Po(po), -s** (*fam.*) behind, rear end
populär' popular(ly)
die **Popularität'** popularity
das **Portemonnaie, -s** wallet
der **Portier', -s** desk clerk
das **Porto** postage
das **Porträt, -s** portrait
(das) **Portugal** Portugal
der **Portugie'se, -n, -n / die Portugiesin, -nen** the Portuguese
portugie'sisch Portuguese
das **Porzellan'** porcelain
die **Post** post office (5W); mail (8W)
der **Postbote, -n, -n / die Postbotin, -nen** mail carrier
der **Postdienst** postal service
der **Posten, -** position
das **Postfach, ⁻er** PO box (8W)
das **Posthorn, ⁻er** bugle
die **Postkarte, -n** plain postcard
die **Postleitzahl, -en** zip code (8W)
die **Postwertzeichen** (*pl.*) postage
die **Pracht** splendor
prägen to shape, influence
das **Praktikum, Praktika** practical training, internship (12E)
praktisch practical(ly) (6W)
die **Präposition', -en** preposition
das **Präsens** present time
präsentie'ren to present
der **Präsident', -en, -en** president
die **Praxis** practical experience; practice

der **Preis, -e** price; prize
die **Preiselbeeren** (*pl.*) type of cranberries
die **Presse** press; **Tages~** daily press
das **Presti'ge** prestige
prima great, wonderful (S4)
primitiv' primitive(ly)
der **Prinz, -en, -en** prince
die **Prinzes'sin, -nen** princess
das **Prinzip', -ien** principle; **im ~** in principle
privat' private(ly) (10E)
das **Privat'gefühl** feeling for privacy
das **Privileg', Privile'gien** privilege
pro per
die **Probe, -n** test; **auf die ~ stellen** to test
probie'ren to try
das **Problem', -e** problem (6W); **(Das ist) kein ~.** (That's) no problem. (6W)
problema'tisch problematic
das **Produkt', -e** product
die **Produktion'** production; **Buch~** book publishing
der **Produzent', -en, -en** producer
produzie'ren to produce
der **Profes'sor, -en** professor (13W)
das **Profil', -e** profile
profitie'ren to profit
das **Programm', -e** program, channel (10W)
der **Programmie'rer, -** programmer
das **Projekt', -e** project
das **Prono'men, -** pronoun
proportional' proportional(ly)
die **Prosa** prose
Prost! Cheers!; **~ Neujahr!** Happy New Year!
der **Protest', -e** protest
protestie'ren to protest
protzen to brag
das **Proviso'rium** provisional state

das **Prozent', -e** percent
die **Prüfung, -en** test, exam (1W); **eine ~ bestehen*** to pass an exam (13W); **bei einer ~ durch·fallen*** to flunk an exam (13W); **eine ~ machen** to take an exam (13W)
der **Psalm, -e** psalm
das **Pseudonym', -e** pseudonym
der **Psychia'ter, -** psychiatrist
die **Psychoanaly'se** psychoanalysis
der **Psycholo'ge, -n, -n / die Psycholo'gin, -nen** psychologist
die **Psychologie'** psychology
psycholo'gisch psychological(ly)
das **Publikum** audience; **Stamm~** regular clients
der **Pudel, -** Poodle
die **Puderdose, -n** compact
der **Pudding, -s** pudding (3W)
der **Pulli, -s** sweater (S3)
der **Pullo'ver, -** pullover, sweater (S3); **Rollkragen~** turtleneck sweater
der **Punkt, -e** point; period
pünktlich on time
die **Puppe, -n** doll
die **Pute, -n** turkey hen
putzen to clean; **sich die Zähne ~** to brush one's teeth (9G)
die **Putzfrau, -en** cleaning lady
die **Pyrami'de, -n** pyramid

Q

der **Quadrat'kilometer, -** square kilometer
der **Quadrat'meter, -** square meter
die **Qual, -en** torment, agony
die **Qualifikation', -en** qualification
qualifiziert' qualified
die **Qualität', -en** quality; **Lebens~** quality of life
die **Quan'tität** quantity
der **Quark** (sour skim milk) curd cheese

das **Quartal'**, **-e** quarter (university) (13W)

das **Quartett'**, **-e** quartet

das **Quartier'**, **-s** (*or* **-e**) lodging

der **Quatsch** nonsense (7W)

die **Quelle**, **-n** source

quer durch all across

die **Querflöte**, **-n** flute

das **Quintett'**, **-s** quintet

das **Quiz** quiz

die **Quote**, **-n** quota

R

das **Rad**, **¨er** bicyle, bike (9W); **~ fahren*** to bicycle (9W)

radeln (ist) *(coll.)* to bike

der **Radier'gummi,-s** eraser

das **Radies'chen**, **-** radish

das **Radio**, **-s** radio (6W)

der **Rand**, **¨er** edge; **am ~e** (**+ gen.)** at the outskirts

der **Rang**, **¨e** theater balcony; **im ersten ~** in the first balcony

der **Rasen**, **-** lawn

sich **rasie'ren** to shave o.s. (9G)

der **Rat** advice, counsel (12E)

raten (rät), riet, geraten to advise, guess

das **Rathaus**, **¨er** city hall (5W)

(das) **Rätoroma'nisch** Romansh

die **Ratte**, **-n** rat

rauchen to smoke

der **Raum** space

räumen to clear

das **Raumschiff**, **-e** spaceship

reagie'ren (auf + *acc.*) to react (to)

die **Reaktion'**, **-en** reaction

die **Realität'** reality

die **Real'schule**, **-n** high school, grades 5–10

rebellie'ren to rebel

rechnen to calculate; **Damit hat niemand gerechnet.** Nobody expected / was counting on that.

die **Rechnung**, **-en** check, bill (3W)

das **Recht**, **-e** right; **Du hast ~.** You're right (12W)

recht: Das geschieht dir ~. That serves you right.

recht-: auf der ~en Seite on the right side

rechts right (5W); **erste Straße ~** first street to the right (5W)

der **Rechtsanwalt**, **¨e** / die **Rechtsanwältin**, **-nen** lawyer (12W)

der **Rechtsradikalis'mus** right-wing radicalism

die **Rechtswissenschaft** study of law

die **Rede**, **-n** speech (15W); **indirekte ~** indirect speech

reden (mit / über) to talk (to / about) (15W)

die **Redewendung**, **-en** idiom, saying

reduzie'ren to reduce

das **Referat'**, **-e** oral presentation (13W); **ein ~ halten*** to give an oral presentation (13W)

reflexiv' reflexive(ly)

das **Reform'haus**, **¨er** health-food store

das **Regal'**, **-e** shelf (6E)

regelmäßig regular(ly)

regeln to regulate

der **Regen** rain

der **Regenschirm**, **-e** umbrella

die **Regie'rung**, **-en** government

das **Regi'me**, **-s** regime

die **Region'**, **-en** region

regional' regional(ly)

der **Regisseur'**, **-e** director (film)

registrie'ren to register

regnen to rain; **Es regnet.** It's raining. (S4).

regulie'ren to regulate

reiben, rieb, gerieben to rub

reich rich(ly) (11W)

das **Reich**, **-e** empire, kingdom

reichen to suffice; **~ bis an** (+ *acc.*) to go up to

der **Reichtum**, **¨er** wealth

reif ripe; mature

die **Reife** maturity; **Mittlere ~** diploma of a *Realschule*

die **Reihe**, **-n** row

die **Reihenfolge**, **-n** order, sequence

das **Reihenhaus**, **¨er** townhouse, row house (6E)

der **Reim**, **-e** rhyme

sich **reimen** to rhyme

der **Reis** rice (3W)

die **Reise**, **-n** trip (7E); **eine ~ machen** to take a trip, travel

das **Reisebüro**, **-s** travel agency

der **Reiseführer**, **-** travel guide; guide book

der **Reiseleiter**, **-** tour guide (12W)

reiselustig sein* to love to travel

reisen (ist) to travel (7E)

der **Reisescheck**, **-s** traveler's check

reißen, riss, ist gerissen to tear

reiten, ritt, ist geritten to ride (on horseback)

die **Reitschule**, **-n** riding academy

der **Rektor**, **-en** university president

relativ' relative(ly)

das **Relativ'prono'men**, **-** relative pronoun

der **Relativ'satz**, **¨e** relative clause

die **Religion'**, **-en** religion

das **Rendezvous**, **-** date

rennen, rannte, ist gerannt to run

renommiert' renowned, well-known

renovie'ren to renovate (15W)

die **Rente**, **-n** pension

die **Rentenversicherung** social security

das **Rentier**, **-e** reindeer

die **Reparatur', -en** repair
reparie'ren to repair
der **Repräsentant', -en, -en** representative
repräsentativ' representative
der **Reservat', -e** reservation, preserve
reservie'ren to reserve (7E)
die **Reservie'rung, -en** reservation
die **Residenz', -en** residence
resignie'ren to resign, give up
der **Rest, -e** rest
das **Restaurant', -s** restaurant (3E)
restaurie'ren to restore (15W)
die **Restaurie'rung** restoration
das **Resultat', -e** result
retten to save, rescue (15W)
das **Rezept', -e** recipe
die **Rezeption', -en** reception (desk)
die **Richtgeschwindigkeit, -en** recommended speed
richtig right, correct (S2); **Das ist genau das Richtige.** That's exactly the right thing.
die **Richtigkeit** correctness
die **Richtung, -en** direction; **in ~** in the direction of
riechen, roch, gerochen to smell
das **Riesenrad, ⸚er** ferris wheel
riesig huge, enormous(ly)
die **Rindsroulade, -n** stuffed beef roll
der **Ring, -e** ring
rings um (+ *acc.*) all around
das **Risiko, Risiken** risk
der **Ritter, -** knight
der **Rock, ⸚e** skirt (S3)
der **Rolladen, ⸚** (roller) shudder
die **Rolle, -n** role; **Haupt~** leading role
das **Rollo', -s** (roller) shudder

der **Rollschuh, -e** roller skate; **~ laufen*** to rollerskate; **~laufen gehen*** to go roller skating
der **Roman', -e** novel (10W)
die **Romanis'tik** study of Romance languages
die **Roman'tik** romanticism
roman'tisch romantic(ally)
römisch Roman
rosa pink (S2)
die **Rös(ch)ti** (*pl.*) fried potatoes with bacon cubes
die **Rose, -n** rose
der **Rosenkohl** Brussels sprout
die **Rosi'ne, -n** raisin
rost rust-colored
rot (ö) red (S2); **bei Rot** at a red light
die **Rote Grütze** berry sauce thickened with cornstarch
(das) **Rotkäppchen** Little Red Riding Hood
das **Rotkraut** red cabbage
rötlich reddish
rot werden* to blush
die **Roula'de, -n** stuffed beef roll
die **Routi'ne, -n** routine
der **Rückblick, -e** review
der **Rücken, -** back
die **(Hin- und) Rückfahrkarte, -n** round-trip ticket (8W)
die **Rückreise, -n** return trip
der **Rückgang, ⸚e** decline
der **Rucksack, ⸚e** backpack
der **Rückweg, -e** return trip, way back
ruck, zuck quickly, in a jiffy
das **Ruderboot, -e** rowboat
rudern to row
rufen, rief, gerufen to call
die **Ruhe** peace and quiet; **in ~** quietly, without being rushed
der **Ruhetag, -e** holiday, day off
ruhig quiet (7W)

der **Ruhm** fame
der **Rumä'ne, -n, -n / die Rumä'nin, -nen** Rumanian
rumä'nisch Rumanian
rühren to stir; **sich ~** to move; **Ich kann mich kaum ~.** I can hardly move.
der **Rum** rum
rund round
die **Rundfahrt, -en** sightseeing trip
der **Rundfunk** radio, broadcasting
der **Russe, -n, -n / die Russin, -nen** the Russian
russisch Russian
(das) **Russland** Russia

S

der **Saal, Säle** large room, hall
die **Sache, -n** thing, matter; **Haupt~** main thing
sächsisch Saxonian
der **Saft, ⸚e** juice (2W)
sagen to say, tell (S2); **Wie sagt man . . .?** How does one say. . . ? (S2); **Sag mal!** Say. Tell me (us, etc.).; **wie gesagt** as I (you, etc.) said
die **Sahne** cream; **Alles ist ~.** Everything is fine.
die **Saison', -s** season
der **Salat', -e** salad, lettuce (2W)
die **Salbe, -n** ointment
das **Salz** salt (3W)
salzig salty
die **Salzstange, -n** pretzel stick
sammeln to collect (9W)
die **Sammelstelle, -n** collection site (15W)
der **Sammler, -** collector
der **Samstag** Saturday (S4); **am ~** on Saturday (S4)
samstags on Saturdays (2E)
der **Samt** velvet
der **Sand** sand
die **Sanda'le, -n** sandal

sanft gentle, gently

der **Sängerknabe, -n, -n** choir boy

der **Satellit', -en, -en** satellite

der **Satelli'tenteller, -** satellite dish

satteln to saddle

der **Satz, ̈e** sentence (1W); **Bilden Sie einen ~!** Make a sentence.

die **Sau, ̈e** dirty pig, *lit.* sow; **Mensch, so ein ~wetter!** Man, what lousy weather!

sauber clean, neat (S3)

die **Sauberkeit** cleanliness

sauber·machen to clean

sauer sour; acid

das **Sauerkraut** sauerkraut

die **Säule, -n** column

die **S-Bahn, -en=Schnellbahn** commuter train

das **Schach: ~ spielen** to play chess (9W)

schade too bad (S4)

schaden to hurt, damage (15W)

der **Schaden, ̈** damage; **Total'~** total loss

das **Schaf, -e** sheep

der **Schäferhund, -e** German shepherd

schaffen to work hard, accomplish; **das kann ich nicht ~.** I can't do it.

schaffen, schuf, geschaffen to create

der **Schaffner, -** conductor

die **Schale, -n** shell, peel

die **(Schall)platte, -n** record

der **Schalter, -** ticket window, counter (7W)

sich **schämen** to be embarrassed

der **Schaschlik, -s** shish kebab

der **Schatten, -** shadow

schätzen to appreciate

schauen to look; **Schau mal!** Look!

das **Schaufenster, -** display window

das **Schaumbad, ̈er** bubble bath

der **Schauspieler, -** actor (10W)

der **Scheck, -s** check (7W)

die **Scheibe, -n** slice; **eine ~ Brot** a slice of bread

sich **scheiden lassen*** to get divorced

die **Scheidung, -en** divorce (11W)

der **Schein, -e** certificate; **Geld~** banknote (15E)

scheinen, schien, geschienen to shine (S4); to seem (like), appear (to be) (14E)

schenken to give (as a present) (4W)

die **Schere, -n** scissors

die **Schicht, -en** level; **die obere ~** upper level (of society)

schick chic(ly), neat(ly) (11W)

schicken to send (8W)

schief crooked, not straight; **~ gehen*** to go wrong

die **Schießbude, -n** shooting gallery

das **Schiff, -e** ship, boat; **mit dem ~ fahren*** to go by boat

das **Schild, -er** sign

die **Schildkröte, -n** turtle

der **Schinken, -** ham

der **Schirm, -e** umbrella

der **Schlachter, -** butcher

der **Schlafanzug, ̈e** pyjama

schlafen (schläft), schlief, geschlafen to sleep (3E)

schlaflos sleepless

der **Schlafsack, ̈e** sleeping bag

die **Schlafstadt, ̈e** bedroom community

das **Schlafzimmer, -** bedroom (6W)

schlagen (schlägt), schlug, geschlagen to hit, beat

der **Schlager, -** popular song, hit

der **Schlagersänger, -** pop singer

die **Schlagsahne** whipped cream, whipping cream

das **Schlagzeug** drums

die **Schlange, -n** snake

schlank slim, slender (11W)

schlau clever(ly), sly(ly); **~ wie ein Fuchs** clever as a fox

das **Schlauchboot, -e** rubber boat

schlecht bad(ly) (S1)

der **Schlemmer, -** gourmet

schließen, schloss, geschlossen to lock, close

das **Schließfach, ̈er** locker

schließlich after all, in the end (15W)

der **Schlips, -e** tie

der **Schlitten, -** sled

das **Schloss, ̈er** palace (5W)

der **Schlüssel, -** key (7W)

der **Schlüsseldienst** locksmith service

das **Schlüsselkind, -er** latchkey child

schmecken to taste (good); **Das schmeckt (gut).** That tastes good. (3W)

schmelzen (schmilzt), schmolz, ist geschmolzen to melt

der **Schmerz, -en** pain, ache; **~en haben** to have pain (9W); **Ich habe (Kopf)-schmerzen.** I have a (head)ache. (9W)

der **Schmetterling, -e** butterfly

der **Schmied, -e** blacksmith

der **Schmutz** dirt

der **Schmutzfink, -en** (dirty) pig

schmutzig dirty (S3)

das **Schnäppchen, -** bargain (8E)

der **Schnee** snow

schneiden, schnitt, geschnitten to cut

schneien to snow; **es schneit** it's snowing (S4)

schnell quick(ly), fast (S3)

der Schnellweg, -e express route

das Schnitzel, - veal cutlet

der Schock, -s shock

die Schokola'de chocolate

schon already (1E); das ~ that's true, sure

schön fine, nice(ly), beautiful(ly) (S4)

schonen to protect (15W)

die Schönheit beauty

die Schrammelmusik (Viennese) music with violins, guitars, and accordions

der Schrank, ¨e closet, cupboard (6W); Gefrier~ freezer; Kleider~ closet; Küchen~ kitchen cabinet; Kühl~ refrigerator

der Schrebergarten, ¨ leased garden

der Schreck shock; Auch du ~! My goodness!

schrecklich terrible, terribly (11W)

schreiben, schrieb, geschrieben to write (S3); ~ Sie bitte! Please write! (S5); Wie schreibt man das? How do you write that?; ~ an (+ acc.) to write to (10G)

die Schreibmaschine, -n typewriter

der Schreibtisch, -e desk (6W)

schreien, schrie, geschrien to scream

die Schrift, -en script; (hand)-writing

schriftlich written; in writing

der Schriftsteller, - writer, author

der Schritt, -e step; pre-unit

schubsen to shove

schüchtern shy

der Schuh, -e shoe (S3); Sport~ gym shoe, sneaker

die Schule, -n school (5W)

der Schüler, - pupil, student

die Schulter, -n shoulder

die Schüssel, -n bowl

schütteln to shake

schütten (in + acc.) to dump, pour (into), spill

der Schutz protection (15W); Umwelt~ environmental protection (15W)

der Schütze, -n, -n rifleman, marksman; Sagittarius

schützen to protect (15W)

der Schwabe, -n, -n / die Schwäbin, -nen the Swabian

(das) Schwaben(land) Swabia

schwäbisch (adj.) Swabian

die Schwäche, -n weakness

der Schwager, - brother-in-law

die Schwägerin, -nen sister-in-law

schwanger pregnant

schwänzen to skip class

schwärmen (von + dat.) to rave (about)

schwarz (ä) black (S2); ~·fahren* to ride (a bus, subway, etc.) without paying

das Schwarzbrot, -e rye bread

der Schwede, -n, -n / die Schwedin, -nen the Swede

(das) Schweden Sweden

schwedisch Swedish

schweifen (ist) to wander, roam; immer weiter·~ to continue wandering

schweigen, schwieg, geschwiegen to be/remain silent

das Schwein, -e pig, pork; scoundrel; ~ gehabt! I was (you were, etc.) lucky!

der Schweinebraten pork roast

die Schweinshaxe, -n pigs' knuckles

der Schweiß sweat

die Schweiz Switzerland (1W)

der Schweizer, - the Swiss (1W)

Schweizer / schweizerisch Swiss

schwer heavy, heavily, hard, difficult (6E)

die Schwerarbeit hard / menial work

der Schwerbehinderte (ein Schwerbehinderter) / die Schwerbehinderte, -n, -n handicapped person

die Schwester, -n sister (1W)

das Schwesterchen, - little sister

Schwieger- in-law; der ~vater father-in-law; die ~mutter mother-in-law; die ~eltern parents-in-law

schwierig difficult (13W)

die Schwierigkeit, -en difficulty

das Schwimmbad, ¨er (large) swimming pool

schwimmen, schwamm, ist geschwommen to swim (9W); ~ gehen* to go swimming (9W)

der Schwimmer, - swimmer

schwühl humid

der Schwund loss

(das) Schwyzerdütsch Swiss-German

ein Sechstel one sixth

der See, -n lake (1W)

die See sea, ocean

der Seehund, -e seal

das Segelboot, -e sailboat

segelfliegen gehen* to go gliding

segeln to sail; ~ gehen* to go sailing

sehen (sieht), sah, gesehen to see, look (3G); Mal ~! Let's see! (13W)

die Sehenswürdigkeit, -en sight (worth seeing), attraction

sehr very (S4)

die Seide, -n silk

die Seife, -n soap

die Seifenoper, -n soap opera

die Seilbahn, -en cable car

sein his, its (7G)

sein (ist), war, ist gewesen

to be (S1, S2, 2G); **Ich bin's.** It's me.; **So bin ich.** That's the way I am.; **Wie wär's mit . . . ?** How about . . . ?

seit (+ *dat.*)   since, for (time) (3G)

seitdem   since then (14W)

die **Seite, -n**   page; **auf ~** on page, to page (S5); **auf der einen / anderen ~** on the one / other hand

die **Sekretär', -e**   secretary (12W)

der **Sekt**   champagne (4W)

die **Sekun'de, -n**   second (S5)

selbst   -self; **~ wenn** even if

selbstbewusst   self-confident (11W)

das **Selbstbewusstsein**   self-confidence

selbstständig   self-employed, independent (11W)

die **Selbstständigkeit**   independence

selten   seldom

seltsam   strange, weird (11W)

das **Semes'ter, -**   semester (13W)

das **Seminar', -e**   seminar paper (13W)

die **(Seminar')arbeit, -en**   term paper

der **Sender, -**   (radio or TV) station

die **Sendung, -en**   (part of) TV or radio program (10E)

der **Senf**   mustard

der **Septem'ber**   September (S4); **im ~** in September (S4)

die **Serie, -n**   series

servie'ren   to serve (food)

die **Serviet'te, -n**   napkin (3W)

Servus!   Hi! / Bye! *(in Bavaria and Austria)*

die **Sesamstraße**   Sesame Street *(children's television program)*

der **Sessel, -**   armchair (6W)

der **Sessellift, -e**   chairlift

setzen   to set (down), put (6W); **sich ~** to sit down (9G); **sich dazu ~** to join sb. at a table

seufzen   to sigh

das **Shampoo', -s**   shampoo

die **Show, -s**   show

sicher   sure, certain (4W); safe, secure (12W); **Ja, ~.** Yes, sure. (9W); **Es geht ~.** It's probably all right.

die **Sicherheit**   safety, security (12W)

sicherlich   surely, certainly, undoubtedly (15W)

sichern   to secure

sichtbar   visible, visibly

die **Siedlung, -en**   settlement, subdivision

der **Sieg, -e**   victory

der **Sieger, -**   victor

die **Siegermächte** (*pl.*)   victorious Allies

siezen   to call each other *"Sie"*

die **Silbe, -n**   syllable

das **Silber**   silver; **der ~schmied, -e** silver smith

silbern (*adj.*)   silver

(das) **Silves'ter: zu ~**   at / for New Year's Eve (4W)

singen, sang, gesungen   to sing (4W)

sinken, sank, ist gesunken   to sink

der **Sinn, -e**   mind, sense, meaning; **in den ~ kommen*** to come to mind

die **Situation', -en**   situation

die **Sitzecke, -n**   corner bench (seating arrangement)

sitzen, saß, gesessen   to sit (be sitting) (6W)

der **Ski, -er**   ski; **~ laufen*** to ski (9W); **~laufen gehen*** to go skiing (9W)

der **Skilanglauf**   cross-country skiing

der **Skiläufer, -**   skier

der **Skilift, -e**   skilift

der **Skorpion', -e**   scorpion; Scorpio

skrupellos   unscrupulous(ly)

die **Skulptur', -en**   sculpture

die **Slawis'tik**   study of Slavic language and literature

der **Slowa'ke, -n, -n** / die **Slowa'kin, -nen**   the Slovak

slowa'kisch   Slovakian

die **Slowa'kische Republik' = Slowakei'**   Slovak Republic = Slovakia

der **Slowe'ne, -n, -n** / die **Slowe'nin, -nen**   the Slovene

(das) **Slowe'nien**   Slovenia

slowe'nisch   Slovenian

so   so, like that; in this way; **~ lala** so so; **~ dass** (*conj.*) so that (13E); **~ ein** such a (7G); **~ so fair**; **~ . . . wie** as . . . as (12G)

sobald'   as soon as

die **Socke, -n**   sock

das **Sofa, -s**   sofa, couch (6W)

sofort'   immediately, right away (11E)

sogar'   even (6W)

sogenannt   so-called

der **Sohn, ̈e**   son (1W)

solch-   such (7G)

der **Soldat', -en, -en**   soldier

sollen (soll), sollte, gesollt   to be supposed to (5G)

der **Sommer, -**   summer (S4); **im ~** in the summer (S4)

das **Sonderangebot, -e: im ~**   on sale, special

sondern   but (on the contrary) (5W,5G); **nicht nur . . . ~ auch** not only . . . but also (3E)

der **Sonderstatus**   special status

der **Sonnabend**   Saturday (in northern and central Germany)

die **Sonne**   sun; **Die ~ scheint.** The sun is shining. (S4)

der **Sonnenaufgang, ̈e**   sunrise

die **Sonnenblume, -n**   sunflower

die **Sonnenbrille, -n** sunglasses

die **Sonnencreme, -s** suntan lotion

das **Sonnenöl** suntan lotion

der **Sonnenuntergang, ̈-e** sunset

sonnig sunny

der **Sonntag** Sunday (S4); **am ~** on Sunday (S4); **Toten~** Memorial Day

sonntags on Sundays (2E)

sonst otherwise, normally; **~ noch etwas?** Anything else?

die **Sorge, -n** worry, concern; **sich** (*dat.*) **~en machen (um)** to be concerned, worried (about) (12E)

die **Sorte, -n** type, variety

sortie'ren to sort

die **Soße, -n** sauce, gravy

die **Souveränität'** sovereignty

soviel' as much as; **~ ich weiß** as much as I know

sowie' as well as (12E)

sowieso' anyway, anyhow (13E)

sowje'tisch Soviet

sowohl . . . als auch . . . as well as

die **Sozial'hilfe** social welfare

der **Sozialis'mus** socialism

sozialis'tisch socialist

die **Sozial'kunde** social studies

der **Sozial'pädagoge, -n, - n / die Sozial'pädago'gin, -nen** social worker

die **Soziologie'** social studies, sociology

das **Spanferkel, -** suckling pig

(das) **Spanien** Spain (1W)

der **Spanier, -** the Spaniard (1W)

spanisch Spanish (1W)

spannend exciting, suspenseful (10W)

sparen to save (money or time) (6E)

der **Spargel** asparagus

die **Sparkasse, -n** savings bank

sparsam thrifty

sparta'nisch Spartan, frugal(ly)

der **Spaß** fun; **~ machen** to be fun (4E); **Das macht (mir) ~.** That's fun. I love it.

spät late; **Wie ~ ist es?** How late is it? What time is it? (S5)

später later; **Bis ~!** See you later! (S1)

der **Spatz, -en** sparrow

die **Spätzle** (*pl.*) tiny Swabian dumplings

spazie'ren gehen* to go for a walk (9W)

der **Spazier'gang, ̈-e** walk

der **Speck** bacon

die **Speise, -n** food, dish; **Vor~** appetizer

die **Speisekarte, -n** menu (3W)

der **Speisewagen, -** dining car

die **Spekulation', -en** speculation

das **Spezial'geschäft, -e** specialty shop

die **Spezialisie'rung** specialization

der **Spezialist', -en, -en** specialist

die **Spezialität', -en** specialty

spezi'fisch specific(ally)

der **Spiegel, -** mirror

das **Spiel, -e** game, play (9W)

spielen to play; **Tennis ~** to play tennis (S5); **Ball ~** to play ball; **Basketball ~** to play basketball; **Dame ~** to play checkers (9W); **Federball ~** to play badminton; **Fußball ~** to play soccer; **Schach ~** to play chess (9W); **Volleyball ~** to play volleyball

der **Spielplan, ̈-e** program, performance schedule

der **Spielplatz, ̈-e** playground

das **Spielzeug** toy(s)

der **Spieß, -e** spit; spear

der **Spinat'** spinach

die **Spindel, -n** spindle

die **Spinne, -n** spider

spinnen, spann, gesponnen to spin (yarn) (11E); **Du spinnst wohl!** You're crazy!

das **Spinnrad, ̈-er** spinning-wheel

der **Spitz, -e** pomeranian

spitze (*adj.*) great, super (10W)

die **Spitze, -n** top

der **Spitzname, -ns, -n** nickname (14W)

spontan' spontaneous(ly)

der **Sport** sport(s) (9W); **~ treiben*** to engage in sports (9W)

der **Sportler, -** athlete

sportlich athletic(ally), sporty (11W)

der **Sportverein, -e** sports club

die **Sprache, -n** language (1W)

-sprachig -speaking

sprechen (spricht), sprach, gesprochen to speak (S3); **~ Sie langsam bitte!** Speak slowly, please.; **~ Sie lauter!** Speak louder. (S3); **Man spricht . . .** They (people) speak . . . ; **~ von** (+ *dat.*) / **über** (+ *acc.*) to speak of / about (10G); **Ist . . . zu ~?** May I speak to . . . ?

der **Sprecher, -** speaker

die **Sprechsituation', -en** (situation for) communication

das **Sprichwort, ̈-er** saying, proverb

springen, sprang, ist gesprungen to jump (11E)

das **Spritzgebäck** cookies shaped with a cookie press

der **Spruch, ̈-e** saying

der **Sprung, ̈-e** jump

spülen to wash dishes

die **Spülmaschine, -n** dishwasher

das **Spülmittel, -** dishwashing liquid; detergent

die **Spur, -en** trace

spüren to feel

der **Staat, -en** state, nation (1E)

der **Staatenbund** confederation

staatlich public; ~ **kon-trol-liert'** state-controlled

die **Staatsangehörigkeit** citizenship

der **Staatsbürger, -** citizen

der **Staatssicherheitsdienst = die Stasi** GDR secret police

das **Stadion, -s** stadium

das **Stadium, Stadien** stage

die **Stadt, -̈e** city, town (1W)

das **Stadtbild, -er** overall appearance of a city

das **Städtchen, -** small town

der **Stadtplan, -̈e** city map (5W)

der **Stadtrand** outskirts (of town)

der **Stall, -̈e** stable

der **Stamm, -̈e** tribe

der **Stammbaum, -̈e** family tree

stammen (aus + dat.) to stem (from), originate (in)

stampfen to stomp

der **Standard, -s** standard

das **Standesamt, -̈er** marriage registrar

die **Stange, -n** pole

stark (ä) strong(ly); **echt ~** (coll.) really super

starren to stare

die **Station', -en** (bus) stop

die **Statis'tik, -en** statistic

statt (+ gen.) instead of (8G); **~dessen** instead of that

der **Stau, -s** traffic jam

der **Staub** dust

der **Staubsauger, -** vacuum cleaner

staunen to be amazed

stechen (sticht), stach, gestochen to prick, sting

der **Stechschritt** goose step

stecken to stick

stehen, stand, gestanden to stand (or be standing) (6W)

stehen bleiben* to come to a stop, remain standing

stehlen (stiehlt), stahl, gestohlen to steal

steif stiff(ly)

steigen, stieg, ist gestiegen to go up, rise, climb

steigern to increase

steil steep(ly)

der **Stein, -e** stone

der **Steinbock, -̈e** ibex; Capricorn

die **Stelle, -n** job, position, place (12W); **an deiner ~** in your shoes, if I were you (13E)

stellen to stand (upright), put (6W); **eine Frage ~** to ask a question

das **Stellenangebot, -e** job opening / offer

sterben (stirbt), starb, ist gestorben to die (11E)

die **Stereoanlage, -n** stereo system

das **Sternzeichen, -** sign of the zodiac

die **Steuer, -n** tax; **Mehr-wert~** value-added tax

der **Steuerberater, -** tax consultant

das **Stichwort, -̈er** key word

Stief-: die ~eltern stepparents; **die ~mutter** stepmother; **der ~vater** stepfather

der **Stiefel, -** boot

der **Stier, -e** bull; Taurus

der **Stil, -e** style

still quiet(ly)

die **Stimme, -n** voice

stimmen to be right / true; **(Das) stimmt.** (That's true. (That's) right. (6W)

die **Stimmung, -en** mood

das **Stipen'dium, Stipen'dien** scholarship (13W)

die **Stirn** forehead

der **Stock, -̈e** stick, pole

der **Stock, -werke: im ersten ~** on the second floor (6W)

stöhnen to complain, moan

der **Stollen, -** Christmas cake / bread with almonds, raisins, and candied peel

stolz (auf + acc.) proud (of) (15E)

der **Stopp, -s** stop

das **Stoppschild, -er** stop sign

der **Storch, -̈e** stork

stören to bother, disturb

der **Strafzettel, -** (traffic violation) ticket

strahlen to shine

der **Strand, -̈e** beach; **~korb, -̈e** beach basket (chair)

die **Straße, -n** street (5W)

die **Straßenbahn, -en** streetcar (5W)

das **Straßenbild** scene

die **Strategie', -n** strategy

strate'gisch strategic(ally)

der **Strauch, -̈er** bush

der **Strauß, -̈e** bouquet (of flowers)

streben (nach) to strive (for)

der **Streber, -** one who studies excessively, grind

strebsam ambitious(ly)

die **Streife, -n** patrol; **~ fahren** to patrol

der **Streifen, -** strip of land

streng strict(ly)

der **Stress** stress; **zu viel ~** too much stress

das **Stroh** straw

der **Strom** electricity

die **Strophe, -n** stanza

die **Struktur', -en** structure; here: grammar

der **Strumpf, -̈e** stocking

das **Stück, -e** piece; **ein ~** a piece of (2W); **zwei ~** two pieces of (2W); (theater) play (10W)

der **Student', -en, -en** student (S5, 13W)

das **Studen'tenwohnheim, -e** dorm(itory) (6W)

die **Studiengebühr, -en** tuition

der **Studienplatz, ⁻e** opening to study at the university

studie'ren to study a particular field, be a student at a university (4E); ~ (**an** + *dat.*) to be a student (at) (4E)

der **Studie'rende (ein Studierender) / die Studierende, -n, -n** student

das **Studio, -s** studio

das **Studium, Studien** course of study (13W)

der **Stuhl, ⁻e** chair (S2, 5W)

die **Stunde, -n** hour, class lesson (S5, 12W); **in einer halben ~** in half an hour (8W); **in einer Viertel~** in 15 minutes (8W); **in einer Dreiviertel~** in 45 minutes (8W)

stundenlang for hours (5E)

der **Stundenplan, ⁻e** schedule (of classes)

stur stubborn(ly)

stürmisch stormy

das **Subjekt', -e** subject

subventioni'eren to subsidize

die **Suche** search; **auf der ~ nach** in search for

suchen to look for (2W); **gesucht wird** wanted

der **Süden: im ~** in the south (1W)

südlich (von) south (of), to the south (of) (1W)

super superb(ly), terrific(ally) (S4)

der **Superlativ, -e** superlative

der **Supermarkt, ⁻e** supermarket (2W)

su'permodern' very modern

die **Suppe, -n** soup (3W)

surfen to surf; **wind~ gehen** to go windsurfing

süß sweet, cute (11W); **Ach, wie ~!** Oh, how cute! (11W)

das **Sweatshirt, -s** sweatshirt (S3)

der **Swimmingpool, -s** pool

das **Symbol', -e** symbol

symbolisie'ren to symbolize

die **Sympathie'** congeniality

sympa'thisch congenial, likable (11W); **sie sind mir ~** I like them

die **Symphonie', -n** symphony

die **Synago'ge, -n** synagogue

synchronisiert' dubbed

die **Synthe'tik** synthetics

das **System', -e** system (13W)

der **System'berater, -** computer consultant

die **Szene, -n** scene

T

die **Tabel'le, -n** chart

die **Tablet'te, -n** pill

die **Tafel, -n** (black)board (S2); **Gehen Sie an die ~!** Go to the (black)board.

der **Tag, -e** day (S4); **(Guten) ~!** Hello! Hi! (informal)! (S1); **am ~** during the day (6E); **eines Tages** one day (8G); **jeden ~** every day (8G); **~ der Arbeit** Labor Day

das **Tagebuch, ⁻er** journal, diary

tagelang for days

-tägig days long

täglich daily (8G)

das **Tal, ⁻er** valley

das **Talent', -e** talent

talentiert' talented (11W)

die **Tankstelle, -n** gas station

die **Tante, -n** aunt (1W)

der **Tanz, ⁻e** dance

tanzen to dance (4W)

tappen (ist) to tiptoe

die **Tasche, -n** bag, pocket (7W); **Hand~** handbag

die **Taschenlampe, -n** flashlight

das **Taschenmesser, -** pocket knife

die **Tasse, -n** cup (2E); **eine ~** a cup of (2E)

die **Tatsache, -n** fact

taub deaf

die **Taube, -n** dove; pigeon

tauchen (in + *acc.***)** to dip (into)

tauschen to trade

das **Taxi, -s** taxi (5W)

die **Technik** technic

der **Techniker, -** technician

das **Technikum, -s** technical college

technisch technical(ly)

die **Technologie', -n** technology

der **Tee, -s** tea (2W)

der **Teenager, -** teenager

der **Teil, -e** part (1E)

teilen to share, divide (13E)

teilmöbliert partly furnished

die **Teilnahme** participation

teil·nehmen* (an + *dat.***)** to participate, take part (in) (13W)

teils partly

die **Teilung, -en** division

teilweise partly

das **Telefon', -e** telephone (6W)

telefonie'ren to call up, phone (8W)

der **Telefonist', -en, -en** switchboard operator

die **Telefon'karte, -n** telephone card (8W)

die **Telefon'nummer, -n** telephone number (8W)

die **Telefon'zelle, -n** telephone booth

die **Telekommunikation'** telecommunications

der **Teller, -** plate (3W)

das **Temperament', -e** temperament

temperament'voll dynamic (11W)

die **Temperatur', -en** temperature

das **Tempo, -s** speed;

das **Tempolimit, -s** speed limit

das **Tennis: ~ spielen** to play tennis (S5)

der **Teppich, -e** carpet (6W)

die **Terras'se, -n** terrace

der **Terrier, -** Terrier

der **Terroris'mus** terrorism

das **Testament', -e** last will and testament

testen to test

teuer expensive (S3)

der **Teufel, -** devil

der **Text, -e** text

das **Textil'geschäft, -e** clothing store

das **Thea'ter, -** theater (5W)

das **Thema, Themen** topic; **Aktives zum ~** *here:* topical activities

der **Theolo'ge, -n, -n / die Theolo'gin, -nen** theologian

die **Theologie'** theology

die **Theorie', -n** theory

die **Therapie', -n** therapy

das **Thermal'bad, ¨er** thermal bath / spa

das **Thermome'ter, -** thermometer

thüringisch Thuringian

der **Tiefbau** civil engineering

der **Tiefbauingenieur', -e** civil engineer

tiefgefroren frozen

die **Tiefkühlkost** frozen foods

das **Tier, -e** animal (11W); **Jedem ~chen sein Pläsierchen.** To each his own; **Haus~** pet

die **Tierart, -en** animal species

tierlieb fond of animals

das **Tierkreiszeichen, -** sign of the zodiac

die **Tiermedizin'** veterinary science

der **Tiger, -** tiger

die **Tinte** ink

das **Tintenfass, ¨er** inkwell

der **Tipp, -s** hint

der **Tisch, -e** table (S2,5W); **Nacht~** nightstand

die **Tischdecke, -n** tablecloth

der **Tischler, -** cabinet maker

das **Tischtennis: ~ spielen** to play ping-pong

das **Tischtuch, ¨er** tablecloth

der **Titel, -** title

tja well (12W)

der **Toast, -s** (piece of) toast

das **Toastbrot, -e** (piece of) toast

der **Toaster, -** toaster

die **Tochter, ¨** daughter (1W)

der **Tod** death

todmüde dead-tired

Toi, toi, toi! Good luck!

die **Toilet'te, -n** toilet (6W)

tolerant' tolerant

toll great, terrific (S4)

die **Toma'te, -n** tomato (2W)

der **Ton, ¨e** tone, note, pitch

der **Topf, ¨e** pot

das **Tor, -e** gate, gateway (14E)

die **Torte, -n** (fancy) cake

tot dead

total' total(ly)

der **Total'schaden, ¨** total wreck

der **Tote (ein Toter) / die Tote, -n, -n** dead person

töten to kill

die **Tour, -en** tour

der **Touris'mus** tourism

der **Tourist', -en, -en** tourist (5W)

der **Touris'tikumsatz** spending on travel

das **Tournier', -e** tournament

die **Tracht, -en** traditional folk costume / garb

der **Trachtenzug, ¨e** parade with people dressed in traditional dress / garb

traditionell' traditional(ly)

tragen (trägt), trug, getragen to carry (3G); to wear (3G)

die **Tragetasche, -n** tote bag

der **Trainer, -** coach

das **Training** training

die **Träne, -n** tear

das **Transport'flugzeug, -e** transport plane

transportie'ren to transport

die **Traube, -n** grape

trauen to trust

der **Traum, ¨e** dream

träumen (von) to dream (of) (11W)

der **Träumer, -** dreamer

traurig sad(ly) (10W)

die **Traurigkeit** sadness

die **Trauung, -en** wedding ceremony

(sich) **treffen (trifft), traf, getroffen** to meet (with) (9W); **Freunde ~** to meet / get together with friends (9W)

das **Treffen, -** meeting, reunion

der **Treffpunkt, -e** meeting place

treiben, trieb, getrieben to push; **Sport ~** to engage in sports (9W)

der **Treib'hauseffekt'** greenhouse effect

(sich) **trennen** to separate (15W)

die **Treppe, -n** stairs, stairway

das **Treppenhaus, ¨er** stairwell

treten (tritt), trat, ist getreten to step

treu faithful(ly), true, loyal(ly)

sich **trimmen** to keep fit

trinken, trank, getrunken to drink (2W)

das **Trinkgeld, -er** tip

der **Trockner, -** dryer

die **Trommel, -n** drum

die **Trompe'te, -n** trumpet

trotz (+ *gen.* / [+ *dat.*]) in spite of (8G)

trotzdem nevertheless, in spite of that (6E)

trüb(e) dim(ly)

die **Trümmer** *(pl.)* rubble; ruins

der **Trümmerhaufen, -** pile of rubble

der **Tscheche, -n, -n / die Tschechin, -nen** the Czech

tschechisch Czech

die **Tschechische Republik' = (das) Tschechien** Czech Republic

die **Tschechoslowakei'** (former) Czechoslovakia

Tschüss! So long; (Good-) bye! (S1)

das **T-Shirt, -s** T-shirt (S3)
tüchtig (very) capable
tun (tut), tat, getan to do (4W)
tünchen to whitewash
die **Tür, -en** door (S2)
der **Türke, -n, -n / die Türkin, -nen** the Turk
die **Türkei'** Turkey
türkis' turquoise
türkisch Turkish
der **Turm, ⁻e** tower (14W); steeple
turnen to do sports or gymnastics
die **Turnhalle, -n** gym;
der **Turnverein, -e** athletic club
die **Tüte, -n** bag
typisch typical(ly) (15E)

U

die **U-Bahn, -en = Untergrund-bahn** subway (5W)
über (+ *acc. / dat.*) over, above (6G); about (10G)
überall everywhere (3E)
der **Überblick** overview
überein'·stimmen to agree
überflie'gen* (hat) to skim
überfüllt' (over)crowded
überhaupt' at all; ~ **nicht** not at all; ~ **kein Pro-blem** no problem at all
das **Überhol'verbot, -e** no passing restriction
überle'ben to survive
überle'gen to wonder, ponder
überneh'men* to take over
übermorgen the day after tomorrow (4W)
übernach'ten to spend the night (7E)
die **Übernach'tung, -en** (over-night) accommodations
überprü'fen to check
überra'schen to surprise (4W)
die **Überra'schung, -en** sur-prise (4W); **So eine ~!**

What a surprise! (4W)
überset'zen to translate
die **Überset'zung, -en** trans-lation
die **Überstunde, -n** overtime
üblich usual, customary
übrig bleiben* to be left, remain
übrigens by the way (15W)
die **Übrigen** the rest
die **Übung, -en** exercise, practice
das **Ufer, -** riverbank
die **Uhr, -en** watch, clock; o'clock (S5); **Wie viel ~ ist es?** What time is it? (S5); **~zeit** time of the day (7W)
der **Uhrmacher, -** watch-maker
der **Ukrai'ner, -** Ukrainian
ukrai'nisch Ukrainian
um- around, over, from one to the other (7G)
um (+ *acc.*) around (the circumference) (2G); at . . . o'clock (S5); ~ **. . . zu** in order to (9G); **fast ~** almost over
um sein* to be over / up; **deine Zeit ist ~** your time is up
sich **um·blicken** to look around
der **Umbruch, ⁻e** radial change
die **Umfrage, -n** survey; **Meinungs~** opinion poll
die **Umgangsform, -en** manners
die **Umgangssprache** collo-quial speech
umge'ben (von) sur-rounded by
die **Umge'bung** (*sg.*) sur-roundings (14W)
umgekehrt vice versa
umher'·sehen* to look around
(um·)kippen (ist) to tip over
um·leiten to detour
umliegend surrounding

ummau'ern to surround by a wall
der **Umsatz** sales, spending
sich **um·sehen*** to look around
der **Umstand, ⁻e** circum-stance
um·steigen* (ist) to change (trains etc.) (8W)
der **Umtausch** exchange
um·tauschen to exchange
die **Umwelt** environment, surroundings (15W)
umweltbewusst environ-mentally aware (15W)
sich **um·ziehen*** to change (clothing), get changed (9G)
der **Umzug, ⁻e** parade; move, moving
unabhängig (von) inde-pendent (of)
un'attraktiv' unattrac-tive(ly)
unbebaut vacant, empty
unbedingt definitely (12E)
unbegehrt undesired
unbegrenzt unlimited
die **Begrenzung** restriction
unbequem uncomfort-able, inconvenient (6W)
und and (S1,2G)
und so weiter = usw. and so on, etc. (5E)
unecht fake
unehrlich dishonest(ly) (11W)
unentrinn'bar inescapable
unerfahren inexperienced
unerwartet unexpect-ed(ly) (14W)
der **Unfall, ⁻e** accident
unflexibel inflexible
unfreiwillig involuntary, involuntarily
unfreundlich unfriendly (11W)
der **Ungar, -n, -n** the Hungar-ian
ungarisch Hungarian
(das) **Ungarn** Hungary
ungebildet uneducated (11W)

ungeduldig impatient(ly) (11W)

ungefähr about, approximately (1E)

ungemütlich unpleasant, uncomfortable

ungenügend insufficient; approx. grade F

ungestört unhindered

unglaublich unbelievable, unbelievably, incredible, incredibly ; **(Das ist doch)** ~! That's unbelievable / hard to believe! (10W)

das **Unglück** bad luck

unglücklich unhappy, unhappily (11W)

unheimlich tremendous(ly), extreme(ly) (14W); **(Das ist)** ~ **interessant'.** (That's) really interesting. (10W)

die **Universität', -en = Uni, -s** *(coll.)* university (5W)

unkompliziert' uncomplicated (11W)

unmittelbar right, directly

unmöbliert unfurnished

unmög'lich impossible, impossibly

unmusikalisch unmusical (11W)

Unrecht haben* to be wrong (11W)

uns us, to us (5G); **bei ~** at our place (3G); in our city / country

unselbstständig dependent (11W)

unser our (7G)

unsicher insecure, unsafe (12W)

der **Unsinn** nonsense (12W)

unsportlich unathletic (11W)

unsympathisch uncongenial, unlikable (11W)

untalentiert untalented (11W)

unten downstairs (6W)

unter (+ *acc. / dat.*) under, below (6G); among (12E); ~ **einander** among each other

die **Unterdrü'ckung** oppression

der **Untergang** fall, downfall

unterhal'tend entertaining

die **Unterhal'tung** entertainment (10W)

das **Unterneh'men, -** company (12E)

unterneh'mungslustig enterprising

das **Unterpfand** pledge (for)

der **Unterricht** instruction, lesson, class

unterscheiden, unterschied, unterschieden to differentiate; **sich ~** to differ

der **Unterschied, -e** difference

unterschrei'ben* to sign (7W)

die **Unterschrift, -en** signature

unterstrei'chen, unterstrich, unterstrichen to underline

unterstüt'zen to support

unterwegs' on the go, on the road

untreu unfaithful

unverheiratet unmarried, single (11W)

unverschämt impertinent

unvollständig incomplete, incompletely

die **Unwahrscheinlichkeit** *here:* unreal condition

unwillig reluctant(ly)

unzerstört intact

unzufrieden discontent

unzuverlässig unreliable, unreliably (11W)

Urgroß-: die ~eltern greatgrandparents; **die ~mutter** great-grandmother; **der ~vater** great-grandfather

der **Urlaub** paid vacation (9E); **der Mutterschafts~** maternity leave

ursprünglich original(ly)

der **Urlaubstag, -e** (paid) vacation day

die **USA = Vereinigten Staaten von Amerika** *(pl.)* USA

usw. (und so weiter) etc. (and so on)

V

der **Valentinstag** Valentine's Day

der **Vampir', -e** vampire

die **Vanil'le** vanilla

die **Varian'te, -n** variation

die **Variation', -en** variation

variie'ren to vary

die **Vase, -n** vase

der **Vater, ¨** father (1W); **Groß~** grandfather (1W); **Urgroß~** great-grandfather; **Stief~** stepfather

der **Vati, -s** Dad

der **Vegeta'rier, -** vegetarian

verallgemei'nern to generalize

die **Verallgemei'nerung, -en** generalization

(sich) **verändern** to change (14W)

verantwortlich responsible

die **Verantwortung, -en** responsibility (12W)

verantwortungsvoll responsible, responsibly

das **Verb, -en** verb; **Hilfs~** auxiliary verb; **Modal~** modal auxiliary; **reflexive ~** reflexive verb

verbannen to ban

verbessern to improve

verbieten, verbot, verboten to forbid, prohibit (15W)

verbinden, verband, verbunden to connect, tie together, link (15E)

verbittert bitter

das **Verbot, -e** restriction

verboten forbidden (15W)

der **Verbrauch** consumption

verbrauchen to consume

der **Verbraucher, -** consumer

verbreiten to distribute, spread

verbreitern to widen

die **Verbreitung, -en** distribution

verbrennen, verbrannte, verbrannt to burn

verbringen* to spend (time)

verbunden in touch, close

die **Verbundenheit** closeness

verdammen to curse; **Verdammt noch mal!** Darn it!

verderben (verdirbt), verdarb, verdorben to spoil

verdienen to earn, make money (12W); to deserve

verdorben rotten

der **Verein, -e** club, association; **Turn~** athletic club

vereinigen to unite; **wieder~** to reunite

die **Vereinigten Staaten (U.S.A.)** *(pl.)* + **die Staaten** *(coll.)* United States (U.S.)

die **Vereinigung** unification (15E)

vereint united (15E)

die **Verfassung, -en** constitution; **das ~sgericht** Constitutional Court

Verflixt! Darn it!

die **Vergangenheit** past; past tense; simple past

vergeben* to forgive

vergehen* (ist) to pass (time); end

vergessen (vergisst), vergaß, vergessen to forget (10W)

der **Vergleich, -e** comparison

vergleichen, verglich, verglichen to compare (11W)

das **Vergnügen** pleasure

die **Vergnügung, -en** leisure time, entertainment; little pleasure, pastime

das **Verhalten (gegenüber + dat.)** behavior (toward)

das **Verhältnis, -se** relationship, condition

verheiratet married (11W)

verhindern to prevent

verhungern (ist) to starve (to death)

die **Verkabelung** connection by cable

verkaufen to sell (2W)

der **Verkäufer, -** salesman, sales clerk (2W)

der **Verkehr** traffic

das **Verkehrsmittel, -** means of transportation

verklagen to sue

verkrampft tense

verlachen: jemanden ~ to make fun of sb.

der **Verlag, -e** publishing house

verlangen to demand

verlassen (verlässt), verließ, verlassen to leave (14E)

sich **verlaufen*** to get lost

verlegen to transfer, relocate

die **Verlegenheit** embarrassment; **jemanden in ~ bringen*** to embarrass sb.

sich **verlieben (in + acc.)** to fall in love (with) (11W)

verliebt (in + acc.) in love (with) (11W)

verlieren, verlor, verloren to lose (11W)

sich **verloben (mit)** to get engaged (to)

verlobt (mit) engaged (to) (11W)

der **Verlobte (ein Verlobter)** / die **Verlobte, -n, -n** fiancé(e) (12G)

die **Verlobung, -en** engagement

verlockend tempting

vermeiden, vermied, vermieden to avoid

vermieten to rent out (6W)

der **Vermieter, -** landlord

vermissen to miss

vermitteln to help find

verneinen to negate

die **Vernichtung** destruction

die **Vernunft** reason; common sense

verrückt crazy (4E)

verschenken to give away

verschieden various, different (kinds of) (10E)

verschlechtern to deteriorate

verschlingen, verschlang, verschlungen to gulp down, devour

verschlossen closed, locked

die **Verschmutzung** pollution (15W)

verschönern to beautify

verschwiegen discreet

verschwinden, verschwand, ist verschwunden to disappear

versichern to insure; **jemandem etwas ~** to assure sb. sth.

die **Versicherung, -en** insurance

der **Versicherungsagent', -en, -en** insurance agent

versinken* to sink (in)

die **Version', -en** version

versorgen to take care of

die **Verspätung** delay; **Der Zug hat ~.** The train is late.

versprechen* to promise (11E)

der **Verstand** reasoning, logic; common sense

verständlich understandable

verständnislos lacking empathy

verständnisvoll with understanding

verstecken to hide

verstehen* to understand (S3); **Das verstehe ich nicht.** I don't understand (that). (S5)

versuchen to try (11W)

die **Verteidigung**   defense

der **Vertrag, ̈-e**   contract

vertragen*   to stand, tolerate

das **Vertrauen**   trust

vertreiben, vertrieb, vertrieben   to chase away

die **Verwaltung, -en**   administration

verwandeln   to change, transform

verwandt   related

der **Verwandte (ein Verwandter) / die Verwandte, -n, -n**   relative

verweigern   to refuse

verwenden   to use, utilize (15W)

verwitwet   widowed

verwöhnen   to indulge, spoil; **sich ~ lassen***   to let o.s. be spoiled

das **Verzeichnis, -se**   index, catalog

verzeihen, verzieh, verziehen   to forgive; **~ Sie (mir)!**   Forgive me. Pardon (me)!

die **Verzeihung**   pardon; **~!** Excuse me! Pardon me! (5W)

der **Vetter, -**   (alternate form for **cousin**)

das **Video, -s**   video

der **Videorecorder, -**   VCR

die **Videothek, -en**   video store

viel- (mehr, meist-)   much, many (3W,10G,12G); **ganz schön ~**   quite a bit; **so ~' ich weiß**   as far as I know

die **Vielfalt**   versatility

vielleicht'   perhaps (3E)

vielseitig   versatile (11W)

vielsprachig   multilingual

viereckig   square

die **Viersprachigkeit**   quadrilingualism, speaking four languages

das **Viertel, -**   quarter; **(um) ~ nach**   (at) a quarter past (S5); **(um) ~ vor**   (at) a quarter to (S5); **in einer ~stunde**   in a quarter of an hour (8W); **in einer Drei~stunde**   in three quarters of an hour (45 minutes) (8W)

die **Vision', -en**   vision

vital'   energetic, vital

das **Vitamin', -e**   vitamine

der **Vogel, ̈**   bird (11W); **Du hast einen ~.**   You're crazy.

die **Voka'bel, -n**   (vocabulary) word

das **Vokabular'**   vocabulary

das **Volk, ̈-er**   folk; people, nation (14W)

die **Völkerkunde**   ethnology

die **Volksherrschaft**   *here:* rule by the people

die **Volkskammer** (GDR)   house of representatives

das **Volkslied, -er**   folk song

der **Volksmarsch, ̈-e**   group-hiking event

die **Volkspolizei** (GDR)   People's Police

der **Volkspolizist, -en, -en** = **Vopo, -s**   member of the GDR People's Police

der **Volksstamm, ̈-e**   ethnic group

der **Volkswagen, -**   VW

die **Volkswirtschaft**   (macro) economics

voll   full(y) (11E); **Ich habe die Nase ~.**   I'm fed up (with it). (10W)

der **Volleyball, ̈-e**   volleyball

völlig   totally

der **Vollzeitstudent, -en, -en**   full-time student

von (+ *dat.*)   of, from, by (3G); **~ . . . bis**   from . . . until; **vom . . . bis zum**   from the . . . to the (4W)

vor-   ahead, before (7G)

vor (+ *acc.* / *dat.*)   in front of, before (6G); **~ einer Woche**   a week ago (4W); **~ allem**   above all, mainly (10E)

voran'·kommen*   to advance

der **Vorarbeiter, -**   foreman

voraus'gehend   preceding

voraus'·sehen*   to foresee

vorbei'-   past, by (7G)

vorbei'·bringen*   to bring over

vorbei'·fahren*   to drive by, pass

vorbei'·führen (an + *dat.*)   to pass (by), guide along (14W)

vorbei'·gehen* (bei + *dat.*)   to pass by (7G)

vorbei'·kommen*   to come by, pass by

vorbei' sein*   to be over, finished

(sich) **vor·bereiten (auf** + *acc.*)   to prepare (for) (13E)

die **Vorbereitung, -en**   preparation

die **Vorbeugung, -en**   prevention

die **Vorfahrt**   right of way

vor·gehen*   to proceed; **der Reihe nach ~**   to proceed one after the other

vorgestern   the day before yesterday (4W)

vor·haben*   to plan (to), intend (to)

der **Vorhang, ̈-e**   curtain (6W)

vorher   ahead (of time), in advance; before, previously

vorher'gehend   preceding; **das ~e Wort**   antecedent

vor·kommen* (in + *dat.*)   to appear (in); **Das kommt mir . . . vor.**   That seems . . . to me.

das **(flache) Vorland**   *here:* tidal flats

die **Vorlesung, -en**   lecture, class (university) (S5); **~sverzeichnis**   course catalog

der **Vormittag, -e**   (mid)-morning; **heute ~**   this (mid)-morning (8G)

der **Vorname, -ns, -n**   first name

die **Vorschau**   preview

die **Vorsicht: ~!**   Careful! (7W)

die **Vorspeise, -n** appetizer, hors d'oeuvre

vor·stellen to introduce; **Darf ich ~?** May I introduce?

sich **vor·stellen** to imagine (12E); **ich stelle mir vor, dass . . .** I imagine that . . . (12E)

die **Vorstellung, -en** performance (10W); idea

der **Vorteil, -e** advantage

der **Vortrag, ¨e** talk, speech, lecture

vor·tragen* to recite

vorü'bergehend temporary, temporarily

das **Vorurteil, -e** prejudice

die **Vorwahl, -en** area code (8W)

vor·wärmen to preheat

vor·ziehen* to prefer (9E)

W

die **Waage, -n** scale, Libra

das **Wachs** wax

wachsen (wächst), wuchs, ist gewachsen to grow (15E); **zusam'men·wachsen*** to grow together (15E)

die **Waffe, -n** weapon

die **Waffel, -n** waffle

wagen to dare

der **Wagen, -** car (8W); railroad car (8W)

die **Wahl** choice, selection

wählen to choose; elect; select

das **Wahlfach, ¨er** elective (subject)

der **Wahnsinn** insanity; **(Das ist ja) ~!** (That's) crazy / awesome / unbelievable! (10W)

wahnsinnig crazy, crazily

während (+ gen.) during (8G); while (conj.)

wahr true; **nicht ~?** isn't it? (S4); **Das kann doch nicht ~ sein!** That can't be true! (7W)

wahrlich (poetic) truly

wahrschein'lich probable, probably (13E)

die **Währung, -en** currency; **die ~sunion** currency union

das **Wahrzeichen, -** landmark

der **Wald, ¨er** forest, woods (7E)

der **Walzer, -** waltz

die **Wand, ¨e** wall (S2)

der **Wanderer, -** hiker

wandern (ist) to hike (9W)

der **Wanderweg, -e** (hiking) trail

wann? when?, at what time? (S4,11G)

wäre: Wie wär's mit . . . ? How about . . . ?

die **Ware, -n** goods, wares, merchandise

warm (ä) warm(ly) (S4)

die **Wärme** warmth

warnen (vor + dat.) to warn (against)

warten to wait; **~ auf (+ acc.)** to wait for (10G); **Warten Sie!** Wait! (7W)

die **Wartungskosten** (pl.) maintenance costs

warum? why? (2E)

was? what? (S2,2G); **~ für (ein)?** what kind of (a)? (2W); **~ für ein(e) . . . !** What a . . . ! (11W)

das **Waschbecken, -** sink

die **Wäsche** laundry; **~ waschen*** to do the laundry

die **Waschecke, -n** corner reserved for washing

(sich) **waschen (wäscht), wusch, gewaschen** to wash (o.s.) (6W,9G)

der **Waschlappen, -** washcloth (fig., coll. wimp)

die **Waschmaschi'ne, -n** washing machine

das **Waschmittel, -** (washing) detergent

das **Wasser** water (2W)

der **Wassermann, ¨er** Aquarius

der **Wasserski, -er** water ski; **~ laufen*** to water ski; **~laufen gehen*** to go water skiing

das **Watt(enmeer)** tidal flats

die **Webseite, -n** Web page

die **Website, -s** Web site

der **Wechsel** change

der **Wechselkurs, -e** exchange rate

wechseln to (ex)change (7W)

die **Wechselstube, -n** exchange bureau

weder . . . noch neither . . . nor (10E)

weg away, gone

der **Weg, -e** way, path, trail (5W); route; **nach dem ~ fragen** to ask for directions

wegen (+ gen. / [+ dat.]) because of (8G)

weg·werfen* to throw away

weh·tun* to hurt (9W); **Mir tut (der Hals) weh.** My (throat) hurts. I have a sore throat. (9W)

weich soft

weichen, wich, ist gewichen to give way to

die **Weide, -n** willow

(das) **Weihnachten: zu ~** at / for Christmas (4W); **Frohe / Fröhliche ~!** Merry Christmas!

der **Weihnachtsbaum, ¨e** Christmas tree

das **Weihnachtsessen** Christmas dinner

das **Weihnachtslied, -er** Christmas carol

der **Weihnachstmann, ¨er** Santa Claus

weil (conj.) because (4G)

die **Weile: eine ~** for a while

weilen (poetic) to stay, be

der **Wein, -e** wine (2W); **Tafel~** table wine; **Qualitäts~** quality wine; **Qualitäts~ mit Prädikat** superior wine

der **Weinberg, -e** vineyard

weinen to cry (10W)

weinrot wine-red

die **Weinstube, -n** wine cellar, tavern

die **Weintraube, -n** grape

weise wise

die **Weise: auf diese ~** (in) this way (13E)

der **Weise (ein Weiser) / die Weise, -n, -n** wise man /woman

weiß white (S2)

weit far (5W)

die **Weite** distance; wide-open space(s)

weiter: und so ~ (usw.) and so on (etc.) **~ draußen** farther out; **Wie geht's ~?** How does it go on? What comes next?

weiter- additional

Weiteres *here:* additional words and phrases

weiter·fahren* (ist) to drive on, keep on driving (8E); to continue the trip

weiter·geben* to pass on

weiter·gehen* (ist) to continue, go on

weiterhin still

welch- which (7G); **Welche Farbe hat . . . ?** What color is . . . ? (S2)

die **Welle, -n** wave

der **Wellensittich, -e** parakeet

die **Welt, -en** world (11E); **aus aller ~** from all over the world

weltoffen cosmopolitan

wem? (to) whom? (3G)

wen? whom? (2G)

wenig- little (not much), few (10G); **immer ~er** fewer and fewer

wenigstens at least

wenn (*conj.*) if, (when)ever (4G,11G); **selbst ~** even if

wer? who? (1G); who(so)-ever

die **Werbung** advertisement (10W)

werden (wird), wurde, ist geworden to become, get (3G); **es wird dunkel** it's getting dark; **Was willst du ([ein]mal) ~?** What do you want to be (one day)? (12W); **Ich will . . . ~.** I want to be a . . . (12W)

werfen, (wirft), warf, geworfen to throw (15W); **weg·~** to throw away (15W)

die **Werft, -en** shipyard

der **Wert, -e** value; worth

wertvoll valuable

wessen? (+ *gen.*) whose? (8G)

der **Wessi, -s** (*nickname*) West German

die **Weste, -n** vest

der **Westen: im ~** in the west (1W)

westlich von west of

die **Westmächte** (*pl.*) western Allies

der **Wettbewerb, -e** contest

das **Wetter** weather (S4)

wichtig important (1E)

wickeln (in + *acc.*) to wrap (into)

der **Widder, -** ram; Aries

widersteh'en* (+ *dat.*) to withstand

wie? how? (S1); like, as; **~ sagt man . . . ?** How does one say . . . ? (S2); **~ bitte?** What did you say, please? (S5); **so . . . ~ as . . . as** (1E); **~ lange?** how long? (4W); **~ gesagt** as I (you, etc.) said

wieder again (S4); **schon ~** already again (S4); **immer ~** again and again, time and again (12G); **Da sieht man's mal ~!** That just goes to show you. (15W)

der **Wiederaufbau** rebuilding

wieder auf·bauen to rebuild

die **Wiedergeburt** rebirth

wiederho'len to repeat (S2)

die **Wiederho'lung, -en** repetition, review

wieder·hören to hear again; **Auf Wiederhören!** Good-bye. (on the phone) (6W)

wieder·sehen* to see again; **Auf Wiedersehen!** Good-bye (S1)

(wieder)·vereinigen to (re)-unite

die **(Wieder)vereinigung** (re)-unification (14E)

wiegen, wog, gewogen to weigh; **Lass es ~!** Have it weighed.

der **Wiener, -** the Viennese

die **Wiese, -n** meadow

Wieso' (denn)? How come? Why? (13W)

wie viel? how much? (S3, 3W)

wie viele? how many? (S3, 3W)

wild wild(ly)

der **Wille, -ns, -n** will; **Wo ein ~ ist, ist auch ein Weg.** Where there's a will, there's a way.

willkom'men sein* to be welcome

willkür'lich at random

die **Wimper, -n** eyelash

der **Wind, -e** wind

windig windy (S4)

die **Windmühle, -n** wind mill

das **Windrad, ̈er** propellor

windsurfen gehen* to go wind surfing

der **Winter, -** winter (S4); **im ~** in (the) winter (S4)

das **Winzerfest, -e** wine festival

wirken to appear

wirklich really, indeed (S4)

die **Wirklichkeit** reality

die **Wirtschaft** economy

wirtschaftlich economical (ly)

der **Wirtschaftsprüfer, -** accountant

die **Wirtschaftswissenschaft** economics; economic science das **Wirtschaftswunder** economic boom (*lit.* miracle)

wissen (weiß), wusste, gewusst to know (a fact) (6G); **Ich weiß (nicht).** I (don't) know. (S5); **soviel' ich weiß** as far as I know

das **Wissen** knowledge

die **Wissenschaft, -en** science, academic discipline (13W); **Natur~** natural science(s) (13W)

der **Wissenschaftler, -** scientist, scholar (12W)

wissenschaftlich scientific(ally), scholarly

der **Witz, -e** joke; **Mach (doch) keine ~e!** Stop joking!

witzig witty, funny

wo? where? (S2,6G)

woan'ders somewhere else

wobei' where

die **Woche, -n** week (S4); **diese ~** this week (8G); **zwei ~n** for two weeks (8G)

das **Wochenende, -n** weekend; **am ~** on the weekend (4W); **(Ein) schönes ~!** Have a nice weekend! (4W)

wochenlang for weeks

wöchentlich weekly (8G)

-wöchig weeks long

woher'? from where? (1W)

wohin'? where to? (6G)

das **wo-Kompo'situm, Kompo'sita** *wo*-compound

wohl *flavoring particle expressing probability*

das **Wohlbefinden** well-being

wohlriechend fragrant

der **Wohlstand** affluence

die **Wohngemeinschaft, -en** = **WG, -s** group sharing a place to live

wohnen to live, reside (1E)

das **Wohnsilo, -s** (*coll.*) (high-rise) apartment (cluster)

der **Wohnsitz, -e** residence

die **Wohnung, -en** apartment (6W)

der **Wohnwagen, -** camper

das **Wohnzimmer, -** living room (6W)

der **Wolf, ⸚e** wolf

die **Wolke, -n** cloud

die **Wolle** wool

wollen (will), wollte, gewollt to want to (5G)

das **Wort, -e** (connected) word; **mit anderen ~en** in other words

das **Wort, ⸚er** (individual) word; **vorher'gehende Wort** antecedent; **zusam'mengesetzte ~** compound noun

das **Wörtchen, -** little word

das **Wörterbuch, ⸚er** dictionary

der **Wortschatz** vocabulary

das **Wunder, -** wonder, miracle

wunderbar wonderful(ly) (S1)

sich **wundern: ~ Sie sich nicht!** Don't be surprised.

wunderschön very beautiful (14W)

der **Wunsch, ⸚e** wish (11W); **~traum, ⸚e** ideal dream

(sich) **wünschen** to wish (4W)

die **Wunschwelt** ideal world

die **Wurst, ⸚e** sausage (2W); **Das ist (mir) doch ~!** I don't care.

das **Würstchen, -** wiener, hot dog (2E)

würzen to season

Z

die **Zahl, -en** number (S3); **Ordinal'~** ordinal number (4W)

zählen to count (S3)

der **Zahn, ⸚e** tooth (9W); **sich die Zähne putzen** to brush one's teeth (9G)

der **Zahnarzt, ⸚e / die Zahnärztin, -nen** dentist (12W)

die **Zahnbürste, -n** toothbrush

die **Zahnmedizin'** dentistry

die **Zahnpasta, -pasten** toothpaste

die **Zahnradbahn, -en** cog railway

der **Zahntechniker, -** dental technician

die **Zange, -n** pliers

zart tender

zärtlich affectionate(ly) (11W)

die **Zärtlichkeit** affection

der **Zauber** magic (power)

der **Zauberspruch, ⸚e** magic spell

der **Zaun, ⸚e** fence

z. B. (zum Beispiel) e.g. (for example)

die **Zehe, -n** toe

das **Zeichen, -** signal, sign, indication

der **Zeichentrickfilm, -e** cartoon, animated film

die **Zeichnung, -en** drawing

der **Zeigefinger, -** index finger

zeigen to show (5W); **Zeig mal!** Show me (us, etc.)!

die **Zeile, -n** line

die **Zeit, -en** time (S5); tense; **die gute alte ~** the good old days

die **Zeitform, -en** tense

zeitgenössisch contemporary

zeitlos timeless

die **Zeitschrift, -en** magazine (10W)

die **Zeitung, -en** newspaper (10W); **Wochen~** weekly newspaper

die **Zelle, -n** cell, booth

das **Zelt, -e** tent

der **Zentner, -** center (100 kilograms)

zentral' central(ly)

das **Zentrum, Zentren** center; **im ~** downtown

zerbomben to destroy by bombing

zerbrechen* to break
zerschlagen* to break, smash
zerstören to destroy (15W)
die **Zerstörung** destruction
das **Zeugnis,-se** report card
die **Ziege, -n** goat
ziehen, zog, gezogen to pull (11E); to raise (vegetables, etc.)
ziehen, zog, ist gezogen to move (relocate)
das **Ziel, -e** goal, objective; destination
ziemlich quite, fairly (6W)
die **Zigeu'ner, -** gypsy
das **Zimmer, -** room (S2)
der **Zimmerkolle'ge, -n, -n /** die **Zimmerkolle'gin, -nen** roommate (13W)
der **Zimmernachweis, -e** room-referral service
die **Zimmervermittlung** room-referral agency
das **Zitat', -e** quote
die **Zitro'ne, -n** lemon (2W)
die **Zitro'nenlimonade** carbonated lemonade
der **Zitro'nensaft, ̈e** lemonade
zittern to tremble, shake
zittrig shaky
der **Zoll** customs; toll
die **Zone, -n** zone, area
der **Zoo, -s** zoo
der **Zorn** anger
zu- closed (7G)
zu (+ *dat.*) to, in the direction of, at, for (purpose) (3G); too (S3); closed (2); (+ *inf.*) to (9G); ~ **mir** to my place
zu·bleiben* (ist) to stay closed
der **Zufall, ̈e** coincidence; **So ein ~!** What a coincidence!
zufrie'den satisfied, content

der **Zug, ̈e** train (8W); **mit dem ~ fahren*** to go by train (8W)
zu·halten* to hold closed
das **Zuhau'se** home
zu·hören to listen (7G); **Hören Sie gut zu!** Listen well/carefully.
der **Zuhörer, -** listener
die **Zukunft** future (12W)
zukunftsorientiert' future-oriented
zuletzt' last (of all); finally
zu·machen to close (7G)
zunehmend increasing(ly)
die **Zunge, -n** tongue
der **Zungenbrecher, -** tongue twister
zurück'- back (7G)
zurück'·bleiben* to stay behind
zurück'·bringen* to bring back
zurück'·fliegen* to fly back
zurück'·geben* to give back, return
zurück'·halten* to hold back
zurück'·kommen* to come back, return (7G)
zurück'·nehmen* to take back
zurück'·sehen* to look back
zurück'·weichen* to withdraw
sich **zurück'·ziehen*** to withdraw
zusam'men together (2W); **alle ~** all together; **~gewürfelt** thrown together
zusam'men·arbeiten to work together, cooperate
der **Zusam'menbruch** collapse
zusam'men·fassen to summarize
die **Zusam'menfassung, -en** summary

die **Zusam'mengehörigkeit** affiliation; solidarity
zusam'men·wachsen* to grow together (15E)
der **Zuschauer, -** spectator (10E)
zu·schließen* to lock
zu·sehen* to watch; see to it
der **Zustand, ̈e** conditions
zu·stimmen to agree
zuverlässig reliable, reliably (11W)
die **Zuverlässigkeit** reliability
zuvor' previously; **wie nie ~** as never before
die **Zuwanderung** immigration
die **Zwiebel, -n** onion
der **Zwilling, -e** twin; Gemini
zwischen (+ *acc. / dat.*) between (6G); **in~** in the meantime; **~durch** in between
die **Zwischenlandung, -en** stop over
die **Zwischenzeit** time in between; **in der ~** in the meantime, meanwhile
(das) **Zypern** Cypres
der **Zypriot', -en, -en** Cypriot
zyprisch Cypriot

English– German Vocabulary

Except for numbers, pronouns, and **da-/wo-** compounds, the English–German Vocabulary includes all ACTIVE words presented in this book. If you are looking for certain idioms, feminine equivalents, or other closely related words, use the key word given and look it up in the German–English vocabulary. Irregular t-verbs ("irregular weak verbs") and n-verbs ("strong verbs") are indicated by an asterisk (*); check their forms and auxiliaries in the list of principal parts in the Appendix.

A

able; to be ~ können*
about (approximately) ungefähr, etwa
above über (+ *dat. / acc.*); **~ all** vor allem
abroad im/ins Ausland
academic discipline die Wissenschaft, -en
to **accept** an·nehmen*
ache: I have a (head)~. Ich habe (Kopf)schmerzen.
acquaintance der Bekannte (ein Bekannter) / die Bekannte, -n, -n
across (from) gegenüber (von + *dat.*)
actor der Schauspieler, -
actual(ly) eigentlich
ad die Anzeige, -n
address die Adresse, -n; **return ~** der Absender, -
advertising die Werbung
advice der Rat
affectionate zärtlich
afraid: to be ~ (of) Angst haben* (vor + *dat.*)
after (time) nach (+ *dat.*); **(conj. + past perf.)** nachdem
afternoon der Nachmittag, -e; **this ~** heute Nachmittag; **tomorrow ~** morgen Nachmittag; **yesterday ~** gestern Nachmittag; **in the ~** nachmittags, am Nachmittag; **every ~** nachmittags
afterwards danach
again wieder, noch (ein)mal; **Could you say that ~?** Wie bitte?; **~ and ~** immer wieder

against gegen (+ *acc.*)
ago vor (+ *dat.*); **a week ~** vor einer Woche
ahead: straight ~ geradeaus
aid die Hilfe
air die Luft
airplane das Flugzeug, -e
airport der Flughafen, ̈
all all-, alles (*sg.*); **That's ~.** Das ist alles.; **above ~** vor allem; **after ~** schließlich; **~ sorts of** allerlei
to **allow** erlauben
allowed: to be ~ to dürfen*
almost fast
alone allein
along (prefix) mit-; **(adv.)** entlang
already schon
also auch, ebenfalls
although (conj.) obwohl
always immer
America (das) Amerika
American (adj.) amerikanisch; **(person)** der Amerikaner, -
among unter (+ *acc. / dat.*)
and und
angry: to get ~ about sich ärgern über (+ *acc.*)
animal das Tier, -e
annoyed: to get ~ about sich ärgern über (+ *acc.*)
another noch ein
to **answer** antworten
answer die Antwort, -en
anyhow sowieso
anyway sowieso
apart auseinander
apartment die Wohnung, -en

to **appear (to be)** scheinen*, aus·sehen*
to **applaud** klatschen
apple der Apfel, ̈
to **apply (for)** sich bewerben* (um)
approximately ungefähr, etwa
April der April; **in ~** im April
architect der Architekt, -en, -en
area das Gebiet, -e, die Gegend, -en
area code die Vorwahl, -en
arm der Arm, -e
armchair der Sessel, -
around (prefix) um-; **(prep.)** um (+ *acc.*)
arrival die Ankunft
to **arrive (in)** an·kommen* (in + *dat.*)
art die Kunst, ̈e
artist der Künstler, -
as wie; **~ . . . ~** so . . . wie
to **ask** fragen, bitten* (um); **to ~ a question** eine Frage stellen
at (the side of) an (+ *dat.*); **(o'clock)** um . . . (Uhr); **(the place of)** bei (+ *dat.*); **(a store, etc.)** bei
athletic sportlich; **un~** unsportlich
attached anhänglich
attention: to pay ~ auf·passen
attractive attraktiv, hübsch
attribute die Eigenschaft, -en
August der August; **in ~** im August

aunt die Tante, -n
Austria (das) Österreich
Austrian (**language**) österreichisch; (**person**) der
   Österreicher, -
author der Autor, -en
available frei
away (**prefix**) ab
awesome: (**That's**) ~!
   Wahnsinn!

B

back (**prefix**) zurück-
bad(ly) schlecht;
   schlimm; **too** ~ schade
bag die Tasche, -n
baggage das Gepäck
to **bake** backen*
bakery die Bäckerei, -en
balcony der Balkon, -s /
   -e
ballet das Ballett
banana die Banane, -n
bank die Bank, -en
banknote der (Geld)-
   schein, -e
barely kaum
bargain das Schnäppchen,-
to **bathe** baden
bath(room) das Bad, ⸚er;
   to take a ~ sich baden
to **be** sein*; (**become**) werden*; **Be . . .!** Sei (Seid,
   Seien Sie) . . .!
bean die Bohne, -n
beautiful (wunder)schön
because (**conj.**) weil,
   denn; ~ **of** wegen (+ gen.
   / [dat.])
to **become** werden*
bed das Bett, -en; ~**room**
   das Schlafzimmer, -
beer das Bier, -e
before vor (+ acc. / dat.);
   (**conj.**) bevor; **not** ~
   (**time**) erst; (**adv.**) vorher
to **begin** beginnen*, an·fan-
   gen*
beginning der Anfang, ⸚e;
   in the ~ am Anfang; **at**
   the ~ **of the week** Anfang der Woche
behind hinter (+ acc. /
   dat.)

to **believe** (**in**) glauben (an +
   acc.); (**things**) Ich glaube
   es.; (**persons**) Ich glaube
   ihm/ihr.; **You better** ~
   it! Und ob!; **That's hard**
   to ~! (Das ist doch) unglaublich! **I don't** ~ **it!**
   Das gibt's doch nicht!
belly der Bauch, ⸚e
to **belong to** gehören (+ dat.)
below unter (+ acc. / dat.)
beside neben (+ acc. /
   dat.)
besides außer (+ dat.);
   (**adv.**) außerdem
best best-; **it's** ~ am
   besten; **All the** ~! Alles
   Gute!
bet: you~! Und ob!
better besser; **You** ~ **be-**
   lieve it! Und ob!
between zwischen (+ acc.
   / dat.)
bicycle das Fahrrad, ⸚er
to **bicycle** mit dem Fahrrad
   fahren*
big groß (ö)
to **bike** mit dem Fahrrad
   fahren*
bill die Rechnung, -en
billion (**US**) die Milliarde,
   -n
bird der Vogel, ⸚
birthday der Geburtstag, -
   e; **on/for the** ~ zum
   Geburtstag; **When is**
   your ~? Wann haben Sie
   Geburtstag?; **My** ~ **is on**
   the . . . Ich habe am . . .
   (s)ten Geburtstag.; **My** ~
   is in . . . Ich habe im . . .
   Geburtstag.; **Happy** ~!
   Alles Gute/ Herzlichen
   Glückwunsch zum
   Geburtstag!
bit: a little ~ **of** ein bisschen
black schwarz (ä)
blackboard die Tafel, -n
blouse die Bluse, -n
blue blau
boarding house die Pension, -en
body der Körper, -

book das Buch, ⸚er
bookstore die Buchhandlung, -en
border die Grenze, -n
bored: to get (**or be**) ~ sich
   langweilen
boring langweilig
born geboren (ist); **I was** ~
   May 3, 1968, in Ulm.
   Ich bin am 3. 5. 68 in
   Ulm geboren.
both (**things, sg.**) beides;
   (**pl.**) beide
bottle die Flasche, -n; **a** ~
   of . . . eine Flasche . . .
boy der Junge, -n, -n
bread das Brot, -e
break (**intermission**) die
   Pause, -n
breakfast das Frühstück;
   (**What's**) **for** ~? (Was
   gibt's) zum Frühstück?;
   to eat ~ frühstücken
bridge die Brücke, -n
bright (**light**) hell; intelligent
to **bring** bringen*; **to** ~ **along**
   mit·bringen*
brother der Bruder, ⸚; ~**s**
   and sisters die
   Geschwister (pl.)
brown braun
to **brush** (**one's teeth**) sich
   (die Zähne) putzen
to **build** bauen, auf·bauen;
   to re~ wieder auf·bauen;
   to be built entstehen*;
   building das Gebäude, -;
   der Bau, -ten
bus der Bus, -se
business das Geschäft, -e
businessman der
   Geschäftsmann, ⸚er
business management:
   graduate in ~ Betriebswirt, -e
businesspeople Ge-
   schäftsleute
businesswoman die
   Geschäftsfrau, -en
but aber; doch; **not only**
   . . . ~ **also** nicht nur . . .
   sondern auch
butter die Butter

to **buy** kaufen
by (prefix) vorbei-; **(prep.)** von (+ *dat.*)

C

café das Café, -s
cafeteria (student) die Mensa
cake der Kuchen, -
to **call** rufen*; **to ~ (up)** an·rufen*, telefonieren; **to ~ (name)** nennen*; **to be ~ed** heißen*
campground der Campingplatz, ⸚e
can können*
Canada (das) Kanada
Canadian (adj.) kanadisch; **(person)** der Kanadier, -
candle die Kerze, -n
capital die Hauptstadt, ⸚e
car das Auto, -s, der Wagen, -; **railroad ~** der Wagen, -
card die Karte, -n; **post ~** die Postkarte, -n; **telephone ~** die Telefonkarte, -n
cardigan die Jacke, -n
to **care: Take ~!** Mach's gut! **Careful!** Vorsicht!
carpet der Teppich, -e
carrot die Karotte, -n
to **carry** tragen*
case: in any ~ jedenfalls
cash das Bargeld; **~ register** die Kasse, -n
to **cash (in) (a check)** ein·lösen
cashier's window die Kasse, -n
cassette die Kassette, -n
cat die Katze, -n
cathedral der Dom, -e
to **celebrate** feiern
celebration das Fest, -e, die Feier, -n
cellular phone das Handy, -s
cent der Cent, -s
center die Mitte
certain(ly) bestimmt, sicher(lich)

certificate der Schein, -e
chair der Stuhl, ⸚e; **arm ~** der Sessel, -
chalk die Kreide
champagne der Sekt
change das Kleingeld
to **change** (sich) ändern, (sich) verändern; **(clothing)** sich um·ziehen*; **(money, etc.)** wechseln, um·tauschen; **(trains)** um·steigen*
channel das Programm, -e
characteristic die Eigenschaft, -en
charming charmant
cheap billig
check der Scheck, -s; die Rechnung, -en; **traveler's ~** der Reisescheck, -s
cheese der Käse, -
chic schick
child das Kind, -er
choice (of) die Auswahl (an + *dat.*)
choir der Chor, ⸚e
Christmas (das) Weihnachten; **at/for ~** zu Weihnachten
church die Kirche, -n
citizen der Bürger, -
city die Stadt ⸚e; **~ hall** das Rathaus, ⸚er; **~ map** der Stadtplan, ⸚e
civil servant der Beamte (ein Beamter) / die Beamtin, -nen
to **clap** klatschen
class (group) die Klasse, -n; **(time)** die Stunde, -n; **(instruction, school)** der Unterricht; **(instruction, university)** die Vorlesung, -en
clean sauber
to **clean** putzen
clerk der Angestellte (ein Angestellter) / die Angestellte, -n, -n; **(civil servant)** der Beamte (ein Beamter) / die Beamtin, -nen; **(salesman)** der Verkäufer, -

clock die Uhr, -en; **o'clock** Uhr
to **close** zu·machen
closed (prefix) zu-; **(prep.)** zu, geschlossen
closet der Schrank, ⸚e
clothing die Kleidung
coat der Mantel, ⸚
coast die Küste, -n
coffee der Kaffee
cola drink die Cola
cold kalt (ä)
cold: to catch a ~ sich erkälten
to **collect** sammeln
color die Farbe, -n; **What ~ is . . . ?** Welche Farbe hat . . . ?
colorful bunt
to **comb** (sich) kämmen
to **come** kommen*; **to ~ along** mit·kommen*; **to ~ back** zurück·kommen*; **to ~ in** herein·kommen*; **That comes to . . . (altogether).** Das kostet (zusammen) . . . ; **Oh, ~ on!** Ach was!
comfortable bequem, gemütlich; **un~** ungemütlich, unbequem
comical komisch
common gemeinsam
compact disc, CD die CD, -s
company die Firma, Firmen; **large ~** das Unternehmen, -
to **compare** vergleichen, verglich, verglichen
to **complain (about)** (sich) beschweren (über + *acc.*)
complicated kompliziert; **un~** unkompliziert
composer der Komponist, -en, -en
concern die Sorge, -n
to **be concerned (about)** sich Sorgen machen (um)
concert das Konzert, -e
condo die Eigentumswohnung, -en

congenial sympathisch;
un~ unsympathisch

to **congratulate** gratulieren

congratulation der
Glückwunsch, ⁻e; **~s!**
Herzliche Glückwün-
sche!; **~s on your birthday!** Herzlichen Glück-
wunsch zum Geburts-
tag!

to **connect** verbinden*

construction der Bau

container der Behälter, -

to **continue** weiter·gehen*,
weiter·machen

contrary: on the ~ im
Gegenteil

convenient bequem

convivial gemütlich

to **cook** kochen

cookie das Plätzchen, -

cool kühl

corner die Ecke, -n

correct richtig

to **cost** kosten

council der Rat

to **count** zählen

counter der Schalter, -

country das Land, ⁻er;
**into the ~(side) / in the
~(side)** aufs / auf dem
Land

couple: a ~ of ein paar

course der Kurs, -e; **(~ of
study)** das Studium; **of ~**
natürlich; **(na) klar**

cousin der Cousin, -s /
die Kusine, -n

cozy gemütlich

crazy verrückt; **(That's) ~!**
Wahnsinn!

to **cry** weinen

cucumber die Gurke, -n

cup die Tasse, -n; **a ~ of
. . .** eine Tasse . . .

cupboard der Schrank, ⁻e

cultural(ly) kulturell

curtain der Vorhang, ⁻e

D

daily täglich

to **damage** schaden

to **dance** tanzen

danger die Gefahr, -en

dangerous gefährlich

dark dunkel

date (calendar) das Datum, Daten; **What ~ is
today?** Welches Datum
ist heute?

daughter die Tochter, ⁻

day der Tag, -e; **during
the ~** am Tag; **one ~**
eines Tages; **all ~ long,
the whole ~** den ganzen
Tag; **each ~** jeden Tag; **in
those ~s** damals

dear lieb-; **Oh ~!** Ach du
liebes bisschen!

December der Dezember;
in ~ im Dezember

to **decide (on / about)** sich
entscheiden* (für /
gegen)

decision die Entscheidung, -en

definitely unbedingt

degree der Abschluss, ⁻e

dentist der Zahnarzt, ⁻e /
die Zahnärztin, -nen

to **depart** (from) ab·fahren*

departure die Abfahrt,
-en

to **depend: That ~s.** Das
kommt darauf an.

dependent unselbst-
ständig

to **describe** beschreiben*

desk der Schreibtisch, -e

dessert der Nachtisch

to **destroy** zerstören

to **develop** (sich) entwickeln; **~ apart** sich
auseinander ent-
wickeln

devoted anhänglich

to **die** sterben (stirbt), starb,
ist gestorben

difference der Unter-
schied, -e

different(ly) verschieden,
anders; **Say it ~!** Sagen
Sie es anders!; **s.th. ~**
etwas anderes

difficult schwer, schwierig

dining room das Esszimmer, -

dinner das Mittagessen,
das Abendessen

diploma der Abschluss, ⁻e

dirty schmutzig

to **discard** weg·werfen*

dishonest unehrlich

to **divide** teilen

divorce die Scheidung, -en

divorced geschieden

to **do** tun*, machen

doctor der Arzt, ⁻e / die
Ärztin, -nen

dog der Hund, -e

dollar der Dollar, -(s)

done fertig

door die Tür, -en

dorm das Studenten-
wohnheim, -e

downstairs unten

to **dream (of)** träumen (von)

dress das Kleid, -er

dressed: to get ~ (sich)
an·ziehen*; **to get un~**
(sich) aus·ziehen*

dresser die Kommode, -n

to **drink** trinken*

to **drive** fahren*; **to ~ on
(keep on driving)**
weiter·fahren*; **to ~ up**
hinauf·fahren*

drugstore die Drogerie, -n

dull langweilig

during während (+ *gen.*)

DVD die DVD,-s

dynamic temperament-
voll

E

each jed-

ear das Ohr, -en

earlier früher

early früh

to **earn** verdienen

earth die Erde

east der Osten; **~ of**
östlich von

Easter Ostern; **at/for ~** zu
Ostern

East German der Ost-
deutsche (ein Ost-
deutscher) / die Ost-
deutsche, -n, -n;
(derogatory nickname)
der Ossi, -s

easy leicht

to **eat** essen*

economy die Wirtschaft

educated gebildet; **un~** ungebildet

education die Ausbildung

egg das Ei, -er

e-mail die E-Mail, -s

employee der Angestellte (ein Angestellter) / die Angestellte, -n, -n

empty leer

end das Ende; **in the ~** am Ende, schließlich; **at the ~ of the week** am Ende der Woche

to **end** auf·hören

engaged verlobt; **to get ~ (to)** sich verloben (mit)

engineer der Ingenieur, -e

England (das) England

English (adj.) englisch; **in ~** auf Englisch; **(language)** Englisch; **Do you speak ~?** Sprechen Sie Englisch?; **(person)** der Engländer, -

to **enjoy** genießen, genoss, genossen; **~ your meal.** Guten Appetit!

enough genug; **That's ~!** Jetzt habe ich aber genug!

to **enter** herein·kommen*

enterprising unternehmungslustig

entertainment die Unterhaltung

entire(ly) ganz

entrance der Eingang, ¨e

environment die Umwelt

environmentally aware umweltbewusst

equal gleich

especially besonders, vor allem

etc. = et cetera usw. = und so weiter

euro der Euro, -s

European europäisch **European Union** die Europäische Union

even sogar

evening der Abend, -e;

this ~ heute Abend; **tomorrow ~** morgen Abend; **yesterday ~** gestern Abend; **in the ~** abends, am Abend; **every ~** jeden Abend; **Good ~!** Guten Abend!

evening meal das Abendessen

every jed-; **~ three years** alle drei Jahre

everything alles

everywhere überall

exact(ly) genau

exam die Prüfung, -en; **to pass an ~** eine Prüfung bestehen*; **to flunk an ~** bei einer Prüfung durch·fallen*; **take an ~** eine Prüfung machen

excellent ausgezeichnet

except for außer (+ dat.)

exchange der Umtausch

to **exchange** um·tauschen, aus·tauschen, wechseln

exciting spannend

to **excuse** sich entschuldigen; **~ me!** Entschuldigen Sie bitte! Entschuldigung! Verzeihung!

exit der Ausgang, ¨e

to **expect** erwarten

expensive teuer

to **experience** erleben

experience die Erfahrung, -en

to **explain** erklären

extremely (loud) unheimlich (laut)

eye das Auge, -n

F

face das Gesicht, -er

fairly ziemlich

to **fall** fallen*; **to ~ in love (with)** sich verlieben (in + acc.)

fall der Herbst, -e; **in (the) ~** im Herbst

false falsch

family die Familie, -n

famous berühmt

fantastic fantastisch, toll

far weit

fast schnell

fat dick; **to be ~tening** dick machen

father der Vater, ¨

fax das Fax, -e

fear die Angst, ¨e

to **fear** Angst haben* vor (+ dat.)

February der Februar; **in ~** im Februar

fed: I'm ~ up (with it). Ich habe die Nase voll.

to **feel (a certain way)** sich fühlen; **How are you (feeling)?** Wie geht es Ihnen? Wie geht's?; **I'm (feeling). . .** Es geht mir . . .; **to ~ like (doing s.th.)** Lust haben* (zu + inf.)

to **fetch** (sich) holen

few einig- (pl.); wenig-; ein paar

fiancé(e) der Verlobte (ein Verlobter) / die Verlobte, -n, -n

field das Feld, -er; **(~ of study)** das Fach, ¨er; **(of specialization)** die Fachrichtung, -en; **(major)** das Hauptfach, ¨er, das Schwerpunktfach, ¨er; **(minor)** das Nebenfach, ¨er

to **fill out** aus·füllen

film der Film, -e

finally endlich

to **finance** finanzieren

to **find** finden*

fine gut (besser, best-), schön

finger der Finger, -

finished fertig

firm die Firma, Firmen

first erst-; **~ of all, at ~** (zu)erst

to **fish** angeln; **to go ~ing** angeln gehen

fish der Fisch, -e

flavoring particle for: admiration aber; **(curiosity/interest)** denn; **(concern,**

impatience, assurance)
doch; *(emphasis)* ja

flight (plane) der Flug, ⸚e

to **fly** fliegen*

floor: on the first / ground ~ im Parterre; **on the second ~** im ersten Stock

flower die Blume, -n

to **follow** folgen (ist) (+ *dat.*); **~ing** folgend

food das Essen; **Enjoy your ~!** Guten Appetit!

foot der Fuß, ⸚e

for für (+ *acc.*); **(since)** seit (+ *dat.*); **(conj.)** denn

to **forbid** verbieten*

forbidden verboten

foreign ausländisch

foreigner der Ausländer, -

forest der Wald, ⸚er

to **forget** vergessen*

fork die Gabel, -n

formerly früher

foyer der Flur

France (das) Frankreich

free frei

French (adj.) französisch; **in ~** auf Französisch; **(language)** Französisch; **Do you speak ~?** Sprechen Sie Französisch?; **(person)** der Franzose, -n, -n / die Französin, -nen

(French) fries die Pommes (frites)*(pl.)*

fresh frisch

Friday (der) Freitag; **on Fridays** freitags; **~ night** Freitag Abend; **~ nights** freitagnachts

friend der Freund, -e

friendly freundlich; **un~** unfreundlich

friendship die Freundschaft, -en

from von (+ *dat.*); **(a native of)** aus (+ *dat.*); **I'm ~ . . .** Ich bin aus . . . , Ich komme aus . . .; **(numbers) ~ . . . to** von . . . bis; **(place) ~ . . . to** von . . . zu/nach

front: in ~ of vor (+ *acc.* / *dat.*)

fruit das Obst

full voll

fun der Spaß; **to be ~** Spaß machen; **to make ~ (of)** sich lustig machen (über + *acc.*)

funny lustig, witzig; komisch

furniture die Möbel *(pl.)*

future die Zukunft

G

game das Spiel, -e

garage die Garage, -n

garbage der Abfall, ⸚e

garden der Garten, ⸚

gate das Tor, -e

gentleman der Herr, -n, -en

genuine(ly) echt

German (adj.) deutsch; **in ~** auf Deutsch; **(language)** Deutsch; **Do you speak ~?** Sprechen Sie Deutsch?; **(person)** der Deutsche (ein Deutscher) / die Deutsche, -n, -n

Germany (das) Deutschland

to **get (become)** werden*; **(fetch)** holen; **(receive)** bekommen*; **to ~ off** aus·steigen*; **to ~ on** *or* **in** ein·steigen*; **to ~ up** auf·stehen*; **to ~ to know** kennen lernen; **to go and ~** (sich) holen; **to ~ used to** sich gewöhnen an (+ *acc.*); **~ well soon!** Gute Besserung; **to ~ together** sich treffen*

girl das Mädchen, -

to **give** geben*; **(as a present)** schenken

glad froh

gladly gern (lieber, liebst-)

Glad to meet you. Freut mich.

glance (at) der Blick (auf + *acc.*)

glass das Glas, ⸚er; **a ~ of . . .** ein Glas . . .

to **go** gehen*; **to ~ by (bus, etc.)** fahren* mit; **to ~ by plane** fliegen*; **to ~ out** aus·gehen*; **to ~ up** hinauf·fahren*

going: What's ~ on? Was ist los?

good gut (besser, best-); **~- looking** gut aussehend

Good-bye! Auf Wiedersehen! Tschüss!; **(on the phone)** Auf Wiederhören!

goodness: My ~! Ach du liebes bisschen!, Ach du meine Güte!

grade die Note, -n

to **graduate** das Studium ab·schließen*

grandfather der Großvater ⸚

grandmother die Großmutter, ⸚

grandparents die Großeltern *(pl.)*

gray grau

great (size) groß; **(terrific)** prima, toll, herrlich, klasse, spitze

green grün

greeting der Gruß, ⸚e

grief: Good ~! Ach du liebes bisschen!

groceries die Lebensmittel *(pl.)*

to **grow** wachsen*; **to ~ together** zusammen·wachsen*

to **guarantee** garantieren

guest der Gast, ⸚e

to **guide along** vorbei·führen (an + *dat.*)

guitar die Gitarre, -n

H

hair das Haar, -e

half halb; **in ~ an hour** in einer halben Stunde

hallway der Flur

hand die Hand, ⸚e

to **hang (up)** hängen

to **hang (be hanging)** hängen*

to **happen** geschehen*, passieren (ist)

happy glücklich, froh; **I'm ~ for you.** Ich freue mich für dich.

hard (difficult) schwer; **~-working** fleißig

hardly kaum

to **have** haben*; **to ~ to** müssen*

head der Kopf, ¨e

healthy gesund (ü)

to **hear** hören

heavy schwer

Hello! Guten Tag!

help die Hilfe

to **help** helfen* (+ *dat.*)

her ihr

here hier

Hi! Guten Tag! Hallo!

high hoch (hoh-) (höher, höchst)

to **hike** wandern (ist)

his sein

historical(ly) historisch

history die Geschichte

hobby das Hobby, -s

to **hold** halten*

holiday der Feiertag, -e

home: at ~ zu Hause; **(toward) ~** nach Hause; **at the ~ of** bei (+ *dat.*); **(homeland)** die Heimat

honest ehrlich

to **hope** hoffen; **I ~** hoffentlich

hoffentlich hopefully

horse das Pferd, -e

hot heiß

hotel das Hotel, -s, der Gasthof, ¨e, die Pension, -en

hour die Stunde, -n; **for ~s** stundenlang

house das Haus, ¨er

household der Haushalt

househusband der Hausmann, ¨er

housemate der Mitbewohner, -

housewife die Hausfrau, -en

how wie; **~ much?** wie viel?; **~ many?** wie viele?; **~ much is / are . . . ?** Was kostet / kosten . . . ?; **~ come?** wieso?; **~ are you?** Wie geht's?, Wie geht es Ihnen?

however aber, allerdings, doch, jedoch

human being der Mensch, -en, -en

hunger der Hunger

hungry: I'm ~. Ich habe Hunger.

to **hurry** sich beeilen

to **hurt** weh·tun*; **My (throat) hurts.** Mir tut (der Hals) weh; **(to damage)** schaden

husband der Mann, ¨er

I

ice, ice cream das Eis

ID der Ausweis, -e

idea die Idee, -n; **(I have) no ~!** Keine Ahnung!

identification der Ausweis, -e

if (conj.) wenn; ob

ill krank (ä)

to **imagine** sich vor·stellen; **I ~ that . . .** Ich stelle mir vor, dass . . .

immediately sofort

impatient ungeduldig

important wichtig

impossible unmöglich; **That's ~!** Das gibt's doch nicht!

in in (+ *dat.* / *acc.*)

income das Einkommen, -

in common gemeinsam

inconvenient unbequem

incredible einmalig, unglaublich

independent selbstständig

individual(ly) einzeln

inexpensive billig

indeed wirklich, doch

industrious(ly) fleißig

influence der Einfluss, ¨e

inn der Gasthof, ¨e

insecure unsicher

inside in (+ *dat.* / *acc.*)

in spite of trotz (+ *gen.* / [*dat.*]); **~ that** trotzdem

instead of (an)statt (+ *gen.*)

intelligent intelligent

interest (in) das Interesse (an + *dat.*)

interested: to be ~ in sich interessieren für

interesting interessant; **really ~** unheimlich interessant

intermission die Pause, -n

internship das Praktikum, Praktiken

to **invite (to)** ein·laden (lädt ein), lud ein, eingeladen (zu)

island die Insel, -n

isn't it? nicht wahr?

Italian *(adj.)* italienisch; **in ~** auf Italienisch; **(language)** Italienisch; **Do you speak ~?** Sprechen Sie Italienisch?; **(person)** der Italiener, -

Italy (das) Italien

its sein, ihr

J

jacket die Jacke, -n

jam die Marmelade, -n

January der Januar; **in ~** im Januar

jeans die Jeans *(pl.)*

job die Arbeit; **(position)** die Stelle, -n

joint(ly) gemeinsam

juice der Saft, ¨e

July der Juli; **in ~** im Juli

to **jump** springen*

June der Juni; **in ~** im Juni

just gerade; **~ like** genau(so) wie; **~ when** gerade als

K

to **keep** behalten*; **to ~ in shape** sich fit halten*

key der Schlüssel, -

kind nett; **what ~ of (a)?** was für (ein)?

kind (of) die Art, -en (von)
king der König, -e
kitchen die Küche, -n
knee das Knie, -
knife das Messer, -
to **know (be acquainted with)** kennen*; **(a fact)** wissen*; **(a skill)** können*
knowledge die Kenntnis, -se
known: well-~ bekannt

L

lab(oratory) das Labor, -s (*or* -e)
lacking: to be ~ fehlen
lady die Dame, -n; **old ~** die Alte, -n, -n
lake der See, -n
lamp die Lampe, -n
to **land** landen (ist)
landscape die Landschaft
language die Sprache, -n
large groß (ö)
last letzt-
to **last (duration)** dauern
late spät; **How ~ is it?** Wie spät ist es?, Wie viel Uhr ist es?
later später; **See you ~.** Bis später!
to **laugh** lachen
lawyer der Rechtsanwalt, ¨e / die Rechtsanwältin, -nen
to **lay (down)** legen
lazy faul; **to be ~** faulenzen
to **lead** führen
to **learn** lernen
to **leave (behind)** lassen*; **~ from** ab·fahren*; **(a place)** verlassen*
lecture die Vorlesung, -en; **~ hall** der Hörsaal, -säle
left links; link-
leg das Bein, -e
leisure time die Freizeit
lemonade die Limonade, -n
to **let** lassen*
letter der Brief, -e

lettuce der Salat
library die Bibliothek, -en
to **lie (to be located)** liegen*; **to ~ down** sich (hin·)legen
life das Leben
light (weight) leicht; **(bright)** hell
likable sympathisch; **un~** unsympathisch
like wie; **just~** genau(so) wie; **s.th. ~** so etwas wie
to **like** gefallen*; **I ~ it.** Es gefällt mir.; **I really ~ it!** Das gefällt mir aber!; **I would ~ (to have)** ich möchte, ich hätte gern
likewise ebenfalls
to **link** verbinden*
to **listen** zu·hören (+ *dat.*); **to ~ to** sich an·hören
little klein; **(amount)** wenig, ein bisschen; **(some)** etwas
to **live** leben; **(reside)** wohnen
living room das Wohnzimmer, -
location der Ort, -e
long (adj.) lang (ä); **(adv.)** lange; **how ~?** wie lange?; **So ~!** Tschüss! Bis später!
to **look** sehen*; **to ~ (like)** aus·sehen* (wie + *nom.*); **to ~ at** sich an·sehen*, sich an·schauen; **to ~ for** suchen; **to ~ forward to** sich freuen auf (+ *acc.*); **~!** Schau mal!
to **lose** verlieren*
loud(ly) laut
love die Liebe; **to be in ~ (with)** verliebt sein* (in + *acc.*); **to fall in ~ (with)** sich verlieben (in + *acc.*)
to **love** lieben
loving liebevoll
luck das Glück; **tough ~** das Pech; **Tough ~!** Pech gehabt!
lucky: to be~ Glück haben*; **I was (you were, etc.) ~.** Glück gehabt!

luggage das Gepäck
lunch das Mittagessen, -; **for ~** zum Mittagessen

M

mad: That makes me ~. Das ärgert mich.
magazine die Zeitschrift, -en
mail die Post
mailbox der Briefkasten, ¨
mainly vor allem
major (field of study) das Hauptfach, ¨er
to **make** machen
man der Mann, ¨er; **(human being)** der Mensch, -en, -en; **gentle~** der Herr, -n, -en; **old ~** der Alte (ein Alter)
many viele; **how ~?** wie viele?; **~ a** manch-
map die Landkarte, -n; **(city ~)** der Stadtplan, ¨e
March der März; **in ~** im März)
market der Markt, ¨e
marmalade die Marmelade, -n
marriage die Ehe, -n
married verheiratet; **un~** unverheiratet
to **marry, get married** heiraten
matter: (That) doesn't ~. Das ist doch egal. (Das) macht nichts.; **What's the ~?** Was ist los?
may dürfen*
May der Mai; **in ~** im Mai
meal das Essen, -; **Enjoy your ~.** Guten Appetit!
to **mean (signify)** bedeuten; **(think)** meinen
meanwhile inzwischen
meat das Fleisch
to **meet (get to know)** kennen lernen; **Glad to ~ you.** Freut mich (sehr, Sie kennen zu lernen); **to ~ with friends** sich mit Freunden treffen*
menu die Speisekarte, -n

merry:~ Christmas! Frohe/Fröhliche Weihnachten!

middle die Mitte; **in the ~ of** mitten in/auf (+ *dat.*); **in the ~ of the month** Mitte des Monats

milk die Milch

millennium das Jahrtausend, -e

minor (field of study) das Nebenfach, ⁻er

minute die Minute, -n; **See you in a few ~s!** Bis gleich!

missing: to be ~ fehlen

Monday (der) Montag; **~ morning** Montagmorgen; **on ~s** montags; **~ mornings** montagmorgens

money das Geld; **to make ~** Geld verdienen; **to spend ~** Geld aus·geben*

month der Monat, -e; **per ~** im Monat, pro Monat; **for one ~** einen Monat

monthly monatlich

monument das Denkmal, ⁻er

more mehr; **once ~** noch (ein)mal; **~ and ~** immer mehr

morning der Morgen; **early ~** früh (morgen); **mid-~** der Vormittag; **this ~** heute Morgen; **tomorrow ~** morgen früh; **yesterday ~** gestern früh; **in the ~** morgens, am Morgen; **every ~** jeden Morgen; **Good ~!** Guten Morgen!

most meist-; am meisten

mostly meistens

mother die Mutter, ⁻

mountain der Berg, -e

mouth der Mund, ⁻er

movie (film) der Film, -e; **(theater)** das Kino, -s

Mr. Herr

Mrs. Frau

Ms. Frau

much viel (mehr, meist-); **how ~?** wie viel?

museum das Museum, Museen

music die Musik

musical musikalisch; **un~** unmusikalisch

must müssen*

my mein

N

name der Name, -ns, -n; **What's your ~?** Wie heißen Sie?; **My ~ is . . .** Ich heiße . . . , Mein Name ist . . .

to **name** nennen*

napkin die Serviette, -n

nation das Volk, ⁻er

natural science die Naturwissenschaft, -en

nature die Natur

nature preserve das Naturschutzgebiet, -e

near (distance) nah (näher, nächst-) **(vicinity)** bei (+ *dat.*), in der Nähe von (+ *dat.*)

neat prima; schick

neck der Hals, ⁻e

to **need** brauchen

neighbor der Nachbar, -n, -n

neither . . . nor weder . . . noch

never nie; **~ before** noch nie

nevertheless trotzdem

new neu; **s.th. ~** etwas Neues; **nothing ~** nichts Neues; **What's ~?** Was gibt's Neues?

New Year's Eve Silvester; **at/on ~** zu Silvester

news die Nachricht, -en

newspaper die Zeitung, -en

next nächst-; **~ to** neben (+ *dat. / acc.*); **What comes ~?** Wie geht's weiter?

nice schön, nett

nickname der Spitzname, -ns, -n

night die Nacht, ⁻e; **to~** heute Nacht; **last ~** gestern Nacht, heute Nacht; **Good ~!** Gute Nacht!; **at / during the ~** nachts, in der Nacht; **every ~** jede Nacht; **to spend the ~** übernachten

no nein

nobody niemand

noisy laut

nonsense der Quatsch, der Unsinn

no one niemand

noodle die Nudel, -n

noon der Mittag, -e; **to-day at ~** heute Mittag; **tomorrow at ~** morgen Mittag; **at ~** mittags; **af-ter~** der Nachmittag, -e

north der Norden; **in the ~** im Norden; **~ of** nördlich von

nose die Nase, -n

not nicht; **~ any** kein; **~ only . . . but also** nicht nur . . . sondern auch; **~ yet** noch nicht; **~ ever** noch nie; **~ at all** gar nicht

notebook das Heft, -e

nothing (to) nichts (zu); **~ special** nichts Besonderes

novel der Roman, -e

November der November; **in ~** im November

now jetzt, nun; **just ~** gerade

number die Nummer -n, die (Ordinal)zahl, -en

nurse (male) der Krankenpfleger, -; **(female)** die Krankenschwester, -n

O

o'clock Uhr

October der Oktober; **in ~** im Oktober

of course natürlich; doch

off ab-

to **offer** an·bieten*

office das Büro, -s

often oft

oh ach; **~, I see!** Ach so!; **~, come on!** Ach was!; **~ dear!** Ach du liebes bisschen!; **~, how cute!** Ach, wie süß!

okay: That's ~. Das geht. Das macht nichts.; **That's not ~.** Das geht nicht.

old alt (ä); **~ man** der Alte (ein Alter); **~ lady** die Alte, -n, -n; **~ people** die Alten; **~ things** das Alte

on (top of) auf (+ acc. / dat.); **(vertical surface)** an; **~ the first of July** am ersten Juli

once einmal; **~ more** noch (ein)mal; **~ in a while** manchmal; **(formerly)** einst, früher

one (people, they) man

only nur; **(not before)** erst; **not ~ . . . but also** nicht nur . . . sondern auch

open (prefix) auf-; **(adj)** **~ auf**, offen, geöffnet

to **open** öffnen, auf·machen

opera die Oper, -n

opinion: to be of an ~ halten von

opposite das Gegenteil, -e

or oder

oral presentation das Referat, -e; **to give an ~** ein Referat halten* (13W)

orange die Orange, -n; **(color)** orange

orchestra das Orchester, -

order: in ~ to um . . . zu (+ inf.)

to **order** bestellen

other ander-; **~s** andere; **the ~s** die anderen; **s.th. ~ (quite different)** etwas (ganz) anderes; **in ~ ways** anders; **in ~ words** also

our unser

out of aus (+ dat.)

over (location) über (+ acc. / dat.); **(finished)** vorbei; **~ there** da drüben

own (adj.) eigen-

P

to **pack** packen

package das Paket, -e

page die Seite, -n; **on/to ~ . . .** auf Seite . . .

pain der Schmerz, -en; **to have ~** Schmerzen haben*

to **paint** malen

painting das Gemälde, -

palace das Schloss, ¨er

pants die Hose, -n

paper das Papier, -e; **(term ~)** die (Semester)arbeit, -en

parcel das Paket, -e

parents die Eltern (pl.)

to **pardon: ~ me!** Entschuldigung! Entschuldigen Sie! Verzeihung!

park der Park, -s

part der Teil, -e; **to take ~ (in)** teil·nehmen* (an + dat.)

to **participate (in)** teil·nehmen* (an + dat.)

partner der Partner, -

party die Party, -s; die Feier, -n

to **pass (an exam)** bestehen*; **to ~ by** vorbei·gehen* (bei + dat.), vorbei·kommen*, vorbei·fahren*, vorbei·führen (an + dat.)

passport der Pass, ¨e

past (prefix) vorbei-; **in the ~** früher

patient geduldig

to **pay (for)** (be)zahlen

pea die Erbse, -n

peace der Frieden

pen der Kuli, -s

pencil der Bleistift, -e

people die Leute (pl.); **(human being)** der Mensch, -en, -en; **(as a whole or nation)** das Volk, ¨er

pepper der Pfeffer

per pro

performance die Vorstellung, -en

perhaps vielleicht

person der Mensch, -en, -en

pharmacy die Apotheke, -n

to **phone** an·rufen*, telefonieren

physician der Arzt, ¨e / die Ärztin, -nen

piano das Klavier, -e; **to play the ~** Klavier spielen

to **pick up** (sich) holen

picture das Bild, -er; **to take ~s** fotografieren

piece das Stück, -e; **(of music or ballet)** das Stück, -e

pink rosa

pizza die Pizza, -s

place (location) der Platz, ¨e, der Ort, -e; **at our ~** bei uns; **in your ~** an deiner Stelle

plan der Plan, ¨e

to **plan** planen, vor·haben*

plane das Flugzeug, -e

plate der Teller, -

platform der Bahnsteig, -e

play das Stück, ¨e

to **play** spielen; **(checkers)** Dame spielen; **(chess)** Schach spielen; **(tennis)** Tennis spielen

pleasant gemütlich; **un~** ungemütlich

to **please** gefallen*

please bitte

pleased: ~ to meet you. Freut mich.

pleasure: My ~. Nichts zu danken!

P.O. box das Postfach, ¨er

pocket die Tasche, -n

police (force) die Polizei; **~man** der Polizist, -en, -en; **~woman** die Polizistin, -nen

pollution die Verschmutzung

poor arm (ä)

population die Bevölkerung

position die Stelle, -n

possible möglich; **That's im~.** Das ist doch nicht möglich!

postcard (w. picture) Ansichtskarte, -n

post office die Post

potato die Kartoffel, -n

pound das Pfund, -e; **a ~ of . . .** ein Pfund . . . ; **two ~s of . . .** zwei Pfund . . .

power die Macht, ⸚e

practical(ly) praktisch

precise genau; **~ly!** Genau!

to **prefer** lieber tun*; vor·ziehen*

to **prepare** vor·bereiten; **~ o.s. (for)** sich vor·bereiten (auf + *acc.*)

present (gift) das Geschenk, -e

preservation die Erhaltung

pretty hübsch

private privat

probably wahrscheinlich

problem das Problem, -e; **(That's) no ~.** (Das ist) kein Problem.

profession der Beruf, -e; **choice of ~** die Berufswahl

professor der Professor, -en

program das Programm, -e; die Sendung, -en

prohibited verboten

to **promise** versprechen*

to **protect** schützen, schonen

protection der Schutz

proud (of) stolz (auf + *acc.*)

pub die Kneipe, -n

public öffentlich

pudding der Pudding, -s

to **pull** ziehen*

pullover der Pullover, -; Pulli, -s

purple lila

to **put (set down)** setzen; **(stand upright)** (hin·)stellen; **(lay down)** (hin·)legen; **(hang up)** (hin·)hängen; **to ~ on (clothing)** (sich) an··ziehen*; **~ up** (auf·)bauen

Q

quarter das Viertel; **a ~ to** Viertel vor; **a ~ past** Viertel nach; **in a ~ of an hour** in einer Viertelstunde; **(university ~)** das Quartal, -e

queen die Königin, -nen

question die Frage, -n; **to ask a ~** eine Frage stellen

quick(ly) schnell

quiet(ly) ruhig, leise

quite ziemlich

R

radio das Radio, -s

railway die Bahn, -en

to **rain** regnen; **It's raining.** Es regnet.

rather lieber; ziemlich

to **read** lesen*

ready fertig

really wirklich; echt

to **rebuild** wieder auf·bauen

to **receive** bekommen*

to **recognize** erkennen*

to **recommend** empfehlen*

to **recuperate** sich erholen

red rot (ö)

refrigerator der Kühlschrank, ⸚e

region die Gegend, -en; das Gebiet, -e

regular normal

relationship die Beziehung, -en

to **relax** sich entspannen

reliable zuverlässig; **un~** unzuverlässig

to **remain** bleiben*

to **remember** sich erinnern (an + *acc.*)

to **remind (of)** erinnern (an + *acc.*)

to **renovate** renovieren

to **rent** mieten; **to ~ out** vermieten

to **repeat** wiederholen

to **report** berichten

reporter der Journalist, -en, -en

to **request** bitten* (um)

to **rescue** retten

to **reserve** reservieren

to **reside** wohnen

responsibility die Verantwortung, -en

responsible verantwortungsvoll

to **rest** sich aus·ruhen

restaurant das Restaurant, -s

to **restore** restaurieren

to **return** zurück·kommen*

return address der Absender, -

(re)unification die (Wieder)vereinigung

rice der Reis

rich reich

ridiculous lächerlich

right rechts, recht-; **(correct)** richtig; **You're ~.** Du hast Recht.; **isn't it (~)?** nicht wahr?; **(That's) ~.** (Das) stimmt.; **~ away** sofort

river der Fluss, ⸚e

roll das Brötchen, -

room das Zimmer, -; **bed~** das Schlafzimmer; **bath~** das Bad, ⸚er (Badezimmer); **dining ~** das Esszimmer, **living ~** das Wohnzimmer; **guest ~** das Gästezimmer; **single ~** das Einzelzimmer; **double ~** das Doppelzimmer, -

roommate der Zimmerkollege, -n, -n / die Zimmerkollegin, -nen

round-trip ticket die Hin- und Rückfahrkarte, -n

row house das Reihenhaus, ⸚er

to **run** laufen*

S

sad   traurig
safe   sicher; **un~** unsicher
safety   die Sicherheit
salad   der Salat, -e
salt   das Salz
same   gleich; **the ~ to you** gleichfalls; **It's all the ~ to me.** Es ist mir egal.
Saturday   (der) Samstag; **on ~s** samstags
sausage   die Wurst, ̈-e
to **save (money or time)** sparen; **(rescue)** retten
to **say**   sagen; **Could you ~ that again? What did you ~?** Wie bitte?; **How does one ~. . .?** Wie sagt man . . . ?
scared: to be ~ (of)   Angst haben* (vor + *dat.*)
scarcely   kaum
scenery   die Landschaft
schedule (transportation) der Fahrplan, ̈-e
scholarship   das Stipendium, Stipendien
school   die Schule, -n
science   die Wissenschaft, -en; **natural ~** die Naturwissenschaft, -en
scientist   der Wissenschaftler, -
second   die Sekunde, -n
secretary   der Sekretär, -e
secure   sicher
security   die Sicherheit
to **see**   sehen*; **Oh, I ~.** Ach so!
to **seem**   scheinen*
selection (of)   die Auswahl (an + *dat.*)
self-confident   selbstbewusst
self-employed   selbstständig
to **sell**   verkaufen
semester   das Semester, -
seminar   das Seminar, -e
to **send**   schicken
sentence   der Satz, ̈-e; **to make / form a ~** einen Satz bilden
to **separate**   trennen

September   der September; **in ~** im September
server   die Bedienung
service (in store or restaurant)   die Bedienung
to **set (down)**   setzen
several   mehrer- *(pl.)*
to **share**   teilen
shared   gemeinsam
to **shave o.s.**   sich rasieren
shelf   das Regal, -e
to **shine**   scheinen*
shirt   das Hemd, -en
shoe   der Schuh, -e; **in your/ his ~s** an deiner / seiner Stelle
shop   das Geschäft, -e
to **shop**   ein·kaufen; **to go ~ping** einkaufen gehen*
short   klein; kurz (ü)
to **show**   zeigen; **That goes to ~ you.** Da sieht man's mal.
shower   die Dusche, -n; **to take a ~** (sich) duschen
siblings   die Geschwister *(pl.)*
sick (adj.)   krank (ä); **~ person** der Kranke (ein Kranker) / die Kranke, -n, -n
to **sign**   unterschreiben*
to **sign up for**   belegen
to **signify**   bedeuten
silly   dumm (ü)
simple, simply   einfach
since (time)   seit (+ *dat.*)
to **sing**   singen*
single (unmarried)   unverheiratet, ledig
sister   die Schwester, -n; **~s and brothers** die Geschwister *(pl.)*
to **sit (be sitting)**   sitzen*; **to ~ down** sich (hin·)setzen
to **ski**   Ski laufen*; **to go ~ing** Ski laufen gehen*
skill   die Kenntnis, -se
skinny   dünn
skirt   der Rock, ̈-e
slacks   die Hose, -n
slender   schlank
to **sleep**   schlafen*
slim   schlank

slow(ly)   langsam
small   klein
to **smile**   lächeln
to **snow**   schneien
soccer: to play ~   Fußball spielen
sofa   das Sofa, -s
soft drink   die Limonade, -n
some   etwas *(sg.)*; einig- *(pl. only)*; **(many a)** manch-; **(a couple of)** ein paar; **(a little bit of)** ein bisschen
somebody   jemand
someone   jemand
something (to)   etwas (zu)
sometimes   manchmal
son   der Sohn, ̈-e
song   das Lied, -er
soon   bald; **See you ~!** Bis bald!; **as ~ as** sobald
sore: I have a ~ throat. Mir tut der Hals weh.
sorry: I'm ~.   Es tut mir Leid.
sort: all ~s of   allerlei
so that (conj.)   so dass
soup   die Suppe, -n
south   der Süden; **in the ~** im Süden; **~ of** südlich von
Spain   (das) Spanien
Spanish (adj.)   spanisch; **in ~** auf Spanisch; **(language)** Spanisch; **Do you speak ~?** Sprechen Sie Spanisch?; **(person)** der Spanier, -
to **speak**   sprechen*; **~ up (louder)!** Sprechen Sie lauter!
special: s.th. ~ etwas Besonderes; **nothing ~** nichts Besonderes
spectator   der Zuschauer, -
speech   die Rede, -n
to **spend (money)** aus·geben*
to **spin**   spinnen, spann, gesponnen
spoon   der Löffel, -
sport(s)   der Sport; **to engage in ~** Sport treiben*

sporty sportlich
spring der Frühling,
  in (the) ~ im Frühling
square der Platz, ⸚e
stamp die Briefmarke, -n
to **stand (upright), be**
  standing stehen*
to **start** an·fangen*
start der Anfang, ⸚e
state der Staat, -en
to **stay** bleiben*
stay der Aufenthalt, -e
still noch
stomach der Bauch, ⸚e
stop (for buses etc.) die
  Haltestelle, -n
to **stop (doing s.th.)**
  auf·hören (zu + *inf.*)
to **stop (in a vehicle)** halten*; **~!** Halt!
stopover der Aufenthalt,
  -e
store das Geschäft, -e;
  department ~ das Kaufhaus, ⸚er
story die Geschichte, -n;
  detective ~ der Krimi, -s
straight gerade; **~ ahead**
  geradeaus
strange komisch,
  seltsam
strawberry die Erdbeere, -n
street die Straße, -n;
  main ~ die Hauptstraße,
  -n
streetcar die Straßenbahn, -en
strenuous anstrengend
strict(ly) streng
to **stroll** bummeln (ist)
student der Student, -en,
  -en / die Studentin, -nen
study das Studium, Studien; **(course of ~)** das
  Studium; **(room)** das
  Arbeitszimmer, -
to **study** lernen; **(a particu-**
  lar field, be a student at
  a university) studieren
  (an + *dat.*)
stupid dumm (ü)
subject das Fach, ⸚er
subway die U-Bahn

such so ein *(sg.)*; solche
  (pl.)
sudden(ly) plötzlich
sugar der Zucker
suitcase der Koffer, -
summer der Sommer, -;
  in (the) ~ im Sommer
sun die Sonne; **The ~ is**
  shining. Die Sonne
  scheint.
Sunday (der) Sonntag;
  ~ early in the morning
  Sonntag früh; **on ~s**
  sonntags
superb super
supermarket der Supermarkt, ⸚e
supper das Abendessen;
  for ~ zum Abendessen
to **suppose** an·nehmen*
sure sicher; doch; **(na)**
  klar; **for ~** bestimmt
surely bestimmt,
  sicher(lich)
surprise die Über-
  raschung, -en; **What a ~!**
  Was für eine Über-
  raschung!
to **surprise** überraschen
surroundings die Umgebung *(sg.)*; **(ecology)** die
  Umwelt
suspenseful spannend
system das System, -e
sweater der Pullover, -;
  der Pulli, -s
sweatshirt das Sweat-
  shirt, -s
to **swim** schwimmen*,
  baden
Swiss (person) der
  Schweizer, -; **(adj.)**
  Schweizer, schwei-
  zerisch
Switzerland die Schweiz

T

table der Tisch, -e
to **take** nehmen*; **to ~ along**
  mit·nehmen*; **to ~ off**
  (clothing) (sich) aus·-
  ziehen*; **to ~ off (plane)**
  ab·fliegen*; **(last)**
  dauern; **to ~ (a course)**

belegen; **to ~ an exam**
  eine Prüfung machen;
  ~ care! Mach's gut!
talented talentiert; **un~**
  untalentiert
to **talk (to)** reden, sprechen*
  (mit); **to ~ about / of** reden über (+ *acc.*) / von
to **taste** schmecken; **That**
  tastes good. Das
  schmeckt (gut).
taxi das Taxi, -s
tea der Tee, -s
to **teach** lehren
teacher der Lehrer, -
to **tear** down ab·reißen*
telephone das Telefon, -e
tell sagen, erzählen (von
  + *dat.*)
tennis Tennis
term paper die Arbeit,
  -en
terrible, terribly furchtbar, schrecklich
terrific toll, super
test die Prüfung, -en; **to**
  take a ~ eine Prüfung
  machen
than *(after comp.)* als
to **thank** danken (+ *dat.*); **~**
  you! Danke!; **~ you very**
  much. Danke schön!
  Vielen Dank!; **~ God!**
  Gott sei Dank!; **~s, the**
  same to you! Danke,
  gleichfalls!
that das; **(conj.)** dass; **so ~**
  (conj.) so dass
the . . . the je (+ *comp.*)
  . . . desto (+ *comp.*)
theater das Theater, -;
  movie ~ das Kino, -s
their ihr
then dann; **(in those days)**
  damals
there da, dort; **over ~** da
  drüben; **to ~** dorthin;
  ~ is/ are es gibt
therefore deshalb, darum
thick dick
thin dünn
thing das Ding, -e
things: all sorts of ~ so
  einiges; **old ~** das Alte

to **think (of)** denken* (an + *acc.*); **(be of an opinion)** glauben, meinen, halten* von; **I ~ it's** . . . Ich finde es . . . ; **I ~ so, too.** Das finde ich auch.; **If you ~ so.** Wenn du meinst.; **Don't you ~ so?** Oder?

thinker der Denker, -

thirst der Durst

thirsty: I'm ~. Ich habe Durst.

this dies-

thought der Gedanke, -ns, -n

throat der Hals, ⁻e

through durch (+ *acc.*)

to **throw away** weg·werfen*

Thursday (der) Donnerstag; **~ evening** Donnerstag Abend; **on ~s** donnerstags; **~ evenings** donnerstagabends

ticket die Karte, -n; **(bus, etc.)** die Fahrkarte, -n; **(round-trip ~)** die (Hin- und) Rückfahrkarte, -n; **~ window** der Schalter, -

to **tie together** verbinden*

time die Zeit, -en; **What ~ is it?** Wie spät ist es? Wie viel Uhr ist es?; **at what ~?** wann?; **in the mean~** inzwischen; **one ~** einmal; **the first ~** das erste Mal; **for the first ~** zum ersten Mal

tired müde

to **(prefix)** an-; **(prep.)** zu (+ *dat.*); an (+ *acc.*); **(a country, etc.)** nach

today heute

together (prefix) mit-; **(adv.)** gemeinsam, zusammen; **~ with** mit (+ *dat.*)

toilet die Toilette, -n

tomato die Tomate, -n

tomorrow morgen; **the day after ~** übermorgen

too (also) auch; **~ much** zu viel; **me ~** ich auch

tooth der Zahn, ⁻e

to **tour** besichtigen

tour guide der Reiseleiter, -

tourist der Tourist, -en, -en

toward the speaker (prefix) her-

tower der Turm, ⁻e

town die Stadt, ⁻e; der Ort, -e

townhouse das Reihenhaus, ⁻er

toxic waste der Giftstoff, -e

track das Gleis, -e

trade der Handel

traffic der Verkehr

trail der Weg, -e

train der Zug, ⁻e, die Bahn, -en; **~ station** der Bahnhof, ⁻e

trained: well-~ gut ausgebildet

training die Ausbildung; **practical ~** das Praktikum, Praktiken

trash der Abfall, ⁻e

to **travel** reisen (ist)

travel agent der Reiseleiter, -

tree der Baum, ⁻e

tremendously unheimlich

trillion (American) die Billion, -en

trip die Reise, -n, die Fahrt, -en; **to take a ~** eine Reise machen

true richtig, wahr; **(That's) ~.** (Das) stimmt.; **isn't that ~?** nicht wahr?; **That can't be ~!** Das kann doch nicht wahr sein!

to **try** versuchen

T-shirt das T-Shirt, -s

Tuesday (der) Dienstag; **~ at noon** Dienstagmittag; **on ~s** dienstags; **on ~s at noon** dienstagmittags

to **turn: to ~ off (radio, etc.)** aus·machen; **to ~ on (radio, etc.)** an·machen

TV (medium) das Fernsehen; **(set)** der Fern-

seher, -; **to watch ~** fern·sehen*

type (of) die Art, -en (von)

typical(ly) typisch; **That's ~ of you.** Das sieht dir ähnlich.

U

ugly hässlich

unathletic unsportlich

unbelievable unglaublich; **That's ~!** (Das ist doch) unglaublich!, Wahnsinn!

uncle der Onkel, -

under unter (+ *acc.* / *dat.*)

to **understand** verstehen*

undoubtedly sicherlich

unemployed arbeitslos

unemployment die Arbeitslosigkeit

unexpected(ly) unerwartet

unfortunately leider

unification die Vereinigung

united vereint, vereinigt

United States (U.S.) die Vereinigten Staaten (U.S.A.) *(pl.)*

university die Universität, -en; die Uni, -s

unlucky: to be ~ Pech haben*; **I was (you were, etc.) ~.** Pech gehabt!

unique einmalig

until bis; **not ~** erst

up (prefix) auf-

upset: to get ~ about sich ärgern über (+ *acc.*)

upstairs oben

usual(ly) gewöhnlich, meistens

to **use** gebrauchen, benutzen, verwenden

used: to get ~ to sich gewöhnen an (+ *acc.*)

to **utilize** gebrauchen, verwenden

V

vacation die Ferien *(pl.)*

various verschieden-

vegetable(s) das Gemüse, -

versatile vielseitig
very sehr; ganz
view (of) der Blick (auf / in + *acc.*)
viewer der Zuschauer, -
village das Dorf, ˸er
to **visit** besuchen; **(sightsee- ing)** besichtigen

W

to **wait (for)** warten (auf + *acc.*)
waiter der Kellner, -; der Ober, -; ~ ! Herr Ober!
waitress die Kellnerin, -nen; ~! Bedienung!
to **walk** zu Fuß gehen*, laufen*; **to go for a ~** spazieren gehen*
wall die Wand, ˸e; **(thick)** die Mauer, -n
to **want to** wollen*, möchten*
war der Krieg, -e
warm warm (ä)
to **wash (o.s.)** (sich) waschen*
waste der Abfall, der Müll; **toxic ~** der Gift- stoff, -e
waste separation die Mülltrennung
watch (clock) die Uhr, -en
to **watch: (TV)** fern·sehen*; **(pay attention)** auf·pas- sen; **(look at)** Sich an·- schauen; **~ out!** Passen Sie auf!
water das Wasser
way der Weg, -e; **by the ~** übrigens; **this ~** auf diese Weise
to **wear** tragen*
weather das Wetter
wedding die Hochzeit, -en
Wednesday (der) Mitt- woch; **~ afternoon** Mitt- wochnachmittag; **on ~s** mittwochs; **~ afternoons** mittwochnachmittags
week die Woche, -n; **all ~ long** die ganze Woche;

this ~ diese Woche; **Have a nice ~end!** (Ein) schönes Wochenende!
weekly wöchentlich
weird seltsam
welcome: You're ~. Bitte (bitte)!, Bitte schön!, Nichts zu danken!
well (adv.) gut; **~ also**, na, ja, nun; **Get ~ soon!** Gute Besserung!
west der Westen; **in the ~** im Westen; **~ of** west- lich von
what? was?; **~ did you say?** Wie bitte?; **~'s new?** Was gibt's (Neues)?; **~'s on . . . ?** Was gibt's im . . . ?; **So ~?** Na und?; **~ kind of (a)?** was für (ein)?
when (at what time?) wann?; **(at the time ~) (conj.)** als; **~(ever) (conj.)** wenn; **just ~ (conj.)** gerade als
where? wo?; **from ~?** woher?; **~ to?** wohin?
whether (conj.) ob
which? welch-?
while (conj.) während
white weiß
who? wer?
whole ganz
whom? wen?, wem?
whose? wessen?
why? warum?, wieso?
wife die Frau, -en
wild wild
to **win** gewinnen*
window das Fenster, -; **ticket ~** der Schalter, -
windy windig
wine der Wein, -e
winter der Winter, - **in (the) ~** im Winter
to **wish** (sich) wünschen
wish der Wunsch, ˸e; **Best ~es!** Herzliche Glück- wünsche!
with (prefix) mit-; **(prep.)** mit (+ *dat.*); **(at the home**

of) bei (+ *dat.*); **~ me (us . . .)** bei mir (uns . . .)
without ohne (+ *acc.*)
woman (Mrs., Ms.) die Frau, -en
to **wonder** sich fragen
wonderful(ly) wunderbar, prima, herrlich
woods der Wald, ˸er
word das Wort, ˸er; **in other ~s** also
work die Arbeit
to **work** arbeiten; **That won't ~.** Das geht nicht.
worker (blue-collar) der Arbeiter, -
world die Welt, -en
worry die Sorge, -n
to **worry (about)** sich Sorgen machen (um)
to **write** schreiben*; **to ~ to** schreiben* an (+ *acc.*); **to ~ about** schreiben* über (+ *acc.*); **to ~ down** auf- schreiben*; **How do you ~ that?** Wie schreibt man das?
wrong falsch; **You are ~.** Du hast Unrecht.

Y

year das Jahr, -e; **all ~ long** das ganze Jahr; **next ~** nächstes Jahr; **Have a good New ~!** Ein gutes neues Jahr!
yellow gelb
yes ja; doch
yesterday gestern; **the day before ~** vorgestern
yet doch; **not ~** noch nicht
young jung (ü)
your dein, euer, Ihr
youth die Jugend
youth hostel die Jugend- herberge, -n

Z

zip code die Postleitzahl, -en

Index

This index is limited primarily to grammatical entries.

Photo Credits

Cover Photos: Left to right: Berlin Holocaust Memorial Opens, May 10, 2005: © Reportage/Getty; Neuer Zollhof, Düsseldorf © Frank O. Gehry/SuperStock; Statue in Munich: © Kevin Forest/Getty RF; Hamburg Main Train Station: © Mollenhauer/Taxi/Getty.

Text Credits